THE CAMDEN TOWN MURDER MYSTERY

DAVID BARRAT

Orsam Books
www.orsam.co.uk

First edition published 2014
Published with amendments 2015
Revised 2017

ISBN: 978-0-9570917-1-9

Typesetting and book design Ken Anderson www.kenandglen.com

Photographic Credits:

Rising Sun © London Metropolitan Archives; Emily Dimmock © Mirrorpix; Robert Wood © Mirrorpix; 29 St Paul's Road © Mirrorpix; 29 Agar Grove (author); P.C. Killion © Mirrorpix; Inspector Neil © Mirrorpix; Emily Dimmock in sailor's outfit © Mirrorpix; Postcards © Mirrorpix; Ruby Young © EMPICS / Topfoto; Arthur Newton © Mirrorpix; Justice Grantham © Illustrated London News Ltd/Mary Evans; Edward Marshall Hall © Mirrorpix; Jury Members © Mirrorpix; Robert Wood in the dock © Illustrated London News Ltd/Mary Evans; George Wood © Mirrorpix; Robert Wood after the trial © Mirrorpix; Robert Wood and Charles Carlyle Wood in 1952 from the private collection of Sheila Wood, reproduced by kind permission of Sheila Wood.

Contents

Chapter One

Mafficking

'Maffick, v. To celebrate uproariously, rejoice extravagantly...'

Oxford English Dictionary, Oxford University Press, 2013

It seemed like the roar of the crowd would never cease. As many as ten thousand people, tightly packed in the streets around the Central Criminal Court in the City of London, cheered their hearts out with unrestrained joy. Most had stopped on their way home from work but a significant number had been there all day, despite the cold winter weather, waiting anxiously for the jury's verdict. When it came at eight o'clock in the evening – not guilty! – the 'boiling, seething, expectant crowd', as one journalist described it, erupted.[1] The effect was said to be 'dazzling, electric, deafening'.[2] A contemporary observer recorded 'Wild tumult, cheers and a general pandemonium.'[3] Hats were removed to be waved in the air; handkerchiefs were tied on sticks; umbrellas were held aloft; strangers shook hands with each other; young men surged forward; women screamed and fainted. To those outside the court it appeared as if, by sheer weight of numbers, 'the strong cordon of police that guarded the folding gates of the main entrance would have been swept up the steps and into the building itself'.[4] With not a little difficulty, the police managed to hold their lines but, for some commentators, the scene was reminiscent of the Gordon Riots of June 1780 when Lord George Gordon led a violent mob to the gates of Newgate in protest against Catholic emancipation. Others were reminded of a happier and more recent event about seven years earlier, in May 1900, when news from South Africa of the relief of Mafeking reached London and virtually every inhabitant of the capital, young and old, was out on the streets celebrating, singing and dancing. Indeed, this thought inspired the use of the relatively new verb, 'mafficking', to describe the reaction outside the criminal court house in December 1907.[5]

But why did the acquittal of a man accused of the brutal murder of a young woman while she slept in her bed in Camden Town cause such an outpouring of delight amongst the populace of London? Why did they sing 'For he's a jolly good fellow' at the top of their voices? Why did they cheer him to the heavens when he emerged, smiling, from the court building after the trial? These were questions even some newspapers of the day found hard to answer; an editorial in *The Globe* said it was 'a little difficult to understand the intense enthusiasm on behalf of the prisoner'.[6] Almost thirty years later, a writer for the *Daily Mirror* referred to 'some never explained reason' which prompted 'a howling mob' to make a hero of the acquitted defendant.[7] For others, it was a simple matter; he was innocent! But that hardly explained the mass hysteria following his acquittal. In fact, while there were certain specific elements relating to the arrest and prosecution of the accused murderer which excited the sympathy of the general public, the extraordinary outpouring of joy following his acquittal can only really be understood in the context of the remarkably low esteem with which the police – especially the Metropolitan Police – was held during 1907.

Only a few weeks before the aforementioned murder – of 22-year-old Emily Elizabeth Dimmock – serious allegations against the Metropolitan Police Force had been made by James Timewell, the secretary of the Police and Public Vigilance Society, during a sitting of a Royal Commission investigating the Metropolitan Police held at the Middlesex Guildhall in Westminster on 31 July 1907. Timewell claimed that police constables 'used every means to secure the conviction of a person charged' and that magistrates were 'misled by the untrue statements of police officers'. Policemen who did not wish to give false evidence were 'encouraged by their superior officers to do so'. As if that was not enough, Timewell said that, to his personal knowledge, it was common for policemen to drink alcohol at all hours and estimated that half of all officers on night duty were 'quite incapable of doing their duty' as a result.[8]

Over the following few months, there was an extraordinary sequence of well-publicised scandals involving individual police officers. On 15 August 1907, two police constables of the S Division of the Metropolitan Police, William Stoodley and Ernest Pink, were found guilty at the County of London Sessions of having stolen a cigarette holder and case, three packets of tobacco and nine cigars from a tobacconist's shop in Hampstead. During their trial they claimed they found a key to the shop and took the items as 'a lark' in order to show the tobacconist how easy it was for people to help themselves. Their defence was rejected by the magistrate who observed that they did not offer this explanation at the time they were arrested.[9] Both constables were sentenced to three months imprisonment.[10] In September 1907, summonses for perjury were issued by James Timewell's Police and Public Vigilance Society against Philip Jenkin and James Adams, constables in the X Division, who had arrested two men, William Church and Ernest Sexton, on a charge of obstruction, for attempting to rescue a violent prisoner they were taking to Paddington Police Station. Church and Sexton emphatically denied the charge, which, they claimed, the constables had fabricated against them, and, as the two arrested men had some corroborating evidence to support their claims of innocence, proceedings were instituted against the constables at Marylebone Police Court. Although they were both eventually acquitted, the proceedings dragged on for some months, culminating in a trial at the Central Criminal Court in November, with the verdict not being announced until 2 December, thus keeping the story alive throughout that time period.[11]

Also during September, Timewell called for a full inquiry following the failure of police prosecutions in what was known as the 'West End flats case'. This involved an attempt to convict three women, Mrs Maud Cooper, Mrs Jessie Crawford and Miss Catherine Goldie, the latter a well-known actress, at Marylebone Police Court, for running disorderly houses at their London apartments. The prosecutions collapsed after a number of respectable witnesses gave convincing evidence that this was not possible. Mrs Cooper's husband, for example, was a government official at the water board who left home for work every morning and returned every evening, yet the supposedly detailed police observation log on the Coopers' home in Langham Street, compiled over a number of days, did not contain any record at all of his coming and going. Mr Cooper described the police evidence as 'a tissue of lies'. The porter at the Coopers' apartment building also testified that the police evidence was 'utterly untrue'. Furthermore, the police were unable to identify any of the numerous prostitutes they claimed to have seen entering the premises. The magistrate, Chester Jones, prepared a report for the Home Office dated 30 September 1907 in which he said: 'I have found great difficulty in accounting for the conduct of the police officers, the evidence was too detailed for me to accept the theory of mere mistake...the only conclusion I could safely come to was that I could not accept the evidence of the police officers in the face of the evidence of Mr Cooper'.[12]

A similar situation arose in the same month involving 71-year-old Esther Bowen, against whom evidence was given by four constables at the Old Bailey as to the alleged disreputable character of her house at 13 Chesterfield Street, St Pancras, which she ran as a private hotel. Against this, however, was the evidence of Canon Miles, Rector of Pangbourne, the Reverend Williamson, Vicar of Bobington; Ernest Boore, the former deputy-registrar of births, deaths and marriages for St George's, Hanover Square; and Francis Marshal, an Australian barrister, amongst other highly respectable witnesses of unimpeachable character, who all stated that they had stayed as guests at Miss Bowen's house and there was no such activity as had been alleged by the police. At the judge's request, Richard Muir, counsel for the prosecution, accepted that the jury should be directed to acquit but, in a remarkable twist, the jury independently decided to bring in a guilty verdict which led to an even more remarkable and almost unprecedented response from the judge who said that in his opinion 'the verdict is entirely wrong' and, to make his point, sentenced Miss Bowen to a mere one day in prison.[13]

At the end of September 1907, Mr Cluer, the magistrate at Old Street Police Court, said of the prosecution against a man accused of attempting to rescue someone being arrested for using insulting language against the police, 'I am sorry to say I do not believe the evidence in this case' as he discharged the prisoner.[14] The North London magistrate, Mr Fordham, discharged two men accused of gambling in an Islington street with the words that the evidence from the police officers in the case 'was not to be trusted'.[15] Other scandals filled the newspapers during September. Three constables were dismissed from the force for breach of duty at Southfields after they left their beats and were found playing cards inside an empty house in the early hours of Sunday 15 September.[16] At virtually the same time, two police officers with the London and India Dock Police were charged with breaking and entering the Great Northern Railway Company's warehouse at Victoria Docks with intent to steal cigarettes and other items.[17] As if all that was not enough bad publicity for the police, the senior magistrate at Marlborough Street Police Court made an order that, to prevent collusion, police officers would no longer be allowed to sit in his courtroom and listen to their colleagues give evidence in the witness box before they gave their own evidence.[18] Shortly after this, the Coroner for West London, Mr Luxmore Drew, made an identical ruling during an inquest in Kensington on a man who had died in a police station after having been arrested for being drunk and incapable. Mr Drew said that the evidence of two constables at the inquest was 'unsatisfactory, and they had contradicted each other' adding that he 'could not understand it'.[19]

Hostility to the police was evident during September 1907 when two police constables in Central London attempted to arrest a violent man called Arthur Haslett who bit a chunk of flesh out of one of the constables' fingers during the struggle to contain him. Despite the fact that the constables were struggling with an obvious lunatic, the *Police Chronicle* reported that 'a very large and hostile crowd had collected and on the way to the police station the officers were stoned'.[20]

Still the bad news kept coming. The *Star* of 1 October 1907 alleged that 'police officials of the G Division may be seen drinking on duty at any hour of the day in out-of-way corners' and made various allegations of police corruption. The *Weekly Dispatch* of 6 October 1907 said that 'police scandals show anything but a tendency to diminish', observing that, at the time, there were 'no fewer than four constables...in custody charged with burglary and theft'. On 16 October 1907, two officers of the N Division, police constables Banks and Smith, were convicted at Essex Quarter Sessions for committing a burglary while in uniform at a tobacconist's shop in Chingford, having been caught red-handed stealing a quantity of cigars and cigarettes, some of which were found concealed in one of the constables' helmets. P.C. Smith was sentenced to hard labour for a year and P.C. Banks to three months imprisonment with hard labour.[21]

This plethora of scandals involving the Metropolitan Police has to be viewed within the wider, national context of police failures and miscarriages of justice. The best example of this relates to events in Great Wyrley, Staffordshire, surrounding a series of horse mutilations which had resulted in the imprisonment of George Edalji in 1903. Edalji had been released from prison in 1906 but there was a widespread belief that he had been wrongly convicted and his case attracted national attention. The normally loyal publication, *Police Review & Parade Gazette*, was critical of the Home Office for its handling of the case in its 6 September 1907 issue saying: 'The Great Wyrley Mystery thickens and darkens and so far its developments are damaging the police in the public estimation', adding that it had no doubt that the Staffordshire police were 'mistaken in their certainty at the time of the prosecution that the prisoner was the guilty man'. The problems in Staffordshire were still attracting national attention when the police arrested a young butcher called Francis Hollis Morgan for some of the maimings but the prosecution against him was withdrawn at the local police court for lack of evidence. In a foretaste of what was to come later in the year, the *London Weekly News* of 15 September 1907 reported that 'a great crowd' which had assembled in the courtroom and outside 'received the news with prolonged cheering, and accorded the released man an ovation'.

There had been so many questionable convictions over the previous few years that parliament had passed the Criminal Appeal Act in August 1907 to establish a Court of Criminal Appeal although this was not entirely to the liking of all the members of the judiciary, with one High Court judge, Mr Justice Grantham, declaring that the Act was 'quite unnecessary'.[22] During the debate on the Bill in the House of Commons, the Home Secretary, Herbert Gladstone, pointed out that 'the constant reiteration' in the newspapers of cases where someone had been convicted in error 'led people to believe that the miscarriages of justice were of every-day occurrence.'[23] During the same debate, however, the Member of Parliament for Kensington North, Henry Stanger, said that he thought that 'the number of innocent persons who were wrongly convicted was often understated'.[24] An editorial in the *Times* referred to 'the demoralizing irregular discussions in Parliament and the press of the verdicts of juries and sentences by Judges' and supported the new appeal court because there were 'many cases as to which public opinion is much excited....that injustice has been done'.[25]

Against such a background of suspicion and downright hostility towards the police from large sections of the public, including members of parliament, there was likely to be sympathy for anyone against whom there was the slightest hint of mistreatment by police officers. If that person was of a good character, from a respectable hard working family, with a venerable elderly father, who was 'betrayed' to the police by his sweetheart, and who was faced with incredible almost unbelievable evidence from prosecution witnesses, then it is probably not so surprising that even an alleged murderer of a defenceless woman could and would be turned into a national hero.

The crowd outside the Old Bailey on the day of the verdict, 18 December 1907

Chapter Two

From Camden to Hertfordshire and Back

'Such beginning, such end.'

William Camden, *Remaines concerning Britaine*, 1636

As the twelve-year-old William Camden lay seriously ill from the plague in Islington in 1563 he could never have guessed that his name would one day be appropriated by a nearby area that would eventually turn into a thriving urban industrial town but was then no more than fields and empty land. Had he known, he would surely have enjoyed the thought. Born, appropriately enough, at the Old Bailey in May 1551, Camden recovered from the plague and went on to become a successful antiquarian and historian, being especially interested in the origins of place names. He spent his retirement living in Chislehurst, Kent, and his mansion there, Camden Place, was named after him. Although Camden died in 1623, Camden Place kept his name alive into the eighteenth century when it was acquired by a former Attorney General and Lord Chief Justice of the Court of Common Pleas, Sir Charles Pratt, who, when elevated to the peerage in 1765, selected the style of 'Baron Camden of Camden Place in Kent'. A little over twenty years later, Lord Camden inherited the rights to farm three hundred acres of land through his wife's mother in an area of London just south of what had long been known as Kentish Town and to the north of the recently created Somers Town in the parish of St Pancras. At the time, the land was a prebendal manor owned by St Paul's Cathedral, and in 1790, not being at all interested in farming, Lord Camden came to a financial arrangement with Reverend Thomas Randolph, the prebendary, whereby he would lease the land out to builders for the development of housing. It was the subsequently built block of houses in six new streets which formed the core of what was to become known as Camden Town. The *Times* of 10 January 1791 reported:

> A lot of ground adjoining the road to Hampstead, part of the estate of Lord Camden, has lately been let on a building lease to three persons of considerable property in the City, who have entered into an agreement to build within a limited time, four hundred houses; to be divided into streets and called Camden Town. The bricks are now making on the spot for the purpose. This, when completed, with other buildings now erecting on that road, will soon join Hampstead to London.

The new streets, which were soon built, required new names and Camden took inspiration from himself and his family. He was also known as Viscount Bayham, with his brother being John Pratt of Bayham; hence Bayham Street is found at the centre of Camden Town and Camden's original family name is responsible for Pratt Street which intersects Bayham Street. His wife's family surname was Jeffreys, which accounts for Jeffreys Street, and his grandfather-in-law was Sir Geoffrey Jeffreys of Brecknock, explaining why Brecknock Road was so named. During 1791 and 1792, a veterinary college was also built in the area, which was then no more than a village, lending its name to College Street.

The area was not without danger. Two years before work started on the creation of Camden Town, there was a brutal murder of an unknown woman in fields leading from Somers Town to Pancras church. The *Times* of 23 November 1789 reported that her head was 'cut from the back part nearly off', with a razor case found nearby. As the woman, who 'appears to have been a gentlewoman', was still wearing her wedding ring, it did not seem that robbery was the motive for this horrid homicide. The next major crime recorded in the area, however, *was* a robbery: of a stockbroker by a highwayman in Camden Town in April 1798; a soldier was arrested for the rape of a 14-year-old girl in the village later that year, while a Hampstead resident was robbed of nine guineas, a watch and gold chain in Fig Lane (now Crowndale Road) in late 1800.

The first significant murder in the region of Camden Town itself appears to have been the shooting of William Joachim of Pratt Place during the evening of 1 June 1808. Mr Joachim had, earlier that day, come into the possession of one hundred pounds in Marylebone and this appears to have been the motive for a robbery which turned into murder. Joachim's body was found in a field leading back to his home, having been killed by a single bullet to the heart, with both his money and watch missing.[26] The man suspected of being the murderer, William Howe, was executed in Staffordshire five years later after murdering another man in Stourbridge by shooting him in the back with a pistol. When he was captured he was found to be in possession of Joachim's watch.[27]

Despite the occasional unfortunate murder, the new Camden Town was an instant success and expanded quickly during the nineteenth century. An 1811 publication commented that 'the buildings now in progress promise, when completed, to render it [Camden Town] an elegant appendage to the western part of the metropolis' and added: 'The houses are in general respectable and regularly built; the crescent terrace and other ranges of building in the upper part of it, are of handsome appearance'.[28] Expansion of the area was assisted by the extension of the Regent's Canal to Camden Town and, subsequently, in 1838, by a new railway line passing through the area, operated by the London and Birmingham Railway, with the opening of a railway station in Camden Town, enabling passengers and goods to be transported cheaply. The *Penny Cyclopaedia of the Society for the Diffusion of Useful Knowledge,* published in 1839, stated that 'Camden Town is now rapidly increasing, and…consists of some streets of good houses'. As more people came to live in this part of London, more new roads were built, including a new road to the east of Camden Town called St Paul's Road, commemorating the fact that the land had originally been owned by the cathedral. For some time, Camden Town was associated with middle class respectability and *Punch* magazine joked in 1845 that 'exports from Camden Town consist ordinarily of Sally-Lunn Tea Cakes' but by the second half of the nineteenth century, as the middle classes moved to the suburbs, it fast became a predominantly lower class area, and Charles Dickens' *A Christmas Carol* has Bob Cratchit living there in some poverty in 1858.

The first murder labelled by sections of the press as 'The Camden Town Murder' occurred in October 1871 when the body of a young woman was fished out of the Regent's Canal, having clearly been beaten and murdered; but her identity could not be established and the perpetrator was never caught.[29] Then, in March 1885, another so-called 'Camden Town Murder' occurred when John Rose, a former patient of Colney Hatch Lunatic Asylum, shot dead a fellow lodger in Caroline Street and, declared unfit to stand trial due to insanity, ended up in Broadmoor. Five years later, in October 1890, there was a third 'Camden Town Murder', although it started off being labelled by the press as 'The Hampstead Murder', when the body of 31-year-old Mrs Pheobe Hogg, a resident of Kentish Town, was discovered in South Hampstead with her throat cut and her wedding ring missing, while the body of her 18-month-old baby daughter was found shortly afterwards in a field in West Hampstead. It transpired that the murder had actually been committed in a house in Priory Street (now Ivor Street) off College Street, in Camden Town, and, following complaints from the well-to-do residents of Hampstead who did not wish to be associated with such a sordid crime, it was re-assigned in the newspapers to the more appropriate geographic area of Camden Town. There was a sensation when a female friend of Mrs Hogg was arrested and charged with the murder. Mary Eleanor Wheeler had evidently been in love with Mrs Hogg's husband and the police found blood and clear signs of a struggle in her house in Priory Street. There were suspicions that someone else was involved to help her move Mrs Hogg's body to Hampstead, and the evidence against Mary Wheeler was circumstantial, with the missing wedding ring never found, but she was convicted at the Central Criminal Court and executed on 23 December 1890. We shall return to Camden Town in due course for the story of this book does not begin there; it commences in the more rural surroundings of Hertfordshire.

The Vicar of Braughing, in Hertfordshire, during April 1871 was the 67-year-old Francis Say who lived in the vicarage with his brother, Henry, a retired major in the Indian Army, and his two unmarried sisters, both in their fifties. According to the 1871 census, he employed four female servants at the vicarage: a cook, a kitchen maid, a parlour maid and a housemaid. The last of these was Sarah Uncle from Great Hadham. [30] She was the 19-year-old daughter of Peter Uncle who had died after an accidental explosion at the relatively young age of 40 in 1865 when Sarah was just 14. [31] He had been pouring some fuel from a can into a bottle near a lighted candle when the fuel ignited, covering him in flames. [32] With help from bystanders, who threw water over him, he was able to walk away from the fire but his injuries were too severe for the medical men attending him to do anything other than try to alleviate his pain and he died ten hours later. Before he passed away, he prepared his will in which he left £100 to Sarah: to be provided to her when she reached the age of 21. [33] The interest on this sum until 1873 (when Sarah would turn 21) was to go to Peter's wife, Maria, for their daughter's maintenance, but this had evidently not prevented Sarah from having to go into service. In doing so, she was following her mother who had been a domestic servant in Shoreditch, East London, when she had married Peter who, at that time, in December 1850, had been a humble labourer living in the area. Subsequently, he and his wife had moved to Hertfordshire, the place of his birth, and he made some money, first as a hay and straw dealer and then as the landlord of the *Royal Oak* public house in Widford, although he lost the licence in March 1861 when he illegally sold spirits to customers. [34] Nevertheless, his profitable hay dealing business continued and the 1861 census shows that he employed two servants. In July 1863, his friend, John Carter, transferred to him the licence of the *Bull Inn* at Great Hadham and it was in the tap room of the *Bull* that the fatal explosion occurred in November 1865. Maria continued to run the public house on her own after her husband's death but, shortly after re-marrying another hay dealer, Samuel Archer, in 1867, the licence transferred to her new husband.[35] Sarah presumably lived with her mother and stepfather in the *Bull* until she went into service in nearby Braughing at some point in or before 1871.

Within two years of the 1871 census, and now presumably £100 richer, Sarah was pregnant. The man responsible for this was Richard Henry Skillin, a 29-year-old fur traders' porter from London, and, on 20 October 1873, Sarah, assuming the position of Richard's wife, gave birth to a girl, Sarah Maria Skillin, at 76 Seymour Place in Marylebone. On the birth certificate, the mother was described as 'Sarah Skillin formerly Uncle' giving the appearance that she was a married woman. There is some considerable doubt about this. In 1866, Richard Skillin had married Letitia Wheadon who had presumably died by 1873 but there is no surviving record of her death or of a subsequent marriage between Richard and Sarah Uncle. Despite this, in 1874, while still living together at Seymour Place, the couple gave birth to another girl, Rosa.[36] Richard Henry then dropped out of Sarah's life as did little Sarah Maria, who almost certainly never knew her father[37] and was evidently brought up by her grandmother, Maria Archer, who left Hertfordshire at some point after 1874 with her second husband to run a pub in Essex.[38]

Two years after Rosa's birth, Sarah was pregnant again, but to a different man. This time it was a 26-year-old carpenter from Bermondsey, South London, called William 'Maynard' Dimmock, the son of a Walworth cab proprietor. The name 'Maynard' came from William's grandmother, originally Mary Maynard before she married William's grandfather (William Dimmock) in 1802, but it was not given to baby William on his birth certificate, being added to his name later in life. Sarah and William's first son, officially called William Maynard, was born on 9 August 1876 in Codicote, Hitchin, where the Dimmocks briefly lived before moving to South London. Although the couple were not married, Sarah was stated to be 'Sarah Dimmock, formerly Uncle' on the birth certificate, ignoring the years she spent living as Mrs Skillin. The same is true of the birth certificate of Esther Elizabeth Dimmock born in Newington, Surrey, in January 1878 and it was not until the autumn of 1879 that Sarah and William decided to wed, their names appearing in the banns to be married at St Mary's church in Lambeth.[39] However, as far as can be established, the marriage did not take place and, despite living as man and wife, it appears that they never actually married in any formal ceremony.

The Dimmocks continued to be a productive couple while living in South London. Sarah gave birth in February 1880 to Henry John (probably named in memory of William's younger brother, Henry, who had died of heart disease, aged 24, the previous month), then, in December 1881, to Thomas James and, in August 1883, to Rebecca Maud. Between these births, however, in December 1881, 3-year-old Esther Elizabeth died of 'congestion of lungs'. By 1881, William had taken up portrait photography and was managing to make a living from this while remaining a journeyman carpenter but, over the next few years, he would describe himself as a 'travelling photographer' on most official documents.

In 1884, the Dimmocks moved from Walworth to rural Standon in Hertfordshire, near Sarah's birthplace of Great Hadham, where, on 11 March, William became the landlord of a beerhouse called the *Red Lion*, situated in

Standon's high street.[40] Sarah was already pregnant again by this time and, on 20 October 1884, produced a daughter, Emily Elizabeth, whose middle name was presumably chosen in Esther Elizabeth's memory, although Elizabeth was also the name of William's mother. Despite now being the landlord of the *Red Lion*, William listed his profession as a 'carpenter' on Emily's birth certificate.[41] This was quite common at a time when running a public house was not a full time occupation. In the 1881 census, for example, the occupation of Robert Ellenby, the then landlord of the *Red Lion* (or the *Lion* as it was listed on the census return) was stated to be a 'Traction Engine Driver', with 'Licensed Victualler' added almost as an afterthought. William Whitaker, the landlord of Standon's *Bell Inn*, an alehouse in the same street as the *Red Lion*, was described only as a 'carpenter' on the same census. This did not necessarily mean that being a licensed victualler was regarded as a lesser occupation and, when Emily was baptized by the Reverend Henry Rose Wetherall, vicar of Standon, on 14 December 1884, William occupation's was entered as 'publican' in the parish register.

A year after Emily's birth, in October 1885, a major tragedy occurred in the Dimmocks' life when little Thomas James was bitten by a mad dog and contracted rabies; he died of hydrophobia, aged 3 years old, in a carriage whist being taken by his father to the Hertford Infirmary. The incident was reported in the local newspaper, which referred to 'Thomas Dimmock, son of William Dimmock, photographer of this village' showing that William was actually regarded more as a photographer in Standon, than a publican or a carpenter. The newspaper also said: 'The mother of the poor child was confined the day previously and considering the shock is progressing favourably'.[42] The confinement was successful and, a few weeks after the tragedy, Sarah gave birth to a boy, Peter, but he died within three months, on 31 January 1886, of 'acute eczema'.[43] This constituted a double tragedy for William because his own father had died just two days earlier of liver failure at the age of 69, and William was present at the death at his father's home in Walworth. There might have been some comfort for him in the fact that he was left a third share of his father's estate of £65, along with his two surviving brothers: Thomas (a private in the Royal Marines) and John (an ostler living in South London).

In between all the deaths, William had to deal with the local sanitary inspector, who reported to the Rural Sanitary Authority in January 1886 that there was 'fouling of the road gulley in front of the *Lion Inn*, Standon'. This was a common problem at a time when sanitation of houses was very basic and there was no public sewage system. Nevertheless, William Dimmock wrote an indignant letter to the authority 'expressing surprise at the contents of a communication he had received from the Authority', and complaining that 'if there was a nuisance, why did their Inspector, who was frequently in the neighbourhood, not call his attention to it'.[44] He also complained that 'the accusation must have been based on a mistaken report or was to be attributed to ignorance of the state of affairs'. In response, the sanitory inspector told the authority that 'hardly a week passed without his calling the landlord's attention to the matter'.[45] In the event, it was decided to allow Dimmock time to remedy the problem which he must have done because there were no further sanitary issues reported with respect to the *Red Lion*.

Meanwhile, the Dimmock family continued to expand and another male Dimmock was born in November 1886, called Arthur Robert. He was baptized in March 1887 with William again described as a 'publican' on the parish register. However, William surrendered the licence for the *Red Lion* in November 1887 and the Dimmocks moved to Hitchin where Sarah gave birth to a girl, Kate, in September 1888, with Walter Ernest being born in August 1889. The latter birth was quickly followed by another tragedy as Kate died in September 1889 of bronchitis aged eleven months – her half-sister, Rosa, being present at her death. During the 1890s, Sarah's remarkable fertility continued with three more children being born: Albert Edward in December 1891, Florence Rose in February 1893 and Frederick in March 1894, but Florence died at the age of seven months after suffering from 'marasmus convulsions'. William's photographic career was, perhaps, not proving as profitable as he had hoped because he was back to describing himself as a carpenter on the birth certificates of these two children (and on Florence's death certificate), although when Albert Edward died of 'broncho pneumonia' aged 4 years in March 1896 he was said to have been 'son of William Dimmock a photographer'.

During the 1870s and 1880s, William appears to have toured England, Ireland and Wales with a limelight lantern, also known as a 'magic lantern', exhibiting photographs with special optical effects, known as 'dissolving views', on behalf of the Indian Female Normal School & Instruction Society and then (from 1880) the Church of England Zenana Missionary Society for whom he was a 'travelling agent'.[46] A zenana was the part of a house set apart for (high caste) Indian women to live in seclusion in residences in India: the word 'zenana' being derived from the Persian word 'zan', meaning 'woman'. It was believed by a somewhat fanatical group of people in England that such women were being treated as second class citizens and deprived of their freedom in India so they dedicated their lives to gaining access to the zenanas in order to educate Hindu women and convert them to Christianity in an attempt to 'improve' their lives. A 'Ladies' Society for Promoting Female Education in the East' was formed in Calcutta with a number of day-schools opened during the 1820s and 1830s, and the Calcutta Normal School (a school to train English and Eurasian girls as mission teachers) was established in 1851 under a committee of English ladies who founded the Indian Female Normal School & Instruction Society. Similar missions in other non-Christian countries, such as China, were also attempted. The society was initially interdenominational but, during the late 1870s, the majority of members were Anglican and wanted to link up with the Church of England Missionary Society. In acrimonious circumstances in 1880, this majority, which evidently included William Dimmock, seceded to form the Church of England Zenana Missionary Society, a decision the dissenting members described bitterly as a 'lamentable desertion'.[47]

Most activists in the movement were women and it is not known why William was actually attracted to this cause. The two sisters of a wealthy Staffordshire timber merchant, Josiah Dimmock, were regular contributors to the society but it does not appear that William was related to them and it is almost certainly a coincidence that William and Sarah would move to Staffordshire in their old age.

William's third brother, Henry, who died of heart disease in 1880 at the age of 24 and whose occupation on his death certificate was recorded as a letter sorter for the post office, had apparently been involved in founding a lay mission in Walworth during the 1870s,[48] so there must have been a certain evangelical zeal amongst the South London Dimmocks. It seems that the work William did for the society was voluntary but the minutes of the General Committee of the Church of England Zenana Missionary Society held on 4 November 1891 reveal that the committee had received a letter from William Dimmock dated 29 October 1891 'pointing out his long service in connection with the society & asking for a small grant to enable him to commence other work'.[49] It was resolved that a grant of £5 would be made to him which must have been very welcome at a time when his wife was eight months pregnant.

Emily Elizabeth Dimmock is supposed to have attended St Mary's National School in Hitchin but, in June 1894, at the age of nine, her studies were interrupted when she was knocked down by a runaway horse and cart owned by a marine store dealer called Henry Malkern at the foot of Hitchin Hill.[50] Malkern noticed that his horse had become restless and jumped off to see what was wrong but it then bolted down the hill and onto the Folly (now called Stevenage Road) where Emily was pushing a pram containing two children, presumably baby Frederick and little Albert Edward. The horse smashed into the pram and knocked poor Emily against a wall, with the wheel of the cart passing over her head while she was lying flat on the ground, leaving her unconscious and causing concussion to the brain.[51] One of the children in the pram was also badly shaken while the other was unhurt. Emily was treated by Dr James Gilbertson, a local registered medical practitioner, and spent the next three weeks in hospital. According to her father, speaking to a journalist from the *North Herts Mail* many years later, the doctors at the hospital told him that Emily would have to go into a lunatic asylum unless someone was able to devote time to look after her twenty-four hours a day. Not wishing such a fate for his daughter, William apparently took care of her at home for a number of weeks and pushed her around in a bath chair until she seemed to get better, although it is possible she never fully recovered.

William remained in Hitchin with Emily and the rest of his family for three years after the accident until about 1897 when Emily was thirteen. At this point, the Dimmocks moved to Bedford where Emily worked at the Swan Hotel as a chambermaid.[52] At the age of fifteen she learnt straw hat work at Mr Elliot's factory at Guildford Street in Luton[53] and, from April 1899, lived for about eight months at Slip End, near Luton, with her younger half-sister, Rosa, who, in July 1898 had married a widowed blacksmith nearly twice her age called Harry Martindale.[54] Rosa was then pregnant and Emily nursed her through her confinement.

From Bedfordshire, Emily, who had developed into a 'fine built girl with slim figure',[55] moved to London with her older sister, Rebecca, who was known to her family by her middle name of 'Maud'. William Dimmock would later say that Maud 'decoyed poor Emily away from her mother and father and a good position she held at Bedfordshire'.[56] Maud was already in a situation as a domestic servant and the pair lived in East Finchley, where Emily took a position as a housemaid. William subsequently transferred to Northampton where he started to manufacture medicated sweets for children's coughs which he sold at a market stall, becoming known as 'Cough Candy' by the locals. He says he lost sight of Emily's whereabouts for a year, 'my son not answering my letters as to her whereabouts'.[57] It is the first sign of a rift within the Dimmock family and there are a number of indications that some of Emily's siblings did not wish their father to know where she was living. However, despite the fact that the 1901 census recorded William as being on his own in Cambridge, while Sarah lived with Emily and two of her sons in St Neots, Huntingdonshire, there does not appear to have been any rift between William and his wife. It seems that William, still calling himself a photographer, was simply staying temporarily at the *Cardinal's Cap Inn* in Cambridge while on business.[58]

Emily escaped from domestic service by falsely telling her mistress in East Finchley that she had been called away to Hitchin by wire to attend to her brother's wife. William complained that, although he wrote a letter to his brother asking about Emily, 'I was ignored, and none of my family told me anything about her'.[59] In fact, Emily ended up back in Bedfordshire in August 1904 and became re-engaged in the straw trade. She learned velvet and felt finishing at a Luton factory (possibly one run by Mr Brown in Cheapside), residing with Rosa at her home in Langley Road. Emily's nickname among fellow workers at Richard Burley's straw hat factory in the Old Bedford Road, where she subsequently gained employment, was 'Tangerine' due to her preference for wearing that colour of trimming on her hat.[60] She was regarded as 'deep and mysterious and there were not many who made friends with her'.[61] She had the habit of taking long weekends off on her own, saying she had been 'up the Thames' or on similar trips. When asked by her supervisor to do something, 'she always had something to say for herself'.[62] At the same time, according to Rosa, 'she always kept good hours and was rarely out after ten'.[63]

Emily's reappearance at Luton appears to have brought her father back to the town. He told a journalist in September 1907:

> One day not three years ago I was at my stall in Northampton when a man came up and said he had seen my daughter Emily in Luton and she was asking where her father was. I went to Luton and found Emily in Langley-street with my sister whom she was nursing. Emily's box was nearly empty; there was only a prayer book and some pawn tickets in it. She had nothing with which to go back to service. I sent for my wife and took a house there, trying to keep in touch with Emily. The house was in High Town and while my wife was there I went back to Northampton.[64]

William appeared to blame Rosa for not looking after Emily and for allowing her box, which should have contained all her clothing and belongings to enable her to function as a servant, to be empty – its contents presumably pawned. After the murder, he chided Rosa by saying 'Why did you not know where she was?'.[65] Emily spent about five months employed as a straw-plaiter in Luton before the work became slack. She pawned her clothes before nursing Rosa through either an illness or pregnancy in November. In the early part of December 1904, she moved back to London ('ran away to London' according to her sister) with one of Rosa's stepdaughters, 18-year-old Lucy Martindale (a child of Harry's former marriage). The flight to London might have been prompted by a fight with the wife of a married man with whom Emily had supposedly been having an affair.[66] It is likely that it was at this stage that she became a prostitute if she wasn't one already – and it seems that her sister, Maud, had been working as a prostitute in London for some time[67] – but she told Rosa and others that she was earning her living from dressmaking in London.

In London, Emily initially lived at the house of a Mrs Roberts at 2 Grafton Place and plied her trade in the Euston Road, an area notorious for prostitution since at least the early 1890s. This road was perfectly positioned, with three mainline stations, King's Cross, St Pancras and Euston situated within it, bringing businessmen and other travellers with money to spend down to the capital from the north of England. In February 1892, a doctor wrote to the local parish to complain that during his rounds he had suffered 'considerable annoyance from the foreign gay women who nightly promenade from St Pancras Church to Gower Street'. He said he had made enquiries and discovered that:

> 9 out of 10 of the so-called private houses or hotels which swarm and abound on the left hand side as you walk up Euston Road from Liverpool Street, Kings Cross, to Gower Street are nothing more or less than fashionable brothels, where the gay women take gentlemen to, and pay, so I am informed from 2/6 to 3/6, 5/- and 10/- for a short time. From the corner of Judd Street to Gower St, St Pancras Church or South side, there are a large number of these gay houses.[68]

In the same month, a local chemist wrote to the Commissioner of Police complaining of the 'nuisance caused by immoral characters who infect this neighbourhood nightly. Their conduct and language being filthy in the extreme'. Another letter, posted in May 1893, from a group of twenty-nine ratepayers to the Board of Vestry of St Pancras, called attention to 'the annoyance caused to the respectable inhabitants of the district, by women of loose character who frequent this road night after night particularly between Gower Street and Endsleigh Gardens on the south side of the road, and who ply their unlawful calling in the most persistent manner possible and apparently without any check being made on them by the proper authorities'.[69] A police report from June 1893 agreed that 'a great many prostitutes frequent the neighbourhood of Euston Road'.[70]

The problem was not resolved and, in September 1900, a Metropolitan Police report recorded that Euston Road 'and in particular that portion in the vicinity of Kings Cross is now…much resorted to by prostitutes'.[71] This ongoing issue brought a complaint from St Pancras Borough Council in January 1901 to the superintendents of Tottenham Court Road and Albany Street Police Stations asking them to deal with 'the large and increasing number of disorderly houses in Euston Road and the adjacent districts, and to the numbers of women frequenting the streets of these localities for the purpose of solicitation for immoral purposes'. A further letter from the Council to the superintendent at Hunter Street Police Station in November 1901 noted that 'complaints have been received by the Borough Council recently that a considerable number of women are again making it a habit of congregating at the corners of streets abutting upon Euston Road and Tottenham Court Roads (sic) who use foul language, accost passers-by for immoral purposes and are a public nuisance'.[72]

Attempts to deal with the problem were hampered by the fact that prosecutions of those who ran brothels were traditionally the responsibility of local councils whereas prosecutions of prostitutes for their behaviour on the streets fell to the police.[73] The police believed that the councils did not want to incur the considerable expenditure of collecting the evidence necessary to prosecute brothel keepers, which would involve undercover police officers (paid for by the council) setting up observation on suspected properties for many days and nights. In September 1902, for example, an internal police report within Tottenham Court Road Station stated: 'There are without doubt a very great number of prostitutes in Tottenham Court Road vicinity and they are on the increase and there is no doubt that this is largely caused by the inaction of the Boro Council with regard to disorderly houses they having only prosecuted two brothel keepers on the sub division during the past six months although 46 suspected brothels exist in the parish of St Pancras within two minutes walk of Tottenham Court Road.'[74] The conclusion of a Hunter Street Police Station report in September 1902 was that, 'Perhaps a more aggressive policy on the part of the Council in the suppression of brothels would tend to abate the nuisance'.[75] Equally, there were no doubt suspicions among councillors that police officers, perhaps being on too friendly terms with prostitutes or their pimps, were not overly interested in dealing with the problem. Even if they wanted to take action, the difficulty for the police was that they could only charge a woman for prostitution if a witness attended at a police station and testified to having been solicited by the woman (which most men did not want to do) or an officer actually witnessed her soliciting a man in the street, which was not a simple matter to achieve. There were also jurisdictional issues due to Euston Road running through two police divisional areas (E and D Divisions) and two boroughs (St Pancras and Marylebone). Everyone blamed everyone else for not tackling the problem.

As a result, very little was done to solve the nuisance to local residents or people simply walking along Euston Road. An art dealer who ran a shop at 109 Euston Road wrote to the Chief Inspector at Scotland Yard on 27 March 1905 to draw his attention to the 'large number of prostitutes along here and consequent following of men, [which] make it impossible for any respectable woman to go out after dark, without being molested'.[76] He complained that his own wife had been harassed a couple of days earlier and no policeman could be found. In November 1905, the Reverend Herbert London, curate of Wimbledon, wrote to the Chief Commissioner of Police to inform him that his eighteen-year-old son was frequently sent on business to Euston Station during the evening but, while there, 'he is continually molested by solicitation.' The curate continued: 'I think that it is nothing short of monstrous that Euston Road should be in such a condition that it is unsafe for any young man to pass along it after dark without being exposed to this annoyance'.[77]

The authorities were spurred into action by the volume of complaints and St Pancras Borough Council became more active in funding prosecutions from 1905 onwards, usually under the supervision of Inspector Thomas Bryson of E Division. A typical operation would involve two constables watching a suspected brothel for three or four days and counting the number of couples to enter and emerge. They would also observe which women had keys to the premises or who was letting them in. If there were a large number of men and women, especially known prostitutes, seen to enter the building, a warrant would be obtained and the inspector would arrest the owner who would be brought instantly before a magistrate at the Clerkenwell Police Court. The usual punishment for a first offence would be a fine of about £20 and costs or, alternatively, a short term of imprisonment.

One of Emily Dimmock's favourite haunts along the Euston Road was a public house, originally built in 1861, called the *Rising Sun*, but known as 'Chapman's' to the locals after the landlord, Fred Chapman. He had become the licensee in 1898 and arranged for the house to be rebuilt, the work being completed in 1899. One of the attractions of the rebuilt *Rising Sun* for prostitutes and their clients would appear to be that there were now seven bedrooms in three floors above the bar. They were designated for the landlord and staff but it is likely that favoured women were allowed to take men up to a spare room, no doubt with a fee paid to the house. It is certainly the case that there was 'a private door in the bar which leads to a place of accommodation' through which prostitutes would pass.[78] This would have been very useful for women staying in lodgings who were unable to bring different men home every night without being kicked out by their landlord or landlady. The authorities appear to have suspected such things were going on; in September 1905, the Commissioner of Police made a complaint about the establishment to the St Pancras Borough Council but the council was unable to obtain evidence that the premises were being used for the purposes of prostitution so no prosecution took place.[79] Emily was on very good terms with Fred Chapman's wife, Alice, and, having purchased a sewing machine, was sometimes employed by her on dressmaking or repairing tasks.

By all accounts, Emily was a successful prostitute with many clients and, as a result, it did not take long for her to be infected with venereal disease, euphemistically known at the time as 'the disorder'. This probably accounts for a story told by her family that, at about this time, her health 'broke down' and she wrote to her brother William, a hedge trimmer in Hitchin, asking if he could accommodate her but, presumably being aware of the cause of her condition, he refused. It is known that, on 16 March 1905, Emily was admitted to the Lock Hospital, in Harrow Road, remaining there for three weeks for treatment before being discharged as an outpatient.[80] The two main forms of venereal disease were gonorrhoea and syphilis and it was noted at Emily's autopsy that she had previously suffered from syphilis but had been cured. Many prostitutes used working names to keep their real names private and Emily became known as 'Phyllis'. Whether there was any light-hearted connection between her choice of name and her disease is unknown although there is an obvious similarity between 'Syphilis' and 'Phyllis'. The only known spelling of her alternative name during her lifetime is 'Phillis' and it is not impossible that this is how she would have spelled it herself if she had ever written it down.[81] In Greek mythology, Phillis, or Phyllis, was the name of a woman who mistakenly believed she had been abandoned by her lover, Demophon, and hanged herself in despair, the gods turning her into an almond tree. It is unlikely, however, that Emily had this story in mind when she chose her new name. One modern writer has suggested the inspiration for the name might have been the then famous fourteen-year-old actress, Phyllis Dare, who had first appeared on stage aged nine in 1899, although she might have been a bit young to have been a role model for the twenty-year-old prostitute.[82] In any event, the full course of treatment for syphilis would have taken about three months and Dimmock had evidently recovered by the summer of 1905 when she was back to work while living at 64 Harrison Street, off the Gray's Inn Road. By this time, Lucy Martindale had returned to Luton; on 5 August 1905 she married 44-year-old Edward Dowsett at the Luton Register Office.

On 9 August 1905, thousands travelled to Portsmouth, Southsea and Portsea to see the combined British and French fleets uniquely on display together at Spithead for a review by King Edward VII. It must have been an extraordinary scene with so many large battleships at sea in one place. Rain, typically, fell that day but 'The weather did not stop the eager crowds who, conscious that they were in expectation of a sight rarely to be obtained, flocked in masses to all available spots from which they could view the spectacle'.[83] It is known that Emily was one of those spectators because she met George Henry Biddle, a 24-year-old signalman serving on board the ceremonial flagship, HMS Victory, at some point during the naval review.[84] Biddle was very much the love of Emily's life for the next fifteen months; she told virtually everyone she knew that she had married him in Portsmouth and took to fancifully calling herself 'Mrs Biddle'. Even her half-sister, Rosa, believed they were married, especially as Emily wore a gold wedding ring and a brooch with a sailor's knot in it. However, Biddle, who was transferred to a reserve battleship, HMS Centurion, at the end of August, was based in Portsmouth and the couple could only meet infrequently, either in Portsmouth or London, when Biddle was on leave, but that was not such a major problem for Emily, considering her lifestyle, and allowed her to continue earning money.

At about this time, Emily moved to 5 Upper Chadwell Street, Clerkenwell, and shortly thereafter, in about September 1905, to 60 Burton Crescent, off Euston Road. At Burton Crescent she became friendly with another prostitute called Gladys Warren whom she had first met in the Euston Road during the previous year. From Gladys Warren we know that one of Emily's clients at Burton Crescent was a Scotsman known only, and tautologically, as 'Scotch Jock' (or possibly, without tautology, 'Scotch Jack') who visited her regularly and generally spent the weekends with her.[85] He contracted some form of venereal disease from her, although she claimed that *he* had given it to her. Emily told Gladys that she was frightened of the man who was angry because (he claimed) she had given him the disease. Another prostitute living at Burton Crescent while Emily was there was Lillian Donaldson, also known as May Campbell, originally from Lancashire.[86] She later recalled a man known as 'Scotch Bob' with whom Emily was acquainted and said she regarded him as Emily's 'fancy man'.[87] On one occasion, Emily told her that 'Scotch Bob' had contracted 'the bad disorder from her'.

Two more clients of Emily's at Burton Crescent, Arthur Thomas Atkins and George Wright, are also both known to have caught venereal disease from her. Indeed, Atkins was still suffering from it after her death in 1907. George Wright was a conductor on a restaurant car of the Midland Railway between London and Edinburgh and used to visit Emily with a colleague, Frank Maidmont, who appears to have been a client of Gladys Warren. Emily went for treatment at the London University Hospital, recovering from the illness again, and remained at Burton Crescent until March 1906 when the landlady, Mrs Thornhill, who was evidently happy to allow Emily to use her room for prostitution, gave up the house. She moved out to 12 Belgrave Street a few weeks before Mrs Thornhill departed, leaving Gladys Warren behind. When she was gone, 'Scotch Jock' showed up asking to see her. Gladys, believing him to be a violent man, refused to reveal her friend's whereabouts and, in response, he threatened to commit an act of violence against Emily, saying that he would 'do her in' because she had given him the disorder.

The house at 12 Belgrave Street was suspected by the council of being used for prostitution from 19 March 1906 onwards and a police report dated 7 April 1906 recorded that 'Four street walkers use the house. The couples are admitted by Mary Fletcher who seems to be the occupier'.[88] It may well be that Emily was one of the four women referred to. According to May Campbell, 'Scotch Bob' continued to visit Emily at Belgrave Street.

At some point in early April, Emily moved into a house at 121 Judd Street where Gladys Warren's 22-year-old lover, William Linehan, kept a brothel in two rooms on the top two floors.[89] However, after only two or three weeks of her presence, on 26 April 1906, Linehan was arrested by Inspector Thomas Bryson, on behalf of St Pancras Borough Council, for conducting a disorderly house. The council had suspected the house was being used for prostitution since 24 February and its register of disorderly houses reveals that the police reported that 121 Judd Street was being used as a brothel 'by six street walkers'.[90] Two police officers watched the premises for six days during which time they recorded seeing fifty-one couples, men and prostitutes, enter the house and forty-seven couples leave. When arrested by Inspector Bryson, a despondent Linehan pointlessly asked: 'Why don't you have them downstairs? They are doing it now.'[91] During a hearing at Clerkenwell Police Court on 27 April before the impressively named magistrate, Edmund Charles Tennyson-d'Eyncourt, Gladys Warren gave evidence in Linehan's defence, claiming that, to her knowledge, the rooms in the property were not used for prostitution. She admitted to being a prostitute herself but said she took men to hotels, not back to Judd Street.[92] Her efforts were in vain as Linehan, who described himself as a 'music seller', was convicted and given the choice of a fine of £15 and £5 costs or two months imprisonment.[93] Not being able to pay the fine, due to 'having no goods', he went to prison.[94]

Also arrested during the raid on 121 Judd Street was a 24-year-old prostitute called Edith Webster who was suspected of running the brothel with Linehan and another man. She appeared separately at Clerkenwell Police Court and was released on her own recognisances but a measure of the type of company Emily was evidently keeping at this time can be seen in the fact that Edith Webster had been charged at Clerkenwell Police Court on 22 March 1906 with stealing a watch and chain to the value of £9, and £12 in cash, from a man called Bernard Bloom at her Judd Street residence.[95] Bloom explained to the magistrate that he had met Miss Webster at one o'clock in the morning in the Euston Road and she had taken him back to her apartment in Judd Street. Instead of the night of pleasure he was expecting, 'three fine fellows' came into his room, attacked him and stole his possessions and money. Bloom, who had presumably learnt a valuable lesson about the ladies of the Euston Road, found a constable and returned to Judd Street where Edith Webster was arrested, although the three fine fellows had escaped.[96]

On 28 April 1906, the very day after Linehan's conviction, the occupier of 12 Belgrave Street, Mrs Alice Mary Fletcher, was convicted at Clerkenwell Police Court of running a disorderly house and fined £5 and £5 costs.[97] Like William Linehan, she had been arrested by Inspector Bryson.[98] That might have been a coincidence but both Linehan and Gladys believed that Emily's indiscreet habit of openly bringing men back to the house was responsible for alerting the police to the activities in 121 Judd Street.[99] Consequently, Gladys fell out with

Emily who thus moved out from Judd Street in May 1906 to a residence at 1 Bidborough Street.

By this stage, Emily had made enough money to purchase furniture in instalments from the Royal Furnishing Company in Essex Road, Islington, enabling her to furnish a bedsitting room in the front parlour on the second floor.[100] William Linehan had submitted to the furniture company a reference on her behalf (presumably before his arrest). While she was living at Bidborough Street, the lease was taken by a former New Zealand criminal, now working as a bricklayer, called Jack Crabtree, who was 44 years old and who was, according to one account: 'Short, squarely built, with fair, rough hair, shaggy eyebrows and loose lips'.[101] According to Crabtree, Emily was frequently visited by a man, whose name he did not know, who beat her up and once took her purse. According to Crabtree's wife, this man was called 'Tom' (although Crabtree would refer to him as 'Scottie'). Crabtree later told police that he heard this man tell Emily that he would 'do her in' and cut her throat for giving him 'the disease'. Despite this, he recalled Emily presenting the man with a silver watch and gold chain as a birthday present.

At the end of June, Crabtree took the lease on a lodging house at 13 Manchester Street and, no doubt because he was happy to accommodate working girls, Emily moved there with him. Another sailor (not Biddle) who had stayed a few nights with Emily at Bidborough Street, helped her move in and put her room straight. Yet another man called for her and advised her not to have anything to do with soldiers or sailors because she might get 'the disorder' from the likes of them. This man also mentioned, with apparent distaste, someone he called 'Big Jumbo', a soldier in the Grenadier Guards, with whom Emily had formed a relationship. He was known as 'Jumbo' Hurst (so-called because he was a little over six foot two inches tall) and, at one point, Emily took him to Luton to meet her half-sister, Rosa, who, believing she was married to Biddle, was shocked at her behaviour.[102] She told her: 'You will play the game with these fellows once too often. You will be murdered if anyone lives to see it'.[103] Rosa could see that Jumbo was a jealous man but Emily appears to have enjoyed toying with his emotions, as with those of other men. Rosa was also aware that Emily wrote to Biddle to say she was enjoying her holiday in Luton with her sister, omitting to mention that she was there with Jumbo. Whilst in Luton, Emily and Jumbo stayed together in a house in Park Street.

Back in London, while Emily was living in Manchester Street, Crabtree was working as a bricklayer on a new building in the Strand for the *Morning Post*. He was employed on the night shift and normally started work at 6:30pm. One evening, however, as he would later tell the police, he was unable to do any work because of heavy rain which had flooded the foundations so he returned home early, arriving back at 7:30pm. If Crabtree's memory was correct, he must have been referring to Friday, 29 June 1906 when an exceptionally violent torrential downpour had arrived over London during the early hours and continued throughout the day.[104] As he entered his house, Crabtree saw a man walking down the stairs from the direction of Emily's room on the first floor. It was the same man who had told Emily not to have anything to do with soldiers or sailors. He says the man caught sight of him and went down to the kitchen in the basement. Crabtree says Emily came down and caught the man by the sleeve as he was negotiating the basement stairs, following which they had a quarrel. Crabtree gained the impression that the man had taken something belonging to Emily because she was saying 'Give it to me then'. He went into the kitchen where Emily was crying and asked her, 'What's all this trouble about?' His wife, who was in the kitchen, told him, 'This man says he has slept with Miss Dimmock on several occasions and that she is only a prostitute'. He also heard the man calling her a whore. Rather dubiously, Crabtree claimed that, until this time, he was unaware that Emily was 'a woman of ill fame', as he put it. A few weeks later, he was doing some work at King's Cross Station and had to leave early in the morning. Before he departed, Emily called him into her room and he saw her in bed with the same man from the kitchen. She asked him if he would pawn a silver cigarette case on her behalf. Crabtree took it in his hand and saw it had a monogram in the centre. Suspecting it was stolen, he asked the man, 'Is this your initials?' to which the man replied, 'Yes'. Crabtree said, 'It's alright, it's yours then' and was prepared to pawn it but the man changed his mind and said he would deal with it himself. Later that evening, Emily told Crabtree that she had, in fact, pawned it.

In late July, Emily went to Portsmouth to see Biddle. While she was away, Scottie called for her. Crabtree recalled that Scottie, 'finding she was gone got very angry swore about her and threatened to do for her' saying that she 'had given him the bad disorder, had ruined him for life', that he was unable to do or get any work in consequence and that 'no one knew how he had suffered [and] that the pain was excruciating'. Also, according to Crabtree:

> He wanted to go into her room and when I would not let him, he produced a razor and opened it and took his handkerchief from his pocket wrapped it around the handle of the razor and waving it about said he would do her in yet I have frequently heard him ask her for money which she has always found for him, at times borrowing it from me.[105]

Crabtree claimed that, on 29 July, he lent Emily ten shillings but then watched her walk down the street and hand the money straight over to Scottie. In an apparently unrelated development, two days later, on 31 July, Crabtree and his wife were arrested by Inspector Thomas Bryson and taken swiftly to Clerkenwell Police Court where they were charged that same day with managing a brothel.[106] The police had been keeping 13 Manchester Street under observation on behalf of the St Pancras Borough Council, which initiated the prosecution, for three days – 27, 28 and 29 July – during which time ninety-one couples had been seen to enter the premises, with some women being seen to go in with different men. Emily was probably one of these women. When Crabtree was told by Inspector Bryson that he was being arrested for keeping a disorderly house, he replied: 'What if I am? We are not the only people in the neighbourhood doing it.'[107] During the hearing at the police court, however, Crabtree denied saying this and put the blame on his lodgers, Mr and Mrs Martin, whom, he claimed, were bringing people into his house without his knowledge. He said he found out on 27 July that they were using his house for immoral purposes and, after trying to stop them, turned them out. He was not believed and was found guilty of the offence, being sentenced by the magistrate, James Reader White Bros, to three months in prison although, as he was on early release from prison from an earlier sentence, his licence was revoked and he would actually spend almost ten months behind bars for the offence. His wife was also convicted and fined £5 with £5 costs.

Emily then moved to 28 Gower Place but not before purloining from Manchester Street a curtain pole and curtains belonging to Crabtree, now safely out of the way in prison. She remained at Gower Place until October 1906. The landlady there was a Mrs Bromley who was told by Emily that her husband was a sailor about to leave for Malta and would be away for two years. This was Biddle who had joined the battleship, HMS Prince of Wales, at the end of May. It was set to sail for Malta in November 1906 and would not return to England until December 1908.[108] Emily explained that, when he returned, they were going to take a small business but in the meantime she would support herself by dressmaking. It was usual for prostitutes to formulate a cover story to explain to their respectable landlords and landladies how they earned a living. Laundress, seamstress, machinist, dressmaker etc. were all common occupations offered up. Seeing that Emily possessed a sewing machine, Mrs Bromley believed what she was told and noted that Emily once received a letter bearing a Portsmouth postmark which seemed to bear out her story of being married to a sailor. Emily took a back room in the house and furnished it herself. According to Mrs Bromley, Emily frequently left the house at noon and did not return until late at night. One day, a cab drew up at the door and a man who bore some facial resemblance to Emily stepped out and was introduced as her brother. She said they were going down to Portsmouth to meet her husband and see him off to Malta. She took her luggage with her and was gone a week. Shortly after her return, she came home late one night with a well dressed, clean shaven, man who looked about twenty-four years old. Mrs Bromley, a respectable woman, refused to allow the man into her house, despite Emily claiming that this was her husband. Mrs Bromley could tell that the man was not a sailor and could thus not be Mr Biddle. The next day, now suspicious that Emily was a prostitute, Mrs Bromley gave her lodger notice to leave and Emily moved back to where she started at 2 Grafton Place.[109]

It is known that, on 9 November 1906, Emily and another girl, who also said her surname was Dimmock (possibly one of her sisters), had their photographs taken at a studio in King's Cross.[110] A few days later they called at the same studio and asked the photographer if he had a sailor's outfit that they could be snapped in. Given that Biddle was about to sail for Malta, which he did on 14 November, it looks like Emily was trying to get a photograph taken to send to him as a keepsake.[111] The photographer said he did not have a sailor's outfit but Emily told him they would borrow one from a man they knew. The girls returned to the shop with a sailor's cap and jumper and were each photographed with the hat while also wearing the jumper over their blouses.[112] The sailor's cap bore the name of the ship, HMS Prince of Wales, which suggests they borrowed Biddle's.[113] But Emily's relationship with the sailor was not to last much longer. It was a familiar story; Biddle was extremely unhappy to find himself suffering from 'the disorder' which he had obviously caught earlier in the year from Emily.[114] He was, in any event, now at sea so that particular relationship was over.

There were plenty of other men for Emily though. While plying her trade in the *Rising Sun* during 1905 she had met a young chap of only 18 years of age, originally from Northampton, who worked as a cook in restaurant cars for the Midland Railway called Bertram Shaw, known as 'Bert' and quite possibly also as 'Bertie'.[115] He was 'a slightly-built, fair man, of medium height, with a pale, thin face and a moustache which is only just perceptible,' and, initially a regular client, he now became her new sweetheart.[116] Emily herself was a tall, slender, attractive young woman with dark brown hair. Those who knew her described her as 'bright and lively' and 'merry and good natured' with 'a pleasing face and quite nice manners'.[117] She was always smartly dressed, usually in her favourite green outfit and pink hat (having evidently discarded her tangerine one), and was said to have 'a sort of rough refinement', being able to hold her own in conversation with those of more education.

On 7 January 1907, the newly formed couple moved away from Euston Road to new lodgings at 50 Great College Street in Camden Town.[118] Emily now claimed to the landlady, Mrs Eliza Maw, that Bert was her husband; she had stopped being 'Mrs Biddle' and had taken to calling herself 'Mrs Shaw'. By doing so, of course, she was taking after her mother who had simply called herself 'Mrs Skillin' before becoming 'Mrs Dimmock', despite the apparent absence of any wedding in either case. To bolster her respectable credentials, Emily told Mrs Maw that her sister, Rebecca Maud, was married to a police officer called Charles Coleman. This was true. The marriage ceremony had taken place on 2 September 1906 in East Finchley, although Coleman, then a gardener, did not join the Metropolitan Police until three months later and the couple now lived in Putney.[119] Mrs Maw recalled Emily as being of 'a very lively disposition, and often played on the piano'.[120] She also had a habit of singing during the day. Her hobby was collecting postcards and she had an album full of them, often sent to her by male admirers.

Meanwhile, a young man turned up at 2 Grafton Place and inquired after Emily. As Mrs Roberts later told a journalist for the *Daily Mail*, she recognised him as a man who had visited Emily one day in November 1906 and taken her for a motor ride.[121] When Mrs Roberts told him that Emily had left her house and married a young man named Shaw (as she believed was the case), he angrily replied: 'That cannot be so, for she is married to a sailor. But if she is living with Shaw I'll find her out, if it takes me years. She has ruined me and I'll do for her.' He repeatedly pressed Mrs Roberts to give her the new address but, as Emily had asked Mrs Roberts not to tell anybody where she was living, she did not reveal it. After the man left, Mrs Roberts met Emily and informed her of the man's threats but Emily laughed and appeared to treat the matter as a joke, as was her manner.

On Easter Sunday (31 March 1907), Emily's brother Henry, a plasterer's labourer living in Luton, visited her in Great College Street. He believed Shaw was engaged to his sister. He thought him to be 'a nice gentlemanly fellow' and felt that the couple were 'much attracted to each other'.[122] Unlike Rosa, he knew that his sister was not married to Biddle although he had heard talk towards the end of 1906 that they would wed. Henry would later tell a reporter that he was invited to his sister's wedding to Shaw (by his other sister, Maud) but never attended and, not having heard anything more about it, assumed that the ceremony had taken place as planned.

A strange incident occurred on 20 May 1907 according to a woman who also lodged at Mrs Maw's lodgings in Great College Street. This was a Mrs Houpsman who said that the woman she knew as Mrs Shaw received a telegram from a man she referred to as 'Uncle' which announced that he would be visiting that evening. On reading it, Emily said, 'Oh what a nuisance, my uncle is coming'.[123] When he arrived and knocked at the door, Mrs Houpsman opened it to find an 'elderly' man, of about fifty, with a beard, moustache and whiskers but was surprised that, when she asked his name, he made no reply but brushed past her and walked straight upstairs to Emily. She thought his behaviour uncouth but Emily told her that he was a man of education with plenty of money, and he certainly played the piano beautifully. He spent about an hour with Emily before leaving with her, presenting her with a sovereign as he always did at the end of his visits.[124] Shortly afterwards, Emily and Shaw were forced to move out of Great College Street after one of the residents, possibly Mrs Maw's husband, Frank, a policeman, saw Emily taking men into her room.[125] However, Mrs Maw would later inform journalists that the couple told her that they were moving because they were going to take a friend of Shaw's, who worked on the railway, as a lodger and therefore required a third room. In any event, they transferred to a 'barracks like' model dwelling at 27 St Pancras Square.

Even stranger events were to occur in Emily's life after Jack Crabtree was released from prison on 24 May 1907. One of the first things he did was to go looking for her in order to retrieve his curtain pole and the money she owed him. It wasn't difficult to find her in the Euston Road and, as he later told the police, he observed her meet a man and take him to the rear of St Pancras Station where they engaged in outdoor sexual intercourse. When they parted, Crabtree saw Emily meet Scottie in the Euston Road and give him something (presumably money) from her purse. She then parted from him and met Bert Shaw; according to Crabtree she took his arm and they walked together to a building at St Pancras Square. The following morning, Crabtree paid a visit to the superintendent of the building, John Bucknall, and found out from him the number of the flat in which Emily and Bert were living. Not one to miss an opportunity, Crabtree informed Mr Bucknall about Emily's character and the superintendent said he would put the couple out at the weekend. Then Crabtree and his wife went to Emily's room and demanded the return of the articles she had taken from him, some of which she returned on the spot. She also promised to repay the money she owed him. After leaving her room and being suspicious of her intent, Crabtree kept observation on the premises and, while doing so, saw Scottie with another man also watching the building. Crabtree gave a boy sixpence to follow the two men but had foolishly made no arrangements to meet him afterwards and could not find him again.

The money Emily had promised to repay Crabtree was not immediately forthcoming so he continued to stalk her in the Euston Road. As she and Shaw had been asked to leave St Pancras Buildings, due to his own actions, he did not now know where she lived but, with his wife assisting him, he tracked her down in the Euston Road again, after the pubs had closed, one Sunday night. She was with the same man he had seen in his basement kitchen back in June. Crabtree approached her and asked for the return of his money. Emily ignored him and walked off with her male companion to St Pancras Station then disappeared into the lavatories while her companion walked through the station. Crabtree's wife went into the ladies' toilet and found Emily hiding behind the door. Emily then went out into the street and caught a bus to Tottenham Court Road with Crabtree following on the same bus. She alighted from the bus at Tottenham Court Road and walked down into a tube station but then came straight out and boarded another bus going back to King's Cross where she joined up with her male friend again. They remained talking for a few minutes but seeing Crabtree was still waiting they boarded another bus with Emily inside the lower deck and the man on top. A determined Crabtree followed them onto the bus and sat opposite Emily. They all travelled as far as the Seven Sisters Road in Holloway where they alighted. Emily and her friend, now totally frustrated at their inability to shake off their pursuer, wanted to give Crabtree into custody to a constable on duty. Emily told the officer that Crabtree was a 'ticket of leave' man (on early release from prison) who was annoying her. The constable, after listening to what both sides had to say, advised Emily to give Crabtree her address so that he would leave her alone for now but Crabtree said there was no point because she would only provide a false one. He told the police officer that he would follow her at a respectable distance and not molest or interfere with her. The constable decided he had no jurisdiction over the matter and left them to it, so Emily and her companion walked over to a coffee stall where they had a cup of coffee before dashing into a hansom cab which drove off, leaving Crabtree behind.

Crabtree, however, would not be defeated. Having discovered that Shaw worked for the Midland Railway he went to see his manager who told him which train Shaw would arrive on. Crabtree waited for it to come in but somehow missed him. Undeterred, he left a note for Shaw, with his address, on a piece of paper supplied by a clerk at the office of the Midland Railway. This resulted in Bert and Emily visiting him at his home where they finally came to an agreement that Crabtree would be repaid in instalments. After this, Crabtree saw Emily frequently in the Euston Road talking to Scottie. On one occasion, when standing with Emily at the corner of Judd Street, he and Emily both saw Scottie walk past with a girl on his arm and Emily became agitated, saying she had a good mind to go up and tear his hat off. Crabtree persuaded her to take no notice, to which she replied, 'Just fancy and I am keeping him'. On another occasion, Emily said to Crabtree (whom she referred to as 'father'): 'Come on and have a drink father to show there is no ill feeling' and he joined her in the *Rising Sun* for a cider. As he left the public house, he bumped into Scottie who asked him if 'the old cow' was inside.

There was yet further contact between Emily and Crabtree (according to Crabtree). She asked if she could speak to him for some fatherly advice and they met by arrangement one day near the Agricultural Hall in Islington. Emily showed Crabtree some letters she had received from a male lover in which she was being asked to leave Shaw and live with him instead because Shaw did not earn enough to keep her. Emily asked Crabtree whether she should leave Shaw; she said she did not really want to because he was very kind and had been good to her whilst she was bad but she was getting tired of the life she was leading in Euston Road and could not live on Shaw's wages. Crabtree's advice is not known but he saw Emily again a few nights later when she said she had torn up all the other man's letters and had decided she was not going to have anything more to do with him.

During July 1907, Emily and Bert moved back to Camden Town, taking two rooms on the raised ground floor at 29 St Paul's Road for eight shillings a week. The rooms consisted of a sitting room, or parlour, at the front of the house and a bedroom in the back room, also used as a kitchen and bathroom, which was separated from the front room by folding doors. Both the front room and the bedroom could be entered by separate doors from the passage on the ground floor. The house, as described by the *Pall Mall Gazette*, was 'semi-detached, with a little front garden and a tree that half conceals a window, with green shutters'.[126] The landlady was Mrs Sarah Ann Stocks, a small 27-year-old woman from Peterborough, married to a railway train carriage cleaner, George William Stocks, who was five years older than her. They lived in rooms on the first floor of the house, and other rooms in the basement, with their two little boys, Charles and George. Mrs Stocks believed that Bert and Emily were newly married; she inspected their rent book which seemed to be in order and had no reason to think that they were anything other than a respectable married couple. She asked Bert why they had left their previous lodgings and he told her that they couldn't stand the noise made by children at that residence, which was, of course, a lie. During the bank holiday weekend at the start of August 1907, Emily and Bert visited Shaw's parents in Northampton – again as Mr and Mrs Shaw – and attended the wedding of Bert's twenty-seven-year-old sister, Ethel, at the Church of St Matthew, on Saturday 3 August. According to Mrs Shaw, Emily was 'a very nice girl, and we all liked her'.[127]

By this time, Bert, who had been working mainly during the day, was assigned the evening train to Sheffield, requiring him to stay overnight in that town, leaving Emily alone in London. This allowed Emily plenty of opportunities to liaise with other men.[128] One such was a 26-year-old unemployed ballroom tent builder of 'irregular habits' called Arthur Harrap who lived with his two married sisters at 61 Arlington Road in Camden Town.[129] Emily visited Harrap in Arlington Road and, equally, Harrap shared Emily's bed at 29 St Paul's Road on at least one occasion at the end of August 1907. It is clear that Harrap was an intensely jealous man who became very attracted to Emily. Maud Coleman, Emily's sister, was told by Emily that Harrap had said to her that if he could not have her then 'no-one else should'.[130]

Harrap was not the only man to take advantage of Bert Shaw's night-time absences. When Robert Percival Roberts, a ship's cook of around 30 years old, who had been paid off in Swansea following a three-month tour of duty at the end of August, and was thus flush with cash when he arrived in London in September, met Emily in the Euston Road during the evening of Sunday 8 September, there was nothing to prevent him being taken to Emily's bedroom after buying her drinks in the *Rising Sun*.[131] He was a 'smooth, light-haired man with a slight moustache' and Emily would not have found his appearance objectionable.[132] They travelled by tram from Euston to Camden Town Railway Station and walked from there to St Paul's Road, arriving at about midnight. Emily opened the front door with her latchkey and they entered the house. Roberts was asked to be careful not to make any noise. He was taken into Emily's front parlour which was fitted up as a sitting room and Emily quietly locked the door after they entered with a key which was on the inside of the door. She then led him into the back room which served as her bedroom. He stayed the night and left at about 7:00am on the Monday morning. Emily's services cost him fourteen shillings (two more than Emily actually asked for) and were evidently satisfactory because he was back, looking for her, in the *Rising Sun* at 6:00pm the following evening. He had to wait for some two and a half hours for her arrival because she walked in at about 8:30pm. Roberts was hoping to secure her company for the entire evening but, to his disappointment, after initially speaking to her when she came in, she approached another man who bought her a drink.

Roberts noticed that this other man was about five foot eight inches in height, clean shaven and dark haired with 'a very long thin face and a scowling expression'. He thought he had some pimples on the lower part of his face. He estimated that he was about 23 or 24 years of age. This man was Robert Thomas George William Wood who was, in fact, 30 years old, having recently celebrated his thirtieth birthday.

A contemporary sketch
of Bert Shaw

Emily Dimmock

Chapter Three

Enter the Man Hunted

'This slim young fellow…with his long, delicate hands and tapering fingers, with his deep-set, cavernous eyes and glistening eye-balls, his high cheek bones, his broad mouth with its twitching lips.'

Hall Caine, describing Robert Wood, *Daily Mail*, 20 December 1907

Robert Wood was, in many ways, a regular guy. He liked cricket and football – supporting Fulham, newly promoted to the then Second Division – enjoyed the company of women, smoked Egyptian cigarettes, played billiards, drank beer and seemed to be well liked by those who knew him. In other ways, he was quite extraordinary; the man was a remarkably talented artist, with what might be said to be an artistic personality, not quite of the world but above and far beyond it.

He was born in Edinburgh on 17 August 1877.[133] His father, George, was a compositor for the *Scotsman* newspaper who had married Margaret Cavers, a domestic servant, in June 1861, but she had died in June 1880, aged 37, of pulmonary tuberculosis, or consumption of the lung, when Robert was only two years old.[134] Nevertheless, Robert always had an image of his mother as 'a handsome woman, of great charm, culture and talent'.[135] In her memory, Robert at some point added 'Cavers' as one of his middle names; he would later refer to himself as Robert William Thomas George Cavers Wood, or sometimes just Robert Cavers Wood, but this was not how he was named on the register of births in the Edinburgh district of St Andrew. When he was a baby, Robert's hand was accidentally burnt, causing his little finger to be permanently crooked and useless while his third finger was damaged and scarred. Self-conscious of this in later life, he tended to wear a glove or hide his left hand in his pocket.[136] Before he was born, Robert's parents had lost five children through illness, with the most recent death, that of six-year-old George Thomas Wood, having been on 20 July 1877, less than a month before Robert's birth. He did, however, have one surviving older brother, Charles Carlyle Wood, and George left Edinburgh, taking both boys to London (St Pancras) in 1881 along with their nursemaid, Mary Hogg, who George made his second wife.[137] Prior to leaving Scotland, George had supplemented his income with a touch of journalism by writing some sports book reviews (he obviously had a passion for sport like his son) along with the odd obituary for the *Scotsman*[138] (and Robert always preferred to describe his father as a journalist) but in London he reverted to being solely a compositor, working for Spottiswoode & Co based at New Street Square, off Fetter Lane.[139] In May 1889, when the Woods were living at 39 Tonbridge Street, St Pancras, Mary gave birth to James George, a half-brother to Robert and Charles.

Virtually everything that is known about Robert Wood's life in London comes from his own accounts, as told in two separate articles for the *Evening News* and *Weekly Dispatch* after his trial in December 1907. He said that 'at the usual early age' he was 'packed off' to 'Thanet Church School' by which he was referring to the local Thanet Street National School for Boys.[140] It did not take boarders; all its pupils, including Wood, lived with their parents at home. The school, situated in Burton Crescent, near Judd Street, was opened in May 1873 but faced a number of challenges, including lack of proper text books, and children who could neither read nor write. The headmaster's log book for 5 May 1873 states: 'I find it deplorable that many of the scholars are in a deplorable state, as to the first rudiments of education some of them are unacquainted with the letters of the alphabet, have no notion of writing of figures'.[141] Robert presumably started at the school at the age of six, in 1883, although the admissions records for this period have not survived. One of his teachers might have been a Mr Flinders who, according to the headmaster, writing in the log book in June 1885, 'so frequently takes the corporal punishment of the scholars into his own hands that it causes many troubles with the parents'.[142] Robert, however, claimed that he never got into any serious trouble at school and that both masters and pupils liked him. In fact, he described himself as 'exceedingly popular'.[143]

A government inspector's report in January 1886 found the condition of the school as 'very unsatisfactory' with 'faults of discipline, instruction and registration' but things changed quickly with the appointment of a new headmaster, William Cleaver, in July 1889 and, very early in his tenure, a report of the diocesan inspector noted that 'Mr Cleaver's skilled and able teaching has at once produced a complete change in this school…The school is now excellent, the order being perfect and the boys throughout the school are thoroughly interested in their work'.[144] Although Mr Cleaver had improved the boys' behaviour, that of the masters was not always beyond reproach. John Thomas Ward, a teacher at the school, made an appearance at Westminster Magistrate's Court in October 1889 on a charge of threatening to cut his wife's throat following a dispute caused by the fact that she had allowed their lodger ('a well known actor') to owe fifty shillings in back rent.[145] He was quickly replaced.

The boys at Thanet Street school were taught reading, writing, arithmetic, scripture, geography, music and poetry but an entry in the headmaster's log book of 16 October 1890 records that the school 'commenced teaching drawing' on that day and, according to Robert, it was his skill at drawing (which he believed he had inherited from his mother) that ensured he won the highest prize in the school for all-round ability and good conduct. It is possible this was awarded on 17 December 1891 when the vicar distributed the prizes and certificates for that year.[146] At this time, Robert would have been fourteen years old and, having passed the highest standard – there being seven standards for the boys to attain – he says he left the school and was introduced by the headmaster (presumably Mr Cleaver), to a friend of his, Dr Wilfred Kent Hughes, an Australian surgeon then employed at St Bartholomew's Hospital. Dr Kent Hughes had helped form the Australasian Students' Club on an informal basis in 1889 and then formally in 1891. It was designed for the growing number of students from Australia and New Zealand who were then studying subjects such as law and medicine at universities in England.[147] Its aim was to allow them to 'keep in touch with each other and have a definite meeting place' where they could benefit from an 'interchange of experiences'.[148] Wood took employment at the club which was based at New Stone Buildings in Chancery Lane. In his later newspaper account, he did not specify the exact nature of his job, saying only that his duties were 'not arduous' and that he had little to do, but it has been assumed by later writers that he was a steward and this is probably correct, although Wood also says that he was 'greatly trusted with money' suggesting that he might have assisted the club's treasurer.

The finances of running a club for Australasian students in central London during the 1890s were tight. In early 1892 the club only had forty members, each paying an annual subscription of two guineas, making a total income of £202, but the rental for the club's room at Chancery Lane was £100 a year which did not leave a great deal for salaries and other expenses.[149] As a result, it relied on donations from wealthy Australians for its continued existence. The Australian newspaper, the *Advertiser* of 22 March 1892, was sceptical about the club's prospects of survival, noting that, of half a dozen Anglo-Colonial clubs which had started in England during the previous decade, none had lasted more than a year. The newspaper felt that the long-existing Colonial Institute took care of most needs of visitors from Australia. However, membership of the club increased to seventy-six by the summer of 1892 and it seemed like Dr Kent Hughes' club might buck the trend. Unfortunately, however, a banking crisis in Australia erupted in the spring of 1893, when the accounts of the Anglo-Australian Bank were found to be untrue, and Charles Staples, the bank's managing director, was convicted of fraudulent conduct and sentenced to five years imprisonment, with the bank's auditor and its accountant also receiving prison sentences. More bank suspensions followed causing the Australian economy to collapse and the London club could not survive. Dr Kent Hughes returned to Australia at the end of 1893.

Wood obviously needed another job. Whilst working at the club he had been studying art and doing anatomical related drawings, presumably for Australasian medical students. He claimed to have met the Islington born artist and war correspondent, Frederic Villiers, but never explained in what capacity. When his brother drew his attention to an advertisement placed by John Richard Corsan, the proprietor of a glass decoration company called The London Sand Blast Works, requesting a youth with artistic ability, Wood applied for the job and was accepted after impressing Mr Corsan with his original artwork. He initially earned a few shillings a week designing for glass but was soon promoted to figure work, art decoration and designing posters and advertisements, providing him with a better salary. At the same time, he submitted a series of humorous sketches to a comic paper and was delighted to receive a cheque for more than twenty-two shillings when they were accepted and published. However, although he created a few more sketches for publication and was apparently asked to do more, he let the opportunity pass him by. In his own words: 'it is part of my temperament to let things drift. Sometimes I am overcome by a feeling of inertia. What does anything matter?'[150] In about 1894, when he was seventeen, William Morris supposedly expressed an interest in seeing his work and Wood took a few specimens to him at his office while he was engaged in designing a carpet. The great artist, who was then about sixty years old, spoke encouragingly to Wood, giving him some advice and there was apparently some talk of Wood assisting him but it came to nothing.

By his own account, Wood went on to lead a bohemian lifestyle as a young man, staying out late at night and making friends everywhere 'regardless of their station in life'.[151] He met a slim, pretty, young woman called Ruby Young one evening in 1904 as she was crossing the Euston Road, near the tube station. According to Ruby, by her own later account of the meeting: 'He was crossing the road at the same moment and evidently looked back at me; for, a few seconds after, he turned back and was at my side speaking to me.'[152] Wood, interested, bluffed that he thought he knew her from somewhere but Ruby, in her 'pleasant, musical voice' told him he was mistaken.[153] Nevertheless, the introduction having been made, Wood asked Ruby to join him for a glass of wine and they walked over to the nearby *Rising Sun* where they got on so well that a three-year relationship commenced, with the couple meeting up almost every day. They did what lovers do: went for walks, spent evenings at the music halls and theatres and frequently went rowing together, an activity they both enjoyed. Sometimes Ruby, who lived in Liverpool Street, near King's Cross Station, would visit for tea at Wood's house, 129 King's Cross Road, where he lived with his father, stepmother and stepbrother before they all moved to nearby 12 Frederick Street, but usually the lovers would go out to tea shops and restaurants together. As gifts, Wood bought Ruby a small white English fox-terrier puppy, which she called 'Prince', and a little black kitten she named 'Sweep'. He liked to use her as a model for his drawings: 'I was never tired of sketching her', he told the *Weekly Dispatch*, 'She inspired me, she appealed to me. Her features lent themselves to my artistic perception and mine was fired'.[154] Ruby was proud of being an artist's model and this is how she would describe herself, claiming to have a number of 'artist patrons' who would employ her. Wood regarded his time with Ruby as 'happy days', full of laughter, and referred to her as 'the girl I loved best in the world, a girl who had an indescribable influence over me, for whom I would have done anything'. At one point, early in their relationship, Ruby said to Wood, 'Bob, if there is anything that I can do for you at any time to show you that I love you, just tell me, and I will do it for you'. Although she could not have known it at the time, Wood would indeed ask her to prove her love for him one day – and ruin her entire life in the process.

Christmas of 1906 was spent together but their meetings became less frequent after Ruby moved out from the King's Cross area to Earl's Court on 21 January 1907. Nevertheless, they would still see each other once or twice a week; Ruby would visit Wood at his workplace at lunchtime or meet him in the evening. On Saturday afternoon, after watching Fulham at nearby Craven Cottage, Wood would take the opportunity to visit his sweetheart at her new lodgings. As a sign of his continuing affection, he presented her with a ring which had previously been worn by his stepmother who had died of heart failure in the St Pancras Infirmary at the age of fifty on 14 February 1907. Ruby understood this to be an engagement ring but the relationship came to an abrupt end in July when she heard that Wood had been living for a fortnight with a friend of hers called Pansy. According to Wood, Pansy 'certainly had a very fine figure' and he was 'an immediate appreciator of her attractions' which he was evidently unable to resist.[155] Understandably, Ruby was not too happy about this and effectively broke off the relationship, although Wood would claim, nonchalantly, and somewhat coldly, that she was not away long enough for him to notice her absence.

In August, Wood went to Bruges for his annual holiday and it was there that he bought a number of postcards, some of which he posted to friends, including Ruby, and the remainder of which he brought back with him to England. Shortly after his return, he met Ruby accidentally in Cranbourn Street, near Leicester Square. She asked about his holiday and they walked together for about half an hour but parted without their former relations being restored.[156]

Overshadowing their relationship was the fact that Ruby was a prostitute who had been convicted at Marlborough Street Police Court for soliciting. In a 1908 letter to the editor of *Reynolds's Newspaper*, Ruby explained that this arose because she stopped to look at a broken down motor bus while walking home down Regent Street. A man asked her what had happened and she naturally told him what she knew. She then walked to Piccadilly to catch a bus, at which point she was stopped by a police constable who said he had seen her talking to a man and instructed her to accompany him to Marlborough Street Police Station. Ruby protested that she had only been replying to the man's question but it was to no avail and the next morning she found herself in court, crying, without, she claimed, knowing what was happening. Told that she must pay a fine of twenty shillings or go to prison, a friend of hers covered the fine and she put it all down to experience. It was an unlikely story but not one that was completely beyond the bounds of credibility. In June 1906, a notorious and well publicised incident had occurred after a police constable arrested Ellen Hitchcock, a 28-year-old married woman who lived in Camden Town, and charged her at Highbury Police Station with behaving in a disorderly manner and using obscene language in Upper Street, Islington. The constable claimed he had seen Mrs Hitchcock speak to three different men – itself enough for a woman to be arrested at that time – and that when he cautioned her she used 'a foul expression'. She claimed before the magistrate at Clerkenwell Police Court that just one man had stopped to speak to her and that he was an old friend, recently returned from India, where he had been for four years. When she tried to explain this to the constable he simply took her to the police station. In normal circumstances, Mrs Hitchcock would have been convicted of disorderly conduct on the word of the officer alone but it just so happened that her arrest had been witnessed by a local councillor walking back home from the National Liberal Club with two of his friends, one of whom was a member of the London County Council, while the other was the election agent to the local member of parliament. All three men gave evidence that they heard the police officer tell Mrs Hitchcock that he was arresting her for accosting men and that, despite Mrs Hitchcock replying in a quiet, civil way, he violently marched her off to the station, shaking her from one side of the pavement to the other in a bullying manner. A letter was also provided to the magistrate by the man to whom Mrs Hitchcock spoke in the street, corroborating her story. Mr D'Eyncourt, the magistrate, decided that the constable had made a mistake of the type 'constables were apt to make', acting hastily and using unnecessary force. The case was dismissed and a question was raised in the House of Commons about the issue by the M.P. for Islington on 9 July 1906.

So Ruby's explanation for her conviction was not entirely unbelievable but she would privately admit to the police that she sometimes led 'an irregular life' and police inquiries revealed that she solicited in Piccadilly, Charing Cross and Leicester Square. Wood said that Ruby admitted to him that she was a prostitute in about 1905 after having denied it 'consistently and persistently'.[157] He said his reaction was that he felt 'heartily sorry' for her and tried to get her some commercial work, or a position as a hospital nurse (which she had previously been in Liverpool), but was unsuccessful. Despite Wood's account, the suspicion must be that Wood met Ruby in the Euston Road while she was working as a prostitute and that he very well knew her line of work from the start. However, both Ruby and Wood independently tell us that the first meeting was innocent and, while they both would have had their reasons for wanting to do so, there is no evidence to contradict them.

It took a lot for George Wood to miss work through illness. The only time he had ever taken any substantial sick leave was in early 1868 when he broke his jaw bone, the result of a violent storm in Edinburgh which threw him against some railing spikes, one of which became impaled in his neck.[158] He was then off work for four weeks.[159] On Monday, 9 September 1907, Mr Wood, now seventy years old, had an attack of gouty eczema in his foot and, in great pain, not being able to stand, was forced to leave work early and take to bed at home. Later that evening, his son, Robert, entered the *Rising Sun*. Emily was not there and he asked two of her friends, Florence Smith and Ellen Lawrence, if they had seen her but they said they had not. Florence Smith asked him, 'Are you going to treat us?' and he graciously bought them drinks, saying in jest, 'Don't tell Phyllis, she might be jealous'. When Emily appeared about half an hour later, she walked straight to a musical box at the bar, probably an automatic piano.[160] Automatic pianos were shaped like ordinary pianos and were popular in public houses at the time, being set in motion by the dropping of a penny in a slot to play a selection of popular tunes.[161] Emily asked Wood for a penny to put in the machine; he gave her the coin and the two of them chatted for about forty-five minutes. Wood found the conversation agreeable, believing that his companion had 'some intelligence'.[162] Robert Roberts, who, despite suffering from a slight cold, for which he had purchased some ammoniated tincture of quinine from a chemist across the road, had been waiting patiently for Emily's arrival in order to enjoy another night of pleasure with her, stared hard at Wood, wondering who he was, and Wood stared hard back. Wood bought Emily a drink and asked for an Egyptian cigarette but had to make do with a Turkish one because the *Rising Sun* did not sell the Egyptian variety. He and Emily left the *Rising Sun* together at about 9:15pm, telling Smith and Lawrence that they were going to the Holborn Empire. Lawrence saw them catch an omnibus in the Euston Road and they were absent for about two hours, returning to the *Rising Sun* at some point shortly after 11:00pm. When asked by the women what they had seen at the Holborn Empire, Emily replied that they had not gone there after all but had been to a pub at the corner of Hampstead Road and Euston Road called the *Adam and Eve*.

Ellen Lawrence would later say that she thought Emily was scared of her companion (although that might have been with hindsight) and claimed that Emily had passed some uncomplimentary remarks about him to her. Wood and Emily remained talking in the *Rising Sun* until shortly after midnight when they again left the bar together. Roberts naturally thought that this meant he would be spending the night alone but Emily returned to him about twenty minutes later and he gratefully accompanied her to 29 St Paul's Road where he again spent the night with her, this time at a slightly increased cost of sixteen shillings. In her bedroom, while undressing, Emily removed a postcard from her bodice and showed it to Roberts, saying, 'That is from the man you saw me with just now'. Roberts noted that the postcard contained a request to meet the author in the *Rising Sun* and was signed 'Alice'. Emily explained that it was signed 'Alice' so that the man with whom she was living should not know it was from another man.

Roberts could not get enough of Emily. He was back in the *Rising Sun* again on the Tuesday evening, 10 September, waiting for her. Emily walked in at about 8:00pm and he took her to the Euston Music Hall, at her request. After that evening's performance was over, they returned to the *Rising Sun* for some drinks and, at about 12:30am, travelled once more to 29 St Paul's Road where Roberts spent the night. On the Wednesday morning, Roberts heard the postman knock at the front door and soon afterwards there was a knock on the bedroom door (the one which opened onto the passage), following which two letters addressed to 'Mrs Shaw' were pushed under it. Emily collected them and opened them both in Roberts' presence. One was an advertisement from a ladies' tailor and the other was a three-page letter from a 'Bertie' in which the author requested Emily to 'Meet me at 8 o'clock at The Eagle tonight'. The *Eagle Tavern* was situated at the corner of Camden Road and Great College Street, opposite what was then known as Camden Town Railway Station (now called Camden Road Station). Emily said: 'I mustn't keep this, I must burn it'. She lit a match, burned the letter and threw it into the fireplace. When Roberts asked her why she had done this, she replied, 'It's better that my young man shouldn't know that I receive letters'. She explained that the letter came from the man Roberts had seen her with in the *Rising Sun* on the Monday evening. He had wanted to come home with her (for sex), she said, but had no money, although he had said he would pay her at the end of the month when he collected his wages and he promised to recover her things out of pawn at the same time. She also told Roberts that he was very jealous of other men who knew her and that she had 'better meet him that night'. Roberts then left Dimmock at 8:30am, paying her a reduced rate of twelve shillings, and returned to his lodgings in the Euston Temperance Hotel at 173 Euston Road.

Despite having slept with Emily for three nights in a row at a total cost of forty-two shillings, Roberts was eager for more. He spent the whole of Wednesday evening in the *Rising Sun* hoping that the woman he knew as Phyllis would show up but she never did. Frank Clarke, a *Rising Sun* regular and out-of-work draughtsman who had recently served a six-month term of imprisonment in Wormwood Scrubs for stealing a watch and two gold scarf pins,[163] had seen Roberts and Emily together on previous nights and asked where the lady was. Roberts replied, 'I know where to find her. She is at the *Eagle*, Camden Town'.[164] Clarke was also a fellow lodger of Roberts at the Euston Temperance Hotel and the two men returned to their lodgings together, shortly before closing time, at 12:15am.

The letter inviting her to the *Eagle* was not the only one Emily received on Wednesday 11 September. Bert's mother, Sarah Ann Shaw, wrote to confirm a visit to see her son and the woman she believed to be her daughter-in-law. Shaw's parents had met their son's supposed wife several times in

Northampton and Emily had been trying to encourage Mrs Shaw to visit them in London. She had written a letter to Shaw's sister a few days earlier saying, 'Tell ma to hurry up and come while the weather is nice'.[165] And, indeed, after a fairly disappointing summer, the weather was splendid. The weekend of 7/8 September had been warm and sunny, with temperatures up to 72 degrees Fahrenheit and the *Daily Chronicle* of Monday 9 September informed its readers that an anticyclone had arrived over the United Kingdom 'bringing with it a more settled condition of weather than this country has experienced since Easter'. Mrs Shaw wrote back to say that she would be coming down on the Thursday morning train from Northampton. This was probably the 7:45am train arriving at Euston at 9:35am (although she could equally have caught the 8:20 arriving at Euston at 10:25 or, more sensibly, the 8:45 fast train, arriving at 10:10). As her son would still be on his way back from Sheffield, and she did not know the way from Euston to St Paul's Road, the plan was that Emily would meet her at the station.

The weather remained fine and sunny, with temperatures hitting the high seventies, and Emily spent much of a hot Wednesday afternoon washing her clothes in the wash-house adjoining the kitchen in 29 St Paul's Road and gathering up linen in the yard. She was wearing a brown velvet skirt and a light blouse and had curling pins in her hair. In the evening, she popped into the kitchen to speak to Mr and Mrs Stocks and said to George Stocks: 'I have to go out and buy a lamp'. She was heard to leave the house at about 8:15pm.

At about nine o'clock in the evening, Lilian Raven, the barmaid of the *Eagle Tavern* in Camden Road, about 720 yards, or ten minutes walk, from 29 St Paul's Road, saw a young woman with a man sitting in the saloon bar. She particularly noticed the woman because she had metal curling pins in her hair, beneath her hat, which was unusual. She did not know the names of the couple but it was, in fact, Robert Wood and Emily Dimmock. Another man came in and had a drink then turned to leave. As he did so, he saw Wood and said something like, 'Hello! What are you doing here?'. This man was Joseph Lambert, a bookseller, who had known Wood for almost two years through lodging with one of Wood's colleagues in Gower Street. After shaking hands, Wood said he was doing some business in that part of town. He introduced Lambert to his companion as 'a merry girlfriend'. Emily, for her part, apologised for her appearance, saying, 'You really must excuse me for being so untidy. I have just run out to meet him', pointing to Wood. Lilian Raven also heard her say to Wood, 'Fancy your making me come out like this'. Wood bought some drinks for his friends – a stout and bitter for Lambert and a small Bass for Emily – and while he was at the bar doing this, Emily said to Lambert, 'He is a nice boy'. The three of them chatted for about ten minutes and Lambert left. About half an hour later, Miss Raven saw Wood and Emily leave together.

The following morning, Mrs Shaw arrived at Euston carrying with her a large bunch of freshly cut country flowers and some fruit. She was surprised that her supposed daughter-in-law was not at the station to greet her as planned. She waited a considerable time before concluding that she must have missed her and set off for Camden Town, asking directions from a policeman en route.[166] Finally managing to find her way safely to 29 St Paul's Road at about twenty minutes past eleven, she knocked at the front door and Mrs Stocks answered. The landlady had already attempted to summon Emily at 9:00am, as she usually did, by rapping on her door but, getting no answer, assumed she must already have gone out to meet her mother-in-law. Mrs Shaw knocked on the door of the room her son was renting but there was no response. She waited in the hall for about ten minutes before Bert arrived. He was, in his mother's words, 'thunderstruck' that Emily was not with her but figured that she had gone to Euston and the two women had somehow managed to miss each other

After checking the doors to his front room and bedroom, and finding them both locked, Shaw initially set off with his mother to Euston, having asked Mrs Stocks that, if Emily returned while they were away, she should tell her where they had gone.[167] Within a minute or so, however, he had second thoughts and came back to the house with the idea of kicking in his front room door.[168] This prompted Mrs Stocks to look for a key which she thought might fit the lock.[169] Managing to find one which worked, she gave it to Shaw who unlocked the door which led into his sitting room. He entered the room, followed gingerly by Mrs Stocks, while Mrs Shaw waited outside. Bert could immediately see that something was wrong. All but one of the drawers of his chest of drawers had been pulled out and some of their contents, mainly clothes, were scattered over the floor. One of his two razors was, unusually, perched on top of the chest of drawers. Considering the disordered state of the room, it must have been with some trepidation that Bert approached the folding doors which separated the sitting room from his and Emily's bedroom. He found them locked but this time he was not prepared to wait until a key was found. He used his strength to force the doors open and stepped into the bedroom. It was dark in there – the shutters of the window were closed – and Bert could only see a heap of bedclothes on the bed. He pulled them aside and found Emily's naked body lying motionless on the bed. She was lying on her left side with her left arm behind her back and her right arm on the pillow. Despite the poor light, he could see that her throat was cut.

A few moments later, having barely recovered from the shock, Bert ran out of the room to tell his mother, 'She's dead – as dead as a doornail'. Mrs Shaw ventured into the sitting room but was too upset to go as far as the bedroom. She also did not notice much, although she remembered seeing a scrubbing brush and bucket on the floor, and some sewing which looked as if it had been cast aside.[170] Bert ran into the street to locate a policeman and found P.C. Thomas Killion in Camden Square, bringing him back to St Paul's Road. It was now about five minutes to twelve. According to Killion's written statement: 'I saw deceased on the bed, she was lying on her face with her left cheek on the pillow, her left arm was bent at right angles over her back and her right arm stretched forward. She was lying in a pool of blood, the whole of the bedding being saturated with blood. She was quite nude. I placed my hand on her shoulder and found her to be quite cold'. He sent for a doctor and remained in the bedroom with Bert until the arrival of more police officers from Somers Town Police Station.

By a strange coincidence, the longstanding resident of 27 St Paul's Road, John Lewis, had died six days earlier of a cerebral haemorrhage at the age of sixty-four, and his body was being taken to be buried by the undertakers at the very moment the additional officers arrived. This caused some confusion because, believing that the body of Emily Dimmock was being removed, the officers rushed into the wrong house. Eventually they located the correct address and were joined at about one o'clock by the divisional surgeon, Dr John Thompson, a 72 year old whose surgery was located at 70 Oakley Square in nearby Somers Town. At this stage, the police at the scene believed they were dealing with a case of suicide but, on examination of the body, the doctor discovered that the cause of death was a deep cut in Emily's throat which had almost severed her head from her body. It was clearly not a self-inflicted wound and he informed the officers present that they were dealing with a case of murder. A message was sent to the local detective inspector to attend the scene.

Robert Wood

P.C. Thomas Killion

The Rising Sun (in 1927 but as it would have looked twenty years earlier)

and its location

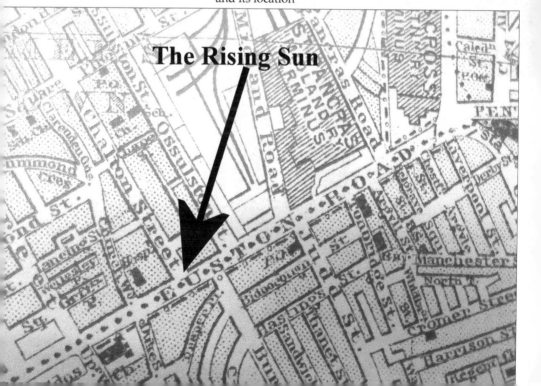

29 St Paul's Road in September 1907

And now Agar Grove pictured in 2013

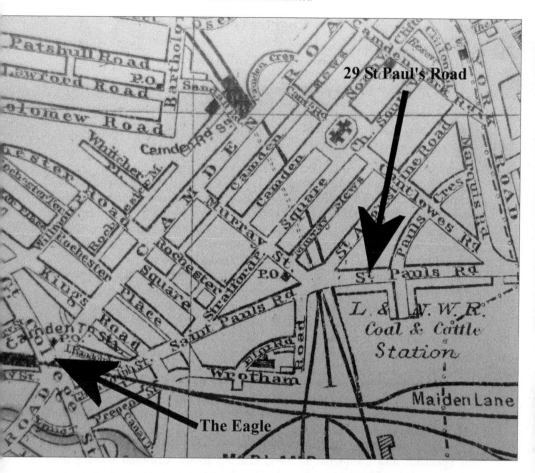

Map of Camden Town showing the locations of 29 St Paul's Road and the Eagle

Chapter Four

Enter the Manhunter

'Aim like the cunning fowler, close one eye,
that you the better may your game espy.'

John Webster, *The White Devil*, 1612

Detective Inspector Arthur Fowler Neil was, according to one crime reporter who knew him in his prime, 'a tall lean man' who was 'tireless physically and mentally'.[171] Another description was that he was a man 'with rough hair and a somewhat aggressive face.'[172] He had been born on 31 December 1867 in Lewisham. His father, Frederick, was then the gardener at Hither Green Lodge, owned by retired Major-General Thomas Townsend Pears who was the military secretary at the India Office.[173] Frederick had married the Lodge's housemaid, Emma Talbot, in 1861 and Arthur was their fourth son. Emma's mother was originally Mary Fowler before she married John Talbot, to become Mary Talbot, and Mary's surname lived on as Arthur's middle name. His parents could not have known how appropriate it would be: a fowler was a hunter of game and, as a Metropolitan Police detective, Arthur was to become a hunter of men (indeed his autobiography would be entitled *Forty years of Man-hunting*).

The Neil family was forced to move to Dorking in about 1877 after Major Pears had retired from the India Office and taken a smaller home in Putney. At the age of ten, Arthur went to school in Dorking, leaving at the age of thirteen. After brief employment as a stable boy, footman and baker boy respectively, he joined the Metropolitan Police's P Division on 7 May 1888, initially patrolling in Peckham and Camberwell. He graduated to the Criminal Investigation Department in 1892 and transferred to Lambeth four years later where he won promotion to detective sergeant. From October 1900 he worked in Southwark as part of M Division and became involved in a major murder investigation during October 1902 with regard to George Chapman in what was known as the Borough Poisoning Case. Neil was handed a report into the sudden death of Chapman's mistress, Maud Marsh, and two of his former mistresses, Elizabeth Taylor and Mary Spink, which concluded there had been foul play. Chapman was the licensee of the *Crown* public house in Borough High Street and, after reading the report, Neil apparently made a late night visit to that establishment to check if Chapman was still there. In his autobiography he would claim that he could see Chapman's silhouette through the upstairs window looking very busy and concluded that he was preparing to flee. Neil reported to his superiors, and Chapman was arrested the following morning. A thorough investigation into Chapman's life commenced and Neil spent many hours in Somerset House searching the marriage registers to prove that he did not marry the women he claimed were his wives. Chapman was convicted of murder at the Old Bailey in March 1903 and subsequently hanged. Detective Sergeant Neil, along with Inspectors Godley and Kemp, who were in charge of the investigation, were commended by the Old Bailey trial judge, Mr Justice

Grantham, 'for promptitude, skill and ability displayed in apprehending a man for murder, also for the manner in which they procured and placed the evidence before the court'.[174] Neil was rewarded with a payment of fifteen shillings.

Following his success in the Chapman investigation, and now a rising star within the Metropolitan Police Force, Neil was promoted to Local Inspector for Y Division on 11 May 1904. This involved a major upheaval in his life. Having spent his entire career until then in South London, he was now responsible for crime in the area of North London covering Kentish Town,

Detective Inspector
Arthur Fowler Neil

Caledonian Road, Somers Town, Holloway, Highgate and Wood Green and consequently moved from his home in Peckham to a new address in Upper Holloway.

In January 1905, Neil was faced with a curious murder confession made by a 25-year-old labourer who lived in Kentish Town. Arthur Ransley walked into Great Marlborough Street Police Station and volunteered the information that two years earlier he had murdered a woman at a coffee house in St Pancras. He said he had met the woman in Euston Road and went with her to the Blue Lamp Coffee House, 174 Seymour Street, at about 11:00pm during the evening of 15 April 1903. There were rooms to let and the couple went to bed; Ransley strangled her and left. The case was referred to Inspector Neil who investigated the matter and discovered that a 37-year-old married woman called Emma Elizabeth Rice of Gloucester Road, St Pancras, had indeed been found dead in the coffee house during the morning of 16 April 1903. A post-mortem had been conducted which concluded that she had died from 'Syncope involving broncho-pneumonia and valvular disease of the heart' and, at the subsequent inquest, a verdict of death by natural causes was returned by the jury. Despite Ransley's confession, the police decided to offer no evidence against the prisoner who was discharged at Clerkenwell Police Court by Mr D'Eyncourt.

No explanation for their action was provided by the police but it is likely that, in the face of the coroner's verdict, it was felt there was no chance of a conviction, with the only evidence of murder being the confession. However, Ransley was said to have been sober and rational when he made his confession and it is strange that he would confess to a crime, two years after the event, that no-one had even believed had been committed in the first place. The fact that he claimed to have met Mrs Rice in the Euston Road suggests, if true, that she was working as a prostitute. Furthermore, the so-called 'coffee house' at 174 Seymour Street was a well-known brothel. A register of disorderly houses kept by the Town Clerk's Department of the St Pancras Parish during 1894 records that 174 Seymour Street was 'ostensibly a coffee house but no business of that kind is carried on'.[175] Between 6 and 30 March 1894 the police observed 140 couples enter and leave the establishment. A man and two women were arrested and convicted at Clerkenwell Police Court on 13 April 1894 for running the house as a brothel.[176] Just over ten years later, on 5 August 1904, the same register (now kept by the St Pancras Borough Council) recorded that 'well known prostitutes' were seen to take men to 174 Seymour Street and, once again, 'no legitimate business' of a coffee house was done there. Prosecutions were not initiated on this occasion because, in September 1904, it was reported that all furniture had been removed from the building which was now empty. On the face of it, therefore, Ransley's story made sense. Signs of strangulation can be difficult to detect if not suspected during a post-mortem and it may be that the pathologist was mistaken. Alternatively, Mrs Rice might have died of heart failure during a vigorous bout of love making and Ransley thought he was somehow responsible. In any event, no action was taken and Ransley was free to invite other women for coffee if he so wished.[177]

A couple of months later, in March 1905, Frederick Charles Joyce, a 24-year-old carman and porter, attempted to cut the throat of his former sweetheart, a servant called Mabel Martin, at Bayham Street, Camden Town. As he fled the scene being chased by an angry crowd, he fell off a passing van onto which he had clambered to assist his escape, suffering serious injuries, and needed to be carried into Clerkenwell Police Court on a chair. He made a full confession to Inspector Neil, explaining that he had wanted to marry Mabel but one of her friends had advised her against it so she declined, which infuriated him. He took a knife which he found in his sister's house and stuck it in Mabel's throat but lost his resolve when he saw the blood; and Mabel, treated by the divisional surgeon, Dr Thompson, was able to recover from the attack. Joyce, who defended himself during his trial at the Old Bailey, was sentenced to ten years penal servitude by Mr Justice Channel on 3 May 1905.

A few weeks later, Inspector Neil put his man-hunting skills to good use when he tracked down a burglar called Henry Fear who, with an accomplice, broke into a house in Camden Road and stole jewellery to the value of £5 belonging to a man called George Jay. Neil arrested Fear in Hendon while Fear's accomplice, George Sergeant, was arrested by Neil's colleague, Detective Sergeant Gale, in Grafton Road, Kentish Town. At the end of 1905, those same skills were put to use again after a dying man, John Skinner, superintendent of the mental ward of the St Pancras Workhouse, identified a former inmate called Edward MacQuire as the man who had shot him in Tufnell Park with a Webley revolver. Neil set about tracing MacQuire who had gone into hiding and found him within twenty-four hours. MacQuire turned out to be an unbalanced individual who hated Skinner and was found guilty of the murder at the Old Bailey on 14 March 1906; but the jury held him to be not responsible for his actions and Mr Justice Grantham ordered him to be detained at His Majesty's pleasure, whereupon he was sent to Broadmoor.

On 12 September 1907, while Emily Dimmock's dead body was still lying on her bed in St Paul's Road, Inspector Neil was at the Central Criminal Court for the trial of Mary Ann Dearman, whom he had charged five weeks earlier for the manslaughter of her husband, Alfred, in Enfield. Following much abuse and violence directed towards her, Mrs Dearman had fired a 'patent horse killer' into Alfred's back, killing him instantly. One of Neil's colleagues described Alfred in court as 'a thorough, blackguard, the most filthy tongued man I had ever heard'. Mrs Dearman was found guilty under extenuating circumstances but recommended to mercy by the jury. The judge, Mr Justice Bray, agreed and sentenced her to a mere three days in prison which entitled her to immediate release amidst cheers from spectators.[178]

As a result of his attendance at this trial, Inspector Neil was late to arrive at 29 St Paul's Road. He received a telephone message while at the Old Bailey at five minutes past two and went with Detective Constable Frank Page to the crime scene, arriving shortly after 3:00pm. He would later describe what he saw:

> The house was in great confusion….the chest of drawers in the girl's room presented every appearance of having been rifled, but I found three rings in the drawers….There were two razors in the front room, - one on the top of a chest of drawers and the other in the drawer of a sewing machine….One of the razors was very old and rusty.[179]

Detective Constable Page would later say that he observed a picture postcard album with a green cover lying open on a chair near the window of the front room which had a partly raised venetian blind. He would claim that he saw postcards lying loose in the album and several scattered on the floor. Inspector Neil then went into the bedroom where he met Dr Thompson and Chief Inspector Coleman who was also present. According to Neil:

> The Chief Inspector, Doctor Thompson and myself examined the body and found the deceased lying on her stomach perfectly nude; her left cheek was lying on the pillow, her left arm at right angles across her back, her legs drawn up & her right arm stretched forward across the pillow; both hands were clenched. She had a gash about six inches long across her throat, the wind-pipe being almost severed. It was clean cut and had apparently been caused by a very sharp instrument. She had apparently sustained no other injury and there was no sign of any struggle having taken place.[180]

Neil noted that the bed was saturated with blood which had soaked through the bedding to the floor. In addition, Emily's left hand, which had apparently been drawn out and placed across the back by the murderer, was 'full of blood'.[181] It initially appeared to Dr Thompson from the disarrangement of the bedclothes that, contrary to Inspector Neil's first impression, there *had* been a struggle but he quickly came to the conclusion that he was wrong and that the murderer had used the bedclothes and pillow, and 'anything else he could lay his hands on' to wrap round Emily's head and mop up the blood.[182] In the end, he was sure that she had been killed where she was found. There was bloody water in a wash basin in the bedroom which also contained a bloodstained white cotton petticoat on which the murderer had evidently wiped his or her hands. A nearby towel hanging on a rail was perfectly clean. Dr Thompson saw two spots of blood on a table cloth and a spot or two of blood on a jug by the side of the basin although not on the handle of the jug. There was no trace of any blood in the sitting room.

The inspector's first step in the investigation was to take a statement from Bert Shaw who confessed to him that Emily had been a prostitute when he met her although he claimed that she had given up that life since they had been together. More importantly, he was able to inform Neil what property was missing. Quite a lot had been taken: a silver cast pattern chain with a white metal matchbox attached, a small glass charm, a silver cigarette case, Emily's dark green leather purse (which Shaw believed contained five shillings although it might have been more), her gold watch and a nine carat gold, so-called, wedding ring together with a keeper ring (which helped to keep the wedding ring on the finger).[183] Her wedding ring and keeper ring had been last seen by Shaw on her fingers, and she had been wearing her watch, so it appeared that the murderer had prized these items from her dead body.[184]

Three keys had also been taken: the keys to the front door, the sitting room and the bedroom's folding doors. The only key to remain in the lock was a key to the bedroom door leading into the outside passage (as opposed to the bedroom's folding doors which led into the sitting room). Statements were obtained from Mr and Mrs Stocks who both said they heard nothing during the night and could throw no light on Emily's death. All they could tell the inspector was that they believed Emily had left the house at some point after 8:00pm on the Wednesday evening. Alice Lancaster, a middle-aged widow who occupied a room in the house, was also spoken to but she said she had heard nothing either.[185]

The next step was to establish what was known about Emily on the streets and a team of four detectives: Alfred Ball, George Osborne, Frank Page and Charles Goodchild made immediate enquiries and quickly established that her regular haunt was the *Rising Sun*. This was followed by a visit to that establishment.

News of Emily's death had spread very quickly across Camden Town and St Pancras. The *Morning Leader* reported 'a gaping and awestruck' crowd which stood in St Paul's Road during the afternoon of 12 September while Emily's body was brought down into the street, along with the bloodstained clothes and mattress, and placed into an undertaker's van, before being driven off to the St Pancras Mortuary. Word of the murder had reached the ears of Robert Roberts while he was drinking in the *Rising Sun* during the afternoon and, conscious that he would be suspected of involvement in the crime, he declared that he would stay there all night until the police came. They arrived during the evening and Roberts stepped forward to say that he had spent the Sunday, Monday and Tuesday nights with Emily but had not seen her on the Wednesday evening and had nothing to do with her death. He was taken to Somers Town Police Station where he made a statement about the letter from 'Bertie' that Emily had shown him in which a request had been made for her to meet the writer at the *Eagle* at 8:00pm on the Wednesday evening (although he would later refer to seeing a time of 8:30pm for the intended assignation), before the letter had been burnt on the fire.

The police went straight to the *Eagle* and spoke to the barmaid, Lilian Raven, who was at that time asleep in bed. She was woken up and shown a photograph of Emily but, in her sleepy state, did not recognise her. More helpfully, a search of the hearth and fire grate in Emily's room on the Friday morning by Detective Sergeant Osborne located two small fragments of a document which appeared to support the story Roberts had told. The fragments bore the writing, '...ill you...ar...of...th...E....Town...S...Wednes...has...ill... excuse...good...fond....l....mon' which was felt by police to be consistent with a letter from a man to a woman asking, 'Will you meet me at the bar of the *Eagle* public house, near Camden Town Railway Station, 8.30 tonight, Wednesday?' (followed by a mention of someone having been ill, possibly asking the woman to excuse handwriting, concluding with the words 'goodbye...fondest love' and a reference to money).

Curiously, there was no mention in Roberts' statement of the postcard signed by 'Alice', featuring a drawing of a rising sun, which he would later testify that Emily had plucked from her dress and shown him before putting it away in the top left hand drawer of her chest of drawers. Yet, he must have mentioned it to the police because, the next day, Detective Sergeant Herbert Milton accompanied Roberts to Emily's front room at 29 St Paul's Road with the specific purpose of searching for it. Sergeant Milton removed the contents from each drawer, and carried out a thorough search of other parts of the room, but was unable to locate it. In his statement, Roberts also told the police about the man he had seen in Emily's company on the Monday night in the *Rising Sun*. His description of the man was that he was 23 or 24 years of age, about 5 foot 8 inches, very dark complexion and hair, clean shaven with a very long thin face and a scowling expression. Roberts also said he had 'a few pimples' on the lower part of his face.

Roberts' alibi for the night of the murder was checked with Mrs Amelia Lesage, the proprietor of the Euston Temperance Hotel, who recalled that she had let Roberts and Frank Clarke in through the front door at 12:30am on the Thursday morning and, as they were her last guests to return, she locked up afterwards. Clarke also corroborated Roberts' story and said that he breakfasted with him at 10:00am as usual. Inspector Neil was satisfied that Roberts had nothing to do with the murder but was very interested in the man he had described.

The national newspapers reported the news of the murder on the morning of Friday 13 September. The *Daily Chronicle,* under the headline 'MYSTERIOUS TRAGEDY' was rather well informed about the circumstances of the crime. It reported that Emily's naked body was 'lying face downwards, completely covered up by the bed clothes' (only partially correct because Dimmock was lying on her side) and that the door of the bedroom was found locked on the outside and the key of the street door was missing. It also reported that 'the drawers and cupboards in the room had been ransacked and a number of valuables had been stolen'. The *Morning Advertiser,* under the headline 'TERRIBLE TRAGEDY', said that 'Detective Neil of the Y division, and other officers made a thorough search of the room, and found that a chest of drawers which stood there had been ransacked, together with other articles of furniture which were likely to contain things of value', adding that a washstand containing a bowl of water was 'found to be covered with blood and there were indications that someone had washed his hands, and further, on Mrs Shaw's clothes were marks as if the person had utilised them for wiping his or her hands'.

The *Morning Leader* had been making its own enquiries and spoke to the resident of 31 St Paul's Road, Mrs Mary Ann Levesque, a widow, who claimed to be a light sleeper but had heard nothing at all during the night. Her terrier was supposed to be so alert it would bark loudly if it heard a cat crawling along the wall outside the house but it was silent all night. She said that 'Mrs Shaw' had been doing some washing during the afternoon and had put her head out of the window and smiled merrily, saying what a beautiful day it was. She later heard her playing the piano and singing in the parlour. She added that she occasionally saw her go out in the evenings wearing a cap (which Mrs Leveseque assumed was her husband's) and, with a little basket on her arm, would run down to Murray Street to do some shopping.[186] Mrs Levesque said she never saw Emily come home in the evenings with another man. However, the newspaper, whose headline was 'TERRIBLE LONDON

MURDER MYSTERY', had established that Emily had been a prostitute before she met Shaw. The *St Pancras Gazette*, with the headline, 'SENSATIONAL TRAGEDY AT ST PAUL'S ROAD', spoke to Mrs Stocks who, it reported, 'was almost prostrate with grief'.

The exclusive of the day, however, undoubtedly appeared in the *Daily News*, whose reporter claimed to have located a neighbour who had seen Emily walking down St Paul's Road a little before midnight in the company of a 'short, dark individual who wore a bowler hat and a dark suit'.[187] If true, it was a crucial piece of evidence but the police never obtained a statement from anyone to this effect. The same newspaper also reported that the police 'have in their possession a crumpled up note or letter which was found in the deceased's room under the bed early this afternoon' and it wrongly stated that an address was on this document. It is not clear if this was supposed to be the burnt pieces of paper found in the fire or was a totally false report.[188] In addition, it reported another lead, claiming that, on Monday night, Emily had been 'in a neighbouring hostelry with an elderly man'. Its edition the following morning would say that this man was referred to by Emily as 'Uncle' and had given her presents of jewellery and articles of personal adornment.

During the Friday, the police continued their enquiries into Emily's life in London, checking at her previous known addresses and attempting to identify men with whom she associated. Emily's sister, Maud Coleman, mentioned Arthur Harrap as someone who had threatened Emily but he could not immediately be tracked down. Police spoke to his landlord and landlady at 61 Arlington Road, Mr and Mrs Pitt, but they were unable to say whether Harrap was at home on the Wednesday night. Eventually, however, he was found at 61 Arlington Road and voluntarily made a statement (now lost) which was verified by the police as proving that he was not in Emily's company on the night of her death. Another associate of Emily was a man known, by remarkable coincidence, as Bert Wood, another cook on the Midland Railway, whose full name was William Herbert Wood.[189] It was established that this Wood spent the evening playing billiards with a colleague at the *Golden Lion* public house in King's Cross during the night of the murder and did not leave until after midnight, being seen arriving at his lodgings in Kentish Town by a fellow lodger at 1:30am. The police also considered a 23-year-old man of 'eccentric habits', only going out at night, who had lodged at 29 St Paul's Road with his mother, Mrs Moore, until the middle of August. It transpired that the man only went out at night because he was too ashamed of the poor condition of his clothes and the police were satisfied that he never knew Emily.

Up in Wellingborough, Emily's father had seen the reports in the London newspapers while he was in the local library and realised that his daughter was the victim. He informed the Northamptonshire police that he did not know if either of his daughters who resided in London (Emily or Maud) were aware that he was living in Wellingborough, which confirms that relations with his children were not good. He said that he had received a letter from his son, Henry, in about November 1906, informing him that Emily was going to marry a sailor in Portsmouth and had heard no more about her until he saw the news of her murder in the papers. Independently, Emily's brother, Harry, a plasterer's labourer, learned of the murder when his workmates read the Friday morning papers over breakfast and noticed that the surname of the murder victim matched his own, the newspapers having quickly established that Mrs Shaw's real name was Emily Dimmock. Initially he thought they were joking and took no notice, only realising they were being serious when they asked him if he had a sister in London.

At the London Sand Blast Decorative Glass Works in Gray's Inn Road, ornamental glass designer William Moss, who had read the newspaper reports, casually mentioned to his colleague, Bob Wood, 'There's another one of those unfortunate women has been done to death', referring to the deceased as 'Phyllis'. Wood replied, 'I'm not surprised at that kind of thing happening as they never know who they are taking home'. It was the type of banal conversation that was no doubt taking place between workers in offices and factories up and down the country but it would play on Wood's mind over the next few days.

At Kentish Town Police Station, Inspector Neil drafted his first report on the Dimmock case which was dated 13 September 1907. It was written for his immediate superior, Superintendent Louis Vedy, who would forward it to the Assistant Commissioner of the Criminal Investigation Department, Sir Melville Macnaghten. In terms of the time of death, Neil wrote only that Dr Thompson found that 'the woman had been dead for some hours'. He added that the cause of death was 'a deep clean cut in the throat about 6 inches long which almost severed the wind pipe'. He reported that he searched the bedroom for the murder weapon 'but could find nothing whatsoever'. There are three important aspects regarding the inspector's report in respect of what he did *not* include. Neil said nothing about any postcards and did not mention Emily's postcard album. Nor did he say anything to indicate that the loss of items from the property was anything other than a genuine theft (albeit that he did say robbery was not the primary motive) and there was no suggestion by Neil that the murderer was searching for something. He did not even mention the three rings on which he would soon place reliance to suggest that an attempt had been made to fabricate a burglary. He also made no mention of the fact that Emily was found with curlers in her hair. All of these issues were to assume great importance later and it is curious that Neil found no place for them in his first report.

The evening papers on Friday 13 September were building up the story. The front page of the *Evening News* carried the headline 'CLUE IN MURDER MYSTERY' and claimed that fingerprints in blood found upon some of the bedclothes had been photographed and sent to Scotland Yard. This story was completely false and was known to be so later that day when the police confirmed that smudges found on the victim's clothes were 'useless as clues'.[190] The newspaper also reported that the crumpled piece of paper supposedly found under the bed, as reported in the *Daily News*, did not provide any material assistance to the investigation. At the same time, it had two new snippets to report. Firstly, it claimed that on Wednesday afternoon a 'big man' called at Emily's house and went in to see her but was not seen to leave. Secondly, it stated that the only place Emily was well known was at the local public house, the *Murray Arms*, situated at 25 St Paul's Road, where Emily was said to have been a frequent visitor, accompanied by a number of different men, including 'an elderly man of respectable appearance who was noticeable for his beard'. The landlady of the *Murray Arms* was said to have reproved Emily and her companion for their conduct. Unfortunately for the newspaper, both of these stories turned out to be essentially untrue. The 'big man' who was said to have called at Emily's house was later discovered to have visited another house in the street; and Lewis Griffiths the licensee of the *Murray Arms* issued a statement on the Saturday making clear that Emily was not 'an habitué' of his public house and had never been expelled for disorderly conduct. However, he did not say that Emily had *never* visited the *Murray Arms* and it seems that one of her companions *was* a elderly man with a beard (known as 'Uncle') as confirmed by Mrs Haupsman to journalists on the Friday. Interestingly, the *Star*, which repeated the *Daily News'* story, also reported that the police were said to be of the opinion that 'robbery was the motive for the crime'.

Saturday morning's newspapers increased the sensation, with the *Daily Mirror* and *Daily Mail* both publishing the photograph of Emily taken in a sailor's costume in November 1906. It was such an unusual outfit for a woman to be wearing that it caught the nation's attention. It certainly caught Robert Wood's attention and it dawned on him that Emily's picture would no doubt be seen by Joseph Lambert. He knew that Lambert was a friend of William Moss – the two men had previously lodged together at 44 Gower Street – and he was troubled by Moss's interest in the case, as expressed to him the day before. If Lambert discussed the case with Moss, he might mention that he had seen him (Wood) with Emily in the *Eagle* on the night of the murder, something Wood had so far not told anyone. He would come up with a plan to deal with this before the end of the following week.

The *Daily Mail* reporter had also tracked down Mrs Roberts of Grafton Place and she told him about Emily's motor ride with a man who had later said: 'if she is living with Shaw I'll find her if it takes me years. She's ruined me and I'll do for her'. Mrs Roberts informed the reporter that the police had

already asked her if the man was 5 foot 10 inches in height, pale, clean shaven, face rather pimply and sickly looking with a short chin and wearing a navy blue coat and bowler hat, thus revealing the description of the man they were seeking. She replied that the description matched with the exception of the height. She thought the man who had threatened Emily was 5 foot 7 inches. It is not clear why the police apparently told Mrs Roberts that their suspect was 5 foot 10 inches considering that Robert Roberts, the ship's cook, estimated the height of the man he had seen with Emily as two inches shorter. The notion of a man in a blue coat (or suit) and bowler hat was to be a continuing theme during the investigation and it is Mrs Roberts who is the earliest known source of this, albeit that she was passing on to the *Daily Mail* what

Emily Dimmock in sailor's outfit

she had supposedly been told by the police. The original source may be Robert Roberts but he included nothing in his written statement about what the man he saw in the *Rising Sun* with Emily was wearing.

The *Daily News*, having interviewed Mrs Maw and Mrs Houpsman from Emily's former residence in Great College Street, mentioned the telegram that Emily had received from the man she called 'Uncle' and told the story of how he had visited her one day. The *Daily Mirror* claimed that detectives were attempting to locate this 'middle-aged bearded man'. It was also reported in that morning's papers that a Mrs Watson, supposedly a friend of Emily's, had informed the police that Emily had, some months ago, received an abusive and threatening anonymous postcard bearing a Portsmouth post mark.[191] The content of the postcard was reported as: 'Do not be surprised if you hear of a murder being done. You have ruined my life and I may do it soon'. It was said that Emily passed it off as a joke at the time. This story has some credibility to the extent that Mrs Watson also informed the *Star* that Emily was known to her friends as 'Phyllis', a fact which had not been reported until that time, which at least suggests that she probably did know Emily (although it does not mean that her story was true) but the postcard she described was said not to have been found by police in Emily's flat. Mrs Watson also told the *Star* that she saw Emily on Wednesday night at about 9:30pm at King's Cross with three men who wanted her to go to Scotland with them but she refused and the men went away. This story does not appear to have been investigated by the police and the Metropolitan Police file in the National Archives contains no mention of it. Mrs Watson was not called as a witness at any public hearing. Another of Emily's friends told the *Daily Mirror* that 'Sometimes her companion was a man with a black beard from forty-five to fifty years of age. I have seen them together on at least three occasions.' This man, who was also presumably the man known as 'Uncle', was supposedly spotted going in and out of 29 St Paul's Road with Emily. A resident of St Paul's Road said 'He was a big man, broad-shouldered, stealthy looking' and the newspaper added that he was 'of medium height, with dark hair and eyes, and a very dark beard and moustache', noting that, when seen in the neighbourhood of St Paul's Road, he was 'attired in a grey suit and a tail coat'. There is no indication of this in the Metropolitan Police file, and the man called 'Uncle', if he existed, was never identified.

Although the *Daily Chronicle* did not have a photograph of Emily, it had the best scoop of the morning. It stated in an article on the murder that 'Miss Dimmock had an appointment with a mysterious acquaintance, and it seems clear that she kept it'. The article went on to explain that 'Some days ago she received a postcard from a man asking her to meet him on that night at Camden Town Railway Station. That postcard the police have been unable to discover, and the probability is that she destroyed it'.[192] So, although the story appears to mix up the letter requesting a meeting on the night of the murder at the *Eagle* (near Camden Town Railway Station) which Dimmock had put on the fire (but the police had found fragments of), and the postcard requesting a meeting at the *Rising Sun* (in the Euston Road) two nights before the murder, which was indeed missing, it was still obviously based, either directly or indirectly, on some actual information from the ongoing police investigation. At the end of the article, the source of this story is said to be 'a sailor' (obviously Roberts) and it is stated that Emily told him that she had received a postcard from a man, whose Christian name he (Roberts) believed was 'Bertie', asking her to meet him that night. Emily was said to have spoken freely about the appointment but the sailor, not being interested, paid little attention to what she said. Less impressively, the same newspaper also reported that a neighbour had seen a man, wearing a black coat and bowler hat, run up the stone steps of number 29 St Paul's Road and enter the house at seven o'clock on Thursday morning but it later transpired that this was, in fact, a sighting of Shaw returning home at eleven.[193]

Perhaps the most interesting fact to emerge from the Saturday papers was that some of them had clearly been briefed that robbery was not considered to be the motive for the murder. The *Morning Advertiser*, for example, stated that 'So far as the idea of robbery is concerned, little weight is attached to this, for even though the woman's few trinkets were missing and the drawers were found opened, it is felt that this was part of the plan of the murderer, who was really actuated by a feeling of jealousy'; and it repeated later in the article that 'the police pay little or no attention to the fact that a robbery was committed. This they regard as a blind for the motive actuating the committal of the crime'. The *Daily Mail* suggested that the police believed that the murder was committed by one of Emily's old lovers and that the jewellery and purse was probably taken for the purpose of 'making it appear that robbery, and robbery alone, was the motive for the crime'. The *Evening News* also dismissed the significance of the missing valuables, claiming that, 'the importance of them has been exaggerated in some quarters' while adding that Shaw was unable to swear they were even in the house at the time of the murder. The paper had actually managed to secure an interview with Shaw who was said to be 'in an attitude of complete dejection'. He was quoted as saying:

> Nothing has been found out about it yet and there is no clue to the murderer as far as I know. I have given her photographs to the police and they may trace somebody through them. I don't know though. I can't say anything as to who could have done it. I can't think of anyone.[194]

Nevertheless the *Evening News* listed three supposed suspects. One was the elderly man with a beard who Emily was supposed to call 'Uncle'. Another was a 'seafaring man' with whom Emily had quarrelled and who had allegedly threatened her. He was not named but, later in the article, Emily was said to have been living in Portsmouth in 1905 with a 'seafaring man with whom she quarrelled and of whom she is said to have been living in fear'. This can only have been a reference to Biddle, although there is no evidence that he ever threatened her. It would appear that the press simply assumed that the threatening postcard with a Portsmouth postmark, which Emily was said to have received, had been sent by the man from Portsmouth with whom she had lived in 1905. Until this point, Biddle had not actually been mentioned by name in the newspapers but the *Evening News* said that Emily's sister, Rosa, believed that Emily was married to 'a sailor named Biddell (sic) at Portsmouth last September'. The third suspect listed by the *Evening News* was a 'short dark man, wearing a bowler hat' who had supposedly invited Emily to leave Shaw and 'who was with her in St Paul's-road on the night of the crime'. This was the same suspect originally mentioned by the *Daily News* on 13 September.

Also in the evening of Saturday 14 September, the *Star* claimed that Emily had worked hard as a needlewoman for the wife of the landlord of a public house 'at King's Cross' whom she had made 'a confidant' and, although this woman was not named, it was clearly Mrs Chapman of the *Rising Sun*. According to the *Star*, Mrs Chapman had provided police with the description of a man with whom Emily came into the public house on Wednesday night but this must be the wrong date because Emily was not seen in the *Rising Sun* on the Wednesday. Interestingly, the *Star* commented that 'detectives are now believed to be working along one particular line, and it is significant that inquiries in Gray's-inn-rd immediately followed the statement of the landlady.' Such inquiries might actually have been a result of a claim by Ellen Lawrence that the man seen with Emily in the *Rising Sun* on the Monday night had been seen on a number of occasions in the *Pindar of Wakefield* in the Gray's Inn Road, including once with Emily Dimmock.

The Sunday papers were full of the murder, with *Lloyds Weekly News* publishing a new photograph of Emily in more feminine clothing than a sailor's outfit. At the same time, it claimed that 'Certainly robbery was not the primary object of the crime', on the basis that the value of the missing property was estimated at not more than £3. It may be noted that Inspector Neil had written in his report of 13 September that 'I am satisfied that robbery was not the primary object of the crime' and the similar wording of this with what was stated in the *Lloyds Weekly News* story strongly suggests that the newspaper had a police source. Rosa Martindale had been interviewed by a number of journalists and 'Jumbo' Hurst was much mentioned because of the time he spent with Emily in Luton. Rosa was quoted as saying that Jumbo 'made her [Emily] several presents and I thought they were to be married'. She added that 'I often warned her of what might happen if she played with the feelings of any man in the way she did'. Bert Shaw was quoted as saying 'I don't know what to think about it; but it is a cruel murder. I pray God they will find out someone'.[195] Mrs Stocks was clearly also speaking to reporters as the *People* had discovered that she recalled Emily leaving number 29 at 'about nine o'clock' on the Wednesday and 'that was the very last she saw or heard of her'.[196] The *People* had also apparently uncovered another threat to Emily by three men who had visited a house 'off Seymour Place' where, they said, Emily had once lived, and one of them was supposed to have growled menacingly, 'I will have my own back, if I have to wait years for it', although it may be that the paper was confusing the story of what happened at Grafton Place as reported by Mrs Roberts.

Meanwhile *Reynolds's Newspaper* had spoken to Mrs David, the manageress of the *Murray Arms*, in an attempt to clarify stories of Emily's visits to that public house. Mrs David was quoted as saying:

> She used to come occasionally of an evening, shortly before the house closed, and always with a man – generally a stranger. The couple used to drive up in a cab, which they discharged outside. I remember the first time I saw her, it was about two months ago; she was with a man whom I took to be her father. In the evening she used the saloon bar...In the morning she would come into the public bar for a bottle of stout, which she would take away with her. Not on one occasion did she drink it in the house. At these times she would wear a man's cap, an apron and had her hair in crackers, just like any ordinary working man's wife. As for ordering her out of the house, or having her thrown out on account of her behaviour or that of her companion, I never had any occasion to do such a thing. She was always most quiet and well behaved.[197]

Although this comes from a newspaper, and for that reason must be regarded with caution, it is a potentially very important piece of information in that Mrs David refers to Emily regularly having had her hair 'in crackers' i.e. curlers. As we shall see, Inspector Neil became convinced that Emily would not go out in such a state but Mrs David's recollection suggests that she did. It is, of course, possible that Mrs David had mis-identified one of her customers as Emily but at least some corroboration of her story is found in the fact that she said that Emily would wear a man's cap, while Mrs Levesque told reporters that she occasionally saw Emily wearing her husband's cap. The timeframe of Mrs David's story also fits because Emily had only moved into St Paul's Road some two months earlier which would explain why she started visiting the *Murray Arms*.

In addition to interviewing Mrs David, the journalist from *Reynolds's Newspaper* had also been speaking to a potentially important, but unnamed, witness, said to have been a friend of Emily's for three years, described as 'a young woman', who claimed to have seen the deceased woman in the saloon bar of the *Rising Sun* between 9:00 and 10:00pm on Wednesday night.[198] She said Emily was in the company of a man who, from his bearing, appeared to be a soldier or sailor and whom she described as 'about 5ft. 8 in. in height... wearing a blue serge jacket suit and bowler hat'. It was a familiar description. The unnamed friend said that, seeing Emily was in conversation with the man, she did not speak to her. However, we know that Emily was not in the *Rising Sun* on the Wednesday night so this report must have been erroneous.

The *News of the World*, claiming that Detective Inspector Neil and his officers 'were confident of effecting the arrest of the murderer', provided a description of a man supposedly seen with Emily on the night of the murder (but possibly they meant a night before the murder) as follows: 'He is of average size, and was wearing a dark blue serge suit, and a bowler hat several sizes too large. He has very deep sunken eyes'.[199] The newspaper also correctly reported that an unnamed sailor (obviously Robert Roberts) had been able to show the police that, despite being on friendly terms with Emily, he was not in her company on the night of the tragedy.

Clearly the press was all over the Dimmock case but how was the police investigation progressing? Not terribly well is the answer but at least some new witnesses had come forward over the weekend. Two men, Henry Sharples and Frederick Harvey, presented themselves at Kentish Town Police Station in Holmes Road and made a statement to the effect that they had seen Emily, who they knew well, in the Euston Road (near the *Rising Sun*) at just after midnight on the Wednesday night/Thursday morning with a big, well built, fair haired, man of about five foot nine or ten inches (certainly taller than Emily who was not short) wearing a blue suit.[200] He looked like a man they had seen with Emily in the *Rising Sun* on the Sunday night who had been smartly dressed, also wearing a blue suit and a bowler hat. Robert Roberts had, of course, met Emily on the Sunday night in the *Rising Sun* but not until after 10:00pm so it was possible that she had been with the man in the blue suit earlier in the evening. Sharples was certain that the woman they saw on the Wednesday night was Emily because, as she walked past, he raised his hat to her in recognition. The actual statements that Sharples and Harvey gave to the police appear no longer to exist and are certainly not on the Metropolitan Police file at the National

Archives but the two men gave evidence at the Old Bailey, and at the inquest, which presumably matched the evidence in their statements. The remarkable thing about the description of the man they said they saw with Emily is that it was very similar to the description of the man the police apparently told Mrs Roberts the previous day that they wanted to find. It will be recalled that Mrs Roberts told a *Daily Mail* reporter that two detectives asked her if she knew anything of a man about five foot ten inches in height wearing a navy blue coat (albeit not a suit) and a bowler hat.

At the same time as Sharples and Harvey were telling police what they knew at Kentish Town Police Station, Robert Henry McCowan, an unemployed carman who lived in Hawley Street in Kentish Town, was telling Detective Sergeant Ball at Somers Town Police Station in Platt Street that, early in the morning of Thursday 12 September at about 4:55am, having left his home at 4:40am, he was walking down St Paul's Road on his way to seek work at a bread company in Brewery Road when, while looking out for his friend, Richard Coleman, who lived nearby and often accompanied him to work, he saw a man emerge from number 29 and walk down the steps and then briskly along the pavement, in the opposite direction to himself, towards the *Murray Arms* public house. He said that the man had a bowler hat and appeared to be well dressed, wearing a dark overcoat with collar turned up, and 'walked with a swaggering gait'.[201] He estimated he was about 5 foot 7 or 8 inches in height and was 'stiffly built' with broad shoulders. McCowan did not catch sight of his face but thought that he would recognise his walk again. He could have had no idea of the controversy that was soon to surround him in relation to this evidence.

From a post-mortem examination conducted on the Saturday afternoon, Dr Thompson apparently informed Inspector Neil that Emily's last meal consisted of fish and potatoes.[202] This led Neil to send out a large team of officers to all fish bars, restaurants and catering houses in the St Pancras area, along with a photograph of Emily for identification purposes. No useful information was obtained although one Sydney Alberts, proprietor of a fried fish shop at 85 King Street, Camden Town, believed that he served Emily and a male companion (whom he described as 'a man-o-wars man') with fish and potatoes at his shop at about 9:30pm on Wednesday 11 September.[203] Curiously, however, when Dr Thompson gave evidence at the inquest a few weeks later, he stated that Emily's last meal included 'lamb, potatoes and stout' and he said almost exactly the same thing in a subsequent written statement when he described her last supper as consisting of 'lamb, potatoes and some liquid possibly stout'.[204] When giving evidence at the Old Bailey, he said that he found indications of mint, as though from mint sauce, as well as potatoes and bread but made no mention of fish (or lamb for that matter) although he did use the phrase 'among other things' to indicate that there was more in the stomach. It is hard to believe that communication between the doctor and the inspector had gone so badly wrong that the extensive enquiries at the fish shops were conducted on a false basis but, unless Dr Thompson deliberately avoided mentioning fish when he prepared his written statement and testified at both the inquest and the Old Bailey, this appears to have been what happened. We may note that Inspector Neil said at the Old Bailey that on the table in Emily's room, he noticed a lamb or mutton bone, a glass which had apparently contained stout, a bottle about half full of stout and two plates which were packed with knives and forks 'as if they had been put there in a hurry'.[205] He also said that his attention was drawn to some mint-sauce in a cup in the cupboard. The suggestion was that Emily had shared a meal of lamb and mint sauce with someone, washed down with a glass of stout, on the night of her murder. No further attempts appear to have been made by police to trace the 'man-o-wars man' – presumably referring to a brawny naval type – described by Sidney Alberts.[206] The existence, or otherwise, of fish in Emily's stomach remains uncertain but unlikely in view of Dr Thompson's evidence.

Enquiries made of local cabmen for sightings of Emily were equally unfruitful. Neil had learned that she frequently travelled in cabs, when she could find a man to pay for her (which supports what Mrs David told *Reynolds's Newspaper* about Emily and her companion arriving at the *Murray Arms* in a cab), and he wanted to ascertain if Emily had taken a cab on the night of her murder. Despite extensive enquiries, none could be found but the police did manage to locate a cabman called Richard Taylor who was passing through St Paul's Road at about 1:10am on the Wednesday night/Thursday morning, towards his stables at Wilson's Yard, Highbury, when he was hailed by a man standing on the opposite side of the road to where Emily lived and took him to Thornhill Road in Islington. Taylor described his passenger as about 35 to 40 years of age, height 5 foot 5 or 6 inches, fair hair and moustache, dressed in a dark jacket, light trousers and black bowler hat with a fresh appearance, looking as if he had recently washed. He said that, although he passed through St Paul's Road almost nightly, it was a very unusual thing to pick up a fare there. This man was set down near a livery stable. Enquiries were made with houses in the neighbourhood of Thornhill Road with a view to locating the man Taylor described but the police got nowhere.

Could this man have been the murderer? The police might have disregarded him on the basis that they believed Emily was murdered later than 1:00am but this was never positively established. Dr Thompson stated on the first day of the inquest into Emily's death that, when he arrived at St Paul's Road (at about 1:00pm), her body was 'quite cold and rigid', with rigor mortis having set in. For that reason, he thought she might have been dead for seven or eight hours, which would place the time of her death at between 5:00 and 6:00am.[207] However, estimating time of death based on a combination of body temperature (which Dr Thompson does not even appear to have taken) and the onset of rigor mortis is an extremely unreliable method because so many factors can affect the rate of heat loss from a dead body and rigor mortis can set in at any time from immediately after death to seven hours later and remain for up to forty-eight hours.

Upon further consideration, the doctor came to the conclusion that Emily was murdered 'about three hours after she had partaken of food' but estimating time of death from stomach contents is an even more unreliable method due to the fact that different digestive systems pass food from the stomach to the intestines at different speeds. Dr Thompson appears to have applied a general rule of thumb that a stomach empties completely about four hours after a meal. It is known as a fact that the digestive system comes to a halt at the moment of death so, if the stomach of a dead person has emptied three quarters of its food contents (as Emily's had, according to Dr Thompson[208]), then it might naturally be concluded that death took place about three hours after the last meal. However, while Dr Thompson would not have known it at the time, subsequent advances in forensic pathology have shown that the general rule of thumb he applied is totally inaccurate and the simple fact is that there is no way that any sensible conclusion as to the time of death could have been drawn from the contents of Emily's stomach. To add to the uncertainty, it is not even known what time she ate her last meal. Later at the inquest, Dr Thompson informed the coroner that he had 'made inquiries' as a result of which he understood that Emily usually took dinner at between eleven o'clock and midnight which, if she had done the same on the Wednesday evening, would place her death, according to his methodology, at between 2:00am and 3:00am (although he said only 3:00am at the inquest) but no actual evidence was ever produced as to Emily's eating habits, let alone the time she ate on the Wednesday.[209] At the Old Bailey, the doctor repeated his evidence that Emily was murdered about three hours after she had eaten food (adding that it might be four hours) but did not go on to mention that he understood her normal time of eating dinner was in the hour before midnight. Under cross-examination he said that he did not think that Emily had been dead more than nine hours when he saw her (at 1:00pm) which would mean that she was murdered no earlier than 4:00am but he did also say (during his evidence-in-chief) that he could not definitely say how long she had been dead.[210] Although Dr Thompson ultimately appears to have believed that death occurred at around 4:00am, the basis of his belief is not scientifically correct. No doubt the doctor felt that he had to express an opinion – it was certainly expected by everyone involved in the case that he would do so – but it was simply not possible for him to provide an accurate, or even approximate, time of death.[211] Consequently, it is by no means impossible that Emily was murdered at 1:00am or earlier so that the man who caught Richard Taylor's cab could have been the killer.

On Sunday 15 September, the police took a statement from Frank Clarke, who had been drinking with Roberts in the *Rising Sun* during the evening of Monday 9 September. He gave a description of the man he saw with Emily which was different in some material respects to the description provided by Roberts. Clarke said the man was 'a short man', about 30 years of age, dark, clean shaven, with a face marked as if with disorder, wearing an old felt hat, dressed in mixture trousers, black coat, a tie and high collar with turned down corners and had very prominent ears. Clarke said that there was a round of drinks called for, 'about the payment of which there was some question', and the man was excited through drinking. He said that he saw 'the short dark man' again in Euston Square coming from the direction of Seymour Street towards Hampstead Road at about 11:15am on the Thursday morning. He had seen him previously in the *Rising Sun* during the past four months and he 'particularly attracted my attention by the way he hesitated in paying for drink he ordered'. Clarke added in his statement that this man:

> appeared to be well known by the majority of the loose women in the vicinity of the *Rising Sun*. He was of a very nasty temper and appeared to do a small business in "specialities" among the women. I have seen him in the Euston Road also in the Euston Tavern with girls.[212]

It will be recalled that Roberts said the man he saw with Emily on the Monday night was five foot, eight inches, slightly taller than the average male height in 1907,[213] yet Clarke described him as 'small'. Roberts estimated the man's age as 23 or 24 (but, as the man he saw was clearly Robert Wood, this estimate was wrong: Wood being 30, although he looked younger). Roberts said nothing about a dispute over payment of drinks or the man being excited through drinking so it would appear that they were describing different individuals. At the Old Bailey, however, Clarke said that the man he had seen with Emily was Robert Wood and he picked him out of a line-up. He claimed to have seen Wood in the *Rising Sun* several times. However, he was never cross-examined as to his claim that the man he saw was 'short' (whereas Wood, at 5 foot 7 or 8 inches, was of average height) nor that the man he saw had a face marked as if with disorder, whereas Wood's skin was clear (at least at the time of his arrest and trial).[214]

Anyone reading the papers on the Monday morning, 16 September, would have been confused as to how the investigation was progressing. According to the *Daily News*, the police were 'Baffled by Camden Town Crime' and they were 'still without a clue' according to the *Tribune*, whereas the *Daily Mirror* referred to 'important developments' and stated 'AN ARREST PROBABLE'.[215] The *Daily Chronicle* was even more positive, predicting: 'ARREST IMMINENT'. But the police were, in fact, no nearer to making an arrest than they had been on the day of the murder.

The *Daily Mail* of 16 September had some new scraps of information. It accurately reported that, on receiving the letter (from 'Bertie') on Wednesday morning, Emily had said (to the man she was with, who was not named but was obviously Roberts), 'This is a nuisance. I have to meet a man who is very jealous of me'. It also mentioned a clue which the police were said to regard as important that:

> Some time ago, on information supplied by Dimmock, a man was sentenced to a term of imprisonment. She has several times told her friends that this man, who is now free, had threatened to have revenge on her, and that she went in some fear of him.[216]

If this was true – and the police would presumably have known – the identity of the man was never revealed. There is nothing in the Metropolitan Police file to suggest that Emily was a police informant although it will be recalled that William Linehan and Gladys Warren appeared to blame her for Linehan's conviction and two month term of imprisonment.

Another potentially important piece of new information appeared in the *Daily News* on the Monday. The newspaper claimed that a man sought by the police had come forward and managed to prove that he was not with Emily on the night of the murder but admitted to being an acquaintance of hers. He was said to have given the police 'very valuable information concerning the girl's habits and associates' and from this and 'other sources' the police had secured 'new evidence that the dead girl was seen by a female friend in the company of a man near King's Cross Station before ten o'clock on the night of the crime'.[217] The *Daily News* also asserted that the description of the man tallied with that of the man believed to have been seen with Emily in the vicinity of St Paul's Road on the Wednesday night (i.e. the 'short, dark individual who wore a bowler hat and a dark suit' it had first mentioned on 13 September). According to the *Daily Chronicle*, however, the various stories that had been told of Emily having been seen in the company of men of varying descriptions had 'yielded practically nothing upon which the detectives could work'.[218] It also claimed that the difficulties faced by the police were enhanced by the fact that it was not uncommon for Emily to be seen with at least 'half a dozen men in one night'. The *Daily Mirror* had an exclusive, reporting that a postcard album found at St Paul's Road was proving 'of considerable assistance' to the police because it contained numerous postcards from soldiers and sailors who were friends of Emily.[219] This was the first public mention of the postcard album.

At 11:00am on the morning of Monday 16 September, the inquest commenced at the St Pancras Coroner's Court, located in a picturesque old burial ground at the back of St Pancras Gardens, behind St Pancras Station, in Cambridge Street. The coroner was the elderly Dr Danford Thomas who had conducted the inquest into the death of Pheobe Hogg seventeen years earlier which, as we have seen, was the previously labelled 'Camden Town Murder'. Danford Thomas was not very well, being unable to write with his right hand and was rather deaf too. He would die three years later, in the middle of the next so-called 'Camden Town Murder' inquest, regarding the death of Mrs Crippen. According to the *Daily News*, admittance to the court, which could only accommodate about thirty members of the public, was refused to all except those who were involved in the case but, for an hour before the opening of the inquest, large numbers of curious spectators gathered round the court while others 'craned their necks in the endeavour to peer through the mortuary windows but a large canvas covering successfully baffled inquisitive sightseers'.[220] During the proceedings, Henry Dimmock, Emily's brother, formally identified the body as that of his sister but could offer no explanation about her death. Bert Shaw, ironically wearing a blue serge suit that day, explained how he found the body but was in for a shock as Inspector Neil closely cross-examined him about his knowledge of Emily's prostitution. Shaw admitted that he knew she had been a prostitute before he met her but claimed he had no idea she was still bringing men home. Neil did not believe him and thought he 'winked' at such habits. In the police file, he would later set out some calculations on the basis of Shaw earning 18 shillings a week (which he had been for most of the time he was living with Emily). He knew the Shaws were paying eight shillings a week for rent, two shillings and sixpence for the hire of a piano, one shilling and threepence for furniture and one shilling and sixpence for a sewing machine which totalled thirteen shillings and threepence a week, leaving only four shillings and ninepence a week for food and other expenses, which Neil did not believe was enough to live on, thus concluding that Shaw knew that Emily was earning money for them both through prostitution. There was, however, a slight flaw in Neil's calculations because he did not factor in any income that Emily might have received from her sewing work. Shaw said in his statement that she had 'been earning money as a dressmaker' and, furthermore, for the previous three months he had in fact been earning 27 shillings a week (and was apparently giving Emily 20 shillings, or £1, a week). On the other hand, Neil wrote that it was 'well known' that Emily had bought Shaw several suits of clothes since he had been living with her and it would have been hard for Shaw to have believed this could have been afforded without the proceeds of prostitution.

Mr Danford Thomas, however, remarked that the fact Shaw had introduced Emily to his parents suggested that he believed she had 'reformed a little'.[221] Shaw did, however, admit at the inquest that he and Emily had been turned out of St Pancras Square after Jack Crabtree complained to the superintendent that Emily owed him money and had been bringing men home.

At the end of the first day's proceedings in the St Pancras Coroner's Court, Inspector Neil informed the coroner that Emily's chest of drawers had been ransacked 'by someone who was looking for something' although he did not say what.[222] He also mentioned that there were 'three rings there which were not touched'. Clearly Neil had some ideas about what the murderer had been doing but did not elaborate. However, he did officially exonerate Shaw from any blame. The inquest was then adjourned for a fortnight to allow police enquiries to proceed.

The evening papers of 16 September carried reports of the inquest but the *Evening News* had some interesting new information about the 'short dark man' previously identified as one of three possible suspects in its edition of 14 September. It stated that one of its journalists had learned that this man was 'morbidly jealous' of Emily and had used threats towards her in the hearing of one of her female friends, once declaring that she should not live to serve another man as she had served him. Emily was said to have confided that she was afraid of him. He had also supposedly tried several times to tempt her away from Shaw and was believed to be with her at 'a hotel' on Monday night (presumably a reference to the *Rising Sun*). Most importantly, in addition to being 'short' and 'dark', the man was described as, 'Of sallow complexion, with low forehead and deep-set eyes....usually wore a dark blue suit and bowler hat'.[223] According to the *Evening News*, the 'short dark man' was now the main suspect in the police investigation. As the description of this suspect did not particularly match the descriptions provided to the police by Robert Roberts and Frank Clarke, it would appear that the *Evening News* had an independent source – apparently a female associate of Emily's – who had not given a statement to the police.

During the afternoon of the following day, Tuesday 17 September, Emily's funeral was conducted at the St Pancras Cemetery in East Finchley. Thousands lined the route of the procession which began in Kentish Town Road at the premises of the undertakers, the Economic Funeral Company, as a hearse and two mourning carriages drawn by black horses, followed by three hansom cabs, carried Emily's polished elm coffin to its place of rest – an unmarked grave which was no more than a mound of earth covered with turf.[224] There were eight wreaths from friends and family. Bert Shaw was there, as were three of Emily's brothers and some of her sisters. Robert Roberts also attended the funeral and discussed the case with Emily's friends, including May Campbell, or Lillian Donaldson, who was now Mrs Lillian Pohl, having married a commercial clerk called George Pohl at the St Pancras register office nine months earlier. She mentioned that she had some information about the murder but her new husband did not want her to go to the police.

At about the same time as the funeral ceremony, a rumour spread that there had been an arrest but this proved unfounded. According to the next day's *Morning Leader*, what had happened was that a man was found who was known to have quarrelled with Emily and was asked to go to Kentish Town Police station to give an account of his movements, which he did. The newspaper reported that he went home after an interview lasting nearly two hours with Inspector Neil and other officers engaged in the case. There is nothing about this in the police file in the National Archives but the *Marylebone Times* reported that 'on inquiry it was ascertained that though a certain man had been apprehended upon information, he had completely satisfied Inspector Neil and his colleagues as to his movements on the night of the murder, while having admitted being in the woman's company on the Sunday, Monday and Tuesday nights'.[225] This was obviously a reference to Robert Roberts but he was not known to have quarrelled with Emily and had, in any case, satisfied police as to his movements on the day after the murder, a full five days earlier. It may be that the *Morning Leader* was partly referring, in garbled form, to Arthur Thomas Atkins, one of the men who caught venereal disease from Emily. He voluntarily presented himself at Somers Town Police Station after hearing enquiries were being made about him and said that he returned from work to his lodgings at 42 Cumberland Market, Camden Town, at 10:00pm and left for work at 5:45am the following morning. This was corroborated by his landlady and a fellow lodger. Nevertheless, to make absolutely certain, Atkins was seen by Robert Roberts, Florence Smith and Ellen Lawrence who all confirmed that he was not the man seen in Emily's company in the *Rising Sun* on the Monday before the murder. He was thus eliminated from the inquiry.

While this was going on, Inspector Neil was concentrating on arranging an interview with Jack Crabtree in Pentonville Prison. On 18 September he applied for a Home Office order for himself and Sergeant Ball to be allowed to visit Crabtree. This was immediately granted and Neil found himself face to face with Crabtree in Pentonville the following day. Considering Crabtree's importance to the case it is worth looking very closely at this man.

Chapter Five

The Utterly Despicable Jack Crabtree

'...a disorderly house keeper, a convicted horse thief, a liar, a bully and everything that is ignoble and base.'

Edward Marshall Hall K.C. on Jack Crabtree, *Morning Leader*, 16 December 1907

John William ('Jack') Crabtree was born in Kirkgate, Huddersfield, on 17 December 1859. His father, William Crabtree, was a chimney sweep who had married a Yorkshire lass called Grace Rawson, in Keighley, Bradford, on 28 February 1859. William was himself the son of a chimney sweep, John Crabtree, originally from Hull, who had set up business in Keighley. At the time, chimney sweeps were under pressure from the authorities to stop illegally employing young boys, in breach of legislation such as the Chimney Sweepers and Chimneys Regulation Act of 1840, which prohibited anyone below the age of twenty-one from cleaning chimneys. New sweeping machines were supposed to be used for narrow chimneys but these were expensive and did not work in many properties, especially those with old houses. The law was not very well enforced and the temptation to continue to use child labour was too great for most chimney cleaning businesses to ignore. If everyone else was doing it there was no profit margin in paying adults or purchasing machines. Some employers of children were, however, arrested and convicted. The *Leeds Times* of 23 July 1859 reported that a William Crabtree, Chimney Sweeper, was charged at Huddersfield Magistrates' Court with, 'allowing a boy, nine years of age to ascend and descend a chimney for the purpose of sweeping it'. The report stated that Crabtree had bought a chimney sweeping business from a man named Wright and the boy came with the business. The magistrates fined Crabtree £5 and ordered the boy to be handed back to his father. In the following month, the *Bradford Observer*, recorded that a John Crabtree, Master Chimney Sweeper of Keighley, was fined £5, with sixteen shillings costs, at Bingley Petty Sessions, for allowing a boy called John Broadhurst to sweep a chimney in the dwelling house of Joseph Chatburn of Keighley 'contrary to the Act of Parliament'.[226]

It cannot be stated for certain that the Crabtrees referred to in these press reports were the father and grandfather respectively of our Jack Crabtree but the likelihood is that they were indeed the same people. In any event, the difficulties faced by chimney sweeps in England, who traditionally used children, would have affected them, and more legislation, being pushed by Lord Shaftesbury, with larger fines and longer terms of imprisonment for non-complying employers, was on the way in the form of the Chimney Sweepers Regulation Act of 1864. The sweeps were not terribly popular around the country. Shaftesbury referred to the 'great cruelty and suffering' entailed upon children with 'cases of disease and mutilation' when speaking in the House of Lords in 1856, and stated that 'many children were crippled in early life and rendered wholly incapable of earning a livelihood...while these children were handed over to absolute and unqualified slavery, it was impossible they could receive the first rudiments of education'.[227] Being a chimney sweeper was hardly a glamorous job and the *Morning Post* of 19 March 1862 commented that 'There are certain occupations which, however, advantageous or necessary they may be to the community at large, we can never be brought to look upon with favour....chimney sweeps may be estimable citizens, but scarcely desirable travelling companions'. It might have been this sort of negativity that prompted William and Grace Crabtree to consider emigrating and starting a new life in a faraway country.

They were not the only ones. The colonies were crying out for all forms of labour. Financial inducements were offered to those with the right skills. The *Yorkshire Gazette* of 17 May 1862 referred to 'emigration mania' and claimed that 'there has never been such facilities afforded for emigration as there are at present'. It pointed out that there were numerous active emigration committees 'anxious to secure the services of any number of able-bodied men and women and prepared to offer them any amount of good wages the moment they land at whatever colony it may please them to fix upon as their ultimate destination'. South Africa, Canada, Australia and New Zealand were receiving boatloads of hopeful workers escaping from the drudgery, dull work, poor conditions, low pay and drab weather of British industrial towns. As the *Yorkshire Gazette* concluded: 'It is for the intelligent mechanic or agricultural labourer to consider whether it is better for him to stay here but two degrees moved from penury in hard times like the present, or by emigrating make an attempt to secure that wealth which is so difficult to acquire in over-populated countries'. Samuel Browning, an Auckland resident, sang New Zealand's praises in a letter to a friend which was published in the *Bury Times* of 19 July 1862, saying: 'We have warm winters that scarcely require a fire on any of the coolest days of the year; delicious summers; rivers; harbours; timbers; mines, rich soils, a land teeming with poultry, eggs, butter, honey, and the choicest European fruits; whilst our cattle, horses and sheep are rolling in fat in rich meadows close to Auckland'. Balanced against a lifetime of cleaning dirty chimneys in Yorkshire, it was probably not a very difficult decision for William Crabtree to decide to sail off to this dream land which truly seemed to be flowing with milk and honey.

Accordingly, William and Grace, together with their two-year-old son, boarded The Roman Emperor at Plymouth on 22 December 1862 destined for New Zealand. It was a long voyage, lasting almost 100 days, during which time little John William celebrated his third birthday, and the ship finally arrived at Lyttleton on 30 March 1863. William initially started his new life as a carpenter in St Albans in the district of Christchurch and became a father again in 1865 with the birth of another son, Charles. In 1869, still in St Albans, Grace gave birth to a girl, Mary Jane, and, in about 1872, the Crabtrees moved to Knightstown, Canterbury, where they had a second girl called Emma. Shortly after this, William became a storekeeper, running a grocery store and bakery in Knightstown. Young Jack appears to have assisted his father in this business. In April 1879, he married Elizabeth McTaggart in Ashburton, stating his profession as 'Grocer and Baker'. However, he also falsely stated his age as twenty-one when he was really only nineteen, thus committing his first criminal offence. His second was in January 1880 when he was convicted of cruelty to a horse by not feeding it, although he appears to have escaped any serious punishment. William and Grace gave birth to another son, David, in February

1880 but things started to go wrong for them about this time. In March 1880, William was sued for payment by one of his suppliers and, unable to find the money, his furniture was put up for public auction by court order.

In the following month, Jack was sentenced to a month's hard labour at the Christchurch Resident Magistrate's Court for 'revolting cruelty to a mare'.[228] His horse was left to linger with a broken leg which rotted away. It was found eating wood and gnawing boards from the house. Jack claimed that the horse did not belong to him, being part of a bankrupt estate, but he was not believed and the magistrate, when sentencing, 'spoke strongly of the revolting inhumanity of the prisoner'.[229] Things got worse for Jack in July when a warrant was issued on a charge of committing a breach of the Marriage Act 'by making a false declaration as to age before the Registrar'.[230] He was eventually arrested in December.

Meanwhile, in January 1881, William and Grace were charged on three counts of fraudulently conveying a section of land in an attempt to avoid bankruptcy. Grace was arrested but William had fled and was believed to be hiding in Rangitikei. The *Star* of 8 January 1881 reported that 'A son of accused expressed his willingness to become bail and proffered certain deeds, but the Bench declined to accept him as bail at all'. Five weeks later, the same paper stated: 'On Saturday afternoon the property in the bankrupt estate of the now well known William Crabtree which has been the subject of a large amount of litigation recently was sold by order of the trustees Messrs H Matson and Co.' The property consisted of 'about 1 road, 21 perches with a shop, bakehouse, and three cottages thereon, situation in High Street Knightstown. It was sold in four lots and realized £617 10s'.[231] Jack was also having financial problems and was himself made bankrupt by the Supreme Court of New Zealand on 15 July 1881.[232]

During the remainder of the year, Jack was arrested for no less than four separate offences but was convicted of none of them. In August 1881, he was alleged to have left a horse exposed to the weather in a paddock where it was found in such a state of hunger and exhaustion that it had to be shot. However, at the magistrate's court, Jack denied that the horse was his, claiming he had lost his own mare and was in the process of trying to catch it, after he saw it galloping down the street, when he was arrested by a constable in plain clothes. It was an unlikely story but his wife gave corroborating evidence in his defence and the case against him was dismissed.

In November 1881, Jack was arrested for stealing a horse worth £15 from a George Holt. His defence on this occasion was that he did not steal the horse but was in the habit of accompanying the local pound keeper's son on his rounds for the purpose of driving wild or unsecured horses to the pound and he had simply found Holt's horse loose in the road. This did not match with the evidence of Mr Holt who said that he had left the horse in his yard with a well secured gate. Late at night, he said, his attention was attracted by a noise in the yard and he saw his mare being directed out of the gate by Jack Crabtree on horseback. He called out to him to stop but Crabtree did not respond. Holt gave chase and found Crabtree with his horse, and two others, which he said he was taking to the pound. When Crabtree refused to hand back the horse, Holt called a policeman and had him arrested. Although Holt's evidence strongly suggested that Crabtree was using his association with the local pound to release horses onto the street for him to then impound (or steal), Crabtree was given the benefit of the doubt and released. However, the magistrate commented on 'the discreditable state of affairs the evidence had disclosed and requested the police draw up a statement of the case and submit it to the local authority controlling the pound in question'.[233]

Jack's third escape from punishment in 1881 was when he was found not guilty of stealing items worth one pound and ten shillings from Peter Jack on 1 November. Peter Jack's landlady was Crabtree's mother-in-law and she had called in bailiffs to take possession of his goods after he had not paid the rent. For some reason, Crabtree accompanied the bailiffs and appears to have helped himself to a muffler, a smoothing iron, a piece of lace and a pair of boots, although Crabtree's mother-in-law claimed that Peter Jack had told Crabtree he could take the items and do what he wanted with them. Peter Jack's wife reported the items missing on 4 November and they were found in Crabtree's house (which was the same property Peter Jack had previously rented) sixteen days later. When arrested and charged by Detective O'Connor with stealing them, Crabtree said 'all right'. He claimed in court, however, that he had no intention of stealing the articles which, he said, had been left in the house by Peter Jack and he had found them there along with some rubbish when he took possession. Dismissing the case, the local magistrate said that 'as the articles were left in the house he would give prisoner the benefit of the doubt this time but he would recommend him not to sail so close to the wind in future'.[234] Nevertheless, Jack was arrested again at the end of November for horse stealing and appeared in Christchurch's Supreme Court on 3 January 1882 but, still sailing extremely close to the wind, was once again acquitted after the Crown Prosecutor offered no evidence.

Jack's first experience of fire occurred in September 1882 when a kerosene lamp was knocked over by a young girl in a cottage occupied by a Mr O'Donnell in Queen Street, Sydenham, in Christchurch. The flames spread to a six-roomed house owned by Jack. The New Zealand *Star* of 15 September 1882 reported that 'Mr Crabtree's house was mortgaged in the No 3 Building Society for £100 and insured by the society for £200, the original amount of the mortgage...Mr Crabtree's loss is estimated at £250'. Perhaps assisted by the money from the insurance company, but mainly with a loan from the Colonial Bank of New Zealand, Jack bought a bakery store at Anderson's Bay in Dunedin and employed three people to assist in its running. It did not last long. At midnight on 30 March 1884, the store, together with Jack's four-roomed house, was burned down to the ground. The premises and furniture were insured for £560 with the Standard Fire and Insurance Company. This was a large sum but, before Crabtree could get his hands on any of it, the Colonial Bank of New Zealand called in its loan and forced the sale of his horse, cart and harness as well as his baker's tools and a ton of flour and he was then made bankrupt in June 1884 when the local miller demanded payment for goods supplied. At about the same time, a drapery store that Jack also owned in Christchurch burned down. He was clearly very unlucky with fires.

The failure of his bakery and drapery businesses seems to have led Jack to make a living from the proceeds of prostitution. The New Zealand *Star* of 14 August 1884 reported that the Linwood Town Board in Phillipstown, Christchurch, had received a petition signed by twenty-eight residents of

Strickland Street and its vicinity 'to remove an evil arising from the occupants of houses belonging to Mr Crabtree and Mrs McTaggart, being persons of ill-fame'. The newspaper also stated that a by-law dealing with the matter had been framed and would be enforced as soon as possible.[235] A month earlier, Jack had been charged again in the Christchurch Magistrate's Court with cruelty to a horse and was remanded on bail with a surety of £50. Times appear to have been desperate for Jack who was reduced to stealing ducks. He appeared at Christchurch Magistrate's Court in September 1884 accused of purloining a drake valued at nearly five shillings from one Georgina Ambrose who said that the lock of her fowl house had been picked and there was a false key lying on the ground near the door. Clearly aware of the character of her neighbour, she suspected Crabtree immediately and went to his place, where she saw a drake which she was certain was the one that had been stolen. Crabtree said that the drake belonged to his mother-in-law whose adopted teenage son, Robert McTaggart, gave evidence in support. During the proceedings, Ms Ambrose cried out, 'It's my drake sir!' to which the Bench replied, 'We think so too, take it and go away".[236] However, as there was no evidence of larceny, the case against Crabtree was dismissed. So far he had got off very lightly for his various breaches of the law but this was to change after he went on a mini crime spree later in the year.

On Monday, 20 October 1884, a plumber called Harry Flavell, while working at a house in Fendalton, a suburb of Christchurch, noticed that a number of building materials, worth about £30, which had been left on site over the weekend, had gone missing. It was noticed that there were wheel marks as if a horse and light cart had entered the property. The crime was initially unsolved although a neighbour of Crabtree's in Sydenham, Mary Jane McMillan, heard a trap stop at Crabtree's place, followed by a noise like a tin rattling, during the night of Sunday 19 October between 11 and 12 o'clock. The next morning she saw some galvanised iron and tools in her shed. Jack Crabtree told her he had got a bargain for the iron. He said he had paid five pounds and ten shillings for it and was going to build a verandah. Ms McMillan had no reason to disbelieve what she was told and was happy for her shed to be used to store her neighbour's goods.

Nearly two months later, on Wednesday, 10 December 1884, one William Moir reported to police that nine horses had been stolen from his paddock at Papanui. Telegrams reporting the theft were circulated to police stations around the country and a report was received from Rakaia police that nine horses, answering the description of those stolen, had been spotted being driven to an auctioneer's house in Timaru, to be put up for auction on Saturday 13 December by a man whose name was believed to be Crabtree. A police detective – Austin Kirby – was dispatched to the town and located Crabtree on the Great South Road, although, when challenged, Crabtree claimed his name was David Gray. The detective told 'David Gray' that he matched the description of a man who had put some horses up for auction and he was asked to accompany him to the auction house, which he willingly agreed to do. The two men were crossing the road when, separated by a passing cart, Crabtree took his chance and fled. Having been one of 'Canterbury's prominent athletes' in his younger days,[237] he was quickly able to put some distance between himself and the officer. He ran straight into the *Royal Hotel* and dashed through the bar and several rooms, ending up in a nursery, where he knocked over a nurse and baby who were obstructing his path, before raising the nursery window and jumping out. However, the hotel owner, Mr Spillane, had given chase and managed to catch up with the intruder on the veranda, tripping him up and clinging onto him, despite Crabtree attempting to trap the hotel owner's leg by pulling the window frame down on it. At this point, Detective Kirby joined the struggle and overpowered Crabtree before handcuffing and arresting him. The detective charged him with stealing a number of horses belonging to Mr Moir in Christchurch, to which Crabtree replied, 'I know myself better than to give you any information'.[238]

When news of Crabtree's arrest reached police in Christchurch on 15 December, a search was conducted of his house in Queen Street, Sydenham, where detectives found five lengths of pipe, two pieces of lead, and over twenty sheets of galvanised iron in a back shed behind the cottage. These items all matched the description of the property stolen from the house in Fendalton. A further search was conducted of a second property owned by Crabtree in Strickland Street, Phillipstown. This resulted in the discovery of more stolen articles. Elizabeth Crabtree was arrested, but said, 'I won't go with you. I don't know anything about it. I have never been out at night with my husband'.[239] Nevertheless, she and her husband were jointly charged with stealing various saws, planes and chisels, twenty sheets of corrugated iron, seventy-three feet of galvanised iron piping, two dozen small pieces of bends, two pieces of lead, two strips of solder, eighty-three feet of match-lining, one force pump, a part of a pipe threading machine, two pairs of gas tongs, two floor cramps, one air vessel, five taps and two stopcocks. The total value of the property discovered was about £12 out of a total value stolen of £30. Jack was, in addition, charged with the theft of Mr Moir's horses.

The Crabtrees appeared together before a magistrate on 23 December 1884 and the *Star* newspaper reported that: 'The interest taken in the cases was shown by the large crowd of people which assembled to listen to them'. During the hearing, 16-year-old Robert McTaggart, who lived in the house at Strickland Street, gave evidence that Jack Crabtree went out every night on his horse and cart, with Mrs Crabtree accompanying him on some evenings. After their nocturnal journeys, he would notice items in the house that he had never seen before. He told the court he did not like to live in the house 'on account of this going out at nights'. However, he also admitted that he had 'kept company with bad women', explaining that there were prostitutes living next door and that Mrs Crabtree had asked him to do some work for them. At the end of the day's hearing, the magistrate said that there was no evidence against Mrs Crabtree who, he said, had not acted independently of her husband so she was released. Jack, however, was committed for trial on two charges of horse stealing and four of larceny of building materials.

During his trial, before Justice Johnson at the Christchurch Criminal Court on 5 January 1885, Jack was described by Detective O'Connor as 'a thief and consorter with prostitutes'. He pled guilty to all the charges but, despite this, was sentenced to a surprisingly large total of thirteen years penal servitude, with the judge saying that it was 'monstrous to find a man of twenty-four years of age going out every night in his cart stealing as he went, and then winding up the year by stealing eleven horses'.[240] The New Zealand *Tablet* of 23 January 1885 commented laconically:

A more complete, clever, well organised rascal has not been before the court for many years. Did he want to add a verandah to his house? Mr Crabtree went forth by night seeking verandahs in the course of erection. They and the tools lying about disappeared at once. Goods of all kinds likely to be useful to people who have fundamental objections to buying anything, got into the habit of crowding Mr Crabtree's premises, and stowing themselves away in lofts apparently inaccessible and, therefore, apparently non-existent. As for horses, they never could keep out of this extraordinary man's power.

The 'extraordinary man' was sent to Lyttleton Gaol but had served little more than a month behind bars before he made his first dramatic escape attempt on 25 January 1885. While working in a prison gang, supervised by armed guards, at Sticking Point, he took his opportunity while another prisoner had accidentally hurt his foot. With the warders distracted, Crabtree removed his shoes and sprinted up a bank and then along the main road, stripping off his prison clothes as he went. One of the warders fired his rifle but missed and Crabtree made a twenty-foot jump down the bank on the other side. He got as far as a mile away from Sticking Point but it was an extremely hot day, with the sun beating down, and, pursued hard by members of a nearby naval artillery corps, plus the entire Lyttleton police force, he quickly became exhausted. When a second bullet nearly hit him, he lost heart, collapsed to the ground and was captured. With his feet badly cut from walking on sharp rocks, he required the support of two warders to help him back to the prison. The authorities felt that, as Crabtree had been 'considerably knocked about' in his escape attempt, a severe penalty was not necessary and he was cautioned without further punishment. However, he was transferred to the supposedly more secure Mount Cook Gaol in Wellington, arriving on 26 February 1885.

It did not take Crabtree long to plan his first escape from Mount Cook, where he somehow managed to obtain a chisel, gimlet and double-bladed knife. Pretending to be sick, he was allowed to remain alone in his cell where he worked on the wall, nearly succeeding in cutting a hole the size of a man's body. However, an alert warder became suspicious when he found Crabtree sitting up in his hammock with his back oddly positioned against the cell wall. When instructed to stand up, Crabtree declared that he had such an attack of rheumatism that he could not move. The gaoler was sent for and ordered the man to be forcibly removed. Crabtree reportedly exclaimed, 'It's all up with me now', and a search of his cell located the tools and the hole in the wall. Beneath his bed, blankets were found sewn together in classic fashion, designed to facilitate an escape over the exterior prison wall. Crabtree was brought before a magistrate on 26 March 1885 charged with attempting to escape and with being in possession of prohibited articles. A newspaper report said he admitted the charges but 'exhibited the utmost indifference'.[241] He was sentenced to thirty days confinement in irons and seven days of bread and water.

Meanwhile, Crabtree's wife was also making the news. Along with her mother, Anna McTaggart, she was convicted at Christchurch Magistrate's Court of assaulting a bailiff, one H.E. Boardman, at the house in Strickland Street on 21 March 1885. Mr Boardman was there to take possession of goods in lieu of a debt but, at the hearing, he admitted to having a few drinks with the five or six women who were in the house (suggesting it was being used as a brothel). After he had been there some two hours, he was hit on the back of the head with a shovel before Mrs Taggart whacked him with a claret jug and, for good measure, Mrs Crabtree smacked him round the face with a bundle of receipts for the furniture he was attempting to remove. Dazed, he then ran for the door and was pushed out into the street by the ladies. The magistrate declared that Mr Boardman had acted 'most injudiciously' in accepting drinks in the first place and his behaviour was said to be 'very unbecoming an officer of the court' but Mrs Crabtree and Mrs McTaggart were nevertheless fined £2 each for the assault.

Crabtree's two escape attempts in 1885 were merely dress rehearsals for the big one. Despite the warders of Mount Cook Gaol having strict instructions to keep him under close observation, early on Sunday, 30 January 1887 he used surreptitiously obtained tools to remove the hinges from his cell door which allowed him to squeeze out through the opening. He then managed to access the prison yard from where, using the old trick of blankets sewn together, he scaled the prison wall and dropped into the street below. When the escape was discovered, a warder, who was supposed to check Crabtree's cell every half an hour but failed to do so, was sacked, which might have been unfair because Crabtree was probably assisted by a prisoner in the adjoining cell who kept watch during the night and tapped a warning whenever the warder approached. Crabtree was described as 'a dangerous man to be at large' – on what basis it is not clear – and a reward of £20 was offered for his capture.

He was only at large for four days and nights. There were fifty men on his trail and his description was put out in the newspapers. To survive and escape capture while on the run, he broke into various houses and stole clothes (to replace his prison garb) and jewellery (which he sold). He was spotted in a passage near Molesworth Street in Wellington at 11:00pm on 1 February and ordered out by a local resident who received the reply, 'For God's sake leave me alone!'[242] He then jumped a garden fence and ran away when the resident approached. He was caught the following evening when a woman reported that she had seen a man on the lawn of her brother's house. A detective arrived and saw a well dressed man in a black suit wearing an expensive overcoat and gold chain. He recognized him as the escaped prisoner and called on him to surrender, something which surprised Jack so much that he immediately dropped to his knees without offering any resistance. The detective pulled out his revolver as a precaution but Crabtree was armed only with a vast quantity of stolen jewellery, including 'bracelets, rings, studs, earrings and valuables of all descriptions'.[243] The first thing he said to the detective was 'I will die in gaol after this'. He claimed not to have eaten for two days and was so overcome by his efforts that a cab was required to carry him to the police station. When he was brought to the Wellington Magistrate's Court the following day, his legs and feet were reported to be swollen and battered and he seemed to be 'in rather a weak condition'.[244] He said that his intention had been to obtain some food and goods to enable him to escape to the country and start a new life.

Once safely back in custody, Crabtree was charged on various counts of housebreaking during his escape as well as being charged with escaping from prison but, in an interesting twist, the charges were deferred while he became a prosecution witness after police charged a local dealer and his wife with handling stolen goods. Crabtree gave evidence that, on the night after he escaped from prison, he spoke to Joseph and Elizabeth Trenery and, claiming he was 'hard up', sold them a silk handkerchief for sixpence. He claimed that he informed the pair that he had some 'plunder' which he had got 'on the cross' (meaning in dubious circumstances) and asked them if they would be interested in buying it. On receiving a positive reply he went out and stole some clothes and silver goods which he brought back the next evening, asking for five pounds but accepting twenty-five shillings. He gave a receipt for the money in the name of 'William Knowles'. During the proceedings against the Trenerys, it was put to Crabtree by their Counsel that he was giving evidence on behalf of the prosecution in return for a lighter sentence but he denied this, claiming that two or three more years in prison made no difference to him. By all accounts, he produced quite an entertaining performance as this extract of his cross-examination by Mr Skerrett, counsel for the defence, reveals:

> **Mr Skerrett:** Were you anxious to please the police by identifying the accused as the man you sold the goods to?
> **Crabtree:** Not at all.
> **Mr Skerrett:** Now, don't be in a hurry.
> **Crabtree:** I'm not in a hurry; I've plenty of time (laughter in court).
> **Mr Skerrett:** On the evening when you went to the shop were you not rather anxious?
> **Crabtree:** Well, no.
> **Mr Skerrett:** You knew the police were on your track?
> **Crabtree:** Oh no, they were not on my track. I'd passed one of them a few minutes earlier (laughter in court).
> **Mr Skerrett:** Well you knew they were looking for you?
> **Crabtree:** Why, I was talking to one of them only a couple of hours before, so there was no fear on that score.
> **Mr Skerrett:** Well you wanted to get your business done quickly and get home before you met another policeman?
> **Crabtree:** I had no home at the time (laughter in court).
> **Mr Skerrett:** You did not take any notice of this man?
> **Crabtree:** Yes, like I'm taking notice of you now. It would be a funny thing to turn my back to a man when talking to him.

Like any good performer, Crabtree mixed his comedy with pathos and, when accused by Mr Skerrett of burning down his own houses three times, he responded 'in a voice broken by emotion and with tears in his eyes as well as in his voice' that he had been rendered penniless by each fire, pointing out that the last two fires had occurred in his absence from home.[245] In full flow, Crabtree continued, as summarised by the *Poverty Bay Herald* of 9 July 1887:

> Then, he had a thoroughbred mare, in a foal to a well known sire, which he kept in his paddock. The mare broke her leg but he kept her alive for the sake of the foal, and [when] the police got hold of this fact, a charge of cruelty to the mare was brought against him and he was sent to prison for a month. All his insurance money from the last fire, £700 in amount, had gone to his creditors and he was now penniless and disgraced. No sooner out of gaol was he, than the hounding down by the police commenced. Then he got embittered and reckless, and the devil of retaliation entered into him and he went – no was driven – to the bad and to his present position.

It was an interesting explanation of his journey to prison but one which omitted to mention that his conviction for cruelty to a horse, for which he had given a different explanation at the time, was not his first and his decision to turn to robbery was hardly explained by police persecution. Nevertheless, the trial judge, Mr Justice Richmond, commented that 'ill-luck seemed to have strangely pursued the young fellow and to have marked him as a victim' and the press seemed sympathetic to Crabtree's 'harrowing recital', referring to the 'extremely severe and disproportionate sentence which he is now working out'.[246] In the end, however, despite the combination of jokes and sob-stories, Crabtree was not convincing enough as a witness for the prosecution, which was unable to prove that the Trenerys knew the goods were stolen, and they were acquitted. It would not be the only time that Crabtree was a key witness in an unsuccessful prosecution. To make matters worse, he was sentenced to an extra three years in prison for his escape attempt from Wellington Prison. However, the sympathetic press reports of his life story seem to have succeeded in winning him public support, and a petition was got up on his behalf which resulted in his sentence being reduced from a total of sixteen years to ten years. However, now transferred to Auckland Gaol, Crabtree was given a hard time, being placed in solitary confinement and stripped twice every day when being searched for concealed tools. He was not allowed any writing materials or even cups of tea. It was enough to drive a man mad and, indeed, Crabtree did seem to be losing his mind. Early in 1888 he developed symptoms of lunacy, claiming that his wife and friends were conspiring to deprive him of his property and, certified insane by a gullible doctor, he was transferred to a lunatic asylum. As a consequence of his supposed illness, the governor of Auckland remitted the remainder of his sentence and he was handed over to the care of his parents who were living in Auckland.

He was, of course, faking madness. Within a few years of his release, in 1891, with financial assistance from a relative, he opened a grocery store in Lefroy, near Launceston in Tasmania. Inevitably, it burned down to the ground. The cause of the fire on 13 September 1892 was unknown but the store and its contents were insured for a total of £900. As usual, Crabtree was in financial difficulty at the time and, during the following month, with history enjoying a game of repeating itself, he was made bankrupt for a failure to pay his creditors. No insurance money was paid out but, instead, the highly suspicious insurance company offered a reward of £150 for information as to how the fire started. At the same time, during his examination for bankruptcy, an allegation was made that he had been selling stock at cost prices; this was an old trick associated with the long firm swindle whereby a new company is established and goods are obtained on credit and sold cheaply to undercut any competition, with the suppliers never being paid, before the founders of the company disappear with all the money. The same trick could also work if a shopkeeper burnt his store and its contents, reclaiming the value on insurance, having actually sold all the stock at rock bottom prices. Another allegation made against Crabtree was that he had shipped out his stock to an associate in Melbourne before the fire, despite claiming that it had all been destroyed in the flames.

No action was taken by the police at this stage but, at the start of 1893, Crabtree was engaged in an audacious long firm fraud. He found a front man with no criminal record called Henry Thompson who appeared in Wellington representing himself as a wealthy businessman with capital and, consequently, managed to obtain credit with several merchants. With an associate of Crabtree's called George Goode from Auckland, Thompson set up a shop in Molesworth Street, Wellington, which was, ironically, the very street in which Crabtree had been spotted while on the run from prison. Business was brisk and three additional shops were opened in Featherston, Masterton and Greytown respectively, using paid managers who thought they were being employed in a genuine business. Large numbers of goods purchased on credit were sold at bargain prices and everything went well until the credit needed to be paid but wasn't and the merchants realized they had been cheated. The police were called in and arrested Crabtree and Goode (Thompson having fled) in April 1893 and charged them with obtaining over £1,000 by false pretences. The case went to the Supreme Court but it was a very complicated prosecution, involving complex financial aspects, and it was difficult to prove that the defendants were doing anything illegal. Consequently, in July 1893, the crown prosecutor decided not to proceed with the charges against Crabtree and Goode, who were set free. Thompson was, however, made bankrupt and, never one to miss an opportunity, Crabtree claimed £108 from the Official Assignee in bankruptcy of Thompson's estate on the basis that these were unpaid wages but the claim was rejected (the decision being upheld on appeal).

Meanwhile, Jack's father, William, who had spent some time in the army, had settled in Launceston where he worked as a contractor. In 1894 he was embroiled in an extraordinary legal action after a woman called Elizabeth Smith claimed to recognize him as her husband, Thomas Smith, who had deserted her and their seven children, running off with an Emma Crabtree, over thirty years earlier. So convinced was she that William Crabtree and Thomas Smith were the same person that she not only attempted to sue him for maintenance and desertion but had 500 copies of a handbill printed and circulated in which she alleged that William was her long lost husband. He was forced to sue the woman for libel and, in court, was able to prove his identity with official documentation but Mrs Smith, quite unable to face reality, continued to believe he was her husband. A few months later the real Thomas Smith was found working as a miner in Hokitika and William was able to close that strange chapter in his life.

In about 1897, William went into business with his son, Charles, and son-in-law, Thomas Rawson, who had married his daughter Mary Jane, to create a grocery store at St John Street in Launceston called Rawson & Crabtree. Of course, where there was a Crabtree store there was always the likelihood of a fire burning it down and, lo and behold, in August 1898, with their stock insured for £600, a fire did destroy the store. At the subsequent inquiry into the cause of the fire, William Crabtree was asked if his son, the notorious New Zealand criminal and suspected arsonist, had any involvement in the business but he denied it, claiming that he and his son were not on good terms. The inquiry was inconclusive and an open verdict was returned. This allowed Rawson & Crabtree to conduct a fire sale, which they did at the end of August 1898, in a new store in York Street, advertising that they had £1,000 worth of groceries to clear in one week.

By the end of the century, we can say for certain that Jack was not involved in his father's grocery business because he had left the southern hemisphere and sailed to Ireland where, on 9 February 1899, he married a woman called Emily Cavan at the Belfast Register Office. What had happened to his first wife, Elizabeth, is not known – it would not be a huge surprise if the marriage to Emily was bigamous – but a report in the *Launceston Examiner* as early as November 1892 had stated that Jack was 'a single man'.[247] On the 1899 marriage certificate, Crabtree claimed to be a widower, so presumably Elizabeth had died. From Ireland, Jack returned to the county of his birth, settling in Wakefield, Yorkshire. While in Auckland Gaol, he had 'picked up the art of stone cutting' after the prison authorities put him to work cutting fancy stones and one newspaper of the time commented that he 'works them as well as any of the old hands'.[248] Putting these skills to use, he worked, notionally at least, as a bricklayer in Wakefield. It was not long, however, before the locals started to miss their goods. A musician called Joshua Fox Taylor wondered what had happened to an organ he owned, while a retired pawnbroker called Peter Hebden was unable to locate his bicycle. A wagonette belonging to John Armitage, a bricklayer, went missing one evening in September 1901 and, a couple of weeks later, was found in Jack Crabtree's possession in Hull where he was arrested. Crabtree initially appeared normal to the arresting police officers, speaking in a rational manner but then, suddenly, 'threw himself into a passion' and refused to be put into a cab. Four officers were required to carry him to the police station. When subsequently put on a train back to Wakefield, he became quite violent; and he refused to say anything during a committal hearing, where he had to be physically restrained in the dock by two constables. Asked if he had anything to say as to why he should not be remanded, he glared at one of the constables holding him while making frantic efforts to free himself.[249] The *Sheffield Daily Telegraph* described his behaviour as 'extraordinary and violent'.[250] Crabtree was no doubt pretending to be mad in order to avoid having to answer any questions about his past. He would not have wanted the British police to know he was a famous New Zealand criminal and, in this, he was successful; they never found out.

Further charges were placed against Crabtree on the basis that he had procured some furniture on the hire system which he never paid for.[251] The Chief Constable of Wakefield, Thomas Middleton Harris, said that he had converted the furniture for his own use 'but unfortunately for him, he had two wives and one of them gave him away'.[252] What this means is not known and is, perhaps, a reference to his two wives, Elizabeth and Emily. If so, and she was still alive, it must have been Elizabeth who gave him away because he remained with Emily for the rest of his life. During his jury trial, before Sir Thomas Brooke at Wakefield Quarter Sessions on 14 October 1901, Crabtree refused to plead and said nothing but 'forty-seven'.[253] What he meant by this is not clear. Perhaps he was trying to claim he was 47 years old, although he was then only 40. According to a journalist writing for the *Wakefield Express*, Crabtree 'gazed vacantly about the court and not another word could be drawn from him, and he appeared to be wholly imbecile'.[254] The surgeon at Wakefield Prison, Dr Clarke, gave evidence that Crabtree 'has refused to speak or answer any questions but I think he could if he were willing', adding that, in his view, Crabtree was able to understand the proceedings against him. Despite not having the advantage of knowing that Crabtree had previously pretended to be mad while at Auckland Prison, the jury quite rightly decided that he was feigning insanity and convicted him of larceny, with the judge sentencing him to a term of three months imprisonment. A further charge of having stolen 'a large quantity of furniture' was not proceeded with, nor were charges of 'feloniously taking and converting to his own use as bailee' the organ and bicycle of Messrs Fox Taylor and Hebden respectively.

Jack served his time in prison but was not a reformed character upon his release. In August 1903, a resident of Gateshead, George Davis, found that his pony and cart had gone missing while, at the end of September 1903, another Gateshead resident, William Laws, noticed that his stable had been broken into, with the lock having been taken off the door. His horse, cart, several horse collars, some harnesses and hay and corn, having a total value of £50, had been stolen. He notified the police and a description of the horse and cart was circulated to nearby police forces. It was somewhat unfortunate for Jack that Wakefield's Chief Constable, Thomas Harris, was driving out of the town with his wife and family and saw him riding towards Leeds in a horse and cart which matched the description of the one stolen from Gateshead. The Chief Constable, remembering Crabtree from the 1901 incident, took a short cut to the police station. There he rounded up a number of constables and a dramatic pursuit ensued, with Crabtree turning sharply and thrashing his horse to gain speed as the police followed in a variety of hastily sequestered vehicles; the Chief Constable hopped into a tradesman's conveyance, four constables squeezed into a cab and one conducted the chase on a bicycle. Outnumbered and out horse-powered, Crabtree was quickly cornered but he did not give up easily. He jumped from the cart and ran at top speed, chased by Wakefield police force's finest for over a mile across fields, before he was finally captured in some gardens. On being arrested he said breathlessly, 'Yes, you have me all right'.[255] The cart was searched and the collars and harnesses were retrieved along with other stolen items including ten chisels, one lamp, a pair of boots, a saddle, two sacks, two pairs of spurs, a bridle, two trap spanners, two blacking brushes, a hard broom, a waterproof coat, a bicycle lamp, a bicycle pump, a body brush, a number of cooking utensils and sundry clothing. A bunch of skeleton keys was also found in Crabtree's possession.[256] Police investigations discovered that Crabtree had also stolen George Davis' pony and cart and it transpired that he was wanted in Lancashire and Keighley for stealing a horse and trap in both those places too. After appearing at Wakefield Police Court on 2 October 1903, Crabtree was handed over to the Durham authorities.

During his trial at the Durham Assizes on 19 November 1903, at which he pleaded guilty, Crabtree claimed to be 'a victim of circumstances'. He said he had been working in Newcastle when a 'society man' (i.e. a debt collector for a loan society) stopped him and asked for some money he was owed. Then a friend said to him, 'Jack, will you come and steal a horse with me?' and, in dire need of money to pay the society man, Crabtree agreed. The trial judge, on circuit from London, was not impressed and, commenting that he hoped Crabtree would come to the conclusion that thieving did not pay, sentenced him to three years penal servitude.[257] The name of the judge was Mr Justice Grantham; and it would certainly not be the last encounter between the two men.

Jack did not serve the full three years. He was released on license nine months early in March 1906 and, although he did not, as far as we know, return to thieving, he took the lease on 1 Bidborough Street and, subsequently, 13 Manchester Street, where, as we have seen, Emily Dimmock was living, and ran these properties as brothels before being convicted at Clerkenwell on 31 July 1906. He was sentenced to three months for that offence but, as his licence was also revoked, he ended up serving a total of nearly ten months in prison, being released on 24 May 1907. In between chasing Emily across St Pancras for the money and items she stole from him, Jack was keeping another brothel at 30a Argyle Street in St Pancras. However, the police had it under observation for a week from 31 July. They noted that five prostitutes used the house, being let in by Crabtree, and saw fifty couples enter. Crabtree was observed stopping couples leaving the property whenever constables passed by. He was arrested by Inspector John Rouse of E Division on 20 July and appeared before Mr Bros the next day in the Clerkenwell Police Court where he was charged. In his defence, Crabtree denied keeping the house as a brothel and put the blame on another woman called Mrs Turner who lived in the house. He told the magistrate: 'Things were not what they might have been so I gave Mrs Turner notice and she has left'.[258] Admitting that he had previously kept 'a house of ill fame', he also said: 'Some girls still come and try to get in but I refuse them and tell them I won't get into any trouble'.[259] Jack's wife, Emily, gave supporting evidence about Mrs Turner being sent away but it was to no avail and Jack was once again found guilty of brothel keeping; this time he was sentenced to four months imprisonment with hard labour.[260] Consequently, he was locked up in Pentonville Prison when Emily Dimmock was murdered.

On 18 September 1907, Inspector Neil wrote the following memo:

I beg to report that John William Crabtree was sentenced at Clerkenwell Police Court on 21st ult to 4 months h.l. for keeping a brothel.

It is thought that this man might be able to throw some light on the murder of Emily Dimmock which was committed in the night of the 11th inst at 29 St Pauls Road, Camden Town. It is believed that he is now undergoing sentence at Pentonville prison. I would therefore respectfully suggest that a Home Office order be applied for another officer and myself to visit Crabtree.[261]

The next day, his order granted, Neil interviewed Crabtree in HM Prison Pentonville. At this stage, he knew about Crabtree's convictions at Wakefield and Durham in 1901 and 1903 respectively but had absolutely no idea of his past exploits in New Zealand and Tasmania and, in fact, he never would know. Crabtree's silence following his arrest in 1901 had worked; his life history was not investigated.

During the interview, Crabtree told Inspector Neil all about the man whose name he said he did not know (but whom he would later call 'Scottie') who had not only beaten Emily up but had threatened to cut her throat for giving him 'the disease'. He related how the man had once turned up at his house with a razor, asking for 'Phyllis' and saying that he would 'do her in'. Crabtree said he had seen letters from the man to Emily asking for money. In one of the letters, the man referred to a doctor's surgery at Camden Town where he wanted Emily to meet him and, in another, he asked her to meet him in the saloon bar of the *Eagle* Public House in Camden Town. In another of the letters, he said he saw a reference to a silver watch and nine carat gold chain that Emily had bought the man as a birthday present. Furthermore, when Inspector Neil showed him a photograph of the fragments of paper that had survived the fire in Emily's room, Crabtree said that the handwriting matched the handwriting in the letters.

Neil asked Crabtree how he had managed to see these letters and the prisoner answered that when Emily went to Portsmouth she gave him the keys of her door and her box, asking him to forward some things in her box to an address at Portsmouth. He explained that, while he was going through her box to obtain these items for her, he read some of her letters and took possession of them. He also took some from a drawer in her sewing machine. He said that the reason he took possession of her letters 'was because she had written giving a woman I know as Big Nell permission to sleep in her room and use her things'. This does not seem to explain why he felt entitled to take her letters but he went on to inform the inspector that, when Emily returned from Portsmouth, he told her he had taken the letters and she asked him to keep them for the time being but he was arrested three days later and so never had the chance to return them. Inspector Neil was obviously interested in the whereabouts of these letters and Crabtree told him they were in a box in the possession of his wife who had the key to that box. Crabtree described the man who had written the letters and threatened Emily as follows:

> age about 26, height 5 ft 4 or 5 inches, complexion sallow, dark hair, very slight brown moustache, small eyes very close together, small features, hair stands up from well brushing, slight build, pimples on face, slovenly in walk; dress dark suit, wide brimmed hard felt hat, flattish on top, shabby genteel appearance.[262]

It is interesting that Crabtree used the word 'sallow' to describe this man's complexion, a word which had appeared in the Evening News to describe a suspect only three days earlier. Both men were also said to be short and, although Crabtree did not mention the colour blue, he described a man in a dark suit wearing a wide brimmed hard felt hat, compared to the Evening News' suspect wearing 'a dark blue suit and a bowler hat'. Most bowler hats are narrow brimmed but it is possible for them to be wide brimmed – and they are certainly hard felt hats – so it would appear that Crabtree was describing a man in a bowler hat and, thus, his description was not inconsistent with the description of the man in the Evening News. The only other information Crabtree was able to provide about this man was that 'he had a mother and father' (by which he presumably meant that both his parents were still alive) and that he was of the opinion that he lived in the vicinity of Camden Town. Crabtree said: 'I always had an idea that he would sooner or later murder her, for when he threatened her he seemed so determined.'

Crabtree also told Inspector Neil about how he tracked Emily and Bert Shaw down after he was released from prison and eventually retrieved the money he was owed. He said that he had seen the man he had mentioned watching Emily's premises at St Pancras Square with another man whom he described as 'a tall fair man, slightly built with braid on his waistcoat and wearing blue cloth trousers'. Finally, Crabtree told Neil that he knew another man Emily used to be friendly with, who lived with her, but, he said, 'I know very little of him'. However, his wife had pointed this man out to him in Euston Square and he told Neil that he thought she could provide more information. Mrs Crabtree was spoken to by officers but it is not known if she provided any information because no formal statement was taken. However, we know from a subsequent report of Inspector Neil that she confirmed that since her husband had been in prison she had seen the man who threatened Emily; but he could not be traced. An 'exhaustive search' was also conducted to locate the letters Crabtree said he had left in his wife's possession but that proved unsuccessful.

Contemporary sketches of
John William Crabtree (left)
and Emily Crabtree (below).

Chapter Six

Investigation

'It is impossible for an officer engaged on an investigation to be too careful and accurate in his enquiries.'

Metropolitan Police General Orders for 1907

In addition to the unnamed man described by Crabtree, the police had another lead. A postcard addressed to Emily at the post office at 136 Judd Street (where she had letters sent because she moved around so much) had been found in her apartment from someone called 'William' at the Royal Naval Hospital in Chatham. It was apparently dated 25 August 1907. The police were interested in this postcard because they suspected that 'William' might be in hospital suffering from venereal disease contracted from Emily and thus might hold a grudge against her. The police were also particularly interested in sailors. A Metropolitan Police report dated 19 September stated that 'Suggestions have been made which render it desirable that her [Emily's] naval acquaintances should be traced as far as possible'.[263] Enquiries were made at the RN Hospital by the Kent Constabulary, and specimens of handwriting were tested, but they were never able to locate the author of the 25 August postcard, although further investigation led police to believe he was called William Buddell.

A new witness also presented herself on 19 September. Emily's former housemate from Burton Crescent, May Campbell, or Mrs Pohl as she had become, now living in Finsbury Park, gave a confused statement to two police constables of the E Division. She said that she saw Emily (whom she knew as 'Phillis') on Tuesday evening (10 September), the day before her murder, at about 9:30pm, near a 'rubber shop' by the *Rising Sun* (which she referred to in her statement as 'Chapmans').[264] Emily told her that she had to meet a gentleman friend in the *Rising Sun* at 11:30pm but she could not make this meeting because she had an appointment to meet another man called Tom at Camden Town Station at 9:45pm and, if she did not keep that appointment, 'it would be the worse for her'. This is interesting because it mirrors the information first published in the *Daily Chronicle* on 14 September (and subsequently repeated in other newspapers) that Emily had received a postcard from a man asking her to meet him at Camden Town Railway Station. It is not impossible that May Campbell was the original source of this information but it is just as likely that she had read it in the newspapers and incorporated it into her story to the police.

In any event, May Campbell explained that Tom was also known as 'Scotch Bob'. She described him as 'about 5 foot 7 inches, very dark eyes, shadowy, nasty, pimply face'. She said she had seen him dozens of times. She went on to say that she met Emily again at 7:00pm on Wednesday 11 September (the night of her murder) and Emily said to her: 'I have not much time to stay, May, because I must meet this friend. I feel so frightened. I am afraid of him because he is a desperate man and you know who I mean'. Campbell replied that she did not know, to which Emily replied: 'You do, it's Scotch Bob'. Campbell said she met Emily again on her own about an hour later and asked where her friend was. Emily said curtly, 'Mind your own business' and walked off with a female friend (who Campbell believed was called 'Maggie'). Two hours later, at about 10:00pm, Campbell said she saw Emily again in the street with a man wearing a dark overcoat who, from a distance, looked like Scotch Bob.

There are some obvious problems with May Campbell's statement. On the Tuesday evening, Emily was known to have been with Robert Roberts all evening from 8:00pm until 8:00am the next day so it would not appear possible for her to have spoken to May Campbell in the street at about 9:30pm. It also does not seem likely that Emily would have had two additional appointments for that same evening. Further, if Emily was supposed to meet Scotch Bob at 11:30pm on the *Tuesday* night then why did she say 'I must meet this friend' on the *Wednesday*?[265]

However, there is a second statement made by May Campbell in the police file in which she tells a slightly different story. This is a statement made at Hunter Street Police Station to Detective Inspector James Stockley of E Division on 20 September in which she says that, at about 9:15pm on the evening of Tuesday 10 September, she met Emily in the Euston Road – not having seen her for many months – and stood talking to her for twenty minutes, being told that she was going to see Mrs Chapman of the *Rising Sun* about some needlework. Emily also said that she was getting on very well and was living with a railway cook. However, she admitted that she was due to meet a sailor who had been staying with her for 'three nights' while the cook was at work. Campbell thought Emily looked worried and said so, which prompted the reply, 'I am all right but I have had a postcard that has worried me', although she gave no more details and they parted. There is no mention of any meetings later that evening other than the meeting with the sailor (i.e. Roberts). Campbell then says that she saw Emily again the next day, Wednesday 11 September, not at 7:00pm as mentioned in her first statement, but at about 4:00pm in the High Street in Camden Town (later clarified in oral evidence to have been 'about half past four'[266]) at which time Emily told her she had received a letter that morning requesting her to meet a gentlemen friend, called Tom, or 'Scotch Bob', at Camden Town Station at 9:45pm that evening. The letter said that Emily had to go to the meeting or 'it would be worse' for her. At one point in her statement, Campbell says that Emily had told her that 'Scotch Bob' had contracted 'the bad disorder' from her and was afraid he would hurt her for it; but elsewhere in the same document she says that Emily told her that she got 'Scotch Bob' locked up for six months and he had only been out of prison ten days which is why she was worried something would happen. In any event, she said that she had shown the letter to the sailor who was with her that morning and then burnt it.

That was not the end of May Campbell's story for she claimed to have met Emily again that evening at 9:00pm near the St Pancras Goods Station in the Euston Road when Emily said, 'I am going to meet my friend at Camden Town station at 9.45'. An hour later, at 10:00pm, she saw Emily again but she was shaking and seemed flustered. In later oral evidence, she would say that Emily was 'in a terrible way, and was trembling'.[267] Campbell asked where her friend was and Emily said he had gone to the lavatory. Then a man in a dark overcoat emerged from the toilet and May Campbell recognised him as 'Scotch Bob'. She said she knew 'Scotch Bob', who was a betting man, from when she lived with Emily. 'Scotch Bob' used to visit her (Emily) and take her out until at least January 1907, at which time May Campbell got married and moved away. She said that Emily and 'Scotch Bob' walked off together towards King's Cross. That was not the last she saw of the pair though. She said she spotted them again at 11:00pm walking down Euston Road as if coming from the Euston Music Hall. They crossed in the direction of St Pancras Road and headed towards Camden Town. Her best description of 'Scotch Bob' in this statement was: 5 feet 7 inches, very dark, clean shaven, sunken dark eyes, dirty pimply face, wearing a dark overcoat with velvet collar and carrying a walking stick and brown gloves.

May's story had improved in some respects. Emily was now no longer due to meet two men on the same night she was with Roberts but she was still supposed to have spoken to Campbell outside the *Rising Sun* at a time when she was with the ship's cook. There was clearly some overlap between her story about a letter being received by Emily on the Wednesday morning to arrange a meeting in Camden Town and the story told by Roberts but it is known that Campbell had spoken to Roberts at Emily's funeral and she might have incorporated some of his story into hers. As mentioned above, some elements of the story about Emily having arranged a meeting with a man at Camden Town Railway Station had been reported in the newspapers so this could also have affected her evidence. One thing that was consistent in both her statements was that she saw Emily with a man who resembled 'Scotch Bob' at 10:00pm on the Wednesday night. This suggests that she was the 'girl friend' mentioned by the *Daily News* of 16 September who had seen Emily in the company of a man near King's Cross 'before ten o'clock' on the Wednesday. Although May Campbell said she saw the couple in the Euston Road, near the *Rising Sun*, she also said she watched them walk towards King's Cross, so that fits with what was reported. Of course, it is possible that she had read this in the newspaper and incorporated it into her story with other bits of information she had read and remembered but the fact that the police seem to have taken her seriously and took her statement twice is suggestive that she was the original source.

At about the same time as May Campbell was telling police about 'Scotch Bob', Gladys Warren (claiming to be William Linehan's wife and thus giving her name as 'Gladys Linehan') was informing them of a Scotsman she knew as 'Scotch Jock' (or 'Scotch Jack') who used to visit Emily frequently while she lived in Burton Crescent. She said this man worked in the nurseries in Enfield, presumably as a garden labourer, and was associated with racing men, being involved in betting. She described him as 'a very violent man who threatened to do her [Emily] in' because she had given him the disorder. She told police he was about 35 years old, 5ft 10 inches in height, with a pale complexion, blotchy face and heavy moustache. However, she had not seen Emily since about May 1907 (when she had met her in Islington).[268] There is no statement of William Linehan on file but he would later say that he had heard that she had been threatened by a Scotsman called 'Jock' in Argyle Square and had run away from him as a result.[269]

Meanwhile, the newspapers were reporting a new suspect for Emily's murder. A man had been found in the early hours of Friday 13 September on Tottenham Marshes with his throat cut and bleeding slightly. He was taken to the Prince of Wales Hospital in Tottenham where he said that he was a former soldier turned labourer, called Henry Clark, a resident of Tottenham, aged

34 years old. Attempted suicide was then a criminal offence but he admitted cutting his throat with a razor which was still on the marshes. A police officer subsequently located the razor in a pool of blood near to where Clark had been found. According to the newspaper reports, Clark's hands were soft and well maintained while his speech showed that he was an educated man, all of which seemed to contradict his claim to be a labourer but these reports were never officially confirmed. *Reynolds's Newspaper* claimed that Clark was 'well-connected' but had been 'a failure in life's battle'. It said his relations were in business in Nottingham and he was married but lived apart from his wife.[270] Although the cut to Clark's throat was deep and had severed his windpipe, he initially did quite well in hospital and seemed to be recovering but he died on Wednesday 18 September after pneumonia set in. An inquest on 19 September recorded a verdict of 'Suicide whilst temporarily insane'. His death certificate stated that the cause of death was 'Felo-de-se (cut throat)'. The connection between Clark and the Camden Town murder was first made in the morning papers on 20 September 1907. According to the *Daily News*: 'The Central News learns that the detectives in charge of the Camden Town murder case only recently came into possession of the information which leads to the supposition that Clark is connected with the Camden Town crime. They have been looking for a man whose description corresponds in several particulars to that of Clark'. Clark was described as about five foot seven inches in height, dark hair and complexion, some freckles, a grizzled black moustache and grey/blue eyes. He had a tattoo of an arrow piercing a heart on his forearm. At the time he was found with his throat cut, he was wearing a blue flannel suit with narrow grey vertical stripe, a blue Oxford shirt, blue muffler with zig zag white stripe, rusty lace boots and blue cloth cap.[271] Interestingly, he had been living in lodgings at Rowton House, King's Cross, at the time of his death, only a few minutes' walk away from the *Rising Sun*. An investigation by *Reynolds's Newspaper* discovered that Clark's habits were 'peculiar' in that he was 'out all day, returning to the house late at night' but their reporter was unable to establish whether Clark slept at Rowton House on the Tuesday or Wednesday before the murder.[272]

Despite the fact that the newspapers on Friday 20 September were suggesting that the Camden Town murderer might have committed suicide, Robert Wood was sufficiently concerned that the investigation into Emily Dimmock's death might lead police to him that he arranged two meetings during the morning in order to create a false alibi for the night of Emily's murder. Firstly, he sent a telegram to Ruby Young at Earl's Court asking her to meet him that evening at 6:30pm at their regular meeting spot outside a boot makers at 121 High Holborn, on the corner of Southampton Row, called Phit-Eesi's, also known as Abbott & Sons. He then telephoned Joseph Lambert – the man who had seen him with Emily in the *Eagle* during the evening of 11 September – arranging a meeting for between 7:00pm and 8:00pm that evening to discuss 'something to do with the Camden Town affair'. According to Lambert, Wood told him that his colleague, William Moss, had mentioned the affair to him and that he (Wood) should be able to clear himself (although from what he did not specify). Lambert did not want to discuss the matter over the telephone and Wood initially said he would probably be round to see him on Saturday, before they agreed on a meeting later that evening.

Ruby kept the appointment at 6:30pm and met Wood outside Phit-Eesi's, from where the pair walked to the nearby Lyons restaurant for some refreshment. Wood came straight to the point:

'Ruby, if any questions are put to you, will you say you always saw me on Mondays and Wednesdays?'

'Why?' replied a puzzled Ruby.

'Will you do so?' pressed Wood, ignoring her question.

'Yes,' said Ruby compliantly and to ensure she did not forget, Wood wrote 'Mondays and Wednesdays' on one side of a card while, on the other, he noted that they should meet on the following Monday when he would take her to see a show at the Prince of Wales theatre. He gave Ruby the card and the two of them left the restaurant and walked up New Oxford Street then down Charing Cross Road. Leaving Ruby at Leicester Square tube station at about quarter past seven, Wood walked back in the direction he had come to Westell's, a booksellers at 106 Charing Cross Road, to see Joseph Lambert who worked there. Wood appeared to Lambert to be particularly concerned that William Moss might start asking questions about the Camden Town murder. He said to him: 'If Mr Moss says anything to you about it, you might tell him that we met and had a drink, but leave the girl out', by which he meant Emily, adding that he could clear himself but for the sake of the business he did not want to be drawn into the matter.

'That will be all right' said Lambert innocently.

'So far as you are concerned,' continued Wood conspiratorially, 'you know nothing about it at all'.

He then left.[273] It was a surprisingly determined attempt by Wood to cover his tracks but not a very well thought out one. On the one hand, he was creating an alibi that he had been with Ruby Young in Central London on Wednesday 11 September, yet, on the other, he was attempting to persuade Joseph Lambert to say that he had seen him on his own in the *Eagle* in Camden Town on the same night.

On the Monday morning, Ruby received from Wood the following postcard:

Sweetheart,

If it is convenient for you, meet me as before, Phit-Eesi's at 6.30 & we will have tea together & then to the theatre, which I hope will be a little ray of sunshine in your life.

Goodbye.

As before, Ruby kept the appointment and Wood took her to the Prince of Wales theatre, near Leicester Square, to see a performance of *Miss Hook of Holland*, a popular musical comedy. At the end of the evening, Wood said 'Mondays and Wednesdays, don't forget' and then went home by tube, with Ruby taking the omnibus from Piccadilly Circus.

The newspapers that day had reported that the police had 'thoroughly satisfied themselves' that suicide victim Henry Clark had no connection to Emily's death and were supposedly aware of his motive for committing suicide, although it was never publicly stated and we do not know today what it was. It would be reported a few days later that two witnesses who had seen Emily with a man were taken by detectives to the mortuary where they declared that

Clark did not resemble the man they had seen with her. There is no mention of Clark in the Metropolitan Police file on the Dimmock case so it is not known to what extent, if any, the police involved in the investigation considered him as a suspect. All that can be said is that a man living in King's Cross committed suicide by cutting his throat with a razor within 48 hours of Emily Dimmock's murder by having her throat cut, possibly by a razor. The *Tottenham & Edmonton Weekly Herald*, however, was scathing of the 'London papers' for their 'usual readiness to accept a sensational story' and claimed that any connection between Clark and the Camden Murder was 'disproved'.

At the same time as dismissing the notion that the suicide victim, Henry Clark, was involved in the murder, the newspapers were publishing what they called an 'official description' of the man wanted by police. It first appeared in the *Daily Mail* of Saturday, 21 September 1907 as follows:

Age twenty eight to thirty
Height about 5ft 7in
Sallow complexion
Dark hair
Clean shaven
Peculiar appearance about the eyes
Pimples on lower part of the face and neck
Dressed in blue serge suit and old fashioned bowler hat
May be known by the name "Bert"
Known to associate with a certain class of women
Is believed to have been for a time in a certain hospital

At this time, the police had at least six descriptions of men who could be considered prime suspects: (1) the man ('Bertie') seen with Emily by Roberts (and Clarke) on the Monday before her death, (2) the man seen with Emily in the Euston Road by Sharples and Harvey on the evening of her death, (3) the man seen by McCowan apparently leaving 29 St Paul's Road in the early hours of 12 September, (4) the man ('Scottie') identified by Crabtree who had threatened Emily, (5) the man ('Scotch Bob') identified by May Campbell who had threatened Emily and (6) the man ('Scotch Jock') identified by Gladys Warren who had threatened Emily. The possibility had to be considered that these were all the same individual. In a report to his superiors written at the end of September, Inspector Neil, while sceptical of May Campbell's identification for reasons to be discussed later (and not even mentioning the man seen by Gladys Warren), said that Crabtree's description 'certainly agrees with that of the man who was seen [by Roberts] in the public house, and referred to as "Bert"'. This is a surprising comment because Crabtree described a small man of perhaps 5 feet 4 inches (at best 5 feet 5 inches) whereas Roberts described a man of about 5 feet 8 inches, a considerable difference.

The description published in the *Daily Mail*, despite being described as 'official', does not appear to have been released officially by the police but some of the characteristics appear to have been derived, possibly indirectly, from police sources.[274] Let us take each aspect of the description individually:

Age
Daily Mail – 28 to 30 years old

Roberts estimated the age of the man he saw as 23 or 24. The man Clarke saw was supposedly aged 30. Neither Sharples/Harvey nor McCowan were apparently able to estimate an age. Crabtree said that the man he knew was 26. May Campbell did not estimate an age for 'Scotch Bob' while Gladys Warren said her 'Scotch Jock' was 35. With the exception of Clarke, none of the witnesses described a man in the 28-30 age range so this does not fit the suspect in the *Daily Mail*. Curiously, in his report at the end of September, Inspector Neil attributed an age of 26 to Roberts' suspect and was perhaps confusing Roberts' description with what Crabtree had told him.

Height
Daily Mail – 5 foot 7 inches

Roberts estimated the height of the man in the *Rising Sun* at about 5 foot 8 inches, Clarke described the man as 'short', Sharples/Harvey said 5 foot 9 or 10 inches for the man they saw, McCowan said about 5 foot 7 or 8 inches for the man emerging from number 29 in the night. Crabtree said 5 foot 4 or 5 inches for the man who threatened Emily. May Campbell said 5 foot 7 or 8 inches for 'Scotch Bob' while Gladys Warren estimated 5 foot 10 inches for 'Scotch Jock'. Another curious feature is that Inspector Neil's report stated that the man Roberts saw was 5 foot 7 or 8 inches but, while Roberts said 'about 5 foot 8 inches', this was both McCowan's and May Campbell's evidence so, again, perhaps Neil was confused. But clearly 5 foot 7 inches would not have been far from any description compiled by the police at the time.

Complexion
Daily Mail – 'sallow'

The only police witness who used the word 'sallow' to describe a suspect's complexion was Crabtree. The dictionary definition of 'sallow' is 'sickly yellow or pale brown'. Roberts said the man's complexion was 'very dark' in his statement but Gladys Warren said 'Scotch Jock' had a 'pale' complexion. No other witness provided a description. Once again, Inspector Neil's summary of Roberts' evidence in his report is questionable. He claimed that Roberts had described a 'sallow complexion' but he had, in fact, said pretty much the direct opposite. As we have seen, though, the *Evening News* of 16 September had been the first to mention a suspect's 'sallow' complexion and this might have been the source of the *Daily Mail*'s information. However, it will be recalled that the *Daily Mail* had been told by Mrs Roberts on 13 September (and published the information the next day) that the police were looking for a man with a 'sickly looking' face.

Hair
Daily Mail – 'dark hair'

Roberts said 'dark' as did Clarke and Crabtree. No-one else mentioned hair specifically.

Facial Hair
Daily Mail – 'Clean shaven'

Roberts said 'clean shaven', Crabtree said 'very slight brown moustache', Gladys Warren said 'heavy moustache' so Roberts' description is likely to be the ultimate source of the *Daily Mail* suspect's description.

Eyes
Daily Mail – 'peculiar appearance'

The only witness who said anything about a suspect's eyes looking peculiar was Crabtree who described the man he knew as having 'small eyes very close together'. May Campbell, however, said that 'Scotch Bob' had 'sunken dark eyes' which might have carried the same meaning as 'peculiar'. Inspector Neil also summarised Roberts as saying that the man he saw had 'sunken eyes' despite nothing of the sort appearing in his written statement. It must have been more than coincidence that the *News of the World* had used the expression 'very deep sunken eyes' when it had described on 15 September the man the police were looking for.

Skin
Daily Mail – 'Pimples on lower part of the face and neck'

Roberts: 'He had a few pimples on the lower part of his face'. Clarke: 'face marked as if with disorder'. Crabtree: 'pimples on face'. May Campbell: 'pimply'. Gladys Warren: 'blotchy face'. This is something that the witnesses appear to agree on. The *Daily Mail* had reported on 14 September that Mrs Roberts had been told by police that the man they were looking for was 'rather pimply' so this information was publicly available. However, only Roberts had referred to the pimples being on the lower part of the man's face so he was presumably the ultimate source of this information.

Clothing
Daily Mail – 'Dressed in blue serge suit and old fashioned bowler hat'

This is the most intriguing aspect to the *Daily Mail*'s description. As we have seen, an almost identical description appeared in the *Evening News* of 16 September which referred to a 'dark blue suit and bowler hat' worn by a 'short dark man' who was said to have been with Emily on Monday night. Yet, no witness mentions in any surviving police statement that the man they saw was wearing a blue or serge suit ('serge' being a durable, twilled fabric). However, Inspector Neil's report of 30 September (i.e. after the publication of the *Daily Mail*'s description) said of the man Roberts had seen in the *Rising Sun*, 'To the best of Roberts' belief he was...dressed in a dark or blue serge suit with a rather old fashioned felt hat'. This is remarkably close to the *Daily Mail*'s description (and the description in the *Evening News*) but it does not appear at all in Roberts' statement in which he says nothing at all about what the man he saw was wearing. It is, of course, possible that Roberts privately mentioned the blue serge suit and old fashioned felt hat to Inspector Neil after he made his statement and it was not recorded in writing but this certainly should not have happened. Harry Sharples also appears to have told police that the man he saw with Dimmock at midnight before her murder was wearing a blue suit and bowler hat.

In respect of the suspect's clothing, it should be noted that there was a sighting of Emily Dimmock during the afternoon of the day of her murder that we have not yet mentioned. No statement recording this sighting appears in the Metropolitan Police file in the National Archives but, according to Inspector Neil's 30 September report, three apparently independent witnesses claimed to have seen Emily walking arm in arm with a man, between 3:00pm and 4:00pm, in Somers Town during the afternoon of Wednesday 11 September. These witnesses were: a furniture remover called Mr Clarke of 60 Seymour Street, a woman called Mrs Wolton of 8 Pancras Square and Gladys Margaret Bucknall, the 18-year-old daughter of the superintendent of the model buildings where Emily had lived with Shaw before moving to St Paul's Road (and thus not likely to have made a mistake in identifying her). Inspector Neil summarised the description of the man they all saw as follows: 'a tall fair man dressed in a blue serge suit and bowler hat and of a smart gentlemanly appearance'. In addition, he said that this 'somewhat answers' the description given by Sharples and Harvey. So the origin of the man in the 'blue serge suit' appears to have come from *these* witnesses. There is no actual evidence other than Neil's report that Roberts ever saw a man in a blue serge suit. He certainly never said he did in writing.

Name
Daily Mail – 'May be known by the name "Bert"'

The source of this is obviously Roberts from his memory of the letter Dimmock showed him on 11 September and was included in his statement (although his first recollection was that the name was 'Bertie'). This information had appeared in the papers over the weekend of 14/15 September and was public knowledge.

Miscellaneous
Daily Mail – 'Known to associate with a certain class of women and believed to have been for a time in a certain hospital'

It wasn't hard for anyone who had read about the murders to conclude that the suspect was likely to associate with prostitutes, although it is possible that the source of this part of the *Daily Mail's* information was Frank Clarke's statement in which he said that the short dark man he saw with Dimmock on Monday night was 'well known by the majority of the loose women in the vicinity of the *Rising Sun.*' More interesting is that the suspect was supposed to have received hospital treatment, evidently for venereal disease. There had been no public indication at the time that Emily, or any suspect, had suffered from venereal disease. Mrs Roberts' story, that a man had claimed that Dimmock had 'ruined' him, had been reported but it was not clarified what this meant. Crabtree, Campbell and Warren had all informed police that their suspects had suffered from the disorder while Frank Clarke said that his suspect's face was marked 'as if with disorder'.

Overall, considering the number of differences from the information known to the police, it would seem that the *Daily Mail's* description was not provided directly to the newspaper by the police. The likelihood is that it was compiled from a combination of earlier press reports, witnesses they had spoken to and police sources and, perhaps, one of those police sources confirmed its accuracy, hence the 'official' tag. Inspector Neil was asked by the defence, during the Old Bailey trial, about the descriptions of the supposed prime suspect which had appeared in the newspapers and responded by saying that the press were getting their own information. However, the Metropolitan Police file reveals that the *Daily Mail's* description of the suspect was regarded as an accurate one by the police themselves.

At 11:40pm on Sunday 22 September, the Liverpool Police sent a telegram to the Metropolitan Police (whose amusing telegram address was 'Handcuffs') stating that a man from London matching the description of the suspect in that day's *Lloyds Weekly News* (which was an exact reproduction of the *Daily Mail's* description) had taken lodgings in Liverpool the day before but had disappeared after the landlord questioned him about his departure from London. Inspector Neil, who was working late, initially had difficulty in getting hold of a copy of *Lloyds Weekly News* but eventually managed to obtain one the following morning. In a report written once he had read the newspaper article, he stated that 'the published description was that of the man seen in the Rising Sun Public House Euston Road in company with the deceased on the evening of 9th inst', so that, as a result, 'There is some reason to believe that man may be identical with the murderer'. Thus, he sent a telegram back to the Liverpool police informing them that the 'man described in the newspaper' was indeed a suspect and that, if found, he should be asked to account for his movements on the evening of 11 September (although he was never traced).

At the same time, information was coming in from Chatham police that, at 7:00pm on 23 September, a sailor had arrived at New Brompton Station, in Gillingham, Kent, in 'an excited condition' while, 'trembling violently', carrying two bundles wrapped in black silk handkerchiefs which he tied together with rope and forwarded to one Mrs Tuck in Norfolk. When questioned about his excited condition he was said to have replied, 'So would you if your chum was taken for the Camden Town Murder and this is his clothing I am forwarding on, he hasn't got half a chance'. The bundles were then put on the 7:33pm train to London and the sailor walked away.

Detective Frank Page was the lucky officer who was sent to Gillingham on the 5:18am train from Kentish Town on Tuesday morning with instructions to trace the suspicious parcel. He discovered that it had been received in London at 9:30pm the previous evening and forwarded to Liverpool Street Station before being carried on the 5:08am train that morning for Walsingham, Norfolk, where it was due to arrive at 9:45am. Page asked the Norwich police to visit Mrs Tuck, who turned out to be the sailor's mother, in order to await the delivery of the parcel. When it was opened, all it contained was 'some soiled linen evidently sent to be washed, three pairs of discarded sailors serge trousers, a woollen scarf, a quantity of tea, two razors and two table knives'. There was nothing in the appearance of any of them to raise suspicion.

At the same time, a statement was taken by Chief Inspector George Mitchell of the Chatham police force from the source of the original police report who turned out to be a newsagent called George White. He said he was waiting at New Brompton Station for the newspapers to arrive from London when he was asked to tie some bundles for a stoker who was unable to do it himself because his hands were shaking. After he assisted in securing the bundles, the stoker, who appeared agitated and shaking all over, invited him for a drink in the nearby railway hotel. During the ensuing conversation, he said:

> I am on the Hawker and they came and pinched my chum for the Camden Town affair this afternoon. Two 'tecs...came on the ship, handcuffed him and took him off. It was him right enough, there ain't no doubt about it. Poor devil, it was him, he married her years ago. The chap has been demented on the ship

all the time he has been aboard, and the captain knew all about it. They kept him under control and would not let him go on leave.[275]

George White asked the stoker what his friend's name was but he would not tell it, only saying mysteriously, 'You will see all about it in the papers in the morning'. After the drink, the stoker left the hotel and Mr White was sufficiently troubled by what he had heard to report the conversation to the Chatham police, hence the subsequent report to the London police.

The stoker was quickly tracked down. His name was Bedford Tuck and he was on HMS Swiftsure, not the Hawker, which was docked at Chatham Dockyard. When questioned, he claimed that he had only been passing on a rumour to George White that two detectives had arrested a man on HMS London for Emily Dimmock's murder. The ship's police confirmed that Tuck was 'given to telling imaginative tales' and it was established from the ship's books that Tuck was on board the Swiftsure on 11 September, so that line of enquiry turned out to be a dead end.

Another lead came from an overheard conversation by a detective inspector on top of an omnibus that Emily's murderer was a sailor with whom she had lived in Portsmouth (something that easily could have been derived from the newspapers) and that a prostitute by the name of 'Glenull' who lived at 116 Vauxhall Bridge Road was supposed to be in possession of more information.[276] The matter was treated seriously enough for Sergeant Osborne to make enquiries with the occupier of this address, as well as with various local tradesmen and neighbours, but no woman by the name of Glenull could be located. Furthermore, to the extent that the story was supposed to refer to the sailor Henry Biddle, it was established by Inspector Neil that Biddle was with his ship (HMS Prince of Wales) in the Mediterranean on the night of the murder.

While all this was going on, the Sunday papers were reporting a dramatic development. 'LONDON MAN SURRENDERS' screamed *Reynolds's Newspaper* above a story that a man had given himself up to police at High Wycombe in connection with the Camden Town murder. However, within the same story, the papers were also reporting that the police doubted that the man had anything to do with the crime. The *News of the World* claimed that the man hailed from a district 'not a mile from the girl's usual haunts' but thought he was drunk and thus seeking 'transient notoriety'. According to *Lloyds Weekly News*, the man in question was overheard by a constable discussing the murder in a suspicious manner and was asked to explain himself at a police station but was able to establish his innocence of any connection with the crime. Nothing appears in the Metropolitan Police file to suggest the man even existed.

One man the police certainly did believe existed was the man who had an appointment with Emily on the night of her murder and both *Lloyds Weekly News* and the *People* revealed that Emily had received a letter from an unknown man making just such an appointment. This information was said to have come from the police and both newspapers claimed that Emily stated that 'she was somewhat afraid of the man in question, and he was jealous of her, but that she intended to keep the appointment', something which Robert Roberts would later give exactly the same evidence about. The papers also said that Emily had been seen by one witness with a man 'in a public house about half-past eight on the Wednesday night' and by another witness three hours later, with the police said to 'have no doubt' that it was the same man who wrote the letter. In fact, the police had no witnesses who had seen Emily with a man in any public house on the Wednesday night and only May Campbell and Sharples/Harvey claimed to have seen her with a man that night.[277]

In the absence of any hard news of their own to report, the *Weekly Dispatch* had dug out a 'famous' but unnamed retired detective to opine on the difficulties facing Scotland Yard, while also setting out his theory about who committed the murder. Having ruled out robbery as a motive, on the basis that it was inconceivable that anyone would kill a woman for the sake of just three pounds, the ex-detective said that there were three alternative motives: jealousy, revenge and madness, of which he favoured revenge. He believed that Emily's killer was a man 'under whose protection she had once been living' who bore her a grudge. He thought she might have met him by accident on the night of her death and, having no suspicion that he harboured murderous thoughts against her, had taken him back to St Paul's Road. The former detective thought that the only chance of the police finding the killer was if he made a mistake in disposing of the keys or articles of jewellery which he had taken from the house. Even if the detectives on the case knew his identity, he felt that it would be virtually impossible to prove his guilt to the satisfaction of a jury. In this respect, he claimed that the police knew the identity of the person responsible for the unsolved murder of a prostitute who had been found dead, with her throat cut, in Great Coram Street on the morning of Christmas Day 1872, who 'slipped through our fingers after his arrest' (clearly meaning a man called Hessel who had been arrested by the police but was undoubtedly innocent*), and also of 'Jack the Ripper', who 'died in a lunatic asylum', but that they did not have enough evidence to secure a conviction in either case. His conclusion, therefore, was that Emily's assassin 'will probably get away' and he doubted whether Detective Inspector Neil, whom he knew to be 'one of the smartest officers in London', could hope to bring the murderer to justice. His one suggestion to Neil was to work more closely with the press because he felt that 'Journalists are often able to discover things which the police have missed' and he believed that 'A little publicity is often of great use'. Although he could not have known it at the time, there would soon be some quite dramatic co-operation between the police and the press in the attempt to catch the murderer of Emily Dimmock.

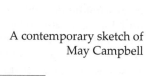

A contemporary sketch of
May Campbell

---

*   See Appendix 1

Chapter Seven

Discovery and Disclosure

'As I waited I thought that there's nothing like a confession to make one look mad; and that of all confessions a written one is the most detrimental all round. Never confess! Never, never!'

Joseph Conrad, *Chance*, 1913

Wednesday 25 September was the hottest day of 1907, with the temperature in London reaching a sweltering 80 degrees fahrenheit. The *Daily Chronicle* called it 'extraordinary'.[278] Inside 29 St Paul's Road, Bert Shaw was preparing to move out of the apartment in which Emily had been murdered in order to take a smaller, and cheaper, room within the same house. He was emptying the chest of drawers in the living room when, hidden within the folds of a newspaper lining in one of the drawers, he found a postcard addressed to 'Mrs B. Shaw', bearing a 'NW' postmark with the time and date of 4:00am, September 9, 1907. The text of the postcard, written in a violet coloured pencil, read:

> *Phillis Darling,*
> *If it pleases you*
> *meet me at 8.15 pm*
> *at the*
> *[sketch of a rising sun]*
> *Yours to a cinder,*
> *Alice*

Recognising its significance, Shaw immediately passed the postcard on to the police. It did not take long for a newspaper to get hold of the story, albeit in garbled form. As the first rain fell in London for eighteen days, the *Daily Chronicle* of 26 September informed its readers that a 'missing post card has come to light' and 'it contains a portrait of the man for whom the police are actively searching'. The man in the portrait, also said to be a 'photograph', had supposedly already been identified by two witnesses as being the man seen with Emily on the night before the crime was committed and had been involved in an argument with one of them. In fact, there was no portrait or photograph on the postcard; on the front was a figure of an Oriental woman holding a child. Interestingly, the suspect was said by the *Daily Chronicle* to have been seen in Euston Square on the morning after the crime was committed. This was something only said to police by Frank Clarke. The newspaper also reported the message on the postcard as being 'Meet me to-night at 8 in the Rising Sun' which was not quite correct.

From a superficial examination, the police believed that the handwriting on what would become known as 'the rising sun postcard' matched handwriting on three other postcards found in Emily's postcard album. These postcards, which were assumed to have been sent to Emily for her to add to her postcard collection, were blank in the text box and the only handwriting on them (in pen) was of the address. They were dated 2 January 1907 (bearing an indistinct, but possibly London, postmark), 9 January 1907 (bearing a Brighton postmark) and 19 August 1907 (bearing a Windsor postmark) respectively. The two January postcards were addressed to 'Mrs Shaw' at 50 Great College Street while the August postcard was, like the rising sun postcard, addressed to 'Mrs B Shaw' at 29 St Paul's Road. On 27 September, a decision was taken at the highest levels of Scotland Yard to circulate to the press a facsimile of these three postcards, together with the critical rising sun postcard, in the hope that, upon publication, a member of the public would recognise the handwriting. Accordingly, Sir Melville Macnaghten, the Assistant Commissioner of the C.I.D., sent photographic copies of the four postcards to a number of London newspapers, including: the *Daily Chronicle, Daily Express, Daily Mirror, Daily News, Morning Leader, Evening News, Star, Reynolds's Newspaper, Lloyds Weekly News, People* and *News of the World,* along with a letter stating that the postcards were 'believed to have a direct bearing' on the case of Emily's murder. Sir Melville requested that 'any person recognising the handwriting should at once communicate with New Scotland Yard'. The aforementioned newspapers all published the rising sun postcard – some published all four – during the weekend of 28/29 September. It was an unprecedented form of co-operation between the police and the press.[279]

It was noted by some newspapers that there were differences in the characters on the postcards but this was said to have been an attempt to disguise the handwriting. The *Daily News* expressed the opinion that 'there can be little doubt' that the author of all four postcards was the same person. The *Daily Mirror* thought there was 'a striking resemblance' between the postcards and supposedly showed them to a handwriting expert who opined that 'they were written by an educated person of some force of character' with 'a quick nervous temperament'.[280] The *Evening News* on the Saturday evening suggested that the sketch of the rising sun revealed a man 'of considerable artistic ability'. It also noted that 'In every quarter, in train, on omnibus and tramway-car, in office and shop the reproduced postcards are being scanned and the writing compared'. By the Sunday morning, the public was even more excited by the rising sun postcard as the proprietors of the *News of the World* offered a £100 reward to anyone 'who brings them such information as will enable the police to identify the writer'.

One person who viewed a reproduction of the rising sun postcard in the newspapers on the Saturday morning was William Moss of the London Sand Blast Decorative Glass Works. He did not actually recognise the handwriting, although it seemed familiar to him, but he said to his colleague, Robert Wood, 'The fellow who wrote that postcard can draw' to which Wood replied disingenuously, 'Yes, I think he can'. Another employee at the Glass Works that Saturday morning was the foreman, Jack Tinkham. He had seen the facsimile of the rising sun postcard in the *Daily Mirror* and, unlike Moss, immediately recognised the handwriting as being that of Wood's, whom he had known for fourteen years. He saw Wood at about ten or eleven that morning.

'Have you seen the paper this morning Bob?'

'No Jack' replied Wood. 'Why?'

'There is a reproduction of a postcard which is supposed to be a clue to the murder at Camden Town and it looks like your handwriting. Here take a look,' said Tinkham, showing Wood the newspaper, 'have you seen this before?'

'No. Why?'

'You wrote that postcard, Bob.'

'Quite right, Jack', confessed Wood, adding, 'I acknowledge writing that postcard and if you will have patience I will tell you how I came to write it.'

Wood then told Tinkham a story he would relate many times.[281] He said he first saw Emily, whom he only knew as 'Phyllis' (or 'Phillis'), at the *Rising Sun* on Friday 6 September. The only reason he was there, he explained, was because he wanted to buy some stamps at Euston and, while walking down Euston Road at about 9:45pm, he bumped into someone whose name he was not sure about (but thought it was 'Hulme') whom he had met a few years earlier at a London Sketch Club supper.[282] Hulme asked Wood to join him for a drink and they walked together to the nearby *Rising Sun*. Hulme bought some drinks and, while they were talking, Wood caught Emily Dimmock's attention. She jokingly came up to him to ask for a penny to put in the gramophone. He willingly gave her the money and she chatted to him in a playful and friendly way. Meanwhile, Hulme was engaged in conversation with a 'man with a dog' but suddenly turned to Wood, shook his hand, said goodnight and left the bar. Then a boy hawker came into the public house with some postcards he was trying to sell. Emily was about to buy one but Wood stopped her, saying they were common and inartistic. Instead, he showed her a postcard he had acquired during his recent holiday in Belgium at the end of August. She was much taken by it, thinking it was pretty, and asked him to send it to her in the post. He wrote on the postcard the first thing that came into his mind. It arose, he said, out of a conversation with Emily in which he mentioned that he might not see her again and she said, 'Oh, but you said to your friend that you might look in tomorrow or some other night', so he wrote something about meeting her again in the *Rising Sun* but, before he could sign it, she said, 'Don't put your name, put my friend's name', pointing to a stout friend called 'Alice' who was sitting beside her. She explained that she did not want to 'create a storm' at home if her 'old man' saw a postcard addressed to her from another man. Wood then wrote her name and address on the postcard at her dictation. Not having a halfpenny stamp on him, he put the card into his pocket and thought no more about it. He left Emily at the *Rising Sun* at about midnight.

The following day he was on his way to the offices of the Gas, Light and Coke Company in Camden Road at about 7:30pm to enquire about purchasing a gas fire when, by pure chance, he met Emily in Great College Street, near Camden Town Railway Station. She said, 'Hello, what are you doing this way?' and they went into the *Eagle* (although Wood said he did not then know the name of the pub) where they chatted for a short time. She asked him why he had not sent her the postcard. He told her that he had the card in his pocket and promised to post it to her, which he did later that night or the following morning. Before this, Wood went to the Gas Company's showroom with Emily and she waited for him outside while he spoke to a salesman. It was near closing time and Wood arranged to call back in a week's time to choose a stove (although, in the event, he did not do so because his brother's wife had learned that the rooms underneath her apartment at 43 Museum Street might become vacant and it might be possible for him to move in there, causing the notion of buying the gas fire to be abandoned). He re-joined Emily in Camden Road and they walked together to a linen draper's shop in Park Street off Hampstead Road. Emily entered the shop and, while Wood waited in the street, he saw a friend, Harry Mason, with his wife and children. Wood explained he was waiting for a girl to come out of the shop and the Masons moved on before Emily emerged. As Emily was a long time in the shop, Wood motioned to her that he was moving on. She came out of the shop and told him that she was late herself and had to meet someone at St Pancras. So Wood left her at about 8:30pm and made his way to the St Pancras Public Baths in Whitfield Street off Tottenham Court Road to wash.

The third and final time Wood told Tinkham he saw Emily was in the *Rising Sun* on Monday 9 September at about 9:00pm but she was flitting about between various men, seeming to know everyone in the bar. On leaving the premises, he saw her walking up Euston Road with a man who had a limp or some form of hip problem. She left this man and came over to speak to him (Wood), saying something like, 'What about the drink I left?' Accordingly, they both returned to the *Rising Sun* where Emily finished her drink. She then went over and spoke to one of the men in the bar before returning to Wood. She said that she did not like the man she had just been speaking to but would have to return to him because it would be to her financial benefit. However, she agreed to walk a little way with Wood and they strolled up to St Pancras Church near the fire station where she was accosted by three or four horsey-looking male friends and she left Wood to join them. That, he said, was the last he ever saw of her.

Having told his story, Wood said to Tinkham, 'You know me well enough Jack to know I could not commit such a crime. There is no secrecy in it at all but don't mention this to anybody else at present. My dad is in very poor health of late and if it gets to his ears that I am in any way connected with this affair I believe the blow could knock him over'. Tinkham promised he would say nothing about it and Wood no doubt hoped that was the end of the matter. However, when he returned home for work, his stepbrother questioned him about the similarity of his handwriting and that of the rising sun postcard. Wood replied that it was like his handwriting but did not admit that it was his. Instead, he sought out his brother, Charles. The two men were very close; in 1905, Charles had named his first son Robert after his younger brother. Wood admitted to Charles and his wife, Bessie, that he was the much sought after author of the postcard. He repeated in full the story he had told Tinkham as to how he had come to write it. Charles advised his brother to go at once to Scotland Yard but Wood claimed that he was too busy in the office, doing the work of his principal who was away at the time. Charles, therefore, suggested that the next best option was to deposit a letter at the Poste Restante at St Martin's Le Grand, a branch of the post office which held mail for collection for a short period on behalf of named recipients, usually travellers, who had no fixed address for delivery. Consequently, the following letter (containing some dating errors evidently not spotted by Charles, who was otherwise an eagle-eyed and extremely competent professional proof reader) was written late on Sunday, 29 September 1907, from the address of 43 Museum Street W.C. (Charles' home):

> We, the undersigned, make this statement and place it in the charge of the Poste Restante at St Martin's le-Grand, in order to safeguard our good faith in the matter should our course of action be impeached. We, the first two signatories, are aware from his own full avowal that the postcard signed "Alice" published in the newspapers of Sept 27 (sic) and 28 by desire of the police, in order to obtain information in the "Camden Town Murder

Case" is in the handwriting and was written by Robert Wood of 12 Frederick-street. We jointly are anxious to assist the police in every way possible: but we are also anxious to avoid the publicity and personal trouble occasioned by an immediate communication. Having regard to the non-reliability of the newspaper theories and comments, and being quite satisfied of Robert Wood's bona-fides and that his contribution to the matter can aid but little, we consider it wise to await the results produced at the adjourned inquest on September 29 (sic): and while trusting that the intervention of Robert Wood may thereby be made unnecessary, at the same time we determine should not satisfaction arise from the inquest, to make the avowal of Robert Wood without delay.

      CHARLES CARLYLE WOOD
      BESSIE M. WOOD
      ROBERT WOOD

It goes without saying that this was an unusual course of action to adopt. Wood's later explanation was that the letter 'was intended to be opened in the event of the police calling on me for an explanation as to the postcard, to show that I had not concealed the fact that I had written it'. However, as he did not inform the police he had written the postcard, in effect concealing his authorship from the authorities, the letter served no real or proper purpose; it was hardly an example of assisting the police 'in every way possible'. Moreover, Charles Wood could have retrieved the letter at any time so that its contents need never have been known by anyone other than the signatories. The excuse for the non-disclosure – that Wood wanted to avoid the 'publicity and personal trouble' which would be caused by telling the truth – was not terribly convincing. It was by no means inevitable that there would have been any publicity if Wood had stepped forward to speak to the police – the press did not have quite the close relationship with them at the time that they developed in subsequent years – and it would have been quite possible for the police to have informed the newspapers that they had eliminated the writer of the postcard from their enquiries without naming him. It is true that Wood might have gone to some personal trouble by making a statement about his activities but it was a murder inquiry after all and Emily Dimmock had been put to not a little personal trouble when she was murdered.

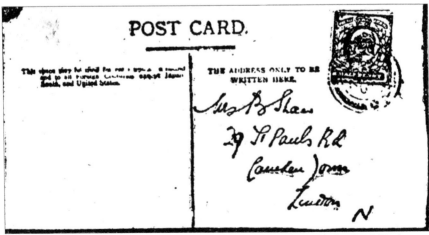

The four postcards addressed to 'Mrs [B] Shaw' circulated by Scotland Yard to the press (the rising sun postcard is the one at the bottom of the next page)

Shaw

50 Great College Street

Camden Town

N.

POST CARD

Mrs Shaw
50 Great College Street
Camden Town
London

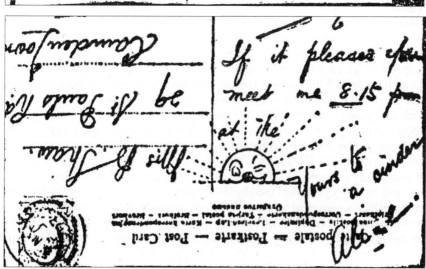

6

If it please you
meet me 8.15 pm
at the

Yours to a cinder

Carte postale — Postkarte — Post Card

Chapter Eight

Scoops and Suspects

'Always suspect everybody.'

Sampson Brass, quoting 'Foxey', in *The Old Curiosity Shop* by Charles Dickens, 1841

With public attention focused on the publication of the postcards, a tremendous scoop by the *People* was barely noticed. Their reporter had spoken to someone who had supposedly dealt with the police investigation 'from a semi official point of view'. This person had told them that the assassin was known to the authorities as Joseph, or 'Scotch Joe'. While not quite right – their source appears to have misheard or misremembered the name of either 'Scotch Jock' (or 'Scotch Jack') or 'Scotch Bob' – it was the first public naming of the prime suspect. It is clear that the paper's source did have genuine information because the *People* was able to exclusively inform its readers that the police had found a scrap of burnt paper in the fire in Emily's room bearing a few words which were believed to be in the murderer's handwriting and which matched the handwriting on the postcards.

This was not the only juicy information that the *People* was able to provide. It also stated that the police had received an anonymous communication from a woman who knew a prostitute friend of Emily's who, the anonymous informant believed, would be able to give the police 'important information', explaining that she had not wished to come forward 'having since her acquaintance with the victim married respectably'. This woman, labelled by the newspaper as 'Mrs X', had been contacted by police and 'after considerable trouble and pressure brought to bear on Mrs X' she had informed them that she not only met Emily with a man on the night preceding the murder but had spoken to her and knew by name the man she was with at the time. The newspaper said that this was 'the man who is being searched for high and low' adding that 'it is curious that he has since the crime been absent from his accustomed haunts'. It is hard to see how 'Mrs X' could be anyone other than May Campbell, a.k.a. Mrs Lillian Pohl, and this is the only indication we have that her information to police might not have been provided voluntarily.

The *People* also repeated what it said was the official description of the suspect but with a few small modifications, namely: 'aged 27 to 30 [previously it had been 28 to 30], of sallow complexion, dark hair, peculiar grey eyes [this was the first mention of the eyes being 'grey'], clean shaven, with chin and neck disfigured with pimples'. No mention was made here of the suspect's height and the paper added the comment that 'He is known as an undesirable character'. This may be compared to a description which appeared in the following morning's *Daily News* which said the police were searching for 'a man of some thirty years of age, and 5ft. 8 or 9in. in height, with dark complexioned face and sunken eyes [who] usually wore a dark suit and black bowler hat'. Its own additional comment was that 'If the police conclusions are correct this man is not unknown to certain Metropolitan prisons'. This would, in fact, appear to be the newspaper's own conclusions and there is nothing in the Metropolitan

Police file to indicate that the police were looking for someone with a known criminal record.

These two new descriptions followed one that had appeared exclusively in Saturday's *Daily Chronicle* which stated that the man being hunted by police was 'about thirty years of age, 5ft 8in in height....has a long, thin, dark, blotchy face and sunken eyes....wearing a blue serge suit, a bowler hat, with a somewhat high crown, a "double" collar and dark tie.... a man of good education and of "shabby genteel" appearance.' The fact that the next sentence in the article stated that 'Detective-Inspector Neil, assisted by Sergeants Ball and Goodchild, is working most energetically...' might indicate the source of the newspaper's information. Inspector Neil was specifically asked about this at the Old Bailey but denied having had anything to do with it. As we have seen, though, the phrase 'sunken eyes' was one that was used by Neil in one of his reports. Only Gladys Warren had referred to the suspect as having a 'blotchy' face, while 'shabby genteel' was a phrase only Crabtree had used but he was locked up in prison and thus could not have been the journalist's source. For those reasons it does appear that the police, if not Inspector Neil himself, had been feeding information to the *Daily Chronicle*.

Another little nugget of information in the weekend papers, buried among the sensation of the postcards, was a report in the *Evening News* on the Saturday claiming that an important witness at the resumed inquest would be 'a man named Clark' with whom Emily spent some of Monday and Tuesday evening and to whom she showed the postcard signed 'Alice' and confided fears about 'the dark man'. This appears to confuse Frank Clarke with Robert Roberts but shows that the paper was getting information from someone with knowledge of the police investigation. It added that other witnesses would be women who had known Emily intimately during the last three years, one of whom had stated that the dark man wanted her to leave Shaw. At the same time, the *Illustrated Police News* said that two men had been taken separately from a public house, with one being interrogated by Detective Inspector Neil and the other by Detective Inspector Stockley, but both were released. This sounds like a belated reference to Roberts and Clarke but the paper went on to say that the interviews produced some new information and one result 'has been the issue of a warrant for the arrest of a certain man on a much less serious charge than that of murder'. Nothing in the Metropolitan Police file supports such a notion. Equally curious was the fact that the paper referred to a 'strange story' which, it said, had reached the authorities in connection with the disposal of a bracelet taken from Emily Dimmock's room but that 'in the interests of justice' it was not advisable to go into details. What that was all about, if anything, has never been revealed.

Late in the evening on Sunday 29 September, Harold Ashton, a reporter for the *Morning Leader*, called at the offices of the Criminal Investigation Department of Scotland Yard to present them with a cunning theory he had developed that the author of the four postcards was 'a racing man' and 'without doubt a follower of race meetings'. He pointed out that 2 January 1907, the date of the postmark of the earliest card, was the first day of racing after a long spell of wintry weather. He thought that the postcard with the Brighton postmark was dated 9 August 1907 (although, as it was addressed to Emily at 50 College Street, it was almost certainly dated 9 January) while the Brighton races were held on 6 to 8 August, moving to Lewes, near Brighton, on 9 to 10 August. The postcard with the Windsor postmark of Monday 19 August corresponded with the fact that the Windsor races were held on Friday 16 and Saturday 17 August, with many racing people staying in Windsor over the weekend until the Monday. So far, almost so good, but then Mr Ashton destroyed his credibility with the police by claiming that the rising sun postcard of 9 September, posted in North London, bore a Doncaster postmark; and he saw a connection between this and the fact that the Doncaster Autumn meeting began on 10 September. To add to the theory, Mr Ashton thought the rising sun postcard had been purchased in France (it was, in fact, from Belgium) during the Chantilly autumn meeting in the first week of September. Ashton had planned to publish this theory in the *Morning Leader* but his mistake about the Doncaster postmark was quietly drawn to his attention by Scotland Yard and he sensibly let the matter drop.

On Monday 30 September, with no hard news to report, the *Daily Chronicle* introduced a supernatural element into the story. Believing that Scotland Yard had called in a clairvoyant who was taken by detectives to Emily Dimmock's house, it claimed that: 'After a short inspection of the room, the clairvoyant lay down on the bed where the dead body was found, and apparently sank into a trance....he began to speak in a rapt, tense voice....he proceeded to give a startlingly vivid description of the actual commission of the crime; pictured in detail the appearance of a certain man and concluded by exclaiming, in answer to a question, "the man you want is on his way to Melbourne"'. Other newspapers did not need much prompting to follow up the story; that day's *Evening News* contacted Dr Abraham Wallace, a 'well known spiritualist' of Harley Street who told their reporter that the use by Scotland Yard of a clairvoyant was 'a step in the right direction and might have an important bearing on criminal investigation in the future'. Needless to say the whole story was nonsense. Inspector Neil was far too sensible to have anything to do with charlatans pretending to be able to speak to dead people and a firmly worded denial of the story was issued within hours.[283]

The police had, in fact, been busy interviewing the living. A man called Albert Arnold had been accused by a neighbour of committing the murder. He was known to have associated with prostitutes and had been treated for venereal disease at the Lock Hospital. Inspector Neil interviewed him and arranged for him to be viewed by Robert Roberts to ascertain if he was the man he had seen in the *Rising Sun* on the Monday before the murder. Roberts confirmed he was not the man, and Arnold denied even knowing Emily Dimmock. There was no evidence to the contrary and Inspector Neil was satisfied that he had nothing to do with the murder. Another man who had contracted venereal disease was eliminated from the inquiry – even though he had been a client of Emily's and had caught the disease from her – because he had a rock solid alibi. This was George Wright, conductor on a restaurant car of the Midland Railway, who had left London on the 11:40am train to Edinburgh on Wednesday 11 September and did not return to London until late on the Thursday.

Another of Emily's clients, but one who appears to have avoided contracting any diseases from her, was William Melvin, a glass and scientific instrument maker, who lived in Clerkenwell Road and who, according to the police, was 'a single man fond of drink and associates with loose women'.[284] He was able to satisfy the police that, at the time of the murder, he was at home with his parents in Hendon from an early hour. William Linehan, who appears to have blamed Emily for his arrest and conviction for keeping a brothel at 121 Judd Street, said that he was at home the whole evening of 11 September with 'his wife', Gladys, in South London and this was corroborated by his landlady.

Others eliminated from the inquiry by the police included: a suspect put forward by Inspector Stockley called William Russell who was a betting man and a pimp but seemed to have an alibi for the night of the murder, a Scotsman called Jack Carr (suspected of possibly being 'Scotch Jack') who had known Emily in East Finchley but who was believed to be living in Belfast and had not been seen in London for the past two years and William Tetlow, a client of one of Emily's prostitute friends, who claimed to have been at home all night on 11 September. Tetlow initially interested police because he matched the description of the man seen by Sharples and Harvey after midnight on the night of the murder but he was then seen by unnamed 'witnesses' (presumably Sharples and Harvey) who failed to recognise him. Tetlow was a former Grenadier Guardsman and, according to information held at the archives of the Grenadier Guards, was a little over 5 foot 9 inches in height, weighing 140 pounds, possessing a 38 inch chest, with fresh complexion, grey hair and fair hair.[285] In exonerating him, Inspector Neil described him as a 'respectable young fellow' which was no doubt true, and he had married a woman (Lily Jeeves) in 1906, but a little over three years after the murder, on 30 January 1911, he was convicted at Marylebone Police Court for assaulting two men and fined twenty-five shillings.[286] The police also considered 'Jumbo' Hurst, the soldier with whom Emily had formed a relationship and holidayed in Luton, but, on the basis that he had since married and had not been seen in the neighbourhood of St Pancras for a considerable time, was not given a great deal of attention.[287]

At the resumed inquest in a crowded courtroom on the Monday morning, Dr Thompson gave further evidence about the murder. He said he wanted to make it clear that whoever committed the crime raised Emily's head with their left hand while she was asleep and managed to cut the bed with a knife (or razor) while doing so, showing that the head was not raised far. It was now that he put forward his theory that death had taken place at about 3:00am based on the contents of Emily's stomach. This was the first time he had estimated a specific time of death in public. In reply to a question from Inspector Neil, he said that Emily's last meal included lamb, potatoes and stout which, for reasons previously mentioned, must have surprised the detective who had authorised extensive inquiries at fish shops. The doctor had some more important information to impart but, before he did so, all women were ordered to leave the court. In their absence, he was able to safely impart that he had found some sort of evidence of sexual activity before Emily's death. This was considered too delicate a fact even to be reported in the newspapers but some did include a report of the coroner's summary of the doctor's evidence when he (the coroner) said: 'That makes it perfectly clear that it was a man who was there that night and not a woman'.[288] One would naturally assume this means that the doctor had found semen and, as if to confirm this, nine days later he prepared a statement for the police in which he stated that 'At the special request of the Assistant Commissioner [Sir Melville Macnaghtan], I have made examination and am of opinion that a man had had connection with her [Emily] prior to her death'.[289] However, he would later state in evidence that he had examined Emily's body with a microscope 'for the purpose of seeing whether sexual connection had taken place within an appreciable time' but 'failed to detect spermatozoa', finding only 'a quantity of mucus'.[290] This suggests that the doctor had made the basic mistake of confusing vaginal or cervical mucus with semen in his visual examination and misled the coroner but corrected his evidence after using a microscope.

In what one newspaper described as a 'Sherlock Holmes deduction', Dr Thompson also stated at the inquest that 'The front part of her hair was done in curling irons, which she had done before going to bed' from which he deduced that the murderer was 'someone familiar with her who was with her when she prepared for bed'.[291] Answering a question from a juryman, the doctor confirmed that Emily had suffered from 'a disease' at some point in her life.[292] At the close of proceedings, the coroner adjourned the inquest for another fortnight at the request of Scotland Yard and then directed some comments to the public at large, saying that, while the police acknowledged that the press and other persons who call themselves 'amateur detectives' had rendered 'valuable assistance in the matter', he wanted say to those individuals who wished to assist the police that they should 'not to rush off to a newspaper with every little bit of information but go at once to Scotland Yard and tell the police what they know if they know anything'. This clearly reflected some official frustration that journalists were getting information on the case from witnesses before the police.

On the same day as the resumed inquest, Inspector Neil sent the Assistant Commissioner at Scotland Yard a detailed thirty-five page handwritten report on the progress of the investigation which he had obviously been working on for a number of days. Sir Melville Macnaghten described it as 'painstaking and comprehensive'. According to the *Daily Mirror*, two days earlier, it had been emphasised by the police that, in circulating the postcards, 'it was not implied that the writer of the cards was the murderer; in fact, he might be an innocent man'. What is clear from Neil's report of 30 September, however, is that the inspector had narrowed his inquiry down to just one man: the author of the postcards, who was also believed to be the man seen with Emily in the *Rising Sun* on the Monday before her murder. 'I and my officers are of the opinion', wrote Neil in his report, 'that the murderer will not be traced until this man is found and every possible effort is being made with that object in view'. The inspector's thinking was heavily influenced by a belief that this man was 'a man of whom she [Emily] was very much afraid, that she feared harm from him, and would have preferred not to meet him but was afraid of the consequences if she did not'.[293] From the evidence of the postcards, the earliest of which was dated January 1907, Neil believed that the suspect had known Emily from at least the beginning of the year and, from the fact that her hair was in curling pins, concluded (like Dr Thompson) that her killer 'was on good terms' with her and this would explain why she allowed herself to go to sleep while he was still in the room.

The evidence of Sharples and Harvey about the man they saw with Emily in Euston Road after midnight was considered by Inspector Neil but he wrote that he was 'not inclined to place a great deal of reliance on what they say'. This was on the basis that if Emily had been in Euston Road, in the vicinity of the *Rising Sun*, at closing time, she would have been seen by some of her 'numerous acquaintances'. He also believed that Emily was not likely to have been near the *Rising Sun* without going into that establishment. For the same reason, Neil did not place a great deal of weight on May Campbell's evidence that she had seen Emily late at night on the Wednesday near the *Rising Sun* with 'Scotch Bob'.

Neil noted that every suspect had been seen at a police station by one or all of Robert Roberts, Frank Clarke, Edwin Smeeth (the barman in the *Rising Sun*) and also by Florence Smith and Ellen Lawrence, referred to by Neil as 'the two prostitutes', in order to ensure that they were not the man seen with Emily on the Monday. The suspects were all also asked to provide a sample of handwriting to compare with the handwriting on the postcards. Neil believed that the author of the postcards had written the letter to Emily, seen by Roberts, making an assignation at the *Eagle* on the night of the murder. He assumed that Emily had met the man there and taken him back to her apartment where they had shared a meal and then engaged in sexual intercourse (as, at that time, Dr Thompson's conclusion was that such intercourse had occurred). Subsequently, Emily went to sleep and was murdered by her companion, either because she had given him venereal disease in the past or she had refused to leave Bert Shaw in order to live with him; the supposed motive was not spelt out in the report.

Surprisingly, Inspector Neil made no reference in his report to the notion that the murderer must have been searching for something. Despite the discovery of the rising sun postcard five days earlier, Inspector Neil still did not draw the attention of his superiors to the fact that the general disorder found at the scene of the crime suggested that the murderer had conducted a frantic search to locate that postcard in the knowledge that his handwriting would be a major clue as to his identity. It was not until a week later, in very different circumstances, that the inspector would file a report in which he stated that it seemed 'as if the murderer had been searching for something' and even then he did not say what it was. Yet, it was certainly Inspector Neil's view that, in order to disguise the purpose of this search and make it look like a robbery, or to throw the police off the scent as to the true motive of the crime, the murderer took a few trinkets of no value. He must have believed that he only needed to find the author of the rising sun postcard and he would have the murderer.

But there was no sign of the prime suspect. The general public was offering suggestions to the police but nothing was coming through of any use. A 44-year-old solicitor called Francis Clutton, of the firm Ivan Brown & Clutton, was accused in one letter from a member of the public but having found nothing to connect him to the crime the police believed that it had been sent 'in spite'. One report in a newspaper which seemed promising was that a clerk employed in the office of a 'well known London establishment' had provided Scotland Yard with letters in his possession 'showing that the writer of the postcards and his correspondent were the same person'.[294] This suspect had held a position as a commercial traveller with a London firm and had moved to Watford earlier in the year but had supposedly disappeared in mid-September. It is not clear if there was any truth in this story and there is no evidence to suggest that the police ever took it seriously. It must have seemed to Inspector Neil that the murder enquiry would end in frustration without even the identification of his prime suspect.

Then, finally, a breakthrough!

A contemporary sketch of Dr John Thompson

Chapter Nine

Arrest

'It was, to my mind, just a piece of unexpected business, to which I had no choice but to attend.'

Robert Wood, on his arrest, *Weekly Dispatch*, 29 December 1907

At about twenty minutes past eight during the evening of Sunday 29 September, after having posted the letter to the Poste Restante, Robert Wood paid a visit to Ruby Young in Earl's Court.

'Ruby, I'm in trouble' were his first words.

'I know you are' replied Ruby, holding out her newspaper containing a facsimile of the rising sun postcard, 'this is your handwriting'. She had seen the reproduction of the postcard in that day's *News of the World* and had written a letter to Wood about it which she had not yet posted.[295]

Wood immediately admitted that he had authored the postcard which began 'Phillis darling' but denied having written any of the other three which had been published.

'What are you going to do about it?' asked Ruby.

'Have patience and I will explain all to you' said Wood who then related to Ruby the same story he had told both Jack Tinkham and his brother about Emily Dimmock asking him to write her a postcard in the *Rising Sun*. Once again, he claimed that he last saw Emily on Monday 9 September when he left her with some 'horsey' looking men by St Pancras Church. 'I was with my brother Charles the whole of the Tuesday night' he told Ruby 'but I was by myself on Wednesday, out walking alone, and therefore cannot prove where I was'. Consequently, he emphasised the need for Ruby to provide him with an alibi saying, 'Now will you be true to me and say that I was with you on that Wednesday night?'

'Why should you want me to say I was with you on Wednesday night?' queried Ruby.

'Well, trust me and be true, your word and my word will stand against the world', answered Wood optimistically.

Ruby was not terribly happy and said she did not want her name in the papers because it would hurt her mother. Wood reassured her by saying, 'If your name gets besmirched in any way through me, if I get out of it I will take you right away and marry you'. Still not convinced, and protesting that she did not want to marry him, Ruby suggested he go to the police and explain to them how he came to send the postcard and where he was on Wednesday but Wood said, 'I cannot do that because I have no-one to prove where I was'. He emphasised once more that he had been out walking that night and arrived home before midnight but had not spoken to anyone and was thus effectively without an alibi. Nevertheless, he assured her that he would go to the police and persisted in asking her to 'be true' by saying she was with him on the Wednesday.

Eventually, after being reminded that she had once said she would do 'anything' for him, Ruby promised that she would do as he asked and the couple walked to Earl's Court Tube Station where Wood told Ruby he was happy because she was going to keep her word. They both caught a train and Ruby travelled as far as Piccadilly Circus – presumably to start work by walking the streets – while Wood continued to Holborn, saying he was going to see his brother. Before parting, Ruby said that if she told police she was with him on Wednesday it might get her into trouble but Wood repeated his mantra: 'Your word and my word will stand against the world'. However, Ruby suspected that the alibi was destined to fail. In reality, she had been with a gentleman friend, presumably a client, from half past eleven at night on the Wednesday evening to the following morning. If the police investigated this, there was a good chance they would discover her actual whereabouts.

On the Monday, when Wood went back to work, the poste restante letter served a useful purpose for him in reassuring John Tinkham that he had taken proper steps in the matter. He told Tinkham that he had spoken to his brother who had said, 'Bob there's only one course for you to pursue and that's the straight course. You must make a clean breast of it'. As a result, he informed Tinkham, he had written a statement signed by himself, his brother and his brother's wife which had been 'posted to the authorities at the proper quarter'. Tinkham naturally assumed that the statement had been sent to the police, whereas all Wood had effectively done was to post a letter to himself.

Wood and Ruby met again on Tuesday 1 October at lunch time at the house of Wood's brother in Museum Street, where Wood always took his lunch on Tuesdays. In a private moment, Ruby mentioned to Wood that she was worried because she thought she would be challenged as to where she was on the Wednesday night and the man she was actually with might come forward with the truth. A frustrated Wood said, 'Oh very well, if you don't want to be true, don't' to which Ruby replied reassuringly, 'Very well, I will be true. I have given you my word and I won't break it'. Bessie Wood, Charles' wife, was present during the lunch and Ruby proved her loyalty and willingness to lie for Wood when Bessie mentioned that it might be important for her brother-in-law to establish his movements; Ruby said: 'Well I can answer for him on the Wednesday night'.

The next day, Wood and Ruby met in the Gray's Inn Road and had lunch together at the Express Dairy in Hart Street, Bloomsbury, where Wood again asked Ruby if she would be true and, now irritated by his persistence, she told him, 'Yes, I will be true but don't keep bothering me; it's getting on my nerves'. That night, Ruby met a 37-year-old architect and landscape artist, James Stewart Campbell McEwan Brown, a man she would describe as her 'friend' but someone, she said, she had not seen for two years, and the likelihood is that he was one of her clients. She did not even know his first name, calling him only McEwan Brown.[296] By pure coincidence he had been born in Camden Town in 1870 and was now living in Bournemouth but (presumably) visiting London. Ruby met him near Bond Street and they stopped for a chat and a walk during which she confided in him, without mentioning Wood's name, that she knew the author of the postcard everyone was talking about and had been asked to provide a false alibi for him. She asked for his advice as to what she should do and he, naturally, told her to speak to the police. Ruby hesitated but agreed to meet him again within the next couple of days.

On the Thursday evening, between 8:00pm and 9:00pm, Wood visited Ruby at her flat near Earl's Court. She asked to be released from her promise which immediately made Wood suspicious, saying, 'You have been speaking to somebody about it. You have allowed somebody else to influence you. It is clear you do not love me', to which Ruby replied, 'I don't love you now'. 'If you don't want to be true' said Wood, 'say so now and I'll say goodbye'. Ruby confessed to Wood that she had indeed told a friend the whole story, causing Wood to exclaim, 'Oh well, you love somebody else!' Ruby replied by saying, 'I love nobody', to which a confused Wood asked, 'Not even me?' and Ruby answered, 'No'. Ruby explained that her friend had advised her not to comply with Wood's wishes, pointing out the possible consequences of providing a false alibi to the police. Wood was not concerned about this and attempted to reassure Ruby by once again repeating that their joint word would stand against the world. Appearing to accept this, Ruby simply replied, 'I will be true' and the pair then concocted a story about what they were supposed to have done on the crucial Wednesday evening of 11 September. They agreed to say that they had met after work for tea at Lyons, walked afterwards from Holborn up to the West End and had parted at the Brompton Oratory at, or shortly after, 10:30pm that night. After the false alibi had been devised on that Thursday evening, Wood left Ruby's apartment at about 10:00pm.

In the meantime, McEwan Brown had passed on what Ruby had told him to a young journalist friend, George Dilnot, the crime reporter for the *Weekly Dispatch*. Dilnot, McEwan Brown and Ruby Young all met together in a Regent Street restaurant called *Gambrinus* during the afternoon of Friday 4 October, although Ruby did not then know that Dilnot was a journalist.[297] After a short conversation, during which Ruby produced some postcards and letters that Wood had written to her, Dilnot left the restaurant and telephoned Inspector Neil. Dilnot was able to tell him that the author of the rising sun postcard had finally been traced.

Events then moved swiftly. Neil dashed to central London with Sergeant Ball and met Ruby Young outside Piccadilly Station at about 5:00pm. A plan was subsequently hatched so that when Ruby met Wood after work, shortly after 6:15pm in Gray's Inn Road, Inspector Neil and Detective Sergeant Ball were watching.[298] The detectives must have been delighted to see Ruby approach a man wearing a blue serge suit and a hard felt bowler hat. Ruby and Wood walked together towards Holborn followed by the two police officers.

'You see that man over there,' whispered Wood to Ruby, pointing to Inspector Neil, 'I believe he is a detective.'

'Take no notice' Ruby replied.

At that moment, Inspector Neil stepped forward and placed his hand on Wood's shoulder.

'Mr Wood?'

'Yes.'

'I am a police inspector and I wish to speak to you.'

'Certainly.'

'I do not wish the lady to hear. Kindly step this way'. The inspector and Wood moved to one side and Neil continued: 'I have been making certain inquiries as to the murder of Emily Elizabeth Dimmock at 29 St Paul's Road, Camden Town, on the night of 11 September, and some postcards have been found which were sent to her by a man with whom she was acquainted, and from my inquiry I have reason to believe that they were written by you, and that she was known to you as "Phyllis"'.

'Quite right' said Wood, coolly, 'There is no mystery about the card. I only wrote one of them, the one with a sketch of the rising sun on it. I know nothing about the others.'

'We cannot discuss the matter here; you had better come with me', said Inspector Neil as Sergeant Ball hailed a cab for Highgate Police Station, 'I shall have to detain you pending inquiries as to your movements on the night of 11 September, which was the night of the murder, as I have reason to believe you know something about it'.

'Very well,' replied Wood, 'You will allow me to wish my young lady goodbye before I go?' Turning to Ruby he said magnificently, 'Goodbye my dear; don't worry, I have to go with these gentlemen. If England wants me, she must have me. Don't cry, but be true.' Ruby immediately picked up on Wood's code and, as he was ushered into the cab by the two police officers, called out tearfully, 'Leave that to me!'

In the cab, on the way to the Police Station, Wood repeatedly told the detectives that he had made no secret of the postcard and had told his brother about it, something which did not impress Inspector Neil at all. Wood explained that his brother had advised him to go to the police but, he said, 'I was busy in the office with the work of my principal, who was away at the time' which is why he and his brother came up with the plan of writing the letter to the Poste Restante at St Martin's Le Grand. Wood urged the inspector to obtain the letter 'to show that I did not conceal the matter'. Under caution, he also told Inspector Neil: 'I only met the girl by accident on the Friday night before she was murdered, and I consider it very hard to be drawn into the matter, as I know practically nothing about it. If one has a good name, you do not care to be mixed up in matters of this sort. I do not think my evidence would help or make much difference to the case'. Inspector Neil told him that the allegation was that the person who wrote the postcard had an appointment at the *Eagle* public house in Camden Town between 8:00 and 9:00pm because Emily Dimmock had received a letter on the Wednesday morning in the same handwriting as the postcard. Wood replied, 'Well I never wrote anything to her but the postcard, which was sent quite by accident'. He then told Neil the same story about how he came to write the postcard as he had told Tinkham, his brother and Ruby Young.

Upon arrival at Highgate Police Station, Wood was searched by D.S. Ball who found a violet coloured pencil in the same shade as the pencil used to write the rising sun postcard. Wood was also carrying seven unused picture postcards similar to the rising sun postcard. Following the search, Inspector Neil told Wood that, if he wished to make a statement concerning his movements when the murder was committed, he would make full enquiries about it. In response, Wood said, 'I want to tell you the truth about the whole matter' and then made a full but not frank statement. Although he admitted to having spoken to Emily in the *Rising Sun* on Monday 9 September, when explaining where he had been on the Wednesday, the last day Emily Dimmock had been seen alive, he said:

On leaving business I went straight home, had tea, and a wash, and walked up to Holborn with my sweetheart who had called for me. Her name is Miss Ruby Young and she stays at 80 Finborough Road, Earl's Court. We strolled along towards 'Phiteesis' and had tea in Lyons, two doors from 'Phiteesis'. We always went to the smoking room, as having had tea myself, the tea room was for her benefit rather than mine. We remained there until about 8 or 8.30 pm. We went (I think) along Kingsway, the Strand and through the West End to Hyde Park. We remained there and in the vicinity until (I should think) about 10.30pm. We then strolled up Brompton Oratory where I bid her good night, and returned by tube to Holborn. I then walked home from there and arrived as near as I can recollect, about midnight.

None of this was true. Wood had, of course, been with Emily Dimmock in the *Eagle*. From his earlier discussion with Ruby Young, Inspector Neil was perfectly aware that Wood was lying but he said nothing for the moment. Wood then added to his statement the claim that 'the postcard I have referred to [i.e. the rising sun postcard] is the only thing in the form of writing, either in postcard or letter, that I have ever sent to deceased'. The inspector was sure Wood was lying about this too, having compared the handwriting on the fragments recovered from the fire in Emily's room with the rising sun postcard, but he continued to bide his time before confronting the prisoner.

Wood also included in his statement that he had first heard of the murder from Mr Moss, who mentioned the name 'Phyllis' on Friday 13 September. He admitted that he saw the photographs of Emily in a sailor's costume in the weekend newspapers and, although he did not recognise her, he knew that 'it must have been the girl I met'. However, he kept quiet because he did not think his association with her 'would reflect credit upon me' and had 'a great objection to the publicity' so he 'decided to have nothing to do with the matter'.

Under the rules existing at the time, as Wood had volunteered a statement, the police were not allowed to ask him any questions (other than by way of minor clarification) so Wood was put into a cell, given some tea and allowed to rest. Meanwhile, Inspector Neil, with two colleagues, left Highgate to visit George Wood at 12 Frederick Street, arriving a little after 11:00pm. Despite the darkness, the inspector could surely not have missed the fact that Wood's home was in plain sight of King's Cross Police Station, a few yards away in King's Cross Road. The most sought after man in London was living a minute from a police station in the heart of the King's Cross area and he had effectively been invisible! Putting any such thoughts aside, the inspector explained to the old man that his son, Robert, had been arrested for Emily Dimmock's murder and told him that he must search the house. Before doing so, he asked him if he could say what time Robert usually came home at night. Mr Wood replied: 'He comes home to tea first and after tea he goes out again. He comes home at all times. He generally comes in and fetches the clock and says goodnight'.

'Can you speak of any particular night?' asked the inspector.

'No, sometimes we are asleep'.

'I want you to tax your memory back to the eleventh of September and say if you can recollect if he was at home that night or what time he came home'.

'No, that would be impossible. I cannot recollect any particular night'.

Inspector Neil then commenced a search of Robert's bedroom which was situated on the ground floor and Neil noticed a brown mixture overcoat of the

Chesterfield shape amongst several lots of clothing hanging behind the door of the room. He searched through the coat pockets but found nothing. A couple of razors were located in the room (subsequently found to contain no trace of blood) as well as forty-two unused postcards but nothing of any significance. At this point, Robert's stepbrother, James, came home and Inspector Neil explained what was going on and asked if he could remember whether he had seen Robert on Wednesday 11 September but James could not recall.

The search and questioning complete, Inspector Neil departed from Frederick Street but he had made one crucial mistake. He had failed to take a written statement from either George or James Wood as to their recollection of events of 11 September and, in particular, the fact that they could not recall what time Robert had come home that evening. At the time, though, Inspector Neil undoubtedly went to bed on the Friday night very happy that Wood had no alibi, believing that he had solved the case of his career.

During the night, however, the inspector's sleep might have been troubled by the thought that he had not looked up Wood's chimney; perhaps his prisoner had hidden the murder weapon, or the stolen jewellery, in there. First thing next morning, on Saturday 5 October, two officers were sent back to 12 Frederick Street. George Wood told them that his son's room had already been searched the previous day but they said they were looking for 'something else'. One of them put his hand up both chimneys in the house but, as Mr Wood later told the Old Bailey to laughter, all he found was soot.

Later that same day, Inspector Neil interviewed Ruby Young at length and she confirmed that she had not been with Wood at all on Wednesday 11 September. Not only that, but she provided a detailed written statement in which she set out exactly how Wood had tried to persuade her to deceive the police with a false alibi. For the purposes of handwriting analysis, she also provided the police with a number of letters and postcards that she had received from Wood. At 3:00pm, Detective Constable Page went to the Poste Restante General Post Office with Charles Carlyle Wood and retrieved the letter deposited by the Woods. About two and a half hours later, at 5:30pm, Robert Roberts and Frank Clarke were brought to Highgate Police Station, deliberately chosen by Inspector Neil because it was well away from Camden Town and the prying eyes of reporters. Robert Wood was placed in a line-up comprising fifteen other men. Such line-ups were governed by Metropolitan Police Regulations as to Identification, dated 12 July 1905.[299] These stated as follows:

Whenever it is necessary to effect the recognition of an accused in police custody by persons competent to identify him, every precaution will be taken that such identification is carried out fairly, the following directions being carefully observed.
(a) The officer in charge of the case against the prisoner, though present, will take no part in the particular proceedings connected with the identification, which will be carried out by the officer on duty in charge of the Station or Court.
(b) The witnesses must not be allowed to see the prisoner before he is placed with others for the purpose of identification, nor should they be shown photographs or be assisted by verbal or written description of him.
(c) Before the witnesses are brought into the presence of the prisoner, he

should be placed among a number of persons, eight or more, if practicable, for purposes of identification. In selecting such persons care is to be taken that they are as far as possible of similar age, height, general appearance and class of life as the prisoner. Police Officers must not be utilised for this purpose.

(d) The accused should then be invited to stand where he pleases among them and not be allotted a special position. He will also be asked if he has objection to take to any of the persons or arrangements made. If he desires to have present at the identification, his solicitor, or any friend actually in attendance, no objection is to be made by the Police, whose chief care it must be to see that the proceedings are so conducted that it cannot be subsequently alleged that they were otherwise than fair and straightforward.

(e) The witnesses should then be introduced one by one for the purpose of recognising the accused, and they should be asked to touch the person they identify. On leaving they will not be allowed to communicate with other witnesses who are in waiting. The accused is to be permitted to change his position if he so desires after each witness has left.

(f) Every circumstance connected with the identification is to be carefully noted down by the Officer who carries it out, whether the accused be identified or not, and care must be taken when a witness fails to recognise the accused that the fact is recorded as carefully as when he is identified; the names and addresses of those who fail to identify, as well as those who identify, being taken down. Any statement made by the prisoner should be recorded at once and read over to the officer in charge of the case in the prisoner's hearing. The prisoner is to be invited to sign such statement.

(g) The officer carrying out the identification will make an entry of the same in the Occurrence Book as soon after as possible.

There was never any allegation made against Inspector Neil that the witness identification line-ups breached these rules and Wood never made any complaint about the way they were conducted even though he did not have a solicitor or friend present, as he was allowed. However, he did make the point that, not only was he dressed in a blue serge suit, like the much publicised prime suspect, but one of the men in the line-up had immediately worked out that he must be the man arrested for the Camden Town murder. He would later say that 'This at once created an electric atmosphere in which I was at the centre, and of course, it was impossible to miss'. He would subsequently draw a brilliant sketch which showed him in his blue suit and bowler hat sticking out like a sore thumb in the line-up with everyone looking in his direction, and perhaps there was an element truth in this.[300]

Both Roberts and Clarke identified Wood as the man they saw with Emily in the *Rising Sun* on Monday 9 September but, as Wood had already admitted that he had been there with her in his signed statement, this was not terribly significant or controversial. The third witness brought to identify Wood came from Pentonville Prison. It was Jack Crabtree and he proved to be a little difficult to handle. After walking along the line he immediately realised that the man he claimed had threatened Emily with a razor was not in the room and said, 'There is a man here who knew Phyllis Dimmock, but the man I have referred to in my statement is not here'. Inspector Neil asked him to pick out the man he had referred to who knew 'Phyllis' but he refused, saying, 'No, I came here to identify another man, and I shall not pick this man out'. Inspector

Neil insisted and, eventually, Crabtree relented and picked out Wood as being a man who knew Emily. However, he refused to make a written statement confirming his identification and was taken straight back to prison.

A few minutes later, after the identification process was completed, Inspector Neil dropped a bombshell upon Wood. He told him he had spoken to Ruby Young while he was in custody.

'Well, Mr Wood' said the inspector, 'your story has been disproved by Ruby Young. She says you were not with her on the night of September 11'.

Wood's response was casual but also disingenuous: 'If the young lady denies that I was in her company', he said, 'I cannot help it. One cannot be correct on all such small details, but I have told you the truth and I cannot do more'. He would later write that Neil's words 'took all the fight out of me' and that Ruby's betrayal of him 'seemed so utterly impossible. Yet it had happened'.[301] He simply could not understand why Ruby was not 'true', despite her promises.

Inspector Neil had one more card to play. He produced a photographic reproduction of the burned fragments recovered from the fire in Emily's room and (not being allowed to ask any questions) said to Wood, 'This is a photograph of a portion of the letter making the appointment for a man to meet the deceased woman on the night of her death'. In saying this, he was going further than the evidence of the virtually indecipherable fragments really allowed. Nevertheless, he was in full flow and continued: 'I believe it to be in your handwriting and, as you have been identified as an acquaintance of the deceased for some months prior to her death [this was a reference to Crabtree's identification] and, as your father and brother are unable to say whether you were at home on that night or not, I shall charge you with wilfully murdering her'.

Wood did not comment on the murder charge but his reaction to the photograph of the fragments was that 'The handwriting is certainly like my own; in fact, I should call it a good imitation.' It wasn't until he was in the witness box at the Old Bailey that he would admit that it was, in fact, his handwriting.

At 8:15pm on the Saturday, Wood was taken in a cab from Highgate to Kentish Town Police Station by Detective Sergeant Arthur Mitchell. During the journey, he struck up a conversation with the officer and said: 'One of your colleagues made a remark that he does not trust any girl, and after what I have heard this evening, I am inclined to think the same. My girl was with me last night when Mr Neil came up to me; she shed tears and said "Leave it to me". Well after that one is apt to make a big bloomer isn't one?' Upon arrival at Kentish Town, Wood was formally charged with Emily Dimmock's murder. Naively, he asked if he could provide any further explanation but it was a little too late for that.

Ruby Young

'A Memory of Highgate' by Robert Wood, 1907

Chapter Ten

Newton to the Rescue

'Should an advocate defend a prisoner who he knows is guilty?....my reply: No-one is certain of anything.'

Arthur Newton, in 'Twenty Years Among Criminals and Others', *Cassell's Saturday Journal*, 21 March 1908

The newspapers did not report the arrest until Sunday morning, and then only *Lloyds Weekly News* and the *News of the World* carried the story. Surprisingly, considering that its reporter was involved in securing the arrest, the *Weekly Dispatch* was still asking its readers if they could identify the handwriting of the postcard. However, that newspaper had an extraordinary exclusive of its own. It claimed to have seen the diary of one of 'two men recently questioned by police' who 'will swear that he knows the man who was with Miss Dimmock at ten o'clock on the night she was murdered'. Neither of the men said to have been questioned by police was identified but the supposed diary entry for Wednesday 11 September was reproduced with redactions as follows:

> Saw ———. Had drink. Remarked as to Dimmock. ——— said, "She has an appointment at the Eagle, Camden Town." ——— wanted to go; I dragged him back.

This purported diary entry, which was never referred to by anyone ever again, only makes sense if the diarist was Frank Clarke and the blank name was that of Robert Roberts, who obviously knew that Emily would be at the *Eagle*, having seen the letter from 'Bertie'. However, Clarke never claimed to know who was with Emily on the night of her murder so that particular element of the *Weekly Dispatch* story is dubious. But if this was a genuine extract from Clarke's diary it is particularly interesting because it shows that Roberts was so keen to meet up with Emily again that he seriously contemplated going over to the *Eagle* and had to be restrained from doing so by Clarke.

However, the dramatic story of the day was obviously Wood's arrest and, despite the fact that the identification process was far from complete, *Lloyds Weekly News* did not hold back from publishing a sketch of Wood nor did it refrain from describing him as 'a man of about twenty-nine years of age, 5ft 8in. in height, having a long, thin, dark face and sunken eyes'. No-one who had been following the case would have failed to miss the similarity of this description with that of the prime suspect and, for good measure, the newspaper added that 'When arrested he was wearing a blue serge suit, with "rolled" collar and bowler hat'. It is not clear if the newspaper's reporter had actually seen Wood or was getting his information from the police but the reporter was certainly well informed, knowing that Wood had already been identified at Highgate Police Station by a number of witnesses 'as a man who had been in the murdered girl's company some days before the crime'. It also knew that he had been charged at Kentish Town Police Station the previous evening and that none of the items missing from Emily's room had been recovered. Somehow the paper's reporter was also aware that the police had been 'working most energetically, sometimes far into the night'. An element of balance was provided by quotes from George Wood, to whom the paper's reporter had managed to speak. The old man said that his son was 'a gem of a fellow' who 'wouldn't hurt a fly' and that, 'Frequently at night he would be hard at work at home designing posters and so on'. By contrast with what he had told Inspector Neil late on Friday evening, Mr Wood now said that before his son went to bed he would always look in and say goodnight and, 'As far as I remember he did so on the Wednesday night in question'. The consequences of Inspector Neil's failure to take a written statement from George Wood were already becoming evident. Moreover, Wood's father said that, when he woke up at about half past seven, he saw his son sitting at breakfast in his room and, 'He seemed as bright as ever, chatting quite cheerfully'.

The *News of the World*'s reporter claimed to have seen Wood arrive at Kentish Town Police Station on Saturday night, or at least had spoken to someone who had seen him arrive, for he described Wood as looking 'a little worried, though his attitude had been one of indignation'. He also offered a description of Wood as 'of average height, his complexion very dark. His nose is prominent, his eyes sunken.' This was another familiar description although, it has to be said, in all photographs of Wood it is striking that his eyes are indeed 'sunken'. The newspaper had also established that Wood described himself as 'an artist and painter of pictures'.

One other story appeared in the Sunday papers, having been taken from the local Hertfordshire press. This was that William Dimmock had told local journalists that Rosa Martindale had informed him that, at 3:00am on the morning of the murder, she had been awakened by the striking of the clock and saw a vision of her sister, Emily, at her bedside. Not only that, but she also saw the figure of a man and, when continuing her dream (because she evidently returned to sleep), saw him board a train and then a ship. This story had first appeared in the *North Herts Mail* of 3 October after William had made clear to that paper's journalist that Rosa saw 'the figure of Jumbo' and she was sure he was the man who did it. No doubt it was pure coincidence that this story of Rosa seeing a vision at 3:00am emerged three days after Dr Thompson had publicly estimated the time of death as about 3:00am. And Rosa had not mentioned any such vision when she spoke to a *Daily Mail* journalist on 18 September. In fact, it is clear from William's interview in the *North Herts Mail* that Rosa only mentioned her 'vision' to him after he had blamed her for Emily's death because she let her go back to London; he told the reporter that he had said to her, 'She will shortly haunt you'. Rosa replied that she had already seen Emily in the spirit and told him about her vision. She did not expect her little story to feature in the newspapers and was said to have expressed 'some surprise and indeed slight annoyance that her strange experience had become public' when asked about it by a journalist from the *Luton News*. To him, she told a long and elaborate story about the visitation, at the end of which the sceptical reporter suggested that 'the excitement caused by the painful tragedy, and the suspense, pending the capture of the murderer that followed, might be in some way connected with the dream' to which Rosa is said have 'smiled and remained unconvinced'.

Back in Kentish Town Police Station, the police were very busy on the Sunday. A number of witnesses were ferried into the station to identify their prisoner. William Linehan and Gladys Warren (still calling herself 'Gladys Linehan') both picked out Wood in a line-up with nine other men as someone they said was an acquaintance of Emily's from as far back as about April 1906. Linehan said he used to see Wood with Emily in the *Rising Sun* (but had not seen him since the start of the year) while Gladys said she had known him (but had never spoken to him) for 'about twelve months', i.e. since about September 1906, but was 'certain' that she had frequently seen him in Emily's company in the *Rising Sun* during the time she and Emily were living at 121 Judd Street. As she and Emily had only lived at 121 Judd Street in April 1906, she must have meant that she had known Wood for about eighteen months, not twelve. More specifically, she said that when she and her 'husband' left Judd Street in July 1906, she 'often' saw Wood with Emily in the *Rising Sun*. Perhaps more importantly, Gladys Warren now made no mention of 'Scotch Jock' (or 'Scotch Jack') in her statement – not even confirming that Wood was not him – despite the fact that her first statement had focused on Scotch Jock's threats to Emily.

Edward Smeeth, the assistant manager of the *Rising Sun* (brother-in-law of the licensee, Fred Chapman, having married his sister, Alice), identified Wood as a man he had seen beckon Emily Dimmock in the *Rising Sun* on Friday 6 September, followed by her rising from her chair and walking towards him; this was the night Wood said he had written the rising sun postcard although Smeeth said that he 'did not see any writing done'.[302] Smeeth also said that he saw Wood leave the bar with Emily on Monday 9 September but, significantly, could not remember with any certainty having seen Wood before 6 September. Florence Smith (a.k.a. Emily Stewart) identified Wood as a man she saw with Emily Dimmock in the *Rising Sun* on both Friday 6 September and Monday 9 September and she gave a statement to the police in which she said 'I noticed when the deceased was in the company of prisoner on the Monday night she appeared nervous of him'. Ellen Lawrence also 'at once recognised' Wood as a man she had seen at both the *Pindar of Wakefield* and the *Rising Sun*. In fact, it seems that Wood recognised her first, saying: 'Good morning' to her before she picked him out of the line-up.[303] A window cleaner called Albert Miller, who had been friendly with Emily for about two years before her death, picked out Wood as a man he had known for about a year as 'a frequenter of Euston Road', or, in plain terms, as a man who associated with prostitutes. He gave a statement in which he said that he remembered one night a year earlier in the *Rising Sun* when Emily was with 'Jumbo' Hurst and suddenly looked scared because she saw Wood peering into the bar but nevertheless went out to him, although Wood supposedly ran away when 'Jumbo' – a man mountain by all accounts – chased after him.

Jack Crabtree's wife was also brought to the Police Station on the Sunday but she failed to pick out Wood; in fact, she picked out another man entirely in the line-up. She subsequently explained in a written statement that she was expecting to identify a man she knew as 'Tom', to whom Emily used to give money and whom she had heard threaten to 'do her in'. She said that 'Tom' was of similar appearance to Wood except that he had a small dark moustache. The man she picked out in the line-up resembled Tom but she said she was 'satisfied he is not the man I mean'. Inspector Neil would later say that Mrs Crabtree told him privately that the man she picked out was an acquaintance of Emily's; but he was released from line-up duty before his identity could be established. Despite her failure to pick out Wood from the line-up, Mrs Crabtree nevertheless provided a written statement to the police in which she said that she recognised Wood as a man who once called on Emily at 1 Bidborough Street in June 1906 and then three times at Manchester Street afterwards. Her evidence, however, would never be used.

As it was for the police, Sunday was a busy day for Wood, having been taken back and forth from his cell to attend the identification parades. In his typically affable way, he made friends with the police constable, Harry Brooker, who was guarding him. They chatted about cricket and football, quite possibly discussing Fulham's defeat of Chesterfield by five goals to nil at Craven Cottage the previous day, with Charlie Millington, their new signing from Aston Villa scoring two goals. According to Wood, Brooker 'sympathised and spoke most kindly to me in my cell'.[304] At about 9:15pm, Wood asked Brooker, 'Why do they want me out there so many times?' The constable explained the reason for the numerous identification parades and then, according to Brooker's evidence at the Old Bailey, Wood said, 'If it comes to a crisis I shall have to open out'. During his trial, Wood hotly disputed that he ever said this and he called Brooker's evidence 'undoubtedly false'.[305] On the contrary, it was undoubtedly true – Brooker had no reason to make up such a statement and, if he was going to incriminate Wood, he would surely have fabricated something far more damaging. It is clear that Wood was not being open with the police at the time, especially regarding his claim to have been with Ruby Young on the night of Emily's murder, so there would have been nothing inconsistent in implying that he was holding something back and saying he would 'open out' in a crisis. Apparently, the fact that Brooker had been so kind but had 'betrayed' him by giving evidence against him greatly upset Wood and he would later describe Brooker's evidence about this as, 'The most bitter moment during the whole time I was on trial for my life'.[306]

Late on Sunday night, a police officer made yet another visit to 12 Frederick Street. After considering all the available evidence, it seems that Inspector Neil had decided Wood must have been the man seen by McCowan emerging from 29 St Paul's Road on the morning of 12 September. According to McCowan, that man had been wearing an overcoat. Inspector Neil had seen an overcoat in Wood's room when he conducted the search but had not seized it as evidence. A constable was sent to retrieve it but, in order to conceal from Wood's family the true reason for his visit, was instructed to say that Wood was feeling cold in his cell and required his coat. It was given to him but there would be a conflict of evidence between the Woods and the police about where it was found. Both George and James insisted that the overcoat was taken from a drawer, whereas Inspector Neil was sure he had seen it hanging on a peg behind Wood's door during the search on Friday. It was not a terribly important point but, if the coat had been on the door, it might suggest that Wood was in the habit of wearing it at the time while, if it had been hidden away in the drawer, then it was probably not being used.

On the morning of Monday 7 October, the London newspapers were full of the story of Wood's arrest, about which they were all very well informed. The *Daily Mirror* published a very detailed account of Wood's arrest including the role of Ruby Young in passing her information to a *Weekly Dispatch* reporter. It even included the details of Wood's alibi for the night of the murder in meeting

Ruby after work on Wednesday 11 September and ending up at the Brompton Oratory. In fact, it virtually reproduced Wood's statement to the police in its entirety. In addition, the paper published a fragment of a letter written by Wood to Ruby Young which concluded with the loving salutation, 'Yours to a cinder', just like the rising sun postcard. Wood's stepbrother, James, was quoted as saying that Wood was 'a methodical man' who usually came home at about 6:30pm and then worked on his posters after tea before going out at about 8:00pm, returning about midnight at which time he used to enter James' bedroom to take up his alarm clock and say 'goodnight'. Crucially, James said, 'He did not miss a single night. If he had, of course I should have remembered it, and wondered what was the matter'. He did not mention that the alarm clock had only been in his room since Monday 9 September so this apparent habit was only three days old at the time of the murder. Most of the papers carried a full account of the arrest as well as Wood's explanation of how he had met Emily Dimmock in the *Rising Sun*. James had clearly been speaking to many reporters. The *Tribune* claimed that James had said that Robert 'came home between 10:30 and 12:30 on the night preceding the murder, and came down to breakfast as usual the next morning'. So, despite having told the police that they could not remember if they had seen Robert on the night of 11 September, both his father and stepbrother were now telling journalists that they had, in fact, seen him that night.

While Londoners were digesting the news of Robert Wood's arrest, his brother Charles made his way to 23 Great Marlborough Street – the offices of Arthur Newton & Co, solicitors.

Arthur John Edward Newton was the most well-known defence solicitor of his day. Born in 1860 to a wealthy family – his father was an actuary and manager of the Legal and General Life Association – he had qualified as a solicitor at the age of twenty-three. He set up initially as a sole practitioner in an office in Lincoln's Inn Fields but this was not successful and two years later, with a slightly younger, newly qualified solicitor, Frederick Freke Palmer, started a joint practice called Newton & Palmer in Great Marlborough Street, virtually next to Marlborough Street Police Court. The office location was good but obtaining the firm's first instruction proved to be difficult. In order to gain an edge over the competition, Newton ensured he was in his office all of Saturday and on Bank Holidays, when other lawyers had left for the country, waiting for someone in urgent need of legal representation to appear. This paid off for him when he was asked late on a Saturday afternoon in early 1886 to defend a man's son who had been arrested for assaulting an old woman; Newton was basically the only solicitor the man could find. The case looked hopeless; the boy's job was to deliver coal but he had become annoyed by an elderly lady on his round and hit her in the face with a lump of his black wares. Nevertheless, under questioning by Newton in court, the woman was forced to admit that the boy had always been well behaved in the past and that she knew of no reason why he should have hit her. Newton was fully aware from his initial consultation that his young client had been irritated by the woman because she always asked for the largest lumps of coal, which is why he had hit her with one of them, but he put forward a fabricated argument to the magistrate that it had all been an accident.[307] After the boy's employer bore witness to his excellent character, the young prisoner was acquitted. Outside the court afterwards, Newton heard the boy say to the old woman, 'Done you in the eye, old girl' but he had no qualms about defending someone he knew was guilty. Most of the time, though, he had an unwavering belief in his clients' innocence and it was this that made him such a successful defence lawyer. With what was referred to as 'a sledgehammer approach', he would challenge every aspect of a prosecutor's case, however small, in terrier-like fashion, determined to find the flaw which he was always certain in his own mind must exist.

Following his success in the lump of coal case, Newton's legal practice went from strength to strength. In February 1887, he and Frederick Palmer took on their first big murder case, known as 'The Hoxton Murder', when they represented Thomas Currell who had gone into hiding after his sweetheart, Lydia Green, was shot dead: his photograph having been published in the newspapers before his subsequent capture and arrest. The trial at the Old Bailey was before Mr Justice Grantham who summed up heavily against the prisoner, despite the absence of motive, and it was Grantham who sentenced him to death after the jury found him guilty. Newton always felt that the fact that Currell was unable to go into the witness box to give evidence in his own defence – the law not allowing this at the time – was the key factor in his conviction. However before his execution, Currell confessed that, high on drugs and drunk on alcohol, he had indeed murdered Lydia but could not explain why he had done it.[308] Newton petitioned the Home Secretary for a reprieve on the basis that his client 'was not really in his right senses at the time he took the life of the unfortunate woman' but the petition was refused.

Despite the setback, Newton's practice remained profitable – although he and Frederick Palmer went their separate ways in the summer of 1887 – and the re-named law firm of Arthur Newton & Co became very busy, usually operating in Marlborough Street Police Court, with a growing, and occasionally wealthy, client base. When Lord Arthur Somerset found himself in a spot of bother after the discovery by police of a male brothel he had frequented at 19 Cleveland Street in London's West End, it was to Arthur Newton he turned for assistance. Although not officially a client of Newton's – he fled the country before he could be arrested so did not need legal representation – Lord Somerset bankrolled the defence of two of the individuals involved in the scandal, George Veck and Henry Newlove, neither of whom would have been able to afford Newton's services on their own. More than this, fearing arrest for sodomy and corruption of minors, Somerset also paid Newton to arrange for some of the key potential prosecution witnesses to 'disappear' by leaving the country. Unfortunately for Newton, one of those witnesses went to the police and the solicitor's questionable activities were uncovered. Newton was eventually arrested and sentenced to six weeks in Holloway Prison in May 1890 for attempting to pervert the course of justice. He was not happy in jail and complained that he was 'treated as an ordinary convicted criminal prisoner, both with regard to food, prison clothing and bedding'.[309] He petitioned for release on the basis that dust from his cell was causing problems with his eyes and that he was suffering from various other health problems. The petition was not successful and he served his full sentence. Despite this, and possibly due to his new friends in high places, Newton was not disbarred by the Law Society and continued to practice as normal after being released from prison. This annoyed one newspaper which commented furiously that 'If a man like this is to remain on the roll of solicitors, we must forthwith consider the advisability of taking from the Incorporated Law Society the privileges which they at present possess'.[310] The Law Society did not lose any privileges and Newton was no doubt well rewarded for his efforts on behalf of Lord Somerset; the 1891 census shows that he employed no less than six domestic servants at his country home in Surrey.

In September 1893, Newton was already being described by *Vanity Fair* as 'the most widely known criminal solicitor in London' (although a couple of possible exceptions were mentioned) and featured in its 'Men of the Day' series.[311] He was said to have 'a good appearance' which contrasted with other police court advocates and although 'not eloquent', he was 'lucid' and 'courteous'. His first major success in a national murder case came in 1894 when he and the barrister, Edward Marshall Hall, defended Marie Hermann, a 43 year old prostitute, charged with the murder of 71-year-old Charles Stephens at 51 Grafton Street, Fitzroy Square. Although found guilty of manslaughter and sentenced to six years in prison, she avoided the gallows and Newton would later say that he regarded this as one of his 'most successful' cases because it seemed inevitable to everyone that she would be convicted of murder after she had been caught red-handed with Mr Stephens' body in her trunk, which she had personally transported from Grafton Street to a new address in Upper Marylebone Street, and had then confessed to killing him with an iron bar. Newton was always proud of the fact that his own cross-examination of the police medical expert at Marlborough Street Police Court proved that Stephens had been attacked from the front (consistent with self-defence by his client) rather than from behind. His biggest failure, in his own mind, was his defence of an unmarried mother, Louisa Masset, convicted of the murder of her 3-year-old son in 1899 despite claiming that she had given her child up to two women who offered to look after him. Newton had some secret information about Masset; he had discovered that she had written a letter to the father of their child, telling him that if he did not fix a date for their marriage she would kill their son and commit suicide. Not only that but he encouraged the man to throw the letter onto a fire so the police never saw it.[312] Nevertheless, Newton firmly believed in Masset's innocence so that her conviction and subsequent execution, despite a petition to the Home Secretary signed by 1,000 people, was a great disappointment to him.

Masset had taken the opportunity provided by the 1898 Criminal Evidence Act to give evidence in her own defence but it had not prevented her being found guilty by the jury which heard her. The decision as to whether a prisoner should give evidence and allow themselves to be cross-examined was now one of the biggest that a solicitor had to advise on. Newton's experience of the Currell case meant that he tended to favour his clients giving evidence in their own defence but they could not be forced to and he could do nothing when his client, Samuel Dougal, charged with the murder of 60-year-old Camille Holland, in what was known as 'The Moat Farm Murder', 'absolutely declined' to go into the witness box.[313] Newton would later say that Dougal's 'fate was sealed' by this refusal.[314] His defence, that a revolver he had been carrying had gone off accidentally, was not believed and he was convicted at Chelmsford Assizes before Mr Justice Wright.

It was Newton's reputation as the best defence solicitor in London which no doubt caused Charles Wood to go straight to him to ensure his brother's escape from the gallows. Newton recalled him as a 'small man' who was 'waiting for me one Monday morning when I arrived at the office and he was in a state of great agitation'.[315] Charles asked the solicitor if he could give his immediate attention to a matter of much importance and put all his other work aside. Robert Wood was due to appear later that day at Clerkenwell Police Court so Newton, after agreeing to take the case, needed to move fast. The first thing he managed to establish was that Wood's employers were prepared to put up a massive sum of £2,000 in bail. Considering the lack of direct evidence against Wood, Newton was hopeful that he could secure bail for his new client – despite this being highly unusual in a murder case – although he was extremely annoyed to learn that Wood had given a statement to the police. His view was that it would be impossible for anyone to remember what they had been doing on one particular night three weeks earlier and he knew that any mistakes would be held against Wood. At the same time, unknown to Newton, Wood knew perfectly well where he had been on the evening of 11 September and had gone to great lengths to put together a false alibi. Nevertheless, from his initial examination of the case, Newton could see that, while Wood had written a postcard to the deceased woman, there was no evidence at all connecting him to the murder.

Inspector Neil was also fretting over the lack of evidence against Wood but the one man who might have seen the murderer had not yet attempted to identify the prisoner. Thus it was that Robert McCowan was brought to Kentish Town Police Station in the morning and Wood was once again removed from his cell to participate in another identification parade. McCowan did not instantly pick out Wood from the line-up, which is not surprising because he had not seen the face of the man who had supposedly emerged from 29 St Paul's Road in the early hours of 12 September. However, all the men were asked to walk around and McCowan then identified Wood from his 'swaggering gait'. In a statement taken by the police shortly afterwards, McCowan said 'I identify him from his back appearance and peculiar swing of the arm when walking.' He said nothing about recognising Wood from his build, despite the fact that he had previously said the man he saw emerging from number 29 was 'stiffly built with broad shoulders'. This was not surprising, considering that Wood was of slender build.

Three other witnesses were also brought by the police to the identification parade during the morning: Lilian Raven, the barmaid from the *Eagle*, an unnamed barman from the same public house and May Campbell. Neither Lilian Raven nor the barman picked anyone out. May Campbell failed to identify Wood in the first instance although it seems she was allowed a second chance and did then pick him out. In fact, something seems to have gone wrong with this particular parade. Each witness should have been brought in to view the line-up and then taken straight out without seeing the identifications of the other witnesses. However, Robert McCowan would say at the Old Bailey that May Campbell, Lilian Raven and the barman of the *Eagle* all saw him identify Wood. If this had been after they had made their own identifications it would not have been too bad (and Miss Raven failed to identify Wood in any case) but McCowan said he also saw May Campbell pick out Wood after he, himself, had touched him on the shoulder. If Campbell saw McCowan pick out Wood and McCowan saw Campbell do the same thing then something must have gone wrong somewhere. In the end, it did not really matter because May Campbell's services were no longer required by the police and she was not called as a prosecution witness. Inspector Neil had no faith in her evidence, believing that her description of 'Scotch Bob' was one that somebody had given her. At the Old Bailey, he said 'I do not think she could identify anybody if she spoke the truth'.

To bolster his case against Wood, Inspector Neil also arranged for a second, and more detailed, statement to be taken from Robert Roberts in which Roberts added some new information regarding what Emily had confided in him about Wood. He now said that Emily had told him on Sunday 8 September, after Wood had left the *Rising Sun*, that 'I am glad he has gone, I am afraid of him'. He also said that, when back at number 29, Emily had told him that 'he was a young fellow she had known for a long time, that his people were well off and that he received his salary once a month, and that he always wanted to be going home with her, but that she wouldn't have him as he only got his money once a month.' There is little doubt that Roberts had told the police that Emily had said of the man in the *Rising Sun* that his parents were respectable – Inspector Neil's report of 30 September records that Emily told Roberts that the man 'was connected with good people' – but one wonders if Roberts, who had already been paid a total of £8 by the police, would have included this type of information in his new statement had it turned out that Wood had been unemployed. Roberts had also not previously mentioned that he had been told that the man had known Emily for 'a long time' and, as it happens, this evidence happily matched that of other witnesses such as Jack Crabtree, William Linehan and Gladys Warren. For good measure, Roberts added that when Emily showed him the letter (from Wood) asking for a meeting at the *Eagle* on the Wednesday, she told him 'that she didn't want to meet him but she had better go'. Roberts' statement of 7 October also put in writing for the first time his recollection that Emily had taken the rising sun postcard out of her bodice and showed it to him.

At this point, Inspector Neil had become convinced that Emily's hair being in curlers was a key factor in the case and Roberts' statement confirmed that, on the nights he slept with her, she did not have her hair in curlers (showing that it was not her practice to use them at night). Neil would obtain additional statements from both Mr and Mrs Stocks confirming that Emily had her hair in curling pins before she went out between 8:00 and 9:00pm on Wednesday 11 September. Roberts also confirmed that she wore a nightdress when she slept with him, although his information only increased the mystery as to why, if she had slept with her murderer, she was not wearing a nightdress, but was wearing curlers, when she was found by Bert Shaw.

Later that afternoon, on 7 October, Wood, still wearing his blue serge suit, was brought to Clerkenwell Police Court – practically opposite Wood's residence of 12 Frederick Street, adjoining King's Cross Police Station – before the magistrate, James Bros. This gave journalists a chance to get a good look at the suspect for the first time. The *Daily Mail* described him as 'twenty-eight years of age…slight in build and about 5ft 8in. in height…pale complexion and black hair, and clean shaven' pointing out that 'The two noticeable features of his face are his deep set eyes and his rather long and sharp nose'.[316] The *Daily Chronicle* said he was 'a dark, clean-shaven man', with 'deep set, coal black eyes, a somewhat pointed nose, and well lined forehead, square at the temples.'[317] According to the *Morning Leader*, he was 'a thin, sallow-faced young man, of medium height. His hair is black and limp; his eyes are dark and deep-set; his nose is long and sharp'.[318] Wood was also reported to be looking anxious and drawn although he smiled occasionally to friends and family in court. He would later describe himself that day as 'cold, hungry, untidy and miserable through lack of sleep'.[319] Arthur Newton, by contrast, was confident that he could do what no-one else thought possible and secure bail for his client so that he could walk out of the court, cross the road and be home for tea. After Inspector Neil outlined the details of the arrest, the detective was cross-examined by Mr Newton and agreed that Wood had 'emphatically denied his guilt from first to last'. Mr Newton then asked the magistrate for bail saying, 'I think it will be shown to you hereafter that a very serious mistake has been made'. He pointed out that Wood had 'never denied he wrote the one postcard' but then pushed his case much too far by claiming 'He has made a frank statement of the matter'. Inspector Neil was not going to let that kind of comment pass. 'No', he said, 'his statement has already been disproved'. Newton tried a different tack:

'Well I don't want to argue the matter' he said; of course he didn't. 'I say that from the time of this occurrence this young man's whereabouts could have been known at any time.'

'No, sir' said the inspector.

'But he has been working continuously' protested the solicitor.

'He may have been', said Neil calmly, 'but I did not know it'.

'There are many things not known to the police' retorted Mr Newton. 'Don't you say that this man has been at his place of business?'

'That was not known to the police' repeated the inspector.

'Perhaps they ought to have found out' said Mr Newton sarcastically, if lamely.

At this point, the magistrate, described by Wood as 'the very essence of refinement', interjected and asked if the police opposed bail. Inspector Neil responded in the affirmative. Newton then played his trump card, offering bail in two sureties of £1,000, adding that the police would know where to find Wood if they needed him. Not many criminal defendants were able to offer such a large sum in bail in 1907 and Wood later wrote that the amount mentioned 'seemed to stagger everybody else'.[320] In addition, Newton was able to draw the magistrate's attention to the fact that Wood had been in continuous work with his firm for twenty years and was, thus, not a flight risk. For a moment it actually seemed possible that the magistrate would relent and grant bail. But Inspector Neil had his own trump card to play.

'I may say that this morning Wood has been placed with a number of men and identified as a man seen coming from the house on the morning of the murder'.

The *Daily Mail* reported that, on hearing this statement, Wood 'turned towards his friends at the back of the court and smiled' although he later stated that 'When Neil declared that I had been seen leaving that poor murdered girl's house my emotions cannot be adequately expressed. I was astonished – astounded – aghast'.[321] Arthur Newton's reaction is not recorded but he was clearly taken by surprise at hearing the news and was immediately suspicious as to how the police had suddenly managed to pull this particular rabbit out of a hat. Inspector Neil, was, of course, referring to McCowan's identification of Wood and, partly as a result of the way he learnt of it, from that day onwards Newton never wavered in the belief that there was something inherently wrong, indeed corrupt, with McCowan's evidence.

Following Inspector Neil's information, Mr Bros said, 'I know nothing about the case one way or the other, except what I have heard today. I must leave that until after hearing the case opened by the Treasury'. Mr Newton still thought he could change his mind. With reference to the poste restante letter, he said, 'It is inconceivable that if he had a guilty mind he would make a record of this affair of the postcard as he has done' but it was too late and the magistrate refused bail, deciding instead to remand Wood for eight days.

According to the *Daily Mail*, Wood 'smiling at his friends, then left the dock'. After being provided with some tea in the court building he was put into a cab and taken to Brixton Prison where he would spend the next two months.

Following the hearing, there was some more good news for Inspector Neil as Joseph Lambert, alerted by a newspaper placard which mentioned Wood in connection with the murder, came forward to inform the police that he had seen and spoken to Wood in the *Eagle* on the night of 11 September and that he was in the company of a woman who resembled Emily Dimmock.[322] Not only that but Wood had implored him not to mention the woman if asked.

On Wednesday 9 October, Dr Thompson prepared a written statement in which he possibly solved the mystery – considering her apparent preference for wearing her chemise in bed – of Emily being found in the nude. Despite Inspector Neil having said that there were no other injuries to Emily than her cut throat, the doctor noted that there was a cut to Emily's right elbow but he thought this was an accidental cut by the murderer, made 'after death *when removing the clothes*' (emphasis added).[323] Unfortunately, the doctor did not explain why he thought the murderer had removed Emily's clothes or for what purpose he (or she) had done so. Nor did he state precisely what clothes he believed Emily was wearing at the time. Due to the natural position she was found in, Dr Thompson believed she was asleep at the time of death, which suggests he thought she had been wearing her nightdress, but he made no mention in his statement of any nightdress or chemise being cut. He only referred to having found Emily's petticoat in a basin which he believed the murderer had used to wipe blood from his hands.

Arthur Newton

Chapter Eleven

Trail of the Parnther

'Among the black catalogue of human offences, there is not, indeed, any that more powerfully affects the mind, that more outrages all the feelings of the heart, than the crime of suicide.'

Forbes Winslow, *The Anatomy of Suicide*, 1840

Amidst the excitement of Wood's arrest, the emergence of a new suspect for Emily Dimmock's murder was overlooked by most of the press and remained overlooked for more than the next one hundred years.

An hour or two before Wood's arrest on Friday 4 October, a letter-card was posted to the editor of the *Morning Leader* from somewhere in North-West London. When it arrived at the newspaper's offices in Stonecutter Street, near Fleet Street, the following morning it bore the postmark 'London, NW, 5.30 p.m., 4 Oct '07'; the 'NW' postmark included the area of Camden Town and Euston. The letter-card was not written or typed but comprised words and letters cut from newspapers and then gummed onto the card, which read as follows:

CAMDEN TOWN MURDER,

THE   MURDERER

committed suicide

at

CARDIFf

12 SEPT.

The anonymous author was evidently making reference to Charles William Parnther, aged 26, whose body had been found separated from its head shortly before dawn on 12 September 1907 by a railway employee on the Great Western Railway 'down' line near the Sanatorium Road Level Crossing about a mile and a half west of Cardiff Station.

The news of this apparent suicide was barely reported in the London daily newspapers but the *Globe* of 13 September carried a small paragraph about it, entitled 'GRIM RAILWAY MYSTERY', directly below its report of the Camden Town Murder. The story read as follows:

> The decapitated body of a middle-aged man was found on the Great Western Railway at Cardiff yesterday morning. On him was found a postcard bearing the address 21, Montpelier-road, Kentish Town, which led to the man's identification as Charles Parnther, a jeweller's traveller, of Lessingham-avenue, Upper Tooting. Mr Parnther was to have been married shortly, the prospective bride being Miss Appleton, to whom the postcard was addressed. Miss Appleton saw her fiancé on Sunday, and he arranged to meet her on Monday with a view to purchasing some furniture for their home, which was practically

complete. He failed to keep the appointment. Mr Parnther had been staying in a leading hotel in Cardiff. It is a mystery how he came to be at the spot where his body was found.

Under the headline 'TOOTING TRAGEDY', that afternoon's *Star* also carried the story on the same page as its lengthy report of the discovery of Emily Dimmock's murder. Other London newspapers did not report the story and it was not mentioned again until the *Morning Leader* received the anonymous letter on Saturday 5 October. Even then, none of the other papers mentioned the receipt of this letter. It appeared to the world that Emily's murderer had been arrested and all attention was focused on Wood so that hardly anyone was interested in the allegation against an obscure individual no-one had heard of. Upon investigation, though, it is evident that Parnther's suicide was as mysterious as Emily Dimmock's murder.

Charles William Parnther was born on 24 September 1880 at 10 Dale Road, Kentish Town, the son of railway clerk, John William Parnther, who had married a domestic servant called Annie Fisher from Addlestone, Surrey, in 1879. The 1881 census shows that John William Parnther and his wife and child were still living at 10 Dale Road but the family subsequently moved to St Albans, Hertfordshire, where they gave birth to a son, Arthur, in 1883, and a girl, Annie, who was born in 1886. Mr Parnther did not survive to be included in the 1891 census; he died on 31 January 1890 of tuberculosis following a '2 year exhaustion', according to his death certificate. His death was at a residence in Embankment, South Chelsea, to where the Parnther family had evidently moved. Charles was just 9 years old when he lost his father. After her husband's death, 33-year-old Annie Parnther relocated to her home town of Addlestone with her children and the 1891 census records her living in Chapel Road with a 27-year-old boarder, a harness maker called George Appleton. In the following year George Appleton and Annie Parnther moved to Clarence Road, Camden Town, and were married in St Pancras, so Charles had a new stepfather at the age of eleven. He also had a new school as he and his brother Charles were enrolled at Great College Street School in Camden Town.[324] It is either a pure coincidence or (possibly) the key to the entire mystery that Great College Street School was the local school for children living at St Paul's Road and the surrounding area; indeed, quite a number of pupils at the school while Charles Parnther was being taught there lived in St Paul's Road, including at numbers 21, 23 and 33. Although he could not have lived in the area for more than nine years – by 1901 the census of that year shows that the Appletons, including Charles, had moved to Camberwell in Surrey – he must have made a number of friends in the Camden Town area.

At a young age, during the 1890s, Charles started work as an office boy at the Royal London Friendly Society, an insurance firm in the City of London. He subsequently worked his way up to become a clerk in the firm.[325] His brother, Arthur, who was also a clerk at the time, joined the army in 1902. Charles remained an insurance clerk and continued to live with his mother and stepfather who moved at some point to Lessingham Avenue in Tooting. Whilst living there, Charles was a volunteer member of the St John Ambulance Association.[326] His stepfather, George, taught him how to play draughts and, discovering he had a talent for the game, Charles joined the Streatham and

District Draughts Club, being elected club secretary in 1906. The relocation of several members from Streatham caused this club to be disbanded so Charles then joined the Balham Draughts Club and, while representing it, was one of the prize-winning competitors in both the 1906 and 1907 Annual Draughts Championships. Other draughts players said he was a man of 'cheery disposition' who 'endeared himself to all with whom he was brought in contact'.[327]

By this time, Charles' family life had become a little complicated. His stepfather was the son of Timothy and Elizabeth Appleton who lived in Albury, Surrey. However, Elizabeth Appleton died of peritonitis in March 1868 when George was four years old. Timothy remarried in 1869 to Jane Brookfield, a former governess of the National Infant School in Newbury, and the couple had five children, one of whom was Florence Kate Appleton, born in 1878. However, the new Mrs Appleton died in flames in 1884 at the age of 42, after accidentally knocking over a paraffin lamp at home late at night, when Florence was six, and Timothy died the very next year of tuberculosis at the age of 45. So Florence was left orphaned and ended up at St Margaret's Orphanage School for girls in East Grinstead with her younger sister, Gertrude, who died at the school in 1895, aged 14, after a severe bout of diphtheria while suffering from a kidney disease. At the age of 23, Florence, who would be described by the press as 'a pleasant, attractive girl', was in service as a housemaid for a barrister in Paddington but at some point she must have been introduced to Charles Parnther, presumably by her stepbrother, because she became engaged to him.

While still living with his parents, Charles took an apartment in a three-storey building at 21 Montpelier Road, Kentish Town, and began furnishing it in preparation for the marriage; he planned to live there with Florence after the wedding, which was due to take place on Saturday, 14 September 1907 at the Holy Trinity Church of Kentish Town. Florence moved into the apartment in early September. For a few weeks prior to this she had been confined to hospital with a 'severe illness' although its precise nature is unknown.[328] In the spring of 1907, Charles had also been ill, suffering from a kidney problem according to his stepfather, and was supposedly operated on for an abscess on the kidneys. However, he was said to have been in good health and spirits when he left his office for a three-week holiday, including his wedding, on Friday 6 September, and 'replied gaily to the good wishes expressed generally for his future happiness'.[329] After the marriage, the newlyweds intended to leave Waterloo on the Sunday morning for a honeymoon on the Isle of Wight. According to his mother and stepfather, Charles was looking forward to his wedding 'with eager pleasure' and he and Florence were said to have been 'on the most loving terms' by their landlady at Montpelier Road.[330] Over the weekend, however, Charles appeared to his mother to be a little run-down due to having done extra work at the office in preparation for his holiday and he declined an invitation to accompany Florence on a walk, suggesting that she go with her sister, Cissie, instead. On the morning of Monday 9 September, Charles took breakfast with his family in Tooting and appeared to be in excellent health. The plan was for him to collect his wedding suit and then meet up with Florence so they could purchase a drawing room suite, the last item of furniture they needed to complete the furnishing of their new apartment. However, Charles did not turn up for the appointment and Florence never saw him again.

Instead of buying furniture, it seems that Charles, who had £8 in his pocket, caught a train from Paddington to Cardiff Station. He arrived at the Angel Hotel in Cardiff on the same day, saying he had come from London. He had no luggage and had not been seen by staff at the hotel before. Apparently, he paid his bill and checked out on the Tuesday morning. Nothing is really known of his movements during the next two days but press reports in Cardiff newspapers immediately after his death stated that he was 'alleged to have spent most of his time since Tuesday in the company of two women, who live in Saltmead, Grangetown'.[331] Saltmead was a well-known red light district and the suggestion appears to be that Parnther spent his last two days on earth with a couple of prostitutes.[332] However, this report was not confirmed and nothing appears to have been said about it at the inquest.

He was found by William Workman, a porter for the Great Western Railway before 6:00am on Thursday 13 September. The precise time was never established. Initial press reports said he was found at 5:20am while the official Cardiff Police record of the inquest noted a time of 5:30am. However, after the inquest, it was also reported that the body was, in fact, discovered at 5:50am. In any event, the head, which was completely separated from the body, was inside the rails on the down line while the body was lying outside, on the north side facing Victoria Park. This suggested that he had walked onto the track from the north side before lying down on the rails in front of a speeding train. Press reports stated that the body was 'very warm' when found.[333] A pair of spectacles and a pipe was lying a yard or so from the body. The dead man was wearing a gold watch and chain and a pair of gold sleeve links but the only money he had on him was a halfpenny. A postcard found on the body was to be of great assistance for the police in quickly establishing his identity; there was not, apparently, any explanation for Parnther's disappearance or suicide on it but it was addressed to Florence at 21 Montpelier Road. Florence had already been to the police on the Tuesday after her fiancé went missing and was said to be 'in a terrible state' over his disappearance.

During Thursday 13 September, the police in Kentish Town were fully occupied investigating Emily Dimmock's murder but this is hardly an excuse for their failure to notify Charles' parents of his death. It was, in fact, a newspaper reporter from the Cardiff *Evening Express* who made the journey to Tooting to break the news to his mother who was 'overwhelmed with grief' when told. George said to the reporter that he could not understand what could have taken 'Charlie' to Cardiff. The news was also conveyed to Florence who was said to have become 'almost distracted with grief'.[334] Continuing his enquiries, the *Evening Express* reporter spoke to Charles' employers in case something at work had contributed to his apparent suicide but they checked and found everything was in perfect order.

The inquest took place on Friday 13 September. George Appleton made his way to Cardiff to identify the body and gave evidence but could offer no explanation as to why his stepson would have wanted to kill himself. However, although he had told reporters that Charles had been perfectly happy when he had last seen him, if a bit tired, he informed the coroner for Cardiff that his stepson 'had been depressed of late and had been treated by a doctor for kidney trouble'.[335] A local doctor gave evidence that, aside from the head being completely severed, there were no other injuries apart from a slight bruise on the wrist. He said death must have been instantaneous. The jury did not find a formal verdict of suicide but would only conclude that Parnther was 'found dead' with 'no evidence to show how he got on the line'. In his summing up, however, the coroner said that 'deceased had evidently put his head on the line and that a passing train had cut it off', adding quite unnecessarily that, 'No man in his sound mind would have done such a thing'.[336]

That would have been the end of that story had the *Morning Leader* not received the strange anonymous letter-card in October. Out of consideration for his family, the *Morning Leader* did not name Parnther but drew attention to his description, which was as follows: age 26, dark hair, about five foot six inches in height, wearing a light grey suit, brown overcoat and a brown bowler hat.[337] The newspaper compared this description to the so-called 'official' description of the suspect for the murder of Emily Dimmock and noted a number of similarities. It will be recalled that the prime suspect was believed to have 'once been in hospital' and the newspaper pointed out that Parnther had been operated on for his kidney problem. The paper then asked 'why did this young man fly from his sweetheart and his friends five days before his wedding; why did he go to Cardiff; and why did he choose such an extraordinary hour of the morning for the act of suicide?' These were all relevant questions and the inquest had answered none of them.

The arrest of Wood seemed to cause the newspaper to lose interest in the Parnther story – and it was never even mentioned by any other London papers.[338] The *Morning Leader* said the letter-card had been shown to the authorities at Scotland Yard but there is not a single mention of it in the Metropolitan Police file nor is there any sign of an attempt to investigate it. The Welsh newspapers, by contrast, did take an interest and raised the matter with the Cardiff police who were dismissive of any connection between the two matters. A Detective Little, said to be in charge of the case, claimed that it would have been impossible for Parnther to have been Emily Dimmock's murderer 'because he had evidently been killed on the line long before the murder was committed'.[339] The problem here, though, was that the Cardiff inquest had not fixed the time of Parnther's death and the time of Emily's murder is unknown – although the Cardiff police no doubt assumed it to have been around 3:00am as reported in the London newspapers. A further reason put forward was that 'other members of the police have information that Parnther was in Cardiff the night before his body was discovered on the line'.[340] This would be conclusive if true but it is strange that such information was not put before the coroner at Parnther's inquest. Some doubt is cast on the detective's claim by the fact that Inspector Rankin of the Cardiff force told a reporter for the *Western Mail*, 'I cannot see how there can be any connection between the two matters for the man whose body was found on the railway had been stopping at the Angel Hotel.' Yet the local reporters, who had spoken to the staff at the Angel Hotel, appear to have established that Parnther checked out of the hotel on the Tuesday morning. Seeing two different members of the same force offering what look like different reasons to dismiss the possibility of Parnther being the Camden Town murderer is curious. It may be that they were taken by surprise by the sudden interest in a suicide which they do not appear to have investigated with any vigour in the first instance. In any event, it was suggested by the Cardiff police that the letter-card accusing Parnther might have been sent by 'the murderer or a friend of his' in order to divert suspicion. Alternatively, it was speculated that someone might have read the report of Emily Dimmock's murder in a newspaper on the same day as a report of Parnther's suicide and 'being struck with the coincidence and with certain particulars common to the description of the suspected murderer and the suicide made up the story and sent it in [to the *Morning Leader*].'

To their credit, the Cardiff journalists did not let the matter rest with the police response. The *Western Mail* reporter spoke to the landlord of the flat at Montpelier Road (presumably the husband of the landlady who had already spoken to a reporter). He said that Charles saw Florence almost daily and 'the whole circumstances of his life precluded the possibility of his having any entanglement with a woman like Mrs Dimmock'. The same reporter also made enquiries 'in the neighbourhood' (of Tooting, presumably) and discovered that Charles Parnther's character was 'beyond reproach' and that he was 'a model son and a faithful sweetheart'. Finally, the *Western Mail* reporter raised the matter with Charles' mother and stepfather but, not surprisingly, they were 'too much upset' and 'very little could be gained' although they 'briefly repudiated' the notion that Charles could have committed the Camden Town murder.

And that was that. Robert Wood had been arrested. The police were not looking for anyone else in connection with Emily Dimmock's murder and the curious allegation about Charles Parnther was forgotten. But could there have been any truth in it? The individual who sent the letter-card had certainly gone to a lot of trouble. Cutting words, letters and numbers from a newspaper and gumming them onto a card is more akin to a ransom note after a kidnapping than an allegation relating to a dead man. If someone had read about Parnther's suicide in the newspaper on the same day as they had read the news of the Camden Town Murder, noticed that Parnther was connected with Kentish Town (because of the letter addressed to Florence he was carrying) and then sent a letter to the *Morning Leader*, there was absolutely no reason for that person to have disguised his or her handwriting. It was not illegal to offer a suggestion as to who might have killed Emily Dimmock and the author of the letter could have provided a genuine name and address without any difficulty. If the author was known to Charles Parnther and his family, and thus had some private information, it might have been different so we need to consider whether the allegation could be true.

The obvious problem with the notion of Parnther being Emily's murderer is with the timing of events. If Parnther's body was found at either 5:20am (as suggested in initial press reports) or 5:30am (as noted in the police report of the inquest), then he could not possibly have been the Camden Town Murderer. We know that Emily Dimmock was alive, in the *Eagle*, between 9:00 and 10:00pm. Her movements after this are uncertain but she was evidently murdered at some time between 10:00pm on the Wednesday evening and 11:30am on the Thursday morning. Without a motor car,[341] the only way anyone could have murdered Emily in Camden Town and have arrived in Cardiff before daybreak in September 1907 was by catching the 1:00am train from Paddington – the previous train out of London departed at 9:15pm. However, the 1:00am train was timetabled to arrive at Cardiff at 5:30am. It was then scheduled to depart Cardiff at 5:34am on its way to Bridgend, passing through the Sanatorium Road Level Crossing (where Parnther's body was discovered), before terminating at Swansea at 7:00am. As the train from Paddington did not arrive at Cardiff

Station until 5:30am, it is self-evident that Charles Parnther could not have been on that train if his body was found a mile and a half west of Cardiff station at 5:30am, or earlier. If he was not on that train then he simply could not have murdered Emily Dimmock. That would be the end of it but for a report in the *South Wales Daily News* on 14 September 1907, following the inquest, that William Workman deposed to finding the body on the railway 'at 5.50 on Thursday morning'. The *Morning Leader* repeated this information when it revealed the existence of the letter-card on 7 October.

Even if Parnther's body had been found at 5:50am it would still be highly unlikely for him to have made the journey from Cardiff Station to the Sanatorium Road Level Crossing, and to have committed suicide, inside twenty minutes. But it was not impossible. A serious failure of the inquest was that no attempt was made to establish which train killed Parnther although, on the assumption that he died between 5:30 and 5:50am, it would presumably have been the London train which severed his head from his body; there could not have been many other trains, if any, running through Cardiff at that time of night.[342] In other words, Parnther would have had to have alighted the train at Cardiff and then, having a four-minute start while it sat at the station, beaten it in a race to the Sanatorium Road Level Crossing in order to get ahead of it to lay his head down on the line. He could not possibly have walked such a distance at sufficient speed. A tram or cab might, theoretically, have been able to get him there before the arrival of the London train but it would have been a real stretch. And it is not certain that the time of 5:50am which appeared in the *South Wales Daily News* was correct. Another newspaper, The *Evening Express & Evening Mail* of 13 September 1907 reported that William Workman stated that he discovered the body at 5:20am, although, if that was the case, it is odd that the official police note of the inquest recorded a time of 5:30am. Perhaps the acoustics in the coroner's court were poor, or someone coughed while Workman was giving his evidence, and different people heard different things; or '5:50' could have been a simple typographical error in the *South Wales Daily News*.

It is also quite possible that Parnther died some time before his body was discovered although, as it was said to have been very warm when found, it could not have been *too* long beforehand. Yet, despite all this, we cannot entirely rule out the possibility that Parnther was on that London train and, if the author of the anonymous letter-card was speculating on the basis of something read in a newspaper, he or she got lucky that even today the claim that Parnther was the Camden Town Murderer cannot be categorically disproved, even if it seems unlikely. The letter-card's author would also have had to have been very lucky, or otherwise quite well informed on the facts of the case, that Parnther's movements on 11 September had not been established at the inquest. The entire charade of cutting out bits from newspapers to gum onto the card would have been a waste of time if Parnther had been seen at any time in Cardiff during the evening of 11 September. None of the London daily newspapers reported any details from the inquest although it has to be said that the local Tooting press did carry reports taken from Welsh newspapers which would have revealed to an interested reader that little was known about Parnther's activities in the day prior to his death.

Regardless of whether Parnther was involved in Emily Dimmock's murder or not, there are a number of puzzling issues regarding his suicide (and despite the inquest jury's non-committal decision, it clearly *was* a suicide). The main mystery is why he felt he had no alternative but to take his own life. Having told reporters that his stepson was perfectly happy in the days before his disappearance, George Appleton gave evidence at the inquest that he was depressed but did not say what about – only mentioning that he had had a kidney operation, but that presumably solved the problem with his kidneys. In the absence of any financial difficulties or fraud at work, the suicide can surely only have been connected to Parnther's pending marriage. While everyone said he was looking forward to the wedding, his actions suggested otherwise. With just five days of single life remaining until he married Florence, he deliberately went to Cardiff without telling her where he was going. Something was seriously wrong and we can only guess as to what it could have been. Was Charles secretly homosexual? Or did he simply not love Florence? Certainly, if he felt marriage to Florence was impossible because he was not in love with her, he would have been in a very difficult position. The brother of the bride was his own stepfather and upsetting his stepfather would mean upsetting his mother. Perhaps he could see no way out of an unwanted wedding and a loveless marriage. Considering the circumstances and timing of his disappearance that seems to be the most likely reason for the extreme measure taken by Parnther in Cardiff.

At the same time, everyone who knew them said that Charles loved Florence and it would have had to have been an extremely good act by the former to keep this up for the years they were said to have been engaged. Could the key to the mystery lie in the fact that Charles and Florence were both ill during 1907? What if Charles contracted venereal disease from a prostitute and then passed it on to Florence? Under those circumstances he might have been so wracked with guilt that he felt he could not continue living. While there is no hard evidence to support this theory, we should bear in mind the initial (albeit unconfirmed) reports that Charles had been seen in the Saltwood region with two women, presumably prostitutes, after arriving in Cardiff. That might explain another baffling mystery connected with the case: why did Charles go to Cardiff of all places? There was no reason that anyone who knew him could think of why he would travel there, and he had no obvious connections with the area. If he had secretly met a Welsh prostitute in London he might have decided to spend his last days on earth with her, knowing she had returned to Cardiff. Alternatively, he might have been aware of Cardiff's reputation for prostitution and chosen the city as his destination for that reason. Reverend Frederick Brotherton Meyer, the evangelical minister of Christ Church, speaking in early 1908, suggested that there were two and a half thousand 'fallen women', and as many as two hundred disorderly houses, in Cardiff.[343]

According to George Appleton, Parnther left London with £8 in his pocket but was found with only a halfpenny. The money spent on his train fare to Cardiff and hotel bill would not have come close to £8. One night at the Angel Hotel could not have been more than £2 at the most (and probably much less) while a single, second class, train fare from London to Cardiff was 16 shillings (or 25 shillings and sixpence if he had decided to treat himself to first class travel).[344] That still leaves a good £4 unaccounted for. We have seen that Emily

Dimmock charged Robert Roberts less than £1 a night so Charles would have had plenty of money available to spend on prostitution had he so wished and, indeed, it might explain where most of his money went. Alternatively, or in addition, he could have caught the return train to Paddington for which the second class fare was just under £3. If Emily Dimmock was the prostitute who had given him venereal disease, perhaps he made his way to Camden Town – an area he was very familiar with – met up with her without letting her know anything was wrong, accompanied her to her apartment, where he cut her throat because she had totally ruined his life, and then returned to Cardiff where, in despair, and horrified at what he had done, he laid his head down on the railway tracks in front of the train that had carried him there. The location he chose, of the Sanatorium Level Crossing, might simply be because it was the only place in Cardiff where it was possible to access the railway tracks without being seen. As to why he chose to kill himself in such a bizarre way – the fear he must have felt in placing his head on a steel railway line in darkness, miles from home, with a speeding train approaching, does not bear thinking about – the reason for this can never be known but presumably he had some kind of death fantasy about a suicide of this type as opposed to a rather more straightforward hanging or leaping off a bridge. It may be a pure coincidence that Emily Dimmock was also decapitated (or almost so) by her killer.

The notion that Parnther was the Camden Town Murderer does not, however, explain why he would have searched Emily's apartment and taken a number of her possessions, as the murderer appears to have done. Initial press reports wrongly described Parnther as a 'jeweller's clerk' but this was evidently *not* because he was carrying jewellery taken from Emily's room; his possessions were listed in full during the inquest and they did not include anything removed from St Paul's Road. Most likely, a journalist spoke to someone in London over the telephone and misheard 'insurance clerk' as 'jeweller's clerk'.

Overall, then, it seems highly unlikely that Charles Parnther murdered Emily Dimmock. In which case: who took so much trouble to disguise their handwriting and send the anonymous letter-card to the *Morning Leader*? One assumes it was not the newspaper itself attempting to boost publication (as might have been the case with some of the Jack the Ripper communications); had someone from the *Morning Leader* wanted to do that they could surely have come up with something more sensational. It might have been a friend of Parnther's who had suspicions and did not wish his handwriting to be recognised by the dead man's family. Alternatively, as the Cardiff police suggested, it might have been Emily Dimmock's murderer attempting to divert suspicion from him or herself.

Could it have been Robert Wood who sent it? Leaving aside the question of whether or not he murdered Emily Dimmock, it is clear that he was under both pressure and suspicion on 4 October due to his handwriting having been widely published in the newspapers. In fact, he was the *only* person under suspicion. If someone else was the murderer, they were under no suspicion at all; the police were totally focused on finding the author of the rising sun postcard so there would have been no need for the murderer, if anyone other than Wood, to draw attention to a new suspect. Moreover, there is no obvious reason why such a communication would have been sent by the murderer (assuming it was someone other than Wood) on 4 October. There had been nothing in any newspapers about Parnther since 21 September, when some of the weekly Cardiff and Tooting newspapers reported details of the inquest from the previous week, and the national and London newspapers had been silent about the suicide since 13 September, not even reporting the inquest. For that reason, it is hard to see what could have prompted *anyone* (other than Wood) to send the letter-card two weeks after anything had appeared about the Cardiff suicide in the press.

In this respect, the timing of the posting of the letter-card on Friday 4 October is particularly interesting. Only the day before, an already suspicious Wood had been told by Ruby Young that she had confided to a third party that he had written and sent the rising sun postcard to Emily Dimmock. As a result, Wood must have felt under very great pressure that his identity would soon be revealed to the police. He thus had even more reason to take drastic action to throw the police off the scent. Others, like Jack Tinkham and Joseph Lambert, also knew the truth and Wood could not have been sure they would refrain from speaking to the police. The heat was on Wood and it would surely have suited him if the press and police considered Charles Parnther as a new suspect.

No-one had more reason to disguise their handwriting than Robert Wood whose script had been reproduced in virtually every national newspaper. Consequently, it would have made perfect sense for him to cut out words and numbers from newspapers rather than write a letter in longhand. He could have prepared the letter-card and posted it in Euston or Camden during his lunch hour to avoid a 'WC' postmark on the letter (considering that Wood both lived and worked in the Western Central area). The Friday he was arrested was a day he did not meet Ruby Young for lunch, having done so on the Tuesday and Thursday of that week.[345] It is clear from those lunch meetings that he was free to leave his office in Gray's Inn Road during the afternoon. So he had the motive and the opportunity to create and post the letter-card. However, as the authorship of the letter-card was never investigated by the police, we will never know.

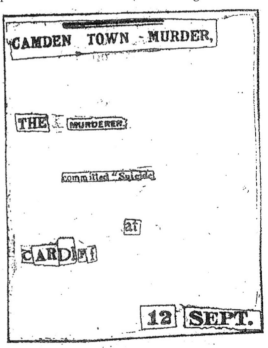

The anonymous letter-card received by the
Morning Leader in October 1907

Chapter Twelve

Inquest

'At this stage I still felt unconcerned.'

Robert Wood, describing his feelings during the inquest, *Weekly Dispatch*, 29 December 1907

The Sunday papers after Wood's first court appearance went into overdrive. The *Weekly Dispatch* published a sketch of Ruby Young by Wood on its front page although, presumably at her request, Ruby's name was not mentioned at all by the newspaper and she was simply referred to as Wood's 'sweetheart' or 'a certain girl'.[346] This was pointless, not only because Ruby was obviously going to be a witness at Wood's trial but also because the *Daily Mirror* of 7 October had already named her: both as Wood's sweetheart and as the woman who had identified his handwriting to the police. In fact, the *Daily Mirror* (owned by the same businessman who owned the *Weekly Dispatch*) had been the first to publish the sketch of Ruby Young in its Saturday edition and it too had decided not to mention her name on that occasion, calling her the 'postcard lady'. The *Weekly Dispatch* was, however, now able to boast of its role in arranging a meeting between 'the girl' and Inspector Neil, taking credit for the arrest. Newton, who realised the value of good publicity in the press for his client – the jury would be drawn from newspaper readers after all – had clearly been speaking to the *Weekly Dispatch* because it reported that Wood had expressed his confidence to his solicitor that he would be acquitted. However, according to his solicitor, writing many years later, Wood took little interest in the preparation of his defence, spending all his time in prison sketching, and said gloomily, 'It does not matter very much if I am wrongly convicted and they hang me, they only rid the world of a fellow able to use a pencil and draw a few sketches'.[347] Nevertheless, he was said by the *Weekly Dispatch* to be 'fairly cheerful' in Brixton Prison, where he had a private cell, and 'eats heartily'. In addition, Wood was described in a positive light by the newspaper as 'an extremely clever artist' who was 'highly thought of by his employers'.

Lloyds Weekly News was not to be outdone and published an exclusive, surreptitiously taken, photograph of Wood sitting in the dock at Clerkenwell Police Court. The *People* meanwhile had managed to establish that the identification of Wood as the man seen leaving number 29 St Paul's Road, which had caused 'a great sensation' when it was mentioned by Inspector Neil at the police court, was only by his 'peculiar walk' and that the witness in question could not recognise him by his face. It claimed that the police 'now realise that their present evidence is hardly sufficient and that more must be obtained if they are to connect the present prisoner with the crime'. It went on to say that, despite Wood being in custody, the police were 'diligently continuing their inquiries' and, moreover, 'watching several other men very carefully in case the evidence against Wood should break down'. There is no indication at all of any of this in the police file. It seems unlikely that the police, and Inspector Neil especially, doubted their own conclusion that Wood was the guilty man.

Certainly, for Inspector Neil, everything must have pointed to Wood's guilt. To his great satisfaction, his theory that the author of the rising sun postcard was the murderer seemed to have been proved by the lies Wood had told him about his whereabouts at the time of the murder and by his convoluted attempts at creating a false alibi. The evidence he had obtained suggested that Wood and Emily had been involved in some sort of relationship and that Wood was jealous of her other male companions. Knowing that Emily had her hair in curlers when she went out to meet Wood in the *Eagle*, and knowing that her hair was still in curlers when she was found dead the next morning, the inspector must have felt it was hardly likely she would have gone out again to meet anyone else in that state after seeing Wood. Surely Wood had gone back to 29 St Paul's Road and shared a lamb dinner with Emily before they went to bed and, in some kind of jealous rage, murdered the prostitute in her sleep. Inspector Neil did not have a murder weapon but that was a minor detail. He must have believed that Wood had searched through the drawers and postcard album in an attempt to retrieve the rising sun postcard in order to destroy it so that he would not be connected with Emily, but unable to find it, had covered up the search, or his motive, or both, by stealing Emily's purse and a few low-value trinkets which he had probably then thrown away. Everything seemed to fit and it is hard to believe that he spent any energy considering other suspects at this stage.

On Monday morning, all attention was focused again on the St Pancras Coroner's Court where Wood was brought from Brixton Prison in a closed carriage, guarded by two warders. According to that day's *Evening News*, crowds of people 'surged round the gates of the coroner's court' but they did not see Wood who was brought in through a back entrance in Battlebridge Road. When the gates were opened, 'there was a great rush to the interior of the court' but, with an army of press reporters needing to be accommodated, there was room for only a few members of the general public.[348]

A new addition to the cast of performers in the proceedings was the barrister, Sir Charles Mathews, an actor's son, who was instructed by the Treasury Solicitor's Department, then responsible for conducting criminal prosecutions, commonly referred to just as 'the Treasury'. According to the magistrate, Sir Charles Rentoul, in his 1944 autobiography *This Is My Case*, Mathews had 'a somewhat melodramatic style of advocacy' and, unusually for a top advocate, his voice was 'squeaky and high pitched'. However, he was said to have a trick of lowering it to a whisper and 'hissing a question like a snake' so that, according to the *Oxford Dictionary of National Biography*, his impact on judges could be 'mesmeric'. One observer noted that, when dealing with a hostile witness, 'he became a terrier shaking a rat'.[349] In appearance, he was a small man with a slim figure and feminine face, punctuated by eyeglasses worn low on his nose, but, as an extremely experienced lawyer, having been called to the bar some thirty-five years earlier, he brought some gravitas to the inquest, ensuring that a police officer was no longer questioning the witnesses.

The star attraction of the resumed inquest, however, was Ruby Young, appearing in public for the first time. She came dressed in black, as if in mourning, with her face covered by a veil, which she was gently asked by the coroner to lift, and much of her evidence was punctuated with sobs, causing the coroner to invite her to sit down in the witness box. During her examination, she explained to Sir Charles Mathews how Wood had asked her to provide him with a false alibi for Wednesday 11 September and, moreover, had told her he had been walking by himself during that evening. This was obviously damaging evidence for Wood but it was perfectly true. Nevertheless, Arthur Newton asked Ruby, 'Might you not have seen Wood on the evening of Wednesday 11th?' thus giving the clear impression that his client's instructions were that her evidence was wrong. As if to suggest that Ruby was being untruthful in the witness box, he also asked her if she had not told Wood's sister-in-law that she was with Wood on the night of the murder. Ruby admitted that she had, but explained that this was all part of her backing of Wood's false alibi. It even prompted the coroner to ask Ruby if she was sure she was not with Wood on the night of the murder; she confirmed she was certain she was not.

In further cross-examination by Arthur Newton, Ruby gave helpful evidence for Wood, emphatically agreeing that he was of 'a kind, loveable nature'. On the balance of her evidence, therefore, Ruby should have been treated as a helpful witness for the defence. That she was not might be explained by the fact that Wood had not been entirely frank with his solicitor and was maintaining that the alibi evidence in his statement was true (and, thus, that Ruby was lying) but, regardless of this, Arthur Newton was not a man who gave a great deal of thought to big picture strategy. His natural instinct was to undermine the credibility of every prosecution witness. He therefore extracted from Inspector Neil the information that Ruby Young was a prostitute. This could have been disastrous for his client's defence. Wood's explanation at trial for not telling his family or police that he was with Emily Dimmock on the night of her murder, and for going to such lengths to create a false alibi, would be that he did not want it known that he had spent time with a prostitute but here was Newton causing it to be revealed that Wood's own sweetheart was a prostitute! It wasn't a particularly sensible strategy. The police or prosecution were hardly likely to make it public that one of their key witnesses was a prostitute so, if Newton had not asked the question, it would probably never have been brought into the open. In the end, more out of luck than judgement, it did not cause any harm to Wood but it could have been a critical mistake.

In order to contrast Ruby's character with that of Wood, Mr Newton invited Inspector Neil to state that Wood had an unblemished character but the inspector surprised the solicitor by saying, 'I have made inquiries and would rather not say'. In fact, Inspector Neil's belief as to Wood's character had been outlined in an internal police report dated 8 October, in which he had written that 'from my enquiries I am satisfied he [Wood] spent a good deal of his spare time in dissipation'. Mr Newton reminded Neil that he had agreed at the Clerkenwell Police Court that Wood had been known in the district as 'a respectable man for twenty years' but Neil said that this was only what he had believed at the time.

Mr Newton's day went from bad to worse as Joseph Lambert appeared in court to state that not only had he seen Wood with Emily in the *Eagle* on the night of her murder but that Wood had subsequently asked him to 'leave the girl out of it' and pretend that he had not seen her. Lambert was a witness whose credibility Mr Newton could not undermine and, in cross-examination, he only invited him to confirm that Wood had given him to understand 'most emphatically' that he could clear himself (which Lambert was happy to do). Mr

Newton did, however, question Bert Shaw at some length, firstly pointing out apparent contradictions in his previous evidence as to whether he knew that Emily was still living as a prostitute and then asking him if anyone could prove that he was in Sheffield on the night of the murder. Robert Roberts was also questioned by Mr Newton as to whether the police were paying him, causing Roberts to admit that he was indeed being kept by the police in order to be available as a prosecution witness rather than go back to sea. Mr Newton was also involved in a heated exchange with Roberts as to whether he was drunk at the time he gave his statement to the police on the evening of 12 September. Roberts denied it, saying he had only had about five or six drinks between 5:30pm and 11:00pm and was, moreover, mainly drinking ginger beer after having had a few liqueurs.[350] Mr Newton did not seem convinced but Edward Smeeth provided a written statement to the police in which he confirmed that Roberts frequently drank ginger ale or ginger beer and was 'a very sober man' whom he had never seen drunk.

As for Wood, he was said to be cool and collected and 'absolutely at ease' during the proceedings. Outside of the court, the same could not be said of William Linehan's 24-year-old sister, Agnes. As William Linehan and Gladys Warren emerged from the court building at 2:00pm (not having been called to give evidence that day), Agnes punched Gladys on the back of the neck 'with some force' while shouting that it was her fault that her brother had been brought into the murder case.[351] She was arrested for assault by Detective Constable Alfred Grosse and brought that same afternoon before Mr Bros at the Clerkenwell Police Court to whom she explained that she and her mother had done everything they could to keep William away from company such as Gladys Warren. She said that her mother, on her bended knees, had asked Gladys to give up her son and had thought the two had separated as a result. She was so horrified to see them together when she passed the coroner's court that she could not contain herself and assaulted her. Mr Bros advised Agnes to have no more to do with William or Gladys and bound her over to keep the peace.[352]

Another witness who was at Clerkenwell that day, and who was also not called to give evidence due to lack of time, was Mr Jack Crabtree. At the end of the day's proceedings, before being sent back to prison, Crabtree approached Inspector Neil and Sergeant Ball and said that if they would come and visit him in prison he would tell them what he knew of Wood's acquaintance with Emily Dimmock. It was an offer the inspector could not resist and arrangements were made with the Home Office for a second visit whereby Neil and Ball would see Crabtree 'alone and unrestricted as to time'. [353]

The following day, Mr Bros agreed to a request by a Treasury representative to remand Wood for another week, with the police court proceedings stayed until the inquest was concluded. Wood, when brought to the police court, was 'very pale' and 'cadaverous looking' but also 'quite self-confident and nodded smilingly to acquaintances in court'.[354] It was only a quick visit to Clerkenwell before he was taken back to Brixton.

Over in Pentonville, on 17 October, Jack Crabtree provided a long statement to Inspector Neil and Sergeant Ball. Whereas in his first statement of 19 September he had concentrated on describing the man who had threatened Emily and had mentioned in passing another man Emily used to be friendly with, of whom he knew 'very little', Crabtree now suddenly seemed to know a great deal about this other man. He told Inspector Neil the story of Emily quarrelling with a man who called her a prostitute at 1 Bidborough Street and then, some days later, at Manchester Street, being asked by the same man to pawn a silver cigarette case while he was lying in bed with Emily. It was the same man who was with Emily as he chased her across North London one night trying to get his money back from her. The same man, he said, warned Emily not to have anything to do with soldiers or sailors because she might get the disorder from them and mentioned a soldier called 'Big Jumbo'. Most significantly, Crabtree said that this man had written letters to Emily in June or July 1907 (which she had shown him), asking her to leave Shaw for him. According to Crabtree, this man was none other than Robert Wood (although he did not previously know his name). Furthermore, he recognised Wood's handwriting, saying the handwriting he saw on the letters was the same as that on the rising sun postcard and the name 'Phyllis' was spelt 'Phillis' as on the rising sun postcard. He even wrote on a piece of paper the same style of handwriting as he claimed to have seen on the letters. He also said that one of the letters sent to Emily concluded with the words 'Yours to dust', similar to the phrase 'Yours to a cinder' on the rising sun postcard.

We need to pause here to consider Crabtree's evidence. If what he was saying was true, then not only was it the case that Wood had enjoyed a long and close relationship with Emily, stretching back to 1906, but he had also been making strenuous efforts to persuade Emily to leave Bert Shaw and live with him instead during the weeks before her murder. Her evident refusal to do so could have been the motive for that murder. However, apart from the fact that Crabtree had initially said that he knew 'very little' of the other man with whom Emily was supposed to have been friendly, there is a problem with Crabtree's version of events. At the end of his first written statement on 19 September, having been shown by Inspector Neil the fragments recovered from the fire, he said, 'The writing shown me by Insp Neil I believe is the handwriting of the man I have described'. Now, there is a slight ambiguity because this sentence was immediately preceded by one in which Crabtree said that 'There was another man she used to be very friendly with and who did live with her from what my wife has heard but I know very little of him' (followed by the comment that his wife, who had pointed the man out to him in Euston Road, might know something about him). So it is not totally impossible that Crabtree was talking about *this* man's handwriting. However, from the context of the statement it is obvious that Crabtree was actually talking about the handwriting of the other man who had threatened Emily (i.e. the man he would later call 'Scottie'). This was the only man Crabtree had described in his statement and he compared the handwriting Inspector Neil showed him with the handwriting of 'the man I have described'. Furthermore, Crabtree had claimed to have seen this man's handwriting on letters he had taken from Emily's box while she was in Portsmouth in 1906 so it only made sense for him to be speaking of the handwriting of the man who had threatened Emily because he had not given any indication that he had seen the other man's handwriting at any stage prior to 1907.

On Crabtree's version of events, therefore, he had, remarkably, managed to read letters written to Emily by both the men he knew to be friendly with her and they must have had virtually identical handwriting because he said at separate times that they both resembled the handwriting of the man suspected of the murder. In both cases, the letters no longer seemed to exist. In respect of the first man's letters, Crabtree said he had given them to his wife but they could not be found by the police. In respect of the letters supposedly written by Wood, Crabtree said he had given them back to Emily and she told him she had torn them up and was going to have nothing more to do with the man. So there were no documents to support what Crabtree was saying and, without any corroboration, his evidence must be treated with extreme caution. His stories about Wood had only been mentioned to Inspector Neil after Wood had been arrested and charged, and after Crabtree had seen Wood in an identification parade. It is true that he had managed to pick out Wood in the line-up on 5 October but Crabtree was so crafty and cunning that one would not be surprised if he had managed to work out which man was the prime suspect and picked him out so that he would remain useful to the police. There was money to be made from helping the authorities and Crabtree knew it.

Buried away in a Home Office Register of Cases passed to the Treasury Solicitor, held at the National Archives, is an entry containing reference to a report dated 2 November 1907 regarding 'John William Crabtree, a prisoner in Pentonville Prison'. The entry reads as follows:

> Ref: on petition from Crabtree asking for some reward on account of certain information given by him in connection with the Camden Town Murder case (R v. Wood) and on other grounds.[355]

The report was submitted to the Treasury Solicitor 'for observations' but unfortunately it has not survived and it is not known if any reward was ever provided to Crabtree. It would be particularly interesting to know what 'other grounds' were put forward as part of Crabtree's case for a reward because it seems as if he was supplying other information to the police. The fact that Crabtree was secretly angling for some money in return for what he told Inspector Neil emphasises the fact that his evidence needs to be treated with extreme caution.

The Sunday papers on 20 October 1907 concentrated on reporting the inquest proceedings but the *People* claimed to have some new information from 'special inquiries'. It said that one of its reporters had interviewed 'a young woman who was one of Emily Dimmock's closest friends'. Until recently this woman had apparently lived in the neighbourhood of Euston Road but, since the murder, had moved to the vicinity of Victoria, near Westminster, out of fear that she would be required to give evidence and 'desiring to avoid publicity'. According to the newspaper:

> She states that she knows the man in custody well, having frequently seen him in the company of her dead friend. The last occasion upon which she declares she saw him was on the eve of the murder when Wood entered the Rising Sun, and knowing her to be a close acquaintance of Dimmock's asked, 'Have you seen Phyllis?' She replied in the negative and they entered into conversation the gist of which is in our possession, but which, for obvious reasons we withhold for the time being, and then left. Subsequently, so she declares, Wood returned and found Dimmock in the bar. Eventually they left the Rising Sun together.[356]

The friend's evidence sounds suspiciously like that of Florence Smith (a.k.a. Emily Stewart) who lived at the time of the murder in Arlington Road (in Camden Town, not Euston Road). Florence told police that, on the night of Friday 6 September (not the night of the murder), Wood spoke to her and said, 'Have you seen Phyllis?' and she replied, 'No, not tonight'. On the night of the murder, Wood met Emily in the *Eagle* and, the night before that, Emily was with Robert Roberts in the *Rising Sun* so this information does not appear to be worth a great deal. For the record, Florence Smith told police that she only saw Wood in Emily's company twice, on that Friday and then on Monday 9 September.

The *People* also seems to have become carried away about the supposed motive for the crime, saying that 'a very unusual motive' was to be advanced by the prosecution. Apparently, 'it will be sought to establish that neither robbery nor even jealousy was the cause' but instead 'whoever the murderer proves to be will be shown to have been [of] a peculiar diseased state of mind well recognised by medical experts in physiology'. In support of this extravagant claim, the paper referred to the fact that Ruby Young had been asked two questions in writing by Sir Charles Mathews at the inquest, to which she replied in writing, and those questions and answers had not been referred to in open court nor were they published in any newspaper reports of the inquest proceedings. Only the jury had been allowed to read them. However, we now know that the questions Ruby was asked in writing were as follows:

> On any occasion or occasions when you had intercourse with the prisoner have you worn anything or have you been undressed?
> At whose instance?

These questions were clearly directed at the fact, for which Dr Thompson had already provided an explanation (completely ignored by the police), that Emily Dimmock had been found in the nude, despite having kept her chemise on each night when sleeping with Roberts: the point apparently being to establish that Wood preferred sex with a naked woman – something which does not seem to fall into any known category of perversion. Ruby's answers were that intercourse with Wood was 'Always dressed, expect on one or two occasions' (which seems stranger than being undressed) and that she could not say at whose request this was. So Wood, unusually, did not seem to have any particular penchant for sex with naked women and the whole point fell away.

On the same day, the *News of the World* carried a letter it had received from Ruby Young who was said to be 'Deeply distressed by unfounded rumours that have reached her ears'. It was being said that Miss Young had taken the newspaper's reward of £100 for identifying Wood as the author of the rising sun postcard. In response, she wrote: 'I have not received a penny from any person at all. It is against my nature to accept money of such a nature (blood-money, as it is commonly called) and these statements have been most distressing, and have added to the miseries of my unhappy position'. It was the first sign that Ruby Young's character was under attack outside of the courtroom but her letter seemed to have little or no impact. Many people continued to believe that she had received the newspaper's one hundred pounds of 'blood money'.

On Monday 21 October, the inquest continued and Wood was again driven into the back entrance of St Pancras Coroner's Court as hundreds of people clamoured for admission a full hour before the arrival of the coroner. Newspaper reports drew attention to Wood's remarkable coolness as he listened to the proceedings while sitting cross-legged between two warders, 'his hair brushed back from his forehead and his chin resting on his delicately shaped hand'.[357] The initial focus of the evidence related to his identification as someone who had known Emily Dimmock for some time before her murder. It was all rather vague though. Ellen Lawrence said she had seen Wood speaking to Emily once, inside the *Pindar of Wakefield*, during the spring of 1906 and recalled that Emily asked her not to speak to her at the time because the man she was with (i.e. Wood) 'did not care to see her associating with other women'.[358] Gladys Warren claimed to have seen Wood and Emily walking together in the street at some unspecified time in 1906 but, when asked by Mr Newton if she had seen Emily with other men, became coy and claimed she could not recall. William Linehan probably gave the strongest evidence of former relations between Wood and Emily, saying that he had seen the two of them together in the *Rising Sun* on four or five occasions between about March 1906 and February 1907. On the other hand, Edward Smeeth, who had assisted in the management of the *Rising Sun* for eight years, said he had never seen Wood and Emily together before Monday 6 September (although he had seen them both separately in the house over the past few years). Florence Smith hadn't seen Wood before 6 September, despite having been friends with Emily for two years.

It was common ground that Wood had been in the *Rising Sun* with Emily on Friday 6 September so the witnesses who saw them together on that occasion did not add much that was damaging to Wood in this respect. However, Ellen Lawrence claimed that when Emily saw Wood in the *Rising Sun* on Monday 9 September she said, 'There is that ——— again' (the censored word was not reported in any newspapers so we don't know what it was but one would guess at 'bastard' although it could, of course, have been worse). Both she and Florence Smith said that Emily seemed 'very nervous' of Wood but, when the coroner pressed Florence on the point, she admitted that this was only her imagination and Emily had not said anything to this effect. When looking back on the night with hindsight it is quite possible that, in the belief Wood was Emily's murderer, both Ellen Lawrence and Florence Smith viewed Emily's non-verbal responses to Wood in a different light than they did when they were with her at the time in the *Rising Sun*.

One additional witness who claimed to have seen Wood with Emily in about September 1906 was the window cleaner, Albert Miller. Mr Newton asked him sarcastically, 'Is your story that twelve months ago you saw the prisoner pop his head through a public house door and you never saw him again till you identified him at the police station?' Mr Miller confirmed this was indeed what he was saying but it was, by definition, a very weak identification and proved very little in any case. He said that Emily went out to speak to Wood for a minute. The involvement of 'Jumbo' Hurst in leaving the bar with the intention of fighting Wood had to be dragged out of him by the coroner.

Of rather more significance was the evidence of the *Eagle's* barmaid, Lilian Raven. Although she could not actually identify Wood, she told the inquest that, on the night of 11 September, she saw a young woman in the saloon bar, with her hair in curling pins, speaking to a man (and then the couple had a drink with a second man who left the bar). At this stage, Wood had not admitted to being with Emily in the *Eagle* on the night of her murder so this was useful evidence for the Treasury, especially as Joseph Lambert had already sworn that he had left Wood with Emily in the *Eagle* that night. Most importantly, Miss Raven said that the man and the woman left the *Eagle* together. Although not mentioned in court, Miss Raven had explained to the police nine days earlier the reason for her initial failure to remember the woman by saying: 'I saw a photo on the night of the 12th Sept 1907 but I was in bed when it was shown to me and rather sleepy at the time and did not recognise it but I have seen the photo today and I think it is very like the girl.' In her statement, she also explained that she took notice of the woman's hair because: 'it is so unusual to see anyone with curling pins in their hair at that time of the evening and especially sitting down in the saloon bar'. While the circumstances of her suddenly remembering seeing Emily in the bar may seem suspicious, she was certainly telling the truth, although Wood would later deny that he left the *Eagle* with Emily.

Without doubt the most important evidence of the day given on behalf of the police was provided by Robert McCowan, making his first public appearance. Described by one reporter as 'short, dark, somewhat grizzled',[359] he described how, when passing through St Paul's Road in the early hours of 12 September, he saw a man – since identified by him as Robert Wood – wearing a hard hat and long overcoat 'come out of the gateway of number 29 and walk at a quick pace in the opposite direction'. He admitted that he could not view the man's face but noticed that he 'walked with a peculiar motion of the shoulders'. It was not yet daylight (although it was starting to get light) but he was clearly able to see the man, who was about two yards away from him, because the 'electric standards were blazing along the road at the time'. On the subject of light, there was a chink of it for the defence when the coroner asked, 'You did not see the man coming down the steps?' to which McCowan replied, 'No; he had come out of the gate when I turned round'. This was different to what he had said in his statement so the coroner pressed him to say if he was sure that the man had come from number 29 and McCowan replied 'Yes'. A juror then asked if there was sufficient light for him to see the house number to which he replied, 'I have no doubt about the house'. Yet, if he did not see the man come out of the gate then it was obviously possible he did not come from number 29 at all.

As McCowan had stated that the man he saw was taller and broader than himself, Mr Newton motioned to Wood to stand up in the courtroom and asked McCowan, 'Do you say he is broader than you are across the shoulders?' It was evident to everyone in the courtroom that Wood's shoulders were very narrow but McCowan was reluctant to concede the point. (Mr Newton later asked Inspector Neil if he would describe Wood as 'a man with broad shoulders' and Neil was forced to accept that he would not, calling him 'square shouldered' instead but the inspector would, conveniently, confirm that he had noticed something unusual about the prisoner's gait.) Suspecting a police stooge, Mr Newton asked McCowan, 'When did the police first come to you?' It was a trick question based on Newton's belief that McCowan had been asked by police to provide false alibi evidence but McCowan responded that *he* went to the police on 14 September.

In an article on the case published in the *Sunday Express*, some seventeen years later, Newton wrote that he thought to himself at the time 'I don't like the look of this man' so he instructed his clerk to follow him from the court and make enquiries. These enquiries do not appear to have amounted to anything but, two days later, Newton received an anonymous letter which read:

> That man McGowan (sic) is a copper's nark, and I can tell you all about him. He is not a carman. I swear he has never done a stroke of work for twenty years. Before he went to the police he was in rags and trodden down boots and he had a dirty, scraggy, beard. Now, sir, he is dressed up by the police and goes about boasting that he is being paid 12s 6d a day. I swear to you sir, that man was not in St Paul's-road at all that morning. I have suffered innocently, and I don't want to see Mr Wood put away falsely.[360]

Newton commented that he usually ignored anonymous letters but, on this occasion, he was 'very struck with the contents which harmonised with my own suspicions' and gave the impression to the readers of the *Sunday Express* that it was all true. However, while McCowan was paid expenses of three shillings to attend the inquest, there is very good reason to doubt the main allegations in the letter. McCowan was certainly in St Paul's Road on the morning of 12 September and there was corroborating evidence of this from Richard Coleman, a van driver living in Camden Town, who did odd pieces of work for the same bread company that McCowan was on his way to that morning. He said he often met up with McCowan in the morning to go to the V.V. Bread Company in Brewery Road in search of work and he recalled seeing him at the company's yard the day before he heard the news of Emily Dimmock's murder. Like most people, he would have heard this on Friday 13 September so he must have seen McCowan in the morning of Thursday 12 September. As a result, there can be no real doubt that McCowan was seeking work as a carman with the bread company on the Thursday morning and the route from his house to the bread company would have taken him through St Paul's Road.

We know that McCowan was born in Plomesgate, Suffolk, in 1854, the son of a river pilot, and married Mary Palmer, also of Suffolk, in 1882. The 1891 census records that he was still living in Suffolk with two children, Lily aged 6 and Florence aged 4, working as a farrier (repairing horses' hooves). In 1894, however, when his third daughter, Elizabeth, was baptised he had moved to Islington where he was now employed as a coachman. By 1901 he was living at 2 Hawley Street, St Pancras, with five children and his occupation on the census return is given as 'Baker, carman'. This is entirely consistent with the fact that he claimed in 1907 to have been employed as a commission agent by the Aerated Bread Company for twelve years and with his claim to have been attempting to obtain work as a driver with a bread company on the morning he saw the suspect in St Paul's Road. Hawley Street, where McCowan was still living in 1907, was north-west of St Paul's Road and Brewery Road is at the east end of it, so it would have been perfectly natural, and indeed sensible, for him to be walking along St Paul's Road on his way to the V.V. Bread Company. The claim by the author of the anonymous letter that McCowan had not done any work for the past twenty years would appear to be false and, it may be noted, McCowan would say at the Old Bailey, without challenge, that he had spent sixteen years in the army.

Just as McCowan was undoubtedly in St Paul's Road, it is fairly certain that he did see a man that morning – but just not the murderer. The strange thing about Arthur Newton's 1924 article is that it suggests that the allegations made by the anonymous author were true. Yet the defence would eventually produce the man they believed McCowan actually saw in St Paul's Road that morning. Thus, McCowan's claim to have been in that road was perfectly consistent with the defence case. Furthermore, the idea that McCowan was asked by the police to come forward in order to incriminate Wood is contradicted by the fact that McCowan gave his written statement to the police two days after the murder, long before Wood was arrested. It was typical of Newton to take any point which appeared to be in his client's favour – even long after a case was over – without thinking very deeply of how it fitted in with the overall picture.

Another conspiracy suggested by Mr Newton – but this time in the coroner's court – was that it was only after Wood's arrest that the police came up with the theory that the murderer had searched through Emily Dimmock's postcard album in order to remove all evidence of his past relationship with Emily. According to Detective Constable Page, described by the *Morning Leader* as 'a young and promising Scotland Yard man', it looked as though someone had 'gone through' the album 'as if searching for something'. His reasoning was that there were 'four or five postcards which had been sent through the post lying on the floor'. The fact that the album was on a chair near the window with open shutters also suggested to him that someone had been using the light coming through the window to look at the album. Mr Newton asked D.C. Page if he had made a report to his superiors about the postcard album on or about 12 September but the officer said he had only filed such a report for the first time earlier that day (although this report is not in the Metropolitan Police file in the National Archives). In response, Mr Newton exclaimed, 'Ah! So when the case was fresh in your mind, you didn't suggest for a moment that the album had the appearance of being hastily gone through by somebody?' According to the reporter for the *Daily Mail*, Page replied to this question by saying 'No'. However, the reporter for the *Morning Leader*, indicated that the witness made no response and Newton repeated the question saying, 'Did you then say a word with regard to the album giving you that impression?' to which D.C. Page replied by saying quietly, 'I did', which would appear to be the direct opposite of his previous answer, if the *Daily Mail* reporter is to be believed. In any event, Sir Charles Mathews asked Inspector Neil if he had seen the open album on the chair that afternoon. Neil said he had and that 'personally I formed the opinion that some cards had been taken out'.[361]

That seems to deal with that but there is a major problem with the police evidence. When later asked about the album, Bert Shaw, who was the first person into the room, would say that it was normally kept on a small table in the front room but after the murder he found it 'lying open on the sewing machine'.[362] So how did it get from the sewing machine onto a chair? The obvious answer is that someone – perhaps one of the police officers in the room before the arrival of Inspector Neil and Detective Constable Page – moved it there. And if that is the case, then the postcards lying on the floor around the chair must have fallen out at the same time. Bert Shaw certainly never said anything about seeing any postcards on the floor. If the album was on the sewing machine, this does not necessarily negate the police theory that the murderer used the light from the window to view the album because Shaw explained that the sewing machine was close to the window in the front room. Nevertheless, if Neil and Page suspected from the start that someone had rifled through the album, it is strange that they did not ask Bert Shaw about it when he gave his statement. In fact, the album was not mentioned in any surviving police document until after Wood's arrest. This was in a report submitted to Scotland Yard by Inspector Neil on 8 October when he wrote that it appeared that the murderer had been 'searching for something' and that 'everything in the room was in its usual position except a postcard album which had apparently been searched through'. Yet, Neil had said nothing about the album in his long report of 30 September, or about the murderer searching for anything, despite the fact that the rising sun postcard had been found by then and it was such a glaringly obvious possibility that the author of the postcard, then suspected of being the murderer, might have been looking for it in the album and the chest of drawers. Constable Killion made a written statement on 12 September in which he stated that 'The room was in disorder and the contents of drawers were scattered over the floor', while Inspector Neil said in his written report of 13 September that 'The drawers of a chest of drawers were pulled out and placed on the floor, the clothing and other things out of them being scattered about the room and everything was in confusion'. Neither of them mentioned anything about the postcard album and there was no explicit suggestion in either document that the murderer had been searching for something specific. If the thought had occurred to the police at any time between 12 September and 8 October that the murderer had rifled through the postcard album, they did not seem to appreciate the significance of this, hence its location was not properly recorded. It was only after Wood's arrest, in the knowledge that he was the author of the rising sun postcard and had provided a false alibi (making him look like the guilty man), that the police thought it necessary to put into writing that the postcard album had the appearance of being searched through. To that extent, Mr Newton had a decent point.

At the close of the police evidence, Mr Newton stated that he intended to call a number of witnesses not called by the Treasury, emphasising with misplaced optimism that he was 'quite confident that after hearing all the evidence the jury would have an entirely different view'. One of these witnesses was May Campbell and it was her revelation about 'Scotch Bob's' threats against Emily Dimmock that stole the headlines of the next day's newspapers from Robert McCowan and his supposed sighting of the murderer. This was to be her only public appearance in the case and sketches of her by court artists show her to have been young and pretty. She elaborated on her written evidence by saying that Emily told her that she had got Scotch Bob six months in prison 'for assault' and that he had 'threatened to cut her head off'.[363]

The interesting thing about May's claim that Emily was responsible for a man being locked up in prison for six months is that it corresponds with what had been stated in the *Daily Mail* of 16 September 1907 which, it will be recalled, said that, on information supplied by Emily, a man had been sentenced to 'a term of imprisonment'. While it is possible that May Campbell had read this story at the time and incorporated a fictional version of it into her evidence, or was the original creator of the tale, it might equally have been something Emily told her (although whether Emily was telling her the truth at the time is another matter).

A six-month custodial sentence for assault could have been imposed by a magistrate for an assault on a woman or child, or on a police officer in the execution of his duty, but a charge of assault could also have been referred up to the Sessions if it was serious enough. Emily supposedly told May Campbell that the man she was responsible for convicting had been released from prison ten days prior to their meeting on 10 September, i.e. 31 August 1907, but it is unlikely any prisoners were released from a six-month sentence on 31 August 1907. A six month sentence was for six *calendar* months so that anyone convicted on 28 February 1907 would have been released on or about 28 August 1907 if they served their full term.[364] Furthermore, prison rules in force at the time rendered prisoners eligible for release after serving five-sixths of their sentence, as long as their conduct was good.[365] Thus, someone released from a six-month sentence on 31 August 1907 would be expected to have been sentenced five calendar months earlier, on 31 March 1907, but that was unlikely because it was a Sunday. Prisoners were also not released on a Sunday which means that no-one was released from prison on Sunday, 1 September 1907. From the evidence of the Habitual Criminals Register for 1907, prisoners sentenced to six months imprisonment in the last week of March 1907 were released on either 3 or 4 September 1907. In short, May Campbell's belief that someone serving a six-month prison sentence was released ten days before 10 September is unlikely to have been literally correct which could be said to undermine her evidence, although it is always possible that she misheard what Emily had told her.

Inspector Neil considered May Campbell's claim that Emily was responsible for sending a man to prison for six months and, in response, stated in his report of 30 September 1907: 'We have never heard from anyone except Campbell that deceased ever charged anyone and no record of her having done so has been discovered'. It has to be said that this is strangely worded because it ignores the possibility of Emily having been an informant as opposed to the victim of an assault, otherwise known as the complainant, or prosecutrix, in any proceedings. It also indicates an uncertainty on Neil's part, whereas one would expect him to have been able to confirm it one way or the other.

An extensive search of surviving police court records in the North London area, and of newspaper reports where those records do not survive, together with records of the County of London Sessions, produces only one individual convicted of assault or a similar charge and sentenced to six months imprisonment in the period between 28 February and 31 March 1907 who thus might have been released on, or shortly before or after, 31 August 1907.[366] This was Patrick Hurley, a 45 year old labourer, with a previous conviction from 1906 for assault, convicted at the North London Sessions on 27 March 1907 for maliciously wounding a woman called Elizabeth Gladman (with his sentence stated to commence from 26 March). He would presumably have been released from prison in the first week of September 1907 but there is nothing obvious to connect him with Emily Dimmock.

There are two individuals of a little more interest who were sentenced to six months for assault in early April 1907 and would thus almost certainly have been at liberty at the time of Emily's murder.[367] The first was a 26-year-old labourer called William Phillips who was part of a fifty-strong gang which assaulted Police Constable Henry Lester of the Y Division in Seymour Street, Somers Town, during the evening of Sunday, 31 March 1907. The gang was being loud and disruptive in the street and P.C. Lester asked one of their number, William Churchwood, to behave himself, at which point Churchwood kicked him in the eye and others in the gang followed up the attack. Phillips struck the constable around the head with a belt until he became unconscious. Assistance for the constable quickly arrived and Churchwood was arrested at the scene but Phillips and the rest of the gang fled.[368] However, on the day that Churchwood first appeared at Clerkenwell Police Court (1 April), Phillips was supposedly found 'outside the court' and arrested and brought before the magistrate with Churchwood.[369*] Two days later, along with a third member of the gang who was involved in the assault, Phillips was convicted of grievous bodily harm to the police constable and sentenced to six months hard labour, despite denying he was present at the incident, while Churchwood and the other man each received three months.[370]

On the face of it, there is nothing to connect Emily Dimmock with William Phillips and it is only the location of the assault, in Seymour Street, where Emily was supposedly seen on the last day she was alive, that arouses any interest in the matter. The police either got lucky in finding Phillips outside Clerkenwell Police Court or they found him on information supplied and, if Emily had been responsible for this, it might have caused Phillips to hold a grievance against her but without any evidence there is no point in speculating further.

At the North London Sessions held in April 1907, there was only one man convicted of assault (grievous bodily harm) and sentenced to six months imprisonment. His name was Roland Small, aged 21, a gardener by occupation, working in the grounds of 'Heathlands', a large estate near Hampstead Heath owned by Hildebrand Harmsworth, the brother of Baron Northcliffe, the proprietor of the *Daily Mail*. Small, who lived with his parents at 5 Golden Square, Hampstead, had previously been convicted in 1904 for an unprovoked assault on two brothers, Henry Charles Allen and George Allen, and was known by police to be part of a street gang.[371] His conviction on 10 April 1907 was for a ferocious attack on a widow called Emily Hampton two months earlier. Mrs Hampton said at the trial that she met Small in the street during the evening of Saturday, 10 February 1907 and he asked her 'to go to his place' to which she replied 'I don't care to' but, as she did then accompany him to a greenhouse on Harmsworth's estate, it seems that she might have been supplementing her meagre income, which was stated in court to have come from doing 'daily work', with prostitution. Shortly after entering the greenhouse, Small became 'rough and violent' and 'made advances' to her. She tried to escape but the door was locked. Small threw her on the ground and assaulted her before saying, 'If you don't give me a shilling I'll kill you'. Mrs Hampton told him she did not have a shilling and tried to open the door but Small hit her in her right eye so hard that the medical man who later examined her thought it would need to be removed in order to preserve the sight of her left eye. Small also kicked her in the leg, breaking it. Her screams attracted the attention of Harmsworth's butler who rescued the unfortunate victim while Small fled the scene.[372]

As the only people who knew where the key to the greenhouse was kept were Small and Harmsworth's head gardener, Small was a prime suspect for the assault. He was quickly located by the police and brought to the workhouse infirmary where Mrs Hampton was being treated for her injuries; she identified him from a line-up of twelve men as her attacker. His defence in court was that it was a case of mistaken identity but he was not believed and was taken from the North London Sessions at Clerkenwell to Wormwood Scrubs.[373]

On the face of it, while Small might have the profile of a potential murderer, there is nothing in his conviction which can be linked with Emily Dimmock. It was fairly straightforward for the police to have worked out who was responsible for the assault on Emily Hampton and they do not appear to have needed an informant to help them. At the same time, there is one intriguing potential connection between Roland Small and Emily Dimmock. In the Metropolitan Police file on the Dimmock case at the National Archives is a mention of a payment of £1 to a Frederick Clifford. A report by Inspector Neil dated 10 October 1907 stated, 'I understand that Local Inspr Stockley, E Division, advanced the sum of £1 for an informant named Frederick Clifford in connection with the case'. There is no indication, however, as to precisely what information was provided by Mr Clifford. The only other mentions of Inspector Stockley in the file are in connection with the suspect William Russell and the witness May Campbell, the latter of whom was said by Neil to have 'come forward through local inspector Stockley'.[374] It may be that Clifford provided some form of information in respect of one or both of these two individuals, in which case there is clearly no connection between Small and Emily. However, while there is insufficient information to be able to identify this Frederick Clifford, it is interesting that a man of the same name was living at the home of Roland Small's parents, 5 Golden Square, at the time of the 1911 census.[375] His occupation was stated to be a 'jobbing gardener' but, until September 1905, he had been a police constable, at which time, after twenty-three years of service in the force, and no doubt looking forward to collecting his pension within a year or two, he was forced to resign when he was certified by the Divisional Surgeon as 'suffering from the effects of recent drinking and unfit for duty' after being found absent without leave from his patrol.[376]

If the Frederick Clifford who was living with the Small family in 1911 was the same man who was awarded £1 for the information he gave to Inspector Stockley in 1907 it would be an extraordinary coincidence if there was no connection with Roland Small, a man who just happened to have been sentenced to six months in prison for an assault and, as he would have served exactly five months of his sentence on 10 September 1907, was probably released only a day or two before Emily's murder.[377] While we would have to conclude, in that case, that May Campbell had misunderstood a number of things Emily had said to her, especially about her being responsible for Small's imprisonment, he might still have had a motive for the murder if, as May Campbell also claimed, the man had caught venereal disease from Emily. Although Small lived in Hampstead, and there is nothing to connect him with the Camden Town area, it should not be forgotten that Emily had initially lived and worked in East Finchley, within walking distance of Hampstead, and might have got to know Small at that time. Also, while he was born in Hampstead, Small's maternal grandfather, Charles Stewart, was originally from Scotland (although his mother was born in Northampton) and when he (Roland) appeared at the police court charged with the attack on Emily Hampton, the local newspaper referred to him as 'Robert Small'.[378] There is nothing to suggest that this was anything other than a journalistic error but it could have prompted his friends to jokingly call him 'Scotch Bob', although this is, admittedly, unlikely.

For completeness, it should be noted that there is a record of an 'Emily Dimmock' being given a reward by the police of ten shillings in April 1907 for some unknown form of assistance she provided within the Y Division. The official Police Orders circulated on a daily basis to Metropolitan Police stations (which were not available to the general public) for 23 April 1907, after setting out a number of police officers commended, listed the following payments to members of the public under the heading of 'Commendations and Rewards':

D. Edward Allsop 15s

J. Charles Harris £1

T. Arthur Fagg 7s 6d

W. Alfred Wilkinson £1

X. Frank Weedon 10s

Y. Emily Dimmock 10s

" Thomas Maynard 10s

(E.F.W.)

T. Stanley Mason 10s

The initials E.F.W. stood for Edwin Frederick Wodehouse, the Assistant Commissioner of the Metropolitan Police, who would have approved the payment. The letters on the left-hand side represent police divisions and, during April 1907, the Emily Dimmock living with Bert Shaw was under the jurisdiction of Y Division at 29 St Paul's Road. If she was the Emily Dimmock who received the ten shillings this could, in theory, correspond with May Campbell's story as some kind of reward for the arrest and conviction of someone, such as Roland Small. However, the rewards listed for private individuals in the Police Orders were for assistance provided to the police other than supplying information. A typical reason for such an award, especially of such a small figure as ten shillings, was for assisting a police constable in trouble – for example blowing his whistle while he was in a fight, struggling to arrest someone, or otherwise calling for help.

There were at least two other women called 'Emily Dimmock' living within the Y Division in 1907. On 14 April 1907, a 26-year-old woman, Emily Chamberlain, married a butcher called William Dimmock in Kentish Town to become Mrs Emily Dimmock so it could conceivably have been her who received the reward. A much better candidate, however, is the 43-year-old wife of box packer, Joseph Dimmock, originally Emily Willis, who lived at 6 Grove Street, Eden Grove, in Holloway, which was in the Y Division. This Emily Dimmock actually gave evidence in Clerkenwell Police Court on 2 April 1907.[379] She did so as a witness for the defence on behalf of two of her neighbours: dustman William Curtis, and his wife Sarah, of 33 Eden Grove, who had been charged with assault on a man called Morgan. Mrs Dimmock gave evidence that Mr Curtis was not present at the alleged assault while saying that Mrs Curtis was there but did nothing. She said it was Curtis' sister-in-law who was to blame and Mr and Mrs Curtis were discharged. As she was a defence witness, her appearance in court does not directly provide an explanation for any police reward and the records of Clerkenwell Police Court for 1907 are incomplete so the nature of the assault witnessed by this Emily Dimmock is not entirely clear but there is reason to believe that Morgan might have been a police officer and Emily Dimmock might have blown his whistle to call for assistance.[380] Another reason why this Emily Dimmock may be the Emily Dimmock referred to in the Police Orders is because the resident of 1 Grove Street at the time was Alexander Maynard whose 17-year-old son was called Thomas Maynard. It will be noted that a Thomas Maynard was also awarded ten shillings within Y Division at the same time as Emily Dimmock. His payment might have been completely separate to Emily Dimmock's, so that he had nothing to do with her, but the fact that an Emily Dimmock and a Thomas Maynard lived in the same street (assuming Thomas still lived with his parents at this time) is quite a coincidence, bearing in mind the appearance of both those names together in the Police Orders.[381] On this basis, Thomas Maynard might also have assisted a police officer in the same incident. If, however, it was the subsequently murdered Emily Dimmock who received a police reward, this would be quite explosive and important information but one would have expected this to have been mentioned in one of Inspector Neil's reports and, in all the circumstances, the likelihood is that it was a different woman of the same name, especially as the Emily Dimmock living with Bert Shaw preferred to call herself Mrs Shaw rather than Miss Dimmock.

Now, returning to May Campbell's evidence at the inquest, it may be noted that the shortened form of Robert is 'Bob' and Bob Wood was originally from Scotland, speaking with a Scottish accent, so he could, in theory, have been 'Scotch Bob' but this was never seriously considered by the police. He had not spent any time in prison for a start and he did not have a 'dirty, pimply' face as described by May Campbell. Certainly, the Treasury did not place any reliance on her evidence. Sir Charles Mathews asked her in cross-examination if she was sure she had seen Emily on Wednesday afternoon in Camden Town when Emily told her she had received a letter that morning from 'Scotch Bob' requesting a meeting at 9:45pm. When May said that she was, indeed, sure of this, Sir Charles asked if Emily's hair was done. May said 'Yes, roughly'. Sir Charles responded: 'Then, if there are three witnesses who say that the deceased at that time was in 29 St Pauls-road and that her hair was not done, what do you say?', producing the answer, 'I believe my own eyes sir'.

As it happens, Sir Charles Mathews was not being entirely fair to May Campbell. The three witnesses he was evidently referring to here were Bert Shaw, George Stocks and his wife, Sarah Ann. But George Stocks did not come home from work on the Wednesday until 6:00pm (when he said he saw Emily in the wash house) so he was in no position to say that Emily was at home with her hair not done at around 4:30pm, which was when May Campbell said she spoke to Emily in Camden Town. It is true that Mrs Stocks had told the coroner earlier in the day that during the afternoon of September 11 Emily was cleaning her room and that she 'more than once saw Dimmock, who was washing some linen'. Her belief, which she had only set out for the first time in a statement provided to police four days earlier on 17 October, was that Emily was 'at home the whole of that day' and 'washing all afternoon' but it is hard to see how she could be certain her lodger did not slip out at any point.

In this respect, it is worth looking at the development of Mrs Stocks' evidence in a little more detail. In her first statement of 12 September, she said that she spoke to Emily in her kitchen between 8:00pm and 9:00pm and then, on 8 October, after Wood's arrest, at the request of the police, added a sentence saying, 'When I saw her between 8 and 9pm her hair was in curling pins'. On 17 October, a week before the resumed inquest, she was spoken to again by the police who now, belatedly, realised the significance of Emily's movements during the day and, in response to their new questions about the events of the afternoon, she said:

> I was cleaning my bedroom and between 2 and 4pm I saw the deceased several times and spoke to her. After Shaw left to go to his work at 3pm (sic) I again saw deceased several times, she came in and out of my kitchen and went into the garden and gathered some clean linen which she had previously washed. I am absolutely certain she did not leave the house during the afternoon and early evening.

That makes it hard to argue that Emily could have visited Camden Town that afternoon but Mrs Stocks was attempting to recall a period of a few hours more than one month earlier. She was evidently not with Emily all afternoon; could she really be certain she had not gone out for an hour or so?

Bert Shaw said in his statement of 12 September 1907: 'Yesterday, 11th, I was at home from 11.30am until 4.30pm. Dimmock was at home all the time. I went out leaving her at home'. Consequently, even if Bert Shaw was correct, despite Mrs Stocks' supposed certainty when she was asked about it almost five weeks after the murder, there was no direct evidence as to Emily's whereabouts, or the state of her hair, in the ninety-minute period from 4:30pm to 6:00pm. It will be recalled that three people (never called to give evidence at any court) claimed to have seen Emily in Somers Town between 3:00pm and 4:00pm on the Wednesday. While the timings of this sighting do not precisely match the time we know that Emily could have slipped out without being missed, it was surely possible for Emily to have been in Camden Town and Somers Town at some point after 4:30pm and to have returned to St Paul's Road by 6:00pm without either Shaw or Mr and Mrs Stocks being any the wiser. If May Campbell had said she saw Emily at Camden Town at 5:00pm, instead of half an hour earlier, it would have been quite plausible. Furthermore, if Mrs Stocks was correct in saying that Bert Shaw left for work at 3:00pm that day (although, in an earlier statement, she said that his normal time of departure was 4:30pm) this would open up the timings and mean that all four witnesses who claimed to have seen Emily outside St Paul's Road between 3:00pm and 4:30pm could have been right.

At the same time, there were obvious problems with May Campbell's story. Although it was not yet admitted by Wood, we know that he wrote the letter to Emily (as seen by Roberts) asking for a meeting on the Wednesday night; so, unless Emily received two letters that day requesting a meeting that evening, it would seem that May Campbell was either confused or lying when she said Emily told her she had received a letter to meet 'Scotch Bob' in Camden Town at a quarter to ten. Her behaviour at the identification parade was also the subject of criticism. Having initially said that she could not recognise anybody, she picked out Wood from the line-up as the man she called 'Scotch Bob', but, when asked by Sir Charles if Wood was 'very dark, clean shaven, with sunken eyes and dirty, pimply face', as she had described 'Scotch Bob', she replied

'Yes', prompting the caustic comment from the barrister (presumably in respect of the 'dirty, pimply face' aspect of the description): 'That shows how accurate you are'.

Still, everyone was talking about 'Scotch Bob'. Even before May Campbell had stepped into the witness box, Mr Newton had prepared the ground by asking William Linehan about him, and confused him in the process. Although different newspapers carried differing reports of the cross-examination, it is clear that Linehan knew nothing of any 'Scotch Bob' who had a pimply face but he *had* heard Emily speak of a 'man named Jock', explaining that 'she called every Scotchman Jock'. However, when Mr Newton subsequently asked a poorly worded, leading question: 'Did she ever tell you "Scotch Bob" had threatened to do for her?', Linehan replied 'Yes'. But he was clearly agreeing on the basis that Newton's 'Scotch Bob' was the same as his 'Scotch Jock'. This muddied the waters and most people in the courtroom probably believed that Linehan was corroborating May Campbell's evidence about 'Scotch Bob'. It may well be that they were talking about the same person but Linehan had no idea. After he said he knew nothing about Emily being responsible for the man getting six months imprisonment, remarking 'this is all new to me', the coroner asked him, 'When was the last time you saw Scotch Jock?' to which he replied, 'I never saw him'. So he was in no position to give any direct evidence about the man. Curiously, Gladys Warren was not asked at all about either 'Scotch Bob' or 'Scotch Jock' (or 'Scotch Jack') at the inquest despite her having told the police that she knew the latter and despite the fact that she had given the police a description of him which included a 'blotchy face'. One piece of information William Linehan was able to confirm, however, was that he knew May Campbell and that May Campbell knew Emily Dimmock.

The second witness called to the inquest by the defence was none other than Jack Crabtree, direct from Pentonville Prison. For obvious reasons, Mr Newton wanted the court to hear all about the man who had threatened Emily but his first question did not go too well. 'Was Miss Dimmock visited at Bidborough Street by a man who was not Wood?' he asked, to which Crabtree gave the answer, 'Well, Wood did visit her there', bringing the sharp rebuke from Mr Newton of 'I was not asking you that!' Subsequently, Crabtree told the story Mr Newton wanted to hear. He informed the court:

> There was another man whose face was covered with a rash. On one occasion I heard Phyllis scream and I went upstairs. The man picked up a fender and threw it at me. He was in the habit of knocking the woman about. One night he took a purse from her. There were quarrels between them. I once heard him say he would cut her throat. I told him on one occasion that I would not allow him to go to the house, whereupon he took a handkerchief from his pocket, wrapped it round the handle of a razor and said he would do both Phyllis and me....The man was always tormenting Dimmock for money. She bought him a gold chain and paid £6 10s for it. He told me that he was in great pain, and mentioned that he had been put to great expense, and was angry with her.[382]

Crabtree had not actually mentioned the story of the man throwing the fender at him to Inspector Neil but the rest of the story was reasonably consistent with his written statement. He also related the story he had already told the inspector of seeing the man who had threatened Emily watching St Pancras

Building (where Bert and Emily were living) and Emily later pointing him out saying something like: 'Look at the man I keep'. Asked what he thought of the man's threats, Crabtree said he thought they were made with the object of extorting money from Emily.

After Mr Newton had extracted these helpful stories from Crabtree, it was time for Sir Charles to cross-examine on behalf of the Treasury. He was fully aware of the contents of Crabtree's recent witness statement and directed his questions to Crabtree's knowledge of Wood's relationship with Emily. Crabtree related the stories he had told Inspector Neil for the first time four days earlier about the quarrel between Wood and Emily in 1906, the discussion about the pawning of Wood's silver cigarette case and the fact that he had heard Wood say to her that if she was visited by soldiers and sailors he would have nothing to do with her. He also told how he had seen letters addressed to 'Phillis darling', just like the rising sun postcard, and that the letters 'r', 's', 'p' and 'h' on the postcard resembled those on the letters addressed to Emily that he had seen.

The decision to call Crabtree having somewhat backfired, Mr Newton attempted in re-examination to bring the subject of discussion back to the man who 'used to knock Phyllis about' and he managed to squeeze out a very useful admission from the witness that this man 'very much' resembled Robert Wood (apart from a light moustache and 'stiff hair that stuck up straight'). Crabtree denied that he had made a mistake of identification but it is self-evident that, if Emily had had a relationship with a man who looked like Wood, it could easily have been that man the other witnesses had wrongly identified as Wood in Emily's company.

A little more information about the man who had threatened Emily with a razor was provided by Crabtree in the witness box. Pressed as to whether he knew the man's name, he said he had heard him called 'Mr Dimmock' but also 'Mr Wilson'. This has to be viewed with even more caution than we would normally view anything Jack Crabtree says because he had told Inspector Neil on 19 September 'I cannot tell you his name' and it is strange that he was suddenly able to throw out the name of 'Wilson'. However, Emily Crabtree was also called to give evidence and, as she had told Inspector Neil on 6 October at Kentish Town Police Station, she related her belief that the man who had frequently visited Emily Dimmock and had threatened to 'do her in' was called 'Tom'. So between Mr and Mrs Crabtree we have a complete name for this violent man: Tom Wilson.

It will be recalled that May Campbell told police on 19 September that the man she called 'Scotch Bob' was also known as 'Tom'. Could she and the Crabtrees possibly be talking about the same man? Well, both men were said to have had pimples and, as Mr and Mrs Crabtree each confirmed that their 'Tom Wilson' resembled Wood, while May Campbell had (eventually) picked Wood out of the identification parade saying he was 'Scotch Bob', they evidently both looked similar. The main difficulty in concluding that they must be the same man is that Crabtree had described a small man of only five foot and four or five inches, whereas May Campbell said 'Scotch Bob' was of average height at about five foot and seven or eight inches, which was roughly Wood's height. Also, although May Campbell's description of 'Scotch Bob' was very vague, she said he was 'clean shaven' whereas, according to both of the Crabtrees, 'Tom Wilson' was supposed to have had a moustache.

Emily Crabtree's own credibility was undermined somewhat by her admission that she 'identified as Tom a man who is not Tom at all'. We also know that she gave supporting, and certainly false, evidence on behalf of her husband when he was charged with keeping a brothel at Clerkenwell Police Court. It does not seem to have been possible, however, for her to have colluded with Jack to come up with a false story about the existence of this man. Under prison rules in force at the time, she would not have been allowed visits to Jack in Pentonville, nor would she have been allowed to correspond with him in writing, until after four months of his sentence had expired (which would not be until 31 November).[383] In any event, she could not have known that May Campbell had named a man called 'Tom' so it cannot be entirely ruled out that 'Tom Wilson' and 'Scotch Bob' were one and the same person.

After Wood was remanded again at Clerkenwell, the inquest continued on Monday 28 October. For the first time in public since his arrest, Wood was not wearing his blue suit, having changed into a smart, well-cut, dark grey suit but was said to be 'as cheerful as ever'.[384] His brother offered him a notebook and pencil but he apparently declined the gift, saying, 'I must not have it. I am not allowed'.[385]

Over the past week, Mr Newton had been carefully considering Robert McCowan's claim that the man who had emerged from 29 St Paul's Road was wearing an overcoat. It occurred to him that, if he could establish that Wood was not wearing an overcoat during the Wednesday evening, his client could not have been the man seen leaving number 29. Joseph Lambert was, therefore, recalled to the inquiry and asked by Mr Newton how Wood was dressed when he saw him in the *Eagle*. Lambert had to think for a minute before saying, 'In a dark blue suit'. Had he any overcoat on? 'No' said Joseph Lambert, 'and he was not carrying one either'. In that single question and answer, although the effect would not be felt until the trial, Mr Newton had virtually cleared his client of murder!

Mr Newton called a further two witnesses who had provided statements to the police but who had not been called to give evidence on behalf of the Treasury: Henry Sharples and Frederick Harvey. They told the coroner about the man they saw with Emily in the *Rising Sun* on Sunday 8 September being smartly dressed, thick-set and wearing a blue suit.[386] But he was not, they said, either Robert Wood or Robert Roberts. Sharples said that he thought he saw this man with Emily again after midnight on the Wednesday in the Euston Road, midway between Chalton Street and Oussleton Street, shortly after he emerged with Harvey from a nearby restaurant, but, critically, he could not be absolutely sure it was the same man. He was, however, sure it was Emily whom he knew 'very well'. Harvey also said he saw Emily but did not particularly notice the man she was with that night. Although their evidence was vague, if they had truly seen Emily Dimmock around midnight on the Wednesday with a man taller than her (Wood was slightly smaller than Emily according to Lambert's evidence) then the fact that Wood had been seen with Emily in the *Eagle* a few hours earlier was of much less significance.

Also called to give evidence by Mr Newton was William Moss who said he had seen Wood at work constantly between the night of the murder and his arrest during which time his appearance and conduct had been 'quite normal'. Furthermore, the books of the London Sand Blast Works showed that Wood had turned up at work at the usual time every day.

The final witnesses called by Arthur Newton were Wood's father and two brothers. Charles Carlyle Wood said that his brother was 'a splendid character...a kind hearted, well conducted young man' and the reason Wood had not wanted to 'publish the facts outright' was because 'it would be showing to his family his association with such a woman'. More importantly, he confirmed that he had not seen his brother wearing his overcoat during the last few months; 'it was not his custom' he said, 'he kept it in a drawer in his room'. Sir Charles Mathews took a strange tack in cross-examination, asking him if his brother was 'emotional' or 'hysterical' which Charles denied in strong terms. However, Charles did admit that his brother had told him (untruthfully) that he had met Ruby Young for tea on the night of the murder.

Wood's father, George, was called next to the witness box. An impressively ancient-looking man with a huge white beard and rather deaf, he said that he had been confined to his house on 9 September with gouty eczema. He remembered his son coming home at about midnight on Wednesday 11 September (without an overcoat) and popping into his room for the alarm clock. He knew the date because he had accidentally knocked over a bottle of liniment his doctor had given him for his bad foot. He saw his son the next morning for breakfast and he was as cool, calm and collected as usual. During cross-examination, he admitted telling Inspector Neil that he could not say what time his son usually got home but that it would frequently be very late, at a time when he (George) would be asleep in bed. However, he firmly denied being asked by the inspector what time his son came home on the night of 11 September or telling him that he could not remember. As he stepped down from the witness box he moved observers in the court by gripping his son's hand and saying 'Bob' affectionately.[387]

Finally, James Wood said that he remembered his half-brother coming in on the Wednesday night and saying goodnight to him. He knew it was a Wednesday night 'Because of the broken bottle; and the previous night my two brothers came home together, which was unusual'. This was a reference to the fact that Robert and Charles had spent the evening of Tuesday 10 September together, first at the Holborn Public Library, then at a barbers' shop, then at Charles' home in Museum Street before evidently returning together to Frederick Street. James shared a room with his father so he was also able to recall the alarm clock being collected.

After James stepped down from the witness box, Mr Newton declared that he did not propose to call the accused 'because he is not on trial here, and I don't propose that he should be examined here'. This was his right although, when arguing for bail in front of Mr Bros back on 7 October, he had intimated to the magistrate that Wood was going to give evidence at the inquest so his non-appearance was somewhat of a disappointment to everyone in the court.

Before the coroner summed up the evidence, Inspector Neil was recalled by Sir Charles Mathews and asked to confirm what he had been told by George and James Wood about Robert Wood's movements on the night of the murder. The inspector stated that when he spoke to them on 4 October neither of them could recall any details about this at all. He was asked by Mr Newton why he did not request them to sign statements to that effect. Neil replied, 'I understood the father was ill and I wished to do the thing as quietly as possible. I made notes in my notebook.' Curiously, he also said that he had 'no material' to produce any statements. Mr Newton asked him to expand on this, saying, 'Do you mean you had no paper?' but the inspector gave the answer, 'No, Mr Wood told me he could not remember that night, and he told me nothing about it'. Even if George Wood could not remember anything at all, this was sufficiently 'material' (if that is what the inspector meant) so that Neil should have asked the old man to record this absence of recollection in a written statement and got him to sign it. The same is true for James Wood. The inspector's claim that he had 'no material' suggests he was groping around for some kind of explanation for what was evidently a major failure on his part, probably caused by over-confidence in the evidence against Robert Wood and a belief that his own notes (written up after his conversations with the Woods at Frederick Street) would suffice.

After a break for lunch, Mr Danford Thomas summed up the case for the benefit of the thirteen members of the jury. His starting point was the partly burned letter, fragments of which were found in Emily Dimmock's fire. There was, he said, 'no doubt' that this letter, apparently inviting Emily to the *Eagle*, was in the same handwriting as the handwriting on the rising sun postcard which Wood had admitted to writing and, furthermore, 'Undoubtedly Wood was in the *Eagle* public house with the deceased on the night of the murder'. The coroner drew attention to Wood's attempts to obtain a false alibi from Ruby Young and the fact that he had then made a statement to the police which was untrue. Critically, he said that it was 'difficult to believe' that anyone but Wood had gone home with Emily that night. At the same time, he rather surprisingly thought that the plan of sending a letter to the Poste Restante showed that Wood 'did not in any way desire to conceal his part in the matter' and, quite correctly, said that Wood 'is known as a respectable young man'. However, he told the jury that he knew of two instances (the unsolved Great Coram Street murder of 1872 being one*) where a man went home with a woman and 'suddenly, in some revulsion of feeling, savagely murdered her'.[388] Regarding Wood, he said that there was 'certainly, perhaps, a little jealousy on his part' noting that he wanted to go home with Emily and that 'she put him off on three nights for the more wealthy seaman'. His own view was that Wood ought to be tried but ultimately it was for the jury to decide and the members of the jury retired to consider their verdict at about 3:20pm. Rumours quickly circulated around the courtroom that they would not directly accuse Wood of murder. After fifteen minutes the jury returned and gave a unanimous verdict:

> We find that the deceased, Emily Dimmock, met her death by wilful murder, and that the evidence we have received is sufficient to commit the accused for trial.

The rumours were true and the jury had not actually produced a finding that Wood had murdered Emily. After clarifying with the foreman of the jury that they wished for Wood to take his trial for Emily Dimmock's murder, the coroner stated, in case anyone was in any doubt, 'That is a verdict of wilful murder against Wood'.

On hearing this, Ruby Young, who was sitting by herself in the corner of an ante room, fainted and a doctor had to be called to revive her. According to the *Daily Telegraph* reporter, 'For a moment she gazed round, unable to grasp

---

* See Appendix 1.

where she was and then, suddenly recognising those near her, she burst into tears, sobbing hysterically'. Meanwhile, an old woman leaned over towards Wood and patted him on the shoulder, saying: 'Goodbye if I don't see you again'. An unshaken Wood replied, 'But you will see me again' causing the old woman to mutter 'God bless you' while dabbing a handkerchief to her eyes. As he was led from the courtroom by his prison guards, Wood was heard to say quietly, 'It's really too bad of Neil to persist in what he's been saying today. It isn't humanity!'[389]

According to the *Daily Telegraph*'s correspondent, the large crowd outside the coroner's court 'received the decision of the jury without exhibiting any feeling' but reporters for the *Morning Leader* and *Weekly Dispatch* perceived that the sympathies of 'most of them' were 'manifestly' with Wood as demonstrated by the fact that they groaned when Ruby Young emerged and 'an unpleasant scene was prevented by that young lady being spirited away quietly out of the crush'. The coroner, however, agreed with the jury's verdict and commented optimistically that it would be more satisfactory for Wood to be able to go before a tribunal to establish positively whether he was guilty or not. Before the close of proceedings, the jury commended all the police involved for the way in which they had conducted their inquiries and this was endorsed by the coroner. Nothing was said about Neil's failure to take written statements from George and James Wood.

An hour after the hearing concluded, a large crowd was still waiting outside the coroner's court and, as Wood was driven off in a cab back to Brixton Prison, many people ran after the vehicle shouting 'cheer up Bobbie' and 'keep your pecker up'. He had already started to win the hearts of the British public whereas witnesses who had appeared for the Treasury, such as Robert McCowan, Gladys Warren and Ruby Young could now only expect to receive death threats.

D.	Edward Allsup	...	...	...	...	...	15s.
J.	Charles Harris	...	...	...	...	... £1	
T.	Arthur Fagg	...	...	...	...	...	7s. 6d.
W.	Alfred Wilkinson	..	...	...	...	... £1	
X.	Frank Weedon	...	...	...	...	...	10s.
Y.	Emily Dimmock	...	...	...	...	...	10s.
"	Thomas Maynard	...	...	...	...	...	10s.
							—(E.F.W.)
T.	Stanley Mason	...	...	...	...	...	10s.

Extract from Police Orders of 23 April 1907 showing a payment of ten shillings to an Emily Dimmock (National Archives)

Chapter Thirteen

Police Court

'I was the "star turn," if such an expression is permissible.'

Robert Wood, describing the response to his appearance at Clerkenwell Police Court,
Weekly Dispatch, 29 December 1907

Although the jury's verdict at the inquest meant that a trial was inevitable, the Treasury Solicitor was required to obtain a formal committal of Wood from a magistrate. This meant that there was wasteful duplication between the coroner's inquiry and the magistrate's hearing but nothing could divert the legal system, which required the continuation of the police court proceedings, from its course. Even illness on the part of Mr Bros, which caused those proceedings to be delayed for over a week, could not stop them but it would take a further month to reach the same decision that had already been made at the inquest. Clerkenwell Police Court was far too busy dealing with local drunks, prostitutes and petty criminals to set aside a single block of time to hear the charges against Wood so special half-day hearings were held on 6, 12, 13, 14, 22 and 28 November and then, finally, on 4 December when Wood was committed to the Central Criminal Court for trial. Much of the evidence produced at the police court simply, and rather pointlessly, repeated what had been said at the inquest but some new features did emerge.

Dr Thompson was asked by Mr Newton if he would agree that the deep wound to Emily's throat showed that she was murdered by 'a person of great physical strength' to which he replied, 'No, I don't think he need have been that'. This widened the number of possible suspects although, at the same time, the doctor did say that 'considerable force' had been used to cut the throat. He also attempted to reconstruct the murder, saying that the murderer had been at the back of Emily Dimmock, 'one hand placed on the head, perhaps grasping the hair on the forehead, the head raised a little, but very little for fear of rousing her – no doubt she was asleep at the time – and the instrument slipped under the head, which was just lifted sufficiently for the purpose'.[390] In support of this conclusion, he noted that in lifting Emily's head, while holding the instrument, the murderer had cut a pillow as well as the tick of the bed.

One brand new witness for the Treasury was a handwriting expert, Charles Ainsworth Mitchell, a Fellow of the Institute of Chemistry, a member of the Society of Public Analysts and the author of a 1904 book, *Inks and their Manufacture*. Unlike many such experts of the time, he appears to have been quite competent.[391] He testified that the handwriting on the rising sun postcard was the same as on the fragments recovered from the burnt letter found in Emily Dimmock's fireplace and that the pigment of the pencil which wrote them also matched. He had apparently established that the other three postcards initially thought by the police to have been written by the same author, and published in the newspapers, were in a different hand. Probably the most interesting thing about his appearance in court was the fact that he was (very gingerly) cross-examined by Mr Newton who asked him if he had previously given evidence in a court of law. The expert replied that he had only done so twice, once in July of that year and once in 1903. Mr Newton also asked him how many documents had been provided to him by the Treasury to examine (five) and whether he had been handed a number of documents and asked to pick out five (he was not). Although the expert's opinions were not directly challenged, it would have seemed to experienced legal observers that Mr Newton was lining up a possible future attack (at trial) on Mr Ainsworth Mitchell on the basis that he was not sufficiently experienced and had given answers the Treasury wanted. At the conclusion of the police court hearing, however, Mr Newton admitted that Wood had written both the postcard and the letter, thus rendering Newton's entire, albeit brief, cross-examination of the expert redundant. Before Ainsworth Mitchell had given his evidence, Mr Newton had objected to Robert Roberts stating his (non-expert) opinion that the handwriting on the rising sun postcard was the same as on the letter shown to him by Emily Dimmock. This was a reasonable enough objection, albeit one that was overruled by Mr Bros, but, in the process, Mr Newton stated that there was 'no evidence before the court that the letter was written by the accused, that it was sent by him, or that it had ever come to his knowledge'.[392] The obvious inference is that Wood did not confess to his solicitor that he had written the letter until after Ainsworth Mitchell had given evidence.

Another admission by Mr Newton during the police court proceedings was that Wood had been in the *Eagle* on the night of the murder. After Joseph Lambert's clear evidence that he had met Wood and Emily in there, any attempt to deny this would have been unsustainable. There was, however, no admission that Wood had met Emily before Friday 6 September; and Ellen Lawrence, Florence Smith, Gladys Warren and William Linehan were all closely challenged as to their evidence that they had seen the pair together before that date. None of them would be shaken in their stories but, after intervention from the magistrate, and having initially repeated her evidence from the inquest that she could not recall, Gladys Warren conceded that she had seen Emily with at least six different men during the time they were friends.

The star of the show, apart from Wood, was undoubtedly Robert McCowan, whose presence was felt even when he wasn't in court. Every witness who knew Wood was asked if he walked in an unusual way, as McCowan had claimed he did at the identification parade. Joseph Lambert, Jack Tinkham and William Moss all denied that Wood had a swaggering gait or anything similar and Mr Newton declared that he could produce sixty-five more of Wood's acquaintances who would all say the same thing. Inspector Neil, on the other hand, said in the witness box on 14 November that he had noticed that Wood walked with a 'quick jerk of the shoulders'. Other than referring to Wood's 'peculiar swing of the arm', McCowan had never previously explained what he meant by 'swaggering gait' but, at the police court eight days later, on 22 November, he said that it involved 'a sharp jerk of the shoulder'. Over the next few days, his evidence was much derided by the general public. Ruby Young, herself the subject of much adverse comment, empathised with his isolated position as the only person (outside of the police) to have noticed anything unusual about Wood's manner of walking. In support of her fellow prosecution witness, she provided a written statement to the police on 30 November saying that Wood had 'a decidedly peculiar walk'. By way of explanation she elaborated:

'He generally places his left hand in his pocket when walking and swings his right hand from his side to the front of himself thus causing a movement of the shoulder more than with most men when walking, if both hands are free this is more apparent.' For good measure she also observed that he tended to turn up the collar of his overcoat in cold weather (just like the man seen by McCowan). Returning to the issue of his gait in the police court on 4 December, Ruby said, 'He has a walk unlike that of anybody else...If you are walking with him, or he is coming towards you, you do not notice it so much, but if you are behind him you see that he has a walk of his own...he puts his left hand in his pocket and jerks his right shoulder forward. His brother Charles has a walk similar to him, but not so brisk'. Considering the emphasis on his walk during the proceedings, it is rather a shame that newspaper reporters did not provide regular commentary about it as Wood entered and left the courtroom. The *Morning Leader's* correspondent, however, did report on 13 November that 'the prisoner entered the dock with customary jaunty gait'.

McCowan was very much in Mr Newton's mind when he cross-examined Inspector Neil at the police court and the anonymous letter he had received was clearly the inspiration behind his line of questioning. Apparently believing the allegation that McCowan had virtually been a tramp, with 'a dirty, scraggy, beard', before transforming himself into a respectable police witness, Mr Newton asked Neil if McCowan had worn a beard and had been 'of dirty-looking appearance' when he first saw him.[393] The inspector replied 'No'. Not to be derailed, Mr Newton then asked when McCowan had last been in work and if he had ever had regular employment. Inspector Neil rather took the wind out of the solicitor's sails by saying that he believed McCowan had been eleven years in one situation and it was not long ago since he was in regular employment. It transpired (from McCowan's evidence) that he had spent seventeen years in two jobs. Inspector Neil also denied that McCowan was being kept by the police 'and by no-one else as far as I know'. So much for the anonymous letter but Mr Newton never lost faith in it, as revealed by his *Sunday Express* article of 1924.

Mr Newton had rather more success when cross-examining McCowan over his claim to have been able to see the man exiting number 29 St Paul's Road with the assistance of the electric street lighting. Fully justifying his expensive fees, Mr Newton had established with the Electric Light Department of St Pancras Borough Council that the street lights in St Pauls had been turned off at 4:39am so that it was impossible that they were alight at 4:55am, when McCowan claimed to have been walking along St Paul's Road. Mr Newton set his trap by asking McCowan, 'You swear there were two electric lights in the street when you saw this man?' and McCowan fell head first into it by saying 'Yes'. 'If I were to tell you they were both extinguished before that time' said Mr Newton, barely resisting a lick of the lips, 'what would you say?' McCowan said he would deny it but he was obviously shaken, especially when Mr Newton then asked him if he was aware that the St Pancras Borough Council had recording instruments which showed exactly when the lamps were extinguished. He confessed that he did not know this and, although he stubbornly continued to claim that the lights were on, he was already starting to have second thoughts; soon after leaving the courtroom he would go out and walk from his house to St Paul's Road in order to check his timings. The problem for McCowan was that he had claimed in his statement to police that, when he reached Brewery Road, he heard a Cattle Market clock strike five and, as Brewery Road was only a short walk from 29 St Paul's Road, it was difficult for him to adjust his timings without contradicting his entire story.[394] Consequently, his evidence that he had seen Wood in the glare of the (non-existent) electric lights became the subject of widespread ridicule.

Giving evidence at the police court was also an unpleasant experience for Ruby Young. Now that she was doing more than speaking of Wood's false alibi, by corroborating McCowan's evidence as to his manner of walking, she was fair game; and Mr Newton took the gloves off. With no real thought as to the possible consequences, he asked her directly if she was a prostitute but she refused to answer on the grounds of irrelevance. She was, however, forced to accept that she had been convicted of accosting at Marlborough Street Police Court. Although Inspector Neil had already confirmed she was a prostitute during the inquest, it was still a very public humiliation for the young woman. Yet, she coped. Within days of giving evidence, she sat for a new portrait photograph which was published in both the *London Weekly News* and the *People*, receiving a total payment of £7 for doing so.

At the close of the evidence on behalf of the Treasury, Mr Bros made clear that it was a case that had to go to trial, causing Mr Newton to decide not to call any of the five witnesses he had lined up on behalf of Wood. It is not known who these would have been (although George and James Wood were certainly two of them) but the Treasury had not called either Jack Crabtree or May Campbell, so these two characters played no part in the police court proceedings. As the Treasury had now not called Crabtree at the inquest or at the police court, it seemed that his evidence was simply not believed by them.

Deprived of his witnesses, Mr Newton nevertheless addressed the magistrate in a last desperate attempt to have Wood freed. In doing so, he made a number of concessions. He said that he would not deny that Wood wrote either the rising sun postcard or, more importantly, the fragments of the letter and that it was no part of his case to deny that Wood had an assignation at the *Eagle* with Emily Dimmock at about 10:00pm on the night of the murder (although the evidence was that it took place earlier than this). However, the key point he wanted to make was that he could prove that Wood was back home at midnight so that, with the time of death being placed at around 3:00am, it was basically irrelevant that Wood was the last man known to have been with the deceased. He supposed that the prosecution at a trial would say that Wood must have slipped out after midnight and returned to Camden Town but he contended that this showed 'clearly how people allowed their minds to run riot' and pointed out that Wood's manner was unchanged when he was seen the morning after the murder. The magistrate, he said, was being asked to believe that 'this young man of inoffensive character, this young man of kind, amiable disposition, suddenly, without any motive, became a fiend and murdered this unfortunate woman'. Sir Charles Mathews had asked, when opening for the Treasury, 'May not the robbery have been a fake adopted by the assailant? May not the assailant have thought that it would be prudent to leave behind an apparent motive for his crime?' According to Mr Newton, however, 'It was obviously a low, common, vulgar, foul, murder for the sake of gain, as was suggested by the theft of jewellery.' Warming to his theme, Mr

Newton continued, 'Never, so far as I know, has a man been put on trial on unsubstantial and circumstantial evidence, without any motive.' He was able to point to another suspect (i.e. 'Scotch Bob'), saying, 'Now there was a man who had contracted a terrible disease from the woman, and that, of course, would supply a very strong motive to such a person.' Against Wood, he said, 'the only evidence was that he had tried to avoid a scandal.' Consequently, Mr Newton asked Mr Bros not to send 'this very respectable young man' to trial but his pleading was to no avail; Mr Bros said that a jury needed to decide the issues so Wood was formally charged with Emily Dimmock's murder and 'fullered', the slang term for being fully committed to trial.

While the proceedings were in progress at Clerkenwell Police Court, there was a little drama being played out at the Mansion House Police Court. When charged with being a lunatic on 13 November, a man from Ilford called John Linn, who had shown signs of insanity while being treated for a hernia at St Bartholomew's Hospital, told the magistrate, Sir Horatio Davies, that he had proof Wood was innocent of Emily Dimmock's murder. It seems that Linn had overheard one James Pitcher, another patient in the hospital, wondering aloud if a female neighbour of his, who was regularly visited by a sailor, was Emily Dimmock. For some reason, as a result of this, Linn got it into his head that the sailor was guilty of murdering Emily and that Wood was, therefore, innocent. The magistrate was satisfied that Linn was of unsound mind but he thought it prudent to inform the police of his allegations. In view of the fact that the report had come from Sir Horatio, Inspector Neil personally carried out the subsequent investigation, discovering from James Pitcher that the woman he had mentioned was not, in fact, Emily Dimmock. After speaking to Linn's doctors, the inspector quickly, and correctly, concluded that Linn was insane and no further action was taken.

So there was nothing to prevent Wood going forward to trial but there was still one more hurdle for the Treasury to overcome. The case had to go before a grand jury for a 'true bill' to be found against Wood at the opening of the sessions at the Central Criminal Court on 10 December. The City Recorder, Sir Forrest Fulton, outlined the case against Wood whom he described as 'aged 28, artist, superior education' although he was, as we now know, actually 30 years old. The recorder said that it was 'a case of most serious description' and that the circumstances were such that 'it is necessary that it should take considerable time to investigate'. Ignoring, or unaware of the evidence of Dr Thompson at the police court, Sir Forrest said that the injuries 'must have been caused by a man of considerable power and strength'. As to the appearance of robbery, he said that it seemed 'impossible that mere robbery of paltry trinkets could have been the motive for murder by a man like Wood' but he pointed out that 'there might be a suggestion that they were taken to suggest a robbery'. Ominously for the prosecution, he added that 'The motive of the murder is undisclosed by any documents or evidence I have yet seen'. However, the grand jury only needed to agree that there was a prima facie case against Wood and the recorder stated that 'there was an abundance of evidence to justify the jury in returning a true bill in order that the case might be fully investigated'. It was rare for a grand jury to throw a case out at this stage and it did indeed find a true bill against the prisoner.

In advance of the trial, Arthur Newton had taken advantage of the fact that Wood's fees were being paid by his employers and instructed the expensive Sir Edward Marshall Hall to conduct Wood's defence. He was one of the most famous barristers in the land but, oddly enough, he first came to national prominence in a court case not through his own success as an advocate but as a result of his wife's death at the hands of a conman. Albert Laerman had pretended to be a doctor and performed an illegal abortion on Mrs Grace Ethel Hall which killed her. As a result, Laerman was charged with murder and found guilty of manslaughter before Mr Justice Grantham at the Central Criminal Court on 2 August 1890. The lead prosecutor was none other than Charles Mathews. Marshall Hall was not the father of the unborn baby; he had been separated from his wife and she had taken a lover. The whole affair was mired in scandal and the official proceedings of the Old Bailey deemed the details of the case as not fit for publication.

At the time of his wife's death, Marshall Hall was enjoying a growing reputation as a barrister-at-law in Brighton and the south-east but grabbed wider attention when he was instructed by Arthur Newton to defend Marie Hermann in 1894 and somehow managed to help her escape a murder conviction, making a powerful appeal to the jury in his closing speech. The *Brighton Gazette and Sussex Telegraph* of 9 June 1894 spoke of his 'brilliant defence' in that case and said that he was 'fast coming to the front in his profession'. It described him as 'an indefatigable worker' who 'fights his clients' causes with dogged persistence'. Not only that but he had a 'fine physique' and was 'one of the handsomest men at the Bar'. Lewis Broad, in his 1958 book *Advocates of the Golden Age*, similarly described him as 'a finely built man, standing over six feet high, handsome of face, gifted as an actor, with expressive features and a voice of admirable tone' while Sir Charles Rentoul praised his 'figure and gait of an athlete' and his 'finely shaped head, silver hair, piercing eyes and aquiline features'. He was also said to be 'generous and great-hearted' but also 'hot-tempered, truculent and egotistical'.[395] If there was one aspect of Marshall Hall's character, however, that singled him out above his contemporaries, it was his almost complete lack of fear of the formidable judges he faced on a daily basis, combined with an effortless ability to treat them with both respect and disdain at the same time. 'I am perfectly content to leave the matter to your Lordship. I have absolute confidence in your Lordship' he might say to a judge, while the laughter in court would betray the meaning of his words to be the direct opposite.

It was his very fearlessness, however, which almost caused his downfall in 1901 when he unwisely stood up to a roasting in the Court of Appeal from Lord Justice Mathew, who described a remark in one of his closing speeches during a libel action as 'shocking'. The resulting damage to his reputation and loss of instructions over the next six years nearly bankrupted him and, in May 1907, he was forced to auction off his silver collection at Christies, although the £5,000 he received for it was adequate compensation. By this time he was slowly building up his practice again. Most of May 1907 was spent unsuccessfully attempting to defend one of nine Guardians of the Poor of West Ham Union accused of corruption in a long trial at the Central Criminal Court. His client, Lewis George Hill, was sentenced to two years imprisonment with hard labour but the most notable aspect of the trial was that one of his two juniors was John

Wellesley Orr, a 28-year-old barrister originally from Lancashire, who features later in this story.

In June 1907, some 'classic' Marshall Hall advocacy could be seen in his cross-examination of a police officer at the County of London Sessions when defending Joseph and Ellen Down who were appealing a conviction for assisting in the management of a brothel near Regent's Park. Sergeant Lovelock and Constable Hodder had supposedly kept watch on the Downs' residence over a period of eight days, recording forty-eight couples admitted to the house. Marshall Hall tormented the sergeant, first pointing out that he had given evidence in no less than fifty-eight similar cases and that 'It is a curious fact that in all of the cases you have been in, the number of couples in a week is always somewhere between 40 or 50'.[396] Sergeant Lovelock was unsure about this but Marshall Hall reminded him that the magistrate at the Marylebone Police Court had commented that 'It strikes me there are always about 40 or more couples'. The barrister then asked the sergeant if he had ever made a mistake: 'I may have done' came the reply and Marshall Hall was happily able to provide an example, reminding Lovelock that he had previously cross-examined him in a case where he and P.C. Hodder had both sworn positively that a man was carrying out business as a bookmaker in a public house in Piccadilly when he was, in fact, a respectable jeweller. Despite this, the police officers insisted that their observations of the Downs' residence had been correct and the conviction was upheld.[397]

In between Wood's appearances at Clerkenwell Police Court during the first two weeks of November 1907, Marshall Hall was busy defending a stockbroker, Charles Wilbraham Perryman, on various charges of fraud at the Central Criminal Court. One of his juniors for the trial was none other than Sir Charles Mathews (Marshall Hall, being a silk, outranked him) but their joint efforts were unsuccessful and their client was sentenced to two years behind bars. Junior Counsel for one of Perryman's business associates, who was also found guilty of fraud, was Mr Wellesley Orr.

A week before the start of Wood's trial, Marshall Hall found himself at Chelmsford Assizes defending farmer Herbert Wyndham Stride on a charge of stealing pheasants' eggs. He was again unsuccessful in his efforts and Stride was convicted. The judge at this trial was the 72-year-old Mr Justice Grantham, a cantankerous old man and a notorious reactionary, known for outlandish remarks, such as 'It is time that some of these publicans were strung up by the neck' and 'A husband in certain circumstances is entitled to box his wife's ears'. As we have seen, Justice Grantham was also an outspoken opponent of the forthcoming Criminal Court of Appeal. At the same time, he had shown himself to be on a prisoner's side on at least one famous occasion when his nagging doubts as to the guilt of the unfairly persecuted Alfred Beck played a part in Beck's eventual acquittal and pardon; he held off from sending him to prison after he was convicted in 1904 which allowed time for further investigations, resulting in the innocent Beck being released. Like Marshall Hall, Justice Grantham would soon return to London for the biggest show in town.

A contemporary sketch of Robert McCowan

A contemporary sketch of Sir Charles Mathews

Chapter Fourteen

Trial

'It has been a live page torn ruthlessly from the quivering book of life – a page, therefore, that necessarily contains contradictions in character, evasions, passionate vices and virtues, extreme peril and hazardous escape.'

The Tribune, commenting on the trial of Robert Wood, 19 December 1907

The Central Criminal Court of London was a brand new building, less than a year old, having replaced the previous Sessions House known as the Old Bailey. It was not to everyone's taste, with a grumpy Justice Grantham, unhappy with a noisy ventilation and poor heating system, saying, 'the sooner this place is pulled down the better'.[398] But there was another issue with the new court: what to call it? For many, the answer was both simple and obvious: The New Bailey! Thus, the *Evening News* of 11 December 1907 carried the headline 'Arrangements for Wood's Trial at the New Bailey' while the *Daily Mirror* of 12 December stated that the 'Trial of Young Artist Wood Opens at New Bailey To-day'. Most newspapers, however, continued to refer to the more traditional Old Bailey but there was confusion about it in the public mind and even in the minds of those involved in enforcing the law, as evidenced by an exchange between a constable and officials at the Guildhall Police Court in September 1907. The constable, in giving evidence, said he arrested a prisoner 'at the door of the New Bailey' and was corrected by the Chief Clerk who said, 'You mean Old Bailey'. The constable stood his ground, insisting he meant the New Bailey, and the Alderman, Sir Vesey Strong, chipped in with the conclusion 'Oh, never mind, call it the Central Criminal Court!' producing laughter in court.[399] According to the legal journal, *Law Notes*, however, to refer to the new Central Criminal Court as the 'New Bailey' was 'hopelessly wrong'.[400] The journal pointed out that the old court was named the Old Bailey after the street in which it stood and, as the new court remained in the same street, it should still be referred to as the Old Bailey.

The trial of Robert Wood commenced in the number one court of what we can conclude was indeed the Old Bailey on 12 December 1907. It was expected to last three days but went on for double that amount of time. The court had never seen such a demand for admittance and the Under Sheriff was reported to have been inundated with applications. The public gallery could admit between 250 and 300 people but this was nowhere near enough to satisfy the numbers who wanted to attend. It was not just ordinary members of the public either; plenty of celebrities wanted to follow the trial at first hand. Two famous actresses, Gertie Millar and the beautiful Lily Elsie, had already visited Clerkenwell for one of the hearings at the police court as had the novelist and playwright, Hall Caine, whose new version of *The Christian* – which took the issue of prostitution as one of its themes – had been one of the most talked about plays of the year after being staged at the Lyceum Theatre in September. Hall Caine was present at the Old Bailey for most of the trial and other famous personalities who attended included George R. Sims (writer and playwright),

Seymour Hicks (actor and playwright), Frank Curzon (theatrical manager), A.W. Pinero (playwright), H.B. Irving (actor), Mrs Beerbohm Tree (actress), Gerald de Maurier (actor) and a number of members of parliament.

Although Wood had been safely locked up in Brixton Prison since 7 October, his voice had been heard by the British public during November through his art. On 13 November, an artistic journal, *The Sketch*, had published two 'clever drawings' by Wood (as they were described by the *Star*), one of which was reproduced in the *Star* of 13 November and the other in the *People* of 17 November. Accompanying the drawings was a letter dated 6 November 1907 from Wood's brother which stated, in terms bordering on *sub judice*, 'These are the work of Robert Wood, who is falsely charged with the Camden Town crime, and they have been executed by him in Brixton Prison within the past day or two'. The text of this letter was also reproduced in the *Penny Illustrated Paper and Illustrated Times* of 23 November. The *News of the World* on 17 November also carried a sketch by Wood which directly impinged upon the legal proceedings. It was Wood's brilliant drawing, mentioned earlier, of himself in the police line-up at Highgate, looking thoroughly conspicuous in his suit and bowler hat with other men in the line-up looking straight at him. Anyone reading the *News of the World* that day would have understood how someone could have picked Wood out from the line-up even if they had never actually seen him before. So Wood was not only being shown to be a talented artist but the concept that he was innocent was being subtly, or not so subtly, implanted in the public mind.

On the eve of the trial, the *Star* had some exclusive information about 'an important new witness' who was likely to be called to give evidence on behalf of the prosecution, stated to be the man known as 'Scotch Bob' or 'Scotch Jock'. This information was accurate to the extent that a Scottish kitchen porter called Alexander Mackie had, a few days before the start of the trial, supposedly seen mention in a Glasgow newspaper of the fact that 'Scotch Bob' was said to be acquainted with Emily Dimmock and had immediately travelled to London to make a statement to the police, confessing that he was known as 'Scotch Bob' and was acquainted with the deceased. That statement does not survive in the Metropolitan Police file and it is unclear if he was also claiming to have been known as 'Scotch Jock'. Mackie said he had not been in London since September 1906 and had been working as a kitchen porter in Scotland at the time of Emily's murder. He was in court on the second day of the trial and was described as 'a sturdy, heavy featured young man'.[401] As he could not have committed the murder of Emily Dimmock, due to a cast iron alibi from having been working in Scotland at the time, his appearance was very helpful to the prosecution in that it focused attention back on Wood as the prime suspect.

The trial of *Rex v. Wood* commenced at 10:30am in the number one court of the Old Bailey. The prisoner was called and a smartly dressed Wood walked confidently up the stairs to the large dock 'with his hands in his coat pockets' and a warder on either side of him.[402] According to the reporter for the *Pall Mall Gazette*, he seemed, at first glance, 'curiously unconcerned' as he 'leaned easily on the rail of the dock and surveyed the scene around him'.[403] The *Star's* reporter noted that he had 'a faint smile flickering over his sharp features, and faced the Court with serene, but keen, composure'. Asked by the Clerk of Arraigns how he pleaded to the charge of murder, Wood replied 'Not guilty, sir' in what one newspaper described as 'a pleasantly-toned clear voice' but another preferred to call 'quiet but firm tones'.[404] The jury was then sworn while Wood stood in the dock 'with his left hand in his coat pocket and the right resting on the ledge of the dock'.[405] Marshall Hall attracted some comment amongst the press reporters by, unusually, challenging two jurors who were both forced to step down, with no explanation provided for the objection.[406] The twelve jurors that were sworn became the subject of some adverse comment from the press. The *Daily Mirror*'s reporter described them, harmlessly enough, as 'plain, unpretentious, matter-of-fact looking citizens' but the journalist from the *Evening News* was rather more severe, remarking that they were 'very ordinary-looking citizens who appeared to be wondering how the shop was going while they were away'.[407] This piece of journalism was to bring a stern rebuke next day from the judge who called it 'a very great insult' towards men who 'sacrifice a great deal of their time in assisting in the administration of justice and who, I am sure, are not ashamed to say that they are leaving their shops behind...while they are doing their country's work'. The judge clearly thought they looked like shop owners too.

After a two-hour opening speech from Sir Charles Mathews, during which Wood sat in the dock 'with his legs crossed, and one hand in his coat pocket', the first of thirty-three prosecution witnesses took to the stand.[408] It is in the cross-examination of these witnesses, or at least the key witnesses from the thirty-three, that Marshall Hall has earned much of his reputation as the most successful defence barrister of his day but, as we shall see, he was not always as effective as he has been portrayed. His greatest success, however, was undoubtedly in neutralising the evidence of Robert McCowan.

Since his appearance at the police court, McCowan had timed his walk from his home in Hawley Street to St Paul's Road, discovering that he could manage the distance in eight minutes rather than the fifteen he had originally estimated. Consequently, he claimed that he must have seen the man with the swaggering gait at 4:48am in the glare of the street lights. This did not assist his cause because the defence called evidence from William Brown of the Electric Light Department of the St Pancras Borough Council which proved that the street lights were turned off at 4:40am at the latest (consistent with what Arthur Newton had told McCowan at the police court).[409] Surprisingly, Marshall Hall asked Brown 'Is it possible they could have been alight at 4.55?' to which Brown answered 'No' and then again in re-examination he asked him the same question: 'Could the lights possibly have been lit at five minutes to five?' to which Brown responded 'No, it is quite impossible'. For such a highly paid and respected barrister as Marshall Hall, who now needed to establish that the lights were off at 4:48, it is astonishing that he asked the wrong question twice. It was left to the rather more alert judge to ask 'Could they have been alight at 4.48?' to which the man from the lighting department said 'No.'

Having dealt with the time of the incident, the next part of Marshall Hall's cross-examination of McCowan did not quite work. McCowan had described the morning of 12 September as 'drizzly, thick, muggy' but the defence team had established from the weather records that no rain fell in London that day. Marshall Hall was ready to pounce on the discrepancy but McCowan explained that, where he came from, 'drizzly' did not actually involve rain falling. Marshall Hall sounded incredulous but could not challenge it, not having evidence to hand about the Suffolk dialect. He moved on quickly to a problem with McCowan's statement.

When Sergeant Ball took the statement, he had written that McCowan said, 'I looked round and saw a man coming down the steps of number 29'. McCowan's evidence-in-chief had been that he heard footsteps behind him and 'turned and saw a man leaving the gate and going down the road' – in which case he had not seen him coming down the steps. His response to this discrepancy was that, when he signed his statement (which had been read over to him by Sergeant Ball), he was 'not so fly' (or alert) as he was now that he was being cross-examined in court and said that 'I did not listen particularly to what was read over to me'. This allowed Marshall Hall to score his first big point, asking with scorn, 'Have you no regard for human life?' and then, with astonishment, 'Thinking a man you were going to identify was a murderer, you took no notice of what was read over to you?'

Furthermore, Marshall Hall managed to establish from McCowan that he did not know that the man with the swaggering gait, whom he had supposedly seen coming out of a gate in St Paul's Road, had come out of the gate of number 29. Asked, 'You did not see the number that morning?', McCowan replied, 'No, I saw in the papers that the number of the house was 29'. This was the most extraordinary response from the witness. Having previously sworn to the coroner that he was sure the man he had seen had emerged from number 29, he was now admitting that he only gleaned the house number from the next morning's newspapers. So the man he saw might have come from any house in the street. McCowan had obviously assumed that, having seen a man walking in the street at that time of the night (or morning), he simply must have been the man who murdered Emily Dimmock. Marshall Hall subsequently managed to get McCowan to confirm that he had not seen the man exit the gate but had only assumed he had done so because he heard the gate click, something he had never mentioned before. Marshall Hall then asked, 'Did you see the man come out of number 29?' and McCowan replied, 'No, I saw him after he was out'. It was a remarkable shift of evidence from such an important prosecution witness.

The other controversial aspect of McCowan's evidence attacked by Marshall Hall was in respect of the build of the man with the swaggering gait. As McCowan had said this man was of 'stiff build with broad shoulders', Marshall Hall invited Wood to stand up in court and challenged McCowan to describe him as broad-shouldered, bringing the response 'He has broader shoulders than I have'. Marshall Hall then famously, and rhetorically, asked him if he would describe a bluebottle as an elephant because it is bigger than a fly. It was an attention grabbing question but he wasn't being entirely fair to McCowan. A few minutes earlier, while dealing with the build of the man with the swaggering gait, Marshall Hall had asked, 'Was the man as broad across the shoulders as yourself?' to which McCowan had replied that he was 'a trifle broader than myself'. So when Marshall Hall subsequently asked the witness if he would describe Wood as broad-shouldered, McCowan's response that he had 'broader shoulders than I have' was precisely to the point because this is how he had described the man with the swaggering gait. At the same time, it was not a direct response to Marshall Hall's question and no-one else in court, including the police, would have described the slim Wood as broad-shouldered. In fact, when Detective Sergeant Ball was asked directly in the witness box if Wood was broad-shouldered he said, 'I should describe him as a rather slight man' although he hastened to add that he was 'broad-shouldered in proportion to size', whatever that meant. McCowan himself grabbed at a lifeline by suggesting that the overcoat worn by the man might have made him appear bigger than he actually was; so Wood was asked by the judge to put on his overcoat in court but it made no difference.[410]

Concluding his cross-examination of McCowan, Marshall Hall advanced a theory that he had been able to identify Wood in the identification parade at Kentish Town because he had read the newspaper accounts of the police's prime suspect having worn a blue serge suit and Wood was the only man wearing one. McCowan's response was that he had not read a newspaper description of the suspect before identifying Wood and, moreover, that there was another man wearing a blue serge suit in the line-up whom he did not select. When Marshall Hall put it directly to McCowan that he was either mistaken or lying about his evidence, this produced an indignant denial from the witness, followed by a string of complaints that he had received threatening letters, that the phrase 'blood money' had been chalked on his door and that his children had been bullied at school. 'In future', he said, 'even if I actually saw with my own eyes a man getting his throat cut I do not think I would give evidence again'. This brought a blustered response from the judge that 'If any more of this kind of thing goes on I shall do my best to find out where it comes from', although how he proposed to do this was not made clear and his powers to do anything about it were limited at best. After McCowan said in cross-examination that he had worked for the Aerated Bread Company for twelve years and had served in the army for sixteen years, leaving with the best possible character, Marshall Hall, sensing that the jury might have sympathy for him, decided that it would be a good idea to clarify that he had not actually attacked McCowan's integrity, commenting that 'The best man in the world might be an untrustworthy witness'.

McCowan was evidently an unreliable witness but Arthur Newton's theory, based on the anonymous letter, that he was a police stooge was dead in the water. Indeed, when it came to his speech to the jury at the close of the prosecution case, Marshall Hall submitted that McCowan made an 'honest mistake' (although he also described his evidence as 'the flimsiest and most unsatisfactory evidence ever put before a jury in any Court of justice in the world'). During his cross-examination of McCowan, Marshall Hall had started to question along the lines of what might be called Newton's theory of duplicity, asking him when he had last loaded a bread van for the V.V. Bread Company, presumably expecting the answer to have been 'never'. On being told that it was, in fact, on the morning of 11 September, the day before the murder, that line of questioning was immediately dropped.

As for who it was that McCowan had seen in St Paul's Road during the early hours of the morning of 12 September, the answer was provided by a broad-shouldered seventeen-year-old ticket collector employed by the City and South London Railway who lived at number 26 St Paul's Road. His full name was John William Westcott (although he was known as William Westcott). After discussing the case at a photographic shop, he had been persuaded by the photographer to provide a statement to Wood's lawyers, which he did on

Sunday 15 December, two days after McCowan had given evidence at the trial. He said that, although he was supposed to be at work at King's Cross tube station at 5:00am, with the first train due at 5:35am and the first ticket collection a few minutes later, he usually left his house at 4:55am and arrived a little late at the station. As long as he arrived by quarter past five he explained, he would still be booked in as having arrived at five o'clock.[411] The walk from St Paul's Road to King's Cross took him about twenty minutes which enabled him to arrive at work by 5:15am and thus avoid being disciplined for lateness. On the morning of 12 September, he said he left his house at five minutes to five as usual and saw a man walking in the direction of Brewery Road (where the V.V. Bread Company was situated). He was a little suspicious of this man, being worried that he might steal the poultry and pigeons he kept at the back of the house, but he could not stop because he was already late for work. Most significantly, Westcott told the Old Bailey, 'I am conscious that I have a peculiar walk....After watching the man I started off at a swinging walk. I always swing my arm when I am in a hurry'. By way of further, and perhaps alternative, explanation he said that he was an amateur boxer and had been told that 'a swing of the arm is good for the chest' hence his peculiar walk. As if to put the icing on the cake of his identification of himself as the man McCowan had seen, he added that he was dressed in a long dark blue overcoat, with his collar turned up, and wearing a bowler hat at the time.

In some ways, Westcott's evidence was almost too perfect. It was, without doubt, remarkably convenient for Wood. Against Westcott, it could be said that he failed to provide a convincing answer as to why he had not come forward before 15 December, despite knowing (as he admitted) of the coroner's inquest and the police court proceedings. On the other hand, there was no challenge from Sir Charles Mathews that Westcott lived at 26 St Paul's Road and worked the early shift at King's Cross Station. Had he been lying about this, it would certainly have been exposed after reports of his testimony were published in all the local and national newspapers, not to mention that it would have been easy for the police to check. Moreover, some corroboration of his address is provided in the 1906 and 1908 electoral registers which show that Thomas Westcott, William's brother, resided at 26 St Paul's Road. This information is confirmed by the 1911 census which states that Annie Westcott, a widowed boarding house keeper, was living at 26 St Paul's Road with two of her three sons, Thomas and Albert; William had presumably moved elsewhere by this time. Westcott's evidence was also corroborated by a fellow resident of 26 St Paul's Road, Francis George Varney, who not only said that he woke Westcott up at 4:15am on the morning of 12 September but that 'I have noticed that Westcott has a jerk of his shoulders and a peculiar twitching movement when he walks fast'.[412]

So we have a broad-shouldered man with a peculiar walk wearing an overcoat and bowler hat leaving his house in St Paul's Road at precisely the time that McCowan (initially) said that he saw a broad-shouldered man with a peculiar walk wearing an overcoat and bowler hat in St Paul's Road. If ever there was a case closed, this is it. The only real discrepancy is that number 26 was on the opposite side of the road to number 29, some 260 yards away, but it was both dark and early in the morning and it was clear that McCowan did not really have a good grasp of exactly which house the man had emerged from:

his evidence evidently being corrupted by what he had read in the newspapers the next day. Until he learnt of Emily Dimmock's death, he would have had no reason to think again about the man he saw in St Paul's Road and, after the passage of 24 hours, could easily have muddled up in his head precisely where in the road he was at the time he saw him. He did not give his statement to the police until Saturday 14 September by which time 48 hours had elapsed and any images he had retained of the man with the swaggering gait were probably already fast disappearing from his memory.

The irony is that McCowan amended his evidence to say that he was in St Paul's Road at 4:48am, when Westcott appears to have left his house at 4:55am, the exact time McCowan originally claimed he saw the man. The explanation for this may be that the clock McCowan used to check the time he left his house in Hawley Street was slow and he really left at 4:47am or thereabouts, rather than 4:40am as he believed. This would, of course, mean that the street lights must have been turned off at the time of the sighting, despite McCowan's certainty that they were on when he saw the man.

An alternative explanation, which allows the lights to have been on, is that Westcott left 26 St Paul's Road fifteen minutes earlier than he claimed in court in order to get to work on time. The documentation at King's Cross Station presumably showed him as being booked in at 5:00am which, if (despite Westcott's evidence) was a true record of his time of arrival, must have meant that he left his house at about 4:40am, when the street lights could have been on. One has to wonder if he really did depart at that time but, at Arthur Newton's prompting, gilded the lily by saying that it was 4:55am in order to correspond with McCowan's evidence (at least as it had originally been). For, in truth, there was even less reason for Westcott to be able to recall the events of the early hours of 12 September when he gave his statement to the defence, over three months later, than there was for McCowan when he gave his statement to the police a couple of days later. Westcott might have seen a man walking along the road on one occasion and thought he looked suspicious but how could he be so sure it was on 12 September? And, even if he accurately remembered seeing a man on this date, how could he be sure he left his house at 4:55 that particular morning? By 15 December, Wood was at the height of his popularity and many people were desperately hoping he would be acquitted. For that reason, Westcott might have been perfectly happy to assist in the process of ensuring his acquittal by agreeing that he was in St Paul's Road at 4:55am on 12 September and saw McCowan on his way to work.

Ultimately, Westcott's memories are not really important. His true importance to the case is the simple fact that he lived in St Paul's Road and had to leave for work in the early hours, between about 4:40am and 4:55am, in order to reach King's Cross at some time between 5:00am and 5:15am. This was unchallenged by Sir Charles Mathews, which it would certainly not have been if it had even been suspected to have been a fabrication. The Metropolitan Police had sufficient resources to investigate the story but there was not even a hint that Westcott was lying about where he lived or worked. Consequently, on this fact alone, Westcott would have to be a prime candidate for being the man seen by McCowan, regardless of whether Westcott remembered the incident or not. We might be suspicious of Westcott's remarkably convenient claim that he had a peculiar walk, which seems to clinch the identification, but, as we have seen, this part of his evidence was corroborated by Francis Varney and, furthermore, Westcott gave a demonstration of his walk to the judge and jury on the floor of the Old Bailey. So there are very good reasons to believe that Westcott was indeed the man seen by McCowan.

When it came to his closing speech on behalf of the prosecution, Sir Charles dealt with Westcott's evidence by completely ignoring it, preferring to ask the jury not to doubt McCowan's story. In doing so, Sir Charles focused on the attacks that had been made on McCowan outside of court, presumably hoping that the jury would thereby be more sympathetic to him, but they were irrelevant to any questions the jury had to decide. As for the attacks made on his credibility in court by Marshall Hall, Sir Charles insisted that they were groundless but said precisely nothing about the possibility that McCowan had simply been mistaken, which he almost certainly was.

That being so, the detailed questioning during the trial to establish whether there was anything unusual about Wood's walk was a waste of time. Yet, for the duration of the trial, it was one of the most important issues in the case, bitterly fought over by both sides. When Ruby Young informed the court that Wood 'walked with his left hand in his pocket and brought the right shoulder forward' she might as well have been accusing him of having committed the murder, such was the outrage that followed. She had support, however, from Inspector William Carpenter of Kentish Town Police Station who had witnessed McCowan's identification of Wood from his walk. He said in evidence that he had noticed that Wood 'had his left hand in his jacket pocket, with his left shoulder forward, and as he walked he swung his right arm'. On the other hand, Wood's entire family, along with his work colleagues, all denied there was anything unusual in his walk and, as at the police court, Marshall Hall claimed that he had sixty-five witnesses lined up who would all say the same thing (but, mercifully, Sir Charles accepted that this was their genuine belief so that they did not need to appear in court).

There might have been an element of partisanship about some of the evidence provided for the defence. James Wood denied his half-brother had a habit of carrying his left hand in his pocket, or at least said he had never noticed it. Charles Wood similarly said he had never noticed such a thing although he admitted it was possible. George Wood, however, told the court that, as a consequence of the two defective fingers on his left hand, his son 'sometimes carried his hand in his left pocket'. This was just as Ruby Young had said, so the only real dispute was whether he brought his right shoulder forward when he walked. In any other context, this would hardly be worth debating but, in the tense adversarial atmosphere of the trial, it had taken on significance far in excess of its real worth. Ruby might well have noticed a slight movement of her lover's shoulder which others had missed but one which was probably better described as 'distinctive' rather than 'peculiar'. Many people have a distinctive walk and, no doubt, did in 1907, but that does not mean they were all in St Paul's Road during the early hours of 12 September.

If Westcott was the man seen by McCowan then the whole issue of Wood's overcoat also falls away. During the trial, however, it remained another hotly contested point, with the prosecution insisting that Wood was the man wearing an overcoat seen by McCowan, despite the fact that Joseph Lambert, a witness for the prosecution, insisted that Wood was not wearing, or in possession of, an overcoat when he was chatting to him in the *Eagle* on the Wednesday night. Lambert was a witness of unimpeachable character so that alone should have disposed of the issue, especially as the prosecution had no counter evidence from anyone that Wood had been wearing, or carrying, an overcoat during the evening of the murder and had to rely on the mere fact that (according to Inspector Neil) his coat was hanging on the door in his room in October which, even if true – and this was disputed by Wood's family – goes nowhere near to proving that Wood had worn it at any time in September. Recognising the strength of the evidence against Wood wearing an overcoat during the Wednesday evening, Sir Charles put forward a desperate theory during his final address to the jury, or rather he asked a ludicrous question. 'As to the overcoat', he said, 'is it not possible that the prisoner took Dimmock home and then returned for his overcoat?' Anything is possible, of course, but one would have to retort with another question: why would Wood, or anyone, have taken Dimmock home and then returned to his own home some thirty minutes' walk away to collect his overcoat before returning to St Paul's Road? It wasn't even as if it was a cold, or even cool, evening which might have made Wood feel it was essential for him to have it. And the question as phrased by Sir Charles was not even complete. Presumably what he was trying to ask was: 'Is it not possible that the prisoner took Dimmock home and then returned to Frederick Street for his overcoat and then returned to Dimmock's home and then killed her?' Not only would it have been strange behaviour but Sir Charles' question actually undermined the prosecution's case which was based in large part on Wood being the last man to have seen Emily alive due to his having met her in the *Eagle*. If the prosecution was now saying that Wood parted from Emily during the evening, after meeting her at the *Eagle*, and returned to Frederick Street, this precisely matched what the defence was saying had happened – except that it was no part of the defence case that Wood ever returned to St Paul's Road (of which there was no evidence). Once it was accepted that Wood had left Camden Town at any point after meeting Emily in the *Eagle* then there was really no more reason to suspect him of killing Emily than any of her other male acquaintances, apart from, perhaps, his subsequent attempt to concoct a false alibi.

Sir Charles must have recognised the problem but there was no way around it. He had no choice but to stick with the theory that McCowan had seen the murderer leaving St Paul's Road and, thus, that the man he saw must have been Wood. If he abandoned this theory, and accepted that McCowan had really seen Westcott, or someone else, or no-one, then he had nothing at all linking Wood with St Paul's Road, which would have completely destroyed his case. Yet, at the same time, he had to concede that Wood did not have an overcoat with him when he met Emily in the *Eagle*. So he had to have Wood leaving the scene of the crime, as it were, before the crime had even been committed, before returning to it, overcoat in hand or over shoulders, in order to see Emily again and kill her. And this scenario did not work.

The battle of wits engaged in by Marshall Hall with McCowan was probably only matched by his crossing of swords with Jack Crabtree. For, yes, the prosecution had decided to call the incorrigible old rogue, now released from Pentonville, to give evidence against Wood at the trial. It must have been a close call. On the one hand, he was a convicted ex-prisoner whom the prosecution knew would be able to speak of another man who had threatened to murder Emily, which was obviously unhelpful to the prosecution, yet he was also able to give direct evidence of a close relationship between Wood and Emily stretching back to early 1906. The existence or otherwise of this long relationship became another central theme of the trial, as it had been of the police investigation. On one view, however, this supposed relationship was wholly irrelevant. Wood could have known Emily for his entire life but that would hardly be evidence that he had murdered her. Equally he could have met her for the first time on 6 September (as he claimed), or even later, and still have killed her. At best, the existence of a physical or emotional relationship between the two before September 1907 would have provided some weak support for the prosecution case on the basis that Wood might have had more of a motive to commit murder. We will deal with the problems faced by the prosecution in establishing a motive later but it is clear that *any* evidence that would support a prior relationship between Wood and Emily was regarded as extremely valuable by the prosecution and they were prepared to risk putting Crabtree in front of Marshall Hall to get that evidence before a jury.

Thus, Crabtree was invited to court number one in order to tell his story of seeing Wood arguing with Emily at 1 Bidborough Street and then of being asked to pawn Wood's silver cigarette case while the couple were in bed together. He also told of seeing Wood at 13 Manchester Street and, for the first time, claimed that Wood had made enquiries after Emily while she was at Portsmouth. He was not, however, asked by Sir Charles Mathews to tell the long story of his pursuit of Emily around north London while she was supposedly accompanied by Wood.

Whether Justice Grantham recognised Crabtree while he gave his evidence is not known but he had, it will be recalled, sentenced him to a three-year term of imprisonment at the Durham Assizes back in 1903. Crabtree's known criminal record in England stretching back to 1901 was the first thing Marshall Hall wanted to ask him about during cross-examination. After establishing that he had spent most of the previous six years in prison, Marshall Hall asked him if he lived an honest life, prompting a smirking Crabtree to respond: 'I have lived for fifty-six years and have only been in prison three times' which produced laughter in court and a rebuke from Marshall Hall for treating the matter with levity, which in turn brought a counter rebuke from Crabtree that Counsel was trying to make fun of him. In fact, Crabtree was playing his own private little game. As he well knew, he had been in prison rather more than three times in his life. It wasn't just that he had been in prison four times in England but he was probably New Zealand's most notorious former prisoner, although no-one in the courtroom was aware of this. He had successfully hidden his real identity and this might be why he ostentatiously claimed he was 56 when he was really only 47. Marshall Hall then asked, 'Has any competent expert ever inquired into your mental condition?' Crabtree answered, 'Not that I am aware of' and Marshall Hall decided to leave it at that. No-one at the time, outside of the defence team, knew the purpose of this question but Arthur Newton had obviously done his research on Crabtree, discovering his attempt to feign madness in Wakefield in 1901 and his subsequent examination by Dr Clarke who had concluded he was faking. Crabtree was well aware of this so it was just another lie he was telling.

Perhaps the greatest success of Marshall Hall's cross-examination, albeit unintended, was in getting Crabtree to confess that the police 'frightened the life' out of him when they visited him for the first time in Pentonville because 'at first I thought they wanted me for the murder'. Although Crabtree was in prison at the time of the murder and thus had a rock solid alibi, this confession might have put an element of doubt into the minds of the jury members regarding the veracity of his evidence on the basis that he might have invented stories about other men to clear himself. Marshall Hall had not even been digging for this answer. He had simply wanted to know how the police had come to see Crabtree in prison and it was in response to this question that Crabtree volunteered the information about having the life frightened out of him. In fact, that information was double edged for Marshall Hall because the real focus of his cross-examination was to elicit the story of the man who had threatened to cut Emily's throat with a razor and there was no point undermining the truth of that story.

For the very first time, Crabtree ascribed a nickname to the man who had previously been known as 'Tom Wilson'. He now called him 'Scottie'. This name had not appeared in either of his two statements nor had it been mentioned in his evidence at the inquest. Faced with this unexpected piece of new information, Marshall Hall asked, 'Do you mean Scotch Bob?' to which Crabtree replied, 'No, this is another one. That is the motor car driver'.[413] It is not entirely clear what Crabtree meant by 'another one'. It is usually assumed to be that he was referring to another Scotsman but Crabtree had never previously said anything about the man being Scottish. The name 'Scottie' obviously suggests someone from Scotland but when Crabtree said 'another one' he might just have meant another suspect.

Although Crabtree's reference to 'the motor car driver' is, on the face of it, ambiguous as to whether he meant Scottie or Scotch Bob, all the reporters who were present in court took him to be saying that Scottie was the motor car driver. The *Times*, for example, reported that 'the witness said he had given the police the description of a man named "Scottie", a motor driver' and the official shorthand record states that Crabtree said 'Scottie is not Scotch Bob; there is another one, a motor driver'. This was the first time Crabtree had mentioned any such thing about his suspect being a motor driver but it is striking that it corresponds with what Mrs Roberts, Emily's landlady at 2 Grafton Road, had told the newspapers back in September (when Crabtree had been in prison and unable to read newspapers). It will be recalled that she said that the man who had threatened to kill Emily had previously taken her for a motor ride. Motorised vehicles had started to appear on England's streets from about 1896 but were still relatively rare in London in 1907, with most forms of private transport still being horse drawn, so it would be quite a coincidence if two different men who had threatened to murder Emily Dimmock had both driven motor cars. It is not, of course, impossible that, since his release from prison, Crabtree had learned of what Mrs Roberts had told the newspapers and adopted her story but there would not have been any advantage to him in doing so because she was not a witness at the trial and what she told reporters had long since been forgotten. During re-examination by Sir Charles, Crabtree said he saw Scottie 'a week ago last Saturday' when he (Scottie) had supposedly said to him, 'Jack, you're a fine chap, trying to put a halter round my neck'.

Asked if he had told the police about this, he said, 'I am not touting for the police. Let them do their own work'.

As it happens, it was another feature of Crabtree's evidence that he was not terribly complimentary about the police. To Marshall Hall he said that 'the police do not tell the truth' and he snapped his fingers, saying, 'I do not care that for the police'. If he ever had any chance of receiving a police reward for giving evidence for the prosecution he probably lost it in that moment. Whereas McCowan was awarded £10 from the Police Informants' Fund after the trial, Crabtree got nothing. He did, however, receive scorn poured down on him by Marshall Hall in his closing speech. 'No one' said Marshall Hall 'can express the horror and contempt I feel for a man like Crabtree' and he called him 'a thing' whose appearance as a witness for the prosecution only went to show the weakness of the prosecution's case. For his own part, in one of the more convincing parts of his evidence, Wood said, 'I hope God will destroy me this moment if I have ever entered a house of his or ever knew him'.

But if Wood did not know Crabtree, had he nevertheless known Emily before September 1907? A string of witnesses were brought to the Old Bailey to say that he had and it was Marshall Hall's job to convince the jury that they were lying or mistaken. It is often said that Marshall Hall was like an actor, and there was certainly an element of the theatrical in his style of advocacy, but it is probably more accurate to say that he resembled a stage magician, attempting to bamboozle his audience with metaphorical sleight of hand and misdirection. It was essential that the credibility of every prosecution witness was undermined in some way, even if they were probably telling the truth. With Ellen Lawrence, who claimed to have once seen Wood and Emily conversing in the *Pindar of Wakefield*, Marshall Hall came up with a novel approach, asking her to explain the origin of her feelings against Wood. When she denied having any such feelings, he asked, 'Then why have you been looking at the prisoner as you have done while giving your evidence?' It was a strange question and Mrs Lawrence responded with reasonable astonishment, saying: 'Good gracious, are not my eyes my own to look round with?' Marshall Hall persisted, saying: 'I am using my eyes, too. Now what is it you have got against him?' Presumably the hope was that by repeating the allegation enough times, the jury would believe it but, if so, he was unlikely to have been successful. He had more success in attacking her character. It wasn't particularly hard because she admitted to having been a prostitute until about 1902. When asked why she went to the *Rising Sun*, she became a little paranoid and complained that Marshall Hall was trying to make her out to be a bad character, to which the barrister famously responded, 'God forbid that I should make you one'. It was a good line but still did not quite explain why Mrs Lawrence should have invented a single meeting between Wood and Emily when she could have told far more extravagant and damaging lies if she had wanted to fabricate a prior relationship between the accused and the deceased.

Of rather more substance was Marshall Hall's point that Mrs Lawrence could not, as she claimed, have seen Wood 'put his head in at the door [of the *Rising Sun*]' and make signs to Emily with his eyes at 'about 7:30[pm]' on the night of Tuesday 10 September because he was with his brother that evening. However, while Wood does appear to have met up with Charles in Theobald's Road at 7:35pm, he could still have popped into the *Rising Sun* at 7:00pm and then made his way to Theobald's Road within half an hour. Mrs Lawrence could hardly have been expected to recall the exact time someone had looked into the *Rising Sun* one night three months earlier so her evidence about Wood's brief appearance was not entirely implausible and it is hard to see why she would have invented such a minor incident.

When it came to Gladys Warren, Marshall Hall found it difficult to demolish her claim that she had seen Wood and Emily together on three occasions in 1906. He began by asking her if she had seen Emily with several different men and she admitted that she had, agreeing (as she had previously conceded) that it might have been at least half a dozen men. He then suggested that she had discussed the case on a number of occasions with William Linehan but she said she had only spoken to him about it once. He had, she said, been a good friend of hers but was not any longer. Marshall Hall's only substantial point was that Ms Warren had seen a description of Wood in a newspaper before she picked him out at Kentish Town Police Station. When asked if she had admitted this before the magistrate, Ms Warren said, 'I might have said that' which brought a deserved rebuke from Marshall Hall: 'You fence with me. Please remember that we are not playing here for small stakes'. In re-examination by Sir Charles, Ms Warren denied that the newspaper description had been in her mind when she picked out Wood but she appears to have been rattled by the suggestion because she changed the subject and gained the sympathy of the judge by informing him that she had been sacked from her position as a cashier by her employer as a consequence of being a witness in the case. She left the witness box without Marshall Hall really laying a glove on her but no-one seemed to have noticed that her evidence in the witness box had been slightly different from what she had said in her second statement on 6 October. In that document, she stated that Wood used to meet Emily 'very often in the *Rising Sun*'. Yet, in the witness box, she said she had only seen Wood and Emily together in the *Rising Sun* once. The other two occasions she claimed she saw them together was in the Euston Road in June 1906 and then, three weeks later, at the corner of Judd Street.

William Linehan had also claimed in his statement of 6 October to have seen Wood and Emily together in the *Rising Sun* and, in the witness box at the Old Bailey, he said that this was 'on four or five occasions' between July 1906 and January 1907. Marshall Hall had surprisingly little to offer by way of challenge in cross-examination, preferring to focus on a seemingly irrelevant allegation that Linehan's employer had complained of his conduct because he had kissed Gladys Warren at the cashier's desk at his place of employment. Linehan completely denied it and the matter was dropped by Marshall Hall but Arthur Newton evidently had a source of information within Pastimes Limited, a recently incorporated company which ran 'amusements' (featuring stereographic photograph machines, often with risqué images) in the Strand, where Linehan was employed as an office attendant. Unknown to everyone else in the courtroom, Newton's son, Reginald, a solicitor at his law firm, had acquired forty shares in Pastimes Limited on 3 October 1907, making him the fifth largest shareholder in the company.[414] No doubt, therefore, there was something in the allegation against Linehan but it is not clear what Marshall Hall was aiming at by bringing it up. It was either a character point against Linehan (although one would have thought his conviction for managing a brothel, which Marshall Hall did not mention[415], would have achieved this more successfully) or Marshall Hall was trying to develop a theory that Linehan and Gladys Warren were involved in some sort of conspiracy against Wood. Either way, Marshall Hall did not enjoy any great success against either witness but perhaps had muddied the waters sufficiently that the jury would not place too much weight on what they said.

If we are looking for a classic piece of Marshall Hall misdirection, however, we find it in his cross-examination of Frank Clarke. One wonders if Clarke needed to be cross-examined at all, since nothing about his evidence-in-chief was damaging to Wood. He simply said that he had seen Wood speak to Emily for about a minute on the night of Monday 9 September but had not seen him on the Tuesday or the Wednesday. As Wood had already admitted speaking to Emily in the *Rising Sun* on the Monday night, Clarke's evidence only corroborated the defence case. The main purpose of producing Clarke for the prosecution seemed to be to provide an alibi for Robert Roberts should the defence try to suggest he was the real killer, with Clarke saying that he and Roberts went together from the *Rising Sun* to the Euston Temperance Hotel in the early hours of Thursday 12 September, arriving at about 12:50am. Yet, Marshall Hall's first questions in cross-examination somehow managed to extract evidence damaging to Wood. Asked about his identification of Wood in the line-up at Highgate, Clarke said that he had seen Wood several times at the *Rising Sun*. This was still not a real problem because Clarke had never previously seen Wood with Emily but Marshall Hall had another line of questioning he seemed determined to pursue. He asked Clarke how long he had known Roberts; Clarke said he had first met him on Sunday 8 September. He then asked if Roberts had been anxious to prove where he was on the night of 11 September but Clarke denied it. This led to the following exchange:

Marshall Hall: Did you hear that he [Roberts] slept with Dimmock on the Monday, Tuesday and Sunday nights?
Clarke: Yes.
Marshall Hall: Did he tell you?
Clarke: Yes.
Marshall Hall: When did he tell you?
Clarke: In the course of a conversation on Wednesday morning, after breakfast.
Marshall Hall: Was that not a curious conversation to hold with a man who had only known you, and you him, for three days – to tell you he had passed the three previous nights in that way?
Clarke: I did not say he said so. He merely said he had been with her.
Marshall Hall: For three nights?
Clarke: No.
Marshall Hall: Why! I put the three nights to you specifically. I know I did, because, getting an answer I had not expected, I put the question again specifically – and put the three nights in the wrong order to mark the question?
Clarke: I did not understand.[416]

At this point, the judge intervened, complaining that he had not understood Counsel's question either. Marshall Hall then lost his composure, saying in a loud voice that he was certain he had mentioned 'the three nights' to the witness, to which the judge responded, 'There is no need to get excited Marshall Hall. I did not follow you either'. Some non-contemporary accounts of this exchange claim that Marshall Hall then requested that the shorthand notes be read out. However, while he certainly claimed that the shorthand notes would support him, it does not appear from newspaper reports of the incident that the notes were actually read out in court.

Marshall Hall remained in an agitated state and asked Clarke, 'Will you base the truth of your evidence on the statement that I did not ask you about those three nights?' When Clarke replied in the affirmative, Marshall Hall sat down and said curtly, 'Then I will never ask you another question'.

What was going on here? It was a confusing situation that no-one, including the judge, appears to have fully understood. As Marshall Hall did not, in the end, develop the point in cross-examination, it is not entirely certain where he was going with it. In his 1929 biography of Marshall Hall, Edward Marjoribanks says that the reason Clarke became defensive during the exchange was because it suddenly occurred to him that he was effectively saying that Roberts had slept with Emily on the Wednesday night (when she was murdered). Marjoribanks even seemed to believe that the judge was well aware of Clarke's supposed slip but pretended not to understand it because his view of the case was 'adverse' to Wood. David Napley, in his 1987 account of the case, offered a similar interpretation but went even further, claiming that in reversing the order of the three nights and saying 'Monday, Tuesday and Sunday' instead of 'Sunday, Monday and Tuesday', Marshall Hall was not simply 'marking' the question as he claimed (whatever he meant by that) but was playing a deliberate trick on Clarke to make him think he had said 'Monday, Tuesday and Wednesday', thus including the night of the murder within the 'three nights'. Consequently, when Clarke agreed that Roberts had told him he had slept with Emily on the previous three nights, this must have included the Wednesday.

Napley was an experienced criminal solicitor but his interpretation of the exchange between Marshall Hall and Clarke simply cannot be right. Nor can Marjoribanks be correct in saying that Clarke had somehow let slip that Roberts was with Emily on the Wednesday night. It is clear from all versions of the exchange that both Marshall Hall and Clarke were speaking about a conversation between Clarke and Roberts on 'Wednesday morning', *before* Emily had been murdered. This does not appear to have been a slip of the tongue because Marshall Hall identified 'the three previous nights' as the Sunday, Monday and Tuesday nights, which only made sense if he was asking about something said on Wednesday. He also made the point that the conversation between Clarke and Roberts was a curious one for two men who had only known each other 'for three days'. As Clarke said he met Roberts on a Sunday, this means that the conversation in question must have taken place on Wednesday, three days later. This was certainly what Sir Charles Mathews understood because, when attempting to clarify the position, according to the *Notable British Trials* transcript, he asked Clarke in re-examination, 'In the course of conversation on Wednesday morning, did Roberts tell you that he had been with Dimmock?' to which Clarke answered, 'Yes, but he did not mention any day'. The official *Minutes of Evidence* note that this conversation took place 'after breakfast' on the Wednesday morning. If Roberts had told Clarke on Wednesday morning that he had slept with Emily for the three previous nights – in fact if he had told him anything at all that morning – it could not have had anything to do with a murder which had not yet occurred.

Even if Marshall Hall had meant to refer to a conversation on the Thursday morning (or afternoon/evening) so that, in asking Clarke to confirm that Roberts told him he had spent 'the previous three nights' with Emily, he was trying to trick Clarke into including Wednesday night, this would have made absolutely no sense. Not only had Marshall Hall defined the previous three nights as Sunday, Monday and Tuesday so that any admission by Clarke must, by definition, have excluded Wednesday night, but Clarke's unchallenged evidence was that he had been with Roberts in the *Rising Sun* all of Wednesday evening and returned with him to their lodgings after closing time so that, from his own personal knowledge, he knew that Roberts had not slept with Emily that night. Marshall Hall was hardly likely to have believed that he could trick Clarke in such crass fashion into making an admission that Roberts was with Emily on the night of the murder.

In order to understand what Marshall Hall was probably attempting to do, we first need to consider what Edward Smeeth, the assistant manager of the *Rising Sun*, had said in his statement to police on 6 October. It was Smeeth who had informed Roberts of Emily's murder early on the Thursday evening and, in his statement, he said that 'on telling him [Roberts] of the murder he [Roberts] immediately said that he had been home with her [Emily] for the three nights preceding Wednesday viz on Sunday, Monday and Tuesday.' Marshall Hall, who would have been provided with the statements of all the prosecution witnesses, no doubt had this in mind when he asked Roberts in cross-examination, 'You knew that the habitués of the Rising Sun knew you had been with this woman on the Sunday, the Monday and the Tuesday nights?' (and Roberts had agreed). One of the first questions Marshall Hall asked Clarke was whether he was a 'habitué' of the *Rising Sun* and Clarke had admitted he went there 'pretty frequently'. In this context, it would seem that the purpose of Marshall Hall's initial question to Clarke about what Roberts had told him was to establish that Roberts had said *on the Thursday evening*, to someone he barely knew, that he had slept with Emily for the three nights preceding the Wednesday (as Smeeth had put it). The reason why this was apparently important to Marshall Hall was because, in his view, it indicated extreme anxiety on Roberts' part that he would be suspected by the police of being the murderer. The defence case was that Roberts was so worried about this that he attempted to frame both Shaw (by falsely claiming that the letter Emily had shown him was signed 'Bert') and, more importantly, Wood (by providing his description to the police). As far as can be ascertained, Marshall Hall's big point was that, in telling Clarke that he had slept with Emily on Sunday, Monday and Tuesday (but not, by implication, on Wednesday), Roberts was revealing just how very anxious he was.

It was not a very good point to begin with and was probably formulated by Marshall Hall while he was on his feet after Clarke had unexpectedly denied that Roberts had been anxious to establish his whereabouts on the night of the murder. Clarke then appears to have ruined it by saying that Roberts had told him *before the murder* that he had slept with Emily. Marshall Hall then had to continue his questions on the basis that Clarke had spoken with Roberts on the Wednesday morning and quickly realised that he was going nowhere with that particular line of questioning. At the same time, Clarke was possibly confused as to what Marshall Hall had asked him. The barrister's first question ('Did you hear that Roberts slept with Dimmock on the Monday, Tuesday and Sunday nights?') was not well worded and did not specify when Clarke was supposed to have heard this information nor who told him. It may be that, when Clarke answered this question, he was referring to what he had learnt after the murder but then, in subsequent answers, switched to explaining what Roberts had told him before the murder, namely that he had slept with Emily. If that was the case, it was little wonder that Marshall Hall became agitated when Clarke appeared to backtrack in saying that Roberts had not mentioned any particular nights but, as Clarke had never expressly said in his own words that Roberts had told him on Wednesday morning that he had slept with Emily on the three nights in question, he was quite possibly not backtracking at all. In any event, Marshall Hall must have regarded the apparent inconsistency as manna from heaven and he sensibly abandoned the flawed point he had intended to make and latched onto this inconsistency instead to demonstrate the unreliability of the witness.

The whole thing was a storm in a teacup but the effect of it was that Marshall Hall had, either by default or design, manufactured a huge dispute between himself and the witness over what had been said. If the jury recalled the mention of the three nights, but not the precise wording of the original question, they might well have thought that Clarke was an unreliable witness who had changed his answer from first saying that Roberts had told him he had slept with Emily on the Sunday, Monday and Tuesday nights to then saying something different, even if that difference was inconsequential. From out of nowhere and nothing, a question mark over Clarke's credibility had been introduced into the proceedings.

Although Marshall Hall dramatically concluded his cross-examination by sitting down and announcing that he refused to ask the baffled witness any more questions, the fact is that he had probably run out of things to ask. Had he known about Clarke's criminal past as a watch thief he would certainly have raised it but this does not appear to have been something that even the prosecution was aware of at the time. In the end, nothing appears to have turned on Clarke's evidence and the proceedings moved on. The following day, however, Marshall Hall apologised to the judge for his outburst, saying that he had not meant to impugn his lordship's hearing but that: 'It was the hearing of the witness Clarke I questioned'. Even that was unfair to Clarke. If the judge had not heard something then why should a witness have been criticised for not hearing the same thing? As we have seen, it was not a question of poor hearing but it should nevertheless be noted that the acoustics in the new number one court of the Old Bailey were very poor and the judge and members of the jury had complained about the humming noise of the ventilation system drowning out what witnesses were saying. At one point, the judge said angrily, 'If you can't have ventilations without noise in this building the authorities should never have been allowed to erect it'.[417] Thus, even if Clarke had somehow misheard a question it would be very harsh to blame him for this.

As the central focus of the questions asked of Clarke was on Roberts, it is not surprising that Roberts himself faced some aggressive questioning from Marshall Hall. It was, in fact, so aggressive that Marshall Hall was forced to declare that he was not accusing Roberts of being the murderer. The defence seemed to have two problems with the cook's version of events. One concerned

Roberts' evidence about the letter Emily had shown him, arranging an appointment at the *Eagle*, the cross-examination of which we shall return to.

The other problem Marshall Hall had with Roberts' evidence was in respect of his identification of Wood as the man he saw with Emily in the *Rising Sun* on the night of Monday 9 September. This was strange because Wood had admitted in his statement to having been in the *Rising Sun* with Emily that night. In that statement, dated 4 October, Wood said that he saw a friend of Emily's who pointed her out to him at the other end of the bar with some men. The friend then caught Emily's eye 'and deceased came over and joined us'. However, Emily 'flitted about a good deal between one and another and seeming to know all'. It is hard, therefore, to understand what was so objectionable about Roberts' evidence on this. It is true that there was a slight difference in his account in that he said (during his evidence-in-chief) that 'Dimmock went straight to him [Wood] and they remained talking together in the bar until a quarter to nine.' He also said that, 'The accused and Dimmock then left together'. According to Wood's version, however, Emily left the bar on her own followed by Wood and he saw her outside speaking to a man who had a short leg or hip trouble. Roberts asserted that 'Dimmock and the accused returned to the public house at eleven and stayed till ten minutes past twelve and then went out together' whereas Wood, admitting that he and Emily went back into the bar, said, 'She finished her drink and went over and spoke to one of the men, and then came out with me'. The man Emily spoke to must have been Roberts because Wood said that Emily told him that she would have to return to him, 'inferring that it was to her benefit monetarily'. Roberts himself said that Emily came back alone a short time afterwards and he went with her to 29 St Paul's Road.

In essence, despite some minor differences in the details, both Roberts and Wood were telling the same story, namely that Roberts was in the *Rising Sun* on the Monday night while Emily chatted to Wood and then Emily and Wood left the bar before Emily came back to Roberts. That being so, it was perfectly understandable that Roberts would have taken note of his rival for Emily's affections, wondering who he was, and, no doubt, Wood had wondered who Roberts was too. As Roberts said in his evidence at the Old Bailey, 'he looked very hard at me, and I looked hard at him'. The description of the man he had given to police on 12 September was a reasonably accurate description of Wood in that he had said he was 'about 5ft 8 in, comp[lexion] and hair very dark, clean shaven with a very thin long face and a scowling expression'. The only element that does not seem to have been correct was Roberts' additional claim that 'He had a few pimples on the lower part of his face'. When asked about this by Marshall Hall, Roberts tried to be clever, saying, 'Pimples do not always stay there' and he was promptly told off by the barrister for arguing. He might have had a point though because there was no evidence one way or the other about the state of Wood's complexion as at 9 September. All we know is that he did not have any pimples when he was arrested by the police almost one month later, at which time any skin issues from early September might have cleared up. It is equally possible that the lighting in the *Rising Sun* was unflattering and, from a distance, Roberts gained the false impression of pimples on Wood's face.

However, it was not so much the pimples that Marshall Hall was concerned about but the similarity between the descriptions provided to the police in their respective statements by Roberts and May Campbell. According to Marshall Hall's biographer, Edward Marjoribanks, it was the young barrister, John Wellesley Orr, who spotted the point when reviewing the case papers. He had noticed that May Campbell's description of 'Scotch Bob' was remarkably similar to Roberts' description of Wood in that she had claimed he was 'about 5ft 7 or 8 inches in height, very dark, clean shaven, sunken dark eyes, dirty pimply face.' Roberts had said nothing about Wood's sunken eyes (although one of Inspector Neil's reports attributed this phrase to him) but in all other respects it was a suspiciously close match. Furthermore, Orr is said to have realised that May Campbell could not possibly have spoken to Emily in Camden Town High Street during the afternoon of 11 September because (according to the evidence of Bert Shaw and Mrs Stocks) Emily was at home all day. Yet, in her second written statement, she had said that Emily had told her, at about 4:00pm on 11 September, that she had received a letter that morning to meet a gentleman friend at Camden Town Station at 9.45pm and that, 'Her friend the sailor was with her and that she showed him part of the letter and then burnt it'. If May Campbell had not been told this by Emily, Wellesley Orr wondered how she could possibly have known it. His conclusion was that Roberts, being anxious that he was, or would be, suspected by police of murdering Emily, must have asked her to concoct a false story to support his account.

There are a number of problems with this, not least with the supposed involvement of Wellesley Orr who was not part of Wood's defence team. Marshall Hall was assisted by no less than three junior barristers, Herman Cohen, Huntley Jenkins and John Rolleston Lort-Williams, so one wonders why Wellesley Orr would have been reviewing any papers on the case. It is true that Wellesley Orr shared the same Chambers as Marshall Hall at 3 Temple Gardens and no doubt 'devilled' for him, by which he stood in for the great man when he was booked to appear in two courts on the same day, but by December 1907 the 28-year-old Wellesley Orr had been a practising barrister for over three years and would appear to have been a little too senior to be acting, in effect, as Marshall Hall's unpaid pupil.[418] Marjoribanks' biography of Marshall Hall was published in 1929, two years after Marshall Hall's death and, although Wellesley Orr himself was still alive at the time, having been appointed stipendiary magistrate for the City of Manchester, the source of Marjoribanks' information is unclear and never appears to have been verified. It may well be that Wellesley Orr did assist Marshall Hall in the preparation of the Wood case – and Marjoribanks certainly knew that Wellesley Orr was not officially briefed, saying that he needed special leave to attend the final consultation with Wood – but there is no independent corroboration of this. The most that can be found in support is a reference in the *Daily News* of 19 December 1907 to Marshall Hall's 'four juniors'. As Marshall Hall only had three juniors, the so-called fourth may well have been Wellesley Orr who had been spotted by a journalist in court. Marjoribanks claims that Marshall Hall acknowledged his debt to Wellesley Orr in his closing speech but, if he did, it went unreported by the press and is certainly not recorded in the *Notable British Trials* transcript.

That is a minor point, however, because the defence team certainly did develop the theory that there was some sort of conspiracy between Roberts and May Campbell. In fact, so important was it believed to be that Marshall Hall opened his cross-examination of the cook on the point. The story of this cross-examination has taken on a mythical life of its own in the secondary literature. In his 1962 book, *The Murder and the Trial*, for example, Edgar Lustgarten described it as 'one of the great forensic coups of history'. He claimed that when Marshall Hall asked Roberts if he knew a woman called May, 'The effect on the ship's cook was extraordinary. His jaw dropped, his fingers twitched; a perceptible tremor shook his bulky frame' and Lustgarten has him stammering 'No, no' in reply. As a result, according to Lustgarten, 'It needed no psychology to tell he was lying'. A nice story but all nonsense. The truth is that Marshall Hall's cross-examination fell flat on its face. Here is what actually happened when he raised the point with Roberts:

> **Marshall Hall:** Did you know a woman named May Campbell?
> **Roberts:** By sight, yes.
> **Marshall Hall:** Have you ever spoken to her?
> **Roberts:** Yes.

So, far from denying that he knew May, Roberts admitted it immediately and had no difficulty in doing so. His jaw did not drop, his fingers did not twitch and his bulky frame did not tremor. The cross-examination continued:

> **Marshall Hall:** When did you first speak to her?
> **Roberts:** I think it was the day of the funeral.
> **Marshall Hall:** Did you talk about the case?
> **Roberts:** It was talked of all over the place.
> **Marshall Hall:** Did May Campbell give you the description of a man who, she said, was known as a friend of Dimmock?
> **Roberts:** Yes.
> **Marshall Hall:** And did that description correspond very much with the description of the accused?
> **Roberts:** It tallied very much.

In other words, Roberts freely and frankly admitted that he spoke to May Campbell at Emily's funeral on 17 September and that they compared descriptions of the man they thought had murdered Emily. He also agreed that he had told her about the letter Emily had shown him and then thrown into the fire. As a result of Roberts' frankness, the idea that there had been any secret collusion between the pair fell away. While it is possible that May Campbell had incorporated Roberts' description into her story when she made a statement on 19 September, she was not a witness for the prosecution at the trial so it did not matter. Roberts had given his first statement to the police, in which he provided a description of the man he saw with Emily, on 12 September, so there was absolutely no question of his being influenced by anything May Campbell had told him. Wellesley Orr, or whoever noticed the point, might well have been correct that May Campbell had learnt from Roberts of Emily's burning of the letter but that was not a factor in any way determining Wood's guilt or innocence. The explosive ammunition that Marshall Hall had been so keen to use on Roberts turned out to be a dud.

Returning to Roberts' evidence about the letter shown to him by Emily, it is clear that the defence did not like this at all and Roberts was cross-examined at length about it by Marshall Hall with the suggestion being that he was lying about its contents. Indeed, it was directly put to Roberts that his evidence about the letter was 'an invention'. The issue was another strange one. Roberts had told the police on the day after the murder about a letter in which the author asked Emily to meet him at about 8:00 or 8:30pm in the *Eagle* on the Wednesday night. It was not until some weeks later that the police established that Emily met Wood in the *Eagle* at about 8:30pm, or shortly thereafter, on the Wednesday night. If Roberts had invented the letter it was an astonishing coincidence that he was able to inform the police precisely where Emily had been that evening. Furthermore, although Wood had initially been reluctant to admit that the fragments of the letter were in his handwriting, Arthur Newton had admitted at the police court that his client was the author. Consequently, Roberts had been able to tell the police that both the author of the letter and the addressee had been in the very place at the very time stated in the letter. In addition, although not mentioned in Roberts' statement, it seems clear that Roberts told the police about the rising sun postcard which at the time was known to no-one else and was hidden at the bottom of a drawer. So his credibility has to be rated as reasonably high.

The defence position was that Emily had shown Roberts, not a letter but a note, scribbled on paper torn from a pocket book. It was pointed out during Roberts' cross-examination that the fragments found in the fire had faint blue lines on them which, it was suggested, would not appear on paper used for a letter. Yet, when Marshall Hall had earlier cross-examined Bert Shaw, he had asked him if he had written to Emily on the day of the murder (which he denied) and whether he signed his letters 'Bert' (which he admitted). A little later in the cross-examination, he asked Shaw, 'As a matter of fact did you not write to her?' (denied) and 'Did you not write to her from Sheffield that night?' (also denied). The only purpose in asking these questions was if it was being suggested that Shaw wrote the letter received by Emily on the morning of 11 September which, it will be recalled, was signed 'Bertie' according to Roberts' first statement. The questions presupposed that the fragments found in the fire were of a letter as opposed to a note. Both Sir Charles Mathews and the judge said they understood that it was being suggested that Shaw had written the letter and Marshall Hall was asked to clarify the situation. After consulting with Wood and showing him the fragments, Marshall Hall stated:

> It might save time if I admit there is no question that the handwriting on the fragment produced is the accused's handwriting. I never suggested that the witness Shaw wrote the letter. While there is no question that the handwriting on the fragment is the handwriting of the accused, I do not admit that it is a fragment of any particular letter or anything of that kind. There is a very great difference between admitting that the fragment is in the accused's handwriting and admitting that the whole of Roberts' story is true. I do not admit that the fragment is part of a letter sent by Wood...I admit and it has already been admitted in the police court by Mr Newton before Mr Bros, that the writing as shown there is Wood's. I am not admitting that the fragments were part of any particular letter. All I say is that the writing on the fragment is the accused's.

One might almost think that the barrister doth protest too much. In the first place, his refusal to admit that the fragments were part of a letter was inconsistent with what Arthur Newton had said to the magistrate at the police court; both the *Times* and the *Islington Daily Gazette* had recorded him as saying that he 'would not deny that Wood wrote...the fragments of the letter'.[419] Furthermore, despite his denials, Marshall Hall had clearly been attempting to suggest that Shaw had written to Emily from Sheffield during the night of 10 September and that it was this letter that Roberts had seen. Unless Marshall Hall had not, until this point, understood his brief, and wrongly believed that Wood was denying that it was his handwriting on the fragments, he must have been about to suggest that the fragments found in the fire were from a completely different document to the one seen by Roberts. In the end, he seems to have abandoned any reliance on this possibility and the defence position became that Roberts fabricated his evidence about the contents of the letter in order to deflect police attention away from himself and towards Bert Shaw. He thus asked Roberts, 'Where did the name "Bert" come from?' followed up by, 'If the object had been to put suspicion on Shaw, the suggestion would have been very useful?' Roberts did not dignify this with an answer but Marshall Hall persisted, asking, 'Did you not know that Bert Shaw was the name of the man Dimmock was living with?' to which Roberts responded that he only knew this after the murder (a rather vague and unhelpful answer considering that he only mentioned the letter to police after the murder). Nevertheless, Roberts eventually agreed with Marshall Hall's thesis that 'If it had been the object to put suspicion on Bert Shaw, the signature "Bert" would have been a good piece of evidence would it not?' One has to question this. The man living with Emily was hardly likely to write her a letter asking to meet her in a local public house and it would be strange if Roberts or anyone else would have thought it would be a good idea to frame Shaw in this way.

The name 'Bert' could also have been a shortened form of Robert, albeit that Robert Wood was known as 'Bob', and this might be one reason why Marshall Hall was so intent on establishing that the entire letter was the product of Roberts' imagination. His big point to disprove its authenticity was in respect of the word 'tonight', said by Roberts to have been included in the letter. Roberts, as we know, had claimed that the letter read: 'Dear Phyllis – Meet me at 8 o'clock at the *Eagle* tonight'. Marshall Hall asked, 'Do you usually when writing on a Tuesday to make an appointment for a Wednesday night, write "Meet me tonight"?' It was not, however, a good point. Anyone writing a letter to someone late on Tuesday, which they knew would reach its intended recipient first thing on Wednesday morning, would surely use the word 'tonight' to mean Wednesday evening without any difficulty. Roberts' answer was to the same effect, as he said, 'Well, people usually write like that don't they'. Marshall Hall also attempted to undermine Roberts' evidence by pointing out that there was writing on the reverse of the fragments found in the fire. Roberts had said that the letter was four pages long and the writing he had seen was on the third page with the fourth blank so there should not have been anything on the other side. However, as Roberts explained to Marshall Hall, he had seen the letter for a very short time and had no reason to memorise the details so he could easily have been mistaken about what page he had seen. In short, there was no good reason to support the defence theory that the story of the letter was a fabrication. It is true that Roberts realised he was a possible suspect, which is why he remained at the *Rising Sun* waiting for the police, but he denied Marshall Hall's suggestion that he was 'in a great fright' when he heard of the murder.

When Wood was asked under oath about the letter it was by far the least convincing part of his evidence. Although admitting the fragments were in his handwriting, he claimed not to be able to remember when he had written the words on the fragments, nor what the words were, nor how the document (whatever it was) came into Emily's possession. He theorised that Emily must have looked through his letters and papers which had probably fallen from his pocket when he pulled out his sketch book in the *Rising Sun* and that she had taken some 'fragments of some little sketches that I was doing in the public house bar'. This reflected what Ruby Young claimed he had told her before his arrest. In her statement of 30 November, she said:

> When it appeared in the newspapers that the police had found some pieces of burnt paper in the fire grate, Wood appeared greatly concerned but said he supposed they must be parts of the pieces of paper he had been drawing and scribbling on when he saw her in the Rising Sun on the Monday. I asked him whether he had written anything to her besides the postcard and he said he had not but that when she asked him in the Rising Sun on Friday evening to write something nice on the card he was to send to her he drew a few small designs on some pieces of paper he had in his pocket and wrote something on and after he had done so she kept them.

That explanation does not seem to match the reality of what was found. There were no designs, drawings or scribbles on the retrieved fragments and it is interesting that Ruby claimed in court that Wood said to her during one of their discussions before his arrest, 'I wish I knew what the bits of paper are that have been found'.

One thing Wood claimed to be certain about in his oral evidence was that the fragments were not part of a letter he had written to Emily because, he said, the only time he had ever written to her was when he wrote the rising sun postcard. He insisted that the fragments were not part of a letter of assignation and he had made no appointment to meet Emily in the *Eagle* on the Wednesday night. Although he admitted for the very first time in the witness box that he had met Emily in the *Eagle* that night, he insisted that this was not a pre-arranged meeting. His answers must have puzzled the prosecution because Arthur Newton had not only admitted to Mr Bros at the police court that Wood had written the fragments of the letter but had also said that 'it was no part of his case to deny that he had an assignation with Dimmock on that night [11 September]'.[420] Sir Charles Mathews attempted to obtain Wood's assistance to decipher the fragments but his efforts were futile as Wood could not explain anything. We will discuss later why Wood might have lied about not having an appointment with Emily but the point for now is that, even if he did send her a letter arranging to meet her at the *Eagle*, this does not necessarily mean that he murdered her.

Before moving on from Roberts' evidence, it has to be noted that the most important part of it was what he did not say – or rather, what he was not allowed to say. Strict legal rules on hearsay meant that he could not tell the jury what Emily had told him about Wood. It will be recalled that, in his written statement, he had said that Emily informed him that the author of the letter had wanted to come home with her but had no money to pay her. He also claimed that she told him that the man was 'very jealous'. In his second statement dated

7 October, he also claimed that Emily said to him in the *Rising Sun*, 'I am glad he has gone, I am afraid of him' and he repeated at the inquest on 14 October that Emily had said she was afraid of Wood.[421] The jealousy point clearly went to the issue of motive but the jury was never told of it. On the one hand, it seems unjust in that a possible murderer has the advantage of silencing his or her victim, and eliminating incriminating evidence, by the very fact of having killed them. On the other hand, leaving aside whether Roberts had correctly remembered what was said to him or was simply making it all up, Emily might not have been telling the truth when she spoke of Wood to Roberts. She might, for example, have been attempting to play the two men off against each other. Certainly, her behaviour in showing Roberts the postcard she had received from Wood (and the letter which, despite Wood's protestations, does appear to have been a letter of assignation) was strange and there can be no doubt that she wanted Roberts to know that she had another admirer who wanted to meet her. As she could not be questioned in court under oath by virtue of having been murdered, it is possible that an injustice to Wood could have been committed had Roberts been allowed to give evidence as to what Emily said to him. Yet, one might feel that justice would best be served by the jury being given all the facts and allowed to make up their minds, with the appropriate caveats being provided. But this was not to be and the prosecution was left without any evidence at all to establish a possible motive against Wood.

The final key witness for the prosecution was Ruby Young and, here, Marshall Hall surprised everyone by taking a relatively gentle approach and not bringing up the topic of her being a prostitute. Nevertheless, Miss Young's evidence about Wood's peculiar walk allowed him to begin his cross-examination on the offensive, drawing attention to the fact she had said nothing about the walk in her first statement or in her evidence to both the coroner and the magistrate until she was recalled to the police court on 4 December. Although he did not explore the point in cross-examination, he would tell the jury in his closing speech that Ruby's late evidence about Wood's walk was 'invented by her in a spirit of revenge' because she had been revealed by Mr Newton in the police court to be a prostitute. The main theme of his cross-examination was to the effect that she was jealous of Wood's relationship with her friend, Pansy, and that this was colouring her evidence against him. Looked at objectively, he was not successful. Miss Young agreed that she was, naturally enough, angry with Wood for cheating on her but denied that she had been jealous and insisted they were always friendly. Marshall Hall then asked two questions in one: 'He knew that you had been jealous of him with regard to Pansy? He knew you had broken it off?' to which Ruby Young answered 'Yes'. She was, no doubt, answering Marshall Hall's second question only but Marshall Hall had cleverly contrived to make it appear that she was agreeing that she was 'jealous'. Perhaps for that reason, most observers seemed to think that Ruby was indeed jealous and that her evidence could be discounted for this reason. Marshall Hall would later describe her evidence about Wood's walk as 'a gross and vindictive lie'.

To Miss Young's face, though, Marshall Hall was politeness itself and the gentle approach bore fruit when he took full advantage of Ruby's affection towards Wood by asking her if she would agree that he was a man 'of a singularly amiable and gentle and inoffensive disposition', to which she readily agreed.

Marshall Hall had a few more tricks up his sleeve. He got Ruby to agree that she had told Wood (and believed it) that if he went to Scotland Yard and explained the circumstances under which he sent the postcard he would be allowed to go free. 'Therefore' he said 'you could not have believed he had committed the murder?' 'No, I could not' she conceded. But his best point was a simple one:

> **Marshall Hall:** With regard to the arrangement which you say you had come to that you should say that the accused was in your company on the night of Wednesday, 11th September, from 6.30 to 10.30, have you ever thought that, having regard to Dr Thompson's evidence, that would be a useless alibi for the murder but a perfect alibi for the meeting of the girl?
>
> **Young:** It did not strike me that it was a useless alibi then.
>
> **Marshall Hall:** But it does now, does it not?
>
> **Young:** Yes, it does now.

Marshall Hall had struck a blow at the very heart of the prosecution's case. Yes, Wood had asked his former sweetheart to provide him with a false alibi on the night of the murder but that alibi only lasted until midnight (which was the time Wood claimed to have returned home after parting from Ruby). If, as the medical evidence seemed to suggest, Emily was murdered between 3:00am and 4:00am then that alibi was of no use for the murder. Although we now know that Emily could have been murdered any time between about 10:00pm on the Wednesday night and 11:00am on the Thursday morning, this was not what was believed by the police at the time. Their theory that McCowan had seen the murderer leaving 29 St Paul's Road shortly before 5:00am only made sense if Emily had been killed within the previous hour or two. He was hardly likely to have hung around in her room for five hours. The combination of the medical evidence and McCowan's evidence meant that it was not open to the prosecution to argue that Wood might have killed Emily before midnight. They were stuck with a time of death at or after 3:00am and, that being so, why would Wood not have ensured that he had an alibi for the time the murder was believed to have been committed? Even if Wood was the murderer and killed Emily before midnight, he would surely have known, from the newspaper reports of the inquest on Monday 30 September, that the medical evidence placed the time of death at about 3:00am.[422] It is true that he had cooked up his alibi with Ruby on the day before this (Sunday 29 September) so that the time of 3:00am would not necessarily have been in his mind at that point. Dr Thompson had said on the first day of the inquest that Emily might had been dead 'seven or eight hours' but not all newspapers reported that he also said that he had arrived at the scene of the crime at 1:00pm; thus, it may not have been entirely clear to everyone what time he was estimating death to have occurred. So it is possible that Wood could have murdered Emily at say, 11:00pm, and, when it came to devising an alibi with Ruby at the end of September, believed that he only needed to account for his time up to midnight. Yet, by 4 October, when he gave a statement to the police, in which he falsely claimed to have parted from Emily shortly after 10:30pm, he must have known this would be inadequate, even if he knew that he had, in fact, murdered Emily before midnight.

One could argue that the real murderer would only believe he needed an alibi for the actual time of the murder and not for the time it was (wrongly) thought by police that the murder was committed. For that reason it is not conclusive but the fact that Wood's alibi was for no later than midnight tends to suggest that his main purpose was to conceal the mere fact that he was with Emily that evening as opposed to murdering her. One thing is certain: if Wood did murder Emily, he must have done so before midnight otherwise his alibi would have been plain daft.

There is one other point worthy of note which emerged from the prosecution evidence at the trial. Initially, Dr Thompson said that he came to the conclusion that neither of the two razors belonging to Bert Shaw was used in the murder because no trace of blood was found on them when they were examined under a microscope. He thought it would be 'difficult' to remove blood from the spaces between the blade and the handle of the razor. However, in re-examination, he conceded that 'If cleaned immediately after death the razor need not have shown any trace [of blood], even under microscopic examination'.[423] This was an astonishing volte-face and meant that one of Shaw's razors could have been the murder weapon, presumably the one found lying on top of the chest of drawers which Shaw said was normally kept inside that item of furniture. We have seen Inspector Neil's evidence that one of Shaw's two razors was old and rusty.[424] However, even this does not appear to exclude it from being the murder weapon. It is clear from Dr Thompson's evidence that the only reason he initially ruled out the razors was because he could not find any microscopic traces of blood on them. There was no suggestion from him that one of them could not have been used as the murder weapon because it was too old or rusty. His view was that the murder weapon was 'most likely' to have been a razor.[425] He said that it would have had to have been tied to make it rigid but, apart from that, a razor certainly could have been responsible for inflicting the wounds on Emily's body and, it seems, one of Bert Shaw's razors in particular could have been responsible.

Contemporary sketches of Ellen Lawrence (left) and Florence Smith (right)

Mr Justice Grantham

Edward Marshall Hall

A contemporary sketch of Lilian Raven

Five members of the Jury

Chapter Fifteen

Witnesses for the Prosecution

'The question is whether you were lying then or are you lying now…or whether you are in fact a chronic and habitual liar.'

Charles Laughton as Sir Wilfred Robarts, in *Witness for the Prosecution*, (1957)

A little over nine years before the murder of Emily Dimmock, a man known amongst the racing fraternity as 'Scotch Bob' was sentenced to five years imprisonment at the Old Bailey for obtaining goods by false pretences and intention to defraud. His real name was Robert Johnston Stevens; he was a 36-year-old publican from Glasgow who was living in Islington at the time of his arrest.[426] His nickname made perfect sense considering he was called Bob and came from Scotland. In the trial of Robert Wood (who was, ironically, a Scotsman called Bob) the man known as 'Scotch Bob' was supposedly a Scotsman called Alexander. In what was the most unsatisfactory aspect of the Wood trial, the prosecution produced Alexander Mackie as their final witness. He volunteered the information on the witness stand that 'They sometimes call me "Scotch Bob"' and admitted that he knew Emily Dimmock. The reason why he was called 'Scotch Bob' by unidentified people was never explained. Although he had no pimples when he appeared at the Old Bailey, he said that he once had a rash on his face which could have been described as pimples. He confirmed that at the time of Emily's murder he had been working as a kitchen porter at the Portpatrick Hotel in Wigtownshire, Scotland. The hotel manager, John Mair, came down to London to state at the Old Bailey that Mackie was definitely at the hotel on 11 September. Four days after that date, he said he discovered that Mackie had stolen some table silver and sacked him. An agreement relating to Mackie's wages, dated 15 September 1907, was produced. Marshall Hall was briefly excited by the fact that the document bore two dates, one at the top being '15.09.07', the other below Mackie's signature being '15.08.07', so perhaps Mackie had been sacked in August and made his way to London, but Mair explained convincingly that the August date was a mistake by Mackie.

By the time Mackie gave evidence in court, Marshall Hall had all but totally lost interest in 'Scotch Bob'. As Mackie could not have murdered Emily there was no point in cross-examining him in any detail to establish the precise nature of his relationship with the victim and, indeed, any attempt to suggest that he had any part to play in the murder would have been self-defeating and risked being regarded by the jury as a desperate attempt to implicate someone other than Wood. As a consequence, Marshall Hall only asked a few questions of Mackie and many more were left unasked and unanswered.

It will be recalled that the only person to have specifically mentioned 'Scotch Bob' to the police was May Campbell. She had said that 'Scotch Bob' was known as Emily's 'fancy man' but Mackie was not asked to confirm that he had any relationship with Emily other than that he knew her. More importantly, May said that Emily told her that 'Scotch Bob' had contracted the 'bad disorder' from her but Mackie was not asked if he had contracted venereal disease from anyone. It is possible that his rash was a symptom of such disease but this was never confirmed in court and Mackie said the rash was the result of an illness contracted in Glasgow, so that seems to rule out the possibility that it was connected with Emily. May Campbell also claimed that Emily told her that she had got 'Scotch Bob' locked up for six months but Mackie was not asked if he had ever been in prison. Nor was he asked if he was known as 'Tom'.

If Mackie's evidence was true, then the fact of the matter is that he could not possibly have been the man known to May Campbell as 'Scotch Bob'. He said that he left London in September 1906 and had not returned until 9 December 1907 when he came to England for the purpose of giving evidence at the trial. Yet, May Campbell said in one of her statements that she saw Emily 'frequently in the company of this man Bob up to January last when I got married'. If May Campbell had seen 'Scotch Bob' with Emily in London in October, November or December 1906 (or January 1907) then, Q.E.D., her 'Scotch Bob' could not have been Alexander Mackie. The police had previously believed 'Scotch Bob' to have been variously known as Bob Machonockie, Robert Bruce and Robert Burn so it is not clear why, other than Mackie's uncorroborated claim to have been 'Scotch Bob', he was believed to have been the man referred to by May Campbell. It may well be that Mackie answered all these questions in a statement to the police which was also provided to the defence, hence Marshall Hall's lack of interest, but, if so, it has not survived and is not in the Metropolitan Police file in the National Archives.

Gladys Warren had spoken of a man she knew as 'Scotch Jock' or 'Scotch Jack' who, she said, was 'a very violent man' towards Emily and had 'threatened to do her in'. Mackie was never asked if he had ever threatened Emily so it is impossible to assess whether he was the man Ms Warren knew. Both Scotch Jock and Scotch Bob were said to have bad skin but May Campbell estimated Scotch Bob's height as five foot, seven inches, whereas Gladys Warren thought he was five foot, ten inches. She also said he had a 'heavy moustache' but May Campbell did not mention any facial hair. Alexander Mackie was clean shaven when he appeared in court.[427] His height is not known. May Campbell offered no estimate of Scotch Bob's age but Gladys Warren said her suspect was about 35 years old. We do not know Alexander Mackie's age but journalists described him as a 'young man'.[428] From sketches by court artists he looks to have been in his early twenties. It is by no means clear, therefore, that Warren and Campbell were describing the same man nor is it clear if either of them was describing Alexander Mackie. Marshall Hall asked Mackie if he knew Harry Sharples and Frederick Harvey (he said he did) but the question was not put as to whether he knew May Campbell or Gladys Warren.

Mackie was one of three prosecution witnesses suspected at some point of murdering Emily who seemed to have had rock solid alibis. The other two were Bert Shaw and Robert Roberts. We have already seen that Marshall Hall cross-examined Shaw on the unlikely basis that he had written the letter to Emily arranging an appointment at the *Eagle*. He also asked Shaw if Emily was frightened of him and whether he would have had any objection to her receiving letters from men. Shaw said that he would have had no objection as long as there was 'nothing in them' and that Emily was not frightened of him. The implication behind the questions was that Shaw had found out about her correspondence with another man and killed her out of jealousy.

Marshall Hall also appeared incredulous that the police had not found the postcard in the chest of drawers, despite believing it was there, and it certainly does seem strange that the newspaper lying at the bottom of the drawer was not properly lifted to check whether the postcard was present. Was it possible that it was not, in fact, in the drawer when the police were searching for it but inside Shaw's coat? Had he found it earlier and realised that, despite being signed 'Alice', his so-called 'wife' was cheating on him with another man? Then (regardless of whether or not he murdered Emily as a result) did he take the opportunity to pretend he had found the postcard in the drawer on 25 September in order that the police could locate the author by his handwriting, thereby diverting suspicion further from himself? This would appear to be what Marshall Hall suspected and the circumstances of the police failure to find the postcard and its eventual discovery were certainly quite remarkable.[429] Yet the police officer who had failed to locate the postcard during the search – who, one would imagine, would have been the most suspicious of its sudden appearance nearly two weeks later – completely accepted that he had missed it. Detective Sergeant Herbert Milton stated that, while conducting the search, he lifted up the newspaper that covered the bottom of the drawers, but nevertheless agreed that it was possible he might have overlooked the postcard despite searching carefully for it. 'Yes, I could have missed it if it had got into the crease of the paper' he said. Privately, the police had no doubt that the postcard was missed as a result of their own incompetence. After the conclusion of the trial, Sir Melville Macnaghten wrote to Inspector Neil's superior officer, Superintendent Vedy, saying, 'With the exception of the search of the room where the victim Dimmock was murdered (and which search I am bound to say was not made with greatness of care) I have nothing but praise for the manner in which this very difficult case was conducted.'[430] If the police themselves accepted that they had made a mess of the search, it is likely that they actually did.

Even if Shaw had found the postcard before Emily's murder, it would have been difficult for him have to killed her considering he was in Sheffield at the time. He was working in the dining car on the 5:42pm train from St Pancras which was timetabled to arrive in Sheffield at 9:17pm.[431] It is true that he could have caught the 11:29pm train back from Sheffield, returning to St Pancras at 4:20am, but Inspector Neil apparently established 'beyond any doubt' that Shaw was in Sheffield on the night of the murder and did not return to London until 10:45am on 12 September.[432] He even obtained a statement from a witness – probably a fellow employee who slept in a house in the same street – who saw Shaw in Sheffield that night, that statement being offered to the defence (although it has not survived).[433] In the face of this, Marshall Hall conceded, 'I accept at once the statement that he was at Sheffield on this particular night', adding, 'My object in asking the questions I did will be seen later' although, more than one hundred years later, if it was not to suggest that Shaw was the murderer, it is difficult to see what he was getting at.

Robert Roberts was another prosecution witness with what appeared to be a rock solid alibi. He was seen by Edward Smeeth to leave the *Rising Sun* with Frank Clarke at about quarter past midnight in the morning of 12 September and the two men were both let into their hotel by the proprietress, Amelia Lesage. Mrs Lesage, a woman in her mid-thirties, was born in Scotland and had married a Frenchman, Edward Lesage, in about 1891, originally living with him in Belfast. The 1901 census shows that Edward was working as a chef in Lancashire but, by 1907, was the proprietor of the Euston Temperance Hotel and, at the same time, a chief officer in the mercantile marine. So Mrs Lesage appears to have been a perfectly respectable woman and she said that she locked up the hotel after Roberts and Clarke came in. Clarke said that Roberts was staying in a room above him on the third floor and that, after a short discussion (on an unknown topic), Roberts went up to his room at about 1:00am. In the morning, the two men breakfasted together in the coffee room at 10:00am.

It is a reasonably solid alibi but would only qualify as rock solid if it was impossible for Roberts to have left the hotel after the doors were locked, about which we have no evidence. Clarke was a convicted thief but, as his evidence was corroborated by Mrs Lesage, this is not so important. Still, there was some interesting information to emerge about Frank Clarke after the Wood trial. In February 1909, he was arrested for stealing three overcoats and a pair of gloves, with a total value of £14, from houses in Houghton Street and Russell Square. There had been forty robberies of overcoats in the neighbourhood and it would seem that Clarke was suspected of being responsible for most, if not all, of them. The items of clothing Clarke was charged with stealing all belonged to women. He was tried at the London Sessions on 9 March 1909 when he pleaded guilty and was sentenced to twelve months in prison with hard labour, which he served at Wormwood Scrubs.[434] The interesting information revealed by the police, either during his trial or following his conviction (the precise timing is unclear but it was reported by the press after the trial), was that he had been interviewed during the police investigation into the murder of Esther Prager, a prostitute who had been found dead from strangulation in lodgings near Russell Square in October 1908. The officer investigating this murder was Detective Inspector James Stockley, who was also involved in assisting Inspector Neil with the Dimmock investigation, and it seems that he became aware that Clarke had lived at the same lodgings in which Prager was murdered, albeit that Clarke had apparently moved out before Prager moved in. There was no mention of Clarke in any newspaper reports of the inquest into Prager's death and one cannot help but think that the fact that the police released this information in 1909, together with a reminder that he was a witness in Emily Dimmock's murder, indicates that they had some suspicion that he was involved in the murder of both Dimmock and Prager but could not prove it.

If we consider that Frank Clarke was a regular at the *Rising Sun* and would surely have known the prostitutes who used that establishment very well, he suddenly becomes an interesting suspect in his own right. In particular, as a friend of Roberts, he knew (as he admitted during the trial) that Emily had been paid to sleep with him so that she must have had some money in her purse. As we have seen, Clarke denied that Roberts told him before the murder that he had slept with Emily on three nights but he might have worked this out himself. In fact, it is possible that the reason for the apparent reversal in his evidence, complained about so vehemently by Marshall Hall, was because he realised the implication of Marshall Hall's comment that it was a strange thing for Roberts to have told him that he had slept with Emily for three nights, namely that it showed he was very close to Roberts and was privy to his secrets. Knowing that

Roberts had slept with Emily for three nights, and knowing Emily's charge-out rate, meant that he would have known Roberts must have paid her more than £2 for her services which, in itself, would have been a tempting sum for a petty thief like Clarke.

It seems likely that Roberts was annoyed with Emily because, despite paying her large sums of money for three nights in a row and being prepared to pay more, she did not show up in the *Rising Sun* on the Wednesday night. While the evidence is not conclusive, reading between the lines it seems that he waited all night for her in the *Rising Sun*, only giving up at, or shortly before, closing time. It is a fact that Emily was a topic of conversation between Roberts and Clarke as they sat drinking together in the *Rising Sun*. In his statement to the police of 15 September, Clarke revealed that Roberts said to him on Wednesday night, 'I know where to find her [Emily]. She is at the *Eagle*, Camden Town'. We have seen that the *Weekly Dispatch* published a diary entry which, if correctly interpreted, appears to reveal that Clarke had to physically drag Roberts back from going to the *Eagle* in an attempt to find (and assault?) Emily. Although the provenance of this diary is completely unknown, it is entirely plausible that such an incident could have occurred and is consistent with what Clarke said in his statement. Frank Clarke was clearly a man who knew how to break into houses so it may be that he was able to break out of the Temperance Hotel. At the same time, Roberts knew where Emily lived. The two of them could have decided to pay the prostitute a visit in the early hours or perhaps Clarke alone decided to rob her. In a drunken state, and angry with her on behalf of his friend, and perhaps, we may conjecture, because she had refused to take him home in the past, could he have slashed her throat?

We know a little bit about Frank Clarke. He was born in Cardiff on 28 December 1883 and his father, Charles Clarke, was a butcher's son who had only recently moved to Cardiff from Devon to run an auction house, shortly before marrying Louisa Bonifant in 1881. As an auctioneer, Charles must have been reasonably wealthy and Frank was educated to a good standard and trained as a draughtsman. By 1901, when Frank was eighteen, the Clarke family had moved to north-west London, with Charles now a farmer at Featherstone Farm in Mill Hill assisted by Frank and his younger brother, Merton. The interesting thing about this is that Emily initially resided in East Finchley, close to Mill Hill, when she first came to London; but there is no evidence that Frank and Emily ever knew each other. By 1906 the Clarkes had moved to Langley Park, also in Mill Hill, but Frank was evidently finding St Pancras a more interesting area of London and travelled there frequently on the Midland Railway. He preferred to do so, however, without paying for a ticket. When challenged by railway inspectors he would offer up a card in the name of 'Evans' while claiming to be in possession of a ticket which he had left at home. On the return journey to Mill Hill Station, he would invariably claim to have boarded at Hendon in order to pay a much reduced fare of only a couple of pence. He even had the nerve to write a letter to the Midland Railway complaining that he was repeatedly being accused of travelling without a proper ticket by a porter at Mill Hill who, he said, seemed to have taken an irrational dislike to him, and he described this porter's conduct as 'scandalous'. However, it was all a bluff; Frank was eventually caught evading his fare and was convicted at Edgware Petty Sessions on 7 February 1906 for 'riding on the Midland Railway between

St Pancras and Mill-hill without having paid his fare, and with intent to avoid payment thereof'.[435] He was fined £2 plus 30 shillings costs. Two months later, in April, he was again caught travelling on a train without having paid his fare, this time falsely claiming to be a season ticket holder on the Metropolitan Railway, probably travelling between Willesden and King's Cross, when challenged. At Willesden Petty Sessions he was fined the rather more hefty sum of £10 plus almost £2 in costs on 2 May 1906.[436]

Before the year was out, Frank was in Wormwood Scrubs, having been convicted and sentenced to six months imprisonment at the North London Sessions on 23 October 1906 for stealing, during July, a gentleman's silver watch and two gold leaf scarf pins valued at £2.[437] Another charge of fraudulently obtaining credit to the value of nine shillings and sixpence was dropped at Marylebone Police Court. His physical appearance can be gleaned from the Home Office Register of Habitual Criminals which states that he was a little under five foot nine inches in height, with a fresh complexion, brown eyes and dark brown hair.[438] In April 1907, shortly after being released from prison, he took up residence at Mrs Lesage's hotel which is where he was living when Robert Roberts showed up in September. At the Wood trial, Clarke claimed to be a commercial clerk although it is quite likely that he was by now a professional thief, especially as he had claimed to be of independent means at Marylebone Police Court in 1906. When released from prison in 1910, following his second conviction for theft, he planned to return to Cardiff (according to the Register for Habitual Criminals[439]) but, ended up with his parents in Hendon, supposedly working for his father as an engineer.

It appeared as if Frank had turned over a new leaf when he was to be found at the end of 1910 sitting on a committee which organised a benefit concert in Hendon for a local 75-year-old railway worker called William Phillips who had become incapacitated due to an accident but was not entitled to a pension. The concert was held at the King's Hall in West Hendon on 20 December 1910 and featured a mixed bag of performers including ventriloquists, comedians, impressionists, jugglers, singers and dancers and was supported by the local magistrate, José Diaz. Over £6 was raised for Mr Phillips but it later transpired that there was £5 of expenses, so it is not clear how beneficial the benefit concert actually was. In any case, it seems that Frank Clarke became excited about this new world of charity fund raising because, in January 1911, he visited two local residents claiming to be collecting money on behalf of the widow and children of a stonemason's labourer called Jennings who had supposedly died of a heart attack. He managed to obtain five shillings from both residents after handing them a subscription list which showed that Mr Diaz was one of the contributors to the charity. But Jennings did not exist and the subscription list was fake. Clarke, who was arrested and charged with obtaining money under false pretences at Edgware Petty Sessions on 2 February 1911, claimed in court that he had been acting in good faith on the instructions of a fellow member of the concert committee, John Millard, to whom he had given the ten shillings. Millard, however, denied that he had anything to do with it and Frank was convicted and sent to Pentonville Prison in 1911 for six months.[440] His father, Charles, who was now working as a debt collector, accountant and estate agent had a close escape the following year when he was sent for trial at the North London Sessions for alleged fraudulent conversion of money he had obtained for a client as a result of his debt collecting service but a grand jury threw the case out in June 1912.[441]

There is nothing in what is known of Frank Clarke's history to suggest he was a potential murderer but he was certainly a thief and it was always thought to be a possibility that the murderer of Emily Dimmock was a common burglar. Shaw gave evidence that the shutters of the windows were usually fastened at night but those in the front room were partly open when he burst in on the morning of 12 September. In a statement made within a few hours of the discovery of the murder, P.C. Thomas Killion said that the windows in the bedroom and the front room 'were both closed and shuttered' although, in view of Shaw's evidence about the partly open shutters in the front room, this could not have been entirely correct. Inspector Neil also recorded in a report dated 13 September that Shaw 'found the windows closed' and, at the inquest, said that 'the windows of the back room were closed and fastened'.[442] Surprisingly, there is no record of whether all the windows were actually locked shut or whether they could have been opened or closed from the outside. It must have been a warm night. Could Emily have left the windows open while she slept which allowed access and were then closed by her murderer?[443] The *Pall Mall Gazette* of 13 September 1907 made an interesting observation:

> The floor that was occupied by the murdered woman is reached from the front garden by a flight of steps. Her bedroom was at the back, and those who favour the robbery theory insist that it could easily have been entered from the back.

So there was, clearly, a contemporary 'robbery theory'. It was quickly quashed by the police theory that the appearance of a robbery was a distraction and it was never really discussed further in the press or even during any of the legal proceedings.

While it is probably true that Emily was not murdered for the sake of the money in her purse and her few possessions, the murderer might easily have taken the opportunity afforded by being alone in her apartment to relieve the deceased of her now redundant goods. Could that murderer have been Frank Clarke? He is certainly the only suspect who seems to have had experience in breaking into houses and we cannot ignore the possibility that he was involved. If he had entered through an open window, he could have closed and fastened the shutters of the window from the inside and left through the front door, making it appear that the windows had been closed all night. More intriguingly, if he entered *and* left the house through the window, then this could explain why the door of Emily's front room (or parlour) was locked and the key missing. Roberts said that when Emily took him into her apartment she locked the door of the front room from the inside. Mrs Stocks' evidence was that Emily usually kept the key to the front door of the house in her purse but left the key to the front room in the lock. However, it may be that, when entertaining a client, Emily put the front room door key in her purse along with the front door key. Consequently, if the purse was stolen and the murderer entered and exited through a window it would account for the door remaining locked. It hardly seems likely that the murderer, on fleeing the scene of the crime, would waste precious time by turning his (or her) back and locking the door when there was no need to do so. By standing in the corridor of the house to lock the door, the murderer would have been putting himself (or herself) at unnecessary risk of being caught. For that reason, an explanation for the murder which does not involve the murderer locking the door has its attractions.

Admittedly, we do not know if it was even possible for anyone to have exited through the open windows of either the bedroom or the front room and then closed both the shutters and the window from the outside. Shaw used the word 'fastened' to describe how the shutters were closed (Inspector Neil referred to them being 'pulled to') but equally the shutters of the front room window were only partially closed or 'half-closed' according to Shaw. At the Old Bailey, Shaw said that 'there was a gap of about a foot' in the shutters. The police theory was that the murderer opened those shutters in order to see what he or she was doing (especially with regard to the photograph album) but, if the murder was committed during the night, in the darkness, it is questionable how much benefit opening one of the shutters would have been. Sunrise was at 5:30am on 12 September but it would have started to get light from about 4:30am so it is possible that opening the shutter at some point after this time might have been of benefit to someone in the room. However, Shaw said that the front room was normally lit by a lamp and that 'There were signs of a lamp having been burnt out' so that might have been how the murderer was able to see. If it was possible to close the windows from the outside then it may be that the reason for the shutter being partially open was because the murderer escaped through the front room window and was unable to close the shutter from the outside. The problem with this theory, though, is that it would surely have been easier to leave the house by the front door than jumping out through the front room window. One could understand a surreptitious exit through the bedroom window at the back of the house but squeezing through the front window into the main street defies logic unless the murderer was trying to create a 'locked room' mystery, which seems unlikely.

Even if the murderer did leave the house through the window, thus ensuring the front room door would be found locked, this would not explain why Shaw found the connecting doors between the front room and the bedroom locked. The murderer clearly moved between the bedroom and the front room to search through the chest of drawers so the door must have been unlocked at some point during the crime. But were the connecting doors actually locked? Shaw certainly believed they were but in the stress of the moment, finding the front room ransacked and believing Emily in danger, he might have assumed the folding doors were locked, just as the front room door had been, when the mechanism was simply a bit stuck. Without an examination of the doors this can only be pure speculation but Shaw seems to have burst through them without any difficulty. Finding Emily dead in the bedroom, he would not have been concentrating on the state of the door even for a second so it is possible he could have been mistaken. He was not asked about this by anyone, so we can never know what he would have said, but the odds are probably against it, especially as the key to the folding doors was missing which suggests that those doors were locked by the murderer from the outside, otherwise it should have still been in the lock where Shaw said it was usually kept.

Another prosecution witness who might have been the murderer was William Linehan. He evidently believed that Emily was somehow responsible for his spending six weeks of a two-month sentence in prison for running a brothel in early 1906 so could have harboured a grudge against her. It would have had to have been a long held grudge though, and one nurtured from a distance, because, by September 1907, Linehan had moved out of St Pancras to Southwark. According to Inspector Neil's report of 30 September 1907, he was at home with 'his wife' during the evening of 11 September, a reference to Gladys Warren who still regarded herself as married to him despite not having been through any form of wedding ceremony. As she had given false evidence in his support in April 1906, it would not be at all surprising if she had provided a false alibi for him but the alibi was confirmed by his landlady so that probably rules him out of contention. The interesting thing about William Linehan, though, is that, like Frank Clarke, he was involved in two major unsolved murder cases in the early twentieth century.

William's sister, Agnes, has already featured in this story, having assaulted Gladys Warren outside the St Pancras Coroner's Court. She had married John Starchfield, a former soldier, then a market porter, in October 1903 and gave birth to a son, John, in June 1904.[444] The marriage did not go well. Starchfield was regularly drunk and he beat his wife who, in response, unsuccessfully attempted suicide by taking salts of lemon (otherwise known as potassium oxalate). That being a crime, she was arrested and charged at the North London Police Court where the magistrate, Mr Fordham, told Starchfield to treat his wife better in the future or 'he would get into trouble'.[445] His words had no effect and Starchfield continued to knock his wife about so that she ran away with her son to be taken care of by the Society for the Protection of Women and Children. A separation order was granted in January 1906 at Marlborough Street Police Court and Starchfield was supposed to give Agnes, who was then pregnant, an allowance of five shillings weekly but he never paid anything and was, consequently, sentenced to twenty-one days imprisonment at Marlborough Street Police Court. At the time he boasted that he would rather do twenty-one days in prison than hand over five pounds to his wife. Further attempts to force him to pay were unsuccessful and there was more misery for Agnes when her second son, Christopher, died of a wasting disease aged two months in April 1906, followed later in the same year by the death of John from pneumonia, caught after a bout of measles.

In July 1907, Agnes took her husband back and they were living together when they had another son, Charles William, in June 1908. He was evidently named after Agnes' two brothers, Charles and William, but his first name was abandoned and he was always called William, or Willie for short. Starchfield was then working as a news vendor but, at the start of December 1908, he left home, taking all of Agnes' money after drunkenly tearing up every article of clothing she owned. He returned a few weeks later on Christmas Day and smashed up all the furniture, causing Agnes to send for the police and apply to Bow Street Police Court where she was granted a summons for desertion and obtained a further separation/maintenance order. Little Willie became ill with bronchitis and Agnes was forced to obtain parish relief to survive.

Starchfield was sentenced to three months hard labour in January 1909 for failing to comply with the maintenance order made against him. At the end of the year he attacked his wife in the street then followed her home claiming that he wanted to see Willie, who was sick again, and insisted that he would not leave until he was allowed to do so. He told her that if she attempted to have him turned out or called the police he would kill both her and Willie. Then he became remorseful and promised to give up drinking if she would take him back for the sake of the child but, when she did, he continued drinking and deserted her again. Times were hard for young Willie too. In January 1910, he was admitted to King's College Hospital suffering from pneumonia then, two years later, caught scarlet fever. In between this, in March 1910, Starchfield was again sentenced to three months in prison for continuing non-compliance with the maintenance order against him.

There was a twist in the story though. On 27 September 1912, the wife-beater, John Starchfield, became an unlikely hero. Shortly after 11:00am on that day, a powerfully built Turkish man called Stephen Titus walked into the bar of the Horseshoe Hotel, Tottenham Court Road, with a loaded revolver and, after ordering a drink, shot dead the assistant manageress and immediately fired a second shot which wounded the barmaid. He then fired four more shots and fled the scene, chased by onlookers, while re-loading his revolver. John Starchfield was at his usual newspaper stand outside Tottenham Court Road tube station when he saw Titus running down the road and joined the pursuit. He caught up with him in Great Russell Street and grappled with the man but was shot in the stomach at close range. Other members of the public assisted in the chase and Titus was eventually overpowered. He was tried for murder and found guilty but insane at the Old Bailey in November, being dispatched to Broadmoor Asylum. Starchfield spent time recovering from injuries to his abdomen and spleen in the Middlesex Hospital, and then in a convalescent home, until May 1913 but was rewarded with £50 by the trial judge; subsequently he was also awarded £1 a week for six months (followed by a reduced weekly sum) from the Carnegie Hero Fund which had been established in Britain in September 1908 with a sum of £250,000 by the Scottish born American philanthropist, Andrew Carnegie, to reward those injured (or the dependants of those killed) in heroic efforts to save human life.

After leaving the convalescent home, Starchfield returned to Agnes but they were unable to live happily together and parted for the last time in October 1913, although friction appears to have remained between the couple over Starchfield's money from the Carnegie Fund which was received directly by Agnes in the form of postal orders. Agnes moved into lodgings in Hampstead Road and tried to earn a living as a tailoress but was unable to obtain work. In November, the unfortunate Willie, now five years old, having recently recovered from a bout of ringworm, was knocked down by a motor vehicle and fractured his collarbone. He was treated at the nearby Temperance Hospital and made a rapid recovery, although he had to wear his arm in a sling for the rest of the year. Agnes remained close to her brothers, Charles and William Linehan, and, on Wednesday 7 January 1914, Charles spent the evening playing with his nephew. William was at this time running a second hand furniture shop in Leather Lane assisted by Charles. The next day, 8 January, while Agnes was visiting a friend, little Willie was sent on an errand to a nearby shop by Agnes' landlady. A few hours later, his dead body was found in the carriage of a train on the North London Railway. The little boy had been strangled.

At the inquest on 29 January 1914 at Shoreditch Coroner's Court, the jury sensationally brought a verdict of murder against John Starchfield as two witnesses said they had seen him with his son on the afternoon of the murder, one in Kentish Town Road and the other at Camden Town Railway Station.

Starchfield was arrested and committal proceedings were commenced against him at Old Street Police Court in what had become known as the North London Train Murder case. On 6 February, William Linehan and his younger brother Charles were both at the police court. For the purpose of being eliminated from the inquiry they were asked to stand up so that they could be identified by Agnes' landlady who said she had seen one of Agnes' brothers visiting Agnes in November. It appears that she had seen William because the brother she described was about 30 years of age (whereas Charles was only 19). Thus it was that Linehan was personally involved in his second major murder case.

The prosecution of Starchfield did not go well for the Crown, despite the appearance in the police court of a third witness who said he saw the prisoner with his son on the day of the murder. His statement had been taken by none other than Inspector Neil. That witness attempted to commit suicide by inhaling gas after he was unnerved by allegations made by Starchfield's lawyer that he had a drinking problem, and the defence managed to create sufficient doubt about the identification evidence of the other two witnesses. Consequently, on the second day of Starchfield's trial at the Old Bailey, the Crown decided to offer no further evidence and Starchfield was formally acquitted on 1 April.

Two months later, a penniless Agnes was arrested for threatening to commit suicide after she was found in tears with a bottle of hydrochloric acid and a letter in her possession in which she said she could not go on living without her son. She also told a police constable who arrested her that she hoped to soon be 'joining the angels'. She was brought before the magistrate at Marylebone Police Court on 23 June where her brother, presumably William, said he was prepared to take care of her. The magistrate, however, thought Agnes was suffering from hysteria and wanted her medically examined but on 30 June she was handed over into her brother's care. Despite this, Agnes was back in court four weeks later after she was summonsed at Marlborough Street Police Court for assaulting a woman in Wardour Street who appeared to suggest she had something to hide from the police. The magistrate, who caused her to be bound over to keep the peace, said she appeared to be 'an excitable and neurotic sort of woman'.

John Starchfield died in the infirmary of the St Pancras Workhouse on 20 April 1916, having been admitted suffering from consumption. Four days later, a handwritten note in a bottle was recovered from the River Thames, off Northfleet, which said 'I, John Starchfield, hereby confess that I murdered my son in 1914' but police enquiries established it was not in Starchfield's handwriting and they concluded it was a hoax. In September 1916, a forty-year-old tramp called John Fitzgerald confessed to Willie's murder but his story did not match the known facts and he was sent to the workhouse. Five years later, in 1921, a man calling himself Zach Tiratzin claimed to have raped and killed Willie but, as there was no sexual assault involved, he was not believed. The murder of Willie Starchfield was never solved.

George Stocks was not considered a suspect for the murder of Emily Dimmock until 1966 with the publication of a book entitled *Marshall Hall* containing a chapter on the Camden Town murder by Nina Warner Hooke and Gilbert Thomas. The authors had noticed that, when being re-examined by Sir Charles Mathews at the Old Bailey as to why he had not heard anyone leaving the house on the morning of Thursday 12 September, Mr Stocks had said, 'At twenty minutes to five my alarm clock went off, and I was awakened by it, but I went to sleep again until twenty minutes past five'. The significance of this for the prosecution was that it would explain how the murderer could have slipped out into St Paul's Road some fifteen minutes after hearing the alarm going off, to be seen by McCowan, without Stocks hearing anything. Hooke and Thomas, however, wondered why Stocks was so tired that he fell back to sleep for forty minutes. He was an engine cleaner employed by the London and North Western Railway and would have needed to be at work on time which, they said, was 5:30am. They pointed out that if he had been liable to oversleep he would have been sacked for unpunctuality so that his drifting back to sleep after the alarm went off must have been an unusual event.

Unfortunately, however, Hooke and Warner got their timings wrong. Stocks only needed to report to his place of employment in Granby Street, off the Hampstead Road, at 6:00am, not 5:30am as Hooke and Warner believed. Granby Street, as Stocks said in his evidence, was twenty minutes away from St Paul's Road. On the morning of 12 September, Stocks said he left his house shortly after 5:30am so must have managed to get dressed (and have a cup of tea, which he said he generally had before he went out) in about ten or fifteen minutes which would appear to be feasible. He told Sir Charles, 'I had to make a rush to get to work by six', but it seems he made it. There is no evidence as to whether he always got straight out of bed as soon as he heard his alarm clock at 4:40am or whether he regularly took the opportunity to go back to sleep, presumably to be awakened by his wife in good time for him to leave his house before twenty minutes to six. Consequently, the point is not quite as good as it might first have seemed.

Hooke and Thomas believed that Mr and Mrs Stocks must have known that Emily was a prostitute and, that being so, speculated that George might have brooded about the 'forbidden joys' of having an attractive and available woman in the house and had 'resentment burning and boiling in him till it erupted into action'. They did not spell out what happened next but presumably they thought he must have crept into Emily's room but was rejected by her, causing him to murder her so that she did not tell his wife what he had attempted to do. Strangely enough, Hooke and Thomas did not mention the best point in favour of Stocks being the murderer: this is that the door of Emily's room was locked. As already mentioned, it makes no sense on the face of it for the murderer to have wasted time, and added to the risk of being caught, by locking the door in the middle of the night. If George Stocks was the murderer, the answer as to why he would have locked the door is simple: the last thing he would have wanted when he woke up early in the morning was for his wife to discover the murder before he left for work. If she did, he would have had to calm her down and go out to find a policeman which inevitably would have made him late for work, which in turn could have cost him his job. Moreover, he would have had to have put on an act of pretending to know nothing about the murder for the entire morning. Far better, he might have thought, for him to get out of the house and leave it for his wife and Shaw, then the police, to deal with the drama of the discovery of his crime.

Against this, if he was the murderer he must have taken Emily's purse and possessions which he would have needed to hide and then dispose of. Taking them back to his room at night would have been a huge risk and it would surely have made more sense to remove nothing other than the door key. Perhaps the temptation of stealing from Emily was too much to resist, especially after seeing how much money she was carrying in her purse.

The fact that the door was locked is also a factor which means we need to look at whether Mrs Stocks could have been the murderer. She said in her evidence that she always knocked at Emily's door at about 9:00am (and tried to do so on the morning of 12 September but, not receiving a reply, assumed she had gone out to meet Mrs Shaw). Had the door not been locked, therefore, she would have been the person to discover the murder. One can easily understand that the murderer would have preferred someone else to do this. Hooke and Warner raised the possibility that the murderer could have been a woman. We have seen that Dr Thompson said that it would not have taken a person of great physical strength to cut Emily's throat so it cannot be assumed that the killer must have been a man. Hooke and Warner put forward Ruby Young as a candidate due to her jealousy that Wood was seeing Emily but this does not really work because Ruby had ended her relationship with Wood and, in any case, if she had been the murderer she would hardly have turned down the opportunity of adopting a free alibi from Wood. Ruby explained that the reason why Wood's alibi would not have worked was because she was with someone else during the Wednesday evening, meaning that her lie could have been easily exposed, and there is no reason to disbelieve that. There might have been many other women annoyed with Emily for sleeping with their boyfriends (or for giving them venereal disease) but, unless that woman broke into Emily's house in the middle of the night, the murderer was unlikely to have been such a woman, bearing in mind that Emily appears to have been murdered in her sleep. While we can envisage Emily sleeping with a male friend or client in her room, she is not likely to have gone to bed in the presence of a furious female visitor.

What about a woman with a key to Emily's room? As the landlady of the property, Mrs Stocks would have had one. In fact, we know she did because that is how Shaw was able to gain entry on the Thursday morning. According to Mrs Stocks, in her evidence at the Old Bailey, 'Shaw tried to open the door, but could not get in without a key, so he borrowed mine'. It is the process by which this key emerged that could potentially be the key to the whole mystery. In an interview with *Reynolds's Newspaper* shortly after the murder, Mrs Stocks said that, finding the door of Emily's room locked during the morning of 12 September, Shaw and his mother started on their way towards Euston to search for Emily but then some 'uncontrollable impulse' impelled Shaw to want to enter his apartment and he talked about bursting open the door. Mrs Stocks asked him not to do this, saying, 'I think I have some keys downstairs, one of which may fit'.[446] In other words, by her own account, it was only when Shaw threatened to kick down the door that Mrs Stocks suddenly realised she might be able to find a key to open it. Had there been no such threat, it appears that she would have allowed Shaw and his mother to wander off to Euston to look for Emily. Could that be because she knew what Shaw would find and wanted to delay the discovery of the awful crime for as long as possible? One would have expected a landlady to know whether she had spare keys to the rooms in her house so the fact that it evidently took some time for her to realise she could gain access to the locked room must be considered a little suspicious.

There is also the curious behaviour of the murderer in, according to Dr Thompson, mopping up the blood from the wound in Emily's throat with her bedclothes and pillows. From a photograph of Emily's bedroom, published in the *Daily Mirror* of 9 October 1907, there appears to have been a large rug underneath Emily's bed. Why would her murderer have cared if some blood dropped onto the rug? If, however, the murderer was the owner of that rug, as Mrs Stocks presumably was, it would have made perfect sense.

If Mrs Stocks was responsible, one can only assume it was because she was furious after discovering the existence of a sexual relationship between Emily and her husband. There is, however, no evidence of this. We know that Emily socialised with Mr and Mrs Stocks because George Stocks said that during the evening of 11 September she sat with them in their kitchen, and he was able to recall what she was wearing that day, suggesting that he had been looking at her. As set out below, there is even some evidence to suggest that he was alone with Emily in her apartment shortly before she left to meet Wood but, at the same time, there is no indication of anything going on between them. There is no point in speculating further but if George found out what his wife had done during the middle of the night, and agreed to help her cover up the crime, it might explain why he was unable to get out of bed when his alarm went off the next morning.

In the context of suspicions arising against Mr and Mrs Stocks it may be instructive to look more closely at their evidence regarding Emily's movements during the evening of 11 September because it is fair to say that there are a number of inconsistencies in that evidence. When questioned by the police immediately after the murder, as recorded in her written statement dated 12 September 1907, Mrs Stocks said she spoke to Emily in the kitchen in the basement on the Wednesday evening 'between 8 and 9pm' when Emily told her she was going out and that 'She went out I believe some time after nine'. When giving an additional statement to the police on 8 October, Mrs Stocks continued to maintain that she saw Emily between '8 and 9pm', adding that her hair was in curling pins and she was not dressed as if she was going out for a walk. She also said that there was 'no time' between then and 'the time I heard her go out' for her to have arranged her hair. When she came to the inquest she said she did not see Emily go out on the Wednesday evening, which was consistent with her written statement to the extent that she only said she heard her leave, but at the police court in November she said that she heard Emily go out at 'about 8.20' so her memory of events had changed from hearing Emily leave 'after nine' to some forty minutes before nine.[447] Furthermore, she now said that she 'last saw the woman alive between seven and eight o'clock' which was, as a range, a whole hour's difference from between eight and nine when she had originally believed she had spoken to Emily in the kitchen.[448] A report in the *Islington Daily Gazette* was more specific, reporting that Mrs Stocks said that the last time she saw Emily was '7.30 or 7.45'.[449] She repeated this at the trial when she also mentioned for the first time that she had seen Emily tidying the rooms upstairs in preparation for Shaw's return home, although she did not specify the time when she saw her doing this. She clarified that Emily came into the kitchen, wearing a brown velvet skirt and light blouse with her hair in curling pins, and then left the kitchen to return to her apartment on the first floor between 7:30 and 7:45pm before she heard the door bang to at either 8:15

or 8:20pm. While this evidence in relation to the timing of events was consistent with her evidence at the police trial it was not consistent with the evidence in her written statement.

George Stocks' evidence also contained a number of inconsistencies. In his written statement of 12 September he revealed that he saw Emily quite frequently in a two and a half hour period after his return from work at 6:00pm. He said he saw her 'several times' in the back yard and then when she came into the kitchen and sat down. He did not say if Mrs Stocks was present in the kitchen at this stage but one assumes not because he recalled Emily saying that she had to go out to buy a lamp whereas Mrs Stocks never mentioned anything like this. After Emily told him she was going out, Mr Stocks says he went up to the first floor to put his children to bed and then saw Emily again at 8:30pm although he does not say where. In his oral evidence at the police court, however, he said that he had some conversation with her at 8:05pm and 'she was then in the front parlour'.[450] This suggests that he spoke to her inside her apartment because no other 'front parlour' has ever been mentioned. It is unclear if Emily had been out and returned, having purchased her lamp, but Mr Stocks said in his statement that Emily now told him she was going to clean up her fender brasses. In his oral evidence at the inquest, he said she was wearing her favourite green costume 'and seemed to be preparing to go out'. In the written statement he said 'I believe she went out but I did not hear her' but in his oral evidence at the police court he said that at about quarter past eight he 'heard the front door slam'.[451] He said the same thing about hearing the door slam at the Old Bailey so it seems that, contrary to what he said in his written statement, he did, in fact, hear her leave the house. It is strange that he could have omitted such a fundamental part of the story from his written statement. Furthermore, it seems that at no time in his oral evidence did he mention Emily telling him that she was going out to buy a lamp or that she was going to clean the fender brasses. It may also be noted that, at the Old Bailey, George said that Emily was wearing 'a light brown skirt and a short jacket' when he last saw her, in distinct contrast to his initial claim that she had been wearing her green costume.[452] As to that, it is hard to see how she could have changed into her green outfit considering that Mrs Stocks said she last saw Emily in her brown skirt and believed there was no time for her to have arranged her hair before she went out, in which case there was also presumably no time for her to have changed her clothes.

It is to be expected that honest witnesses will give inconsistent evidence and that memories will improve or fade with time. Sometimes witnesses will speak to others and incorporate what they have been told into their own story without even being aware that they have done so. Mrs Stocks, for example, might have adjusted the time she believed Emily left the house after discussing the issue with her husband and there would be nothing sinister about this. It is also possible, however, that the inconsistencies identified in their respective stories indicate that the couple were not being truthful. Putting the inconsistencies aside, it does appear that George Stocks was alone with Emily in her parlour at some point shortly after 8:00pm. Nevertheless, the likelihood is that Mr and Mrs Stocks had nothing at all to do with Emily's murder and we are discussing the involvement of a perfectly innocent couple in a ghastly crime. Ultimately, we have to rely on the professional instincts of Inspector Neil and his detectives that there was nothing amiss about the behaviour of the Stocks.

In considering whether any of the prosecution witnesses could have been the murderer of Emily Dimmock we briefly need to mention, for completeness, Jack Crabtree. He had a motive in that Emily had stolen money and a curtain pole from him and there was nothing that Crabtree cared for more than money. The fact that he was in prison at the time of the murder certainly rules him out from personally being involved but he could have paid someone to carry it out. However, although Crabtree did work with accomplices when carrying out his frauds, there is nothing in his known history to suggest he ever employed anyone to use violence on his behalf nor that he was ever violent himself. If Crabtree's evidence against Wood was false it was either because he was playing games with the police or wanted reward money; it was not because he was the murderer.

A contemporary sketch of Gladys Warren

Alexander Mackie ('Scotch Bob')

Frank Clarke

Robert Roberts

William Linehan

Chapter Sixteen

Verdict

'How did it feel when I confronted the jury at the last? Strange as it may seem, I felt inclined to laugh!'

Robert Wood, *Evening News*, 19 December 1907

Marshall Hall's advocacy in defence of Robert Wood is often viewed as a classic of its kind but it did not all run smoothly. One of the most important tasks for the defence was to explain how George Wood was now able to provide an alibi for his son in respect of the evening of Wednesday 11 September when he had told Inspector Neil on 4 October that he could not recollect his son's movements on any particular night. The solution Marshall Hall offered to the jury was that, under the pressure of a visit from a police officer, the old man had not been able to think properly. Thus, in his opening speech, Marshall Hall said:

> It is true that Inspector Neil asked the father as to whether he knew where his son was on the Wednesday night. He replied: "I cannot answer until I think it over". That was the answer of an honest man.[453]

Mr Wood, unfortunately, had not read the script and sang from rather a different hymn sheet when he was examined in-chief by Marshall Hall. It all started off well enough when Marshall Hall asked Mr Wood what the effect of Inspector Neil's visit had been on 4 October and the old man said, 'I became very nervous'. This was precisely what Marshall Hall expected; and he then asked, 'On that night could you at a moment's notice say what happened on the Wednesday?' The answer recorded in the *Notable British Trials* transcript is 'Yes', which would have been a disaster for Marshall Hall, but that might not have been an accurate transcription. The *Star*'s reporter heard George Wood say 'I could not but I did afterwards'. The following exchange then certainly occurred:

> **Marshall Hall:** Can you remember whether Inspector Neil asked you anything about Wednesday night?
> **George Wood:** I forget really what was said.
> **Marshall Hall:** But something was said?
> **George Wood:** Yes.
> **Marshall Hall:** Tell the jury frankly, could you remember then exactly what occurred on 9th, 10th or 11th September?
> **George Wood:** On the night of the 4th October I could remember what happened on the Wednesday.

It was completely the wrong answer. If he could remember on 4 October what happened on the Wednesday then why didn't he tell Inspector Neil? Marshall Hall was too experienced an advocate to draw attention to the issue and moved swiftly on to a different subject. Sir Charles Mathews smelt blood, however, and asked Mr Wood in cross-examination to confirm that he had told Inspector Neil that he could not say what time his son would return home after going out. Mr Wood said it was very likely that he had said this but denied that he had told the inspector that he could not speak of his son's movements on any particular night. Sir Charles pointed out that he had given the opposite impression to the coroner and pressed him further:

Sir Charles Mathews: Do you repeat that you did not tell Inspector Neil that you could not recall any particular night?
George Wood: Yes.
Sir Charles Mathews: All that you could tell him was that it was accused's custom to come in and fetch the clock, but you could not speak to any particular night as sometimes you were asleep?
George Wood: No.

This was the very evidence that Marshall Hall did not want from his witness because it put him in direct conflict with Inspector Neil who was very clear that George Wood had told him that he could not recall what time his son had returned on any particular night, including the Wednesday night. Marshall Hall was perfectly happy to accept Neil's evidence and simply focus on the fact that no-one could have been expected to remember what had happened one night three weeks earlier, especially during a surprise visit from a police officer accusing one's son of murder. When questioning James Wood, he highlighted this difficulty by asking him, 'If you were asked now what took place on, say 20 November, would you be able to say without thinking about it?' and James dutifully answered 'No'.

It was James who explained what had happened the day after Inspector Neil's visit. He told the court that his father had then tried to recall what had happened in the week commencing 9 September and worked out that he had returned home from hospital on the Monday so that it must have been on the Wednesday, two nights later, that his liniment bottle was knocked over, staining the hearthrug. On its own, such a spillage would have meant nothing but George Wood believed the incident helped him fix Wednesday night as the night Robert returned to 12 Frederick Street at about midnight and entered his room in order to collect the clock he had lent him after his own had broken. James also said he was sure that he, too, remembered seeing his half-brother a few minutes before midnight when he made a cheery remark and said 'goodnight', although it took him about a week after the inspector's visit before this recollection came to him. The reason for the delay, he explained in cross-examination, was that he believed his brother would be freed a few days after his arrest so did not bother to concentrate on the issue of his whereabouts on the night of the murder. This was a little odd because he evidently knew his father had been trying his best to work out on 5 October what had happened on the Wednesday yet he gave it no thought himself until about 8 or 9 October.

During cross-examination, James accepted most of what Inspector Neil claimed he had said on 4 October but denied having told the inspector that he was sometimes asleep when his half-brother returned home. On the contrary, he said he *never* went to sleep before Robert's return, although under questioning from the judge he appeared to accept that he did not always know when Robert had returned home.

The sudden realisation by both George and James that they remembered seeing Robert on the Wednesday night when they had clearly told Inspector Neil that they had no such recollection is certainly curious, notwithstanding Marshall Hall's reasonable point that it would have been difficult for them to instantly recall any particular night on demand, and its value is limited. Yet, their evidence nevertheless did have some value and Inspector Neil's failure to obtain written statements, committing their absence of recollection to paper, was obviously a major error.

It should be mentioned that George's evidence was partially corroborated by his doctor, Dr Humphreys, who testified that he prescribed lotion for his patient's gouty eczema and ulceration of the foot on Tuesday 10 September and was then told on the following Monday that the old man had had an accident with the bottle, so prescribed some more. Thus, there was definitely a spillage of the lotion at some point between the Tuesday 10 September and Monday 16 September but this does not really go anywhere to supporting Wood's alibi.

There was, however, independent evidence put forward by the defence that Wood had returned home shortly before midnight on the Wednesday. This came from another resident of 12 Frederick Street: 66-year-old Joseph Rogers, who lived in the basement of the property. He swore he had seen Wood walking down Frederick Street from the direction of Gray's Inn Road and then entering number 12 at about ten minutes before midnight on 11 September. The prosecution were rightly suspicious as to how it was possible for Rogers to be so sure he had seen Wood on a particular evening when he could only have applied his mind to the matter three weeks after the event at the earliest. Yet, Rogers had a decent explanation for this. He said he was a keen fisherman and a member of the Great Northern Brothers' Angling Society through which he had participated in an angling contest on Sunday 15 September. To prepare for the contest, Rogers required bait which he always collected outside his apartment on the Wednesday before any contest taking place on a Sunday. Thus, he was able to state positively that he was in the garden in the front of his house gathering worms during the evening of Wednesday 11 September and that it was then that he saw Wood returning to number 12.[454]

While it might seem strange for a fisherman to be collecting bait so late at night, Rogers had an answer for everything Sir Charles threw at him while, at the same time, exuding 'an air of kindliness and friendliness and good humour'.[455] He said that the preparation of his bait took exactly four days, which is why he was certain he was out collecting lob worms on the Wednesday in preparation for the Sunday contest; any earlier and the worms would not be as fresh as he liked them to be in order to attract fish; any later and he would not have enough time to prepare them. Apparently, the preparation involved scouring the lob worms in milk which required a certain number of days to ensure they were at their optimal condition by the time of the contest. It was not, however, explained why he did not collect his bait during daylight hours although he gave a partial explanation in that he suffered from bronchitis and seldom went to bed before 2:00am. On the whole, though, his answers seemed reasonable and only towards the end of his cross-examination did he become a little defensive when Sir Charles commented, 'You seem to remember Wednesday very well' and, in response, he prayed in aid the fact that his daughter, eight-year-old Louisa, had been ill that day – an unnecessary reference if he had been absolutely sure that he only collected his bait on Wednesdays.

The question was also raised as to whether Rogers could have confused Wood with his half-brother but he said he was able to distinguish them, having known the family for twelve months. Marshall Hall managed to make one of the best jokes of the trial by confirming with Rogers that, although he was a fisherman, not all of his stories were necessarily untrue. His evidence certainly had the benefit that he was a totally independent witness. He had been living at 12 Frederick Street since at least 1898, when his daughter was born, many years before the Woods moved there. It is possible that he was friendly with George Wood because his own father, Frederick, had been a compositor but that in itself does not seem likely to have affected his evidence. We know a reasonable amount about Joseph's life because we can trace him through all the censuses. Although there is nothing in his history to suggest he might have been a perjurer – and Marshall Hall would later describe him as 'one of the most honest witnesses ever called before a jury'[456] – there are a couple of issues thrown up from the records that might make us doubt his honesty.

Joseph was born and baptised as Joseph William Rogers in the City of London in 1837; his first job appears to have been as an errand boy, as recorded in the 1851 census. He was then aged fourteen and living with his parents. By 1861, Joseph had moved to Birmingham where he worked as a gas fitter and married Harriet Jackson from Stockton-on-Tees. For reasons unknown, Joseph's father, Frederick, is described as a 'Baronet' on the marriage certificate when he was no such thing, and, if this was a deliberate lie, as opposed to some sort of clerical error, it was an extraordinary one for someone calling describing himself as a 'gas fitter' to tell. There *was* a fifty-year-old Baronet, Sir Frederick Rogers, alive in 1861 but he and his wife, Georgina, were childless.[457] Joseph and Harriet moved to London, Islington, and gave birth to a girl, Phoebe, in 1867, with Joseph still described as a gas fitter on the birth certificate and in the 1871 census. We then have our first real problem with Joseph because, on Christmas Day of 1872, he married 20-year-old Mary Ann Jackson in Battersea but described himself as a 'Bachelor' on the marriage certificate. What had become of Harriet is uncertain.[458] He also lied about his age, claiming to be 31 when he was actually 34. When he had married Harriet in January 1861 he correctly stated that he was 23 years old so it was not a question of his having lost track of his age as a child like some of his contemporaries. He had also changed occupations and was now a 'Property Maker'. His father, however, was now correctly described as a compositor. In the 1881 census, Joseph's occupation was clarified to be 'Theatrical Property Maker', possibly explained by the fact that his wife described herself as a 'Theatrical professional' in the 1891 census. By this time, however, Joseph, now living in Clerkenwell, had become a jeweller. In 1898, Joseph and Mary Ann gave birth to a girl, Louisa Margaret, and Joseph had reverted to describing himself as a gas fitter. He was then living at 12 Frederick Street and he was still there at the time of the 1901 census when his occupation is recorded as 'jeweller, gold'. However, his wife is now 43-year-old Kate Rogers. What has happened to Mary Ann is not clear, just as it was not clear what happened to Harriet. We know that Joseph was living at 12 Frederick Street in 1907; when he appeared at the Old Bailey in December, he said he was a 'jeweller'.

In his 1911 census return, which Joseph filled in and signed personally, he is still shown to be living at 12 Frederick Street but is working as a street vendor, selling vegetables.[459] Aside from the fact that Joseph now correctly stated his age as 74, there is a curious factor about this return. In the column in which he is supposed to state how long the 'present marriage' has lasted,

Joseph first entered '50 years' which is crossed out and '15 years' has been entered in its place. As he had married Harriet fifty years earlier, in 1861, he evidently became confused, which is understandable, but he could not have married Kate fifteen years earlier, in 1896, because Louisa Margaret's 1898 birth certificate makes clear that he was still married to Mary Ann at that time.[460] So there is something rather unusual in Joseph's life history which might cast some doubt upon his veracity.

Nevertheless, if we take a step back and look at the bigger picture, it would seem to be almost certain that Robert Wood had returned to 12 Frederick Street by midnight regardless of whether he murdered Emily or not. As previously discussed, the false alibi which Wood concocted with Ruby Young lasted only until midnight. He told Inspector Neil that he left Ruby at the Brompton Oratory and travelled by tube to Holborn from where he walked home 'and arrived, as near as I can recall, about midnight'. Had Wood's father, his half-brother and his neighbour all said immediately, when asked by the police, that they remembered him arriving home at midnight we might be suspicious that they were part of a conspiracy with Wood to support his story but their recollections appear to have emerged independently. Without any corroboration of his claim to have returned home after parting from Emily, Wood effectively would have had no alibi for the supposed time of the murder. If he had been with Emily after midnight he would surely have arranged with Ruby that he was with her all night or at least for as long as he had parted from Emily. As he did not, we don't really need any witnesses to be reasonably certain that Wood was tucked up in bed by 1:00am regardless of whatever he had done earlier in the evening.

According to Lilian Raven, Wood left the *Eagle* with Emily at 10:00pm, about ten minutes after Lambert went on his way but, when Wood finally admitted to having been with Emily that night, as he did for the first time in the witness box, he claimed to have left an hour later at around 11:00pm, with Emily remaining in the bar. Of Raven's time estimate, Wood said cattily, 'I do not know how she fixes it'. On his account, he walked straight home to Frederick Street from the *Eagle*. He estimated it would have taken about thirty minutes do so which would be broadly consistent with him returning shortly before midnight.

The notion that Emily must have met another man who killed her was one pushed by the defence which called Harry Sharples and Frederick Harvey, about whom we know virtually nothing. The *Star* described Sharples as 'a clean-shaven young man' when he gave evidence at the inquest and we know that he lived in Wicklow Street, very close to where Wood resided. Sharples claimed to be a commission agent and Harvey, who lived in Islington, said he was a music seller but, according to Inspector Neil, they were nothing more than a couple of pimps. If that was true, it is strange that Sir Charles did not cross-examine them about their occupations. The failure of the prosecution to call them had already been turned into somewhat of a cause célèbre by Marshall Hall. During his opening speech (made after the close of the prosecution's case) he said, 'The Crown has had proof from Harvey and Sharples that at 12.30 the woman was seen in the company of a man who was not the accused. If the Crown condescends to call a man like Crabtree, why not call those men?' Had Sir Charles been able to establish that they were both pimps it would have gone a long way to explaining why their evidence was being ignored by the

Crown. It may be that there was no proof of it or, alternatively, Sir Charles took a decision not to give them a hard time on the basis that they had immediately come forward to give their evidence to the police. It might have looked bad for the authorities had they decided to smear two men who had done no more than their public duty in assisting the police in a murder inquiry. Perhaps for that reason, Sharples and Harvey were very lightly cross-examined, with Sir Charles confining himself to asking the men if they noticed how the woman they said was Emily was dressed and whether her hair was in curling papers or not. Yet, their evidence that they saw Emily with a man who was not Wood after midnight was devastating to the prosecution's case. The reporter for the *Islington Daily Gazette* noted that when Sharples said that he had seen Emily with a man that night, it caused a 'sensation' in the courtroom.[461] In the absence of any serious challenge to their evidence by the prosecution, the jury would have been entitled to acquit Wood on that basis alone.

Nevertheless, Marshall Hall and Arthur Newton evidently decided that they had to put Wood in the witness box. At this stage, he had still not admitted to meeting Emily in the *Eagle* nor had he explained the apparent letter in his handwriting found in the fire. He had also not given a truthful account of his movements on the night of the murder. Thus, despite the fact that McCowan's evidence had now been fully discredited and there was nothing to place Wood at the scene of the crime, the fact that he was the last identified man to have seen Emily alive meant that he still had some questions to answer.

The first of these was very simple. 'Did you kill Emily Dimmock?' asked Marshall Hall of his client in the witness box. The reporter from the *Tribune* described the response to this question as if he was writing a novel. His report in the following morning's edition read:

"Did you kill Emily Dimmock?"

Slowly, even sternly, with an accentuating pause between each word, Mr Marshall Hall puts this question to Robert Wood, the artist accused of murdering Emily Dimmock at 29, St Paul's-road, Camden Town, on the 12th September last. As he speaks counsel leans forward with a look of eager expectation. Surely there was never such a silence even in a court of justice; surely there was never a more memorable moment. It is evening, and a pale light shed somewhat mysteriously from nooks and crannies suffuses the hot, densely-crowded court with a soft yellow light. The judge turns towards the witness box; every eye is fixed in one direction.

Again the question – "Did you kill Emily Dimmock?"

Robert Wood stands silent and motionless in the witness box. The drawn white face might be a mask of wax, but for the hot steady sparkle of those two dark, deeply sunken eyes. The silence palpitates with painful suspense. It is only an instant, but seems an hour. One notices strange little details in a quaint, inconsequent fashion – the loose ends of the man's tie, the trembling beard of his old grey father huddled up in a shrunken attitude on the steps of the jury box, the twist and twirl of the Judge's pen, and the constant rise and fall and flicker of the curiously modulated lights.

"Did you kill Emily Dimmock?"

Suddenly life breathes through the man's disguise of marble. A faint incredulous smile breaks on his lips, the thin white fingers relax, and the arms expand. He turns towards the jury and the smile deepens as his lips move.

"It is – it is ridiculous," he says, and then as though repeating the question in his thoughts, swerves round again towards his counsel and cries out in a loud, passionate voice, "No, no!"[462]

This journalist was the only reporter in the court who appears to have heard Marshall Hall asking Wood the same question three times before receiving a response. Other journalists did not detect any failure of Wood to answer Marshall Hall's question. Take the *Daily Mail* representative, for example, who reported as follows:

"Did you kill Emily Dimmock?" The point-blank question, flung with stern intonation by Mr Marshall Hall, staggered the prisoner with its dramatic suddenness and set the whole court at a thrilling tension.

Wood pulled himself upright, threw out both hands in a kind of gentle expostulation, and for a moment could not find a word. The hushed court waited in an almost painful suspense. Wood turned from counsel to jury and from jury to counsel, seeming to struggle with his feelings, and then they found vent.

"It's ridiculous," he said in a soft, surprised, voice.

Pressed for a direct answer he formally denied the murder, and was breaking into a voluntary statement when counsel checked him.[463]

So here we have an account in which Wood certainly paused before answering his counsel's question but there was no actual failure to answer. The *Daily Telegraph* claimed that 'Wood looked smilingly at his counsel without replying' and it was only when the question was repeated that he said it was 'ridiculous'. Every other newspaper account of the exchange, however, supports the notion that Wood answered the original question by saying it was 'ridiculous', to which Marshall Hall chided him with the instruction 'You must answer straight' prompting Wood to say something like 'It's not true' or 'I did not' or 'The charge is absurd – I did not kill Emily Dimmock' depending on which newspaper one prefers. For the record, the *Notable British Trials* transcript has the questions and answers as follows:

Marshall Hall: Did you kill Emily Dimmock?
Wood: It is ridiculous.
Marshall Hall: You must answer straight. I will only ask you straight questions. Did you kill her?
Wood: No, I did not.

It may be that the truth of the matter lies somewhere in between.

The *Morning Advertiser*'s reporter noted that, in response to the first question, Wood simply shook his head, causing Marshall Hall to enquire 'Did you reply?' Wood then said it was 'ridiculous' causing Marshall Hall to press for a direct response before finally receiving a categorical denial. The reporter for the *Scotsman* offered a little more detail, describing how Wood asked his Counsel, 'Do you really want an answer?' to which Marshall Hall responded by saying, 'Yes, I don't want it to be said I did not put the question'. In other words, it would seem that the question *was* answered by Wood despite a pause and a prompting from his Counsel. The notion that Marshall Hall had to repeat the question before he received a response of any kind would appear to be a myth created by the *Tribune* journalist's melodramatic style of reporting but one that has survived to this day.[464]

Nevertheless, Wood's performance in the witness box during examination-in-chief was certainly a strange one. Asked how he came to know Emily, he turned to the members of the jury and told them in conspiratorial fashion that they no doubt knew what went on in a public house, earning a rebuke from Marshall Hall that he should not speak directly to the jury. When asked to tell the court what happened when he had a drink with Emily on 6 September, he replied that he could not recollect everything and, instead of answering, referred to his written statement, 'which is true' he said. Marshall Hall had to try again before extracting from Wood the story about how he came to write the postcard signed 'Alice'. In answer to the question as to when he made up his mind to induce Ruby Young to provide him with a false alibi, he replied, 'I cannot exactly say' and, when pressed as to whether it was on the day he sent her a telegram asking her to meet him, he replied, 'I suppose that I sent the telegram with the object of seeing her and inducing her to prove an alibi' before turning again to the jury and saying, apparently in order to excuse his poor recollection, 'You see, lately I have been behind prison bars'. When asked why he required a false alibi from Ruby, he answered with a question of his own, saying, 'Is there not a certain amount of disgrace in it?' and then directed a further comment in the direction of the jury, saying, 'It must appeal to the average man that he would like to steer clear of a thing like that'. However, in response to a further question from Marshall Hall, he admitted that he was anxious to conceal the fact that he had been with Emily on the Wednesday night, claiming that he did not wish to be associated with the type of girl who went to the *Rising Sun*.

The essential point made by Wood during his examination-in-chief was that at no time did he do any more than have a drink with Emily and amuse her with his sketch book. As for the night of the murder, he claimed that he met Emily by chance in Camden Road and took her to the *Eagle* before leaving her at 11:00pm and returning straight home. At no time (even during cross-examination when he was surprisingly not asked) did he explain why he was in Camden Town that evening. He was certain he had not written to Emily to arrange a meeting that night, although he admitted that the writing on the fragments of paper found in the fire in her room were in his handwriting. The point was made by Marshall Hall that Wood had only previously been shown a photographic reproduction of the fragments on a different piece of paper to the original, and Wood said that the photograph had 'the appearance of a copy', the implication being that this was why he had been unable to identify his handwriting when first shown the photograph by Inspector Neil.

One of the weaknesses of Wood's evidence was his explanation for why he made such repeated and determined attempts to extract a false alibi from Ruby Young. His claim that he did not want to be associated with someone from the *Rising Sun* was hardly credible considering that he had been in a long relationship with a woman he knew to be prostitute with whom he had shared a first drink at the *Rising Sun*. Furthermore, he had admitted in his statement to chatting with Emily in the *Rising Sun* on other nights; it was only in respect of the night of Wednesday 11 September that he invented a false story. It was patently obvious that the real reason for this was because he did not want the police to know he had been with Emily Dimmock shortly before her murder in case he was suspected of being her murderer. In this respect, Sir Charles did him a favour during cross-examination by leading him to the correct answer in the following exchange:

> **Sir Charles Mathews**: …had you anything to fear from publicity being given to your association with the woman?
> **Wood**: The association was low.
> **Sir Charles Mathews**: And that is all – all the dread you felt?
> **Wood**: That is all.
> **Sir Charles Mathews**: Beyond that, was what you had to fear the fact that you were so late in her company on the night she was killed?
> **Wood**: Well, naturally, that looked very bad.
> **Sir Charles Mathews**: And it was of that that you were apprehensive?
> **Wood**: Yes.

Within the space of two questions, having been gently guided by prosecuting counsel, Wood had gone from saying he was only afraid of his low association with Emily being revealed to the world to confirming that he was, in fact, afraid of being suspected of her murder. Another barrister might have made more of the complete change of position but Sir Charles was too much of a gentleman even to point out that Wood was effectively contradicting his evidence in-chief. Until that point, the impression Wood had given was that he had only wanted to keep his name out of the sordid affair and had no more than a passing and tangential acquaintance with it; but the truth was, as he had now effectively admitted, that he always understood that he was deeply implicated in the matter and had been desperately attempting to create a smokescreen to keep his involvement secret.

Sir Charles' opening to his cross-examination had been more hostile than his questions about Wood's fears. He began by asking Wood if he had made any public admission about having been in Emily's company on the night of 11 September prior to his examination-in-chief the previous day. It seemed to unsettle Wood who answered, 'No sir – oh, public?' The judge intervened, helpfully for Wood, to suggest that there might be confusion between counsel and the witness as to the meaning of the word 'public', before Wood pointed out that he had not, in fact, spoken in public before. This was a little disingenuous because he had informed Inspector Neil immediately after his arrest of his movements on the night of the murder and had denied that he had met Emily that night. However, it was a poorly worded question from Sir Charles. The problem was that he could not ask Wood about his conversations with his own legal team and thus had to try and phrase the question to exclude any private discussions. In doing so, he allowed Wood to muddy the waters by implying that, if he had never spoken in public before, he could not have been lying about anything before.

The next question from Sir Charles also did not go too well for him. He asked Wood if he had denied to Ruby Young, his brothers and Mr Tinkham respectively, that he had been in Emily's company on the night of 11 September but Wood said that he had not done so to any of them. It would seem that Sir Charles had asked the wrong question. It was true that Wood had not denied being with Emily on the night of 11 September to either Ruby Young, John Tinkham or his brothers but only because none of them had asked him if he had been in her company. Ruby had queried where he had been on the Wednesday night but, in the witness box, she said that he replied that 'he could not prove where he was and he gave no proper answer'. In her earlier statement, she had said that Wood told her he was by himself that night but not that he had expressly denied being with Emily. Tinkham said that Wood told him he had met Emily on three occasions, twice at the *Rising Sun* and once in Great College Street, making no mention of seeing her at the *Eagle*, but he did not expressly say he had not been with her on the night of the murder. Neither of his brothers appear to have asked him where he was on the Wednesday night, no doubt believing that he was with Ruby.

The first real success achieved by Sir Charles during his cross-examination of Wood was in respect of the rising sun postcard. Wood agreed that the postcard was, on its face, a letter of assignation but, when Sir Charles asked him if he kept the assignation, Wood dissembled, saying, 'I went to the *Rising Sun* that night, but later'. By this, he meant that he did not arrive at the *Rising Sun* until 9:00pm on the night of the supposed assignation whereas the postcard suggested a meeting at 8:15pm. Pressed by Sir Charles, however, he conceded that he might have arrived earlier than 9:00pm, as other witnesses had testified. At the same time, he denied that it was earlier than 8:30pm but was unable to swear as to the precise time. He also quibbled about other aspects of the postcard. He claimed that his use of the phrase 'if it pleases you' in the sentence 'If it pleases you meet me at 8:15pm at the [Rising Sun]' demonstrated that there was no seriousness attached to the suggestion of a meeting and that it was 'immaterial' to him. It was, according to Wood, 'hardly an appointment'; it was an understanding 'so mild that it was just by the way.' Sir Charles pressed him hard on the point: 'Did you keep the appointment made on the postcard – yes or no?' Wood's answer was 'Not on the Saturday it was intended for, when it was written'. It will be recalled that Wood claimed to have written the postcard in Emily's presence in the *Rising Sun* during the evening of Friday 9 September so he was here saying for the first time that his original intention had been to post the card on the Saturday morning for an assignation at 8:15pm that night. Be that as it may, the fact of the matter is that he posted the card in the early hours of Monday morning and then showed up in the *Rising Sun* before 9:00pm that same day, when he met Emily. He was clearly keeping the assignation requested in the postcard.

That Wood did not argue that Emily would have understood that there was no question of an assignation because she knew that he had written the postcard on the Friday night to add to her postcard collection is extremely revealing. The story he consistently told everyone, both before and after his arrest, was that he wrote something pleasant on the postcard at Emily's prompting in order to make the postcard of value and was supposed to post it to her but forgot to do so until she reminded him of it when he met her by chance in Great College Street on the Saturday evening. If this was true, he would surely have said that Emily would have understood perfectly well that the postcard did not fix an assignation for the Monday night because she knew it was written on the Friday night (in respect of a possible meeting on the Saturday night) and contained pleasantries which had no real meaning. This is very suggestive that he was lying about the circumstances in which the postcard was written. He had simply not worked through in his mind the consequences of his story.

The time that Wood posted the card is also revealing. He claimed that he posted it late on Sunday night, after he left his brother's house, possibly after midnight and possibly as late as 1:00am. The evidence from George Hollamby, a clerk in the Accountant-General's Department of the General Post Office was that the postmark of 4:00am of 9 September on the card proved that it must have been posted between 1:00am and 4:00am on Monday morning. This suggests that Wood, knowing that (because of the highly efficient postal service) the card would arrive at St Paul's Road later that morning, had been determined to lure Emily to the *Rising Sun* that same evening in order to meet him. Wood himself said that he had not been to the *Rising Sun* much before 6 September, telling Sir Charles that he only visited that public house 'very occasionally'. The only sensible reason for his appearance on the Monday evening was because he was keeping the appointment in the postcard.

The judge expressed surprise that Wood addressed Emily as 'Phillis darling' in the postcard supposedly written on the Friday night, considering that he claimed he had never seen her before. Misunderstanding the point, Wood replied, 'She was quite a well-known personage in the bar....You could not be in her company long without knowing her name'. The judge said, 'I dare say she was, but that does not seem to explain how, not having seen her before, you at once addressed her as darling?' Wood's rather feeble response to this was to say, 'It was written to please her, I suppose. The *Rising Sun* company is friendly in a very short time'.

Upon arrival at the *Rising Sun* on the Monday evening, Wood agreed that he offered Florence Smith and Ellen Lawrence a drink and had a 'slight recollection' of saying 'Don't tell Phyllis' when paying for that drink. However, he claimed that it was 'a concoction' that he had told the two women that he and Emily were going together to the Holborn Empire but instead went to the *Adam and Eve* public house at the end of Euston Road. As he explained: 'I could not have addressed them [Mrs Smith and Mrs Lawrence] in that way. I was not sufficiently acquainted with them'. At this point the judge made a very pertinent intervention, observing, 'You were familiar enough to stand them drinks' to which Wood replied unintelligibly, 'Well such things are asked for, but not always in words. I spoke in a friendly way to Mrs Smith, but I do not think I spoke the words to Mrs Lawrence'. He then became a little less certain about his claim that the story of the two women was a concoction. Asked if it was imagination on their part he said 'I should say so. It may be'. Nevertheless he denied asking Mrs Smith if she had seen Phyllis and said he did not beckon Emily towards him on the Friday night as Mr Smeeth had claimed.

The mention of Mr Smeeth's evidence brought a flash of anger from Wood as he railed against the failure of the prosecution to call Fred Chapman, the licensee of the *Rising Sun*. 'I cannot understand,' he said, 'why the manager of the *Rising Sun*, who would be most likely to see everything that has passed in the bar, has not been called...while the barman, who would see least, and had the whole range of the bar to attend to, is called to give evidence against me'. While we have no idea what Fred Chapman did when he was in the *Rising Sun*, it is questionable that he would have had a better view than the barman of what was happening in his bar and one cannot help but feel that Wood's outrage was manufactured to embarrass the prosecution. Whether Fred Chapman had co-operated with the authorities in relation to the murder inquiry is not known but it is hardly likely he would have wanted to be subject to questioning in court about the activities of prostitutes in his establishment. It may be that Wood knew that Chapman had refused to become involved and used this as a way of undermining Smeeth's unchallenged evidence. Marshall Hall had certainly not put it to Smeeth that he was mistaken in saying that Wood had beckoned Emily over to him on the night of 6 September. Moreover, he had been perfectly happy to accept Smeeth's evidence that he had not seen Wood and Emily together before 6 September. Had Wood truly believed that Fred Chapman could have supported his story, his legal team were free to call him as a witness and their failure to do so suggests that they did not think it would be a worthwhile exercise.

The distinguishing characteristic of Wood's cross-examination was undoubtedly his remarkable failure to remember very much that happened during the five days prior to the murder, sometimes expressed with the odd aphorism. Asked what time he left the *Rising Sun* on 9 September, he replied, 'Such an idle hour is carelessly spent' before saying that he could not speak definitely as to the time. Asked if he had slipped out with Emily at any time during the evening he said, 'I might have gone out with her, but I cannot say'. When pressed if he was with her alone for something over an hour he responded, 'You have me again. I cannot say'. Where did he go with her? 'Beyond that I was in her company at the *Rising Sun*, I cannot tell you anything'. Despite alleging that Mrs Smith and Mrs Lawrence had concocted a story that he had told them he had been to the *Adam and Eve* with Emily, he was unable to deny that he had actually gone with Emily to the *Adam and Eve*. 'I cannot say for certain' he said, 'but I do not think I went with her to the *Adam and Eve*' although a few minutes later he said: 'I may have called there that night' and 'possibly' with Emily. The question as to whether he could remember seeing Mrs Smith and Mrs Lawrence together on his return to the *Rising Sun* from wherever he went brought the response 'I have seen them once together, but when or where I cannot say'. He excused his poor memory by saying, 'Probably the cells of Brixton have had some effect'.

His memory of events on the night of Tuesday 10 September, however, seemed to be much better and he was certain he had not put his head in at the door of the *Rising Sun* at some point after 7:00pm and gone away. He said he had his tea that evening between 6:00pm and 7:00pm and then met up with his brother in the opposite direction from the *Rising Sun*. The prosecution case was that he had attempted to attract Emily's attention but failed because the *Rising Sun* was so crowded and that, as a direct result of this, he wrote a letter to Emily arranging to meet her on Wednesday night, well away from the *Rising Sun*, at the *Eagle* in Camden Town. However, if Wood's recollection of the events of 9 September was vague, his recall of what he had written on the paper found in Emily's fireplace was positively amnesic. He simply could not assist Sir Charles in deciphering a single word he had written on the fragments: 'I cannot say what it is' he remarked, 'I can make neither head nor tail of it'. The only thing he was certain of was that it was not a letter he had written to Emily for the purpose of arranging a meeting with her in the *Eagle*. In fact, he said he had not even known the name of the *Eagle* public house at the time. This brought another intervention from the judge who pointed out that he had admitted being in the *Eagle* on Saturday 7 September. Wood insisted that he knew of the public house but not its name.

Yet, despite Wood's inability to decipher any of his own words, he did make some concessions. He agreed that the word 'Town' might have been part of 'Camden Town' and the word 'Wednes' might have been a reference to 'Wednesday 11 September'. Nevertheless, his explanation for the fragments was that they must have been part of 'amusing phrases and sketches' he had written in Emily's presence which she took from him without his knowledge, even though there were no obvious amusing phrases or sketches remaining on them. But Sir Charles had one trump card to play regarding the fragments. He revealed an extremely important piece of information that had never been mentioned before. Among the fragments was a portion of an envelope upon which was the letter 'W'.[465] The correct postal district for St Paul's Road was 'London NW' (although Wood's postcard had used 'London N'). Sir Charles' cross-examination on this point was devastating to Wood's case:

> **Sir Charles Mathews**: Tell me with regard to that 'W'. It is the only portion apparently of an envelope. What do you say to that? Is that your 'W'?
> **Wood**: It may be; quite likely.
> **Sir Charles Mathews**: The printed 'W' you are referring to?
> **Wood**: I am.
> **Sir Charles Mathews**: It is quite likely to be yours?
> **Wood**: Quite.
> **Sir Charles Mathews**: And it looks as though it were part of the envelope upon which you had written the postal district?
> **Wood**: It depends on what course you are following.
> **Sir Charles Mathews**: Might it have been?
> **Wood**: If that were the story to be attached to it, you can put it that way.

Wood's typically oblique answers could not hide the fact that he had been caught out. If there was an envelope among the burnt fragments which also bore his handwriting then the fragments simply must have been part of a letter sent by Wood to Emily. The notion that they were amusing phrases or sketches made no sense if there was an addressed envelope amongst the fragments. Despite this, Wood clung stubbornly to his story. 'I sent no message to her', he maintained, 'that is what I said on the night of my arrest and what I dictated in my statement to the police'. It was obviously untrue and even his ardent supporters realised this. After the trial, Mrs Helen Beerbohm Tree, a famous actress present for Wood's cross-examination, whose sympathy was 'so much with Robert Wood' that she was 'trembling with hope and fear' throughout the cross-examination, wrote an article for *Reynolds's Newspaper* in which she said:

> Time after time I longed to start up and exclaim, "Oh don't say that! Don't say that!" I kept expecting Wood to admit that he wrote that letter, the charred fragments of which he held in his fingers as Sir Charles plied him with questions. Why, I thought, doesn't he own that he wrote it. "We met by appointment on Monday evening. We met again by appointment on Wednesday evening". Why not? These were the words I believed he might have uttered. I was wrong, of course, for he would not admit that he had made an appointment.[466]

It was a very good point. Why did Wood not simply admit what was obvious? After all, Roberts had testified to the contents of the letter being a request for a meeting in the *Eagle* on the Wednesday night. Wood had joined Emily for a drink at the *Eagle* at about the time Roberts said was stated in the letter (although Wood said he met her just outside the bar). Wood had said in cross-examination that he went to the *Eagle* public house so rarely that he did not even know its name. His being there with Emily on the night and at the time Roberts had seen on the letter could not have been a coincidence. Wood admitted that he had been with Emily in the *Eagle* so what was the problem in saying it was a pre-arranged meeting? The answer is probably very simple. Wood had told a blatant lie in his signed statement following his arrest on 4 October when he said: 'The postcard is the only thing in the form of writing that I ever sent to the deceased'. He had already been forced to admit to having lied about having spoken to Emily on the Wednesday night in that statement. Another lie being exposed – or at least him having to admit to another lie – might, he felt, have been a lie too far for the jury. There is sometimes only so much that one's credibility can be undermined.

At the same time, Wood, no doubt, would have been conscious of the fact that if he admitted to arranging a meeting with Emily on the Wednesday night he would have had to explain his motive for doing so; and that motive could only have been that he wanted to have sex with her. Even Marshall Hall ended up accepting that this was what he was up to. Early in the trial, the barrister had become involved in a row with Justice Grantham after the judge had asked Mr Moss if he knew that his friend, Wood, had been living an immoral life with Emily Dimmock. Marshall Hall had strongly objected to the judge's questions, saying, 'With great deference, I only wish, in the interests of justice, to point out that there is not a particle of evidence that the accused ever stayed with the woman, or had any improper relations with Dimmock'. During his closing speech, after Wood's cross-examination, however, he was singing a rather different tune. He said that the jury will have noticed from Wood's conduct in the witness box that he was 'a person of overweening personal vanity'. Indeed, for Marshall Hall, Wood's vanity was 'the keynote to this strange and mysterious case'. He told the jury:

> The accused could not take upon himself, by reason of that vanity, the responsibility of admitting that he had done anything which would cause people who held a high opinion of him to diminish the undivided attention and respect they had for him. If that is the solution of the matter, it accounts for almost every single thing he had done. His ability was such that in his own particular line of business he was a favourite at the works. He did not wish to lose that regard.

In other words, Marshall Hall was effectively saying that Wood had lied about his relationship with Emily, not because he had murdered her, but because he did not want his friends and family to know he had been having sex with a prostitute. Thus, he continued, 'I must strongly impress on you, members of the jury that you are trying the accused for murder, and not for lying or for immorality', adding that 'Though there may be evidence of immorality, there is none of murder'. It was a dramatic turnaround; from initially saying that there was not a 'particle of evidence' of Wood having had a sexual relationship with

Emily, Marshall Hall was now, for all practical purposes, conceding that there had, in fact, been such a relationship. This was despite his client insisting to Sir Charles in the witness box that he had never been home with Emily and had never had sexual intercourse with her.

Wood's memory of events after the murder was almost as bad as his memory of those before it. Did he recall saying to Mr Moss that there had been another of those unfortunate women done to death and that he was not surprised considering that they never knew with whom they went home? 'I do not remember' he said, although he admitted that it was 'quite likely' that he had made such an observation. Did he recall telling Mr Lambert that he could clear himself? 'I do not remember using those actual words' he replied, although, when pressed, accepted that he had used words to that effect. Nevertheless, Wood was prepared to admit virtually all the evidence of the prosecution witnesses relating to his attempts to cover up his association with Emily and create a false alibi for the night of the murder. In his own words, he asked Ruby Young to do him 'a little kindness' by telling the police she had been with him on the Wednesday evening.

The one thing he challenged strongly was Ruby's evidence regarding the nature of their relationship. He was extremely reluctant to admit that she had broken off relations with him in July 1907 owing to his behaviour with Pansy. All he would say was that 'She may have stayed away from me, but she was not away for long. Not long enough for me to notice'. He described her as being 'a little huffy' about Pansy but no more. He also denied that a ring he had given her in February 1907 was an engagement ring, saying it was merely 'something to please her'. However, he agreed that he asked Ruby to be true to him when he was arrested because 'I believed that her word and mine would stand against the world'. It was a revealing insight into his thought process.

When it came to the closing speeches, Marshall Hall, who was not feeling well that day but was determined to continue, was forced to speak first because he had called evidence in his client's defence. He complimented Sir Charles on the 'conspicuous fairness' with which he had conducted the cross-examination but became embroiled in an argument with his opposite number when he said it was 'absolutely unpardonable' for the prosecution not to have called Sharples and Harvey as witnesses. A furious Sir Charles Mathews leapt to his feet to insist that he had offered to call any witnesses Marshall Hall wanted, something that Marshall Hall had evidently forgotten for he immediately withdrew the accusation, and issued a statement of apology after the trial.

Not surprisingly, Marshall Hall took advantage of the exclusion of Roberts' evidence that Emily had told him that the author of the rising sun postcard was jealous of her relationship with Shaw and emphasised the lack of any motive put forward by the prosecution. He characterised the case against Wood as 'flimsy', remarking that 'As far as I can see, the only thing the prosecution have against my client in this case is his asking Ruby Young to tell a lie for the purpose of saving his reputation, which lie he repeated to the police'. Wood, he said, was not being tried for lying and, in any case, the false alibi was 'useless' because 'it did not cover the time of the murder'. He told the jury that the evidence against Wood had been edited by the police 'to an amazing degree' and that they 'dare not hang Robert Wood upon it'. Furthermore, he wanted the charge against Wood 'utterly annihilated' so that 'the lying tongues of persons like Crabtree, Mrs Lawrence and Mrs Smith may not in the future taunt him'. The jury's verdict had to be 'a verdict upon the evidence' he insisted and he was sure that the evidence was not sufficient to secure a conviction.

When it came to the evidence about the postcard and the fragments, however, Marshall Hall's argument became confused and uncertain. He said:

> That postcard, of which we have heard so much, made no appointment on the face of it; and I urge that the fragments found in the fire grate were not part of a letter of assignation. Is it not equally as conceivable as the Crown theory that the murderer, whoever he is, put the postcard where it was ultimately found in order to implicate Wood and direct the guilt on to him? The accused has always maintained that he never wrote such a letter.

Contrary to Marshall Hall's assertion, the postcard most certainly *did* make an appointment on the face of it – 'meet me 8.15' could mean nothing else; Wood's argument had been that it was not intended by him to be an appointment. It was also not 'equally as conceivable' that the murderer placed the postcard underneath the lining of the drawer in Emily's room to implicate Wood; in fact it was a crackpot theory. Placing a postcard where it could not easily be found, even during an official police search of the chest of drawers, was hardly a sensible way of directing guilt towards anyone. Wood had sent the postcard to Emily so it was always going to be in her possession; it would have made no sense for the murderer to hide it in the hope that one day it *might* be found and the author *might* be identified. It may be that Marshall Hall was thinking that Shaw had placed the postcard in the chest of drawers (and that Shaw was the murderer) or, alternatively, he had simply confused the postcard with the letter but, if so, that made just as little sense because burning a letter in a fire was an equally poor way of directing guilt onto someone as hiding it.

Marshall Hall concluded his speech in dramatic style, instructing the jury that if they were satisfied beyond all reasonable doubt that Wood murdered Emily Dimmock then they should find him guilty and send him to the scaffold 'although it breaks your hearts to do so'. However, if they could not honestly and conscientiously say beyond all reasonable doubt that the prosecution have proved their case, 'then I say it will be your duty, as well as your pleasure, to say, as you are bound to say, that Robert Wood is not guilty of the murder of Emily Elizabeth Dimmock'. As he sat down, after speaking for almost two and a half hours, there was some slight applause in court but this was quickly suppressed by the court officials.

Sir Charles Mathews then stood up to address the jury. Arthur Newton would later describe the effect in the courtroom of his speech, saying:

> His voice rose and fell. The atmosphere was tense. One almost felt the presence of death and all eyes were on the speaker whose eloquence thrilled as it never had thrilled before in the Old Bailey.[467]

Sir Charles dealt with the absence of a motive by saying that if the crime had been committed by a sexual maniac it would be apparently motiveless. He drew attention to Wood's many lies and described him as 'a man cool and collected, an extraordinary man whose nerve was such that when from day to day the newspapers were publishing accounts of the murder and he was spoken to about it by his foreman he preserved his calmness and cheerfulness'. According to Sir

Charles, it was this very coolness that marked him out as the murderer. It was, he said, 'a cold-blooded murder' and Wood was an 'unnaturally, dreadfully, singular man, a man with nerves so extraordinary that nothing could move him'. Arthur Newton later recalled seeing Wood flinch; it was the first time he had given any outward sign that he appreciated the danger he was in.[468]

Sir Charles hypothesised that in addition to taking Emily home and then returning to Frederick Street for his overcoat and then (presumably) returning to St Paul's Road, Wood committed the murder while naked, which explained why no blood had been found on any of his clothes. He did not, however, venture to suggest what the murder weapon was or what Wood had done with it, nor did he say what Wood had done with the money and items removed from Emily's room. Like any good prosecutor, he concluded by advising the jury that suspicion was not enough and that, if there was the slightest doubt that Wood had committed the murder, he should be acquitted. It seemed there was a good chance they would follow that advice but, before they would have a chance to do so, the judge would have his say; and most people in the courtroom expected he would join the prosecution in pressing for a conviction.

In opening his summing-up to the jury, Mr Justice Grantham described the trial as 'one of the most remarkable trials that is to be found in the annals of the Criminal Courts of England for many years'. He said that he had tried a great many murder cases but none where a woman had been apparently murdered in her sleep by one blow delivered with great force and without a struggle.

Anyone who had predicted that Sir William Grantham would sum up against Wood must have felt their prediction confirmed when the judge turned to the question of motive and told the jury that they should not assume that the accused was innocent simply because no motive had been established. He pointed out that 'many of the most brutal murders have been committed without any apparent motive'. Furthermore, when he said that Emily must have been murdered 'by a man who was leading a double life… whom nobody would believe to have been guilty of a shocking murder, but would pass in decent society as a highly respectable citizen' before commenting that Wood had clearly been leading a double life, it looked very bad for the accused. When the judge then said that Wood had been spoken of as having an excellent reputation, 'yet he now seems to have been in the habit of frequenting a place where harlots resorted', the hangman might have been justified in preparing his rope.

Regarding the nature of the (circumstantial) evidence against Wood, it became a little more difficult to discern the judge's intentions. On the one hand, he pointed out that 'a large majority of murders have in the past been detected by circumstantial evidence' and informed the jury that he had once tried a case based on circumstantial evidence in which the accused was convicted and subsequently confessed. On the other hand, he stressed that the jury needed to be 'very careful' before they condemned a man to death on the basis of circumstantial evidence. Moreover, he stated, 'Looking at the evidence, I must say that, with the exception of McCowan's, there is no evidence which brings the accused into the company of the deceased woman at all on the morning of the murder, or after he left the *Eagle* public house with her on the night of 11th September'. Wood had, of course, denied that he left the *Eagle* with

Emily, despite the evidence of the barmaid, but the judge's remark still seemed favourable to Wood, especially as he cautioned that the case was one in which the jury needed to be 'doubly careful' not to allow circumstantial evidence to prejudice the accused.

Yet, there were a number of factors which the judge felt weighed against Wood. The most obvious was his own conduct in telling lies and endeavouring to persuade other people to tell lies on his behalf. 'Throughout the history of the case,' said the judge, 'he has lied and been untruthful' and, despite claiming to be innocent, 'he keeps everything from the police and from his own brother'. As a result, the judge felt that there was 'a strong case' made against him. He also concluded that 'there is evidence to show that Wood did know Dimmock before 6th September' and that there was very strong evidence which would justify the jury in believing Roberts' story about the letter Emily had shown him. None of this, however, proved that Wood had committed the murder but the evidence of McCowan, if relied upon, said the judge, 'would justify in finding him guilty'. He pointed out that McCowan's evidence was corroborated to some extent by Ruby Young who agreed that Wood had a peculiar walk but this was also contradicted by witnesses for the defence. In the end, the judge concluded, 'I do not think the evidence is sufficient to justify you in bringing in the accused man guilty...The accused is entitled to the benefit of any doubt there may be and, if there is, to have a verdict of acquittal'. One reporter described the effect of this remark in the court as 'electrical' and that 'A wave of passionate applause' broke out in the courtroom with 'shouts of excited exclamations'.[469] Once order had been restored, the judge added that the jury were free to please themselves and did not need to act upon his view, but everyone in court would have known that they were unlikely to differ from him.

The jury retired at a little before 7:45pm to consider its verdict which did not now appear to be in doubt. Having expected a three-day trial, the jury members were keen to return to their businesses with only a few days to Christmas. They had been kept virtually prisoners in the Manchester Hotel at Aldersgate Street for seven days, living in rooms in a locked corridor, playing cards, chess, draughts, dominoes and billiards after dinner, with only the occasional ride out for some fresh air, including a visit to St Paul's Road on the Sunday for the purpose of examining the position of the electric lights. During those seven days, there had been some developments outside of the Old Bailey. The trial had commenced on Thursday 12 December and three days later, on the Sunday, *Lloyds Weekly News* published, in full, a letter written by Wood to his brother from Brixton Prison written after the first day of the trial. In the letter, Wood stated that he would carry his head high: 'for I have done no grievous wrong'. On the same day, the *Weekly Dispatch* carried five sketches by Wood of witnesses at his trial including McCowan and Ruby Young. His portrait of Ruby also appeared in the *Daily Mail* on the Monday morning. There was nothing derogatory about the sketches but they solidified the impression that Wood was a talented artist: something which could do him no harm. Did talented artists commit murder? The answer was uncertain.

The crowds had gathered outside the Old Bailey from the first day, despite poor weather and plenty of rain. After a young woman who came down the steps with a police officer by her side was mistaken for Ruby Young and 'angrily hooted' by the mob, the police took action and, on the Saturday, when the real Ruby Young arrived at court to give evidence, members of the public were forced to stand on the opposite side of the road to the court house entrance.[470] On Monday 16 December, the *Evening News* estimated that there was a crowd of more than five hundred people outside the packed court. Ruby Young emerged from the building, having attended as a spectator, and was loudly hooted. According to the *Daily Express*, two detectives hurried her to a four-wheeled cab and 'the crowd rushed towards the vehicle with excited shouts'. Before the cab could drive away 'both the cab windows were smashed and the mob was only driven back with extreme difficulty'.[471] By contrast, Marshall Hall was enthusiastically cheered as he walked down the street. When Wood was driven away from the Old Bailey to Brixton Prison in a closed carriage at the end of the court day, the vehicle was immediately surrounded by a large crowd while held up in traffic at Ludgate Hill and three cheers were raised for the prisoner inside.[472] On the penultimate day of the trial, when the defence witnesses were giving evidence, there were estimated to be over two thousand people in Newgate Street. The police had difficulty maintaining order during the lunch hour with 'one or two ugly rushes being made as some of the witnesses were leaving'.[473] Traffic was seriously interfered with and the police sent out for reinforcements to all parts of the city. At 4:00pm, following a false rumour that Wood had been acquitted, one John Pheasant, a market porter, was outside the court drunk while shouting: "Three cheers for Wood! Hooray!" He was told to move on by the police but refused to do so and was arrested, subsequently being fined five shillings at Guildhall Police Court for drunk and disorderly conduct.[474]

By the final day of the trial, on Wednesday 18 December, the crowd was massive, all apparently rooting for Wood's acquittal. According to the *Star's* reporter, 'They came today from all quarters and from all ranks – out of works, City men, suburban shoppers, country cousins, beggars, boys and tramps'. There was an equally massive police presence with City constables trying to keep everyone moving but the crowd just kept getting bigger. No-one inside the Old Bailey, including the judge and members of the jury, could have been oblivious to the mood of the huge crowd and it was obvious that a conviction of Wood could start a riot. It is impossible to say if the outside pressures had any effect on the judge's conclusions, or upon the way the jury viewed the case, but it would be surprising if they had none at all.

Another pressure on the jury was the lateness of the hour. None of them wanted to be stuck in their hotel overnight. At the lunch adjournment earlier in the afternoon, the foreman of the jury had told the judge that they would like to finish the case that day and they were willing to stay late for that purpose, so they were clearly not going to be considering their verdict overnight. In fact, they spent a quarter of an hour making their decision and returned to the courtroom at 8:00pm. It should not be imagined that they were completely seduced by Marshall Hall's performance. We have no information as to what went on in the jury room but in February 1963, Marjorie Jessie Agnew, the daughter of a jury member, Henry Coates Agnew, wrote a letter to the BBC in which she stated that her father told her: 'Marshall Hall was a bully, intimidating witnesses by shouting at them and confusing them'. He also informed her of his belief that it did not necessarily follow that 'because the victim's friends were "publicans and sinners" that they were lying when they gave their evidence'. At the same time, however, Agnew felt that there was insufficient evidence to convict Wood although, coming originally from Scotland, he thought that a 'not proven' verdict would have been appropriate.[475]

The fifteen minutes spent waiting for the verdict was an anxious one for everyone in the courtroom, apart from Wood apparently. Outwardly, at least, he projected the appearance of not having a care in the world as he sat with his pencil in the dock, quietly and coolly sketching, until a warder told him he was not allowed to do this. His rough sketch of Mr Justice Grantham from the dock would be published in the *Daily Mail* a few days later. The time passed quickly, however, and the twelve men of the jury shuffled back into the courtroom along with the judge who, some noticed, was not carrying his black cap.

The Clerk of the Arraigns asked the foreman of the jury if they found the prisoner at the bar guilty or not guilty of the wilful murder of Emily Elizabeth Dimmock. 'We find him not guilty' came the reply from the foreman, who also confirmed it was a unanimous verdict. James Douglas, an American visitor to London who was in the courtroom at the time, described what happened next:

> At the words "Not guilty", a sharp shout of exultation explodes like a mine, as if a button had been pressed. The judge raises his hand, and across the sudden silence is heard the muffled roar of the crowd outside, like an echo of the roar within. It is a superb strange effect, electrically dramatic in its lightning rapidity.[476]

Those standing outside might have had some idea of what had happened during Wood's cross-examination from the early evening papers but, from the reaction of those inside the court, it is clear that he had lost none of his support due to his vague answers and lack of recollection in the witness box. As Douglas' account suggests, the news of the acquittal reached the crowd outside within seconds, prompting the start of some extended mafficking.

As for Wood, he sprang forward and shook hands with Arthur Newton from the dock. Marshall Hall asked for him to be discharged, which the judge immediately allowed, and Wood then slipped out of the courtroom through the ensuing mayhem.

Wood in the dock at the Old Bailey

A contemporary sketch
of Harry Sharples

Chapter Seventeen

More Suspects

'I suspect everyone and I suspect no-one.'

Peter Sellers as Inspector Clouseau in *A Shot in the Dark* (1964) after Basil Rathbone as
Sherlock Holmes in *The House of Fear* (1945)

The point is often made by modern commentators that the police officers who
investigated Emily Dimmock's murder in 1907 were at a major disadvantage
because they did not have the ability to process DNA evidence from the crime
scene. This is true up to a point but it is by no means clear that modern forensics
would have solved this murder. Even if there had been semen at the crime
scene (which the elderly Dr Thompson did not detect, having apparently failed
to test for it until a 'special request' by the Assistant Commissioner, made some
considerable time after the murder, before apparently managing to confuse
semen with cervical mucus), DNA evidence would no doubt have told us with
whom Emily last had sexual intercourse but not necessarily that this man was
her murderer. For the same reason, any hairs or fibres found at the crime scene
which could have been linked to an individual, unless covered in blood, would
only have shown that the person had been in Emily's room. If, for example,
Wood's DNA had been traced on Emily's body, or in hairs on her bed, he would
have been forced to concede that he left the *Eagle* with her and went back to her
room for sex but there would have been exactly the same evidence showing
that he had killed her, i.e. none.

The police in 1907 were fully aware of the value of fingerprints but they
could only capture visible prints, such as marks on glass or in bloodstains,
which would be photographed and taken to Scotland Yard for identification.
They did not yet have the ability to make use of 'invisible' prints.[477] Again,
though, if Wood's fingerprints had been found in Emily's room, it would only
have proved that he had been in her room, the same being true for anyone.
It might have been different if Wood's prints had been found on the murder
weapon but the police were never even able to identify this and it is not clear
if modern day forensics would have been able to do any better in that respect.

Perhaps there was no way of solving this mysterious crime but it is certain
that there were a number of things the police did not do, but could have done,
in 1907. The first of these was to document the crime scene properly with a
statement from every officer who entered 29 St Paul's Road on 12 September.
We only have a statement of Constable Thomas Killion, who discovered the
body, and a report by Inspector Neil of 13 September but Neil did not arrive
until three hours after Killion and, in the meantime, a number of officers
had been inside the rooms. Sergeant Toseland, Inspector Hufflet and Chief
Inspector Coleman are all identified by Neil as having arrived before him (and
there may well have been more, too junior to merit a mention in Neil's report)
yet none of them appear to have provided statements as to what they saw and
touched. Killion's statement itself contains no confirmation that he did not
touch or move anything. Detective Page, who arrived at St Paul's Road at the

same time as Inspector Neil, but did not prepare a statement, was asked by Marshall Hall whether anyone had opened the shutters and put 'the place to rights' during the morning and said, 'No, it had been left just as it was'; but we should not be relying on the oral evidence of an officer three months after the date of the crime to confirm this. It is also quite astonishing that not a single police document notes the existence or otherwise of any food, plates, knives, forks or glasses in Emily's room, despite the importance of the issue as to when, and with whom, Emily ate her last meal. Nor, even more incredibly, is there any documentation regarding the condition of Bert Shaw's razors despite the fact that one of them could have been the murder weapon.[478] For both of these factual matters we have to rely on Inspector Neil's oral testimony – presumably given from memory – some considerable time after the event.

The second thing the police could have done was conduct house-to-house enquiries in St Paul's Road as to whether anyone had seen or heard anything while at the same time putting out an appeal in the newspapers for witnesses or, indeed, for anyone who had known Emily and could provide information about her. Enquiries could also have been conducted during the night, asking anyone who walked along the road if they had done so on 11/12 September. Their failure to conduct such enquiries meant that they completely missed a potentially important witness in William Westcott. Everyone who had to leave early for work in St Paul's Road could have been located and questioned. This kind of thing would certainly happen in a modern murder inquiry and, while police procedures were very different in 1907, the point is that there was nothing from a technological perspective stopping the police from making these enquiries had they so wished. Equally, once Wood had been identified as the author of the rising sun postcard, enquiries could have been made at 12 Frederick Street and questions asked of other residents or neighbours, such as Joseph Rogers in the basement. He saw Wood returning at midnight, looking normal, but, for all the police knew, might have seen him walking down the street covered in blood at 5:00am. They simply never asked him. As we have discussed, Inspector Neil's failure to take statements from Wood's father and half-brother was a mistake that cost the prosecution dearly when it came to the trial. Wood's room was not even searched properly after his arrest and officers had to return the next day to look up his chimney. The police themselves accepted that they had made a mess of the search for the postcard.

A third failure of the police investigation was that loose ends were not tied up. We know, for example, that Roberts told the police that 'the landlady' pushed two letters, including the letter from 'Bertie', under the door on the morning of 11 September because he included this in his statement of 12 September. If Mrs Stocks was asked about this, as she should have been, there was no mention in her statement that she did not collect the post that morning. It was not until shortly before the trial in December that the police established that it was Alice Lancaster who had slipped the letters under the door and then only because she happened to mention it to Mrs Stocks, who passed this information on to them. When Mrs Lancaster was asked by Marshall Hall why she had not informed the police of what she had done, she protested that all she had been asked was whether she had heard any noise during the night of the murder. It was only when the letters were mentioned in the coroner's court that she thought she should tell Mrs Stocks of her involvement. In other words, the police never took the simple step of confirming Roberts' evidence with Mrs Stocks or, if they did, they did not record a negative answer in her statement as they should have done and then question the other residents to establish who had collected the post.

One thing the police certainly could have done is fully document their investigation. There was no shortage of paper or writing materials. It is a little hard to assess how well they did this because the file held at the National Archives is clearly incomplete but, just to give one example, we can say with certainty that Detective Sergeant Herbert Milton did not produce a statement documenting the search of the chest of drawers at 29 St Paul's Road for the rising sun postcard when it would have been a simple matter for him to have done so. Leaving aside the failure of Inspector Neil to collect statements from George and James Wood, and making allowance for the missing statements which we know were taken from witnesses Sharples, Harvey, McCowan, Alice Lancaster and the suspect, Harrap, there appear to be far fewer statements in existence than one would expect from a major murder inquiry. The file contains only fifteen statements dated before Wood's arrest on 4 October, three of which relate to the strange but irrelevant behaviour of Bedford Tuck in Gillingham. The remaining twelve are as follows: Bert Shaw, George Stocks, Sarah Ann Stocks, Robert Roberts, Frank Clarke, Jack Crabtree, P.C. Killion, William Dimmock, Rosa Martindale, May Campbell (x2) and Gladys Warren. All statements taken after 4 October were simply directed at proving Wood's guilt, something which was obviously vital for the police of the day, but are of little assistance in establishing the truth if Wood was innocent. It is true that Inspector Neil's reports fill in some of the gaps although, as previously noted, he often included details in his reports which did not match those in the statements on the file. There are no statements in the file from some key individuals such as Mrs Roberts, Emily's landlady at 2 Grafton Place, or Richard Taylor, the cab driver who picked up a man in St Paul's Road on the night of the murder. Very few of Emily's friends appear to have provided statements. We have the evidence of Florence Smith and Ellen Lawrence, as well as Gladys Linehan and May Campbell, but we know that Emily had at least three other female friends, known as 'Big Nell', 'Little Nellie' and 'Little Annie', the latter of whom may be the 'short dark girl named Annie' who, according to Rosa Martindale, accompanied Emily to Luton with 'Jumbo' Hirst about a year or so before the murder.[479] According to Wood, she also had a friend called Alice, in whose name he supposedly signed the rising sun postcard. Fred Chapman's wife was also called Alice and she was said to have been friendly with Emily and offered her work but no statement appears to have been taken from her or, indeed, from Fred Chapman himself.

All this may be due to an unwillingness to speak to the police by the people with whom Emily mixed but it does not seem that the police tried terribly hard to speak to them. Inspector Neil was happy enough that he had identified his prime suspect from day one: the man seen with Emily in the *Rising Sun* on the Monday night who had, according to Roberts, written a letter to Emily arranging to meet her at the *Eagle* on the Wednesday night. He had sufficient descriptions of this man and did not need to speak to more of Emily's acquaintances. Anyone who did not match the description of the prime suspect was quickly eliminated from the inquiry without, it seems, having statements taken from them to confirm the nature of their relationship with Emily and their whereabouts at the time of the murder. None of this is to criticise the police who were, like all police forces, working hard with limited resources. Inspector Neil and his team appear to have worked extremely long hours but it was a small team, largely comprising himself and six officers. There are always limits to how many individuals can be dedicated to a murder inquiry but the point is that one should not necessarily focus on the lack of knowledge of DNA and other issues of modern forensics. Detective work is not all about Sherlockian deductions from raw data but, if that data is not available, any inquiry is handicapped by lack of basic knowledge of the facts.

Over one hundred years later, can we do any better than the police of the day, relying, as we must, largely on the evidence they collected during their flawed investigation? For, alas, there is no hitherto undiscovered confession, diary or secret document which will assist us in getting to the truth. All we have, in essence, is the Metropolitan Police file, any answers extracted during questioning in the legal proceedings and the newspaper reports from the weeks following the murder, containing whatever reliable or unreliable information the various journalists sniffing around could uncover. With that, and our 'little grey cells', let us at least consider the available evidence.

The first and most obvious question is 'Did Wood do it?' but, frankly, that will get us nowhere so let us re-phrase it: Is it *plausible* that Wood did it?

If Inspector Neil's suspicion was right and Wood was the killer of Emily Dimmock then two personal characteristics of Wood must surely have been relevant factors in causing him to commit murder. The first is his deformed finger which made him wear gloves or hide his left hand in his pocket. The second is his age. Despite having turned thirty in August of 1907, he evidently claimed to be twenty-nine years of age when he was charged by the police for Emily's murder. The official records of the Clerkenwell Police Court state his age as twenty-nine and that information can only have come from Wood himself.[480] Confusingly, the Calendar of Prisoners for the session commencing 10 December 1907 state that he was aged twenty-eight so he must have said different things at different times.[481] Yet, he knew his age perfectly well. The 1901 census, taken at the end of March, correctly recorded him as being aged twenty-three, obviously meaning that he turned twenty-four on his birthday in August of that year. He cannot have lost track of his age over the following six years. One can easily imagine a certain depression surrounding him, even shock, on his thirtieth birthday as he reflected upon his life. Despite his obvious artistic talent, he remained in a poorly paid position as a decorative glass designer while living in small rented accommodation with his father and half-brother. He liked to describe himself as an 'artist', and this is what he called himself in his statement to the police and in the witness box, but this was stretching the description of what he did for a living. As we know, Wood claimed (after the trial) that he could have had plenty of his sketches published but let the opportunity pass him by, giving the impression, not very convincingly, that he was not bothered. Earlier in the year, his sweetheart of three years, herself a prostitute, had broken off their relationship. He attempted to downplay this in the witness box but it seems that he had asked her to marry him and had given her an engagement ring. It is not hard to imagine a man, alone, on his thirtieth birthday, suffering an early mid-life crisis, over-conscious of his deformity, bored with his work and frustrated with life. Would such a man snap if he was rejected by another woman, another prostitute, to the extent that he would kill her?

Before we consider the murder itself we should ask if Wood had known Emily before 6 September as the judge concluded he had. The witness evidence relating to this is by no means conclusive. In his second statement, made after Wood's arrest, Roberts claimed that Emily told him that she had known the man later identified as Wood for 'a long time' and that Wood 'always wanted to be going home with her' but none of this was mentioned by Roberts in his first statement and was all hearsay in any case (and thus excluded from the trial). Only three people had actually seen Wood in Emily's company on more than one occasion, one of whom was the scoundrel, Jack Crabtree, whose evidence needs to be treated with extreme caution, and it will be recalled that he did not mention Wood in his first statement. As we have seen, he spoke of a man with whom Emily used to be friendly but said 'I know very little of him'. After the arrest in October, however, he was full of stories about Wood's relationship with Emily. Considering that Wood was in a relationship with Ruby Young during the spring of 1906, it is unlikely that he was conducting a second relationship with Emily, especially as he avoided contracting any form of sexually transmitted disease, whereas most of her known clients and lovers from this period were not so lucky. The only other two witnesses who said they regularly saw Emily with Wood were William Linehan and Gladys Warren but they were hardly the most honest pair, considering that Linehan had falsely denied running a disorderly house and Gladys had supported him in court. Most importantly, none of Emily's friends, apart from Gladys Warren, saw Emily with Wood at the time they were supposedly conducting this affair. True, Ellen Lawrence said she saw Wood speaking to Emily once in the *Pindar of Wakefield* but this hardly supports the notion that they were in any kind of relationship. Florence Smith had only known Emily since late 1906 so she was not in any position to confirm whether Emily knew Wood earlier in that year. May Campbell, who did know Emily during the Spring of 1906, supposedly saw her with a man she knew as 'Scotch Bob', which nickname could fit Wood, but 'Scotch Bob' was distinguished by his bad complexion and there is no evidence that this ever applied to Wood; in any case, we know that Alexander Mackie admitted to being 'Scotch Bob' albeit without explaining why he was called that. In favour of the notion that Wood had only recently met Emily, it is notable that he spoke to both Ellen Lawrence and Florence Smith in the *Rising Sun* during the week before Emily's murder, yet had never apparently spoken to any of her friends before this. Moreover, Emily was frequently in the *Rising Sun* but the barman of that establishment had never seen her with Wood before September 1907.

Crabtree, Linehan and Warren had, of course, all picked out Wood in an identification parade as a man they had repeatedly seen with Emily. For that reason, even bearing in mind that Wood might have stood out like a sore thumb as he claimed, we cannot entirely dismiss the notion that he had a prior relationship with the murder victim. His denials of this certainly count for little bearing in mind the arrogance revealed by his words to Ruby that their joint word would 'stand against the world', even though that word was a lie. Wood was a man quite capable of telling falsehoods, regardless of how many people were saying the opposite. We do need to be careful about identification evidence though. The example of the Beck case is well known but there was another lesser known case in October 1907 when, in what one newspaper described as 'an extraordinary police blunder', the son of Lord Justice Selwyn, Major Harry Jasper Selwyn, was mistaken for a notorious ex-convict who had failed to report himself to police while on a ticket of leave. As he left the Pavilion Music Hall in Piccadilly in full evening dress, having earlier dined at a nearby restaurant with a female companion, Major Selwyn was 'jostled somewhat roughly by a man in a silk hat and frock coat', who turned out to be a plain clothes detective, and told he must accompany him to the station. When he replied that he would do nothing of the kind, the detective seized his right arm while a uniformed sergeant grabbed hold of his left arm and he was forcibly marched to Vine Street Police Station. There he was searched and placed in a cell and 'subjected to many indignities', before his true identity was established and he was released from custody with a written apology from the Assistant Commissioner who called it a 'most unfortunate mistake'.[482] Major Selwyn was not put into an identification parade but this is just one small example of how easy it could be for mistaken identity to lead to unfortunate consequences.

On balance, the truth of the matter is probably somewhere in between the two extremes of a long-term relationship and no prior contact. Wood is likely to have been familiar with Emily Dimmock from 1906 onwards, having spoken to her now and then in various public houses, just as Ellen Lawrence had observed in the *Pindar of Wakefield*. It is noteworthy that, while Emily was living in Manchester Street, Ruby Young was living less than one minute's walk away in Liverpool Street, both locations being close to the *Rising Sun*. Wood was a frequent visitor to Ruby's home so might easily have become familiar with Emily through seeing her in the street or in nearby public houses and, from the evidence of Smeeth, he undoubtedly visited the *Rising Sun* which, of course, is where he shared his first drink with Ruby. Potentially the most important evidence to support some form of prior knowledge was Florence Smith's claim that Wood had entered the *Rising Sun* on the Friday evening and asked her if she had seen 'Phyllis', showing that he knew her name. However, Wood disputed this and it may be that Mrs Smith was confusing the Friday night with the Monday night because Ellen Lawrence said that Wood asked this question of her and Florence when he came in on Monday. The fact that Florence Smith had never seen Wood before makes her claim that he came up to her to ask her this question on the Friday night problematic, whereas Wood saw the two women speak to Emily on the Friday night so it makes more sense that he would have asked them if they had seen Emily/Phyllis on the Monday.

Ultimately, though, it makes little difference whether Wood had known Emily before September 1907. An extended emotional relationship between the two might have made it marginally more likely that one would murder the other but passions could just as easily be aroused by a short relationship as a long one.

Emily supposedly told Roberts that Wood had wanted to come home with her on the Monday night but could not afford her. It is interesting that Wood revealed details of his salary to the *Evening News* immediately after his trial. He said he was paid a 'retaining fee' of 43 shillings a week but claimed not only that this was to be increased to 57 shillings per week (or £150 per annum) before the end of the year but that he earned considerably more than his retaining fee because he would often 'sit down and do a drawing of an evening for a guinea, and receive additional money from my employers according to the work'.[483] Was his desire to tell the world about his income a result of Roberts' publicised claim that Emily mentioned to him that the man pursuing her had 'no money' until he was paid at the end of the month, albeit that this evidence was excluded from the trial? Perhaps surprisingly, Inspector Neil did not see fit to investigate Wood's finances. Wood himself told the *Evening News* that he had no debts but we do not know if he had any savings or even whether he was paid weekly or monthly. Wood's lack of cash, if there was such a lack, might explain why Emily made disparaging remarks about him to her friends. If he was pressing her for free sex, or sex on account, it might have been the reason why Emily seemed, on occasion, to be afraid of him; only it was not that she was afraid, just irritated by his demands. We know that she charged between 12 and 18 shillings a night which would have been a large chunk of Wood's weekly salary, although cheaper options were presumably on offer. The problem for Wood was that Roberts, his rival for Emily's affections during September, was flush with cash.

Wood had Emily to himself during the evening of Friday 6 September and, by his own account, enjoyed her company. She was, in Wood's words, 'playful' and 'friendly' and he paid for her drinks. The story of how he came to write the postcard to her in the *Rising Sun* that night is a little too unlikely to be believed. One thing it has going for it is that Emily collected postcards, so it is not impossible that she wanted Wood to send her one and gave him her address accordingly, but the message on the postcard surely cannot have been anything other than it appeared: Wood was asking to meet her in the *Rising Sun* at 8:15 on the Monday evening. It seems that he deliberately waited until it was past midnight before he posted the card so it would be postmarked as 11 September and she would know he was asking to meet her that evening when she received it. The obvious reason for signing the postcard as 'Alice' was so that Bert Shaw would not know it was from a man if he saw it. It may be asked how Emily would know who the card was from and Wood's story certainly provides an answer to this. Any other suggestion can only be speculative but Wood must have been sure that Emily would have understood he was the author.

When Wood arrived at the *Rising Sun* on the Monday evening, he asked Mrs Lawrence and Mrs Smith if they had 'seen Phyllis' so he was clearly there with a specific purpose in mind. Ellen Lawrence recalled that Emily asked Wood for a penny to put into the automatic piano – which may have been a mistake because that was how Wood said he first met Emily on the Friday night; but is not impossible that, having asked him for a penny on the Friday, she asked him again on the Monday. If there is one part of Wood's story that certainly cannot be believed it is in respect of what happened next. Ellen Lawrence saw Emily and Wood leave the bar and board an omnibus, having said they were going to the Holborn Empire. She said she noticed that Emily did not want to go with Wood but appeared to have to go and it was then that some uncomplimentary remarks were passed by her about him. Wood's claim under cross-examination that he had absolutely no recollection of where he went with Emily for about two hours that evening was ridiculous and cannot be believed. Had the pair simply gone to the *Adam and Eve*, as they told Mrs

Lawrence and Mrs Smith, there is no reason why Wood would not have said so. For that reason we cannot avoid the conclusion that the two of them went somewhere for sex, presumably back to 29 St Paul's Road.

It was at this point that Roberts' rivalry kicks in because Emily told Wood at about closing time that she was going to have to leave him to join Roberts, it being to her financial advantage to do so. The following night, the likelihood is that Wood did indeed pop his head round the door of the *Rising Sun* as Ellen Lawrence recalled. He saw Emily fully engaged with Roberts, causing him to send her a letter requesting a meeting in the *Eagle*, well away from the *Rising Sun* where she was so popular and difficult to speak to for any length of time because, as Wood himself observed, she 'flitted about' between different men. Emily received the letter while she was with Roberts on Wednesday morning. It is difficult to know why she showed him that letter, and indeed the postcard, other than to make him jealous and attempt to play him off against Wood. Be that as it may, we know for a fact that Emily ended up in the *Eagle* but it is by no means clear that she went there to meet Wood. She told George Stocks at about quarter past eight – roughly the proposed meeting time – that she was going out to buy a lamp and perhaps that is what she attempted to do. The fact that she had curlers in her hair is inconclusive evidence as to her intentions bearing in mind the reported comments of the manageress of the *Murray Arms* that this was how she sometimes came into her establishment but it does not suggest someone dressing up for an evening out. It may be that Wood waited for Emily in the *Eagle* but, when she did not appear, walked towards St Paul's Road and found her in the street on her way to the shops, persuading her to come with him to the public house. Wood's own story was that he met Emily outside the *Eagle* so it is by no means implausible but, if this is what happened, Wood might have felt insulted by Emily's failure to keep the appointment and by the fact that she had not even taken out her curlers for him.

Whatever happened later that evening we can be confident that Wood did not plan to murder Emily. If that was indeed his intention he would have been a complete fool to carry out the plan having accidentally met his friend, Joseph Lambert, in the *Eagle*. As Lambert spoke briefly to Emily, it would have been obvious to Wood that any thoughts he might have had of meeting up with Emily without anyone knowing and killing her before slipping silently away into the night had been completely ruined. Whatever Wood was, he was not a complete fool so we can rule out the idea that he had murder in mind. Instead, he surely had sex in mind.

It is the missing hour that tells us that Wood returned to St Paul's Road with Emily. Lilian Raven's evidence seems to have been entirely reliable. Although she initially failed to recognise Emily as a customer of the *Eagle* from a photograph, her explanation that this was because she was too tired to focus, having been woken by the police, is undoubtedly correct. Everything she said about the events of that evening which could be corroborated by Joseph Lambert was corroborated by him, and even Wood agreed with her account of his conversations with Emily and Lambert. Raven believed that Wood left the *Eagle* with Emily only minutes after Lambert had departed, which means that, despite Wood's feeble protest to the contrary, Wood and Emily probably left at about 10:00pm. As Wood did not return home until shortly before midnight, and the walk home would have taken no more than thirty minutes, this leaves a whole hour, at least, unaccounted for. The obvious and straightforward explanation is that Wood managed to persuade Emily to take him back to St Paul's Road where some form of sexual intimacy took place. They might even have shared some dinner together, although the fact that Inspector Neil's evidence indicates that he saw two plates but only one glass means it is uncertain whether two people did partake of food that night.[484]

As mentioned at the start of this chapter, even if there was DNA evidence to prove that Wood had intimate relations with Emily at St Paul's Road it does not necessarily mean he murdered her. The jury must have suspected that he did go back to number 29 with her – as did the judge and Marshall Hall – but still declined to bring in a guilty verdict. Why would he have killed her? One answer to this question from a psychopathological perspective has been put forward by Nina Warner Hooke and Gilbert Thomas in their 1966 biography of Marshall Hall. They speculated that Wood might have had had a schizoid personality which, together with his church school education and 'repressive Scottish upbringing', meant that, when he woke up in the small hours next to a prostitute, his feelings of 'shame and disgust' caused him to 'destroy the partner of his guilt'.[485] Their only objection to this theory was that he would not have had a weapon to hand but they wrongly believed that microscopic examination of Shaw's two razors had proved that neither of them had been used. As we have seen, Dr Thompson was unable to rule out the possibility that one of them might have been the murder weapon. Yet, this does not appear to be the real problem with their theory. Nothing in Wood's personality suggests he was a repressed individual. On the contrary, he appears to have been a very relaxed chap, at ease with himself and perfectly at home in the surroundings of the *Rising Sun*. Surely the type of man Warner Hooke and Thomas were thinking of would not have publicly described himself as 'a bohemian'. Furthermore, such a theory completely ignores the little bit of evidence which does exist relating to motive, namely Roberts' claim that Emily told him that Wood was jealous.

Crabtree's evidence that he saw letters written by Wood to Emily (in the same handwriting as that on the rising sun postcard) begging her to leave Shaw, if accepted, suggests that Wood's objective was to persuade Emily to live with him but, despite Crabtree's almost convincing recollection that one such letter had been signed off with the very 'Woodian' phrase 'yours to dust', ultimately, we have to disregard it. He would have been more believable had he not previously claimed that he had seen letters written to Emily by 'Scottie' in the same handwriting as that on the rising sun postcard. Even without that, however, it is not possible to believe anything Crabtree says without corroboration because he was clearly angling for a reward for helping to convict Wood.

Nevertheless, taking Roberts' hearsay evidence that Wood was jealous – presumably of Shaw and/or Emily's other clients – we have a starting point to explain why Wood might have murdered Emily. Perhaps, after having sex, he asked her to leave Shaw, ditch Roberts and her other clients and live with him but Emily simply laughed at him. Perhaps she disparagingly mentioned his deformed fingers, thus humiliating him. It may be that, at this point, as Emily lay in bed, drifting off to sleep, her comments festered in Wood's mind and his frustrations with his life reached boiling point. Here he was, an artist – a superior person in every way, in his own mind, to a railway car attendant like Bert Shaw – rejected by a common prostitute; not only rejected but she laughed at him and simply drifted off to sleep while he was pouring his heart out to her, begging her to live with him. We can never prove that anything like this happened but the scenario is not entirely implausible. It seems more likely than one of the most common reasons for men to murder, or attempt to murder, their lovers, namely the thought 'If I can't have her, no-one can'. There are plenty of examples of this from the period but one would have expected some kind of argument, with raised voices, between the couple if this had been the case. As it was, no-one heard anything. There might have been an element of 'If I can't have her, no-one can' in Wood's thinking but, if he did kill her (a big 'if') it is more likely to have been as a result of some ill-conceived insults which caused him to brood and ultimately to snap and behave out of character.

Alternatively, might there have been no motive at all? We only need to cast our minds back to Arthur Newton's former client, Thomas Currell, who freely confessed to murdering his sweetheart but, being affected by drink and drugs, was unable to explain why. We do not know if Wood was an alcoholic or experimenting with drugs in September 1907. None of his family would have said anything to the police if he was but one would have expected any strange behaviour to have been detected by his colleagues at work and, indeed, if he was taking any drugs that caused some kind of psychosis, he would have been unable to function properly in a work environment, which could not have gone unnoticed, so we can probably rule out a motiveless crime.

When we look at the crime scene, it is not hard to conceive of Wood covering Emily's dead body with the bedclothes. Psychologists would tell us that such an action shows that the victim is known to their killer and that the act of covering up the body, especially the face, is a way of that killer attempting to disassociate himself from his actions. Equally, we have no difficulty in picturing Wood, who gave the impression of being a thorough man, cleaning blood off himself as indicated by the bloodstains on the washstand. Even easier to imagine is Wood desperately searching through Emily's postcard album to locate and remove the postcard he had sent her earlier in the week. This was certainly the prosecution theory at the trial with Sir Charles Mathews saying in his opening speech, 'There were indications that the postcard album had been hastily gone through for the purpose, there can be no doubt, of discovering whether a particular postcard was there' and that 'The murderer evidently searched for a card which might be there'.[486] But it wasn't there. Nor would he have been able find the letter she would have received that morning. So he would have searched through the chest of drawers, scattering its contents over the floor, but no trace of the postcard or the letter would have been found. As we know, the letter had been burnt in the fire and presumably Emily had hidden the postcard inside the newspaper lining the chest of drawers so that Shaw would not find it. To that extent, the state in which Emily's room was found is consistent with Wood being the murderer. However, it is a little more difficult to understand why Wood would have taken the silver cast pattern chain, the small glass charm, the silver cigarette, Emily's purse and her watch and rings. If he had simply taken the opportunity afforded by being alone in Emily's room to steal money there would be no problem. Wood was not wealthy and the temptation to pocket the cash that Emily had earned from Roberts might have been too much for him to overcome. But Wood was not a criminal and he would not have had the contacts to sell the stolen goods. The simple act of taking them and carrying them with him in the street greatly increased the risk of his capture, conviction and execution, because the only explanation for having them in his possession was that he was the murderer. Trying to sell them would have been far too risky and they could not have been very valuable in any case.

Why then (assuming Wood murdered Emily) would he have taken Emily's possessions from her room? As we know, Inspector Neil thought he had the answer. He believed that Wood had attempted to create a false trail by staging a robbery to make it look like this was the motive for the murder (and, perhaps, to cover up the search for the postcard). His supporting evidence for this was the three rings he saw in one of the chests of drawers in the front parlour on the morning of 12 September. If it was a genuine robbery, Neil wondered, why would the robber not have taken the rings? Yet, the existence of these rings only begs the question: if Wood (as the murderer attempting to stage a robbery) saw the rings and believed them to be valuable why did he simply not take them? It makes no sense for him to have removed much larger items yet leave the rings which could have been slipped into his pocket. The obvious conclusion, but one which did not seem to have occurred to Inspector Neil, is that Wood (or whoever committed the murder) did not spot the rings in the darkness. If that is the case, however, it calls into question the entire notion of a faked robbery because it was the existence of the rings that put the thought into the inspector's head in the first place.[487]

There are other problems. Let us assume that Wood murdered Emily. We have no problem in also assuming he would have searched in the front room for the postcard (and letter), creating disorder. He might then have thought he needed to cover up the disorder in the room by making it look like the murderer was not after the postcard/letter but looking for valuables. Yet, if he had gone through *that* thought process, surely he would have picked up any postcards lying on the floor and replaced them into the album, which he would have put back where he found it. Despite the police evidence being that there were some loose postcards on the floor and the album was on a chair, it may be that Wood did, in fact, put the album on the sewing machine with all postcards inside and it was a police officer who moved it to the chair and dropped some of them on the floor. It will be recalled that Shaw never said he saw any postcards out of place. While it would make sense that Wood as the murderer of Emily would have replaced the album on the sewing machine after searching through it, this would mean that the main factor at the crime scene that lends support to the idea that Wood committed the murder, namely the appearance of the postcard album being searched, never actually existed.

Furthermore, even if we accept that Shaw was wrong to think that the folding doors were locked when he arrived at the crime scene, it does not make much sense for Wood to have locked the door to Emily's apartment on his way out. Neither Inspector Neil nor the prosecution ever considered the point. It has to be said that the fact of the locked door does not rule Wood out as being the murderer – there was nothing to stop him from locking it – but, if he had wanted the police to think that a burglar had murdered Emily, by locking the door of a room with closed and shuttered windows he was totally defeating that purpose. The obvious question the police would have asked is how the burglar entered the premises so it would have been foolish and self-defeating to lock the door. Of course, had a window been left open by the murderer before departing, the police would have assumed that the killer had entered through the window and, perhaps, would have regarded it as less likely that one of Emily's clients had murdered her. As it was, without any signs of forced entry, it must have been obvious to anyone contemplating a deception plan, especially someone of Wood's obvious intelligence, that the police would think Emily had allowed her killer in – just what Wood would not have wanted them to think. He had, of course, been seen with Emily by Lambert only a few hours earlier and would have had to have been a supreme optimist to have believed that Lambert would never have made the connection once the murder was reported. True, Wood could not have anticipated the huge public interest in the murder, especially the fact that Emily's photograph would be published in all the newspapers, but by simply stealing some of Emily's money and a few of her personal possessions he was hardly going to throw the police off the scent. It was not as if he was a wealthy man whom no-one would ever suspect of theft.

Then consider what he said to William Moss after the murder. According to Moss, 'I remember casually mentioning to him that such a murder had occurred and he made a remark in reply something to the effect that he was not surprised at a woman like that getting murdered for they never knew who they were taking home with them'. That is not at all consistent with a man who had gone to great lengths to try and make the murder look like part of a robbery. On the contrary, Wood was saying to Moss that he assumed that Emily was murdered by one of her clients. The apparent theft of Emily's jewellery was reported in the morning newspapers the day after the murder, so it would have been quite natural for Wood to have speculated that a burglar had been to blame yet he did not do so.

What makes Wood such a good suspect, apart from his attempt to create a false alibi, is the fact that he was the last person known to be with Emily before she was murdered. Yet, we cannot ignore the fact that two witnesses said they saw Emily with a man who was not Wood after midnight. The police and prosecution did, of course, ignore this fact and Sir Charles Mathews, during the course of his closing speech, helpfully provided the three reasons why they did so. According to Sir Charles, 'the woman seen with a man in the Euston Road on the night of the murder by Sharples and Harvey could not have been Phyllis Dimmock, because she would not have been so near the Rising Sun and not go in; because she was not dressed for her calling; and because we know that until a late hour that night the woman was not at the Rising Sun, but some distance away, at the Eagle public-house'. Inspector Neil had given a slightly different reason for disregarding their evidence in his report of 30 September, namely that, had Emily been in the vicinity of the *Rising Sun*, 'she would have been seen by some of her acquaintances, several of whom left the Rising Sun at closing time, when the two men say they saw her'.

None of these reasons are convincing. No evidence was ever provided that Emily always visited the *Rising Sun* whenever she was in the Euston Road and, in fact, if she was already with a man, she would have had other priorities. Moreover, as Inspector Neil observed, it was almost closing time when Sharples and Harvey said they saw Emily so there would have been no point in her visiting the *Rising Sun*. It also seems extremely questionable for Inspector Neil to have concluded that Emily's acquaintances *must* have seen her when they left the *Rising Sun*. We don't even know how many of those acquaintances there were who left the *Rising Sun* at closing time (and, of those, how many spoke to Inspector Neil) and there could be many reasons why any of her friends who did leave the public house at that time would not have noticed Emily, who was simply walking down the street and not doing anything to call attention to herself. As for Sir Charles' claim that Emily was 'not dressed for her calling', an obvious reference to her hair being in curlers, there was no evidence that her hair was in curlers at the time she was seen by Sharples and Harvey. It is perfectly true that Emily's hair was in curlers when she was in the *Eagle* with Wood and she was found with her hair in curlers the following morning but that does not necessarily mean that her hair was in curlers all evening. What if she put her hair in curlers during the day, in preparation for going out that evening, but found herself dragged into the *Eagle* by Wood when she went to the shops, or perhaps she knew she was going to meet Wood and did not wish to take her curlers out yet. Then, as soon as she returned home with Wood she removed the curlers or, having spent an hour with Wood in her room, she wanted to go out again and removed the curlers from her hair for that reason. According to Bert Shaw, it was Emily's habit to keep her hair in curlers during the day, presumably in preparation for going out in the evening, so there would have been nothing unusual in her doing this.[488] The question might then be asked as to why she put the curlers back when she went to bed but this could be explained by the fact that Shaw's mother was visiting the next morning and she wanted to do her hair again overnight. Even if the concept of her putting her hair in curlers twice in one day is far-fetched, we do not have any evidence at all that Emily would not pursue her 'calling' with her hair in curlers. It is true that she commented to Lambert something to the effect of 'fancy making me come out like this' but, to the extent that this was a reference to her hair being in curlers (about which we cannot be entirely certain), it is not consistent with the manageress of the *Murray Arms* seeing her like that in her bar.[489] As for Sir Charles' third point, that Emily was in the *Eagle* on Wednesday night, this was the weakest of all. Lilian Raven said that Wood and Emily left the *Eagle* at about 10:00pm so there was absolutely nothing to have prevented Emily from being in the Euston Road at midnight with another man. Sharples and Harvey both knew Emily and there is no reason for them to have been mistaken. They went to the police 48 hours after the discovery of the murder so the incident was relatively fresh in their minds. The fact that they saw Emily with someone who was not Wood was inconvenient for Inspector Neil because it did not accord with his theory that the author of the rising sun postcard must have been the killer but that is not a good reason to disregard their evidence.

There was even a weak form of corroboration of the evidence of Sharples and Harvey from the three people who, according to Inspector Neil's report of 30 September 1907, saw Emily with 'a tall fair man dressed in a blue serge suit and bowler hat and of a smart gentlemanly appearance' during the afternoon of Wednesday 11 September. We don't quite know exactly what they said to the police because their statements are either missing or were never taken. Inspector Neil disregarded what they said because he was sure Emily was at home all of Wednesday afternoon based on what Shaw and Mrs Stocks had told him but, unless all three of the witnesses who said they saw Emily recanted, it would seem that their evidence was not shared with the defence. Inspector Neil might also have been relying on the fact that no other witnesses saw the tall man in the blue suit with Emily in the *Rising Sun* on the Sunday night but neither Florence Smith nor Ellen Lawrence appear to have been in the *Rising Sun* on the Sunday and Frank Clarke, who was there, said nothing in his statement about what Emily was doing before she met Roberts.

The strongest point against the evidence of Sharples and Harvey is not so much in what they said but who they were. There is no reason to doubt Inspector Neil's claim that they were a couple of pimps, despite the fact that this was never alleged against them in cross-examination, yet, in some respects, the fact that they were pimps but still came forward to talk to the police could be said to enhance their credibility. They were, presumably, the last men to volunteer information to the authorities, so their actions in doing so must have meant they felt sufficiently horrified by the attack on Emily to want to help the police to catch the man who murdered her. Or could they have had another motive for emerging from the underworld?

In the supplement to his 2008 book, *The Camden Town Murder*, author John Barber offers what even he describes as a 'fanciful' theory that there might have been a conspiracy between Mackie, Sharples, Harvey and a few others (who he does not name, but he was presumably thinking of Crabtree) to frame 'Scottie'. This might have been the reason, he suggests, why the two pimps were so eager to step forward and speak to the police. However, the theory does not make any sense. Alexander Mackie said in cross-examination at the Old Bailey that he did not know 'Scottie' and he made no other mention of him during his testimony. Crabtree's description of 'Scottie' was that he was a small man whereas Sharples and Harvey said the man they saw with Emily on the Wednesday night was tall so we can instantly rule out the notion that they were all involved in any attempt to direct blame towards 'Scottie'. If anything, Sharples and Harvey were directing blame *away* from him – and that might even be what they were trying to do.

It will be recalled that, on Friday 13 September, the *Daily News* reported that Emily had been seen by one of her neighbours walking along St Paul's Road, a little before midnight on Wednesday, with 'a short, dark individual'. The very next day, Sharples and Harvey presented themselves at a police station to say they had seen Emily shortly after midnight with a 'tall, fair man'. If, as Barber suggests, their evidence was designed to mislead the police then the only sensible theory is that they wanted to draw attention away from a real, small man to an imaginary, tall one. According to Crabtree, 'Scottie' was five foot four or five and was clearly also a pimp. Could it be that 'Scottie' murdered Emily and, worried by the accurate report in the *Daily News* which alerted him to the fact that someone had seen him with his victim, persuaded his fellow pimps, Harry Sharples and Fred Harvey, to create a fictional 'tall fair' individual for the police to chase? Could the three people who claimed to have seen Emily with a tall, fair man in Somers Town during the Wednesday afternoon also have been part of the conspiracy? On the face of it, a conspiracy involving so many people seems unlikely but this would certainly explain why all the Somers Town witnesses attested that they saw Emily in the street between 3:00pm and 4:00pm even though Bert Shaw was certain she did not leave the house at any time before he left for work at 4:30pm. It would also explain why they, and Sharples/Harvey, all said the man they saw with Emily was wearing a blue suit.

The *Daily Mail* on the Saturday morning had carried an early description of the police suspect from the landlady of 2 Grafton Place, Mrs Roberts, who said that the police told her on the Friday that they were looking for a man wearing a navy blue coat and a bowler hat. She also said that the man was supposed to be five foot ten inches in height but the source of this information remains unknown; it could not have come from Sharples and Harvey because they did not approach the police until the Saturday.[490] Although not included in his statement, Robert Roberts supposedly told Inspector Neil that the man he saw with Emily in the *Rising Sun* was wearing a blue suit and Wood was, in fact, wearing a blue suit and a bowler hat when he chatted with Emily on the Friday and Monday nights before the murder. Plenty of people must have seen Wood in this outfit and a man like 'Scottie' (as described by Crabtree) could easily have picked up the local gossip about it in the *Rising Sun* during the two days after the murder and ensured that his fake witnesses incorporated it into their stories. There is no doubt that Scottie would have wanted as few people as possible to know that he was involved in the murder but he need not have been personally involved in instructing everyone what to tell the police; an associate could have done this for him so that the witnesses need not have known on whose behalf they were providing the false story. Without knowing anything about the character of Mr Clarke, Mrs Wolton and Miss Bucknal – the three people who said they saw Emily with the tall man on the Wednesday afternoon – it is impossible to say if such a conspiracy is credible but it certainly provides food for thought.

Regardless of this, we need to take a good look at 'Scottie', also known as 'Tom Wilson', because he is a serious suspect for the murder of Emily Dimmock; if he ever existed. Because, of course, it was Crabtree who identified him as a suspect and we cannot be entirely certain that he was not a product of the man's imagination. Yet, not absolutely everything Crabtree said was a fabrication. He certainly knew Emily, and his stories about chasing her to recover his money and curtain pole and informing the superintendent of her apartment building that she had been bringing men home were corroborated by Bert Shaw. However, the only other person who gave evidence of even knowing 'Scottie' was Mrs Crabtree, which does not inspire much confidence. If we only had the word of the Crabtrees that Scottie existed then we would probably conclude that he was a fictional character and that the Crabtrees were playing a game with the police. However, there is one thing that lends support to Scottie's existence. Although she was not a witness at any court of law, and there is no surviving witness statement from her, Mrs Roberts told the *Daily Mail* of a man called 'Tom' who had threatened to kill Emily in precisely the same way that Scottie had done in front of Crabtree. We know from Inspector Neil's report of 30 September that Mrs Roberts was indeed Emily's landlady at 2 Grafton Place.[491] In his report of 13 September, the inspector stated that the landlady at 2 Grafton Place 'has been seen and she gives deceased a very bad character stating that since she left the address several men, whom she does not know, have called and complained that they have contracted venereal disease from her and one or two of them have threatened to "out" her if they could find her', presumably meaning to expose her as a prostitute. In this report,

Neil gives the landlady's name as 'Leticia Houpe' (which was presumably an error[492]) but the point is that Neil's report provides official confirmation that Emily was indeed being threatened by a man to whom she gave 'the disorder'. Mrs Roberts' story to the *Daily Mail* was that the man called Tom told her in January 1907 that he would track Emily down, saying 'I'll find her if it takes me years….I'll do for her'. He sounds remarkably like Crabtree's 'Scottie'. It will be recalled that Crabtree told Inspector Neil on 19 September that 'the man I have described called at the house and finding she was gone got very angry swore about her and threatened to do for her…he produced a razor and opened it and took his handkerchief from his pocket wrapped it around the handle of the razor and waving it about said he would do her in yet'. The expression 'do for her' was exactly the same as that remembered by Mrs Roberts as having been used by the man she knew as 'Tom'. Mrs Crabtree also stated that 'This man (Tom) she used to give money to and I have heard him threaten he would "do her in"'. Furthermore, Mrs Roberts said that the man told her 'She's ruined me' and Crabtree said that Scottie accused Emily of having 'ruined him for life'. Crabtree could not have known about the *Daily Mail* article containing the quotes from Mrs Roberts because he was in prison and newspapers were not available to prisoners so the two stories of the two men threatening to do Emily in because she had ruined him were, as far as can be established, completely independent of each other.

There are, however, two problems in concluding that the man spoken about by Mrs Roberts was the same as the man identified by Crabtree. Crabtree's 'Scottie' was threatening to cut Emily's throat in the summer of 1906 but Mrs Roberts said that the man she had heard threatening Emily had taken her for a motor ride in November 1906 and only threatened her in January 1907. She also described the man as being five foot and seven inches compared to Crabtree's 'Scottie' who supposedly stood at no more than five foot and five inches. Yet neither of these points is fatal to the notion that they both spoke to the same man. It was clear from Crabtree's evidence that Scottie was frequently violent towards Emily yet the pair would evidently make up after their quarrels. So it is not impossible that, having been determined to cut Emily's throat in July 1906, when she was in a relationship with Biddle, Scottie tracked Emily down at Grafton Place in November and relations between them were restored. By November, of course, Biddle was at sea and Emily's relationship with him was over, although she appears to have led people to believe she was married to him. According to Mrs Roberts, the man she spoke to at 2 Grafton Place in January 1907 said that he thought Emily was 'married to a sailor'. What seemed to inflame him, however, was that Mrs Roberts told him that Emily was now living with a man called Shaw. In other words, it is possible that what really caused Scottie to want to murder Emily, as much as the fact that she had given him venereal disease, was that she was putting herself out of his control and under the protection of other men. The discrepancy between the height of the man described by Crabtree and the man described by Mrs Roberts could be explained by an inability of one or both of them to estimate heights correctly. It is by no means easy to estimate someone's height accurately, especially when being asked to do so some months after a brief encounter. In the case of Mrs Roberts, she was being told by police that their suspect was five foot ten inches and her estimate in response that he was closer to five foot seven inches might have erred on the tall side as a result. If Scottie had, in fact, been five foot six inches he would only have been one inch on either side of the estimates of Mrs Roberts and Crabtree.

There were a number of other characteristics provided by Mrs Roberts of the man she spoke to. She agreed with the police description that he was 'pale, clean shaven, face rather pimply and sickly looking; clean chin'. According to Crabtree, Scottie was: 'complexion sallow, dark hair, very slight brown moustache, small eyes very close together, small features, hair stands up from well brushing, slight build, pimples on face'. Clearly there are some differences (one was clean shaven the other had a moustache) and some similarities (both were pale or sallow complexioned with pimples). The difference could be easily explained by Scottie having shaved off his moustache by November 2006. The other elements of the descriptions are not inconsistent with each other but do not assist either way in establishing whether they were talking about the same person.

It is not essential to prove that Mrs Roberts' suspect was the same as Crabtree's but it would certainly be helpful corroboration of Crabtree's story if they were the same man. We should also bear in mind what Gladys Warren told the police in her statement of 20 September 1907. As we have seen, she referred to a man called 'Scotch Jock' or 'Scotch Jack' who asked her several times where Emily had gone after she moved out of Burton Crescent and who was 'a very violent man' who had 'threatened to do her in'. Emily was said to be frightened of this man who claimed that she had given him the disorder, which matches what Crabtree had said about Scottie. Again, however, the description given of the man by Gladys Warren was rather different to Crabtree's 'Scottie', especially in respect of his height, which was said to have been five foot ten inches: much too tall it would seem to be the man Crabtree was speaking of. It should also not be forgotten that William Linehan gave evidence that he had heard that Emily had been threatened by a Scotsman called 'Jock' in Argyle Square, albeit that this was obviously hearsay evidence and of limited value.

If Crabtree was telling the truth then Scottie is a strong suspect. It will be recalled that Crabtree claimed that he saw Scottie, together with a 'tall fair man', watching the dwellings where Emily lived in St Pancras Square at some point in late May or early June 1907. He said that he gave a boy six shillings to follow the two men after they saw him and crossed the road but he never saw the boy again, something which at least has the ring of truth about it because it does not seem to be something he would have made up, considering that it only highlights his own incompetence. On that basis, it rather looks as if Scottie was stalking Emily at the time. The interesting thing, however, is that Emily seems to have retained a soft spot for Scottie despite his history of violence towards her. It will be recalled that, according to Crabtree, while standing at the corner of Judd Street with Emily, Scottie walked past with a girl on his arm. Emily drew his attention to it, 'got very excited and said she had a good mind to go and tear his hat off. I persuaded her to take no notice and she said "Just fancy and I am keeping him"'. If this was true, then it was Emily who appears to have been the jealous one in the relationship and still seems to have been giving Scottie money despite living with Bert Shaw. Crabtree said that, after sharing a drink with Emily in the *Rising Sun*, he met Scottie who asked him 'if the old cow was inside'. He also said he saw Scottie talking to Emily on several occasions. It is clear, therefore, that Scottie did not carry out his threat from the summer of 1906 to cut Emily's throat but this is consistent with Scottie being the man who took Emily for a motor ride in November 1906 yet threatened to kill her a couple of months later upon learning she had moved in with a new man.

The precise nature of the relationship between Emily and Scottie is unclear but, if Crabtree is to be believed, he was living off Emily's earnings during the first half of 1906 and she gave him presents, despite regular beatings in return. She also gave him venereal disease. He felt this had ruined his life and caused him to be very angry towards her, especially when he learnt that she was living with other men. Yet, Emily was jealous when she saw Scottie with other women. It is not an uncommon form of abusive relationship. It is perhaps strange that none of Emily's friends seemed to know anything about it but, then again, Ellen Lawrence and Florence Smith were not even asked if Emily had known Scottie; their evidence was directed entirely towards her relationship with Robert Wood.

There are two possible scenarios involving Scottie as the murderer. The first entails him having an accomplice who, because Emily would have refused to meet him (Scottie) alone, courted Emily as a client on the Wednesday afternoon and then met her again in the evening. This would have to be the tall man in the blue suit seen by the three witnesses in Somers Town and the man seen by Sharples and Harvey in the Euston Road (from which it follows that all five witnesses were telling the truth and were not part of a huge conspiracy to deflect attention from Scottie). Having been invited back to Emily's room, the tall man would have opened the front door of 29 St Paul's Road, after Emily fell asleep, to allow Scottie in. While there is obviously no evidence to support this, Crabtree did tell Inspector Neil that Scottie and another man appeared to be watching Emily's premises at St Pancras Square. Crabtree described Scottie's friend as a 'tall fair man' who was slightly built with 'braid on his waistcoat and wearing blue cloth trousers'.[493] In this scenario, Wood meets Emily in the *Eagle* at 8:30pm and goes with her to 29 St Paul's Road at about 10:00pm. He remains in her company until about 11:00pm when he returns to Frederick Street. Emily either decides it is too early for bed or has arranged to meet the tall man in the blue suit and walks down towards Euston (possibly having removed the curlers from her hair).

Or, in the second possible scenario, having parted from Wood and gone back out onto the streets, Emily meets Scottie who persuades her to walk back to St Paul's Road with him. They arrive at about midnight. Emily says that Scottie can stay the night until the house alarm goes off at 4:40am. The couple presumably share some form of sexual intimacy and Emily drifts off to sleep (having put her curlers back in her hair in preparation for Mrs Shaw's visit the next morning). While she sleeps, in either scenario, Scottie carries out the act he has twice threatened and cuts her throat, either with his own razor (the one he waved in front of Crabtree in 1906) or with Shaw's. The depth of the cut, almost severing the neck from the body, reflects the hatred he feels towards Emily for the disease she has given him which, he still thinks, has ruined his life. He might, nevertheless, have asked Emily if she would leave Shaw for him and her answer, that she would not, might have been the final straw. After the cruel murder, he covers Emily's face with a blanket and washes the blood from both the razor and himself in the washstand and then cannot resist stealing all of Emily's money and whatever valuables he can find in the chest of drawers in her front room. He has plenty of underworld connections who will ensure he can sell the items. He then leaves number 29 but, if he was the killer, it will have to remain a mystery as to why he locks either one or both of the doors on his way out.

It will be recalled that at 1:10am, cab driver, Richard Taylor, was hailed by a man in St Paul's Road, opposite number 29, described as 'about 35 to 40 years of age, height 5ft 5 or 6, fair hair and moustache, dressed in a dark jacket, light trousers and black bowler hat'. Both the estimated height and the fact that he had a moustache matches Crabtree's description. However, Crabtree said that Scottie was aged 'about 26' so there is quite a discrepancy there. The interesting part of Taylor's description is that the man to whom he gave a ride 'had a fresh appearance and looked as if he had just washed'. The killer of Emily Dimmock had certainly made use of the washstand and washed himself, so, combined with the fact that Taylor said it was unusual to pick up a fare in St Paul's Road at that time of night, there is some good reason to think that the Taylor's passenger was the murderer.

With both Crabtree and Mrs Roberts identifying a man called Tom as having threatened Emily it may be wondered if anyone with that name was a suspect. The only Tom on Inspector Neil's list of suspects was Arthur Thomas Edwin Atkins, an engineering fitter aged 23, who caught venereal disease from Emily and was referred to on occasion by Inspector Neil as 'Thomas Atkins'. However, this Tom was given an alibi by both his landlady and a fellow lodger for the night of the murder.

Although not an official suspect, there is one other man called Tom (Thomas) who featured in the police investigation – but secretly. On 18 September 1907, Inspector Neil wrote the following memo to his superiors:

> I beg to report that two informants known to me as Thomas Brownlow and Robert Roberts are assisting me with a view to secure the arrest of the murderer of Emily Dimmock. If the men are to be of any value this means a considerable expenditure of money on their parts. I would therefore respectfully suggest that a sum of £6 may be made from the Information Fund for this purpose.

A note on the reverse indicates that £4 was paid to Roberts and £2 was paid to Brownlow. We know all about Roberts' involvement in assisting Inspector Neil but who was Brownlow? The question seems to have occurred to Sir Melville Macnaghten because he wrote a manuscript note dated 10 October 1907 saying 'I should like to speak to Insp Neil about T Brownlow when he is next at C.O. [Commissioner's Office]'. Neil wrote a memo on the same day stating:

> I beg to report that I have advanced further various sums of money to Robert Percival Roberts amounting to £3 in connection with the arrest of prisoner Robert Wood in the murder of Emily Elizabeth Dimmock. He is still out of employment and has been rendering very great assistance. I therefore beg to suggest that a further sum of £4 be granted him from the Information Fund. I understand that Local Inspr Stockley E Division advanced the sum of £1 for an informant named Frederick Clifford in connection with the case while I have received valuable assistance from an informant named Thomas Brownlow who has already received £2. In the circumstances I would respectfully beg to suggest that Clifford receive £1 and Brownlow a further sum of £2 from the information fund.

There is nothing further in the Metropolitan Police file as to who Brownlow was or what 'valuable assistance' he provided to Inspector Neil.

Perhaps surprisingly there is only one 'Thomas Brownlow' who can be identified as living in London in 1907. This was a married carpenter with three children who is recorded in the 1911 census as living at 29 Staple Street in Southwark. He is also shown at this address in the 1909 electoral register. We know that he was also living in Southwark in 1905 because, in this year, his first son was baptised, having been born at the end of 1904 so it is a reasonable conclusion that he was living in Southwark in 1907. Thomas Brownlow had been born in Whitechapel in 1873 and was, thus, aged thirty-three at the time of Emily's murder. His father John, a fish porter born in Yorkshire, had married Eliza Batchelor in London in 1869. John Brownlow appears to have died in 1881 when Thomas was 7 years old and Eliza married a dock labourer called Charles Grafton in 1882. Consequently, Thomas was brought up as Thomas Grafton from 1882 onwards but had changed his name back to Brownlow by 1898 when he married Jane Lucas in Southwark.

Inspector Neil had spent some years in the early part of his career in Southwark so it is possible that he used Thomas as an informant but it is difficult to imagine what possible information an apparently respectable married carpenter from Southwark could have had about the murder of a prostitute in St Pancras. Of course, the fact that only one Thomas Brownlow can be located in London from official records does not mean that there were no other men of that name living there in 1907. There was much geographical movement at the time, with thousands of people coming in and going out of London every year who would not be recorded in the electoral register or picked up in the census taken four years later, so that any number of Thomas Brownlows could have been living in the capital at the time of Emily's murder.

More important than whether this Thomas Brownlow was Inspector Neil's informant is the question of whether the informant by the name of Thomas Brownlow, whoever he was, could have been the 'Tom' who was also Scottie. On the face of it, there is no reason to think so. The only connection is the first name. Crabtree said that his 'Tom' had the surname of 'Wilson' although he also said he was known as 'Mr Dimmock', presumably because of his close relationship with Emily. However, the surname of 'Brownlow' has no connection with Scotland; it derives from the north of England and is most common in Lancashire. There is no reason, therefore, to think that any man called 'Thomas Brownlow' would be nicknamed 'Scottie' and certainly none in respect of the Thomas Brownlow from Southwark who did not drive a motor car for a living as Crabtree's 'Scottie' was supposed to.

Nevertheless, allowing ourselves an indulgent flight of fantasy, let us explore a scenario in which the man called 'Thomas Brownlow' who was Neil's informant was also the 'Tom' known to Crabtree as Scottie. Before doing so, it is important to state that there is absolutely no evidence to support this, and any such theory is akin to a work of fiction but, still, it is too tempting a scenario to ignore because, if it were true, it would explain a great deal.

The one hard fact we know about Thomas Brownlow is that he was assisting Inspector Neil with the investigation by 18 September when Neil mentioned him in a report to his superiors. At this stage, the police were busy tracking down Emily's clients and male friends but they were also interested in Jack Crabtree. The police seemed to know about Crabtree from as early as 16 September. When Bert Shaw gave evidence at the inquest on that day about Crabtree being responsible for the fact that he and Emily were turned out of the dwelling in St Pancras Square, Inspector Neil immediately asked: 'Mr Crabtree was convicted of keeping an improper house was he not?' When Shaw agreed, the inspector was able to force him to admit that he knew that Emily was a prostitute. Two days later, on 18 September, Neil put in a request to the Home Office to be allowed access to Jack Crabtree in Pentonville. The police might have had good records about convicted criminals but it is not clear if they were good enough to have connected Emily Dimmock with Jack Crabtree within four days of the murder. Emily was not mentioned at Crabtree's 1906 police court hearing and, while it might have been possible for the police to have established that Emily had once lived at 13 Manchester Street, and that the man responsible for running that house as a brothel had been imprisoned, it is also possible that it was Thomas Brownlow who was able to tell the police of the connection between Crabtree and Emily Dimmock and that this was why Brownlow was rewarded with two pounds.

If Brownlow was the man who tipped off Inspector Neil to Crabtree then he must have known both Crabtree and Emily. One man called Tom who did know them both (if Crabtree is to be believed) was Scottie. If we accept the premise that Tom Brownlow was the man who informed Inspector Neil about Crabtree, and assume that Brownlow was also Scottie, then it would explain why Inspector Neil appears to have taken no steps to track Scottie down, despite him being a major suspect in the inquiry. He would have known who he was all along. It might also explain why he wrote to his superiors that the description Crabtree gave of Scottie 'certainly agrees with that of the man who was seen in the public house [*Rising Sun*]' when Crabtree had described this man as five foot four or five inches, which did not match any of the other descriptions of the man seen in the *Rising Sun*. Inspector Neil could hardly have failed to notice that Crabtree said that Scottie was a short man but might have omitted to mention this fact in his report to his superiors in an attempt to mislead them into thinking that Scottie was a different person to his informant but the same person as the prime suspect so that no special efforts would be needed to track him down. Even when it was made perfectly clear during the trial that they were different people (and that 'Scottie' was a different person to 'Scotch Bob') Inspector Neil, the great manhunter, seems to have made no attempt to find Scottie. It would not be the first example of a police informant being shielded by his handler. If Scottie/Thomas Brownlow did murder Emily he could have used his relationship with Inspector Neil to deflect attention onto others. Neil would undoubtedly not have believed that Scottie was guilty and would have had no interest in him as a suspect, only as someone who was able to provide him with information about Emily and her acquaintances.

We cannot develop this theory any further and the only thing it really has going for it is that Thomas Brownlow could have been referred to as 'Tom'. If Brownlow was a Scotsman, the idea might have some substance but there is nothing to suggest he was. He will have to remain a mystery man who provided information to Inspector Neil and we may never know what the information was or precisely how he was involved in the story of Emily's murder.

Manuscript note of Sir Melville Macnaghten confirming
payment of £2 reward to Thomas Brownlow (National Archives)

Chapter Eighteen

Aftermath and Aftermyths

'A myth is, of course, not a fairy story. It is the presentation of facts belonging to one category in the idioms appropriate to another. To explode a myth is accordingly not to deny the facts but to re-allocate them.'

Gilbert Ryle, *The Concept of Mind* (1949)

Half an hour after the verdict, the new hero, Robert Wood, stepped out of a side door from the Old Bailey into Newgate Street. He was immediately spotted by his many supporters in the crowd who cheered and surged towards him. Surrounded by police, he dashed into a motor car which had been temporarily loaned to him by the judge for the purpose of helping him escape. Accompanied by Arthur Newton, Wood was driven away at speed in order to get clear of the crowd which unsuccessfully gave chase before dispersing. A little to the west of Chancery Lane, Wood and Newton changed vehicles, hailing a passing hansom cab, while the motor car presumably returned to the Old Bailey to collect Mr Justice Grantham. The cab then turned down Red Lion Street and took Wood home.

George Wood had already emerged from the court house. According to the *Daily News*:

> ...the cheering swelled into a roar, the roar into a shriek, and the old man, leaning on the strong arm of his guardian, was overwhelmed by a human avalanche. For a few minutes he could do nothing but hold out his hand to the hundreds who struggled to grasp it. Tears were running down his cheeks. He was dazed. He spoke not. The strains of "He's a jolly good fellow" and "Auld Lang Syne" swept over the crowd.[494]

The old man, surrounded by a protective cordon of fifty police officers, was shuffled across the road to an Aerated Bread Company tea shop at the corner of Newgate Street where he took some tea with his two sons, Charles and James, while the crowd cheered in the street and he was then transferred up to a balcony above the shop so that everyone could see him clearly. Amidst all the noise, he could be heard to thank the members of the public for their enthusiastic reception of him and 'for the kindness which they have shown to me and my family in this very trying case'. To a *Daily Chronicle* journalist he said, 'I knew Robert would get off...I have been convinced of my son's innocence and I had little doubt that a British judge and a jury see that he got justice.' James Wood stated, 'I was absolutely certain he was not guilty' while Charles' wife, Bessie, was quoted as saying, 'My husband and I were convinced that he was not guilty; he is such a kind hearted man and it would be quite impossible for him to have committed such a terrible crime'. Peter McNeil, a fellow employee of Wood's, remarked, 'He was no more guilty of murdering Dimmock than an unborn babe. He is the most kind hearted chap you could meet, and would do anyone a good turn if he could'. Ruby Young, who had been forced to flee from the Old Bailey under the protection of two police officers, while disguised as a charwoman, joined in the chorus of support for the verdict, saying, 'I have never thought Robert guilty, and my evidence was never intended to indicate that I did'. She also mentioned to a *Daily Mail* reporter, with some justification, that she felt she had been 'treated abominably' despite having told the truth.

Marshall Hall made a short statement saying, 'I have always been convinced of the innocence of Wood. He is certainly a very remarkable man and his coolness and courage throughout have been beyond anything I have ever seen. He was actually engaged in sketching the judge during the absence of the jury'. Wood himself spoke to a *Daily Mail* representative, revealing that he was, in fact, less than cool during the trial. 'To be tried for one's life' he said 'is an experience I can scarcely describe. It is indescribable'. He said that he only sketched to take his mind off the ordeal and that watching the jury come back before they announced their verdict was 'a terrible moment'. His dominating impression of the trial, however, was of 'complete fairness' and he had no complaints with the way the judge managed the proceedings nor with how Sir Charles Mathews prosecuted him. His fondest moment appears to have been when the actress Lily Elsie smiled at him across the courtroom.

Mrs Beerbohm Tree went straight from the Old Bailey to the Marlborough Theatre in Holloway where she was due to recite on stage between the acts of a performance of the comedy play, *Dolly Varden*, in aid of the Great Northern Hospital and the Crippled Children's Christmas Hamper Fund. She broke the news of Wood's acquittal to an ecstatic audience and was reported to have said, 'While the jury were out, we seemed to hold our breath and we hoped, but we feared that the jury would after all —— (cries of "no, no") I was one of those who burst into tears – others burst into cheers…'.[495]

The next morning, newspaper editors offered their opinions on the case and they did not all chime with the public mood. For the *Daily Express*, the 'outburst of unrestrained popular approval' which followed the verdict was 'from every point of view to be deplored'. It said that the result 'tends to make a hero of a young man of somewhat extraordinary character, whose own folly has largely been responsible for the position in which he has been placed, and who has certainly done nothing to make him worthy of the hero worship of a crowd.' The editor of the *Daily News* agreed: 'The scenes yesterday outside the New Bailey' he wrote, 'will give no pleasure to those who take a sober view of this case. We may be glad that Wood has been able to recover his liberty, but at least the story told during the past week is not one to make a wholesale public sentiment regard him as a hero'. The *Morning Leader* was the most trenchant in its criticism of Wood, expressing the view that 'sympathy with him is necessarily restricted by the plain evidence that he brought this penance so largely upon himself' adding that 'But for his own folly, his own mendacity, and certain other aspects of his character which need not be further dwelt upon, Robert Wood would never have been charged with the murder of "Phyllis" Dimmock'.

Other newspapers, however, focused on the weakness of the prosecution evidence. The *Morning Post* believed that 'It hardly amounted to more than the prisoner had been in the murdered woman's company on the previous evening and had some previous acquaintance with her'. It recommended that more training was required for 'those who are in any way responsible for the early stages of a prosecution'. Nevertheless, it still felt the need to inform its readers that a 'not guilty' verdict sometimes 'means that the jury are satisfied that the prisoner is innocent; sometimes it means not quite sure'. *The Globe* stated that 'there was practically no evidence at all to connect the prisoner with the crime' and, along with a number of other newspapers, expressed the view that the conduct of the London police left a lot to be desired, commenting that the failure of the prosecution 'cannot fail to increase the dissatisfaction which for a long time past has been growing with regard to the detection of crime in the Metropolitan district.' For the *Daily Graphic*, 'Nothing making for the prisoner's conviction had been adduced except circumstantial evidence'.

Of commentators on the trial, the journalist and author, Bart Kennedy, was one of the first to be published, with an article in the *Daily Mail*. He was full of praise for the 'splendid advocate', Marshall Hall, but felt that Wood's answers under cross-examination 'all bore the same curious quality…of vagueness and suggestion and indirectness'. The conclusion he drew from the trial was that a man who is being tried for his life should not be put into the witness box because 'the long time of tension has unnerved and broken him'. Indeed, he felt it was 'a most unfair thing' for a defendant to have the option of giving evidence because it has 'a bad effect on the jury' if he fails to take it. 'How is a man who is being tried for his life to do well?' he asked, 'It matters not how innocent he be. He is a nerveless, broken man…One chance word may put the rope round his neck…the very fact of his being innocent will make him all the more halting and stumbling and confused'.[496]

On the same morning, the *Daily News* carried a damning indictment of the criminal justice system by the Member of Parliament for St Pancras South, Philip Whitwell Wilson, writing for the newspaper under the initials 'P.W.W.'. He thought it 'preposterous' that the last word should lie with the prosecution in a criminal trial when the defence called evidence, and 'outrageous' that facts in the prisoner's favour should not at once be stated to the jury by the prosecution. He thought that the judge summed up 'with somewhat frequent inaccuracies on matters of considerable moment' although he did not say what these inaccuracies were and appears to have been the only person to have noticed them. With more justification, he questioned whether the judge should have been dealing with issues of morality. It was a fair point as Justice Grantham certainly had strayed into areas which did not concern him during his address to the jury, such as criticising Wood for frequenting the *Rising Sun* and condemning unmarried couples who lived together. The M.P. was also unhappy with the police's methods of identification. According to Whitwell Wilson, the tactics used by the police against an accused man were simple:

> His description is permitted to leak out and appear broadcast in the newspapers. Then he is "paraded" with other men, taken at random and promptly picked out by the required witnesses. No legal adviser for the prisoner is permitted to be present. The names of the other paraded men do not transpire.[497]

In this respect, the criticisms were not entirely fair. As we have seen from the regulations, legal advisers *were* permitted to be present at identification parades but Wood did not request one. Also, the police could hardly be criticised for circulating a description of their prime suspect in order to catch him. They could not have been attempting to frame a man whose identity they did not even know at the time.

Whitwell Wilson was also suspicious of the late evidence of Inspector Carpenter relating to Wood's supposedly peculiar walk which, he felt, was part of a desperate attempt by the police to secure a conviction. He might have had a point but his best argument was that the type of justice available to Wood who, through the backing of his employers was able to secure representation by Arthur Newton and Marshall Hall, and whose trial was keenly observed by so many reporters and distinguished people of the day, was not available to everyone charged with murder. 'But what,' he asked, 'if the other prisoners who, now or at some future time shall have to face trials without sensation – face these trials without money for an adequate defence – and be confronted with evidence so constructed and pieced together, without the safeguard of an aroused public opinion which helped to save Wood?'. It was a reasonable question to ask. Most other murder trials lasted no more than a couple of days at most and the police and prosecution evidence was rarely challenged as closely as it had been by Marshall Hall and his team during the Wood trial.

Wood evidently spent the day after the verdict writing an article entitled 'My Life' which was published in the *Evening News* on 19 December. While essentially a short biography of his life, he could not resist throwing in a couple of new points to support his innocence. He said that during his recent holiday in Belgium, it was his custom to spend his evenings in a café and send postcards to all his friends and acquaintances so that 'had I known the deceased before my holiday of this year, which was a few weeks before her death, I should most surely have sent her a card or two'. It would have been churlish to point out to Wood that the murderer had the opportunity to remove postcards from her album so that, if he had killed her, he might have sent her any number of cards from Belgium but destroyed the evidence. Wood also wanted to make the point that he had 'never written or spoken a vulgar word to a girl', albeit that this had never been alleged against him. The same newspaper also published a second article by Wood in which he gave his account of the trial and said that his greatest anxiety was that he should have been 'for a moment suspected of being guilty of such an unmanly and cruel act towards a woman'. He protested that, while the company of women fascinated him and he liked to sit with them and be merry, 'this does not necessarily imply any immoral thought or behaviour'. He also stressed that he had no complaint to make against Ruby Young but he turned his relationship with her to his advantage by making the point that he trusted her completely and that 'I would have told her anything there was to tell'. This wasn't quite true because he failed to tell her that he was with Emily Dimmock on the night she was murdered but no-one was cross-examining him now. In this article, he also criticised the way the identification parade was conducted which, he claimed, made it impossible to miss him because of the atmosphere his appearance in the room created.

Wood's articles in the *Evening News* were accompanied by a rather ungrateful editorial, considering that he had given the paper an exclusive, which was not only critical of the fact that Wood 'spent a part at least of his spare time drinking in public houses with fallen women' but that he only had 'his own wicked folly' to blame for most of his problems as a result of his 'perjured evidence' which had led him down a 'crooked path'. He was not believed to be guilty of the crime, however, because his alibi 'which ended at half past ten, would in reality have been useless in the case of a murder which the medical evidence timed some four hours later'. One wonders what the conclusion would have been had the newspaper's leader writer known that the medical evidence as to the time of death was wholly unreliable.

The editorial in that evening's *Pall Mall Gazette* also believed that Wood only had himself to blame for being prosecuted for murder. 'Wood brought his troubles upon himself,' it said, and 'found himself caught in a web of suspicion which he, and nobody but he, had woven for himself'. It disapproved of the fact that, 'From a suspected murderer, Wood has been transformed, transfigured, into a hero of romance' and stressed that 'Mr Wood is no hero: he is only a by-no-means admirable young man, who has got himself into a mess and had the luck to get out of it'.

The next morning brought an essay by Hall Caine entitled 'The Law and the Man: Psychological Study of the Great Trial' which was published in the *Daily Mail*. In a thoughtful piece, Hall Caine was full of praise for the conduct of the trial by the judge, the prosecution and the defence team. Like Bart Kennedy, he came to the conclusion that 'the law which permits a prisoner to testify for himself is hedged round by a thousand dangers' and he was certainly not impressed with Wood's stint in the witness box, saying that 'the case for the prisoner would have been more convincing and inevitably more sympathetic if he had never gone there at all'. For Hall Caine, Wood's 'admission of damning facts, his perpetual impeachment of the truthfulness of other witnesses, his uncertainty about incidents of which he might have been expected to have clear knowledge, would have dealt blow after blow at the stability of his case if the converging lines of circumstantial evidence which seemed to point to him had been able to come ever so little closer together'. Delivering a devastating critique of Wood's performance on the stand, he continued:

> Not once or twice, but again and again, under the searching light of a withering but always temperate cross-examination, the witness was being destroyed by his anxiety to prove too much, by his overweening personal vanity, by his excess of small cleverness, by his little unnecessary flourishes of personal pride, by his want of logical balance, by his apparent inability to distinguish between the facts that were paramount and dangerous to his chances of life, and those that were secondary and only damaging to his reputation.[498]

At the same time, Hall Caine described Wood as 'the most extraordinary person I have ever seen in all the world of men' and was impressed with his 'constant smile of some sweetness and complete self-possession...his cheery and almost jovial manner...his frequent lack of seemly seriousness, of becoming gravity, of conscious responsibility...[and] his calm, confident, imperturbable airs...'. He still felt he was a 'strange' man though.

On the Sunday, the *Weekly Dispatch* carried a long article written by Wood entitled 'My Fight for Life', accompanied by a number of sketches and cartoons drawn by the author. In the article, Wood attempted to describe what he had previously referred to as the indescribable, namely how he felt when he heard the verdict. He said:

> I was not relieved. I felt depressed. I was seized with a sort of shivering fit in the pit of my stomach, though it did not actually affect my composure. I was overwhelmed with sadness. I believe I was the only person who did not rejoice at the result. The accusation and imprisonment have left a mark on me that I

The Camden Town Murder Mystery

fear will be indelible. True, I was victorious in my fight for life, but the bitter remembrance will ever remain with me.[499]

Wood also took the opportunity to inform the readers of the *Weekly Dispatch* that Emily Dimmock was 'not handsome' but, at the same time, she was 'in herself an exceedingly attractive girl' who impressed him as 'a crushed rose that had not lost all its fragrance'. He admitted that there was something about her that attracted him and that it delighted him to see and sit with her. However, he insisted that their relationship was limited to 'banter and lighthearted chat' and that of passion there was 'not an atom!' He excused his poor memory of events during the trial by saying that it was not possible for him to recall all the details of 'the casual meeting' some months after the event. He asserted that there was no reason for him to lie to the readers of the *Weekly Dispatch* and solemnly declared: 'I never saw the girl before that [Friday] night'. As he had done in the *Evening News*, he used his close relationship with Ruby Young as a point in support of his innocence, saying, 'If I had ever done anybody any harm, or if I had ever known Emily Dimmock, Ruby Young would have heard of it'. Towards Ruby, he bore 'no ill feeling whatsoever' while towards Emily: 'I felt, as I do now, heartily sorry for the poor girl' and offered his 'profound sympathy to her people'.

With the *Weekly Dispatch* having exclusive access to Wood, the *People* had to make do with an interview with his brother Charles. He said:

Not the least curious feature of Bob's remarkable coolness of demeanour is that in his earlier years he never exhibited any peculiar power of self-control. On the contrary I used to think he was particularly sensitive, and I believe he is to this day. I have known him when much younger to be so affected by the sight of blood that on cutting his finger he would almost swoon, and I can recall more than one occasion on which distressing surroundings have deeply moved him.[500]

The *News of the World*, meanwhile, carried a Christmas card sketched by Wood in Brixton Prison while *Reynolds's Newspaper* had commissioned an article by Mrs Beerbohm Tree. She revealed her anxiety during the closing moments of the trial:

I was terrified during the judge's summing up. I had trembled for the prisoner during Sir Charles Mathews' speech but when the Judge began in his severe tones to denounce a man leading a double life – and that was in his opinion the kind of life Wood had been leading – my blood ran cold. I thought that Wood was dead. If only the jury could see with my eyes and think with my mind then all would be well. The more I listened the more terribly anxious and distressed I became. But then came the Judge's brilliant last sentence. Oh, what inexpressible relief. I was hardly able to believe my ears, but I knew I had heard aright, for similar relief was apparent on the faces of those near me.[501]

The next morning's *Daily Mail* published a poignant drawing by Wood of a dead man hanging on a gallows, a girl in the foreground kneeling next to her bed with her head in her left hand while holding an unopened letter in her right: a baby, or an angel, possibly cupid, by her feet. Another Wood drawing featured a game of cards between a police officer on one side and Arthur Newton on the other: a little man on the table, presumably Wood himself, being the prize.

One particular sketch by Wood that had appeared in the weekend newspapers attracted the attention of Emily's father and appears to have upset him at the same time. This was entitled 'Lady Diablo of Monte Carlo' and showed a giant of a woman, bearing a certain resemblance to Emily Dimmock, using puppet strings to lift a tiny man wearing a top hat and tails and dangle him in mid-air. On the floor in front of her lie three men whom she had evidently dropped from a height while a string of men queue up for their own turn to be dangled by her. Did this reflect Wood's feelings that he had been used and discarded by Emily? A distraught Mr Dimmock was in no doubt that 'Lady Diablo' was 'supposed to represent my poor daughter' and called Wood's sketch 'fanatical' in a letter to the *Herts Mail*.[502] Mr Dimmock, while emphasising that a man was innocent until proven guilty, nevertheless appears to have believed Wood was guilty of the murder, pointing out that 'One little link was missing from the chain of evidence, otherwise Wood's position was of great danger'. He described Wood as 'the most remarkable man alive' and 'the most strangest of men'. Emily's father also complained that he was not called upon by the police to make a statement and said he was suffering from 'strained depression' caused by answering so many questions about the case from members of the public at his market stall.

After completing his articles for the *Weekly Dispatch* (the second part of which would be published in the 31 December edition), Wood travelled incognito to the south-coast and on to the Isle of Wight for a short holiday with a couple of friends using the alias 'Mr C. Hall'.[503] He was recognised, however by a chambermaid at his hotel who kissed him and told him she was 'so glad you got off'. On returning home, he found hundreds of letters and telegrams of congratulations waiting for him. The criticism of his behaviour continued in the newspapers though. The weekly journal, *John Bull*, in its 28 December issue was the next to declare that Wood was the author of his own misfortune, saying 'Wood has to thank himself for the position which he found himself – just as he has to thank Marshall Hall for extricating him' and it even went so far as to imply that he was guilty of the crime by saying 'the mental pathologist may draw his own conclusions from…the fact of the facile self-assurance and calm of the prisoner under all the fiery ordeal of the trial but the jury have said he is not guilty, and, therefore so be it.'

At the same time, news broke that Wood was booked to appear on stage at three music halls, in Shoreditch, Woolwich and Rotherhithe respectively.[504] Under the title 'Impressions of the Camden Town Murder Trial', the idea was that Wood would create lightning sketches of the key people connected with the case while the audience watched. It had previously been reported, two days after the trial had concluded, that Wood had been offered £325 per week, for two weeks, by Harry Day of Day's Variety Agency, on behalf of Walter Gibbons, to give a five-minute performance at six of Mr Gibbons' London music halls.[505] It was said to be the largest offer ever made to an artist to appear on the London music hall stage. Both Charles Wood and Arthur Newton had agreed to this on Wood's behalf but only if it was for eight weeks instead of two. This was refused by Mr Gibbons and it seemed that the plan had died. Further negotiations had evidently continued over Christmas, however, and agreement was finally reached for Wood to give twice nightly performances, drawing caricatures of the judge and counsel engaged at his trial, at each of the three music halls for two weeks commencing on Monday 30 December, with the option of a third week, in return for £150 per week. Wood was reported as being nervous and quoted as saying:

> I have never done anything of the kind before. It is so difficult to know how I shall feel. But the audience will perhaps excuse a little nervousness. I shall do my best and if the sketching is a success on its merits – well, who knows? My plans to some extent depend on this affair. I cannot say what I shall do in the future. I want a great deal of money to pay for the many expenses connected with the trial. You see, I cannot permit anyone to be out of pocket through me.[506]

At the last minute, however, Wood's appearances were cancelled, with bills placed outside the three music halls stating that he could not appear owing to 'indisposition'. This was not the true reason. What had happened is that the association of music hall artists, known as the Grand Order of Water Rats, had written a letter of protest to Mr Gibbons in the following terms:

> The Grand Order of Water Rats, without going into the merits or demerits of the performances to be given this week under your management by Robert Wood who has so recently become notorious in the Central Criminal Court wishes to protest against this class of entertainment being made in Variety theatres. It has always been the aim of this Order to elevate the music-hall profession and we are glad to see that so many managers today have the same intention. It is felt that the discontinuance of this class of engagement will be better, not only for the bona fide artist, but for every manager whose intention is the advancement of the music hall industry.[507]

The letter had the desired effect. With other artists refusing to perform alongside Wood, Gibbons thought it was better to cancel Wood's appearances than have all his shows ruined. Wood did not seem to be unduly worried about the cancellation, though, telling the *Daily Chronicle*:

> From the beginning I was very loth to go on the stage, and it was only under great pressure indeed that the arrangement with Mr Gibbons was entered into. He spoke so encouragingly to me that after much consideration I accepted his offer. My only desire was to make a little money legitimately in order to meet the expense which my trial involved. I was extremely anxious that my presence on the stage should offend no member of the theatrical profession and I emphasised this to Mr Gibbons, who told me that everything would be right, and advised me to pay no attention to what anybody might say. As a matter of fact, I was so averse to the idea of publicly exhibiting myself that I rejected several larger sums than Mr Gibbons offered...My solicitor, however, was agreeable to my fixing up an arrangement with Mr Gibbons and I did so. [508]

Wood added that he was nevertheless disappointed by the turn of events, saying, 'I have been to considerable expense in buying all sorts of things and I have lately been concentrating all my attention on making my work interesting, and not merely appealing to the spectators as a man who was tried for his life.' Others were positively pleased at the outcome. The journal, *The Bystander*, which felt that Wood was an 'unworthy object of popular applause' because he had 'led not only a double but a treble life, and, not satisfied with lying himself, endeavoured to suborn others to commit perjury in order to save himself', praised the 'legitimate' music hall performers who 'to their eternal credit, appear to have stopped the nauseous exhibition by boycotting him', adding that it had 'sufficient faith in the inherent decency of the nation to believe that he should have been speedily hissed off the stage'.[509]

With Wood blocked from a performing career, he appears to have had thoughts of continuing in journalism following the success of his articles for the *Evening News* and the *Weekly Dispatch*. It was reported in the gossip section of one monthly publication in January 1908 that he was understood to have let Fleet Street know that his initial contracts with newspapers had expired and that 'he is now free to offer his services elsewhere'.[510] He was said to have been surprised at the 'very short duration of his association with the publications which he has represented since his trial' and to have already been involved in 'negotiations with...various newspaper proprietors'.[511] The outcome of his meetings with those proprietors was said to be 'awaited in journalistic circles with quite exceptional interest'.[512] However, he was never to be taken on as a journalist by any newspaper.

Meanwhile, *Reynolds's Newspaper* announced a 'Sensational Development' in the Camden Town Murder Mystery with the police said to be 'working on a new theory'.[513] The newspaper exclusively reported that 'the official view' was now that the killer of Emily Dimmock was also the person who murdered a thirty-year-old Jewish prostitute from Poland called Dora Piernick who had been found lying her on back in bed, wearing only a nightie, with her throat cut, in a house in Whitfield Street, off Tottenham Court Road, in December 1903.[514] Her door was locked, the police having to burst it open, and the key was missing. At the inquest held at the St Pancras Coroner's Court in January 1904, it emerged that Piernick owned £8 worth of gold and silver coins and five rings which were found hidden in her room in a roll of bedding, suggesting a possible robbery motive for murder albeit that the robbery was unsuccessful. However, when the police divisional surgeon, Dr Samuel Lloyd, was asked by the coroner whether the wound was self-inflicted, he answered, 'it has the appearance of being self-inflicted' before adding without any sense of irony, 'On the other hand, it might have been inflicted by someone else'. Nevertheless, he gave his opinion that the wound *was* self-inflicted on the basis that there was no evidence of a struggle. A second medical man, Professor Augustus Pepper, also thought it possible that the wound could have been self-inflicted but noted that there was a line of bruises on one side of the chest, and a huge bruise on the other side, which might have been caused by someone kneeling on the chest. As no weapon was found, one would have thought the ultimate conclusion must have been that it was a murder but the jury returned an open verdict on the basis that there was insufficient evidence to show how the wounds in the throat were caused. Consequently, the case was quickly forgotten but it seemed, for a brief moment at the end of 1907, as if the investigation into Piernick's death would be revived in order to catch the real killer of Emily Dimmock.[515]

However, despite the paper's apparent belief that the police were still actively seeking the person who murdered Emily, there is nothing to indicate such activity in the Metropolitan Police file in the National Archives. On the contrary, Inspector Neil had already reported his opinion to his superiors that 'nothing further can be done in the matter'.[516] He believed that the police had done everything possible 'to secure sufficient evidence to secure prisoner's guilt' and was of the view that, while the jury's verdict had to be accepted, 'morally there can be no doubt of the guilt of the accused man'.[517] The key prosecution witnesses were quietly paid off from the Metropolitan Police Informants' Fund. Robert McCowan and Ruby Young both received £10 each. Robert Roberts was awarded £5. The police officers involved in the case did not walk away empty handed either. Inspector Neil received a £4 reward with Sergeant Ball collecting £3. In justifying these payments, Superintendent Vedy noted that the whole burden of the enquiries fell upon Neil and Ball and that 'no two officers in the force could have done them better'.

After the cancellation of Wood's stage appearances, the national press went quiet about the Dimmock case apart from a short-lived campaign in favour of Ruby Young in *Reynolds's Newspaper*. It started when a woman calling herself 'A Portsmouth Mother' had a letter published on 29 December in which she expressed sympathy for Ruby, adding that Wood 'had only himself to blame for the awful fix he found himself in' and concluded 'I shall read your paper carefully for any news of Ruby Young, and pray that she may lead a peaceful and quiet life'. During the following week, two men wrote to the same newspaper with offers of marriage which were published in its edition of 5 January 1908. At the same time, the newspaper's editor commented that 'The opinion has been held by many people that the mob outside the Central Criminal Court had not sufficient justification for adopting such an extremely hostile attitude towards Miss Young'.

Thus encouraged by some rare support, Ruby provided *Reynolds's Newspaper* with an exclusive article entitled 'Why I "went back" on Robert Wood' in which she explained the circumstances by which she had no alternative but to agree to contact the police, at the same time making the point that 'neither of us would have been in the position we are today if Bob had told me the whole facts from the beginning'.[518] She denied that she had acted out of spite or jealousy and claimed she could have had 'dozens of men who would have willingly shielded me all through my life' but gave them all up for Wood, of whom she had thought the world. Following publication, Ruby received two more offers of marriage, published by *Reynolds's Newspaper* in its 19 January 1908 edition, but her reputation (to the extent she had one) was by no means entirely restored. She probably remained the most hated woman in the country for some time and local children would sing a song suggesting that Miss Ruby Young should be 'hung in the Rising Sun', although they did not necessarily know what it meant.[519]

While Ruby Young sank into obscurity, the same could not be said for Robert Wood who was back at the Old Bailey in April 1908, but this time as a spectator rather than a participant. The cause of his return was none other than Jack Crabtree. He had evidently been a busy man since stepping down from the witness stand in December, having continued to run a number of houses as brothels, including 24 Coram Street, 281 Gray's Inn Road, 25 Liverpool Street, 13 Harrison Street, 14 Tolmer Square and 49 Tonbridge Street. He had been arrested again by Inspector Rouse on 4 March and was sent for trial at the Central Criminal Court by Mr Bros at Clerkenwell Police Court.[520] It seems that Crabtree, assisted by a young woman called Alice Morris, was using each house for a few days before clearing out and moving on to a new one in an attempt to evade the authorities but he was being closely watched and the plan did not succeed. His trial for 'unlawfully keeping, managing and acting and assisting in the management of brothels and maintaining common bawdy houses' took place at the Old Bailey on 6 April before the Common Sergeant, Sir Frederick Albert Bosanquet, and Wood was reported as having attempted to gain admission to the court to watch his old enemy in the dock.[521] Unfortunately, however, the Old Bailey was very busy that day with the opening of a scandalous perjury trial against a 78-year-old woman, Margaret Hamilton, arising out the famous and long running Druce case (involving a fabricated claim that a man called Druce was really the Duke of Portland) and Wood appears to have been unable to enter the public gallery, although he was said to have been present 'in the hall of the court'.[522]

As for Crabtree, he went into the witness box and denied the charges against him but the judge described his defence as consisting of 'the most unblushing perjury' and, having been found guilty, he was sentenced to twelve months hard labour. Upon his release from prison, he made his way to Australia where he went back to his roots by opening a couple of grocery stores in Melbourne. As usual with Jack Crabtree, all was not what it seemed and he had a cunning plan. Having insured the contents of his shop at 85 Brunswick Street in Fitzroy for £620, he spent two weeks removing most of the shop's goods and furniture to a loft he rented in East Brunswick with the help of his young assistant, Charles Shaw (no relation to Bert). The grocery items in the Brunswick Street shop were replaced with dummies, made up to look like genuine goods, such as wooden soap and packets of tea filled with sawdust. During the early hours of Saturday, 19 March 1910, Crabtree and Shaw arranged some wood shavings beneath the staircase in the shop and saturated them with benzine and methylated spirits. Crabtree went out into the yard to put on his clothes, having removed them earlier to avoid spirit fumes being detected on them, before returning to the building. His intention was, of course, to set the shavings alight so that the fire would destroy his shop and he could claim the £600 insurance but his delay in doing so allowed the vapour from the benzine and methylated spirits to fill the shop with a cocktail of beautifully combustible gas. Shaw went upstairs to wait for the fire to start. His assignment was to jump from the verandah once he saw the flames and give the alarm. There was only one final part of the plan left to complete and Crabtree must have been looking forward to spending his small fortune as he struck the match underneath the staircase.

At about 2:20am on 19 March 1910, the area of Fitzroy was shaken by a massive explosion which was heard for miles around. According to one report: 'Everything shook – even the ground trembled. Accompanying the roar was a burst of light that made pale the electric arc lamps in the street. People in the locality jumped from their beds in the belief that an earthquake had occurred'.[523] Others of a more superstitious persuasion pessimistically thought it was 'the long anticipated comet [that] had brought the end of all things'.[524] A constable on his beat several streets away described the explosion as 'resembling half a dozen huge canons simultaneously discharged'.[525] Three brick buildings, including Crabtree's shop, were instantly demolished. Photographs show them as no more than a pile of rubble, looking like a bomb had fallen on them. Amazingly, Crabtree was still alive and conscious, albeit seriously injured and in some distress, embedded in a pile of shattered bricks and mortar. His head was badly burned, his left leg was broken and he had bruises and injuries around his face and shoulders caused by falling debris. When found by the rescuers who rushed to the scene he was moaning 'Let me die! Let me die!'. Dragged from the wreckage, he was taken to Melbourne Hospital. Another miracle was that Mabel Sneddon, a little girl from number 83, who was missing in the rubble, presumed dead, was suddenly discovered after her small voice was heard calling out in the darkness. A heavy beam had fallen in such a position to prevent her from being crushed. Charles Shaw escaped with superficial burns and was taken to St Vincent's Hospital.

The police investigation into the cause of the explosion began immediately during the night and the suspicions of detectives were instantly aroused when they found some of the dummy goods amidst the wreckage. Their next clue was provided by a couple of local children who said they had previously seen Crabtree driving a cart loaded with goods from his shop. It did not make sense to detectives that a shop keeper would take stock *away* from his shop. As usual, Crabtree's criminal plan was so poorly conceived that it fell apart at the first sign of scrutiny. The detectives then went and spoke to Crabtree in hospital. He claimed that the reason he and his assistant had been in the shop during the middle of the night was because they had both been 'marking tins'. Having completed their work, he said, they were tired and went upstairs to bed. When asked how he came to be found downstairs, fully dressed, he replied that 'the explosion must have shot me there'. However, Shaw gave the game away during questioning and revealed the true nature of the insurance swindle. When confronted with this, Crabtree still would not tell the truth. He changed his story and now claimed that, after marking the tins and having a short rest in his bed, he went back downstairs and noticed that some gas was escaping from a stove. He turned off the levers of the stove and found some matches which, for some unexplained reason, he lit and the next thing he remembered he was 'lying under a pile of bricks in the back yard and being pulled out by the police'.[526] He denied having removed any stock from the shop but the police had already found it hidden away in his North Melbourne store and in the loft he had rented in East Brunswick.

Crabtree was all set for another long spell in prison but, this time, the old rogue escaped before being sentenced, having succumbed to his injuries in Melbourne Hospital on 26 March at the age of fifty. The official cause of his death was 'Pneumonia and septic absorption from effects of burns'.[527] Charles Shaw was arrested and charged with unlawfully and wilfully having set fire to Crabtree's shop with intent to defraud. He was found guilty on 25 May 1910 and sentenced to two years imprisonment. It was revealed at his trial that Crabtree had told him that he had 'had other fires' in the past. The Australian police established that Crabtree was the notorious New Zealand criminal but they were completely unaware that he had been a prosecution witness in a major murder trial in England a few years earlier. Likewise, the British police knew nothing of his death in Australia. The Metropolitan Police's Habitual Criminals Register for 1906 contains a manuscript note added on 6 November 1936 which states 'Crabtree presumed dead', showing that they had no idea what had happened to him in Australia.*

Two days after Crabtree's trial at the Old Bailey in April 1908, Wood was back in a courtroom in respect of a murder charge. This time he was there as

* See Appendix 2.

a court artist, having been commissioned by the *People* newspaper. An army deserter, John Francis McGuire, had been arrested on 21 February for the murder of his friend, Miss Emma Sherriff, after her body had been discovered on Southbourne Cliff in Bournemouth the previous day, the cause of death being strangulation. McGuire was in financial difficulty and suspected by the police of killing Miss Sherriff for her jewellery which was missing. When McGuire was brought before magistrates at Bournemouth Police Court on 8 April and again on 15 April, Wood was there to draw him; McGuire passed him a note (addressed to 'Mr Wood') asking 'Can you give me one of your sketches of myself?'. Wood nodded to McGuire and presumably arranged for him to receive one although he remained in custody. Wood's sketches were published in the *People* on 12 and 19 April 1908. McGuire was committed for trial at Winchester Assizes but the jury failed to agree and the prosecution was abandoned, although McGuire was subsequently convicted of desertion from the army at a court martial.

At the end of July 1908 there was a reminder of the mafficking that had accompanied Wood's acquittal when Robert Standish Sievier, editor and chief proprietor of the *Winning Post*, was acquitted at the Old Bailey on a charge of blackmailing the millionaire Jack Barnato Joel, having allegedly asked for £5,000 not to publish certain stories damaging to Joel. The defence case was that Joel had offered to pay the money in order to entrap Sievier into accepting it so that he could therefore be arrested. This line seemed to play well with the general public who offered Sievier their full support and the *Illustrated Police Budget* of 8 August 1908 reported that 'The Sievier trial ended amid scenes of excitement which surpassed even those that followed the acquittal of Robert Wood in connection with the Camden Town Murder'. As with the Wood trial, a crowd of thousands had gathered outside the Old Bailey and there was cheering and singing of 'he's a jolly good fellow' in the streets.[528] Sievier was said to have exited the Old Bailey through the same side door as Wood had done the previous year in order to avoid being mobbed. Once again, however, not everyone could understand the euphoria and one reader of the *Times*, a goldsmith called Millar Wilkinson, harked back to the result of the Wood trial, in a letter to the editor, saying:

> A few months ago a dense crowd assembled outside the Old Bailey. They waited patiently; at last they were rewarded. A young man walked out of the building; then their pent-up feelings broke forth in a series of wild cheering and waving of hats, many rushed forward to shake him by the hand, to at least have the satisfaction of touching him. Was he the saviour of the Empire? Had he saved the national credit? Had he performed a great and glorious deed? No; he had just been acquitted upon a charge of murder.[529]

Mr Wilkinson went on to observe that exactly the same thing had happened with Sievier and asked 'What does all this cheering, all this shrieking, all this hat waving mean?' before concluding 'Whatever may be the cause, the result cannot fail to be regretted by every man'.

After the McGuire trial, Wood appears not to have received any further work as a court artist but he never went back to the glass works. Instead, he seems to have set up on his own as a commercial artist. The 1910 Post Office Directory (which would have reflected information from 1909) includes one

'Robert Wood – artist' with an office at 20 King Street in Covent Garden. Wood's elderly father died in November 1909 but, at this time, Wood was in a relationship of some sort with 20-year-old Annie Louisa Eames. We know this because, on 13 June 1910, Annie gave birth to a baby boy, Gordon, who was Wood's son.

Annie was the daughter of a former police constable, Frederick Albert Eames, who had married Annie Lee on 20 June 1886 in Clerkenwell. She was born on 6 February 1889 and had a sister, Maud, who was two years her senior. The 1891 census records that the Eames family was living at 40 Burton Crescent, St Pancras, which was, by coincidence, only a few yards from Thanet Street School where Wood was then a pupil. Little Annie originally went to Manchester Street School but, in 1897, when her father was living in Tonbridge Street, she was transferred to Thanet Street School for Girls. The 1901 census shows that Annie was living at 4 Seymour Street, St Pancras, with her younger sister Jennie, who had been born in 1892. However, the two girls were not then living with their parents but with a cornet player called Charles Smith, his wife, Alice, and their twelve-year-old son. Frederick had enlisted with the First Royal Rifle Reserve in May 1900[530] and, at the time of the 1901 census, was a corporal residing at the Victoria Barracks, Portsmouth, having left the police force. Only two weeks earlier, on 14 March 1901, his wife had died in the London County Lunatic Asylum of 'Exhaustion from Melancholia' having also suffered from cellulitis of the neck. This explains why little Annie and Jennie were rather abandoned and living with the Smith family at the end of March 1901.

In August 1902, then working as a house painter and decorator, having left the army in May 1901, Frederick fathered a second son, Ernest (his first had died as a baby in 1891), but Ernest's mother was Catherine Eames (said to be 'late Harris formerly Curry'), although there is no known record of any marriage between Frederick and Catherine. In the 1911 census, Frederick, then living in Islington, stated that he had been married to Catherine for 17 years which would have placed their wedding in 1894 but Frederick was then married to Annie, while Catherine Eames (as Catherine Curry) had married Edward Harris on 17 June 1894.

It is not clear why Maud did not feature in the 1901 census but she married Albert Robinson at St Peter's Church, Regent Square, on 5 September 1908 while the couple were living at 119 Harrison Street in St Pancras. She gave her occupation on the marriage certificate as 'Dressmaker'. Her sister, Annie, was a witness at the wedding, as was her father. It is not known when, or in what circumstances, Annie first met Wood but, according to Charles Wood's granddaughter, Sheila Wood, Annie was a nursemaid to Charles Wood's children, Robert and Irene, born in 1905 and 1907 respectively.[531]

Following the birth of their son, Wood's behaviour was very strange. Forty days after Gordon was born (two days before the legally required deadline), Wood registered the birth in the Wandsworth sub-district of Springfield on 23 July 1910 using a false name. He called himself 'Robert Radnor' whose occupation was said to be an 'Advertising Specialist'. Annie was said to be 'Annie Radnor formerly Eames' although the couple were unmarried. Needless to say this false registration was illegal.

At this time, Wood was living in an apartment at Crofton House, 32 Church Street, Chelsea, although Gordon was born, for some reason, at 57a Quinton

Street in Wandsworth. There was a street called Radnor Street near to where Wood was living in Chelsea, which might have been the inspiration for the name, but there was (and is) a forest called Radnor Wood in Shropshire, and this might explain Wood's extraordinary census return in 1911. While still living at 32 Church Street, Wood's census return was completed and signed in the name 'Radnor Wood'.[532] Although he was now aged 33 he still refused to confirm that he had turned 30 and claimed to be just 28 years old. Whether this was all intended as some form of joke by Wood, or was a serious attempt to conceal his identity, is impossible to say at this distance. Nevertheless, he falsely claimed to have been married to 'Annie Wood' (whose age was correctly stated as 22) for two years and again gave his occupation as 'Advertising specialist', adding: 'Designing, printing' which might have been true. No occupation was stated for Annie. Curiously, nine-month-old Gordon Wood (or Gordon Radnor as he was officially named) was not living with his parents when the census was taken. Instead, he was staying as a 'visitor' at the home of a 54-year-old bricklayer called George Henry Gray and his wife Jessie at 16 Headworth Road, Wandsworth. The Grays had two teenage children and one additional 'visitor' living with them: a 6-year-old girl called Alice Shapter, the illegitimate daughter of a 30-year-old domestic servant, Elizabeth Ann Shapter, who was then living with and working for a Mrs Fadelle in Wandsworth's Santos Road.

A census is only a snapshot of what was happening on one particular day in a year so there could be any number of reasons why the Grays were responsible for two illegitimate children on that day but the implication is that Mrs Gray had taken on some sort of (presumably paid) nursing role to look after other people's illegitimate offspring. We can only speculate as to why Annie Eames and Robert Wood were unable to look after Gordon at their Chelsea apartment and it may be that it was impossible for them to do so for some reason.

We also can't say why Wood went to such extreme lengths to hide the birth of his son. It is true that illegitimacy was frowned upon but a false registration of a birth was an illegal and risky act. The normal course would have been for Annie to have registered the boy as her son under the name Gordon Eames with the father's name left blank on the birth certificate and it is unclear why she did not choose this course of action. It may be that Wood wanted to hide his relationship with Annie from his family, while at the same time removing the stigma of illegitimacy from his son, but this does not explain why he switched his false identity from 'Robert Radnor' to 'Radnor Wood' and was entered on the electoral register for Chelsea as 'Radnor Wood' until 1915.

It is clear from the 1911 census that Wood did not abandon Annie and leave her to bring up Gordon on her own and, indeed, four years later, during the middle of the Great War, he finally married her. Their wedding was at the St Martin Register Office, with Wood giving his name as 'Robert Cavers Wood' and stating his correct age of 38 on the marriage certificate. His profession was recorded as 'Press Designer' and the couple were living at 7 Gerrard Mansions which was located at 21-22 Gerrard Street in London's West End. Following the marriage, Wood's name reverted to his correct name of Robert Wood in the electoral register and, on 23 April 1917, Wood and his wife gave birth to a second son, Basil Charles, with Robert, whose occupation was given as 'advertising designer', correctly stated to be the father (in his real name). Subsequently, on 19 January 1926, with Gordon approaching his sixteenth birthday, the false entry in the register was corrected and a new birth certificate issued. Gordon's parents were now stated to be 'Robert Cavers Wood' and 'Annie Louisa Eames now the wife of Robert Cavers Wood', both said to be living in Golders Green. Wood's occupation was now 'Advertising Designer' as opposed to 'Advertising Specialist' as he had stated in 1910. Wood appears to have escaped any punishment for his earlier false registration. The Legitimacy Act of 1926 was introduced for the purpose of allowing parents of illegitimate children to re-register their births, usually with the correct father added where previously it was blank on the register. However, this did not become law until the very end of 1926 so Gordon Wood's re-registration was not carried out under this statute.

With Wood married and his eldest son lawfully registered, there did not seem to be any need for false names so it is rather odd that the 1928 and 1929 electoral registers for the City of Westminster feature one 'Radnor Wood' at his Gerrard Street address. It may be that Wood had built up a professional reputation under this name and so continued using it even after the 1926 re-registration. However, during the 1930s there is no evidence that he used this alias and it seems that he permanently went back to using his real name.

Long before this, Wood's real name was in the spotlight in one of a series of articles written by Arthur Newton in 1908 for *Cassell's Saturday Journal*. 'How I saved Wood' was the modest title of his article published in three parts between 29 August and 12 September 1908. The enemy of the story for Newton was quite clearly Ruby Young. It was she, he said, 'who really caused his [Wood's] arrest' because she told the police that Wood had written the rising sun postcard. According to Newton, 'Some said it was the kiss of Judas – the betrayal of a man by the woman who was his sweetheart', although the relationship was over as at October 1907 so Ruby was Wood's *former* sweetheart (something which never seems to have registered with Newton). At this stage, Newton appeared to be happy to describe the 'kiss of Judas' as a metaphorical kiss to summarise the betrayal but in the third article he said that Ruby had 'by a Judas-like kiss…pointed out Wood, her sweetheart to the police'. This was the beginning of a myth which has persisted to the current day. It was a powerful image for those who believed Wood innocent: the idea that Ruby had identified him to the police by kissing him in exactly the same way as Judas had supposedly identified Jesus to the Romans so that they could arrest and execute him. But it was not true. There was no mention of any kiss by Ruby in Wood's police statement and he never gave any evidence to the effect that there was one. Ruby Young never said anything about kissing Wood when she met him, either in her statement or in her oral evidence. On the contrary, Arthur Newton had asked Ruby during the police court proceedings if she had kissed Wood on the day of his arrest and she said categorically, 'I did not kiss him in the street'. Inspector Neil was asked directly during the trial by Marshall Hall, 'Was there an arrangement that she should kiss him?' to which he answered firmly 'No'. Asked if she did, in fact, kiss him, Inspector Neil was reported as saying 'Nothing of the kind'.[533] Marshall Hall pressed him and asked him if he was sure (he said he was) then if he was quite sure. Inspector Neil confirmed that he was indeed quite sure, adding, 'She came up and they shook hands'. Marshall Hall asked if the handshake had been his 'signal' but Neil said that he had already seen Wood cross the road. That really should have been the end of the matter but it was clearly Newton's obsession that there had been a kiss and he was never able to remove the idea from his mind.

In the 1908 article, Newton also revealed that he was unhappy with the fact that Wood had made an 'elaborate statement' to the police before he was appointed as his legal representative. Indeed, he said that he was 'furious' when he heard about this and protested against it 'in the strongest possible way', considering that the statement was the 'backbone of the evidence against him'. Newton characterised this in a strange way. He said that 'The statement made concerning his actions on a night a month earlier, made to the police with such terrible suspicion resting upon him, might easily have been inaccurate – as it was'. While this is true as an abstract point, it ignores the fact that Wood's statement was deliberately inaccurate, not because of any outside pressure or understandable failure of recollection, but as part of a deliberate design to deceive the police. However, for Newton, there was no case against Wood and he believed that all the police had against him was that he knew Emily. Regarding the question of why Wood did not come forward when he saw the reproduction of the postcard in the press, Newton said 'The explanation was simple. He did not want his sweetheart to know', again missing the fact that Wood had no sweetheart at the time and that Wood's own explanation was that he did not want his family to know of his association with Emily. However, according to Newton, it was Ruby Young's jealousy that caused her to decline to 'save Wood'.

Surprisingly, according to Newton, the 'most important piece of evidence in Wood's defence' was the poste restante letter. He thought it was sufficient to secure his acquittal on its own because it showed that Wood 'concealed nothing from his relatives'. Even if Wood had not concealed from his relatives the fact that he had been out with Emily on the night of the murder, which of course he had, it is hard to see what was so important from a defence point of view about the self-serving letter which could have been withdrawn from the Poste Restante at any time and then destroyed. The fact that Wood confessed to his relatives that he had written the rising sun postcard hardly supports his innocence considering that his handwriting on the card, which had been published in the newspapers, had already given the game away. All the poste restante letter did was to ensure that Wood's identity as the author was protected and kept secret from the police.

Before the last of Newton's three articles was published, a new play in three acts entitled 'Mysterious drama of the Camden Town Murder' was staged at the Assembly Rooms in Whitstable, Kent, on 5 September 1908. Among the small audience of less than a hundred was Sergeant Charles Dengate of the Kent Constabulary who made notes of the performance. His interest was not of a literary or artistic nature. He was there because the play had not been submitted to the Lord Chamberlain for approval, which omission was illegal. The sergeant recorded that the cast included actors representing Robert Wood, Emily Dimmock, Ruby Young and 'William' Crabtree among others. The play opened in a public house with Wood and Emily leaving together followed by the discovery of a robbery and Crabtree shouting 'They know all about it!' Emily was murdered in the second act with the third act being the arrest and trial of Wood. The representation of the trial was not entirely accurate; the 'jury' was comprised of just two men and a woman (whereas, in reality, women could not sit on juries). According to Sergeant Dengate, the judge's summing up in the final act was in favour of a conviction although the jury, as in real life, returned a not guilty verdict. If the sergeant's notes are to be believed, it was not a terribly good production, with very little evident drama or interesting dialogue, but the authorities considered it to be 'a most objectionable play'. Consequently, William Bell, the theatrical agent who staged the play (and who played the part of Crabtree) and, Robert Beal Reeves, the owner of the Assembly Rooms, were prosecuted by the Director of Public Prosecutions at the instance of the Lord Chamberlain at the St Augustine Sessions in Canterbury for performing an unlicensed play. Both were convicted and fined, with Reeves' barrister accepting 'the undesirability of plays in any way representing actual murder cases being performed on the stage'.[534]

The public was reminded of the Wood case again in October 1908 with the murder of prostitute Esther Prager and again in November 1909 when Elizabeth Clark, another prostitute, who falsely told people she was the estranged wife of the Scottish international football player, Bobby Templeton, and called herself 'Lily Templeton', was found murdered in a Brixton flat with her throat cut but with no weapon located at the scene. A witness claimed to have seen the latter victim with a 'short, thick-set' man of foreign appearance shortly before her death, and the description issued by the police of the man wanted for the murder included the fact that he 'walks with a swing'.[535] This excited some interest and the *Daily Mirror* reported that 'A singular circumstance is that the man who committed the Camden Town murder was also described as having a peculiar "swinging" walk and this fact is naturally engaging the close attention of the police'.[536] Noting that robbery did not appear to be the motive for the crime, another newspaper felt that 'the similarity of the circumstances to those attending the death of the woman Dimmock, at St Paul's-road, Camden Town, in September 1907 is remarkable'.[537] A seaman called Frank Vernon confessed to the crime but later retracted his confession and police inquiries showed that he could not have been responsible. The real murderer was never found.

The public was once again reminded of the Wood trial on 30 November 1911 when Sir William Grantham passed away, aged 76, after suffering from double pneumonia accompanied by heart weakness. Not all of the obituaries were kind to the judge; the *Times* of 1 December 1911 commented that he often 'backed his opinion against the evidence' while Harold Ashton, writing in the *Morning Leader*, called him 'A strange man, a man of quick impulses, hasty conclusions (often too hasty as the records of the Court of Appeal will show)' and spoke of his 'harsh' voice: although he also said he had 'a full heart – big and kind'. It is perhaps ironic that Ashton accused Grantham of 'hasty conclusions', considering Scotland Yard's rejection of Ashton's own rather over-hasty theory on the postcards, based on a misreading of the postmark on one of the cards. In any event, the 1907 trial was mentioned in the newspapers as one of Grantham's career highlights: the *Daily Mirror*, for example, saying that 'During his long occupancy of the Bench, he tried many famous cases, among them the Alfred Beck and Camden Murder cases'. Ironically, in the end, it was not the many men he had sent to the gallows that he was remembered for but those he helped to be acquitted.

The Camden Town Murder case next featured in Sir Melville Macnaghten's autobiography, *Days of My Years*, published in 1914, although the man in overall charge of the investigation managed to get some of his facts badly wrong. He claimed that Emily's body was discovered at about three o'clock in the afternoon after her landlady became anxious at finding the door to her room locked and called the police, which was just about wrong in every particular. More worryingly, he stated that a police officer had found the rising sun postcard while conducting a thorough search of the room which, considering that Macnaghten had been critical of his own officers for failing to locate the postcard at the time, seems suspiciously like a deliberate error on his part to conceal a major police blunder. From the way Macnaghten wrote about the case, it is quite apparent that he believed Wood was the culprit, despite the jury's verdict. He highlighted the fact that a letter requesting a meeting had been found in the fire and that Wood was known to have met with Emily at about 10:00pm on the Wednesday. Stressing that Emily's curlers were still in her hair when her body was found, suggesting that she had not planned to go out in the evening, and that Emily's postcard album was lying open 'as if it had been recently looked through', Macnaghten concluded that the murder was committed by a 'sexual maniac' and ruled out robbery or revenge as a motive. Like Sir Charles Mathews, he thought that the murderer had probably stripped naked – which, he claimed, was a 'very usual procedure in these cases' – in order to avoid blood being found on the clothing. As for Wood's acquittal at the Old Bailey, all he had to say about this was that 'a section of the British public thought it fit to regard the suspect as a popular hero' and he preferred to criticise the attempts by members of the public to intimidate the prosecution witnesses rather than any apparent failures by the police to apprehend Emily's murderer.

Wood was then basically forgotten about until 1922 when Arthur Newton wrote a new article on the Dimmock case for *Thomson's Weekly News* in a series of seventeen articles relating to the highlights of his career, followed in short order by two new articles published in the *Sunday Express* in a similar but shorter series in 1924.[538] By this time, Newton had been struck off the Roll and permanently disbarred from practising as a solicitor after having been convicted at the Old Bailey in 1913 of conspiracy to defraud a young Austrian man in a property deal and sentenced to three years imprisonment, of which he served two. He had already been suspended for a year in 1911 for professional misconduct in providing a fake letter to the press, purported to have been written by his condemned client, Harvey Hawley Crippen, from Pentonville Prison. Since his release from prison in 1915, Newton had been carrying on a confidential agency business (the purpose of which was to extricate people from 'all difficulties and embarrassments') although you would not know this from Newton's articles in which he refers to 'looking back over my long career as a solicitor' with no mention at all of the fact that he had not been one for more than ten years.

The article in *Thomson's Weekly News*, entitled 'How I Secured the Acquittal of Robert Wood', is probably most remarkable for the fact that Newton does not mention Edward Marshall Hall despite emphasising how good a prosecutor Sir Charles Mathews was. He claimed that Mathews whispered to him, a few moments before the case began, 'Mr Newton, I am glad you are going to defend this man'. The most interesting revelation was in his account of his first meeting with Wood after he had been charged with Emily's murder. Newton had been told by the police that Ruby Young had contradicted Wood's alibi for the evening of the murder and, he said, 'I hurried off to see him in the cells and told him that unless he searched his mind and realised he had made a mistake I could not hold out any hope of his acquittal'. He then gave the following account of Wood's response to this:

> He walked up and down the cell, cudgelling his brain for a few moments, and then he turned to me and, with a look of satisfaction in his eyes, declared that he believed he had made a mistake after all, and that at the time the murder had been committed he was at home talking to his father, who for the first time in forty years had been absent from his work through sciatica.

If Newton's recollection of the conversation was accurate this can only have been a major piece of play acting on Wood's part. He knew perfectly well he had not made a 'mistake'; his false alibi had been deliberately concocted with Ruby Young over a number of days. The truth, which he does not appear to have confided in Newton at this stage, was that he had been with Emily Dimmock in the *Eagle* at the time he had claimed to have been with Ruby Young. In both the story he had told the police and the one he eventually told to the jury at the Old Bailey, he claimed to have been home at midnight so his answer to Newton had not really progressed matters much further. It would also be remarkable for Wood, who had been required to think about where he had been on the night of Emily's murder since at least the publication of the rising sun postcard at the end of September, to have suddenly refreshed his memory in this brief conversation with his solicitor.

Yet Newton said in his article that he left the interview with a 'feeling of exhilaration' and went straight to Frederick Street to speak to George Wood. He claimed that he told the old man that his son's life depended on establishing an alibi, to which Mr Wood replied that he was sure his son had been with him because he always came to visit him before he retired to his own bedroom. When Newton pressed him to recall any incident to corroborate his recollection, Mr Wood mentioned the fact that he had broken a bottle of liniment and that Robert had noticed a pungent smell in the room. In his article, Newton claimed that he anticipated that the prosecution would ask why the old man had not immediately replaced the liniment bottle the next day considering that it was so important to aid his recovery and, after a period of thoughtful silence, George Wood said (as he would later tell Sir Charles Mathews) that he had not spilt the entire bottle and thus did not obtain more until he required it. One has the feeling from the way he tells the story that Newton had actually coached his witness in how to respond to Sir Charles' questions and, indeed, later in the article, Newton actually refers to the alibi as 'one I prepared for Wood'.

In the first *Sunday Express* article on the Wood case, entitled 'The Mystery Murder of Camden Town', Newton returned to one of his favourite subjects: Ruby Young's supposed 'Judas' kiss. He stated that, on 4 October 1907, Wood emerged from his employer's premises on Gray's Inn Road and that 'As he came out Ruby Young kissed him'. He proudly told his readers that 'This kiss I referred to as the kiss of Judas, as I elicited in cross-examination that she had arranged with the police to betray Wood to them as being the writer of the postcard by kissing him as soon as he came within sight of the officers'. At this time, almost seventeen years after the event, no-one was in any position to challenge Newton's account but, as we have seen, the contemporary records show that the kiss was no more than a figment of his overactive imagination.

Once again though, Ruby was cast as the villain of the piece. According to Newton, 'It was quite evident from her demeanour that she was a jealous, vindictive woman, incensed at the knowledge of Wood's acquaintance with the dead woman'. He also described her as 'The hypocritical Ruby' for having reassured Wood that she would 'be true' when he was arrested but then giving evidence against him. The notion that his former client had put her in an impossible position by asking her to commit perjury on his behalf in a conspiracy which could easily have been exposed by the police, so that she might have been sent to prison, did not seem to have occurred to him.

The hero of the story was partly Wood who, said Newton, 'answered the questions put to him [by the police after his arrest] readily, frankly, and with complete self-possession' although it is hard to see how lying to the police about his whereabouts on the night of the murder, and denying he had been with Emily Dimmock, could be described as being 'frank'. But the real hero was none other than Newton himself who 'destroyed the effect of her [Ruby Young's] evidence entirely' and 'demolished' McCowan during the police court proceedings. He claimed to have conclusively demonstrated at the Clerkenwell Police Court that McCowan had given 'false evidence' against Wood and committed 'deliberate perjury' in order to continue to draw his 'wretched blood-money of over £4 a week' but he had evidently forgotten that Marshall Hall submitted to the jury at the trial that McCowan made 'an honest but a callous mistake'.

Indeed, after so many years, Newton's memory had let him down on a number of important points. He believed, for example, that Wood (who, he stated, was engaged by a firm of porcelain manufacturers designing patterns for china) had met Emily in the *Rising Sun* on the night of the murder, having completely forgotten it was actually the *Eagle*. Thus, in revealing what Wood had told him of his movements that night, he said, 'He had met Phyllis in the Rising Sun; they had a drink or two and then both left separately. He looked in again two or three times, and soon after that he went home'. During the trial, Wood claimed to have gone straight home after parting from Emily, with no mention of looking inside the public house two or three times, so this is potentially an interesting revelation of what Wood might have told his solicitor in private but it may simply be that Newton was confusing the evidence that Wood had (allegedly) put his head round the door of the *Rising Sun* on the Tuesday night with what happened in the *Eagle* on the Wednesday.

In recounting the defence case regarding Robert Roberts' relationship with May Campbell, Newton also made a number of mistakes. He claimed that Marshall Hall cross-examined Roberts on the basis that he and Campbell had jointly invented the existence of the letter that he (Roberts) claimed had been received by Emily from 'Bert' on the morning of 11 September, inviting her to the *Eagle*. While it is true that Marshall Hall suggested to Roberts that his evidence about the letter was an invention, the specific allegation he made in respect of a conspiracy involving Roberts and Campbell was that they had jointly concocted the description of the man they both claimed to suspect of murdering Emily, not that they had put their heads together to fabricate the letter itself. Newton wrote that Roberts had 'turned pale' on being asked if he was in a great fright after hearing of the murder. He also claimed that Roberts went straight to the *Rising Sun* after hearing of the murder 'where he met May Campbell'. However, although Roberts did go to the *Rising Sun* when he learnt the news of Emily's murder (in order to demonstrate that he was not trying to hide from the police), he explained at the trial that he did not meet May Campbell until the funeral and there was no evidence to the contrary.

Newton's account is revealing because it shows that the defence team (possibly inspired by Wellesley Orr) clearly believed that Roberts and May Campbell had put their heads together in the *Rising Sun* on the day after the murder and devised a story whereby Roberts would tell the police that Emily had received a letter from 'Bert', attempting to arrange a meeting at the *Eagle* for later that night, in order to divert suspicion towards Bert Shaw. The supposed plan was presumably that May Campbell would support Roberts by telling police that Emily had mentioned to her that she had received just such a letter. We have already discussed the reasons why this theory does not work and it is worth reminding ourselves that Roberts' story was corroborated not only by the evidence of Alice Lancaster, who had delivered two letters to Emily while Roberts was with her on the Wednesday morning, but also by the fact that Emily *did* go to the *Eagle* that night to meet a man (Wood) and by the burnt fragments of a document indisputably written by Wood found in Emily's fireplace which, while indecipherable, were not inconsistent with Roberts' account. Moreover, if Roberts and May Campbell were going to attempt to throw suspicion on someone through a concocted letter to Emily, it would not have made any sense for that letter to have come from the man she was living with because Bert Shaw would not have communicated with Emily in such a fashion. Nor would it make any sense for May to then accuse 'Scotch Bob' of being the author of the letter considering that, whoever 'Scotch Bob' was supposed to be, it was certainly not Bert Shaw.

The unreliability of Newton's summary of Roberts' cross-examination is demonstrated by his suggestion that Roberts 'crept out [of the witness box] in silence' immediately after admitting that the letter from 'Bert' would have been of assistance had the aim been to throw suspicion on Bert Shaw. It is correct that Marshall Hall asked him, 'If it had been the object to put suspicion on Bert Shaw, the signature "Bert" would have been a good piece of evidence, would it not?' to which Roberts replied 'Yes', but the *Notable British Trials* transcript records that there were a further seven questions from Marshall Hall followed by fourteen questions from Sir Charles Mathews in re-examination at which point the court adjourned for the day. Newton probably saw what he wanted to see but there is nothing in the transcript to suggest that Roberts was reduced to silence by Marshall Hall's question about the letter. In any event, every single witness at the trial left the witness box in silence as witnesses invariably do!

After the first of Newton's articles, the *Sunday Express* issued an apology to a 'Mr Shaw' who was then living at 29 St Paul's Road. The newspaper had published a reproduction of the rising sun postcard (addressed to 'Mrs B Shaw' at 29 St Paul's Road) and it felt the need to clarify that the current tenant of 29 St Paul's Road was 'in no way connected with the recipient of the postcard' and 'regrets that any pain or annoyance should have been caused' to him. The electoral register for St Pancras East reveals that the 'Mr Shaw' in question was Thomas Matthew Shaw who was living at the address with his sister. By this time, the real Mr B. Shaw (Bert), still working as a railway dining car chef, had ventured to Poole in Dorset where he evidently met Margaret Coggan, the daughter of a railway passenger guard. He married her in Poole in August 1913 and appears to have lived there, or possibly in Manchester where he was living at the time, for the rest of his life until his death in 1972. Although not mentioned by the *Sunday Express*, George and Sarah Ann Stocks were still living at 29 St Paul's Road in 1924 and were presumably interested readers of Newton's articles, along with the infuriated Thomas Shaw.

During the following year, there was a glut of resignations of senior police officers amidst rumours of discontent and disaffection at Scotland Yard, and those resigning included former detectives, Alfred Grosse and Arthur Mitchell who had worked on the Dimmock case and reached the rank of inspector. Also retiring was Inspector David Goodwillie; and the *Sunday News* carried a feature telling his life story (without any quotes from Goodwillie himself) which included an account of the investigation into Dimmock's murder.[539] According to the newspaper: 'When detectives – Goodwillie was one of them – searched [Emily's] sordid little room they found several articles missing... Among the things found in the room of the dead girl was a postcard which was to prove a vital piece of evidence in the subsequent trial of Robert Wood'. Just as Sir Melville Macnaghten's memory had failed him, so too the representative from Scotland Yard's Press Bureau, who had undoubtedly given the *Sunday News* its information, had forgotten, or was never aware, that the postcard was completely missed in the police search, only being found by Bert Shaw some days later. The article also claimed that 'Diligent inquiries by Goodwillie elicited the fact that on the night of the murder Robert Wood, a young artist, had been seen in the Eagle public house with the murdered girl'. In reality, of course, the direct opposite was true. The police had totally failed during their inquiries to establish that Wood was with Dimmock in the *Eagle*, the barmaid being unable to help, and it was only when Joseph Lambert stepped forward, having learnt of Wood's arrest from a newspaper placard, that the police were able to confirm that their prime suspect had indeed met Dimmock there that night.

Even worse, David Goodwillie had not been involved in the investigation into Emily Dimmock's murder which was conducted by police from the Metropolitan Police's Y Division whereas Goodwillie, at the time of the murder, had been a detective constable at Scotland Yard. It would appear that Scotland Yard's Press Bureau had confused Inspector Goodwillie with Inspector Goodchild who had retired five years earlier! Certainly, when *Thomson's Weekly News* published Goodwillie's memoirs in sixteen instalments between May to September 1925 there was no mention of any involvement with the Camden Town murder of 1907.

Edward Marshall Hall died in 1927, having been instructed in many more high profile criminal cases after his success defending Wood and, two years later, Edward Marjoribanks, himself a barrister, published a biography of the great man, entitled *The Life of Sir Edward Marshall Hall*, which naturally included a chapter relating to the Camden Town Murder. Marjoribanks had discussed the case with Inspector Neil (whose surname he wrongly spelt as 'Neill' throughout the book) and was sympathetic towards Ruby Young, explaining why she had been forced to give evidence against Wood. He did not think her evidence about Wood's walk was a result of her being vindictive. He was also persuaded by Neil that McCowan was an honest witness but conceded that his evidence was unreliable. Regarding the evidence given in court by Roberts, Marjoribanks claimed to have spoken to an 'eye witness' who told him that Roberts 'looked frightened before he spoke a word', which is odd because Arthur Newton had written in his 1924 article that, when Roberts supposedly 'crept in silence' from the witness box, this was 'in marked contrast to the confidence with which he had entered the box'. Marjoribanks also claimed that Roberts left the witness box 'with perspiration pouring down his face' but, even if that were true, it is understandable considering that Marshall Hall was accusing him of all kinds of things.

In addition to a briefing from Inspector Neil and information from unnamed eye witnesses, Marjoribanks also had access to Marshall Hall's private papers (which appear no longer to be available to researchers) and from these he reproduced a letter to Marshall Hall from Arthur Newton dated 11 December 1907 in which Newton wrote, in the context of a discussion about whether to allow Wood to give evidence, 'We cannot call him. You were perfectly right in every way'. This was apparently in response to Marshall Hall saying that Wood was 'raving mad'. However, Marjoribanks says that Wellesley Orr pressed for Wood to be called and Marshall Hall changed his mind at a late stage.

Marjoribanks did not have access to the Metropolitan Police file nor, apparently, to a transcript of the trial (and presumably used newspaper reports when quoting from cross-examination at the Old Bailey) but his summary of the facts is largely accurate. A few errors nevertheless crept in. He said that the police found the rising sun postcard in a drawer in Emily's room when it was, of course, Bert Shaw who had stumbled across it. He transcribed the postcard as commencing with the words 'Phyllis Darling' when even Crabtree had spotted that Wood had written 'Phillis'. More importantly, he said that the police found Emily's postcard album 'lying on the floor' when they only claimed to have found it on a chair (and Bert Shaw said he had seen it on the sewing machine). Partly as a result of the fact that he believed the album was on the floor with postcards scattered loosely around it, Marjoribanks adopted the police theory that the murderer had been looking for a particular postcard, which in turn suggested that he believed Wood was the murderer. Like Arthur Newton before him, Marjoribanks also wrongly claimed that Ruby Young greeted Wood with a kiss when she met him on the day of his arrest, thus helping to perpetuate this myth.

Marjoribanks also created some myths of his own, the most long-lasting of which was the claim that 'up to this time every prisoner called in his own defence on a capital charge at the Old Bailey had gone to the gallows'. This was completely untrue and was never a claim made by any contemporary observer of the Wood trial. In fact, within a few weeks of the commencement of operation of the 1898 Criminal Evidence Act (on 12 October 1898), which allowed prisoners on capital charges to give evidence in their own defence, a man charged with murder had escaped the gallows on the basis of his own evidence. Walter John Simpson, indicted at the Old Bailey on 21 November 1898 for the wilful murder of his employer, John Paterson, gave evidence in his own defence, claiming that he had fired his revolver at Paterson by accident and, after being cross-examined by Mr Gill for the crown, was found not guilty of murder but guilty of manslaughter and sentenced to twelve months hard labour. Less than a year later, on 26 October 1899, Edouard Marmajou was completely acquitted at the Old Bailey of the murder of his two-year-old son after giving evidence in his own defence. Charles Mathews was one of the prosecutors in that case and another familiar figure was involved in a prisoner's escape from the gallows in November 1903. Mr Justice Grantham was the judge at Durham when Albert Hunt gave evidence in his own defence, charged with the wilful murder of James Coxon Wakefield in South Shields, and was found not guilty of murder but guilty of manslaughter. Alice Bexley was acquitted of the murder of her baby son in March 1906 after telling the jury under oath from the witness box that she discovered her child was dead while on a train from Liverpool Street to Glemsford in Suffolk. There are other examples of prisoners charged with murder and giving evidence in their own defence either being acquitted completely or being found guilty of manslaughter before Wood's trial: it's just that none of them were famous trials which grabbed the headlines.

Perhaps the most influential myth started by Marjoribanks was the story that some years after Wood's acquittal, Marshall Hall was conducting a case in a provincial assize court when a man approached him outside the courtroom and spoke to him as if he knew him. Marshall Hall, having a poor memory for faces, was not sure who the man was but thought it might be Wood and said so. The man replied that his name was not Wood but added 'I'd like you to know I'm doing very well and owe it all to you'. The implication was that it was indeed Wood who was living his life under a false name and wanted to take the chance to thank Marshall Hall for saving his life. However, the overwhelming probability is that, if this incident actually happened, the man was telling the truth and was not called Wood but was another of Marshall Hall's clients. As we know, Wood did briefly call himself 'Robert Radnor' when he registered his illegitimate son's birth in 1910 but, to the extent that he used an alias, he appears to have used the surname Wood, switching between the first names of Radnor and Robert. Nevertheless, virtually every writer who has told the story of the Camden Town Murder concludes with this story, because no-one before had established what became of Wood after the trial.

Marjoribanks' biography of Marshall Hall was serialised in the *Evening Standard* in May 1932 which brought the Dimmock case back into the public consciousness and, in the same year, Arthur Neil, published his autobiography, *Forty Years of Man-Hunting*, which those interested in the murder might have thought would produce some new revelations. Neil had retired from the police force in January 1928 having reached the rank of Superintendent and then took up a position at Wembley Greyhound Racing Track.[540] Unfortunately, his book skipped over the Camden Town Murder case entirely, with Neil referring his readers to Marjoribanks' account of the case (despite Marjoribanks having spelt his name incorrectly throughout). Neil's unwillingness to include any discussion of the case in his book was a clear reflection of his disappointment in having officially failed to solve the crime. He was much happier describing his efforts to arrest and convict the 'Brides in the Bath' murderer, George Joseph Smith, in 1915. However, while it is a shame that Neil did not take the opportunity to reflect on the prosecution of Wood, it has to be said that his book is not the most accurate account of his career. He admitted in the preface that he kept no records, notes or diaries and was relying entirely on his memory but it is hard to believe that this explains his claim to have seen a woman running out of a park screaming 'murder' after she had witnessed Edward MacQuire (who Neil refers to as George McQuire) shoot John Skinner in October 1904, nor his claim to have then been told by the fatally wounded Skinner as he lay injured in the park that MacQuire had shot him. The file on the case in the National Archives reveals that Neil learnt about the shooting from Skinner's brother, an hour and a half after the event, and that the wounded Skinner had been assisted into a cab by two men and made his way home before the police were informed.[541] A number of other stories in the book have the feel of not being quite true so perhaps it is just as well that Neil left the Camden Town Murder alone.

Two years later, the case of Rex versus Wood featured as a chapter in *Six Trials* by Winifred Duke. It contained a fairly straightforward summary of the story of the murder and subsequent trial although Miss Duke wrongly stated that Crabtree introduced 'Scotch Bob' into the evidence. The most notable part of the chapter was Duke's conclusion that Wood was proved to be 'nothing more than an untrammelled liar, a philanderer, a moral coward' and she believed that his exposure as such acted as 'ample punishment and a deterrent'.

In July 1936, a complete transcript of the Wood trial was published in the *Notable British Trials* series which produced renewed interest in the crime. The source of the transcript is not entirely clear and differs in some material respects from the official shorthand record which is in the National Archives and on the Old Bailey website but the main point of interest in 1936 was the fifty-two page introduction by Basil Hogarth. Unknown to its readers at the time, there was an error in the very first paragraph, with Hogarth claiming, as Marjoribanks had done seven years earlier, that the Wood case furnished 'the remarkable precedent of the first instance in which an accused murderer, availing himself of the facilities to give evidence on his own behalf bestowed by the Criminal Evidence Act of 1898, successfully maintained his plea of not guilty'. He also wrongly stated that Emily was born in Walworth (an error he had evidently taken from some newspaper reports and was repeated by later writers) even though Inspector Neil had quickly established that she had been born in Standon. With access to the transcript, however, Hogarth avoided some of the errors Marjoribanks had been guilty of and, for example, he noted Shaw's evidence that Emily's postcard album was on the top of the sewing machine. However, he also stated as a fact that its contents were scattered on the floor when this is questionable (and even the belated police evidence at trial was that only 'several' postcards were scattered on the floor, not the entire contents).[542] Hogarth also seems to have believed that the sewing machine was in Emily's bedroom but Shaw was clear in his evidence that it was next to the window and near the chair in the front room.[543] According to Hogarth, the presence of the postcard album in the bedroom (where it was not), with some of the postcards torn out (of which Shaw had never spoken), 'puzzled Shaw' but Shaw had at no point said that he was puzzled by anything connected with the album. He had not even mentioned it in his statement to the police immediately after the discovery of the murder and it was clearly something he was only asked about much later, after the discovery of the rising sun postcard, when its significance became apparent to the police. His evidence that he remembered seeing it on the sewing machine was given without any additional comment. Hogarth's belief that Shaw was puzzled by it was no more than an inference derived from a misreading of the evidence. Nevertheless, Hogarth felt able to conclude from the evidence of the postcard album, and the disorder in the front room, that the murderer had 'evidently been seeking the [rising sun] postcard'. If that were true then the murderer was obviously Wood but Hogarth failed to notice that he had solved the case, for he concluded his introduction by asking 'Who killed Emily Dimmock?'

Yet Hogarth definitely believed Wood was guilty of the crime. His main reason for this was very surprising because he placed great weight on McCowan's identification of Wood from his walk and dismissed Westcott's evidence. In doing so, he gave three reasons in support, none of which are convincing. The first reason he put forward was that, because Westcott could not identify McCowan, there was no convincing proof that he saw him and 'he may have seen someone else, possibly the murderer'. It is true that Westcott said he was unable to identify the man he saw (which means it could have been anyone, including McCowan) but, in the context of an argument that Wood was the murderer, Hogarth's logic fails because Westcott did not identify Wood as the man he saw either. Secondly, Hogarth said that Westcott's evidence was not forthcoming 'spontaneously' whereas McCowan's was, but the quality of the evidence is at least as important and McCowan certainly failed the quality test; his evidence collapsed under cross-examinations by Arthur Newton and Marshall Hall while Westcott's evidence survived cross-examination by Sir Charles Mathews. Finally, Hogarth said that the man McCowan saw was wearing a hard bowler hat whereas Westcott 'usually wore a cap'. In fact, there was no evidence as to what Westcott 'usually' wore and, while it is true that he was photographed on his way to court wearing a cap, the only relevant question is what he was wearing on the morning of Thursday 12 September 1907. As to that, although not featured in Hogarth's transcript, newspaper reports of Westcott's examination-in-chief state that Westcott testified that, on the morning of 12 September, 'he had his overcoat collar turned up, and was wearing his hard bowler hat'.[544]

Unable to ignore the evidence relating to Wood's alibi, Hogarth thought it was plausible that Wood might have arisen in the middle of the night and returned to Camden Town to murder Emily Dimmock as Sir Charles Mathews had wildly speculated. Quite rightly, in view of his association with Ruby Young, Hogarth found difficulty accepting Wood's claim that he only provided a false alibi to the police because he wanted to avoid social ostracism arising from public knowledge of his relationship with a prostitute but does not consider that the real reason for it (as Wood reluctantly accepted during cross-examination) was because he realised that, as the last person known to have seen Emily alive, it would have looked bad for him to have admitted being in the *Eagle* with Emily only a few hours before her murder.

Hogarth's conclusion, that Wood was probably guilty after all, went down well with some, including the reviewer for the *Daily Mirror* who described Wood as 'cold' and 'callous in demeanor' and asked readers of Hogarth's book to 'Read carefully the evidence here sent forth. Then explain, if you can, that momentary mass hysteria of December, 1907'.[545] This brought a response from one *Daily Mirror* reader who pointed out that many people believed that Wood was innocent and said, 'Surely this was enough to account for the fuss made about him'.[546] Two more letters followed from readers who said they could remember the case and were critical of the 'disgraceful' attacks made on prosecution witnesses, such as Ruby Young and Robert McCowan, by the 'howling mob'.

Another man who well remembered the case was the actor and playwright, Seymour Hicks, who had been present for much of the trial at the Old Bailey and was a regular observer of many criminal trials. He published his memoirs entitled *Not Guilty M'Lord* in 1939 in which he revealed that during the evening after the jury verdict, Arthur Newton had visited him in his dressing room at the Aldwych Theatre, where he was then performing in the musical comedy 'The Gay Gordons' and offered him £500 to write a short sketch for Wood to perform in the music halls. Hicks said that he immediately refused to do anything of the kind (and, of course, the plan then changed to Wood drawing sketches). By this time, incidentally, Newton was dead, having passed away at the age of 70 in October 1930. Of the characters at the trial, Hicks said that he thought that the judge was 'frighteningly hostile' while Sir Charles Mathews (who had died in 1920) was 'at his best' and Marshall Hall was 'brilliant'. In respect of Wood, whom he described as 'weedy looking', he was amazed by his coolness but thought him a bad witness and came to the conclusion that 'three-quarters of his make-up was composed of vanity'. He said he lunched as a guest of Sir Charles Mathews on the final day of the trial and Mathews told him that he believed Wood would be acquitted, regardless of what the judge said in his summing up, because of his father's alibi. Hicks too felt he would have returned a 'not guilty' verdict had he been on the jury. Despite having heard the evidence against Wood in person, Hicks was seduced by Newton's 'kiss of Judas' and repeated the myth that Ruby Young 'had kissed [Wood] so that he might be arrested'.

Developments in Europe and the outbreak of the Second World War tended to divert attention in England from issues relating to unsolved Edwardian murders but older readers of Ernest Raymond's 1944 novel, *For Them That Trespass*, might have had a strange feeling of déjà vu. In that work of fiction, a twenty-two-year-old prostitute called Frances Ketchen, but known to her friends as 'Frankie', is found strangled in her two room apartment in 'Lenten Town' by the man with whom she had been living under the name 'Mrs Heal', a fireman working on the railways called Jim Heal. The story reported in the newspapers was that Heal had returned home from work at 9:30am and discovered the door of his room locked. He borrowed a key from the landlady, Mrs Lillie, and, entering the front room, smashed his way through the locked folding doors into the bedroom. He found Frankie, dead, wearing no clothing except her shoes and a night robe. The room was in a state of disorder; the drawers and cupboards had been ransacked with a number of valuables taken.

All was not as it seemed, however, because Jim Heal had strangled Frankie after he came back early from work and caught her virtually red-handed with another man who had fled in panic upon hearing him returning. Frankie told him that this man was her friend, Herb Logan, a bandy-legged professional burglar who had simply come to say goodbye before taking the train to Glasgow where he had a grocery store to rob. Heal did not believe her protestations of innocence and strangled her in a fit of rage before faking the appearance of a robbery and rushing to his mistress to establish an alibi. Unknown to Heal, the man who had fled was actually a client of Frankie's called Christopher Drew although, to disguise his identity, he had told Frankie his name was 'Kit Marlowe' when he met her in the *White Swan* public house. Drew was an aspiring playwright and poet and, when he learned of the murder from the newspapers, realised that Heal was the murderer but could not go to the police because of the shame and disgrace that would result if his friends and family knew he had been with a prostitute. As Herb Logan had been seen in Frankie's company earlier that evening, and his fingerprints were found in the flat, the police identified him – 'a bandy-legged man' – as their main suspect, causing him to go into hiding with the assistance of his fellow robber, 'Jocko', described by Logan as 'a Scottie and a good bloke too'.

While on the run, Logan formed a friendship with a young girl called Rosie Wareing and confided in her that he was the man the police were looking for. Worried that she might be committing a criminal offence by not reporting this to the police, she tells a friend who tells another friend and she is advised that she could go to prison for life for harbouring a fugitive whereas, if she gives him up to the police, she will collect a £100 reward. So, when she next meets Logan as arranged, Detective Inspector Callow and Detective Sergeant Benstead are waiting. Once Rosie greets Logan they pounce and Callow asks him, 'Your name's Logan isn't it?' Unaware that he has been betrayed, Logan makes a short speech to Rosie, telling her: 'Goodbye Rosie darling...Sorry to disappoint you this afternoon, but I'll be out again in a few days as sure as fate and I'll be looking you up. We'll have a treat...Give us a kiss Rosie'. They are allowed to kiss and Logan is taken away but Rosie does not feel too bad in view of the forthcoming £100 reward. Logan lies to the police in his first statement, attempting to put some distance between himself and Frankie, before finally admitting that he was with the deceased on the night of the murder. He claims that when he left her she was about to see a client who, she had told him, was called 'Kit Marlowe'. During his trial at number one court in the Old Bailey, which commenced on 'a misty October morning', and was an instant newspaper sensation, Logan gave evidence on his own behalf and insisted, during cross-examination by Sir Emsley Hurd for the Crown, that there really was a 'Kit Marlowe'. But the circumstantial evidence against him was too strong; despite the admirable efforts of his barrister, Huntly Frere KC, the jury only took twenty minutes to find him guilty. For reasons which are never made entirely clear, Logan was reprieved five days before his execution by the Home Secretary and sentenced to life imprisonment instead. While in prison, two books are published on the case: a biography of Sir Huntly Frere KC called *Memoirs of a Great Advocate* and a book by ex-Superintendent Callow of Scotland Yard entitled *Forty Years a Detective*. Some years after the murder, Mrs Lillie, the landlady, finds a poem cut from a journal in the folds of a newspaper used to line one of the drawers in Frankie's room. When Logan is eventually released from prison she gives him the poem and he is able to discover that it was published before the murder by Christopher Drew, now a famous playwright. Logan, still convinced that 'Kit Marlowe' exists and must be none other than Christopher Drew, tracks Drew down but, before meeting him, Jim Heal confesses to the murder on his deathbed, having been fatally injured in a railway accident. Logan needs Drew to corroborate Heal's confession but Drew initially denies everything before being filled with remorse that he did not come forward at the trial and confesses that he was with Frankie in the moments before she was murdered. As a result, the story of Frankie's murder becomes a sensation all over again some thirty-one years later. Not all reviewers of the book seemed to appreciate that the story was loosely based on a true story. J.D. Beresford in the *Manchester Guardian*, for example, said in all innocence that 'the book conveys a remarkable effect of being the account of an actual happening' while the *Daily Telegraph* reviewer spoke of the author's 'solid ability to create characters that come to life' apparently unaware that the characters were, on the whole, based on real people.[547]

In 1948, the BBC was planning a radio programme to dramatize the Camden Town Murder as part of a series on famous criminal cases entitled 'Let Justice Be Done' with the actor Alec Ross lined up to play Wood. Of concern to the BBC, as with all programmes of this nature, was whether there were any living individuals who might be affected by the dramatization. Consequently, the scriptwriter, John Gough, sent a memorandum to the BBC's legal department on 15 December 1948 saying 'I think we need anticipate no difficulty at all as far as proprieties are concerned...There will be no trouble about relatives'.[548] Gough had assumed from Marjoribanks' book that Wood had changed his name and disappeared into obscurity. The programme, entitled 'Alibi', was recorded and scheduled for broadcast on the Home Service on Thursday, 3 February 1949 at 9:30pm, being advertised in the *Radio Times* of 28 January.

Out of the blue, a couple of days before the broadcast, a letter dated 31 January 1949 was received from an 'N. Henderson', then staying at the Strand Palace Hotel, claiming to be a relative of Wood and stating that the programme was likely to cause pain and distress to members of Wood's family.[549] The letter also claimed that 'Mr Wood regards it as a very unenviable notoriety in useing (sic) his name – but is more grieved at the possibility of his people being mentioned'. It was noted within the BBC that there was no legal reason to stop the broadcast but that there might be policy reasons not to impersonate real members of the public without their permission. Nevertheless, Stella Hillier, a producer in the Features Department, thought that the broadcast should go ahead and suggested that the BBC should write to Mr Henderson explaining that there was no way that Wood could have been traced for his permission on the basis that Marjoribanks had stated that he had changed his name.[550] Shortly before the broadcast, however, James Wood telephoned the BBC complaining that his half-brother, who was then almost 70 years old, was not happy to be featured in the show and it was decided 'for policy reasons' to pull the plug and replace it with a programme dealing with the story of the building of the Burma railway.[551] A BBC spokesman announced that 'We do not broadcast anything which will cause pain to close relatives of those concerned in past incidents'.[552]

With so little time between the complaints being made and the scheduled broadcast, there was no time to check the authenticity of the man calling himself Henderson, nor of the man claiming to be Wood's half-brother, and this caused some consternation within the BBC during February. James Gough, who felt a little guilty that he had not done enough to check whether Wood was still alive, was curious as to whether any credentials had been checked and a subsequent internal BBC memo referred to Mr Henderson's objection as 'unsubstantiated'.[553] However, the calls were certainly genuine – the Henderson family was related to Betsy Wood, the wife of Charles Carlyle Wood, and it was the real James Wood who had called in to object; although individuals within the BBC became confused in December 1954 when they received a telephone call from Charles Carlyle Wood and appear to have believed that he was the same man as Wood's half-brother to whom they had spoken in 1949. The reason for the 1954 call was that the *Radio Times* had announced in its 29 October 1954 issue that Edgar Lustgarten was planning a series of programmes to feature six well-known trials, including the Wood trial, to be broadcast in the spring of 1955 and Charles telephoned to object to this on behalf of his brother. In the event, the series was never made.

As it happens, by 1954, Charles Carlyle Wood was a very well-connected man, having worked as a proof reader on two books by Winston Churchill: *Marlborough*, a massive four volume biography published over five years between 1933 and 1938, and the second volume of his history of the Second World War entitled *Their Finest Hour*, published in 1949. His abrasive style, finding mistakes everywhere, even when they didn't always seem to exist, annoyed Churchill's publishers which appears to explain why he had been omitted from proof reading work on the first volume, *The Gathering Storm*, but that volume was strewn with errors (for which the publishers were responsible) bringing fresh demand by Churchill for Charles' eagle-eyed services, known by the name of 'Wooding'.[554] According to Churchill, Charles was 'indefatigable, interminable, intolerable'.[555] However, he died in March 1959 of cerebral thrombosis and arteriosclerosis, three years after the death of James, leaving Robert as the only one of the three brothers alive.

Consequently, when history repeated itself, and the BBC advertised another radio programme about the Camden Town Murder case in the *Radio Times* in 1963, it was Robert Wood himself who emerged from the shadows to complain. The programme in question, entitled 'Rex v Wood', was the second in a series about Marshall Hall called 'The Great Defender', presented by Edgar Lustgarten, with each episode dealing with one of his famous cases. This time the BBC made a determined effort to contact Wood's relatives but they had no current contact address for Charles Carlyle Wood. As a result, in May 1963, a letter was sent to his last known address in Golders Green but the envelope was returned unopened, marked 'Not known here'. Further investigations at Somerset House in June produced his death certificate and similar searches were made in respect of Robert Wood but produced no results. An internal memorandum by the programme's producer, Joe Burroughs, stated that it was still believed he had changed his name after the trial and the assumption was that he must have died under a different identity.[556] A notice had appeared in the *Radio Times* during January, March and May of 1963 indicating that the Wood case was to be included in a forthcoming broadcast and no complaints had been received from Wood or any members of his family.[557] Unlike in 1949, Wood was not going to be played by an actor in the broadcast and the BBC's legal team approved the script in August. The programme was thus scheduled to be broadcast on the Home Service on 15 October 1963 as the second episode in the series and featured in the *Radio Times* of 3 October 1963 accordingly.

It came as a shock, therefore, when a letter was received at the BBC on 4 October 1963 from none other than Robert Wood complaining about the broadcast which he objected to on the basis that 'it would be very unfair to my Relatives and "Grand-Children"'.[558] Wood had provided his telephone number and Joe Burroughs called him immediately but could not get past his wife. According to Burroughs, Annie 'was at first hostile and accused us of "raking up dirt to make money"'. She explained that family members did not know of the case but Burroughs countered by saying that, even if they listened to the broadcast, they would not know that her husband was the 'Robert Wood' referred to. He also made the point that the story of the case was available in various printed forms. Annie responded stubbornly by saying that 'her family didn't need that kind of thing and anyway it would be very distressing for Mr Wood himself'. Burroughs told her that she and her husband did not need to listen to it, which did not convince her, but he had more success when he explained that the series was designed to demonstrate how a great barrister like Marshall Hall can help people in need, such as Wood, and she thought this was 'sensible'. Pressing his advantage, Burroughs told her that Wood was a subsidiary character in the programme and was portrayed in as good a light as anyone could be in the circumstances. As a result, Annie, who told Burroughs that she personally liked to listen to programmes about criminal trials, agreed to read the script with Wood and provide their joint comments. Burroughs recorded in an internal BBC memo that: 'I got the impression she was more concerned to stop the broadcast this time because they'd succeeded in doing so before and so "taught the BBC a lesson" than anything else'.[559]

A script was provided to the Woods but the immediate news was bad. Wood wrote a second letter on 6 October saying that 'my wife and I still strongly object to the Broadcast'. He added that they considered it 'in very bad taste – to Broadcast this script while I am still alive'.[560] This time, however, the programme's producer was not prepared to give in so easily. Nothing defamatory was being said about Wood so there was no legal reason why the programme could not be broadcast and, as Wood was not being impersonated, no real policy reason either, although the corporation remained sensitive to complaints from living people about being featured in such programmes. Both Burroughs and the BBC features director, Lawrence Gilliam, felt that they should go ahead with the broadcast regardless, believing that to cancel it now that it had been advertised in the *Radio Times* would draw more attention than if they proceeded. However, the issue went up to the Director of Sound Broadcasting, Frank Gillard, who decided that the broadcast should be cancelled unless Wood agreed to it.[561]

Burroughs, therefore, telephoned Wood again on 8 October to try and persuade him to agree, although he was again only able to speak to Annie.[562] Upon offering to remove all mentions from the script of the name 'Wood' and substituting a 'covering circumulation', Annie spoke to her husband and then told Burroughs that, on such basis, Wood would withdraw his objection.

Ironically, while this was going on, Wood's nephew, Robert Kinnear Wood, the son of Charles Carlyle Wood, was writing a letter to the Director of Programmes at the BBC with his own complaint concerning the forthcoming broadcast about the Wood trial, stating, 'I must point out to you that the man concerned, Mr Robert Wood (my uncle) is still alive and resident in London, and aged I believe 86'. He went on to say that the programme could be detrimental to Wood and requested its cancellation 'in view of his age'. On the very same day, Wood was writing to the BBC to confirm that he did not object to the broadcast on the basis that his name did not appear in the programme or any announcements relating to it.[563] Burroughs was, therefore, happily able to write back to Robert Kinnear Wood on 10 October to inform him that 'we have the permission of both Mr and Mrs Wood to proceed with this programme in a form which is acceptable to them both.'[564] The programme was then broadcast as planned on 15 October but the BBC was careful to refer to it as 'The Camden Town Case' as opposed to 'Rex v Wood' and Wood, who was not mentioned by name, was referred to in the script as 'a young craftsman' instead of a commercial artist.

Had the programme been broadcast sixteen months later there would have been no issues because Robert Wood died at St Luke's Hospital in Chelsea on 17 February 1966 of bronchopneumonia at the age of 88. He was described on his death certificate as a 'Retired Commercial Artist' which was how he liked to think of himself, albeit that he appears to have spent his later working life as a press designer (presumably designing layouts for the press). This was how he had been described on his son's marriage certificate in 1942 when Gordon, then working as a multiple stores manager, had married a multiple stores supervisor (presumably working for the same company) called Mary Hearn, who was then living in Islington. He was married under the name 'Gordon, otherwise Gordon Eames Wood' which must have been a clerical error, with the first Gordon supposed to be 'Gordon Radnor', or perhaps just 'Gordon Wood' – otherwise it makes no sense. Both of his parents were witnesses at the wedding and the address he gave of 13 Embankment Gardens, Chelsea, showed that he was living with them at the time of his marriage. Gordon was the informant stated on Wood's death certificate.

By coincidence, within a few months of Wood's death, Nina Warner Hooke and Gil Thomas published their biography of Marshall Hall entitled, without any unnecessary frills, *Marshall Hall*. For some unknown reason, they claimed that 'Up to a few years ago Robert Wood was alive and living in Australia', not realising that he was actually living in London while they were writing their manuscript. When dealing with the scene of the crime they said, consistent with Bert Shaw's recollection, that Emily's postcard album had been found on the sewing machine but stated that some of the contents had been 'torn out' which went further than the police evidence although Inspector Neil had said at the police court that he thought there were some postcards missing, 'or at least there were spaces empty in which postcards might go'.[565] On this basis, Hooke and Thomas concluded that 'the murderer, whoever he was, searched through the postcard album looking for something he suspected to be there'. They also claimed that the album contained postcards written in the same handwriting as the rising sun postcard which, they said, showed that the writer had been a 'regular associate' of Emily. The postcards they were referring to, however, were the three additional postcards published in the newspapers at the end of September which the police did not, in the end, maintain were written by Wood.

Hooke and Thomas appear to have believed that Wood was guilty, saying that Wood was 'the only possible suspect' once Shaw and Roberts had been eliminated, and they revealed some exclusive information that Marshall Hall, after initially believing him to be innocent, had changed his mind and told his daughter that he thought he had committed the murder after all. At the same time, however, they were the first writers to introduce a new suspect into the equation with their theory that George Stocks might have done it, based on his having gone back to sleep after the early morning alarm went off.

Five years later, in 1971, Gerald Sparrow's book, *Vintage Edwardian Murder*, contained a chapter on the Camden Town murder. For some reason, Sparrow believed that a diary kept by Emily had gone missing during the night of her murder, although no such thing was mentioned in any of the known evidence. He also thought that the police had found the rising sun postcard hidden away 'in one of Phyllis's suitcases' and, at the same time, had noticed a postcard album on the floor from which some postcards were 'missing'. However, the notion that any postcards were missing was no more than a theory of Inspector Neil on the basis that the album contained an unspecified number of 'spaces' in which he thought postcards might have been. In addition, Sparrow appears to be responsible for introducing a myth into the story that Emily's friends told police that one of Emily's regular clients was an 'artist or something' but there is no record of this in any of the police statements in the Metropolitan Police file in the National Archives nor was it stated in evidence during Wood's trial. On the contrary, Inspector Neil's report of 30 September stated that the man they were seeking had vanished and that 'no-one has yet been found who can divulge his name or calling'.

The chapter written by Sparrow is full of a number of odd inaccuracies. The witness McCowan was said to be a 'dust-cart man' (when he was in fact a carman seeking work as driver of a bread van), Charles Wood was described as Robert's half-brother and the trial apparently took place before Mr Justice McCardie.[566] Sparrow claimed that Robert Roberts had picked out Wood in an identification parade after having been given his description by May Campbell even though there was no evidence that Roberts even spoke to May Campbell before his identification of Wood. He also seemed to think that Marshall Hall put to Roberts 'a short note signed "Bert" making an appointment with Phyllis the day before the murder', apparently not realising that this 'note' was the (burnt) letter Roberts claimed to have been shown by Emily which Marshall Hall was denying the very existence of. Perhaps his best touch was to claim that, as Marshall Hall finished his closing speech, 'a fitful winter sun shone through the high windows of the Old Bailey and illuminated his features'. This is somewhat unlikely considering that Marshall Hall sat down at 4:15pm on 18 December 1907, twenty-five minutes after sunset, on a day for which sunshine was in any event recorded as 'nil'.[567]

Annie Wood was still alive when Sparrow's book was published and she survived into the 1980s, dying at the grand old age of 93 in August 1982. It was a pure coincidence that the Metropolitan Police file on the murder of Emily Dimmock was released to the Public Record Office in the following year.[568] Five years after Annie's death, the first entire book devoted exclusively to the Camden Town Murder, called, without frills, *The Camden Town Murder*, was published, although its author, Sir David Napley, did not consult the file in the Public Record Office. Napley was an experienced criminal barrister, but he, too, was confused by the practical effect of the Criminal Evidence Act of 1898, claiming that Wood was the first defendant to give evidence on his own behalf in a murder trial after the passing of the Act. It does not seem to have occurred to him how unlikely it was that in nine years not a single defendant tried with murder had entered the witness box.

In telling the story of the murder, Napley decided to dress it up as if he was writing a novel, requiring him to invent dialogue between the various characters and, where there were gaps in the evidence, reconstruct meetings and events which, he claimed, 'appear likely to have happened'. Consequently, one cannot take the book seriously as a considered analysis of the case. There are no footnotes and it is impossible for the reader to work out what is factual and what has been invented by Napley for dramatic purposes. At the same time, Napley was able to use the transcript from the *Notable British Trials* series and his basic facts of the case are, therefore, reasonably accurate. He even managed to refrain from repeating the false story of Ruby kissing Wood to identify him, tempting though this must have been to include in his semi-fictionalised account.

Napley, however, became seriously undone over the issue of the time of death. Believing Dr Thompson's view to have been that Emily had been dead seven or eight hours when he saw the body shortly after 1:00pm on the Thursday, thus resulting in a time of death of between 5:00am and 6:00am, Napley thought it was 'odd' that Marshall Hall kept repeating that Emily had died between three and four o'clock in the morning. However, while it was true that Dr Thompson had initially indicated that death occurred between five and six in the morning, it will be recalled that he later qualified this at the inquest by estimating a time of death of about 3:00am, based on an examination of Emily's stomach contents and a guess at the time she ate her last meal, before settling, at trial, on no more than nine hours before he saw her, which gave a time of death of not earlier than 4:00am. In view of the conflicting evidence by this witness in different courts, it was perfectly reasonable for Marshall Hall to latch onto the time he did but Napley commented at one point that 'Marshall Hall seems, incredibly enough, to have got the wrong time of death' without pausing to consider whether it was even remotely likely in such an important murder case, with three junior barristers and Arthur Newton (not to mention Wellesley Orr) assisting him, that Marshall Hall would make such a basic error regarding the crucial issue of time of death.

Like others before him, Napley was unable to decide if Wood was guilty of the murder. In one paragraph, he wrote that the murder trial settled 'the innocence of Wood' and then asked, 'Did this trial effectively settle Wood's innocence for all time?' leaving the question unanswered. One thing he felt sure of was that Wood was the man who approached Marshall Hall outside the assize court some years after the trial. He thus wrote that Marshall Hall looked at the man's 'deep sunken eyes and the long artistic fingers'. Marjoribanks, who was the original source of this story, had only written that the man had 'very deep set eyes' and had said nothing about his fingers being artistic or otherwise. It is an interesting example of how a myth gets built up over time as others elaborate on an already elaborate story.

Another writer on the case, Roy Harley Lewis, who also did not consult the file in the Public Record Office for his chapter entitled 'The Role of the Defence' in his 1989 book, *Edwardian Murders*, appears to have been wholly reliant on Marjoribanks for his facts, although he refers to the victim as 'Emily Jane Dimmock' (whereas Marjoribanks did not state her middle name). According to Lewis, the implication of the supposed fact that the murderer was searching for something in Emily's postcard album was 'not lost on the police' which is amusing in its irony considering that the police do not appear to have considered anything about the album as relevant to the case (as opposed to some of the postcards found inside it) until after the rising sun postcard had been found and possibly even until after Wood's arrest. Of course, the belief that the murderer was searching for a postcard is likely to lead one to the conclusion that Wood was guilty and Lewis's assessment was, indeed, that, apart from Wood, there were no other credible suspects. He also fell into the trap created by Marjoribanks of believing that the description of the suspect Roberts provided to the police came from May Campbell when this does not appear to have been possible.

In addition to Lewis' book, the year 1989 also produced a dramatization of the Camden Town Murder case in an episode of *Shadow of the Noose*, a television series starring Jonathan Hyde as Edward Marshall Hall, broadcast on BBC2 on 12 April, in which the Scottish actor, Peter Capaldi, played Robert Wood. The scriptwriter, Richard Cooper, was evidently seduced by the concept of the 'Judas kiss' as Ruby Young was shown kissing Wood in a park in order to identify him to the waiting Inspector Neil so that he could be arrested. During the portrayal of the trial, Wood stood silent in the dock while Marshall Hall asked him three times if he killed Emily Dimmock before finally saying, 'It's ridiculous'. The big twist at the end of programme involved Marshall Hall, having successfully ensured Wood's acquittal, being hit by a sudden flash of realisation as he was leaving the Old Bailey with Wellesley Orr that Dr Thompson had been mistaken as to the time of death and that Emily was murdered well before midnight, meaning that Wood had no alibi and had probably killed Emily after all. The general concept that Emily could have been murdered before midnight was sound enough but the fictional Marshall Hall's reasoning was flawed – he thought Dr Thompson's mistake was in failing to appreciate that it had been a very warm morning when he estimated the time of death from Emily's body temperature and that, adjusting for actual weather conditions, Emily must have been murdered many hours earlier than believed. In fact, Dr Thompson's evidence during the Old Bailey trial as to time of death, as in his written statement, was based on the condition of Emily's stomach and he did not mention the temperature of the body.

Despite the availability to researchers of the Metropolitan Police file, it was not until nineteen years after its release that the first writer made use of the material in the file with the publication in 2002 of crime novelist Patricia Cornwell's *Portrait Of A Killer*, ostensibly a work of non-fiction in the true crime genre, which is not primarily about the Camden Town murder but about the 'Jack the Ripper' murders of 1888. However, without any evidence, or even convincing argument, Cornwell believes that Emily Dimmock's killer was the same man as the much sought after killer and mutilator of prostitutes in Whitechapel nineteen years earlier whom she alleges to be the artist Walter Richard Sickert.

It is certainly true that Sickert was fascinated by the Camden Town murder and, in 1908, he commenced work on a number of paintings, known as the Camden Town Murder Series, which all depict an apparently murdered woman on a bed in a similar type of bedroom to the one Emily was found in. These were first exhibited in June 1911 at the Carfax Gallery in Piccadilly.[569] There is nothing in the paintings, however, to suggest that Sickert had any more knowledge of the murders than could be found in the newspapers and Emily's dead body was covered by the bedclothes when Shaw first saw it, which would thus be how the murderer had last seen it, something which does not feature in any of Sickert's paintings.

Sickert had already been linked to the Whitechapel murders in a 1973 BBC television series which featured his supposed illegitimate son, Joseph, who revealed a convoluted story he had been told by his 'father' as a child that the murders were committed by high ranking freemasons as part of an attempt to cover up a marriage between Prince Albert Edward (the Duke of Clarence) and a Catholic woman, Mary Jane Kelly, one of the Ripper victims. This was followed up in a 1975 book, based on the television series, by Elwyn Jones and John Lloyd entitled *The Ripper File* and then developed further in the following year by Stephen Knight, who named Sickert as one of three men involved in the murders, in his book *Jack The Ripper: The Final Solution*. Cornwell does not adopt the conspiracy theory, believing that Sickert's motive for murdering and mutilating prostitutes was sexual and/or psychological. Her novel approach to solving the crimes has been to attempt to forensically link Sickert to the letters written to the authorities, as well as to newspapers and others, claiming to be from the notorious murderer. Although hundreds of such letters survive, and are generally all believed to be hoaxes, Cornwell concludes that the majority of them were written by the murderer, namely Sickert. Her arguments on this score need not detain us but she dedicates a chapter to showing that Sickert also murdered Emily Dimmock. In doing so, she makes some quite remarkable errors of fact.

Cornwell opens her chapter by mis-identifying the *Rising Sun* as a public house at the corner of Tottenham Court Road and Windmill Street which is, and was in 1907, a different pub of the same name.[570] As a result, her comparison of a rising sun in a 1932 oil painting by Sickert with one etched in glass over the front door of the *Rising Sun* in Tottenham Court Road is misguided. Similarly, the fact that Sickert had studios in a street parallel to Tottenham Court Road and close to Windmill Street, as Cornwell reminds her readers, has less force than Cornwell seems to believe, although it was still only a relatively short walk from Tottenham Court Road to the correct *Rising Sun* in Euston Road. She thinks that Robert Wood gave the rising sun postcard to Emily in the *Rising Sun* on Friday 6 September when the postmark proves that he posted it to her three days later. Having evidently not read any newspaper accounts of the proceedings in the police court, Cornwell wrongly states that handwriting comparisons were 'never made' in the case, so that we have to rely on the evidence of Roberts that the rising sun postcard and the document of which fragments found in the fire had been written by the same person. As we have seen, however, Charles Ainsworth Mitchell gave expert evidence on the subject and, in any event, Wood admitted to having written both documents. Cornwell also claims that 'Bertie' was Wood's nickname, for which there is no evidence, and says that the fragments found in the fire were of 'a postcard' although this was never claimed by either Roberts or Wood himself. More importantly, she says that Wood was 'befuddled' by the fact that the handwriting on the fragments was a 'good imitation' of his, seemingly unaware that Wood admitted in the witness box that it was indeed his handwriting. In the context of her claim that the handwriting was never analysed by an expert, Cornwell appears to leave open the possibility that Sickert had written the letter of assignation to Emily (or 'postcard' according to Cornwell) asking her to meet him at the *Eagle*.

Cornwell's most embarrassing error, however, is in respect of a complete misunderstanding of a police report in the file in the National Archives relating to Harold Ashton's theory that the author of the four postcards reproduced in the national press at the end of September 1907 was a betting man. Cornwell devotes two pages to these postcards because she fails to appreciate that they were addressed to Emily (three of them being in her album) and thinks they were sent to the editor of the *Morning Leader*, possibly by the murderer himself, in the same fashion as the letters sent to newspapers during the period of the Ripper murders, albeit that these postcards were sent before any murder had been committed. Thus, in respect of the postcard dated 9 September, which Ashton believed had been posted from Doncaster during the week of the Doncaster races, Cornwell wonders if Sickert was supplying himself with an alibi in advance of the murder (not that this makes any sense). In fact, as we have seen, Ashton had misread the postmark; the postcard he thought had come from Doncaster was none other than the rising sun postcard which Wood had posted in London on 9 September and certainly had nothing to do with Walter Sickert.[571] Even more embarrassing is that Cornwell seems to think that the postcards were all signed 'A.C.C.' This misunderstanding is derived from a comment in the police report which states that Ashton 'produced photos of four postcards sent to the editor by ACC'. While this point does not advance her case against Sickert, and is thus of no real consequence, it is surprising that someone whose 'knowledge of criminal investigation' is promoted in the blurb on the cover of her book is apparently unaware that A.C.C. denotes the Assistant Commissioner of 'C' branch (Crime), and was a reference to the fact that the Assistant Commissioner at the C.I.D., Sir Melville Macnaghten, had sent photographic reproductions of the four postcards to the editor of the *Morning Leader* in order for them to be published in his newspaper as part of the police strategy to flush out the author.

As for the notion that Sickert was responsible for Emily's murder, there is no supporting evidence for this at all. Cornwell relies partly on the fact that Sickert had a flat in Mornington Crescent, a short walk from Camden Town, but this does no more than help to explain his interest in the crime from an artistic point of view. As it happens, there is a question mark over whether he was even in London when Emily was killed because he visited Dieppe in 'the autumn' of 1907 but the precise date of his departure is unknown.[572] Nevertheless, Cornwell has one more trick up her sleeve, having discovered in the *Evening Standard* of 29 November 1937 what she refers to as 'a short article' – although it was in fact a diary entry (prompted by a forthcoming exhibition of Sickert paintings at the Redfern Gallery) – which mentioned that Sickert was allowed to enter number 29 St Paul's Road and make 'several sketches' of Emily's body.[573] If this had been the case it would have been in breach of the Metropolitan Police's General Orders of 1907 which stated that an officer engaged on a murder investigation 'should take measures to exclude sightseers, or persons with no knowledge of the facts'.[574] Nevertheless, the idea leads Cornwell to wonder if Sickert, having committed the murder, deliberately locked the door of Emily's apartment because he knew that Bert Shaw returned home at 11:30 and wanted to ensure he was passing the house shortly after the body was discovered so that he could charm his way in to sketch the body *in situ* during the few hours before it was removed. She speculates that his true motive in doing this was not to make the sketches but to provide an explanation as to why his fingerprints might have been found in the apartment. While this theory at least has the merit of explaining why the door to Emily's flat was locked (even though it does not explain why the murderer locked the folding doors of Emily's bedroom, assuming that he did so) it seems very unlikely. As previously mentioned, the police in 1907 were only able to locate fingerprints at crime scenes that were visible to the naked eye and they did not, therefore, dust rooms for latent prints.[575] To the extent that they were going to use fingerprints to catch a murderer, they would have had to find them in blood, on the murder weapon or on a surface that only the murderer could have touched, something which Sickert could not have explained away by simply having been present in the flat to do some drawings. His fingerprints would certainly not have been on the relatively small police index at Scotland Yard and the idea that he would have returned to the crime scene in case his prints were found somewhere in Emily's flat is somewhat fantastical. His appearance at the crime scene could only have had the effect of drawing attention to him at a time when no-one suspected his involvement at all. If, by an absolute miracle of detection, his prints had been found somewhere in the room, he would only have had to admit to being a client of Emily's (or he could even have said he visited her to paint her) and no-one would have been able to prove otherwise. In any event, there is no reason to believe that the unsourced story in the *Evening Standard*, some thirty years after the murder, was anything more than a myth derived from the fact that Sickert created paintings of what were supposed to be Emily's dead body. A similarly dubious sounding story says that Sickert used Wood as a model for his Camden Town paintings, some of which include a male figure sitting or standing next to a naked (dead) woman, and at least this has a source – art collector Rex Nan Kivell claims that he was told this by Sickert himself – but, knowing of Wood's evident desire to put the entire episode behind him, the tale is also unlikely to be true.[576]

Like Cornwell, John Barber, whose *The Camden Town Murder* was published in 2007, also makes use of the file in the National Archives but Barber appears to have been pressed for time when he examined it and may not even have handled the actual file; he says that a friend sent him copies of relevant pages. In his book, he notes that Napley refers to a woman called Gladys Warren as a landlady of Emily's and, claiming that her name appears nowhere else, wonders if she was one of Napley's fictional creations. Yet, apart from being mentioned in many newspaper accounts of the case, Gladys Warren features in one of Inspector Neil's reports in which he explains that she was also known as 'Gladys Lineham (sic)' (who Barber knew had lodged with Emily). Barber would also have known who Gladys Warren was had he consulted the *Notable British Trials* transcript in the British Library but he does not appear to have visited that particular institution nor does he seem to have made it to the British Newspaper Library. He was, perhaps, disadvantaged by the fact that the printed shorthand notes of proceedings of the Central Criminal Court were not placed online until 2008 but the hard copy volumes were available in the National Archives under the CRIM 10 series. Barber also says that he could find no trace of McCowan being paid out of the police informant fund when a document in the file in the National Archives shows that he was paid a reward of £10 from the informant fund, albeit that this was after the trial.

Apart from the file in the National Archives, Barber's account of the murder is essentially based on information gleaned from Marjoribanks and Napley, a selection of random press cuttings and a few other bits and pieces, including some correspondence with surviving members of Bert Shaw's family. Ironically, despite revealing that the Shaw family always believed there was a cloud hanging over their head because no-one was convicted of the murder (and thus Shaw could have done it), Barber re-opened the case against Bert Shaw based on a tip-off from his local fishmonger who told him that it was common for shift workers to sign a colleague on if their mate wanted a night off. On that basis, Shaw need not have been in Sheffield on the night of the murder. At this stage, Barber had not yet read the shorthand notes of the trial proceedings and was unaware that the police had a witness who had seen Shaw in Sheffield. When he became aware of this he ruled out Shaw in a subsequent edition.

As for the facts of the case, Barber avoids the trap of claiming that Ruby identified Wood to Inspector Neil with a kiss but falls down on the crime scene by claiming that Emily's postcard collection was in 'albums' which had been scattered around the living room. Until reading the shorthand note of the proceedings online, Barber also believed that Crabtree identified 'Scotch Bob' as his suspect and suspected that Alexander Mackie was another figment of David Napley's imagination. He thinks that a total of four postcards were found by the police in Wood's handwriting, not realising that, after examination by a handwriting expert, the police had come to the conclusion that Wood only wrote the rising sun postcard.

Despite this and a number of similar errors, Barber feels able to conclude that a modern court would find Wood guilty of the murder because he was the only person with the opportunity, time, weapon, method and motive, although in what respect Wood was the only person with access to a weapon is unclear. His thinking appears to be that a modern court, with more knowledge of how difficult it is to accurately estimate time of death, would appreciate that Emily could have been murdered before midnight, which would negate Wood's alibi, but such a court would presumably still require some kind of proof that Wood ever set foot in 29 St Paul's Road and McCowan's identification evidence would surely be as unconvincing today as it was in 1907, if it was even allowed to be put to a jury. With Emily being a prostitute, any number of men could have had the time and opportunity to murder her if she parted from Wood at 10:00pm (or 11:00pm) and spent the rest of the evening soliciting, while the fact that she was known to have transmitted venereal disease to a number of unfortunate clients could have provided the motive, not to mention the way she seemed to play her men off against each other. It is not clear what Barber means by 'method' but if Wood had it then so could anyone.

Before leaving Barber, we may note that he too repeats the myth that Wood was the first prisoner to escape the gallows having given evidence in his own defence. To be fair, he was not the only writer since Hogarth to make this mistake (aside from Napley who, as we have seen, thought Wood was the first accused murderer to have actually given evidence in his own defence). The same claim can be found in, amongst other works, the 1956 book, *Aspects of Murder*, by Thomas Curtis Hicks Jacobs; a 1957 book by William Bixley, who had worked for fifty years as an official at the Old Bailey; the previously discussed 1989 book, *Edwardian Murders* by Roy Harley Lewis; a chapter by Leonard Gribble entitled *In and Out of the Eagle* published in *Still Unsolved* in 1990; a chapter by Jonathan Goodman entitled *Robert and Ruby* in his 1992 book, *Masterpieces of Murder*; a July 1993 article in *True Crime Detective Monthly* entitled 'Camden Town's Mystery of the Rising Sun' and Geoffrey Howse's 2007 book, *The A to Z of London Murders*. It is an extremely persistent myth and without doubt the most common mistake made by writers about the case.

Of the above works, it is worthy of comment that Jacobs distinguished himself in *Aspects of Murder* by claiming that Ruby Young's trouble was 'that she couldn't keep a secret' because 'she was a woman'. He was apparently under the impression that Ruby had told her secret to a female friend in confidence who then told a journalist. As we have seen, however, the truth was not that Ruby let slip the secret due to some kind of compulsive feminine need to gossip but rather that she needed help and advice because of her own precarious legal position caused by Wood's lies. Goodman's chapter in *Masterpieces of Murder* opens with the astonishing assertion that no-one would deny that Wood 'certainly deserved to be hanged' for the murder of Emily Dimmock, regardless of whether he was innocent or guilty. His reason for saying this is not explained at any point although he appears to have believed that Wood was guilty on the highly dubious basis that it was impossible to explain McCowan's identification of him by his walk other than that he actually saw him walking along St Paul's Road in the early hours of the morning of 12 September.

At about the same time as Barber was working on his book, crime writer Jonathan Oates had been examining the file in the National Archives for a chapter on the Dimmock murder in his 2007 book entitled *Unsolved Murders in Victorian & Edwardian London*. His chapter is called 'Did Robert Wood kill Phyllis Dimmock?' and he concludes that he probably did not, mainly on the basis that, had Wood been the murderer, he would have known that the murder was committed in the early hours of 12 September whereas Wood's alibi did not extend past midnight of 11 September: something that would have been a good point were it not for the fact that the murder might have been committed before midnight. His chapter does not get off to a very good start because he says in the first paragraph that Bert Shaw let himself into his lodgings with his latch key, found his bedroom door locked and broke it down, only to find that the chest of drawers had been ransacked, before pulling back the bedclothes and seeing Emily's dead body. The fact that he omits to mention that the locked door to his front room was opened by a key provided by his landlady might be explained by some ruthless editing to keep the story succinct but it does not excuse the mis-location of the chest of drawers which was in the front room, not the bedroom. Things don't get much better in the second paragraph in which Emily is said to have been born in Walworth despite Inspector Neil having done the investigative work and established she was born in Standon, as can be found in one of his reports in the file in the National Archives.

The most questionable statement in Oates' chapter, however, is his claim that some postcards had been 'removed' from Emily's album, 'probably recently and probably by the killer, in order to remove evidence which might incriminate him'. There is no solid evidence that any postcards had been removed from the album and it was not until after Wood's arrest that any mention can be found in the police file of anything unusual in connection with the album, despite the fact that Inspector Neil referred to it in his report of 30 September to say (mistakenly) that the album contained three postcards in the same handwriting as the rising sun postcard. On 8 October, the album was mentioned again in a report by Neil but only to say that it was not in its usual location and had apparently been 'searched through'. It was not until 21 October that Detective Page, who arrived with Inspector Neil at the crime scene more than three hours after Emily's body was found, filed a report (which has not survived) to say that he recalled some four or five postcards being scattered on the floor. This evidence was repeated by Inspector Neil at the police court on 13 November when he said that the album was 'open about halfway and several cards were lying on the floor. There was also one or two loose postcards lying on the page that was open'.[577] It is true that, at the inquest, Neil gave as his opinion that some postcards might have been 'taken out', and he then expanded on this at the police court by referring to 'spaces' in the album which suggested to him that some postcards were missing, but if, as Sergeant Ball recalled, postcards were scattered on the floor, it is hard to see why these were not the ones which had filled the spaces. However, in the misguided belief that some postcards were definitely removed, Oates concludes that Emily's murderer was probably a man she had known for some time who had sent her postcards which he removed after killing her, presumably to protect his identity.

It then gets worse because Oates swallows the story told by May Campbell (whom he refers to as 'Mary Campbell') about Emily having received a letter from a man asking her to meet him at Camden Town Railway Station on the evening of 11 September and he believes that *this* man must have been the murderer. He points out that this letter could not have been the communication Wood sent her because the meeting place in that one was the *Eagle*. It is undoubtedly easy to be seduced by May Campbell's story and to conclude there was a second letter, so it is worth reminding ourselves what May told the police. In her first statement, she said that she met Emily at 9:30pm on Tuesday 10 September (the day before the murder) and Emily said that she had to meet a gentleman friend in the *Rising Sun* at about 11:30pm that night but she could not make that meeting because she had arranged to meet another man at Camden Town Station. May then said that she met Emily again the next evening at 7:00pm and, confusingly, Emily was pressed for time because she was off to meet the man she was supposed to have met the previous night. She told May that this man was Tom, otherwise known as 'Scotch Bob'. We then have to forget about all of that because the story changed in her second statement. May still met Emily on the Tuesday evening – now at 9:15pm – but this time she told her she was on her way to the *Rising Sun* to meet a sailor who had been staying with her for the past 'three nights'. This is problematic because the sailor (Roberts) had only stayed with her for two nights at the time – the Tuesday night was to be his third night. Anyway, Emily did not mention 'Scotch Bob' but told May that she had received a postcard which worried her. When May met Emily again the next day – this time at about 4:00pm – in Camden Town High Street, she told her she had to meet Tom, a.k.a. 'Scotch Bob' at 9:45pm that evening at Camden Town Station. This is where it starts to get seductive because one can easily conceive, as did Oates, that Emily had made a second appointment for the same night and went off to meet Tom after parting from Wood in the *Eagle* (which was located directly opposite the station). It clearly was not Wood to whom she was referring because she told May that she had got Tom locked up for six months and he had only been out of prison for ten days.

Superficially, therefore, it seems plausible that there was indeed a second letter and a second meeting with a man that night. Except that May then went on to state that Emily told her on the Wednesday that she had received the letter arranging the meeting with Tom that morning and that 'Her friend the sailor was with her and…she showed him part of the letter and then burnt it'. This can only have been the letter arranging a meeting at the *Eagle* because it was the only letter read by Roberts. Suddenly the idea that Emily received two letters (or one letter and a postcard), arranging separate meetings, from two different men on the day of her murder, starts to fall apart. When we then throw into the mix the fact that Alex Mackie, by his own admission, was known to Emily as 'Scotch Bob' (albeit never confirmed as the man May Campbell knew by this name), the unreliability of May Campbell's evidence is clear because Mackie was confirmed as being in Scotland during at least the first half of September 1907.

We can imagine that May Campbell might have spoken to Emily at some time (perhaps on the Tuesday as she first told police) about some correspondence Emily had received requesting a meeting at Camden Town Station and then, when she later spoke to Roberts at Emily's funeral, she wrongly assumed that this must have been the same letter as the one he had seen when he was with Emily on the Wednesday morning. Perhaps the man Emily referred to as 'Tom' was actually 'Scottie' and May became confused, thinking this was also 'Scotch Bob'. It is a shame that May was not questioned in any detail about her supposed conversation with Emily but we have to take into account the fact that Inspector Neil believed she was making it all up, as did Sir Charles Mathews, and she certainly had a conversation with Roberts at Emily's funeral so this would explain how she knew certain things about Emily's life. She was obviously weaving facts obtained from Roberts into her story, something she gave away by claiming that Emily had told her that a sailor had stayed with her for three nights when she would have said it was two nights had a conversation about this really taken place on the Tuesday. While some of May Campbell's evidence might have had some basis in fact, we certainly cannot state as a fact, as Oates does, that Emily had two meetings lined up on the Wednesday night.

Following all the interest in the case generated by the one hundredth anniversary of the crime, there was yet another writer who was examining the file in the National Archives. This was Aidan Lawes, then the Academic Publications Manager at the National Archives, and his analysis of the file was published in the December 2008 issue of the now defunct genealogical publication, *Ancestors*. Perhaps the most interesting element in the article is that Lawes attempted to discover the identity of Ruby Young from the 1901 census. He found a Ruby Gladys Young of about the right age (then fifteen years old) who was living with her mother in Croydon. Observing that her mother, Lily, was a dressmaker, who recorded her place of birth as 'Do not know', Lawes wondered if 'family antecedents may have played a role' in Ruby becoming a prostitute.

Further investigation reveals that Lily Young was the daughter of Peter William Campbell Harvey, born in Cornwall in 1797, who had married Mary

Ann Luck in Whitechapel in December 1818 but she died less than two years later at the age of 25. Seven years after Mary Ann's death, Harvey married Jane Jones in Bermondsey but, despite being a Customs officer on a very decent annual salary of £200, he found himself in financial difficulty in 1834 and, as an insolvent debtor, was locked up in Marshalsea Prison before being released in 1838, although bankruptcy proceedings against him rumbled on into the 1840s.[578] The 1841 census shows that Harvey was living with Jane in Camberwell. At some point during the next ten years, Jane died and Harvey married for a third time, to Elizabeth Jones in 1852. If Lily's age was given correctly in the 1901 census then she was born in about 1856, presumably the daughter of Peter and Elizabeth. In 1862, Harvey died of pneumonia in Peckham at the age of 65 leaving effects of less than £20 in his will. What happened next to the six-year-old Lily is not known but there is an intriguing entry in the 1871 census which has a 19-year-old barmaid called Lily Harvey living on her own in a boarding house in St Pancras. If she was born in 1856 she should have been about 15 years old in 1871 but it was not uncommon for people to lie about their age to the census takers. If this Lily Harvey was Ruby Young's mother then it provides a connection with St Pancras, which could explain why Ruby ended up living there. However, the identity of this Lily Harvey is too uncertain to draw any positive conclusions.

What we do know is that Lily Harvey was living in Peckham in August 1872 when she married a mercantile clerk called Arthur Woodfield Young in Camberwell. It is only because she stated on the marriage certificate that her father was Peter William Campbell Harvey that we know anything about her parentage. The following year, Arthur and Lily, who were living in Peckham, gave birth to their first child, Ethel. At this time, Arthur, whose father had been a glass dealer, was a clerk employed by a plate glass company and subsequently became a commercial traveller in the glass trade; this is his occupation given in the 1881 census when he and his family were still living in Peckham. A son, Cecil, was born in late 1882 and their second daughter, Ruby, was born on 12 April 1885.

Ruby's life story took a dramatic twist in March 1895 when she was just nine years old. The Young family was living in Croydon at this time and Arthur, then aged 39, left home for work as normal during the morning of Thursday 28 February. At six o'clock in the evening he sent a telegram to his wife from Cannon Street saying that he would not be home that night but would write to her again the next day. In fact, nothing more was heard from him until Saturday morning when Lily received a parcel containing his watch, chain and ring. Later the same day, the post brought a letter with a Lewisham postmark in which Arthur told her, 'I have for some years past been in a very peculiar state, at times not knowing what I have been doing' and he reminded her of some previous insanity in his family.[579] He told her that by the time she received the letter he would be 'out of this world' and there would be no clues on his body for anyone to be able work out his identity, which he believed would save her an enormous amount of trouble. He asked her to kiss 'the two little ones' and hoped they would soon forget him and bade her farewell. Lily went straight to the police who prepared to institute a search but a pedlar found Arthur's body lying in a field by the side of the road between Ham and Petersham in Surrey on the Sunday morning. An inquest established that Arthur had taken oxalic acid and a verdict of 'suicide whilst temporarily insane' was recorded.

The effect on little Ruby of her father's suicide can only be imagined and, no doubt, there must have been discussion within the family as to what Arthur was referring to in his letter which caused him to take such a drastic step. At any rate, this explains why Ruby was without a father at the time of the 1901 census and, had Aidan Lawes been aware of the full circumstances of Ruby's life, he would probably have been much more confident that this was the Ruby Young who would go on to become a prostitute and meet Robert Wood in the Euston Road, especially if he had known that Ruby revealed in her January 1908 letter to *Reynolds's Newspaper* that she had a stepfather, suggesting that her natural father was dead.

But *is* this our Ruby Young? The main problem in answering this is that we know so little about her; we don't even know how old she was at the time of the trial although she looks from photographs to be in her early to mid-twenties. We do know that she was convicted of soliciting at Marlborough Street Police Court at some point before October 1907 but the pre-1908 records of this court, which would have stated her age, have not survived. We know from Wood's post-trial articles that she was a good rower, and once rowed from Southsea to the Isle of Wight and back, but that does not assist us in establishing her identity. More helpfully, Wood revealed that she had once been a hospital nurse in Liverpool. He also said that she was, at some stage, estranged from her mother, whom he had tried to find on Ruby's behalf. The best clue, however, was provided by Ruby herself in her 1908 letter in which she said that her stepfather 'died last week and was buried on Saturday'. Her letter was dated Thursday, 9 January 1908 so her stepfather must have died in the week commencing 30 December 1907 and been buried on Saturday, 4 January 1908. The problem with using this information to locate Ruby's stepfather, however, is that we don't know his surname. Assuming that Ruby was born with the surname of 'Young', her stepfather's surname was presumably different and so it could be almost any man who was buried on 4 January. There are two additional clues that Ruby provided. During the trial she was asked by the judge where her mother was living at the time Wood was trying to persuade her to give him a false alibi and she said 'King's Cross'. If that was the case, then there is a reasonable chance that her stepfather was also living in King's Cross and died there. The second clue was that Ruby told a newspaper reporter at the Old Bailey on 18 December, 'Like Wood, I have an old father, and I also have a mother, but I have lost all – home, father, mother and everything'.[580] Presumably when speaking about her 'old father', Ruby was referring to her stepfather who was about two weeks away from his death so that we can conclude he was an old man. There is a finite number of elderly men who were buried at the St Pancras and Islington Cemeteries (where we might expect someone who died in King's Cross to be buried) on 4 January 1908 but an initial search of the records has not identified anyone married to a woman with a surname of 'Young' although it is not always possible to confirm this type of information and he may well be hidden in the records.

The real problem with these clues, however, is that none of them seem to fit the Ruby Young from Peckham. We know from the 1901 census that Lily Young, then described as a widow, was living with her two youngest children, Cecil and Ruby, at 46 Beulah Road, Croydon. According to the Croydon Directory, she was still living at that address during the years 1902 to 1909 but there is no mention of any husband. Nor, according to the electoral register for Croydon, is there mention of any males other than Cecil living at 46 Beluah Road during the period. So there is nothing to indicate that Lily Young re-married – her surname appears to have remained unchanged – or lived anywhere other than Croydon during the relevant period. As for Ruby, at the age of 34, on 24 April 1919, she married a 53-year-old widower and wool merchant called James Smith and she died in East Sussex of a cerebral haemorrhage in 1950. Curiously, she married under the name 'Ruby Gladys Yvonne Young' even though her birth certificate confirms that her name was 'Ruby Gladys Young'. Why or when she decided to add 'Yvonne' to her name is anyone's guess. A comparison of Ruby's original signature on her marriage certificate which is held at St Alban's church in South Norwood with her signature on her statement in the file in the National Archives, and letter to *Reynolds's Newspaper,* is inconclusive but, even allowing for the passing of more than ten years, suggests they are probably not the same person. The famous Ruby Young had a very distinctive way in 1907/08 of rounding the letter 'R' at the start of her name which is not replicated in the Peckham Ruby's signature on her 1919 marriage certificate.[581] However, it seems that the ink in the pen was not flowing and Ruby needed to emphasise the 'R' at the start of her name which might have affected her signature. The formation of the capital letter 'Y' in her surname is also obviously different. The 'g' at the end of her name resembles a 'y' in 1907/08 but in the 1919 marriage certificate it is fully rounded. At the same time, both Ruby Youngs add a full stop, or dot, after their signature which is interesting, but by no means unique. In the Metropolitan Police file in the National Archives alone we can find another example of this; Gladys Linehan did the same thing.

If the Ruby Young from Peckham is not our Ruby, are there any more possibilities? Using the clue provided by Wood that Ruby had worked in Liverpool, we do find a Ruby Lilian Young born in Liverpool on 28 December 1889, the daughter of John Victor Young, a Licensed Victualler from Wales, and his wife, Esther. Ruby and the rest of the Young family can be found in the 1901 census when John was the licensee at the Stanley Arms Hotel in Bootle (and is described as 'dumb' in the census) but the entire family, which included five children in addition to Ruby, emigrated to New York in June 1907 and so this Ruby can be ruled out. She was too young anyway and was only seventeen in 1907.

There was also no indication in 1907 that Ruby Young had a middle name. Although it is not entirely reliable, most witnesses at the 1907 trial are listed by their full names, including middle names, in both the *Notable British Trials* transcript and the official shorthand record but in neither of them is Ruby stated to have a middle name. The name 'Ruby Young' was, perhaps surprisingly, not a very common one in England in the 1870s or 1880s, when one would

Ruby Young's signature on her witness statement of 5 October 1907 (National Archives)

Signature of Ruby Gladys Young on her wedding certificate of 24 April 1919 have expected her to have been born, and there are not too many potential candidates. All others can be eliminated, either from having been found to have been married before 1907 or because their father was still alive when the 1911 census was taken.[582] It may be, therefore, that Ruby was born abroad or perhaps even that 'Ruby' was not the name on her birth certificate but was a name she adopted from an early age. It does not appear to have been a 'working name' because this was how she was known to Wood. It may be noted that she believed that it was the news of her conviction for soliciting at Marlborough Street Police Court that killed her stepfather which adds weight to the suggestion that 'Ruby Young' was her real name, although her photograph had been published in the newspapers by this time so her stepfather might have identified her in this way.

She might have been born as 'Robina Young', with Ruby being short for Robina, and there were a large number of Robina Youngs in the correct age range, mainly born in Scotland. One of these, born in Perth in 1886, was living with her uncle in Liverpool in 1891 but she then returned to her family in Perth and her father, John Young, was still alive and living with her mother at the time of the 1911 census. Another Robina Young, who definitely called herself 'Ruby Young', emigrated to Canada in April 1912 and would be good candidate were it not for the fact that her father was still alive, still married to her mother, and died only after she left the country.[583]

There are two additional stories told about Ruby in the secondary literature which are of dubious origin. The first is that she had been seduced by a medical man before she met Wood. This comes originally from Marjoribanks, who had access to Marshall Hall's papers, and is not beyond the bounds of possibility considering that, as Marjoribanks knew, she used to be a nurse and Wood's defence team would probably have been aware of unpublished facts about her; but no actual source of the information has ever been provided. The story certainly appears to have been embellished by Gerald Sparrow who wrote in 1971 that Ruby had been seduced by 'a married doctor' which, he said, accounted for the fact that her family had disowned her and he even provided a supposed quote by one of her parents, namely, 'never darken my doors again'. As we know, Ruby was estranged from her parents and this might have been the reason for it but the suspicion is that Sparrow was speculating. The second story, told for example by Barber, is that Ruby emigrated after the trial. Again, this may be true but, in her 1908 letter to *Reynolds's Newspaper*, she said that she had spent more than four pounds of the reward money she had received from the police on a suite of furniture and a further thirty-two shillings for a single bed. This does not sound like the purchasing actions of someone planning to leave the country any time soon.[584]

The most recent treatment of the Dimmock case is to be found in a 2012 book by Claire Welch called *Unsolved Crimes*, dealing with a large number of murders, said to be 'from the case files of the *People* and the *Daily Mirror*' although, in the Dimmock case at least, this appears to be no more than another way of saying that the information is taken from articles published in those two newspapers. Based on such limited sources, the book presents the opportunity for Ms Welch to introduce some brand new errors into the story; although she kicks off with a very old one, claiming, as is traditional, that the Wood trial was a 'landmark case in legal history' because Wood was the 'first accused man to give evidence on his own behalf following the Criminal Justice Bill (1905)'. This at least has the virtue of having a sensible time frame of two years but there was no Criminal Justice Bill in England and Wales in 1905 and Ms Welch appears to be unaware that a Bill has no statutory force until it becomes an Act of Parliament. As to the date, she might have been misled by a claim in John Richardson's 2007 *The Camden Town Book* in which it is stated that Wood was the first defendant in a murder trial to defend himself in the witness box 'since the Criminal Justice Act of 1905'. It was, of course, the Criminal Evidence Act of 1898 that allowed an accused person to give evidence on their own behalf.

We can deal quickly with the new mistakes in the chapter. Firstly, it is said that 'odd cuts' were found on Emily's knees but Dr Thompson made no mention of any such thing. Secondly, that the letter inviting Emily to the *Eagle* on the night of her murder was 'reportedly from Bert Shaw', although this was only a line of questioning put to Roberts by Marshall Hall. Thirdly, that while the handwriting on the letter proved to be 'similar' to Wood's, the charred fragments 'would ultimately prove indecipherable to the police', Welch apparently being unaware that Wood admitted it was indeed his handwriting on the fragments. Fourthly, that Mrs Shaw was 'less than pleased' about her son's involvement with a prostitute and the visit was 'not a social one' but, in fact, relations between Mrs Shaw and Emily were very good and Mrs Shaw had been invited down to London by her supposed daughter-in-law. Fifthly, Mrs Stocks is referred to as a 'neighbour' rather than the landlady. Sixthly, that Emily's postcard collection had been 'wrecked'. Seventhly, that newspaper reports two days after the murder 'confirmed' that a bloodstained man's handkerchief with a laundry mark had been retrieved from the crime scene along with a crumpled letter found under the bed; while it is true that such things were initially reported they turned out to be false rumours. Eighthly, that bloodstained fingerprints were found at the scene of crime; it is again true that this was reported but Welch was clearly unaware that the reports were wrong because she goes on to say that fingerprinting was in its early stages and it was 'far too soon to use the process'. Evidently, Welch was confused as to why the discovery of the fingerprints did not lead to a conviction (or an instant acquittal of Wood) and concluded that the police at the time must have been unable to identify an individual based on fingerprints when, in fact, they were perfectly able to use them, if only they could find them – which, in this case, they could not. Finally, she says that the rising sun postcard was circulated by Scotland Yard to newspapers at the *Daily Mirror*'s suggestion when this was not claimed by the newspaper at the time and appears to be a misinterpretation of the rather self-important claim in its 28 September 1907 edition that 'The police are anxious to trace the writer [of the rising sun postcard], and the *Daily Mirror* has been called in to help towards this end'.

In any analysis of the Dimmock investigation, which is already complicated enough, the last thing the world needs is more errors to be introduced into the mix and hopefully this book will prevent some of the more persistent ones from being repeated.

George Wood
after the conclusion of the trial

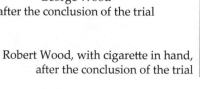

Robert Wood, with cigarette in hand,
after the conclusion of the trial

'Lady Diablo of Monte Carlo'
by Robert Wood, 1907

Robert Wood (left) with his brother
Charles Carlyle Wood, in 1952

Chapter Nineteen

Some Final Conclusions

From Inspector Neil's perspective, the overriding priority from day one was to find the man seen by Roberts with Emily in the *Rising Sun*. Within twenty-four hours of the discovery of the murder, the fragments in the fireplace appeared to confirm Roberts' story that this man had arranged a meeting with Emily in the *Eagle* on the night of her murder. The inspector must have been reasonably sure that this man was the murderer, which was probably why he felt he could safely rule out robbery as the motive. When he said in his report of 13 September that he was satisfied robbery was not the primary object of the crime he did not mention the three rings left in the drawers, which suggests that his thinking was influenced more by what Roberts had told him. He might also have been influenced by the fact that Emily had curling pins in her hair and was apparently murdered in her sleep (indicating someone well known to her), although the curling pins were not mentioned in any police document until 30 September. It took Neil some time to mention the traces of a late night meal for two in Emily's apartment but this also presumably influenced his thinking. He also clearly believed he was dealing with a murder by a man who knew Emily well and of whom Emily was afraid. The absolute focus of his investigation was to find this man. As we have seen, any suspect who did not match the description of the man seen with Emily in the *Rising Sun* on the Monday night before her murder, or who was not positively identified as that man, was eliminated from the inquiry, albeit that his alibi was usually checked first. The inspector must have expected that once the man he was seeking was found all the pieces of the puzzle would fall into place. He presumably thought he would be a known villain, holding a grudge against Emily, probably having caught venereal disease from her and would be someone like 'Scottie' who had previously threatened Emily, so that a conviction would be a fairly straightforward matter. Gathering additional evidence was not the priority. Finding the man was.

Unless Detective Sergeant Milton was lying on oath in the witness box during the trial, it seems that Roberts told police about the rising sun postcard when questioned immediately after the murder because Milton said that he had specifically been instructed to search the chest of drawers for it on the day after the murder. One can only assume that Inspector Neil did not think it was worth recording anything about the postcard in writing because Roberts had told him it was signed 'Alice' and, in the absence of the postcard itself, its existence and relevance to the case was too uncertain to mention. It is nevertheless strange that, knowing there was a missing postcard, nothing was mentioned during the whole time before Wood's arrest about any theory that the murderer had searched the postcard album. The obvious conclusion from this is that the question of whether the murderer had searched through the postcard album was not believed to be important by the police in the days following the murder. Neither the position it was found nor the fact that there were any postcards scattered on the floor was recorded by the police nor did Bert Shaw mention either of these points in his statement. Even after Shaw had located the postcard, which was seen to be in the same handwriting as the writing on the fragments found in the fire, Inspector Neil did not think it sufficiently important to record anything about the album in his long report to his superiors at the end of September.

It was only after Wood had been identified and arrested (on 4 October) that we find the first mention of the album having apparently been searched through by the murderer, i.e. in Inspector Neil's report of 8 October. By this time, the inspector might have been surprised to discover that Wood came from a respectable family and that he had no history of violence or threats of violence against women in general or Emily in particular, but all his suspicions that he was the guilty man must have been confirmed as soon as Wood lied to him about his whereabouts on the night of the murder. The false alibi was exposed immediately thanks to Ruby Young's assistance and, from that point on, the inspector probably viewed the available evidence in a new light. Now believing that Wood was definitely the murderer, his thought process must have been that, as Wood had written the rising sun postcard to Emily (as he admitted), and this postcard had been hidden in the chest of drawers, Wood simply must have been searching the room for that very postcard. Inspector Neil was not the type of officer to fabricate evidence so he must genuinely have believed that the album was on the chair and that postcards were scattered on the floor. However, not only would he have been relying on his memory but, as already discussed, it is possible that the album had been moved before his arrival at the crime scene. A small point which had not even been worthy of mention before Wood's arrest suddenly took on a new meaning.

Something similar happened with McCowan's evidence, albeit to a lesser extent. Prior to Wood's arrest, it is clear that Inspector Neil took McCowan's sighting seriously because he noted in his 30 September report that McCowan was a 'respectable workman' who was convinced that he had seen the murderer coming from 29 St Paul's Road. However, Neil also recorded that he had been unable to corroborate McCowan's evidence and, perhaps most importantly, McCowan did not attend an identification parade until three days after Wood's arrest, along with Lilian Raven and May Campbell. Although Lilian Raven was to become an important witness, her evidence at this stage was that she had not seen Emily in the *Eagle* (and she failed to identify Wood) while May Campbell's evidence had not convinced Inspector Neil; so it seems that McCowan was regarded as one of the less important witnesses at this stage. Indeed, having been identified by Roberts, Clarke and Crabtree, Wood had already been charged with Emily's murder. Had McCowan said that the man he saw in St Paul's Road was not Wood, his evidence would inevitably have been disregarded by the police, although, at the same time, they would have had considerably more difficulty in making a convincing case against their prisoner and he might even have been released on bail by Mr Bros. As it was, McCowan's evidence became so compelling to Inspector Neil that he did not appear to notice that Wood had only given himself an alibi lasting to about midnight of 11 September, even though it was not until almost five hours after midnight that McCowan claimed to see a man emerge from number 29 St Paul's Road.

Regarding the issue of Emily's curling pins, this is far more complicated. Although Inspector Neil collected new evidence concerning the state of Emily's hair after Wood's arrest, this was partly because he received new information from Joseph Lambert that her hair was in curlers when she met Wood in the *Eagle*. For that reason, Mrs Stocks was asked to confirm that she recalled the curling pins when she last saw Emily in the evening. Whereas Inspector Neil had previously only regarded the curling pins as a sign that Emily knew her murderer, they suddenly became indicative of Wood's guilt. If Emily was wearing the curling pins all evening, figured Neil, she would not have gone anywhere after leaving the *Eagle*, meaning she was not the woman seen by Sharples and Harvey at midnight. It has to be said that it is another sign of a poor investigation by Inspector Neil that he did not think of obtaining evidence from Mrs Stocks about the curling pins before he spoke to Lambert, and thus before Wood's arrest. He also never asked Bert Shaw about her custom of wearing curlers and it only came out from him during questioning at court that she normally put curling pins in her hair during the day.

It would be naïve to say that if Wood had immediately admitted to having spent the evening with Emily before returning to his home at midnight, we would today rule him out of having committed the murder. He would still be a suspect but we would surely conclude, with some confidence, that he was probably not guilty of the crime. The evidence about the postcard album is far too uncertain to support a conclusion that the murderer rifled through it in order to search for a postcard and the only sensible conclusion to draw from McCowan's evidence is that he saw William Westcott leaving for work. The other key indication of Wood's guilt, namely that Emily appeared to have been wearing curling pins in her hair all evening and would thus not have seen another client after Wood, can be explained either by Emily putting pins in her hair twice during the day, once to go out for the evening and once before she went to bed, or else by the fact that she *was* prepared to go out with her hair in pins. Alternatively, she could still have been murdered by someone other than a client who obtained access to her room during the night.

The issue of whether or not Emily expressed fear of Wood, as Inspector Neil appears to have believed, is a little complicated but ultimately can be concluded in Wood's favour. The inspector's big point before Wood's arrest was that Emily was 'very much afraid' of the author of the rising sun postcard and 'feared harm from him'. During the trial, the prosecution failed miserably to substantiate this. Joseph Lambert's evidence, on behalf of the prosecution, was that Emily told him that Wood was a nice boy and gave no hint that she showed any signs of being afraid of him. Both Ellen Lawrence and Florence Smith said that Emily 'seemed nervous' of Wood in the *Rising Sun* but it was admitted by Florence that Emily had made no actual complaint about him and there was no evidence from Ellen Lawrence that she had complained to her about him either. If anything, Florence Smith's account of the events in the *Rising Sun* contained in her written statement contradicted the notion that Emily was afraid of Wood because she recorded that, when asked if she had enjoyed her visit to the Holborn Empire with Wood, Emily, who was then sitting with Wood in the *Rising Sun*, 'laughed' and said they had actually been to the *Adam and Eve*, which does not sound at all like a woman in fear.

The only other documented 'evidence' of Emily being afraid of Wood was contained in Robert Roberts' second statement dated 7 October 1907, after Wood's arrest, although Roberts had evidently said something of the sort to Inspector Neil before the arrest because – not only did such a claim appear in the Sunday papers of 22 September (presumably because someone in the police had leaked it) – Neil's report of 30 September 1907 records that Roberts was the source of the claim that Emily was 'very much afraid' of the man she had spoken to in the *Rising Sun* on Monday night (who was also then believed to be the author of the letter she received on Wednesday morning inviting her to the *Eagle*) and 'would have preferred not to meet him but was afraid of the consequences if she did not'. This must refer to a conversation on the Wednesday morning, after the letter of assignation had been received, but, in his statement of 7 October, Roberts only mentioned that Emily had said she was afraid of this man, subsequently known to be Wood, while they were talking in the *Rising Sun* on the Monday night, after Wood had left. There was no mention at all in that statement of Emily saying to Roberts *on the Wednesday morning* that she was afraid of what would happen if she met Wood at the *Eagle* or even that she was afraid of him at all. At the inquest on 14 October, Roberts did appear to say that Emily told him on the Wednesday morning that the man later identified as Wood was jealous of her *and* that she was afraid of him. Yet, in his first statement made the day after the murder, he had only said that Emily told him that this man was 'jealous' and nothing at all was mentioned about Emily being afraid. He was not allowed to give evidence at the Old Bailey about what Emily had said to him, because this was regarded as hearsay, but, considering that Roberts had failed to say anything about Emily being afraid of anyone in his statement immediately after the murder, when his conversations with her would have been fresh in his mind, one has to wonder whether his subsequent evidence was tainted, or influenced, by his conversation with May Campbell at Emily's funeral on 15 September. According to Ms Campbell, in her statements to the police, Emily told her that she was afraid of meeting 'Scotch Bob' because she thought he would hurt her for giving her the disorder and had said 'I am afraid of him because he is a desperate man' and 'it's Scotch Bob and I feel almost afraid to go'. It was only after May Campbell spoke to the police that we hear for the first time that Roberts was saying the same thing (about a different man) and it may well be that the defence suspicions of collusion between Roberts and Campbell were justified in this respect. If Emily was not, in fact, afraid of Wood then not only does a key part of the police case against Wood fall away but it means that one of the main reasons why Inspector Neil was initially so convinced that the author of the rising sun postcard was the murderer had no basis in fact.

We would not, today, place much emphasis on the fact that Wood was acting normally the morning after the murder because we know more about killers hiding their emotions than seemed to be the case in 1907 when a relaxed appearance at breakfast seems to have been considered important, albeit not by the police. It is unfortunate that Inspector Neil did not conduct a thorough investigation into Wood's activities in the week following the murder to establish whether he changed his patterns. If Wood usually went out in the evening but stopped doing so before the rising sun postcard was published this would be suspicious but there is nothing to suggest the inspector even considered the point. He did not, it seems, even check the facts in Wood's statement, other than with respect to his alibi, despite telling him that he would do so or, if he did, everything he found must have corroborated what Wood told him because nothing was ever raised in cross-examination. Wood's foolish insistence that he had been open about being the author of the rising sun postcard because he and his brother had deposited a letter at the Poste Restante clearly played badly with the inspector because he made a point in his statement of 8 October that Wood 'kept repeating' that he had made no secret of the card during the drive to Highgate after his arrest.

It is only because of the lies told after his arrest, along with his attempt to construct a false alibi with Ruby beforehand, that Wood remains the prime suspect today, despite his acquittal by a jury. Yet, while Wood's behaviour after the murder is consistent with him having committed the crime, it is not proof of it and he is not the only suspect. Had Inspector Neil tracked down every individual who had made threats against Emily we could, perhaps, rule out the notion that the murderer was one of these individuals. However, the man identified in the *Daily Mail* by Emily's former landlady, Mrs Roberts, as 'Tom', who visited her residence to threaten to 'do her in', who may or may not have been the same man referred to by Crabtree who threatened to cut Emily's throat, was, it seems, never found. The only man known to have threatened Emily to whom Inspector Neil actually spoke was Arthur Harrap (who, it will be recalled, said that if he could not have her then no-one else would) but he had an alibi. The inspector and his team did well to trace a number of men who contracted venereal disease from Emily but they are unlikely to have spoken to every single such client.

We cannot ignore the evidence of the cab driver, Richard Taylor, that he drove a man from St Paul's Road to Thornhill Road at 1:10am when it was unusual for anyone to hail a cab from there at that time in the morning. As we have already discussed, the man looked like he had 'just washed' which would have been consistent with someone having cleaned himself in the wash basin in Emily's bedroom. We do not know if Taylor was brought to Highgate or Kentish Town to identify Wood but the description he provided did not match that of Wood nor did the time of the man's departure fit with the police theory that the murderer must have left Emily's house shortly before 5:00am, a theory based not only on the fact that it was shortly before 5:00am that McCowan saw a man supposedly exiting 29 St Paul's Road but also because, in the police view, there must have been some daylight for the murderer to have half-opened one of the shutters. Nonetheless, one cannot help but wonder whether Dr Thompson would have helpfully provided a new estimate of time of death starting as early as 1:00am had Taylor identified Wood as the man he saw (and McCowan had failed to do so).

We have also seen that Roberts and Clarke, either jointly or separately, cannot be entirely ruled out of consideration despite the alibi provided for them by Mrs Lesage. However, to the extent that the locking of the door suggests an 'inside job' then Mr and Mrs Stocks, despite their appearance of complete innocence to the police, must be high on the list of suspects. The problem here is that we have to speculate as to any motive either of them would have had to murder Emily when, on the face of it, there was no reason whatsoever for either of them to cause her any harm. The fact that George Stocks went back to sleep after his alarm rang during the morning after the murder is too thin a reason to suspect his involvement but Mrs Stocks' apparent failure to inform Shaw that she had a duplicate key to his room until he was about to break the door down must be viewed as suspicious even if it is not actual evidence against her. Although favoured by crime writer Patricia Cornwell, it seems unlikely, on the state of the known evidence, that the murderer entered and/or exited Emily's apartment through a window but the fact that one of the window shutters was half open may be regarded as a clue, especially if the murder was committed during the hours of darkness and thus not opened to allow in light, as the police theorised. It would seem to be highly unlikely for a normal burglar to cut someone's throat but, with Emily apparently having so many male enemies of the lowest class, it does not seem at all beyond the bounds of probability that one such man broke into her room with the intention of killing her and did so, taking the opportunity of stealing her valuables before fleeing into the night, as Marshall Hall suggested.

With so many other possibilities, even if only theoretical, it is a real shame there was no re-investigation of the crime after Wood's acquittal. The police believed they had their man and no-one was prepared to challenge their basic assumptions. Inspector Neil was a rising star of the Criminal Investigation Department and his boss, Sir Melville Macnaghten, who clearly shared his view that Wood was guilty, despite the jury's verdict, would not have wanted to upset him by suggesting he had messed up the investigation. As the bonus awards of £4 to Inspector Neil and £3 to Sergeant Ball show, rewards for failure are not an entirely modern day phenomenon.

Appendix 1: 35 Years Earlier

Outside the St Pancras Coroner's Court, after the first day of the inquest, on 16 September 1907, the coroner commented to a journalist from the *Star* that Emily's murder reminded him of the murder of a prostitute at lodgings in Great Coram Street, near Russell Square, some thirty-five years earlier. Voluminous papers relating to that murder at the National Archives[585] show that there were indeed a number of striking similarities between the two cases which make it worth describing the Great Coram Street murder in a little more detail.

Harriet Buswell, aged 32, who had adopted the name Clara Burton, was found dead in her bed on the morning of Christmas Day of 1872, her throat having been deeply cut.[586] Her body (but not her face) was covered by the bedclothes while her purse, containing little of value, was missing.[587] When the police investigated her life history it was discovered that, while working in service at a house in Finchley in 1863, she had become pregnant by the coachman and probably turned to prostitution in order to afford a nurse to look after her daughter.[588] At one point, she had lived with a Major Brown, passing as his wife, before forming a relationship with one William Kirby who described her as 'so quick, intelligent, yet so young and with such a fine warm heart'.[589] Kirby had to leave for Hong Kong but he continued to correspond with Harriet (whom he knew as 'Clara') and send her money. She moved to Argyle Street in King's Cross where she lived for four years before an argument with her landlord brought her to Great Coram Street at the end of November 1872. On Christmas Eve, she was seen with a man at a restaurant and, accompanied by a man who may or may not have been the same one she had dined with, bought some fruit at a greengrocer's in Compton Street in the early hours of Christmas Day before returning to her lodgings with a man who was seen, but not clearly, by the landlady. This man gave Harriet ten shillings and she brought the money down to the landlady to keep her happy about the extra guest but, after returning to her room, having said she would spend the night with him, was not seen alive again: the maid finding her dead body at 8:00am. Just as in the murder of Emily Dimmock, the blinds were drawn, while the window was closed and fastened, with no indication of any previous struggle. Some bloodstains were found on a washstand, with blood marks also on a towel, but no murder weapon was in the room.

The police investigation focused on finding the man seen with Harriet during Christmas Eve. A full description of the suspect was circulated on police bills and, remarkably, his most obvious feature was that he had pimples or 'red spots on face'. However, he was also believed to be a foreigner, probably German, and the combination of these two facts made the Ramsgate police suspicious of a pimpled German chemist, Carl Wilhelm Wohllebe, who had been on board a ship travelling from Antwerp to Brazil which had become damaged on the Goodwin sands and had put into Ramsgate for repairs a few days before Christmas. Taking advantage of the unexpected free time, Wohllebe had stayed in a hotel in London, near Tower Hill, on Christmas Eve and the police brought all their witnesses down to Ramsgate, where Wohllebe had returned, to identify the chemist in a line-up. One of the men who volunteered to be part of the line-up was a 31-year-old pastor, Dr Godfried Hessel (a doctor of Divinity), and he was no doubt astonished when the witnesses failed to recognise Wohllebe but picked *him* out (or at least some of them did) as the man who had been with Harriet Buswell on the night of her murder.[590] Despite the circumstances in which Dr Hessel had been identified, and the apparent absence of pimples on his face, the police arrested and charged him, putting together a flimsy case – their only other evidence against him being that, a few days after the murder, back at a hotel in Ramsgate, he had asked a maid for some turpentine (to remove some paint from his clothes) and had also sent some handkerchiefs covered in blood to be laundered. When brought before the magistrate, Hessel was able to prove beyond any doubt that he could not possibly have spent Christmas Eve with Harriet because, although he was staying with his wife in the same London hotel as Wohllebe on Christmas Eve, he was seen by independent witnesses throughout the evening until 11:00pm when the hotel doors were bolted, with a member of staff stationed by them all night so that exit was impossible. In addition, he was brought some camomile tea and rum by the hotel staff shortly before midnight while in bed. On 30 January 1873, at Bow Street Police Court, the case was dismissed by the magistrate who told Hessel he could leave the court without a stain on his character and he was loudly cheered and applauded by the public, both inside the court and on the street. The extraordinary weakness of the case against Hessel had been recognised by everyone except the prosecution; the magistrate's decision was universally applauded by the newspapers which were extremely critical of the police for charging the pastor.

The story did not end there. The police continued to investigate Buswell's murder, considering alternative suspects, but an anonymous letter from Germany re-ignited their interest in Dr Hessel who had been presented by his defence team as 'a clergyman of high character'. The letter, signed by 'Many of the betrayed believers of Dr Hessel', alleged that, in Germany, Hessel was 'profligate and spendthrift' and was regularly 'drunk late at night and early in the morning'. It was said that he suddenly disappeared from Danzig in order to avoid paying his creditors, which was why he was on his way to Brazil in the first place. The letter was passed to the Home Office which asked the Foreign Office to contact the British Consul in Danzig to request a discreet investigation of the allegations. It was a difficult task because it was essential that the authorities were not seen to be continuing to investigate the officially innocent German, not just because of the way it would look back at home but also because of the impact on diplomatic relations with Prussia. Nevertheless, the British Consul reported back that, from the limited enquiries he was able to make, he had heard unconfirmed rumours about Hessel concerning the 'irregularity of his habits' and the 'very low company' he kept, concluding that the allegations in the anonymous letter may be correct and that he quite possibly 'did not leave Danzig with that high character with which he has been credited by his friends and supporters in London.' It may be as a result of this, and the unexplained blood on the handkerchiefs (which could easily have been the result of a nose bleed), that the police never fully believed in Hessel's innocence, despite the fact that, whatever his character, he could not possibly have murdered Harriet Buswell. Whoever did commit the crime was never caught.

Appendix 2: Finding Jack

John William Crabtree has been well known to anyone with an interest in the Camden Town Murder for over one hundred years and I am conscious of being the only person to have identified him as both a notorious nineteenth century New Zealand criminal and the man who caused the Fitzroy Street explosion in Australia. I think it is important, therefore, that I set out how I arrived at the conclusion that John William Crabtree, the prosecution witness in the trial of Rex v. Wood ('the English Crabtree'), is the same John William Crabtree who escaped from Mount Cook Gaol ('the New Zealand Crabtree') and died of self-inflicted wounds in 1910 ('the Australian Crabtree').

Right at the start of my research, having read the English Crabtree's cross-examination at the Old Bailey, I was aware that the man had been imprisoned in England for various offences before 1907. Surprisingly, no-one had ever bothered to research his previous offences in England so the details were not available in any published work and it was a desire to find out more about these crimes that led me initially to 'google' his name. The British Newspaper Archive was not yet online and nothing came up relating to any English criminal but I found a number of stories from New Zealand newspapers about a John William Crabtree's dramatic break-out from prison and sighed wistfully, wondering why I could not be so lucky as to be researching a character with such an exciting history for my book. I did, naturally, consider whether this Crabtree from the 1880s could have ended up on the other side of the world at the Old Bailey in 1907 but articles about him appeared to rule out any possibility of this. The New Zealand *Evening Post* of 26 March 1885, when reporting Crabtree's first escape attempt from Mount Cook Gaol, said that he was aged 25, suggesting that he was born in 1860. The *Manawatu Herald* of 27 April 1893 confirmed this in a short biography which also stated that he had been born in Yorkshire. Considering that the English Crabtree told Marshall Hall in the witness box, 'I have lived for fifty-six years and have only been in prison three times', and I could not then imagine a reason for him to have been lying, I concluded that this Crabtree must be a different person. If he was aged 56 in 1907 then he must have been born in either 1850 or 1851, a difference of at least nine years compared to the New Zealand Crabtree's publicly stated date of birth. Of course, the newspaper could have made a mistake but I figured this was wishful thinking on my part so I therefore concluded that they were different people.

The first breakthrough came when I was in the British Newspaper Library in Colindale searching newspapers for information relating to the English Crabtree's previous convictions. Having discovered from an electronic search of the *Times* newspaper online archive that he had been convicted after the Wood trial in April 1908, I had easily been able to establish the dates of his earlier convictions from the 1908 *After Trial Calendar of Prisoners* of the Central Criminal Court held at the National Archives which, I already knew from previous research, helpfully list the past convictions of all criminals convicted at the Old Bailey. This told me that I needed to check the local Yorkshire newspapers around 14 October 1901 for his first conviction and the Durham papers from around 18 November 1903 for his second and I set aside a day at Colindale for this exercise. I was naturally pleased when I quickly found a short report in the *Durham Chronicle* of 20 November 1903 of Crabtree's trial at the Autumn Assizes. It was interesting to note that the judge was Mr Justice Grantham but what really caught my eye was that the story began 'John Wm Crabtree (51), baker, pleaded guilty to two charges of stealing horses, carts and harness at Gateshead in August and September'. A baker! This rung a loud bell in my head. Had I not seen a story somewhere that the New Zealand Crabtree was a baker? I went straight onto one of the library's computers to check this out and, sure enough, I found the story from the New Zealand *Evening Post* which had mentioned Crabtree's age and saw that it also stated that John William Crabtree was 'a baker by trade'. Surely it was too much of a coincidence that both the New Zealand and the English Crabtrees were bakers. I started to take a much closer look at the New Zealand Crabtree and discovered that he seemed to vanish after 1893. No more was heard of him in the New Zealand or Tasmanian newspapers once he escaped conviction in the long firm fraud case.

Suddenly it seemed possible that he might be the same person after all but what about the thorny issue of his age? Well it seemed that there might be an explanation for that. The *Durham Chronicle* had given his age as 51 when he was tried on 19 November 1903 which, assuming that he turned 52 in late November or early December, corresponded with an age of 56 four years later, just as he claimed at the Old Bailey (and, on checking the *Calendar of Prisoners* tried at the Durham Assizes in 1903, his 'official' age of 51 was confirmed). However, I noticed that the *After Trial Calendar of Prisoners* stated that he was 61 at the date of his conviction for running a disorderly house on 6 April 1908 (and was thus supposedly born in 1848). This was odd. His conviction was less than four months after he had said in the witness box at the Old Bailey that he was 56 and, if that was true, he could not possibly have been any older than 57 by the time of his subsequent conviction in 1908. It looked like there was some uncertainty about his true age even among the British authorities and this was confirmed when, while browsing the National Archives catalogue, I found a remarkably helpful register of habitual criminals which had been kept by the Metropolitan Police. The 1906 register contained a record of Crabtree's conviction for larceny at Gateshead, showing that he had been sentenced on 18 November 1903 and was due to be released early, on licence, on 19 February 1906. It confirmed that his occupation was a 'baker' and also said that he was born in 1852 in Keighley, Bradford. This was almost but not quite consistent with the age Crabtree claimed to be during his cross-examination at Wood's trial but was totally inconsistent with his officially recorded age in the records of the Central Criminal Court for 1908. The only conclusion was that the police somehow realised after the Wood trial that Crabtree had not been born in 1852 after all.

However, Crabtree's new 'official' birth date of 1848 pushed him even further away from 1860 which was not particularly helpful. I was hopeful the new clue that Crabtree was born in Keighley might provide the key to tracing his actual date of birth but, for the moment, my attention was attracted by some vital information about him in the register. There was a physical description. He was said to be five foot six inches in height, with a fresh complexion, light brown hair, blue eyes and, most importantly, 'scar left jaw'.[591] Could I find a description of the New Zealand Crabtree? Fortunately, after Crabtree escaped from Mount Cook Gaol, just such a description was issued and appeared in New Zealand's *Evening Post*. Its 31 January 1887 issue stated:

> Crabtree, who is a native of Yorkshire, is 27 years of age, 5ft 6 in high, of stout build, fair complexion has fair hair, no hair on face, grey eyes, mark of abscess on left cheek, is well made and active.

Things were looking good. The height matched perfectly; the hair and complexion seemed to match; and the slight difference in eye colour between grey and blue could easily be explained by natural changes, or differences in interpretation, especially considering the different light in the two respective hemispheres. The real point of interest was that the New Zealand Crabtree had a mark on his left cheek and the English Crabtree was said to have had a scar on his left jaw. This may not seem conclusive at first blush but the cheek meets the jaw and we will return to this point shortly. For the moment, my next task was to see if I could find John William Crabtree's birth in Keighley. Even if the date of birth he gave the police was false, the location might have been correct. However, despite some possible early candidates, he could not be located, either in 1848, 1850, 1851, 1852 or 1860. Eventually, I found the man who was certainly the New Zealand Crabtree. He was born in Huddersfield, Yorkshire, in December 1859 and confirmation that this was the right man was provided by his mother's name on the birth certificate being Grace Crabtree, formerly Rawson. Crabtree's father had formed a well-known grocery called Rawson & Crabtree and there was sufficient information in the New Zealand and Australian newspapers to confirm that Jack's mother was Grace Rawson.

Until this point, I had not been aware of Jack's exploits in Australia but it was the discovery of his death that was to prove the key to unlocking the mystery of his identity. For a time I had difficulty in establishing that the Australian Crabtree who died in Fitzroy Street in 1910 was the same man as the New Zealand Crabtree, let alone the English Crabtree. There were tantalising references in the Australian press to him being the New Zealand criminal. According to the *Melbourne Advertiser* of 29 March 1910, discussing the death of Crabtree after the Fitzroy Street explosion:

> The police think the deceased is identical with a notorious New Zealand criminal. The gallery of convicted persons contains the portrait of a John William Crabtree who attracted a good deal of attention in New Zealand many years ago and a comparison of the photograph with the features of the dead man showed a remarkable resemblance. On John William Crabtree imprisoned at Christchurch in 1885 were a wen and marks left by an abscess on the left jaw. These were seen on the face of the dead man and very little doubt exists in the minds of the police that Crabtree is identical with the man who on January 5 1885 was sentenced to ten years' imprisonment for horsestealing and three years' for thieving.

This was particularly interesting because it referred to a mark on the dead man's 'left jaw' which precisely matched the information in the Metropolitan Police Register of 1906. If there was official confirmation that the New Zealand and Australian Crabtrees were one and the same then it would be almost certain that he was also the English Crabtree. In addition, the *Wanganui Chronicle* of 29 March 1910 said:

The records of Crabtree, who was a New Zealand criminal, have been received by the police. A photograph though taken 30 years ago, bears a resemblance to the Crabtree who died as a result of the Fitzroy explosion. Copies of the deceased's finger prints are being sent to New Zealand.

Frustratingly, however, there was no further report with any confirmation of the results of the fingerprint test, nor could I locate any photograph, and for a time I thought I would not be able to take it any further and would have to rely on circumstantial evidence that this dead Crabtree had once lived in New Zealand. However, in what felt like a major breakthrough, I managed to obtain the Australian Crabtree's death certificate and this provided official confirmation that the man who died in Australia was indeed the notorious New Zealand criminal because it stated that his parents were John William Crabtree (a grocer) and Grace Crabtree (formerly Rawson). So there was no doubt about it. The fingerprints must have confirmed his identity and we can now officially refer to the New Zealand Crabtree and the Australian Crabtree as a single person, namely 'the Australasian Crabtree'. Knowing that the dead man had a mark on his left jaw meant that the reference to the mark on the 'left cheek' in the 1887 description must have included the area of the jaw which was thus consistent with John William Crabtree's scar on the left jaw noted in the Metropolitan Police register.

A further crucial lead was reported in newspaper reports of the Australasian Crabtree's inquest. His wife was named as Emily Crabtree and *The Age* of 9 April 1910 reported that 'deceased's wife gave evidence of their marriage at Belfast, Ireland, twelve years ago'. A subsequent search of the Irish marriage records produced a wedding on 9 February 1899 (just over eleven years before the inquest) between a John William Crabtree, said to be a bricklayer, aged 32, and Emily Cavan, aged 28. Although the 39-year-old Crabtree was here claiming to have been born in about 1867 we have learnt that we cannot trust the accuracy of his age on any documents and it will be recalled that Crabtree had been arrested back in 1879 for making a false declaration as to his age on his marriage certificate when he married Elizabeth McTaggart. There is enough information on his 1899 marriage certificate to allow us to identify him, although we shall refer to him as 'the Irish Crabtree'. It says under 'Rank or Profession' that he was a bricklayer. When giving evidence before a bankruptcy court in 1892, the Australasian Crabtree said he was 'a bricklayer by trade'.[592] We know that the English Crabtree gave his occupation as a baker when tried in Wakefield in 1903 but he told Inspector Neil in October 1907 that he had worked as a bricklayer on the New Morning Post Building in the Strand in 1906, and Emily Crabtree said in her statement of 6 October 1907, 'I am the wife of John William Crabtree, a bricklayer'. The *After Trial Calender of Prisoners* for 1908 also states that Crabtree's trade was a bricklayer. So that matches perfectly and the Irish Crabtree's father's name is given on the marriage certificate as 'William Crabtree', said to be a builder. We know from both his birth certificate and from reports in the New Zealand newspapers that the Australasian Crabtree's father was William Crabtree, originally a chimney sweep from Yorkshire, who became a grocer in New Zealand. However, on the birth certificates of his children between 1865 and 1872, William's profession is stated to be a 'carpenter' and, during his legal action in 1894 against the somewhat demented Elizabeth Smith who claimed William was her long lost husband, he was described as 'a contractor' which corresponds to him being described as a builder. Furthermore, the Irish marriage certificate appears to bear the actual signatures of John William Crabtree and Emily Cavan. While it would need a graphologist to provide an expert opinion, from a visual comparison of these signatures with the known signatures of John William Crabtree and his wife on their statements in the Metropolitan Police file in the National Archives they would appear to be broadly consistent with each other, allowing for the fact that they were written some eight years apart.

Putting it all together, I concluded that the evidence was overwhelming that the John William Crabtree who appeared as a prosecution witness at the Wood trial was the same as the one who featured in the New Zealand and Australian newspapers before and after the trial. In the absence of any official confirmation or any known surviving photographs of Crabtree, and more than one hundred years later, the evidence can only be circumstantial but it is also undeniable and beyond any reasonable doubt. The timings all fit. Crabtree disappeared from New Zealand in around 1894 and then re-appeared in Wakefield in 1901, having married in Belfast in 1899. There is no record of his being in England at any time before 1899 other than his birth in Huddersfield in 1859. Having been in various degrees of trouble with the law between 1901 and 1908, and presumably released from prison in April 1909 after serving his twelve-month term of imprisonment, Crabtree then next popped up in Launceston in September 1909 when he applied to the Deputy Postmaster General of Australia for a licence to sell revenue stamps.[593] The timing, in other words, is perfect and it is clear from the Metropolitan Police register that the British authorities had no idea what became of the English Crabtree after his release from prison in 1909 because he was regarded as 'presumed dead' in 1936. Everything fits from that perspective and the English Crabtree was both a bricklayer and a baker as was the Australasian Crabtree which, in itself, would be too much of a match to be a coincidence but, in addition, the English Crabtree feigned madness as did the Australasian Crabtree. The physical characteristics also match; both men were five foot, six inches, with light brown or fair hair and grey/blue eyes and with an identifying scar, or mark, on the left jaw. The only discrepancy is in their respective ages but it is a fact that Crabtree gave at least one false age to the authorities while he was in England – he could not have been born in both 1852 and 1848 – and it is, therefore, perfectly credible to suppose that he gave a second one.

It would have been useful if I had been able to find a signature of the Australasian Crabtree. The National Archives of Australia hold a letter dated 13 September 1909 which refers to a letter received from Crabtree dated 11 September 1909 in which, as referred to above, he applied for the licence to sell revenue stamps, but Crabtree's application, which would have borne his signature, does not appear to have survived. However, there is very good reason to believe that the Irish Crabtree is the same man as the Australasian Crabtree and, as mentioned, his signature (and that of his wife) appears to the untrained eye to correspond to the signature of the English Crabtree (and his wife).

For all the above reasons I felt able to conclude with absolute confidence that the four Crabtrees discussed were all the same extraordinary man.

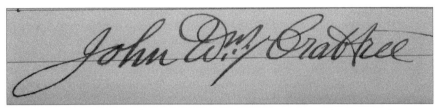

Signature of John William Crabtree on his witness statement of 19 September 1907
(National Archives)

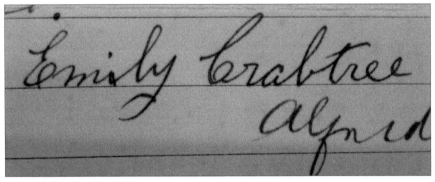

Signature of Emily Crabtree on her witness statement of 6 October 1907
(National Archives)

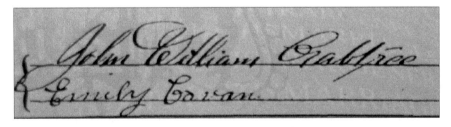

Signatures of John William Crabtree and Emily Cavan
on their marriage certificate of 9 February 1899

Bibliography and Acknowledgments

Places – Acknowledgments

British Library
British Newspaper Library
National Archives
London Metropolitan Archives
Camden Local Studies and Archives Centre
Hertfordshire Archives & Local Studies
BBC Written Archives Centre
Glamorgan Archives
Croydon Local Studies and Archives
St Alban's Church, South Norwood
University of Birmingham, Cadbury Research Library: Special Collections
The School of African and Oriental Studies Library: Archives and Special Collections
The Library of the Royal College of Surgeons
National Library of Scotland
Modern Records Centre, University of Warwick
Essex Record Office

People – Acknowledgments

Don Grant – Sketch Club Archivist
Sheila Wood

Select Bibliography

Primary Sources

National Archives ("TNA")

ADM 53/24996-24999 – Logs of HMS Prince of Wales, 1906-1908
ADM 188/334 – Service Record of George Henry Biddle
BT 31/11894/92555 – Pastimes Limited
CRIM 1/102/4 – Defendant, MacQuire, Edward Charge: Murder
CRIM 1/145/3 – Defendant, Starchfield, John Charge: Murder
CRIM 6/22 – Records of the Central Criminal Court
CRIM 6/80 – Central Criminal Court: Court Books: Third Court, 1904-1910
CRIM 9/54 – After Trial Calendar of Prisoners, 1908
CRIM 10/98 – Central Criminal Court, Minutes of Evidence
HO 45/22269 – Identification parades: procedure
HO 45/22702 – Prison libraries and supply of books and newspapers
HO 45/24442 – Establishment of Press Information Office at New Scotland Yard
HO 45/9994/A46644 – Administration of Metropolitan Police Reward Fund
HO 45/10409/A63109 – Reports on adoption and working of Identification by Finger Prints System (1901-1907)
HO 45/10913/A60340 – Prison Rules
HO 140/213 – After Trial Calendar of Prisoners, 1901
HO 140/223 – After Trial Calendar of Prisoners, 1903
HO 140/250 – After Trial Calendar of Prisoners, 1906
HO 140/258 – After Trial Calendar of Prisoners, 1907
HO 140/274 – After Trial Calendar of Prisoners, 1909

HO 144/477/X24427A – Arthur Newton, Misdemeanour
MEPO 2/293 – Prostitution: complaints about houses and behaviour in Euston Road area
MEPO 2/438 – Disorderly Houses: Allocation of costs
MEPO 2/574 – Noise caused by automatic pianos
MEPO 2/7182 – Reward Fund
MEPO 3/109 – Murder of Harriet Ruswell (sic)
MEPO 3/182 – Murder of Emily Elizabeth (known as Phyllis) Dimmock
MEPO 3/237B – Murder of William Starchfield
MEPO 6/17 – Register of Habitual Criminals, 1906
MEPO 6/18 – Register of Habitual Criminals, 1907
MEPO 6/21 – Register of Habitual Criminals, 1910
MEPO 7/67 – Police Orders for 1905
MEPO 7/68 – Police Orders for 1906
MEPO 7/69 – Police Orders for 1907
MEPO 7/70 – Police Orders for 1908
MEPO 8/7 – General Orders for 1907
MEPO 20/1 – Registers of Murders and Death by Violence
PCOM 6/21 – Registers of Licences
RAIL 253/372 – Paddington – fares and rates
RAIL 936/40 – Great Western Railway: Public Timetables
RG 48/55 – Registration of Births, Deaths and Marriages: Correspondence and Papers
TS 42/25 – Home Office Register: Solicitor to the Treasury
WO 97/4753 – Royal Hospital Chelsea: Soldiers Service Documents 1900-1913

London Metropolitan Archives ("LMA")

EO/DIV2/THA/LB/002 – Thanet Street School Log Book
GLC/AR/BR/22/BA 013683 – The Rising Sun Public House
LCC/EO/DIV02/GRE/AD/001 – Admissions and Discharge Register: Great College Street School
PS/CLE/A/01/002-008 – Court Registers, Clerkenwell Police Court
PS/CLE/B/01/006 – Court Minute Book, Clerkenwell Police Court
PS/CLE/B/01/011-012 – Court Minute Books, Clerkenwell Police Court
PS/CLE/B/02/006 – Court Minute Book, Clerkenwell Police Court
PS/CLE/B/02/014 – Court Minute Book, Clerkenwell Police Court
PS/G/H/A/01/007 – Court Register, Edgware Petty Sessions
PS/MAR/A/01/007 – Court Register, Marylebone Police Court
PS/MAR/A/01/024 – Court Register, Marylebone Police Court
PS/PAN/01/15 – Court Minute Book, St Pancras Petty Sessions Division
PS/PAN/03/02 – Licensing Register, St Pancras Petty Sessions Division

Hertfordshire Archives & Local Studies ("HALS")

PS 18/3/2 – Register of Licences, Petty Sessional Division of Ware, County of Hertford

Glamorgan Archives ("GA")

DCONC 4/1/8 – Cardiff Police Inquest Book

BBC Written Archives Centre ("WAC")

R19/634/1 – Let Justice Be Done, 1947-1948
R19/634/2 – Let Justice Be Done, 1949-1954

R19/1,673/1 – The Great Defender, 1963

Camden Local Studies and Archives Centre ("CLSAC")

JN 20/55E – Register of Disorderly Houses

National Library of Scotland ("NLS")

ACC 4068 (33) & (34) – Minute Books of the Edinburgh Typographical Society's Chapel at the Scotsman's Office 6 May 1858 – 16 Dec 1863 & 7 Jan 1864 – 24 July 1872
ACC 4068 (55-58) – Contribution Lists of the Edinburgh Typographical Society 1851 – 1881
ACC 4068 (87) – Index of the Members of the Edinburgh Typographical Society 1871 – 1881
ACC 11812 (106) – The Scotsman: Contributors Day Book January 1871 – September 1881
ACC 11812 (161-162) – The Scotsman: Wages Books 1857 – 1865
ACC 11812 (163) – The Scotsman: Savings Bank Ledger 1872-1889

Essex Record Office ("ERO")

D/F 182/5/1/5 – Spottiswoode & Co: Apprentices from November 1886 to June 1897

Main Newspapers from 1907

Balham & Tooting News, Bedfordshire Advertiser and Luton Times, Daily Chronicle, Daily Express, Daily Graphic, Daily Mail, Daily Mirror, Daily News, Daily Sketch, Daily Telegraph, Evening Express & Evening Mail, Evening News, Evening Standard and St James's Gazette, Globe, Guardian, Illustrated Police News, Islington Daily Gazette and North London Tribune, Lloyd's Weekly News, Marylebone Times, Morning Advertiser, Morning Leader, News of the World, North Herts & South Beds Journal, Northampton Daily Chronicle, Northampton Herald, Northampton Mercury, Luton News, North Herts Mail, Pall Mall Gazette, Penny Illustrated Paper, People, Reynolds's Newspaper, St Pancras Chronicle, Standard, Star, Sunday Times, The Times, Tottenham & Edmonton Weekly Herald, Tribune, Weekly Dispatch, Weekly Mail, Weekly Standard.

Secondary Sources

Barber, John, 'The Camden Town Murder', *Hertfordshire Countryside*, Volume 57, No. 520, August 2002

Barber, John, *The Camden Town Murder*, Mandrake of Oxford, 2008

Baron, Wendy & Shone, Richard, ed., *Sickert Paintings*, Yale University Press, 1992

Bayley, Wansey, *Venereal Disease: Its Prevention, Symptoms and Treatment*, J&A Churchill, 1924

Bebbington, Gillian, *London Street Names*, B.T. Batsford, 1972

Bixley, William, *The Guilty and the Innocent: My Fifty Years at the Old Bailey*, Philosophical Library, 1957

Black, George F., *The Surnames of Scotland*, New York Public Library, 1946

Bowker, A.E., *Behind the Bar*, Staples Press, 1948

Broad, Lewis, *Advocates of the Golden Age*, John Long, 1958

Butler, Ivan, *Murderers' London*, Robert Hale 1992

Cornwell, Patricia, *Portrait of a Killer: Jack the Ripper Case Closed*, Sphere, 2007

Cresswell, Julia, *Dictionary of First Names*, Chambers, 2009

Crew, Albert, *The Old Bailey*, Ivor Nicholson Watson Ltd, 1933

Daniels, Rebecca, *Walter Sickert and Urban Realism: Ordinary life and tragedy in Camden Town*, The British Art Journal, Volume 3, No. 2, Spring 2002

Dilnot, George, *Great Detectives and their Methods*, Geoffrey Bless, N.D.

Dix, Jay & Graham, Michael, *Time of Death, Decomposition and Identification*, CRC Press LRC, 2000

Douglas, James, *Adventures in London*, Cassell & Company, 1909

Druten, John Van, *Somebody Knows: A Play*, Victor Gollancz, 1932

Du Cann, Richard, *Art of the Advocate*, Penguin, 1993

Duke, Winifred, *Six Trials*, Victor Gollancz, 1934

Eden Hooper, W., *The Central Criminal Court of London*, Eyre and Spottiswoode, 1909

Eeles, H.S., *Lord Chancellor Camden and His Family*, Philip Allan, 1934

Fisher, Sue, *Lust Dust and Cobblestones*, Sue Fisher, 1999

Frasier, David K., *Murder Cases of the Twentieth Century*, McFarland & Company, 1996

Fuller, Jean Overton, *Sickert & The Ripper Crimes*, Mandrake, 2001

Girouard, Mark, *Victorian Pubs*, Yale University Press, 1984

Goodman, Jonathan, *Masterpieces of Murder*, Robinson Publishing, 1992

Glyn Jones, Richard, ed., *Still Unsolved*, Xanadu Publications, 1990

Graham Evelyn, *Fifty Years of Famous Judges*, John Long, N.D.

Hanks, Patrick, Hardcastle, Kate & Hodges, Flavia, *Oxford Dictionary of First Names*, Oxford University Press, 2006

Harris, James C., *The Camden Town Murder (or What Shall We Do About the Rent?)*, Archives of General Psychiatry, May 2008

Hicks, Seymour, *Not Guilty M'Lord*, Cassell & Co, 1939

Hogarth, Basil, ed., *Trial of Robert Wood*, William Hodge & Co, 1936

Hooke, Nina Warner & Thomas, Gil, *Marshall Hall*, Arthur Baker, 1966

Howard, Frederick, *Kent Hughes: A biography*, Macmillan, 1972

Howse, Geoffrey, *The A to Z of London Murders*, Wharncliffe Books, 2007

Jacobs, T.C.H., *Aspects of Murder*, Stanley Paul & Co, 1956

Kahn, Joan, ed., *Trial and Terror*, Hamish Hamilton, 1975

Lambton, Arthur, *Echoes of Causes Célèbres*, Hurst & Blackett, 1931

Lane, Brian, ed., *The Murder Club Guide to London*, Harrap, 1988

Lawes, Aidan, *The Camden Town Murder*, Ancestors, Issue 76, December 2008

Leslie, Mary E., *The Dawn of Light, A Story of the Zenana Mission*, 1868, John Snow & Co

Lewis, Roy Harley, *Edwardian Murders*, David & Charles, 1989

Lustgarten, Edgar, *The Murder and the Trial*, Consul Books, 1962

Macnaghten, Sir Melville L., *Days of My Years*, Edward Arnold, 1914

Marjoribanks, Edward, *The Life of Sir Edward Marshall Hall*, Victor Gollancz, 1929

Matthew, H.C.G. & Harrison, Brian, eds., *Oxford Dictionary of National Biography*, Oxford University Press, 2004

Mills, A.D., *A Dictionary of London Place Names*, Oxford University Press, 2010

Mitchell, Charles Ainsworth, *Science and the Criminal*, Sir Isaac Pitman & Sons, 1911

Moss, A.W., 'Camden Town's Mystery of the Rising Sun', *True Crime Detective Monthly*, July 1993

Murphy, Theresa, *The Old Bailey: Eight Centuries of Crime, Cruelty & Corruption*, Mainstream Publishing Co Ltd, 1999

Napley, Sir David, *The Camden Town Murder*, Weidenfeld & Nicholson, 1987

Neil, Arthur Fowler, *Forty Years of Man-hunting*, Jarrolds, 1932

Oates, Jonathan, *Unsolved Murders in Victorian & Edwardian London*, Wharncliffe Books, 2007

O'Donnell, Bernard, *The Old Bailey and its trials,* Burke Publishing Co., 1950

Raymond, Ernest, *For Them That Trespass*, Cassell & Co, 1944

Rentoul, Sir Charles, *This is My Case*, Hutchison & Co, N.D.

Reynolds, David, *In Command of History: Churchill Fighting and Writing the Second World War*, Allen Lane, 2004

Richardson, John, *The Camden Town Book*, Historical Publications Ltd, 2007

Rowland, John, *Murder Mistaken*, John Long, 1963

Russell, Dora ed., *Best Murder Cases*, Faber & Faber, 1958

Shale, Suzanne, 'Listening to the Law: Famous Trials on BBC Radio 1934-1969', *The Modern Law Review*, Volume 59, Issue 6, 1996

Snyder Sachs, Jessica, *Time of Death: The True Story of the Search for Death's Stopwatch*, William Heinemann, 2002

Sparrow, Gerald, *Vintage Edwardian Murder*, Arthur Baker, 1971

Stone, Austin, *In The Shadow*, John Gifford, 1953

Thomas, Donald, *The Secret Cases of Sherlock Holmes*, Pan Books, 1997

Tickner, Lisa, 'Walter Sickert: The Camden Town Murder and Tabloid Crime' in Helena Bonett, Ysanne Holt, Jennifer Munday (eds.) *The Camden Town Group in Context*, May 2012, http://www.tate.org.uk/art/research-publications/camden-town-group/lisa-tickner-walter-sickert-the-camden-town-murder-and-tabloid-crime-r1104355

Watts, Victor, ed., *Cambridge Dictionary of English Place-Names*, Cambridge University Press, 2004

Welch, Claire, *Unsolved Crimes*, Haynes Publishing, 2012

Whitehead, Jack, *The Growth of Camden Town*, Jack Whitehead, 2000

Wilkes, Roger, *The Mammoth Book of Unsolved Crimes*, Robinson Publishing, 1999

Willey, Russ, *London Gazetteer*, Chambers, 2006

Willey, Russ, *Brewers' Dictionary of London Phrase & Fable*, Charles Harrap, 2009

Websites

www.ancestry.co.uk
www.findmypast.co.uk
www.oldbaileyonline.org
www.britishnewspaperarchive.co.uk
www.ukpressonline.co.uk
www.gale.cengage.co.uk
www.paperspast.natlib.govt.nz
www.trove.nla.gov.au
www.scotlandspeople.gov.uk
www.deceasedonline.com
www.books.google.co.uk
www.youtube.com
http://www.flutewood.org.uk/html/wood.html

Much thanks to my 'proofreading team' of Sidney, Jenita and Rachel

UPDATE - MARCH 2015

By way of a brief update, one further piece of information I acquired after publication was from a 1963 book entitled *From Vine Street to Jerusalem* written by a former police inspector from C.I.D. called Joseph F. Broadhurst. In it, Broadhust says that he knew Robert Wood very well and that: "No-one could think for a moment that he was capable of committing such a dastardly murder". That creates another mystery as to how Wood became friends with a police detective. Broadhurst served in the Metropolitan Police between 1900 and 1924. At the end of 1907, he was transferred from Scotland Yard to Vine Street Police Station and, as far as I am aware, had no connection with the investigation into the murder of Emily Dimmock.

Endnotes

1. *Islington Daily Gazette and North London Tribune*, 19 December 1907.
2. Ibid.
3. *Wellingborough News*, 20 December 1907.
4. Ibid.
5. The *Daily Express* of 19 December 1907, for example, carried a sub-headline: 'MAFFICKING IN THE STREETS'.
6. *The Globe*, 19 December 1907.
7. *Daily Mirror*, 23 June 1936.
8. *Morning Leader*, 1 August 1907. Not surprisingly, the police denied Timewell's allegations but they were widely reported. The Royal Commission, which had been set up in May 1906 in response to two separate complaints against police officers, reported on 19 June 1908 and concluded that the Metropolitan Police operated in 'a thoroughly satisfactory manner' (*Report of the Royal Commission Upon The Duties of the Metropolitan Police*, His Majesty's Stationery Office, 1908).
9. *St Pancras Gazette*, 16 August 1907.
10. *Daily Mirror*, 28 August 1907.
11. Sexton and Church were sentenced to nine months hard labour each for perjury in respect of their evidence against the police officers (*Weekly Dispatch*, 15 March 1908).
12. TNA – MEPO 3/184. The local council investigated and cleared the police of any misconduct in a report dated 31 October 1907 on the dubious basis that the undercover officers had difficulty watching three flats at one time.
13. *St Pancras Chronicle*, 20 September 1907 & *Daily Mirror*, 22 October 1907. There was an even more extraordinary twist some years later in that Miss Bowen, then running a lodging house in Argyle Street, King's Cross, was murdered by suffocation on 8 November 1918, apparently by someone desirous of the £50 she kept hidden in a tin box. Her murderer was never caught (*Times*, 11 December 1918).
14. *Weekly Dispatch*, 29 September 1907.
15. Ibid.
16. *Weekly Dispatch*, 29 September 1907.
17. *London Weekly News*, 29 September 1907.
18. *Evening News*, 30 September 1907.
19. *Weekly Dispatch*, 6 October 1907.
20. *Police Chronicle*, 21 September 1907.
21. *London Weekly News*, 20 October 1907.
22. *Morning Leader*, 15 October 1907.
23. *Times*, 1 June 1907.
24. Ibid.
25. *Times*, 30 July 1907.
26. *National Register*, 5 June 1908.
27. *The Monthly Magazine or British Register*, 1 February 1813.
28. *A Topographical Dictionary of England* by Samuel Lewis, published by S. Lewis & Co, 1811.
29. *Examiner*, 28 October 1871.
30. There are some discrepancies. The Sarah A. Uncle in the 1871 census is stated to be 21 years old. Peter Uncle's daughter, Sarah, was born on 16 August 1851 which would have meant she was 19 at the time of the 1871 census, taken on 2 April. Considering that Peter's daughter was due to gain her inheritance at the age of 21 this is no small matter. Also, the Sarah Uncle in the 1871 census is stated to have a middle initial of 'A', yet Peter Uncle's daughter had no middle name (either on her birth certificate or in the parish register recording her birth). However, it is not uncommon for ages to be wrongly stated in census returns and it is notable that the kitchen maid in the vicarage, whose name is listed directly below Sarah's, is named as Mary A. Cook. It is possible, therefore, that the inclusion of 'Sarah A. Uncle' is an administrative error. The Sarah A. Uncle in the 1871 census is said to have been born in Great Hadham and there is no record of any other Sarah Uncle having been born or baptized in Great Hadham in the period 1848-1852.
31. At the inquest into Peter's death, his wife (who one would have thought would know his correct age) said he was 39 years old at the time of his death. However, the register for the Independent Chapel in Little Hadham held at the Hertfordshire Archives and Local Studies centre shows that Peter was born on 28 March 1825 which made him 40 years old on 7 November 1865. His fortieth birthday on 28 March 1865 was obviously not very memorable.
32. The fuel was naphtha: *Herts and Essex Observer*, 18 November 1865; *Hertford Mercury & Reformer*, 11 November 1865; *Herts Guardian, Agricultural Journal and General Advertiser*, 11 November 1865.
33. Will of Peter Uncle dated 7 November 1865.
34. *Hertford Mercury and Reporter*, 23 March 1861. This followed a conviction for keeping the *Royal Oak* open for the sale of beer after licensed hours despite Peter claiming that his clock showed that he was within time. Maria Uncle gave evidence on his behalf, saying that her husband had been to London

two or three times during the week before the alleged offence and 'their clock was right by London time' – *Herts Guardian, Agricultural Journal and General Advertiser*, 2 August 1859.

35   Kelly's Directory of Hertfordshire for 1869 still has Maria Uncle as the licensee of the *Bull* but Samuel Archer is shown as the licensee in the 1870 edition and remains so until at least 1874. The next surviving edition of the directory, for 1878, shows that the Archers had left the *Bull* and the licensee is one James Carter.

36   On every census in which she appears, Rosa is described as having been born in Great Hadham but this was incorrect. She was born in Marylebone and baptised there on 27 December 1874.

37   When Sarah Maria Skillen (sic), working as a domestic servant, married Albert Craggs in Leyton, East London, in 1891, at the age of 18, she stated on her marriage certificate that her father, Richard Skillen, was 'deceased'. He was, however, very much alive, still living in Marylebone, with four children, having described himself as a 'widow' in the 1881 census and then having married Emma Noyer in 1882.

38   The 1881 census has seven-year-old Sarah Skillen (sic) living with Samuel and Maria Archer at the *King's Head* public house in Thaxted, Essex.

39   Banns were posted on 21 September 1879.

40   HALS – PS 18/3/2. What I have described as Standon's high street was then called simply 'Standon Street'.

41   The address of Sarah Dimmock on Emily's birth certificate was given as 'the Red Lion, Standon', and, in response to speculation that he had run a public house in Hitchin, William told the *North Herts Mail* of 3 October 1907 that 'the only public house I kept was the Red Lion in Standon'. It should be noted that the *Red Lion* was, in official licensing terms, a beerhouse, as opposed to an alehouse. A beerhouse was more restricted in terms of the alcohol it was allowed to sell. Kelly's Directories of Hertfordshire for 1882, 1886 and 1890 only list the names of alehouses in Standon which makes it seem like the *Red Lion* did not exist. William Maynard Dimmock appears in the 1886 directory, described as a 'beer retailer'.

42   *Herts and Essex Observer*, 31 October 1885.

43   Peter was baptized on 13 December 1885 with William entered as a 'publican' on the parish register.

44   *Hertfordshire Mercury*, 9 January 1886.

45   Ibid.

46   *Northampton Daily Chronicle*, 14 September 1907.

47   Annual Report of the Indian Female Normal School & Instruction Society or Zenana Bible and Medical Mission for 1880, School of African & Oriental Studies, Archives & Special Collections: INT/01/02/01/04.

48   *Northampton Daily Chronicle*, 14 September 1907. It is difficult to obtain confirmation of this but the June 1878 issue of *Church Work*, the monthly paper of the Guild of St Alban, refers to Sunday evening services at a Lay Mission in Wadding Street, Walworth, being 'conducted by two earnest young men' and it may be that Henry Dimmock was one of these two men.

49   University of Birmingham, Cadbury Research Library: Special Collections, CEZ/G/C/1/3.

50   *North Herts & South Beds Journal*, 6 July 1894.

51   The contemporary report in the *North Herts & South Beds Journal* does not mention the wheel of the cart passing over Emily's head but William Dimmock said this is what happened in a letter to the press published in the *Northamptonshire Evening Telegraph* of 8 January 1908.

52   *North Herts Mail*, 3 October 1907. It should be noted that Inspector Neil, who was well informed about her life history, believed that Emily took the situation as chambermaid at the Swan Bedford Hotel at the age of 17 in 1901 and remained there until June 1902.

53   *Bedfordshire Advertiser*, 20 September 1907 (for information about Emily's time in Luton with Rosa) and statement of Rosa Martindale (undated) in TNA – MEPO 3/182.

54   Although born as Rosa Skillin and brought up as Rosa Dimmock, Rosa called herself 'Rosa Uncle' on her marriage certificate and left her father's name blank.

55   *Luton Times and Advertiser*, 20 September 1907.

56   *Northamptonshire Evening Telegraph*, 8 January 1908.

57   *North Herts Mail*, 3 October 1907.

58   William and Sarah were together in Staffordshire in the 1911 census.

59   *North Herts Mail*, 3 October 1907.

60   *Bedfordshire Advertiser*, 20 September 1907.

61   *North Herts Mail*, 19 September 1907.

62   Ibid.

63   *Bedfordshire Advertiser*, 20 September 1907.

64   *North Herts Mail*, 3 October 1907.

65   *Hertfordshire Express*, 5 October 1907.

66   The source of this is a report in the Metropolitan Police file in the National Archives by a Detective Constable Joseph Henry Attwood which states that, in about 1905, a married man named Summock was residing with Emily Dimmock in Luton but his wife found them together in the churchyard and gave him a black eye. Summock was said to have then taken a licensed house in a road just off Gray's Inn Road near Camden Town where he was said to have been living until September 1907. However,

there is no follow-up to this report in the file despite the fact that it should have been a simple matter for the police to have tracked down a man called Summock who ran a pub in Camden Town, especially as the surname 'Summock' is extremely rare. The similarity between Summock and Dimmock does make one wonder if Attwood made a mistake in the report.

67   This allegation was made by William Dimmock in a letter to the Northamptonshire press in January 1908 (e.g. *Northamptonshire Evening Telegraph*, 8 January 1908).
68   TNA – MEPO 2/293. The Liverpool Street referred to is not the current Liverpool Street in the City of London but the street currently named Birkenhead Street, opposite King's Cross Station.
69   TNA – MEPO 2/293.
70   Ibid.
71   Ibid.
72   Ibid.
73   This division of responsibility was challenged by the Town Clerk of the Borough of Ealing in December 1906 after the Commissioner of Police wrote to him saying, 'the power to prosecute the keepers of disorderly houses is vested solely in the local authority'. In a letter dated 17 January 1907, solicitors for the Metropolitan Police were forced to make a correction to this statement, admitting that the police *did* have power to prosecute disorderly houses while emphasising that it was 'existing practice' for local authorities to do so and that 'the whole conduct of prosecution in disorderly house cases is in the hands of local authorities in the Metropolitan Police District' (TNA – MEPO 2/438).
74   TNA – MEPO 2/293.
75   Ibid.
76   Ibid.
77   Ibid.
78   This is from the evidence of the *Rising Sun*'s barman, Edward Smeeth, who said he saw Emily walk through the door during the evening of 9 September 1907 (*Minutes of Evidence*, 16 December 1907).
79   CLSAC, Register of Disorderly Houses, JN 20/55E.
80   Report of Inspector Neil dated 30 September 1907, TNA – MEPO 3/182.
81   In a police report dated 13 September 1907, Inspector Neil states that 'she is known to every prostitute in Euston Rd as "Phillis"', TNA – MEPO 3/182.
82   Aidan Lawes, 'The Camden Town Murder', in *Ancestors*, Issue 76, December 2008.
83   *Times*, 10 August 1905.
84   *Reynolds's Newspaper*, 15 September 1907; TNA – ADM 188/334.
85   The confusion about the name is explained by the fact that Gladys Warren's written statement to police dated 20 September 1907 appears to refer to 'Scotch Jack' (TNA – MEPO 3/182) but later references in court were to 'Scotch Jock'.
86   As Lillian Pohl, May Campbell appears in the 1911 census living on her own in Whitechapel, working as a restaurant waitress (while her husband was living with a woman called Minnie to whom he claimed to have been married for two years). On the census return of that year, May stated that she was born in Failsworth in Lancashire (in about 1881) and her marriage certificate states that her father was a colliers' foreman called Joseph Donaldson although it has not been possible to confirm this information. George Colville Pohl remarried in 1919 claiming to be a 'widower' on the marriage certificate.
87   In her second statement to the police, May Campbell said that she lived with Emily at 23 Burton Crescent, although other evidence suggests that the correct address was number 60. Despite this, Inspector Neil wrote in his report of 30 September 1907 that May Campbell 'knew the deceased well having previously lived with her at 23 Burton Crescent'.
88   CLSAC, Register of Disorderly Houses, JN 20/55E.
89   Gladys Warren's evidence about Emily's departure from 12 Belgrave Street is contradictory. In her statement to police of 20 September 1907 she said that Emily left 12 Belgrave Street 'a fortnight before I did'. However, in the same statement she also said that Emily 'lived at Belgrave St about 3 or 4 months and then came to live with me at Judd St'. May Campbell referred to Emily living in Belgrave Street in her second statement but misidentified the address as 23 Belgrave Street. Inspector Neil confirmed in his reports that the correct address was number 12.
90   CLSAC, Register of Disorderly Houses, JN 20/55E.
91   LMA PS/CLE/B/01/006.
92   Ibid.
93   LMA PS/CLE/A/01/002.
94   CLSAC, Register of Disorderly Houses, JN 20/55E.
95   *St Pancras Chronicle*, 23 March 1906; LMA – PS/CLE/B/01/006.
96   The hearing was adjourned to 4 April but Webster was then discharged due to the failure of Bloom to appear at court to continue the prosecution (LMA – PS/CLE/A/01/002). Possibly he had been warned off by Webster's associates.
97   CLSAC, Register of Disorderly Houses, JN 20/55E.
98   LMA – PS/CLE/A1/002.
99   Statement of Gladys Warren dated 20 September 1907 and Report of Inspector Neil dated 30 September 1907, TNA – MEPO 3/182.

100 *Star*, 14 September 1907 and written statement of John William Crabtree dated 19 September 1907 (TNA – MEPO 3/182). They both state that Emily's furniture was from the Islington Furnishing Company in Upper Street but this was denied by that company in a statement published in the *Morning Leader* of 16 September 1907. A document in the MEPO file in the National Archives confirms the correct company name.

101 *Tribune*, 17 December 1907.

102 Interviewed by the *Bedfordshire Advertiser* in September 1907, Rosa Martindale said that her sister's visit to Luton with Jumbo Hurst took place '12 months ago' which would date it to September 1906. In her police statement, however, she said it was '18 months ago' which would place it around March 1906. I have chosen the evidence from the police statement which is most likely to be accurate although other evidence – for example, the statement of Arthur Miller – suggests that Emily's relationship with Jumbo continued to September 1906. One report of an interview with Rosa Martindale suggests that Emily brought another soldier to Luton in September 1906 but this is not mentioned in her statement to the police.

103 Quoted in the *Star*, 14 September 1907.

104 *Times*, 30 June 1906.

105 Statement of John William Crabtree dated 19 September 1907, TNA – MEPO 3/182.

106 PS/CLE/B02/006.

107 Ibid.

108 TNA – ADM 53/24999.

109 *Reynolds News*, 15 September 1907.

110 *Daily Mirror*, 16 September 1907.

111 The HMS Prince of Wales was originally supposed to sail for the Mediterranean on 4 November but mechanical problems led to a delayed departure on 13/14 November (*Portsmouth Times*, 3-17 November 1907).

112 The photographer told the *Daily Mirror* that it was 'about ten days' after 9 November 1906 that Emily came back and another two days after this that she brought a HMS Prince of Wales sailor's cap which would make it the 21 November, a full week after the HMS Prince of Wales, with Biddle presumably on board, had sailed from Portsmouth. It would make more sense if the photograph was taken before 14 November because every sailor with an HMS Prince of Wales cap should have been at sea after that date. It is possible that Biddle was in hospital suffering from venereal disease and was delayed on the voyage but it seems more likely that the photographer's memory as to the dates was at fault. It would certainly make more sense if the photograph with the sailor's cap was taken on 9 November (or earlier) rather than after that date.

113 According to Inspector Neil giving evidence at Wood's trial, the sailor's cap 'belonged to a sailor named Biddle'.

114 From the written statement of Gladys Linehan dated 20 September 1907: 'I also know she gave the disorder to Biddle, a sailor, who used to visit her & who was on the "Prince of Wales". She visited Biddle several times at Portsmouth and on the last occasion he refused to have anything to do with her. This was when she was living at 2 Grafton Place. He would not have anything to do with her because he caught the disorder from her and she had to pawn her watch to get back' (TNA – MEPO 3/182). Given that Biddle appears to have lent Emily his cap on or shortly after 9 November 1906 and HMS Prince of Wales sailed from Portsmouth for Malta on 14 November, any quarrel must surely have taken place at some point between those dates (unless, of course, Biddle was in hospital).

115 The electoral register for 1908 (which probably reflects information as at 1907) has a 'Bertie Shaw' living at 31 Great College Street along with Frank Maw, the husband of Eliza Maw who is known to have been the landlady of Bertram Shaw while he was living with Emily. Shaw and Emily moved from 50 to 31 Great College Street during 1907.

116 *Evening News*, 14 September 1907.

117 *Evening News*, 13 September 1907; *Morning Leader* 13 September 1907; *Lloyd's Weekly News* 15 September 1907; *Weekly Dispatch*, 15 September 1907.

118 It should be noted that Mrs Maw appears to have run lodgings at both 31 Great College Street and 50 Great College Street during 1907. The electoral register confirms that Frank Maw was living at 31 Great College Street during 1907 and Inspector Neil's report of 13 September 1907 states that Shaw and Emily resided at 31 Great College Street between 7 January and June 1907. However, Neil's report of 30 September also states that Emily left 2 Grafton Place and moved to 50 Great College Street before moving to 31 Great College Street. One of the postcards retrieved from Emily's postcard album and postmarked January 1907 was addressed to her at 50 Great College Street confirming that this was the correct address at that time.

119 Charles Coleman joined the Metropolitan Police (V Division) on 24 December 1906 (TNA – MEPO 7/65).

120 *Morning Advertiser*, 14 September 1907.

121 *Daily Mail*, 16 September 1907.

122 *North Herts & South Beds Journal*, 20 September 1907.

123 *Daily News*, 14 September 1907; *Morning Leader*, 14 September 1907; *Morning Advertiser*, 14 September 1907; *People*, 15 September 1907; *Lloyds Weekly News*, 15 September 1907.

124 Emily had two real uncles. From her grandfather's will, we know that her father had two brothers alive in 1886 called Thomas (then a private in the Royal marines, being discharged in 1892) and John. It is not known if they were alive in 1907 but the assumption has to be that the man known as 'Uncle' was a client.

125 This was from 31 Great College Street. It seems that Mr and Mrs Maw, with Emily and Bert, moved from number 50 to 31 and it was only a couple of days later that the lodgers were asked to leave.

126 *Pall Mall Gazette*, 13 September 1907.

127 *Northampton Daily Reporter & Echo*, 16 September 1907.

128 It seems that Emily continued to work as a prostitute for the entire time she was living with Bert Shaw. Ellen Lawrence would give evidence at the inquest on 21 October 1907 that 'about six months ago' Emily was attending the University College Hospital which suggests she had another bout of venereal disease in about March or April 1907.

129 One of his older sisters, Caroline, was married to a copper plate printer called Arthur Lovell. They are recorded as living at 61 Arlington Road in the 1901 census together with Arthur's younger, and then unmarried, sister, Florence.

130 Report of Inspector Neil dated 13 September 1907, TNA – MEPO 3/182.

131 Roberts said he had over £16 in cash when he arrived in London (*Weekly Dispatch*, 17 November 1907). Incidentally, the Minutes of Evidence of the Central Criminal Court for the second session in December 1907 give Roberts' name as 'Thomas Percival Roberts' but he signed his statement 'R. Roberts' and all newspaper reports of the trial gave his name as 'Robert Percival Roberts' or, in the case of the *Daily Chronicle*, 'Robert Percy Roberts' (all of which must have been based on his testimony when asked to state his name) so I have assumed his correct first name was 'Robert' and that the court shorthand writer simply misheard.

132 *Tribune*, 13 December 1907.

133 Scotland's People - Statutory Births 685/02/0858 (the register originally stated the date of birth as 21 August 1907 which was corrected on 18 September 1907). His birth was announced in the *Scotsman* of 18 August 1907.

134 Scotland's People – Statutory Marriages 795/00 0003 and Statutory Deaths 685/02 0413.

135 *Weekly Dispatch*, 22 December 1907.

136 Evidence of George Wood and Charles Wood on 17 December 1907 at the Old Bailey.

137 Wood said that he was 'less than' 3 years old when his father moved to London (*Weekly Dispatch*, 22 December 1907). This is consistent with George Wood's evidence at his son's trial in 1907 that he had been in his present situation in London for 26 years. The 1881 census has the Woods living in Edinburgh so the move to London must have been after this. No record has been located of George Wood's marriage to Mary Hogg.

138 NLS – ACC 11812 (106); George wrote reviews for: *Ruff's Guide to the Turf*, fourth edition, which appeared in the *Scotsman* of 25 December 1879, The *Sportsman's Pocket Book*, twenty-first edition, which appeared in the *Scotsman* of 8 January 1880, *Ruff's Guide to the Turf*, fifth edition, which appeared in the *Scotsman* of 3 May 1880 and the obituary of the late Alexander Mann (a lawyer) which appeared in the *Scotsman* of 17 January 1880.

139 According to Arthur Newton, when questioning Inspector Neil at Clerkenwell Police Court on 7 October 1907, George Wood was 'employed by the King's printers' (*Daily Mail*, 8 October 1907). If this were so, he would have been working for Eyre & Spottiswoode, who were granted the office of King's printer on 27 May 1901 (*London Gazette*, 28 May 1901), having formerly been the Queen's printer, but Robert Wood, who presumably knew the facts, said in his article for the *Evening News* of 19 December 1907 that his father had worked for nearly thirty years for 'the firm of Messrs Spottiswoode and Co'. Despite the similar name, this was a different printing firm, albeit with close historical family connections. The likelihood is that Newton was confused and thought that Spottiswoode & Co was the same firm as Eyre & Spottiswoode – a common mistake – and was thus the King's printers. It certainly would have sounded better in court and was not a material fact so he would not have been too concerned about whether it was right or not. Documentary records of Spottiswoode & Co held at the Essex Record Office confirm that George Wood was employed as a compositor by that company (ERO – D/F 182/5/1/5).

140 It did not officially become a Church School until 1907 but the Church of England played a prominent role in running the school so it was commonly known as one.

141 LMA – EO/DIV2/THA/LB/002.

142 Ibid.

143 *Weekly Dispatch*, 22 December 1907.

144 LMA – EO/DIV2/THA/LB/002.

145 *London Daily News*, 26 October 1889.

146 LMA – EO/DIV2/THA/LB/002.

147 In his account in the *Weekly Dispatch*, Wood erroneously refers to the club as the Australasian Medical Students Club. It was not a club for medical students – all students were free to join – but no doubt there was a disproportionate number of medical student members.

148 Letter from H.B. Allen of the University of Melbourne to the editor of the *Argus* in the *Argus*, 24 June 1891.

Endnotes

149 Ibid.

150 *Weekly Dispatch,* 22 December 1907.

151 Ibid.

152 *Reynolds's Newspaper,* 12 January 1908.

153 The quote about Ruby Young's voice comes from *Lloyds Weekly News* of 15 December 1907.

154 *Weekly Dispatch,* 22 December 1907.

155 Ibid.

156 From newspaper reports of the inquest proceedings on 14 October 1907, it seems that Ruby said that she had lunch with Wood during the afternoon of 11 September 1907. At the Old Bailey, however, she confirmed that she did not see him from the time she parted from him in July 1907 to the time she met him in response to his telegram (i.e. of 20 September), apart from when she bumped into him in August.

157 *Weekly Dispatch,* 22 December 1907.

158 *Scotsman,* 25 January 1868.

159 NLS – ACC 11812 (162).

160 Wood described the musical machine as a 'gramophone' in both his statement to police of 4 October 1907 and during his evidence at trial. Ruby Young and John Tinkham, to whom Wood told the story of his meeting with Emily before his arrest, referred to it as an 'organ' and 'piano organ' (i.e. an automatic piano) respectively in their statements to police. They were not, of course, in the *Rising Sun* at the time but Ellen Lawrence was and in her evidence at the Clerkenwell Police Court on 22 November 1907, as reported by the *Times* and the *Daily Telegraph of* 23 November, she said that Emily 'put a penny in the automatic piano'. However, during her evidence at the trial she referred to the machine as an 'automatic gramophone' so it is not entirely clear if it was a piano or not. For what it is worth, Wood's story as initially reported by the *Daily Mirror* on 7 October 1907 involved Emily asking 'for a penny to place in an automatic piano at the bar' and both the *Weekly Dispatch* and *People* of 13 October 1907, reported the same thing.

161 TNA – MEPO 2/574.

162 Evidence-in-chief of Robert Wood at trial on 17 December 1907 (*Islington Daily Gazette and North London Tribune,* 18 December 1907).

163 TNA – HO 140/250.

164 Statement of Frank Clarke dated 15 September 1907, TNA – MEPO 3/182.

165 *Northampton Daily Chronicle,* 14 September 1907.

166 It was reported (in the *Northampton Daily Chronicle* of 14 September 1907) that this was the same policeman, PC Thomas Killion, who was called to the scene of the crime although he never gave any evidence of this.

167 In Mrs Stocks' statement to police of 12 September 1907, she said that Shaw 'went out to go to Euston but came back again in a minute or two to tell me that if deceased came back I was to say where he and his other had gone' and, at this point, she 'suggested that we should open the door with my keys' (TNA – MEPO 3/182).

168 This comes from an interview with Mrs Stocks in *Reynolds Newspaper* of 15 September 1907.

169 Ibid.

170 Interview with Mrs Shaw in the *Daily Chronicle,* 16 September 1907.

171 George Dilnot, *Great Detectives and their Methods,* Geoffrey Bles, 1928.

172 *Tribune,* 14 December 1907.

173 When Neil came to write his autobiography, he completely omitted to mention that his father was a gardener and said only that he was a county bailiff. It's possible that Frederick did work as a bailiff at some point in his life but all known official documents record him as having been a gardener.

174 TNA – MEPO 7/65.

175 CLSAC, Register of Disorderly Houses, JN 20/55E.

176 Ibid. Those convicted were Ezekiel Hart, Elizabeth Hart (his wife) and Cecilia Gibson.

177 It is not known what happened to Arthur Ransley save that it can be deduced that he was dead by 1911. His parents stated on the census of that year that only two of their children were still alive and their son, Frederick, and daughter, Alice, can both be accounted for so Q.E.D. Arthur must have died, presumably after having emigrated since there is no record of his death in the UK.

178 *Evening News,* 12 September 1907.

179 Evidence of Inspector Neil, *Trial of Robert Wood (a.k.a. Notable British Trials)* ed. Hogarth, 1936.

180 Report of Inspector Neil dated 13 September 1907, TNA – MEPO 3/182.

181 Statement of Dr John Thompson, 9 October 1907, TNA – MEPO 3/182.

182 *Islington Daily Gazette and North London Tribune,* 1 October 1907.

183 *Police Gazette,* 20 September 1907. The *Daily News* of 14 September 1907 tried to be clever by deducing what had been stolen from a list of stolen or missing property circulated to metropolitan pawnbrokers and jewellers by the police on the morning of 13 September. From this, the newspaper concluded that four gold rings, a chain pattern bracelet, a lady's small watch, a silver hair brush, a silver hand mirror and a silver pin tray had been taken from Emily's room. In fact, none of these items belonged to Emily (although some rings and a lady's small watch were stolen from her room) and must have been taken in another robbery.

184 *Evening News*, 12 December 1907 (evidence of Bert Shaw).
185 The electoral registers of St Pancras East for 1907 and 1908 show that an elderly spinster called Martha Inglethorpe was also living at 29 St Paul's Road at the time but there is no mention of her in the Metropolitan Police file at the National Archives.
186 *Morning Leader*, 13 September 1907.
187 *Daily News*, 13 September 1907.
188 The *Evening News* of 14 September referred to 'the crumpled envelope found under the bed, and partly burnt' suggesting that the newspaper was intending to refer to the burnt pieces of the letter found in the fireplace.
189 It was Bert Shaw who informed the police of Emily's association with this man, whom he knew as 'Bert Woods'. Shaw also knew that Arthur Harrap was associated with Emily, according to Inspector Neil's report of 30 September 1907.
190 As reported in the *Daily Mail* of 14 September 1907. However, this news evidently did not reach the *Daily Mirror* which not only reported on 14 September that bloodstained finger prints were on bedclothes, posts and a basin but that the police had also found a man's bloodstained handkerchief bearing a laundry mark. Again, this was not true.
191 In fact, as reported, the postcard bore the post mark of a 'seaside town' but it is evident from the fact that the sender was believed to be Biddle that this was Portsmouth.
192 *Daily Chronicle*, 14 September 1907.
193 The debunking of the story was in the *Evening News* of 14 September 1907 which reported that the neighbour who made the original statement had corrected himself.
194 *Evening News*, 14 September 1907.
195 *Lloyd's Weekly News*, 15 September 1907.
196 *People*, 15 September 1907.
197 *Reynolds's Newspaper*, 15 September 1907.
198 The newspaper actually referred to 'the saloon bar of the Euston public house, which is situated at the corner of Chapel-street' but this was clearly a mistake for Chalton Street and must be the *Rising Sun*. The decision not to name the pub was probably deliberate but the same newspaper also reported on the same day (14 September) that Emily did a quantity of needlework for Mrs Chapman 'proprietress of the Rising Sun public house in the Euston-road'. This was the first public mention of the *Rising Sun* in connection with the crime. The reference to 'a young woman' came in a further mention of this same witness in *Reynolds's Newspaper* of 22 September 1907.
199 *News of the World*, 15 September 1907.
200 The statements themselves are not in the Metropolitan Police file at the National Archives so their contents have been pieced together from a subsequent police report and their evidence at the inquest and trial which, one assumes, reflected their statements.
201 McCowan's statement does not survive in the Metropolitan Police file in the National Archives but it was read out at the inquest on 21 October 1907 (*Tribune*, 22 October 1907) and during the trial on 14 December 1907 (*Evening News*, 14 December 1907). It reveals that McCowan also saw a policeman ahead of him in the distance, walking towards Brewery Road, but his identity was never established.
202 'From the post-mortem examination Dr Thompson was able to inform me that the deceased's last meal was composed of fish and potatoes' (Inspector Neil's report of 30 September 1907, TNA – MEPO 3/182).
203 Neil's report refers to the man as 'Sidney Albert' but I have taken the spelling from the contemporary Post Office Directory.
204 *The Morning Leader* of 1 October 1907 reported that Dr Thompson said at the inquest that, in Emily's stomach, there were 'one or two red pieces that looked like ham'. Despite the red colour matching ham, it is fairly certain that Thompson must have said 'lamb' rather than 'ham', considering that he only refers to lamb in his written statement, and that the reporter misheard what was said.
205 This is from the official *Minutes of Evidence* but does not appear in the *Notable British Trials* transcript.
206 The Scottish publication, *The Day*, of 3 April 1832 described some examples of 'admirable specimens of the man-o-wars-man' with 'their dark and sun tinged faces – their whiskered throats – the open collar displaying to view their muscular bosoms and brawny shoulders – their straw plaited hats, their clean checked shirts and yard wide trousers'.
207 When he later prepared a written statement for the police, on 9 October 1907, Dr Thompson said he initially thought that Emily had been dead 'very likely six or seven hours', TNA – MEPO 3/182. When giving evidence at the Old Bailey he said that 'she must have been dead several hours, seven or eight perhaps' before telling Marshall Hall during cross-examination that he did not think she had been dead 'more than nine hours' when he saw her.
208 At the inquest, Dr Thompson said that Emily's supper was 'about three parts digested'.
209 *Islington Gazette and North London Tribune*, 1 October 1907. In his written statement of 9 October 1907, Dr Thompson said that on the basis that Emily took her last meal at 11:30pm this would bring the time of death 'to about 3am'.
210 One cannot help wondering if the doctor's change of mind regarding the time of death was influenced by Inspector Neil's theory, as expressed in his report of 30 September, that 'the murderer appears to have waited for the first streaks of dawn before completing his work'. This appears to have

been based on two things: firstly, that one of the windows in Emily's front room was half open to let in light and secondly, that McCowan saw a man leaving the crime scene shortly before 5:00am. A time of death of 3:00am was not terribly helpful for the police.

211 See, for example, Snyder Sachs, Jessica, *Time of Death: The True Story of the Search for Death's Stopwatch*, William Heinemann, 2002.

212 Statement of Frank Clarke dated 15 September 1907, TNA – MEPO 3/182.

213 The average height of the British army recruit from 1900 to 1910 was 5 foot, 6.1 inches (*Times*, 10 February 1915).

214 It should nevertheless be noted that one newspaper report, which estimated Wood's height as being 5 foot, 8 inches, nevertheless described him as 'a slight, short young fellow' (*St Pancras Chronicle*, 11 October 1907).

215 This issue of the newspaper also carried the headline 'THE CAMDEN TOWN MURDER MYSTERY'.

216 *Daily Mail*, 16 September 1907.

217 *Daily News*, 16 September 1907.

218 *Daily Chronicle*, 16 September 1907.

219 *Daily Mirror*, 16 September 1907.

220 *Daily News*, 17 September 1907.

221 *Daily Mail*, 1 October 1907.

222 *Evening Standard and St James's Gazette*, 16 September 1907.

223 *Evening News*, 16 September 1907.

224 *Daily Mirror*, 16 December 1907.

225 *Marylebone Times*, 20 September 1907.

226 *Bradford Observer*, 4 August 1859.

227 Hansard, Parliamentary Debates, 4 July 1856.

228 *Evening Post* (NZ), 28 April 1880.

229 Ibid.

230 *Star* (NZ), 18 December 1880.

231 *Star* (NZ), 14 February 1881.

232 *Press* (NZ), 16 July 1881.

233 *Star* (NZ), 5 December 1881.

234 *Star* (NZ), 5 December 1881.

235 Annie Jerome, a neighbour and friend of Crabtree/McTaggart, was convicted of 'keeping a house of ill-fame' in February 1885 (*Star* (NZ), 12 February 1885) and had a number of subsequent convictions for the same offence.

236 *Star* (NZ), 25 September 1884.

237 *The Weekly Press* (NZ), 4 February 1887.

238 *Star* (NZ), 23 December 1884.

239 Ibid.

240 *Press* (NZ), 6 January 1885.

241 *Evening Post*, 26 March 1885.

242 *Evening Post*, 2 February 1887.

243 *North Otago Times*, 3 February 1887.

244 *Star* (NZ), 3 February 1887.

245 *Poverty Bay Herald*, 9 July 1887.

246 Ibid.

247 *Launceston Examiner*, 22 November 1892.

248 *Hawkes Bay Herald*, 10 October 1887.

249 *Wakefield Express*, 12 October 1901.

250 *Sheffield Daily Telegraph*, 12 October 1901.

251 It is possible that this included the missing organ and bicycle but this cannot be confirmed. It would seem that Crabtree had hired both of them and then took them as his own property.

252 *Newcastle Weekly Chronicle*, 21 November 1903.

253 *Wakefield Express*, 19 October 1901.

254 Ibid.

255 *Newcastle Weekly Chronicle*, 17 October 1903.

256 *Yorkshire Evening Post*, 2 October 1903; *Sheffield Daily Telegraph*, 2 October 1903; *Yorkshire Evening Post*, 7 October 1903.

257 *Durham Chronicle*, 20 November 1903; *Northern Echo*, 20 November 1903.

258 LMA – PS/CLE/B02/006.

259 Ibid.

260 Hard labour was not quite as bad as it sounds. Since 1877 it only meant a slightly more arduous work regime for the first 28 days of a prisoner's sentence and then he did exactly the same work as other prisoners for the remainder of the sentence (TNA – HO 45/10913/A60340).

261 TNA – MEPO 3/182.

262 Statement of John William Crabtree dated 19 September 1907, TNA – MEPO 3/182.

263 TNA – MEPO 3/182.

264 This would have been Reynolds & Co, 128 Euston Road, which was a shop selling surgical and rubber goods.

265 The statement in the file in the National Archives, which is handwritten, and not entirely legible, says
that May Campbell met Emily at 7:00pm without specifying a date. Someone else (possibly at a later
time) has written 'Wednesday' afterwards. As Campbell's original meeting with Emily was supposed
to be at 9:30pm on Tuesday, a subsequent meeting at 7:00pm can only have been on the Wednesday
(considering Emily was dead on the Thursday) but the fact that someone needed to write this in suggests that Campbell was confused about the dates. Also, the fact that Campbell gave her statement to
two police constables, who were probably not used to taking statements in murder cases, might have
added to the confusion. It might also be noted that the words 'the fourth' appear next to May Campbell's signature at the foot of the statement, which is torn at the bottom, suggesting that the statement
might have been dated the fourth of a month (which must have been 4 October) but someone has
written 19 September 1907 at the top of statement and I have assumed that this date must be correct.

266 *Reynolds's Newspaper*, 27 October 1907.

267 Ibid.

268 Statement of Gladys Lineham (sic) [Warren], 20 September 1907.

269 *Illustrated Police Budget*, 26 October 1907.

270 *Reynolds's Newspaper*, 22 September 1907.

271 Ibid. A special representative of the newspaper was said to have asked the unnamed female witness
who had seen Emily with a man in a blue serge suit on the Wednesday evening in the *Rising Sun* if
she could recognise Henry Clark's clothes as being those of the man she had seen. The newspaper
reported that she failed to identify the clothes but she said that they belonged to a man of very similar
build to the one she saw.

272 Ibid.

273 It may be noted that, when giving their written statements to the police, both Ruby Young and Joseph
Lambert initially dated their respective conversations with Wood as having taken place within two
days of the murder, i.e. on Friday 13 September, and this dating was repeated at both the inquest and
the police court proceedings. This would have made perfect sense given that, in attempting to cre-
ate a false alibi, Wood appears to have been responding to the fact that his colleague, William Moss,
had commented about Emily Dimmock's murder from newspaper reports on the Friday morning.
It would also explain the apparent urgency of Wood sending a telegram to Ruby and telephoning
Lambert on the same day. However, both Young and Lambert also said their conversations with
Wood occurred *after* the photograph of Emily appeared in the newspapers (which was on Saturday 14
September) although Lambert was less certain. During her cross-examination at the Old Bailey, Ruby
was shown a telegram sent to her by Wood which said 'Meet me 6.30, Phit-Eesi's, to-night – Bob' and
accepted it was dated 20 September 1907 so that this *must* have been the date she met Wood (because
she met him in response to that telegram – and, she confirmed, there were no other telegrams). At the
end of their meeting, she recalled that Wood told her he was going to see Lambert and he left her at
Leicester Square at 7.15pm. Lambert recalled Wood arriving at his shop at 7.15pm so it seems to be
the case that both conversations did take place on 20 September.

274 The *People* of 22 September carried a headline 'POLICE ISSUE DESCRIPTION OF "WANTED" MAN'
and also referred to the description, which it reproduced, as 'official'. However, it was probably pla-
giarising the *Daily Mail* as the papers of the time seemed to copy what the others were saying.

275 Statement of George White dated 24 September 1907, TNA – MEPO 3/182.

276 The detective-inspector who overheard the conversation was Edwin Pollard of 'X' Division (Kilburn).

277 May Campbell said in one of her statements that she saw Emily on her own in the Euston Road near
the *Rising Sun* at about 10:00pm when she was joined by a man who emerged from the lavatory in
that public house but she did not see them together in there at any point.

278 *Daily Chronicle*, 26 September 1907.

279 A handwritten letter addressed to the Central News Agency from someone signing as 'Jack the Ripper' was displayed on bills printed at police stations in October 1888 but was not sent by the police
to the newspapers on that occasion. Criminals, including murderers, had previously been traced
through portraits or photographs published in the press but these had been obtained independently
by the press as opposed to being provided by the police for the aim of catching those criminals.

280 *Daily Mirror*, 28 September 1907.

281 The summary set out is the generic version of the story told by Wood, not necessarily exactly what he
told Tinkham on that day but it is impossible to be certain precisely what Wood told each individual.

282 These suppers were held at 79 Wells Street. According to the Sketch Club's archivist, Wood was not
a member of the Sketch Club but non-members could attend the dinners as guests of members. The
same would be true for anyone called 'Hulme'. The Sketch Club did not have any members called
'Hulme' at the time but there was a member called Robert Hume, a landscape painter living in Fulham who, like Wood, had been born in Edinburgh.

283 A 'leading Scotland Yard official' was quoted in the *Daily News* of 1 October 1907 as saying: 'It is too
absurd. You know our methods; calling in clairvoyants is not one of them'. This did not prevent the
author of the 2008 book, *The Camden Town Murder*, from checking 'the ships to Melbourne' to see if he
could locate a particular suspect. Not surprisingly, he 'came up with nothing'.

284 Report of Inspector Neil dated 30 September 1907, TNA – MEPO 3/182.
285 Email from Lieutenant Colonel C.J.E. Seymour LVO to the author dated 17 July 2013.
286 LMA – PS/MAR/A1/024. Tetlow would subsequently re-join the army during the First World War and be killed in action in France in 1916.
287 According to Inspector Neil, 'J. Hurst', a grenadier guardsman, was stationed at the Tower of London in September 1907. Curiously, however, the archivist of the Grenadier Guards has no record of any soldier called J. Hurst matching the known description of Jumbo (letter to the author from Lieutenant Colonel C.J.E. Seymour LVO dated 9 July 2013).
288 *Star*, 30 September 1907; *News of the World*, 6 October 1907.
289 Statement of Dr John Thompson, dated 8 October 1907, TNA – MEPO 3/182. Just over a week earlier, Inspector Neil had written in his report of 30 September 1907 that 'Dr Thompson states that shortly before her death this woman [Emily] indulged in sexual intercourse'.
290 *Minutes of Evidence* at trial, 12 December 1907.
291 *Star*, 30 September 1907.
292 There had been discussion in the press about Emily's health. In the context of the claim that the prime suspect was 'believed to have been for some time in a certain hospital', *Reynolds's Newspaper* of 22 September 1907 commented that this fact 'lends colour to the theory freely talked of in the district, that the dead woman, about eighteen months ago, was in ill-health'.
293 This was based on what Robert Roberts had told him.
294 *Northampton Daily Reporter & Echo*, 3 October 1907.
295 According to the *Notable British Trials* transcript, Marshall Hall informed the judge that Ruby had seen the postcard reproduced in the *Daily Chronicle* of Saturday 28 September but the *News of the World* published a statement in its 20 October 1907 issue in which Ruby stated that she first saw the reproduction of the postcard in that newspaper on the Sunday. The official *Minutes of Evidence* also record her saying this.
296 She was asked for his first name at the police court proceedings on 4 December 1907 but did not know it. She also denied he was her lover but this does not necessarily preclude him being a client.
297 At the St Pancras Coroner's Court on 14 October 1907, according to the *Weekly Dispatch* of 20 October 1907, Ruby said that she first spoke to a newspaper reporter from the *Weekly Dispatch* on Thursday 3 October (although other papers reported it as Wednesday 2 October). It may, therefore, be that the lunch at the restaurant took place on the Thursday and subsequent events unfolded over 24 hours rather than a few hours on Friday afternoon. This would, of course, mean that Ruby had spoken to both McEwan Brown *and* Dilnot when she met Wood on Thursday evening but confessed to speaking only to a friend. In her evidence at the Old Bailey, Ruby's chronology of events was that she first spoke to McEwan Brown on the evening of Thursday 3 October and then to Dilnot the next day. It is possible that Ruby was feeling guilty about the fact that she had not told Wood that she had spoken to a journalist when she spoke to him on Thursday evening so she gilded her evidence to make it appear that the period between her meeting a journalist and Wood's arrest was very short, and everything happened in a blur, without her having a chance to think.
298 Most accounts only mention Sergeant Ball as being present with Inspector Neil at the arrest (and Wood in his own account of the arrest for the *Weekly Dispatch* of 29 December 1907 referred to a 'small group of four on the pavement' meaning himself, Ruby, Neil and Ball) but the *News of the World* of 6 October 1907 said that Detective Sergeants Goodchild and Osborne were there too.
299 TNA – HO 45/222269.
300 At the same time, according to the evidence of McCowan at trial, the man standing next to Wood in the parade was also wearing a blue serge suit (*Daily Telegraph*, 14 December 1907).
301 *Weekly Dispatch*, 29 December 1907.
302 Smeeth was often wrongly called 'Edwin Sneeth' in contemporary reports.
303 This is from Ellen Lawrence's evidence at the inquest on 21 October 1907.
304 *Weekly Dispatch*, 29 December 1907.
305 Nevertheless, Brooker's evidence was unchallenged at trial when he was in the witness box.
306 *Weekly Dispatch*, 29 December 1907.
307 Arthur Newton, 'Twenty Years Among Criminals and Others', in *Cassell's Saturday Journal*, 21 March 1908.
308 *Pall Mall Gazette*, 19 April 1887.
309 TNA – HO 144/477/X24427A. Although Newton was indeed a convicted criminal, he was in the 'First Class', a classification normally reserved for political prisoners and the like, which should have allowed him special privileges above other convicts. This was the basis of his complaint that he was being treated like an ordinary convicted criminal.
310 *Reynolds's Newspaper*, 29 June 1890.
311 Quoted in *Marlborough Street: The Story of a London Court* by Joan Lock, Hale 1980.
312 *Sunday Express*, 13 January 1924.
313 *Sunday Express*, 20 January 1924.
314 *Cassell's Saturday Journal*, 30 May 1908.
315 *Cassell's Saturday Journal*, 20 August 1908.
316 *Daily Mail*, 8 October 1907.

317 *Daily Chronicle*, 8 October 1907.

318 *Morning Leader*, 8 October 1907.

319 *Weekly Dispatch*, 29 December 1907.

320 Ibid.

321 Ibid.

322 Statement of Joseph Lambert, 8 October 1907, TNA – MEPO 3/182.

323 This was repeated by Dr Thompson during his evidence at trial when he said: 'She [Emily] had a cut on her right elbow, but I think that was done after her death when the murderer was removing the clothes' (Evidence of Dr John Thompson, 12 December 1907, *Notable British Trials* transcript).

324 LMA - LCC/EO/DIV02/GRE/AD/001.

325 *Balham & Tooting Times*, 14 September 1907.

326 *Cardiff Times & South Wales Weekly News*, 14 September 1907.

327 *Balham & Tooting News*, 21 September 1907.

328 *Clapham Observer*, 14 September 1907.

329 *Balham & Tooting News*, 21 September 1907.

330 Ibid; *Cardiff Times & South Wales Weekly News*, 14 September 1907.

331 e.g. *Weekly Mail*, 14 September 1907.

332 Saltmead even had its own murder mystery. Harriet Stacey, a 50-year-old prostitute, of 41 Saltmead Road had been found murdered (by strangulation) in her bed on 7 February 1904. She was 'on her left side with the bed clothes up as far as the shoulders' and a cord around her neck (GA – DCONC 4/1/6). The murderer was never caught.

333 *South Wales Echo*, 13 September 1907.

334 *Evening Express*, 14 September 1907.

335 Official police report of inquest, GA – DCONC 4/1/8.

336 *South Wales Daily News*, 14 September 1907.

337 The newspaper actually said 'brown cap' but George Appleton clarified that Charles had been wearing a bowler hat. Early reports (e.g. *Cardiff Times & South Wales Weekly News* of 14 September 1907) also described Parnther as 'a tall man' although he was subsequently said to be 5ft 6 inches. It must have been difficult to estimate the height of a decapitated body and it may well be that Parnther was taller than this. Army records show that his brother, Arthur, was no less than six foot, three and a quarter inches, in height.

338 There is one exception as the short-lived *Weekly Standard* of 11 October 1907 reported that 'The Cardiff police attach no importance to the rumoured connection of a mysterious case of suicide at Cardiff on September 12 and the murderer of Miss Dimmock'.

339 *Evening Express and Evening Mail*, 7 October 1907.

340 Ibid.

341 Even with a motor car it would not have been easy. The distance by road from London to Cardiff was almost 160 miles, and the maximum legal speed limit was 20 miles per hour, making for an eight hour journey. However, if the speed limit was exceeded and an average of 40 miles per hour was achieved – something that probably would not have been very easy in the cars of the period on an unlit dusty road during the night – it is conceivable that the journey could have been completed within four hours so that someone leaving London at, say, 1:00am, could have arrived in Cardiff at about 5:00am. There is no suggestion that Parnther owned, or had access to, a car so he simply must have taken the train for any journeys he made to Cardiff.

342 Having examined the Great Western Railway timetable for September 1907 (TNA – RAIL 936/40) I have not found any other candidates.

343 *Illustrated Police Budget*, 22 February 1908. The reverend's figures were said to be an exaggeration but the actual numbers are not important – it was the reputation that might have lured Parnther to Cardiff.

344 TNA – RAIL 936/40.

345 Ruby's evidence was that Wood lunched in Museum Street (where his brother lived) every Tuesday and Friday but we do not know if he went there on the day he was arrested.

346 *Weekly Dispatch*, 13 October 1907.

347 *Thomson's Weekly News*, 30 September 1922.

348 *Evening News*, 14 October 1907.

349 *Not Guilty M'Lord*, Seymour Hicks, 1939.

350 *St Pancras Chronicle*, 18 October 1907.

351 LMA – PS/CLE/B/01/012 & PS/CLE/A/01/008 and reported in the *Islington Daily Gazette and North London Tribune*, 15 October 1907.

352 Ibid.

353 TNA – TS 42/25.

354 *The People*, 20 October 1907 and *Daily Express*, 16 October 1907.

355 TNA – TS 42/25.

356 *People*, 20 October 1907.

357 *Evening News*, 21 October 1907.

358 *Star*, 21 October 1907.

359 *Tribune*, 14 December 1907.

360 *Sunday Express*, 3 February 1924.

361 *Daily Mail*, 22 October 1907.

362 This was Shaw's evidence-in-chief during Wood's trial. He also dealt with the postcard album during the police court proceedings on 6 November 1907 but it was poorly reported. According to the *Evening News* of that day (and repeated word for word in the next morning's *Daily Mirror*), Shaw said that the album 'was usually kept…on a small table or beneath the sewing machine, and after the murder it was found lying open on a chair'. However, it is not clear that these were Shaw's actual words. Other newspapers (e.g. the *Daily Telegraph*) reported him saying that the album was 'on the table in the front room' when he left the house on 11 September but mentioned nothing about him saying it was also kept beneath the sewing machine. It may be that, consistent with his trial evidence, he said he *found* it on (or beneath) the sewing machine and the *Evening News*/*Daily Mirror* reporter misheard this and then interposed the police evidence to the effect that it was found lying open on a chair. Under cross-examination from Marshall Hall at the Old Bailey, Shaw was a little less certain whether the postcard album was on the sewing machine or the chair. However, he said that Emily usually kept it in the part of the room where it was found so there was nothing about the position of the album to suggest that the murderer had moved it very far.

363 *Weekly Dispatch*, 27 October 1907 and *Lloyds Weekly News*, 27 October 1907. According to one newspaper, the phrase she used was that he had 'threatened to do her head off' (*Reynolds's Newspaper*, 27 October 1907).

364 From the evidence of the Habitual Criminals Register for 1907, criminals sentenced to six months imprisonment on 28 February 1907 who served their full term actually seem to have been released from prison on 27 August 1907 for some reason.

365 HO/45/10913/A60340; this rule was only introduced on 12 August 1907.

366 The Metropolitan Police Court registers that have survived for 1907 are from the Clerkenwell, Old Street, Marylebone and Bow Street Police Courts. Registers also exist from the Highgate Police Court and the Edgware and Willesdon Petty Sessions. The North London Police Court and Marlborough Street Police Court registers for 1907 have not survived.

367 Two others of less interest are Walter Collins, a 27-year-old labourer sentenced to six months hard labour for assaulting his wife, and James Rowe, a 25-year-old market porter, sentenced to six months hard labour for an assault on a police constable; both convicted at Marylebone Police Court on 9 and 10 April 1907 respectively.

368 *Islington Gazette & North London Tribune*, 4 April 1907.

369 Ibid.

370 LMA – PS/CLE/A/01/006.

371 *Hampstead Record*, 9 April 1904.

372 *Hampstead Record*, 13 April 1907.

373 TNA – HO 140/258.

374 TNA – MEPO 3/182.

375 On the census form his name is wrongly recorded as 'Clifford Frederick'. He was still living at that same address, with the Small family, at the time of his death in 1921.

376 TNA – MEPO 7/67.

377 In the Habitual Register of Criminals for 1907 (TNA – MEPO 6/18), every criminal sentenced to six months imprisonment on 10 April 1907 (and released after five months for good behaviour) was, without exception, released on 10 September 1907.

378 *Hampstead Record*, 16 February 1907 & 23 February 1907.

379 LMA – PS/CLE/B2/009.

380 In the court papers that do survive, there are references to a fight between two men, Morgan and King, with the name of the informant/complainant against Mr and Mrs Curtis given as 'E. Morgan 14Y' which suggests the Morgan involved in the fight was a police sergeant except that '14Y' appears to have been the collar number of a Sergeant Ferrier so the situation is not entirely clear.

381 'Maynard' was, of course, also the surname of Emily's great grandmother.

382 *Lloyds Weekly News*, 27 October 1907 and *Reynolds's Newspaper*, 27 October 1907.

383 Rule 67(3) of the 1899 Prison Rules (HO 45/10913/A60340).

384 *Star*, 28 October 1907.

385 Ibid.

386 Sharples originally said in evidence to the coroner that he saw the man with Emily in the *Rising Sun* on Monday 8 September (although 8 September was a Sunday) and, when pressed by Mr Newton, said 'Yes, it was on the Monday before this job happened'. In cross-examination, however, he said 'It was on the Sunday. I made a mistake when I said Monday' (*Daily Telegraph*, 29 October 1907).

387 *Evening News*, 28 October 1907.

388 The other instance put forward by the coroner was the 'Harley Street murder', when the murdered body of a woman was found in a flour barrel in the cellar of 139 Harley Street in June 1880. She had been killed by being stabbed in the chest some years earlier. Dr Danford Thomas was the deputy coroner who assisted at the inquest. It does not seem to have been a particularly good example of a man murdering a woman in a rage of passion because the motive for the murder was unknown. The

identity of the murderer was never established.

389 *Morning Leader*, 29 October 1907: the *Weekly Dispatch* reporter, however, heard Wood say to someone, '...man's inhumanity to man – you know the rest' which might have been a different interpretation of the same conversation (*Weekly Dispatch*, 3 November 1907).

390 *Islington Daily Gazette and North London Tribune*, 7 November 1907.

391 See *The Islington Murder Mystery*, Orsam Books, 2012, for a brief discussion of this point.

392 *Daily Telegraph*, 13 November 1907.

393 *Daily Telegraph*, 15 November 1907.

394 Statement of Robert McCowan dated 14 September 1907 as read out in court (*Evening News*, 14 December 1907). McCowan would also say that he was booked on at the V.V. Bread Company at 5:05am (*Standard*, 14 December 1907).

395 Rentoul, Sir Charles, *This is My Case*, Hutchison & Co, 1944.

396 *Times*, 4 June 1907.

397 Ibid.

398 *Daily Telegraph*, 19 December 1907.

399 *Globe*, 13 September 1907.

400 *Law Notes*, November 1907.

401 *Reynolds's Newspaper*, 15 December 1907.

402 *Islington Daily Gazette and North London Tribune*, 13 December 1907.

403 *Pall Mall Gazette*, 12 December 1907.

404 *Star*, 12 December 1907 and *Pall Mall Gazette*, 12 December 1907.

405 *Daily Chronicle*, 13 December 1907.

406 One of them was Walter James Reid who may be the same Walter James Reid recorded as living in Harlow, Essex in the 1911 census. His occupation was given as a builder's carman and it may be that both jurors to whom Marshall Hall objected were carmen who might have had sympathy for their fellow carman, Robert McCowan.

407 *Evening News*, 12 December 1907.

408 *Islington Daily Gazette and North London Tribune*, 13 December 1907.

409 It should be noted that Detective Constable Alfred Grosse gave evidence on the first day of the trial suggesting that six electric lights on the line of the Midland Railway, some 100 yards away, might have thrown a glare in the direction of St Paul's Road. These do not appear to have been turned off before 5:00am. So, perhaps, McCowan was confused in his mind between the light produced by the street lamps and the railway lamps. At the start of the trial, Marshall Hall had given Grosse a hard time over supposed inaccuracies in a plan he had prepared showing the positions of the various electric lights in St Paul's Road and the surrounding area, asking him, 'have you ever seen a more misleading plan in your life?' to which Detective Grosse maintained a dignified silence. This exchange was widely reported and history has not been kind to Detective Grosse with most commentators swallowing Marshall Hall's line that his plan was wrong. However, in a little noticed incident during the evidence of William Westcott, two days after the barristers and the jury had visited St Paul's Road, it was reported that Marshall Hall 'apologised to a police officer concerning a remark he had made over a plan' (*Daily News*, 18 December 1907), suggesting that Grosse might have got it right after all. Superintendent Vedy certainly thought he had; on 21 December 1907 he recommended Grosse for a note in favour 'for the manner in which he prepared the plans' (TNA – MEPO 3/182). However, as McCowan had specifically said it was the street lights which illuminated the man he saw in St Paul's Road, any light which might have come from the railway line was not relevant to his credibility.

410 McCowan suggested that if Wood put his coat on 'he would be two inches broader' to which Mr Justice Grantham responded by saying 'If this is going to be pressed I think the prisoner should put the overcoat on' (*Morning Advertiser*, 14 December 1907).

411 This is what he said in evidence. It is possible that he said in his statement that he only needed to be at work by 5:35am because this is how Marshall Hall opened the case for the defence.

412 Some reports call this witness Francis George Barney. It has not been possible to establish which is correct.

413 This answer was reported slightly differently in a number of newspapers but that is how it was quoted in both the *Daily Mirror* and the *Tribune* of 17 December 1907 and seems to be the most likely words used.

414 TNA – BT 31/11894/92555.

415 There did appear to be some sort of attempt by Marshall Hall to dig at whether Linehan had been keeping a brothel in Judd Street; he asked him what rent Gladys Warren paid him (Linehan could not recall) and the name of the landlord (Linehan could not recall it) but, presumably, he was unaware of Linehan's conviction.

416 The wording of this exchange has been compiled from contemporary newspaper reports and from the official *Minutes of Evidence*. It is a little different to the wording in the *Notable British Trials* transcript. In that transcript, it is Marshall Hall who introduces mention of 'Wednesday morning' in one of his questions but this does not make sense because there is no reason for him to have assumed that Roberts and Clarke had spoken on Wednesday morning. The *Daily Chronicle* reporter attributes this to Clarke (and Marjoribanks does the same).

417 *Evening News*, 16 December 1907.
418 Wellesley Orr was called to the bar on 15 June 1904 (*Law List*, 1907).
419 *Times*, 5 December 1907; *Islington Daily Gazette and North London Tribune*, 5 December 1907.
420 *Times*, 5 December 1907.
421 *Morning Post*, 15 October 1907.
422 It has to be said that not all newspapers carried a summary of Dr Thompson's evidence. The *Daily Mirror* of 1 October 1907, for example, did not mention any of the evidence relating to time of death in its report of the inquest. By contrast, the *Daily Chronicle* of the same date carried the headline 'Doctor Fixes the Hour of the Murder'. It is not known what newspaper Wood took but, in fairness, it would not have been impossible for him to have been ignorant of the time of death evidence at this stage.
423 This is from the *Notable British Trials* transcript. The official *Minutes of Evidence* only has Dr Thompson saying that 'A razor might be cleansed by putting it in water and wiping it with the petticoat' but the *Weekly Dispatch* seems to corroborate the *Notable British Trials* transcript, reporting that Dr Thompson said, 'If cleansed immediately after death the razor need not have shown any trace discernible even to microscopic examination' (*Weekly Dispatch*, 15 December 1907).
424 There is some uncertainty in the available transcripts as to whether the inspector was referring to one or both razors. The *Notable British Trials* transcript records Neil saying, 'One of the razors was very old and rusty' whereas the official *Minutes of Evidence* has him saying in the plural, 'They are very old razors and very rusty'. However, the report in the following day's *Times* has the inspector saying exactly the same as in the *Notable British Trials* transcript (*Times*, 14 December 1907).
425 Evidence of Dr Thompson at the inquest (*Star*, 15 September 1907).
426 *Lloyds Weekly Newspaper*, 13 February 1898.
427 *Lloyds Weekly News*, 15 December 1907.
428 e.g. *Daily Chronicle*, 17 December 1907 and The *Morning Leader* of 16 December 1907.
429 It may be noted that Shaw said at the trial that he found the postcard in a different drawer to the one into which he had been told that Roberts had seen Emily put it during the morning of 11 September. In his statement of 7 October 1907, Roberts said that he saw Emily 'go to the left-hand drawer of the chest of drawers in the front room where she placed it [the postcard] with her purse'. During the trial he was a bit more specific, saying that he had seen her put the postcard into the 'left-hand top small drawer' (*Minutes of Evidence*, 12 December 1907) and Shaw confirmed during the trial that he had been told that Roberts saw the postcard being put into 'the top small drawer of the chest of drawers' (*Minutes of Evidence*, 12 December 1907). In a statement to the police after finding it on 25 September, Shaw only said that he found it in 'one of the drawers in a chest of drawers in the front room' but, at the inquest, he gave further information, saying it was in the 'top long drawer of the chest of drawers' (*Evening News*, 14 October 1907) which was presumably different to the top left-hand small drawer. From an unclear photograph of Emily's sitting room published in the *Daily Mirror* of 9 October 1907 it would seem that the chest of drawers had two small drawers at the top of the chest with a single long drawer beneath it (and two rows of drawers beneath that). If the *Daily Mirror* court reporter heard correctly, Shaw said at the trial that he found the postcard 'in the top right-hand drawer' (*Daily Mirror*, 13 December 1907) but he may well have mis-heard because the *Daily Chronicle* of the same day records him as saying it was found in the 'top long drawer'. Neither the *Minutes of Evidence* or *Notable British Trials* transcript provide any assistance in clearing up the confusion because neither of them identify the drawer in which he said he found it. It is a bit of a mystery as to how the postcard supposedly ended up in a different drawer to the one into which Emily put it; but if Shaw always knew where it was supposed to have been put back, and he was making up the story of where he found it, he would surely have claimed he found it in the correct drawer. Interestingly, according to the *Notable British Trials* transcript, Marshall Hall asked Detective Milton during cross-examination, 'You were told by Roberts that the postcard was in the top right-hand drawer?' to which Milton replied 'Yes'. Marshall Hall might have deliberately mis-identified the drawer if he was trying to show that Milton was lying but then one would have expected him to say so after Milton gave his answer. We might be dealing with a transcription error but the *Evening News* of 13 December 1907 appears to corroborate the transcript, reporting that Milton said that he was 'told by Roberts that the Rising Sun postcard was in the top right-hand drawer'. The *Daily Telegraph* reporter heard the same thing and the paper's issue of 14 December 1907 has Milton saying that he was specifically searching for a postcard 'which he was given to understand was in the top right-hand drawer'. On the other hand, the official *Minutes of Evidence* state that Detective Milton told Marshall Hall, 'I was given to understand that the postcard was in the top long drawer' which looks like it might be a more correct transcription of the same evidence even though it is unclear from the context if he was saying that this is what he was told by Roberts or if this was where he understood Shaw had found it. One press report of Milton's evidence has it that Milton 'lifted the paper from the top left-hand drawer and looked underneath but saw no card' (*Standard*, 14 December 1907). The question which elicited this evidence was presumably designed to establish why Milton missed the postcard during the search as opposed to establishing in which drawer he expected to find it. According to the *Minutes of Evidence*, Milton also noted that the 'top long drawer' was on the floor in the front room whereas the others were in their place in the chest (although Bert Shaw recalled there being three drawers on the floor – *Morning Leader*, 7 November 1907). During the Police Court Proceedings, Inspector Neil said that 'the top left-hand drawer of the

chest of drawers had been taken out, and was on the floor' but 'the long drawers had been pulled out but not removed' (*Evening News*, 13 November 1907) which seems to contradict Milton's evidence to the extent that Milton had said that one of the long drawers had been removed. However, in the same report, Neil was asked if he noticed whether 'the top long drawer' was covered with paper, clearly identifying this as the drawer in which the postcard was found. In the *Notable British Trials* transcript Milton is recorded as saying that 'The top drawer was lying on the floor' without identifying it further.

430 TNA – MEPO 3/182.
431 Train timetables from *Northampton Herald*, 13 September – 2007.
432 Report of Inspector Neil dated 8 October 1907, TNA – MEPO 3/182.
433 The fellow employee who slept in Sheffield was referred to by Bert Shaw during his evidence at trial on 12 December 1907 (*Minutes of Evidence*). He said he slept in the house opposite.
434 TNA – HO 140/274 and the *Times*, 10 March 1909.
435 *Hendon and Finchley Times*, 9 February 1906.
436 *Willesden Chronicle*, 4 May 1906.
437 TNA – HO 140/250 and LMA – PS/MAR/A1/007; *Times*, 10 March 1909.
438 TNA – MEPO 6/21.
439 The intended residential address he gave of 192 Newport Road in Cardiff was the address of his father's auction house but his father had moved from Cardiff at least nine years earlier. The likelihood is that he gave deliberately false information to the authorities about his intentions.
440 He was convicted on two counts and sentenced to three months for each to run consecutively: LMA – PS/G/H/A1/007; *Hendon Advertiser*, 3 February 1911; *Hendon & Finchley Times*, 3 February 1911. Clarke appears on the 1911 census as being in Pentonville with his occupation stated as an electrical engineer for a coal colliery.
441 *Hendon & Finchley Times*, 10, 24 & 31 May & 21 June 1912.
442 *Evening News*, 14 October 1907.
443 According to Nina Warner Hooke and Gilbert Thomas in *The Mammoth Book of Unsolved Crimes*, Emily's room had a French window which opened onto the garden to form a convenient entrance for her clients who wished to visit her in secret and that, in hot weather, this window was sometimes left ajar. Where they obtained this information, or whether it is true, is unknown but, as Emily's room was not at street level, it seems highly unlikely that clients would be clambering up the side of the house to get to see her and, as she was living with Shaw, it is far more likely that she brought all her clients home with her, like she did Roberts.
444 Starchfield's actual surname was, apparently, 'Sarchfield', *Times* 16 January 1914. Agnes had known him since she was 15 years old when he enlisted with the King's Royal Rifles and fought in South Africa, being released into the Reserve in 1902 (TNA – CRIM 1/145/3).
445 TNA – MEPO 3/237B.
446 *Reynolds's Newspaper*, 15 September 1907.
447 The *Evening News* of 12 November 1907 reported the time as 'about 8.20' although the *Daily Telegraph* of 13 November 1907 reported that Mrs Shaw said she heard Emily leave by the front door at 'about a quarter past eight'.
448 *Daily Telegraph*, 13 November 1907.
449 *Islington Daily Gazette*, 13 November 1907.
450 *Islington Daily Gazette and North London Tribune*, 13 November 1907.
451 Ibid; *Daily Chronicle*, 14 November 1907.
452 He also said at the Old Bailey that she was not wearing a hat when she left the house whereas Lilian Raven said she was wearing one when he spoke to her in the *Eagle* that evening.
453 *Daily Chronicle*, 17 December 1907.
454 The *Morning Leader* reported events slightly differently from other sources saying that when Rogers was 'scouring his lob worms', he saw the prisoner come home', adding that 'He himself was in the area where he kept his worms'. Is it possible that other reporters misunderstood the meaning of the word 'scouring' and thought that Rogers was searching for worms in the garden rather than preparing them inside his house when he saw Wood return? Apparently not. The *Notable British Trials* transcript is clear that Rogers said 'I got the worms from the garden in front of the house, and I did not go out that night except to get the worms from the garden in front of the house. I was just shutting the cellar door when I saw [Wood] going into house'. The official *Minutes of Evidence* corroborate this, recording Rogers as saying 'I was out gathering worms as usual. I had just put them into the shed and, just as I was shutting the door, I saw [Wood] come up the steps, take the key out of his pocket, open the door, and come in'.
455 *Daily Mail*, 19 December 1907.
456 Closing speech of Marshall Hall at Trial, 18 December 1907.
457 *Dictionary of National Biography*, Volume 17; *A Genealogical Heraldic Dictionary of the Peerage and Baronetage of the British Empire* by Sir Bernard Burke, Harrison, 1862.

458 It may be that Mary Ann Jackson was related to Harriet Jackson but it has not been possible to confirm this. They were certainly not sisters. Harriet's father was John Jackson; Mary Ann's father was William Jackson.

459 Yet, when he died the following year, aged 75, his occupation was described in his death certificate as 'a working jeweller'.

460 No record of Joseph's marriage to Kate has been found (nor has any record been found of the deaths of Harriet or Mary Ann).

461 *Islington Daily Gazette and North London Tribune*, 18 December 1907.

462 *Tribune*, 18 December 1907.

463 *Daily Mail*, 18 December 1907.

464 Having said this, Seymour Hicks, who was present at the trial, wrote in his autobiography that, in response to Marshall Hall's first question, Wood 'did not deign to reply' and, only when pressed, did he say 'It is ridiculous'. But Hicks' book was published in 1939, more than 30 years after the trial, and his recollection might have been influenced by others.

465 Detective Sergeant Osborne had said in his evidence that he found 'a letter and envelope', partly burnt, in the fire but had not mentioned the postmark on the envelope.

466 *Reynolds's Newspaper*, 22 December 1907.

467 *Thomson's Weekly News*, 30 September 1922.

468 Ibid.

469 *The Tribune*, 19 December 1907.

470 *London Weekly News*, 15 December 1907.

471 *Daily Express*, 17 December 1907.

472 *Daily Mail*, 17 December 1907.

473 *Morning Post*, 18 December 1907.

474 *Star*, 18 December 1907.

475 BBC Written Archives Centre ("WAC") – R19/673/1, 1963.

476 James Douglas, *Adventures in London*, Cassell & Co Ltd, 1909.

477 A process of developing invisible (or 'latent') fingerprints was perfected by the San Francisco Bureau of Identification but not until 1912 (*Police Chronicle*, 7 September 1912).

478 No document in the Metropolitan Police file, including Bert Shaw's statement, even mentions Shaw's razors.

479 'Big Nell' was referred to by Crabtree in his statement of 19 September. Edwin Smeeth confirmed to Marshall Hall that he knew 'Little Nellie' and 'Little Annie' who 'used to go about with Phyllis Dimmock'. It is not known if Marshall Hall was told about 'Little Annie' and 'Little Nellie' by Wood or by Arthur Newton from his own enquiries.

480 LMA – PS/CLE/A/01/008.

481 TNA – HO 140/258.

482 *Weekly Dispatch*, 27 October 1907; *Lloyds Weekly News*, 27 October 1907.

483 *Evening News*, 19 December 1907.

484 The *Evening News* of 13 November 1907 reports Inspector Neil saying at the police court that there were indications that two persons had partaken of supper and that 'On the table there were two plates, knives and forks, two glasses which had contained stout'. However, this evidence appears to have been wrongly reported. The *Weekly Dispatch* of 17 November 1907 notes that the inspector was asked if there was only one glass to which he replied 'one only' but also records him as saying there were 'two plates'. In his evidence at the Old Bailey, as recorded in the *Minutes of Evidence*, Inspector Neil also said he only saw 'a glass' which had contained stout and 'knives and forks' with no mention of any plates.

485 *Marshall Hall* by Nina Warner Hooke & Gil Thomas, 1966, Arthur Baker Limited.

486 Opening speech of Sir Charles Mathews at trial, 12 December 1907 (*Notable British Trials* transcript).

487 Another possibility is that the rings had no value. Although he described them as 'gold rings' (probably 9 carat), Inspector Neil never actually said that they were valuable and they were referred to as 'worthless' by Marshall Hall during his closing speech.

488 Evidence of Bert Shaw at the trial, 12 December 1907 (*Minutes of Evidence*).

489 There is, it is true, an element of ambiguity about precisely which time of day Mrs David saw Emily in the *Murray Arms* with her hair in curlers. To the *Reynolds's Newspaper* journalist, she said that Emily used to drink in the saloon bar in the evenings whereas, in the mornings, she would purchase a bottle of stout which she would take away with her. Then she said: 'At these times she would wear a man's cap, an apron and had her hair in curlers' so that it is not clear if the word 'times' is supposed to incorporate both the evening and morning visits or just those in the morning. Yet, even if Emily would not go drinking in the saloon bar during the evening with her hair in curlers, Mrs David's statement shows that she definitely left her house in that state and if she was prepared to do so in the morning, when it was light, there seems to be no reason to think she would not do the same in the evening when the darkness would have provided more cover.

490 It is not known when the three people who saw Emily in Somers Town spoke to the police but, even if it was on the Thursday, it is very unlikely that they were responsible for the police believing the killer was a tall man because there was nothing at that time to suggest that the man they saw was the killer.

491 The electoral register for 1907 also shows a 'William Roberts', presumably the landlady's husband, living at 2 Grafton Place in 1907.
492 Quite possibly this was a reference to Letitia Houps, who appears to have been the sister-in-law of Frederick Houps, who, according to the electoral register, was living at 19 Grafton Street in 1907. Letitia's husband was Herbert Houps and the 1871 census shows that he had a twin brother called Frederick Houps.
493 Statement of John William Crabtree dated 19 September 1907, TNA – MEPO 3/182.
494 *Daily News*, 19 December 1907.
495 *Daily Chronicle*, 19 December 1907.
496 *Daily Mail*, 19 December 1907.
497 Ibid.
498 *Daily Mail*, 20 December 1907.
499 *Weekly Dispatch*, 22 December 1907.
500 *People*, 22 December 1907.
501 *Reynolds's Newspaper*, 22 December 1907.
502 *Herts Mail*, 2 January 1908. The *Herts Mail* did not publish the letter in full and other extracts can be found in the *Northamptonshire Evening Telegraph* of 8 January 1908.
503 *Weekly Dispatch*, 31 December 1907.
504 *Weekly Dispatch*, 27 December 1907.
505 *Daily Chronicle*, 20 December 1907.
506 *Weekly Dispatch*, 29 December 1907.
507 *Daily Chronicle*, 31 December 1907.
508 Ibid.
509 *The Bystander*, 8 January 1908.
510 *Illustrated Police Budget*, 11 January 1908.
511 Ibid.
512 Ibid.
513 *Reynolds's Newspaper*, 29 December 1907.
514 It may be noted that Dora Piernick and her husband, Mendel, had been convicted at the Old Bailey in February 1903 of conspiracy to procure a young Polish girl for immoral purposes at a house in Fitzroy Square. Mendel was sentenced to two years in prison while Dora received a sentence of six months. She was not long out of prison, therefore, when she was murdered at the end of the year.
515 The *Illustrated Police Budget* of 4 January 1908 claimed that the police had a suspect for Piernick's murder having found her keys in the pan of a water closet. It said it knew the identity of the last owner of the keys 'though at the moment it is not thought advisable to apprehend him'. The newspaper continued: 'Though public policy prevents us from saying more to-day, our readers may feel assured that in a very early issue more will be revealed, and can feel confident that sooner or later, and probably sooner, the murderer of Emily Dimmock and, possibly of Dora Piernick also, will be arraigned before our tribunals'. Needless to say, nothing more was heard of this.
516 Report of Inspector Neil dated 21 December 1907 (TNA – MEPO 3/182).
517 Ibid. A similar message appears to have been given out to the press behind the scenes, as reflected in a comment in the *Northamptonshire Evening Telegraph* of 21 December 1907 that criticism of the CID for failing to solve so many recent murders (including Emily Dimmock's) was 'not fair to the police' because, in regard to some of them, 'they are morally certain…as to the authorship'.
518 *Reynolds's Newspaper*, 12 January 1908.
519 Letter to the *Daily Mirror* from Mrs M.J. Cornish, 18 February 1986.
520 LMA – PS/CLE/B2/014.
521 *Daily Chronicle*, 7 April 1908.
522 *Holborn Guardian*, 10 April 1908.
523 *Otago Witness*, 30 March 1910.
524 *Adelaide Advertiser*, 21 March 1910.
525 *The Evening Star* (Au), 1 April 1910.
526 *Otago Witness*, 30 March 1910.
527 Register of Deaths in the District of Melbourne East in the State of Victoria stating the verdict at inquest held by Vivian Tanner, Coroner, on 8 April 1910.
528 *Times*, 31 July 1908.
529 *Times*, 3 August 1908.
530 NA – WO 97/4753.
531 http://www.flutewood.org.uk/html/wood.html.
532 A curiosity about this census return is that the signature of Radnor Wood does not match the known signature of Robert Wood and the handwriting on the rest of the return does not appear to be Wood's.
533 *Standard*, 14 December 1907.
534 *The Kentish Gazette and Canterbury Press*, 3 October 1908.
535 *Times*, 30 November 1909.
536 *Daily Mirror*, 30 November 1909.

537 *Exeter and Plymouth Gazette,* 19 November 1909.
538 *Thomson's Weekly News,* 30 September 1922; *Sunday Express,* 3 February & 10 February 1924.
539 *Sunday News,* 12 April 1925.
540 *Police Review & Parade Gossip,* 16 March 1928.
541 TNA – CRIM 1/102/4.
542 At the inquest, Detective Constable Page was more specific, saying that there were 'four or five' post-cards on the floor (*Illustrated Police Budget,* 26 October 1907). Inspector Neil had also said at the police court that there were 'some postcards upon the floor' and that 'one or two cards lay loose on the open album' (*Weekly Dispatch,* 17 November 1907).
543 Hogarth might have been confused by a report of the inquest proceedings in the *Daily Express* of 22 October 1907 which stated that Detective Constable Page said that he found the postcard album 'lying across a chair near the window in the bedroom where the murdered girl lay' but this must have been confusion on the part of the journalist. Inspector Neil confirmed in his evidence at the Old Bailey that the sewing machine stood in the front room 'on the right opposite the opening of the shutters and the chair was beside that'.
544 *Morning Advertiser,* 18 December 1907; *Daily Chronicle,* 18 December 1907. The *Daily Telegraph* records Westcott as saying, 'I went off with a swing, as I saw in the paper, I thought that described me with collar turned up and bowler hat on'. Marshall Hall also asked him to put on 'his hat' and the official shorthand record states that, during his examination-in-chief, Westcott said he was wearing the coat he wore on the morning of 12 September and he turned up his collar and 'put on his hat', not his cap.
545 *Daily Mirror,* 23 June 1936.
546 *Daily Mirror,* 24 June 1936.
547 *Manchester Guardian,* 15 December 1944; *Daily Telegraph,* 1 December 1944.
548 WAC – R19/634/1, 1947-1948.
549 WAC – R19/634/2, 1949-1954.
550 In actual fact, Marjoribanks had not said this – it was implied in the story about Marshall Hall's exchange with the man he thought was Wood – but Hogarth had categorically stated that Wood changed his name after the trial and this had probably added to the confusion.
551 *Manchester Guardian,* 4 February 1949.
552 *Daily Express,* 4 February 1949.
553 WAC – R19/1,673/1, 1963.
554 *In Command of History: Churchill Fighting and Writing the Second World War* by David Reynolds, Allen Lane, 2004.
555 Ibid.
556 WAC – R19/1,673/1, 1963.
557 The notice, which was identical in all three cases and which requested any living relatives of anyone affected to contact the BBC, was in very small print in the listings section and would not have been easy to spot by any reader of the *Radio Times.*
558 WAC – R19/1,673/1, 1963.
559 Ibid.
560 Ibid.
561 Ibid.
562 In fact, Burroughs had not received Wood's letter of 6 October at this stage but he had received the script Wood had returned and was thus aware that he had not approved.
563 The letter was actually written by Annie but signed by both Robert and Annie, the latter signing as 'Ann Wood' (WAC – R19/1,673/1, 1963).
564 WAC – R19/1,673/1, 1963.
565 *Weekly Dispatch,* 17 November 1907.
566 Marjoribanks referred to Mr Justice McCardie during his account of Wood's trial (saying that the judge had told him that Marshall Hall had the power to terrify a witness) and this seems to have con-fused Sparrow into thinking that McCardie was the trial judge.
567 *Daily Express,* 18-19 December 1907; *Tribune,* 19 December 1907.
568 The file was opened on 1 January 1983 according to the Information Management and Practice De-partment of the National Archives. It was originally closed for 100 years but a decision was taken in 1975 for it to be opened after 75 years (from 1907).
569 *Daily Telegraph,* 22 June 1911.
570 The *Rising Sun* frequented by Emily Dimmock at 120 Euston Road still exists and is now called *The Rocket.* Cornwell's *Rising Sun* was in 1907, and remains, at 46 Tottenham Court Road.
571 Cornwell notes that the police had recorded in their report that Ashton was wrong about the post-mark on the postcard and that it was marked 'London NW' but this does not seem to prevent her from speculating that Sickert might have sent it to pretend he was attending the Doncaster races.
572 According to Sickert expert, Wendy Baron, he 'had probably arrived in Dieppe by the time of the murder' but this would seem to go further than the evidence truly allows (*Sickert Paintings* ed. Wendy Baron and Richard Shone, 1993, Yale University Press).
573 The same story can also be found repeated in *The Artist,* Volume 14, No. 6, of February 1938 and it made its way into some of Sickert's published newspaper obituaries which stated that Sickert 'gained

admission to the house and did a number of drawings of the body' (*Yorkshire Post & Leeds Mercury*, 24 January 1942); and that he 'got permission to see the murdered woman lying on her bed' (*Advertiser* (Adelaide), 26 January 1942).

574 TNA – MEPO 8/6.

575 Officers were advised to look for fingerprints on 'Window frames, glass bottles, tumblers, polished articles of furniture, silver and plated goods and candles' (General Orders for 1907, MEPO 8/6).

576 See *Sickert Paintings* ed. Wendy Baron and Richard Shone, 1993, Yale University Press. Sickert appears to have used two male models during the series, one of whom looks nothing like Wood but the other could be him in theory.

577 *Evening News*, 13 November 1907.

578 *London Gazette*, 28 November 1834; *Morning Post*, 23 December 1834; *London Gazette*, 29 January 1836; *London Gazette*, 12 May 1837; *London Gazette*, 26 October 1838; *London Gazette*, 22 January 1839; *London Gazette*, 19 April 1839; *London Gazette*, 13 April 1841; *London Gazette*, 2 July 1841; *London Gazette*, 16 November 1841; *London Gazette*, 16 June 1843.

579 *The Standard*, 9 March 1895.

580 *Evening News*, 18 December 1907.

581 There are two written statements apparently signed by Ruby Young in the Metropolitan Police file, one dated 5 October 1907 and a further statement dated 11 October 1907. The signature on the 5 October statement corresponds closely with the signature on her letter of 9 January 1908 to *Reynolds's Newspaper*. The signature on the 11 October statement is different to the other two and the distinctive 'R' is formed differently but not in the same way as on the 1919 marriage certificate.

582 One Ruby Young who seemed like a good possibility because she was from Southampton, which would be consistent with rowing on the Solent, was born in 1886 so was potentially the right age, but married a man called John House in November 1906 when the real Ruby Young was in a relationship with Wood, and gave birth to a boy in the summer 1907, so it cannot be her.

583 Her signature also exists on a Canadian Arrivals form for 1924 but is very faint on the microfilmed copy on Ancestry and, while there are some similarities, does not seem to match Ruby Young's known signature.

584 There is a record of a 'Ruby Young', aged 27, sailing alone from Glasgow to Canada on the Cassandra on 20 April 1912 but no further information about this woman is currently known.

585 TNA – MEPO 3/111 to 115.

586 The police initially believed she was 26 years old. Her death certificate gives her age as 28 – which was the age her brother attributed to her – but her birth certificate confirms that she was born on 4 February 1841 and thus 32 years old at the time of her death.

587 The *Star* of 17 September 1907 commented on the disappearance of two earrings, two brooches and a shilling that 'It does not seem to have occurred to the detective intellect of the day that [the murderer] might have taken these trinkets in order to suggest falsely that robbery was his motive'.

588 The coachman was supposed to have been called 'Burton', hence Harriet's adoption of that surname, but when police investigated they discovered that he was probably William Gifford who, nevertheless, denied being the father of the child.

589 TNA – MEPO 3/114.

590 There are different versions of how Wohllebe and Hessel came to be identified. I have adopted the version in the *Daily Telegraph* of 31 January 1873, a cutting from which appears in TNA – MEPO 3/110. I assume this to be correct.

591 Denoted as 'Sc l jaw' under 'Marks'. The equivalent 1907 register also mentions the scar on the left jaw but also refers to a scar on his forehead which was, thus, presumably created at some point during 1906 or 1907.

592 *Launceston Examiner*, 22 November 1892.

593 National Archives of Australia, P234 1909/4581.

Also by David Barrat

**The Islington
Murder Mystery**

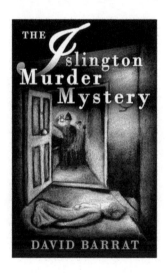

**Published by
Orsam Books**